ENGLISH PHILANTHROPY

1660–1960

ENGLISH PHILANTHROPY

1660 - 1960

DAVID OWEN

CAMBRIDGE, MASSACHUSETTS

THE BELKNAP PRESS OF

HARVARD UNIVERSITY PRESS

LONDON: OXFORD UNIVERSITY PRESS

IN MEMORY OF

BYRD TUTTLE OWEN

PREFACE

THE ORIGIN of this volume lies in the decision of the Ford Foundation in 1955 to sponsor a series of studies of modern philanthropy. This design coincided with my own plans for a sabbatical year in 1955–56, and I was asked to undertake a survey, rather general in scope, of English philanthropy, which might serve as a background for more detailed investigations of the American experience. The bulk of the research was done in the course of that year, though it was supplemented by further work in the United States and in the summer of 1960 by another visit to Britain.

That nearly a decade should have gone by since the issuing of the original commission was to be neither expected nor desired. Two factors have been largely responsible for the length of time taken to produce this book. On the one hand, since 1957–58 I have found myself with heavier academic duties than I had contemplated, and these necessarily curtailed my leisure for study and writing. But also — as seems almost a constant in such enterprises as this — the topic proved even broader and more involved than, in my innocence, I had supposed, and the short cuts, though these have been followed wherever practicable, less usable. What has emerged is a selective survey, more detailed at some points, I suspect, than the Foundation had in mind, but superficial at others. Plainly a great deal is left unsaid. Numbers of problems remain to be worked out, and numbers of individual figures still merit special study.

I have, of course, profited immensely from counsel and other assistance generously given by individuals in England and the United States. Members of the Nathan Committee — the late Lord Nathan, Miss Eileen L. Younghusband (who provided me with a set of the unpublished minutes of evidence and other Committee material), and Miss J. H. Lidderdale, secretary of the Committee — were both cordial and helpful, and Sir Donald Allen, also a member, made available to me documents in his office on the establishment of the City Parochial Charities Foundation. I am happy to acknowledge, too, the aid of officials of various organizations and institutions based on London, who took time to explain their work to me and answer my questions: Mr. R. E. Peers of King Edward's Fund; Mr. W. A. Sanderson of the Nuffield Foundation; Mr. Walter Prideaux, Clerk of the Goldsmiths' Company; Mr. David Jones of the Family Service Units; Mr. Mark Fineman of the Jewish Board of Guardians and Mr. V. D. Lipman, the

Board's historian; Mr. Patrick Howarth of the Royal National Life-Boat Institution; Miss Margaret Stilliard, Miss Margaret E. Brasnett, and Major General C. B. Fairbanks of the National Council of Social Service. Mr. J. C. G. Pownall, former Chief Charity Commissioner, satisfied my inquiries about aspects of the Commission's work, and Professor Helen Cam, Mr. John Bowle, and the Headmaster of Taunton's School, Southampton, supplied me with information on special topics.

In another category it is pleasant to recall the understanding assistance of Mr. A. E. J. Hollander of the Guildhall Library and the hospitality extended by the Family Welfare Association (formerly the Charity Organisation Society). During the bitter month of February 1956 the Association's splendid library proved a comfortably warm refuge, as well as a rich source of material. I only regret that I have not been able to view some of the record of the Society with less qualified enthusiasm. Professor and Mrs. T. S. Simey and Miss M. Penelope Hall joined with Mr. A. G. S. Priestley of the Liverpool Council of Social Service in introducing me to Merseyside philanthropy, and Mr. L. E. Waddilove of the Joseph Rowntree Memorial Trust contributed not only information on York charities but also wise counsel on other aspects of my study. I must also acknowledge with gratitude the help given me in Cambridge by Dr. G. Kitson Clark and Mr. T. C. Nicholas of Trinity College, Mr. A. N. L. Munby of King's, the Master and Bursary of St. John's, Mr. James Grantham of Downing, and Mr. R. S. Hutton, Goldsmiths' Professor of Metallurgy, Emeritus. The Masters of St. Catharine's and Magdalene kindly sent me copies of their Commemoration of Benefactors pamphlets.

On this side of the Atlantic I find myself under heavy obligation to my Harvard-Radcliffe graduate seminars for the years 1956–60. These, more often than not, had to do with some aspect of charity history. Without mentioning individuals by name, I can simply say that at points I have drawn on the work of a half dozen of them. This is also the place to acknowledge the impeccable typing of Mrs. Doris H. Carlin, the editorial assistance of Mr. Donald J. Wilcox, and the helpful editorial counsel of Miss M. Kathleen Ahern of the Press. Professor R. K. Webb of Columbia University read the entire manuscript with extraordinary care and understanding; he has saved me from a good many errors of fact and interpretation. Finally, this book would not have been written without the interest of the Ford Foundation, which not only suggested the subject but made it possible for me to remain in England for a half-year longer than I had planned. The Foundation, and especially Mr. F. Emerson Andrews of the Foundation Library Center and the Russell Sage Foundation, who has served as representative of the Ford Foundation in connection with the book, merit more than this conventional word of thanks. He has read the entire manuscript and has made a number of helpful suggestions, particularly on the treatment of modern foundations in Chapter XX.

The size of this study has prevented the inclusion of a formal bibliography.

The first citation of each work, however, gives a complete reference. Where a book has been published in more than one city — say in London and New York — I have simply recorded the place of publication of the copy I have used.

David Owen

John Winthrop House
Harvard University
September 1963

CONTENTS

INTRODUCTION

INTRODUCTION

I N A N early chapter of *Middlemarch,* Mr. Casaubon, exhibiting what was
in truth a less than minimal interest in the question, concedes philanthropy
to be "a wide field." The phrase is, of course, unexceptionable, but to one
familiar with the "wide field" it gives little intimation of the vastness and complexity of English charitable enterprise. Unless the investigator takes himself
firmly in hand, he will be carried far off the main path — into an exploration of
social work, assorted reform movements, early socialism, state social policy, and
even such an unlikely domain as church finance. It is not easy to decide what
constitutes philanthropy, what topics must be included, and what may be safely
left out.

Though its considerable length may suggest the contrary, this book takes a
rather limited view of its topic, one that will perhaps seem to others wayward
and even wrongheaded. Without attempting to set up a precise definition of
philanthropy, we may stress at the outset that a primary test applied here is
pecuniary. This study has little to do with good works, personal service, or labors
in the public interest, save as these were accompanied by substantial contributions
of money from individuals and groups. What is of primary concern here is the
benefactions of Englishmen which went to create and support a network of services for the mitigation of poverty, disease, infirmity, and ignorance. To this tradition of voluntary action for the improvement of the common life modern English
history owes some of its special flavor.

The theme has held relatively little appeal for historians. Although special
aspects have been dealt with occasionally and although one or two pioneering
studies appeared years ago, Professor W. K. Jordan's recent multi-volumed work
on Tudor-Stuart charities was the first major attempt to examine the contributions made voluntarily by Englishmen to their community.[1] His evidence pictures an extraordinary outpouring of wealth from the merchant aristocracy and
gentry, and shows, also, the reliance which the Tudors placed on private charity
as a solution for major problems of their society. Tudor legislation on poverty,
notably the Poor Law of 1597/1601, was designed as an ultimate resource, to be

---

[1] The essential volume is the first: W. K. Jordan, *Philanthropy in England, 1480–1660* (New York,
1959). Of earlier studies one ought to mention B. Kirkman Gray, *A History of English Philanthropy*
(London, 1905).

invoked only if the situation should exceed the capacities of private philanthropy. Through it all the main burden was, in fact, borne by benevolent citizens rather than by a state system. Not only did these Englishmen establish endowments and institutions for preserving the lives of and rehabilitating the poor throughout the country but, on an astonishing scale, they founded grammar schools and provided, in various ways, for improving their own communities. Altogether this was a dramatic acceptance of social responsibility by numbers of private citizens, many of them affluent and successful, others of only modest fortune. In the course of it, these donors not only helped to ease the country through a hazardous and complex transition but they also contributed to the "fashioning of an ethic of social responsibility which was to be the hall-mark of the liberal society."[2]

Though it deals with a similar theme (and begins nominally at his concluding date), this volume is not designed as a sequel to Jordan's monumental study. As a casual glance at the contents will indicate, the scope is necessarily wider and the evidence leads to no such precise conclusions as he is able to draw. This study rests, in general, on familiar printed materials, original and secondary, and it makes no pretense to exhaustive coverage. It offers a survey, admittedly uneven and perhaps a bit vagrant, of English philanthropic effort (dealing with Scotland only incidentally) from the late seventeenth century to the present. This is its official scope. In fact, however, the emphasis falls heavily on the period from the economic revolution of the late eighteenth century to the First World War (Parts I and IV are hardly more than prologue and epilogue to the main sections). During these years Englishmen continued to follow the tradition established by their Tudor-Stuart forebears, founding institutions of both familiar and novel sorts for the betterment of their common life and banding together in voluntary organizations to deal with problems that emerged in their changing society.

Before the opening of the period with which this book has to do, English charity had already taken on the dignity of a national tradition. To the formation of this tradition, Jordan suggests, a good many factors had contributed — among them the Protestant social ethic, a new sense of national consciousness and national obligation, a pervasive desire to emulate the charitable acts of others — and the merchants and gentry, few in numbers but alert and farseeing, responded splendidly to the challenge. Before the end of the sixteenth century the tradition had been well established and was spreading from these strategic classes throughout English society. To give or leave something to the community — a fund for the poor, an almshouse, a grammar school — came to be expected of the more prosperous Englishmen. By the early sevententh century, Professor Jordan asserts, "the failure of a London merchant to settle some substantial and conspicuous charitable trust or gift was generally regarded as little short of shocking unless there had been a grievous wasting of the estate because of age, ill-health, or commercial misfortune."[3]

---

[2] Jordan, *Philanthropy in England*, p. 143.
[3] *Ibid.*, p. 153.

In the late seventeenth and early eighteenth centuries, Englishmen grafted a new technique on to their philanthropic tradition. Although they continued to give or leave considerable sums of money as individuals, they also discovered increasing merit in collective activity. Inspired, very likely, by the joint stock business ventures of their age, groups of Englishmen arranged to pool their efforts in voluntary societies dedicated to mitigating particular evils or accomplishing special charitable aims. Since much of the charity capital of the age went into this relatively anonymous "associated philanthropy," it is difficult to judge whether the eighteenth century marked a rising or a subsidence in the philanthropic current. Not only did a good deal of money reach worthy causes in the form of annual subscriptions, but large individual bequests came, far more commonly than in Tudor-Stuart times, without trust restrictions. Such benefactions might be treated by the charity as cash income and would tend to disappear from the permanent record. In some measure, then, both the form and the direction of giving were altered during the first century covered by this book. Certainly the most conspicuous monuments of early and mid-eighteenth century philanthropy were the amazing chain of charity schools and the numbers of hospitals (in the modern sense of "hospital") in London and provincial cities. Both of these, in some degree, were achievements of the new-style associated philanthropy.

If the tradition of social responsibility was established at an early date, it was also reinforced by newer currents. No one can miss, for example, the impact of the Evangelical Revival on men's notions of their obligations to their fellows. The compulsions of Calvinist social ethic, with its stress on stewardship of one's wealth, had much to do with developing habits of giving in the first place, but the late century revival altered the impulse to charity and imparted new energies to it. Throughout the history of English philanthropy religious motives appear strikingly — in secular as well as in directly religious philanthropy (largely ignored in this volume), in the gifts of individuals and in the activities of organizations. The Younghusband Report of 1959 could point fairly enough to the pervasiveness of religious inspiration in the voluntary undertakings from which the public services studied in the Report, without exception, had taken their rise.[4]

The evangelical current coincided in time, roughly speaking, with the economic revolution and the population explosion that began in the latter half of the eighteenth century and so decisively conditioned nineteenth-century history. The social situation, critical enough in all conscience, recalled in some respects the conditions that prompted the outpouring of benevolence in the Tudor-Stuart age. A mounting population, cities growing almost catastrophically, an economic mechanism that was being revolutionized, though jumpily and erratically, and a social structure that often showed signs of grave strain, sometimes almost intolerable strain — small wonder that gloom about the country's prospects peri-

[4] *Report of the Working Party on Social Workers in the Local Authority Health and Welfare Services* (H.M.S.O., 1959), Par. 1031.

odically haunted those concerned about such matters. At times, indeed, there was reason to believe the country condemned to a permanent labor surplus and to doubt whether the output of British factories and farms could provide for the Englishmen who, after the turn of the century, were increasing at the rate of around 14 per cent a decade.

A principal weapon of the nation during the age of intermittent crisis was private charity, which attempted to grapple, sometimes hopefully, sometimes desperately, with the evils of the new industrial-urban society. One must not exaggerate. The problems of this society were only dimly understood, and the remedies prescribed owed not a little to motives that in retrospect seem curiously mixed. Most middle- and upper-class Englishmen accepted "the poor" as a given and permanent element in the social structure, a large stratum from which only a few would rise in each generation. The vast majority must make their own terms with the inevitable and carry their burdens without becoming dependent on others. To assist them unduly was simply to pauperize, a word with terrifying implications for the Victorians. Yet, when all reservations have been made, private individuals and groups did finance hospitals, organize schools, arrange to visit the poor in their homes, and found societies to practice an infinite, indeed disconcerting, variety of good works. And in the course of it all, philanthropists contributed something — in some instances a good deal — toward relieving tensions in English life.

But who were these philanthropists? Generalizations about modern English philanthropists as a class do not come readily and are admittedly suspect. In their social origins, the sources of their wealth, their motives, and their charitable interests, the group exhibits an almost incredible variety. Broadly speaking, as would be expected, major donors come out of a financial, commercial, or industrial background. Fortunes from the new factories, however, did not reach the world of charity immediately. In the early nineteenth century not only did the demands of the business itself and the ambition of founding a family preclude large gifts to philanthropy — at least that appears to have been the reasoning of successful entrepreneurs (with some notable exceptions) — but beyond these considerations it also took time to assimilate the new men into the older tradition. Those who were without children (for example, Thomas Holloway and Josiah Mason) might lay out large sums, and others with a strong religious bias (Richard Reynolds) might give more than generously. It was well along in the century, however, before substantial amounts came to philanthropy from industrial entrepreneurs.

Nor did aristocrats write their names large on the tables of philanthropy — again with some important exceptions. Since this was expected of them, they carried on the traditional local charities faithfully enough. By mid-century, indeed, the great estates seem to have been devoting between 4 and 7 per cent of their gross income to uses that may be loosely described as charitable.[5] Peers

---

[5] F. M. L. Thompson, *English Landed Society in the Nineteenth Century* (London, 1963), p. 210.

would often contribute considerable sums for special and nonrecurring purposes, and aristocratic names, of course, appeared on numbers of subscription lists and figured among the officers of charities. Yet the aristocratic class cannot be thought of as a genuinely creative force in the philanthropy of the age. Altogether, one who attempts to collect Victorian philanthropists is likely to return with a mixed-bag — bankers, merchants, professional men, some aristocrats and country gentlemen, and, as the century moves along, increasing numbers from industry.

While philanthropists added their benefactions to the national pool, other Victorians and pre-Victorians agitated (with only moderate success) for more efficient employment of the mass of charitable trusts inherited from the past. The major instrument of Tudor-Stuart philanthropy, Jordan has emphasized, was the charitable trust, the gift or bequest made in perpetuity for charitable purposes. English law is relatively indulgent toward benefactions made in trust for purposes that are legally charitable, and throughout the modern age the practice of making benefactions in this fashion has continued to be an important technique for financing good works. In its charitable trusts, certain Victorians were convinced, their age possessed an asset of incomparable value and one that could be made more fruitful if it were only properly administered. These endowments might, indeed, serve as the basis for some of the services admittedly needed by British society.

Throughout the century, therefore, there was controversy, sometimes recessive, sometimes emerging into the open, about the degree of public regulation to be applied to these thousands of charitable trusts. In the 1820's and '30's they were inventoried in great detail, and in the 1850's the Charity Commission was created to oversee them (though armed with considerably less power than had been called for). From the Commission arose frequent demands for an increase in its regulatory authority, and equity lawyers occasionally appealed for a liberalization of charity law. Yet in general, with the exception of two categories of charity, the situation remained unchanged from the passing of the Charities Act of 1860 until the Act of 1960 finally brought a degree of clarification.[6]

The distinctive modern technique, however, was the charitable society. Throughout the nineteenth century, especially, such organizations multiplied at a fantastic rate, to the mixed admiration and embarrassment of observers. Few social needs failed to call forth their own agencies: disease, poverty, vice, delinquency, old age, and other afflictions of the human condition all had their special organizations, in some cases numbers of them. These were, of course, of all kinds, large and small, silly and sensible, well established and struggling. Their numbers were so great, their activities so overlapping, and their policies sometimes so lax as to inspire repeated protests and at least one major effort (in the charity organization movement) to rationalize their procedures. Yet it would be ungracious to withhold praise from this outpouring of voluntary labor and money. The

---

[6] The two categories of charity handled more drastically were the endowed schools (Chapter IX) and the City of London parochial endowments (Chapter X).

motives that lay behind it may have been exceedingly complex — humanitarian impulses, religion, social aspirations, or, perhaps most important, simply the fact of belonging to "a culture which regards such actions as worthy" [7] — but there can be no doubt that this demonstration was almost unique in modern history. The Nathan Committee was not stretching the point when it described the attempt to create by private effort a series of universal social services as "one of the magnificent failures of our history." [8]

Beyond doubt it was a failure, however magnificent. In the course of the century, as it became plain that production had won out over population growth and as the realities of life in an industrial society defined themselves more clearly, men began to readjust their social thinking. Charitable agencies, with their improved techniques of casework, could do much for individuals — and here their contributions continued to be indispensable. They could give vital service in particular situations. But when the problem was seen as one that, in essentials, had little to do with the actions of individuals, their adequacies and their failures, then the shortcomings of private charity lay exposed. To help individuals handle the unavoidable and grinding poverty of their lives with what success they could, even to assist them in meeting their special crises, was one thing; to ask why and whether destitution and the evils associated with it were necessary in modern society raised a different order of issue. As men's views of what constituted a tolerable minimum became less restricted, it grew obvious that the major social tasks lay well beyond the resources of private charity, however ambitious its aspirations and devoted its performance. During the late century, an age whose commitment to individualism as a social philosophy was weakening and whose perspectives were being altered, numbers of individuals, more or less influential, were doubting the validity of mid-century answers to problems of destitution and public welfare. Henceforth, indeed, it became only a matter of time until the State would move, cautiously or decisively, into areas previously occupied by voluntary agencies.

An underlying theme of the present study has to do with this dual importance of private charity — on the one hand, its role as a pioneering force, pointing the way to action by the State, and, on the other, its ultimate inadequacy when measured against the requirements of industrial-urban society. The indebtedness of the state welfare services to voluntary experimenting has often been stressed. In the 1930's, PEP could point out that "Practically every public social service in operation today has its roots in some form of voluntary provision," [9] and, from the beginning, those responsible for the statutory services have acknowledged their indebtedness to the dedicated imagination of their voluntary predecessors. For example, in the House of Lords debate in June 1949 on "voluntary action

---

[7] Jordan, *Philanthropy in England*, p. 144.

[8] *Report of the Committee on the Law and Practice Relating to Charitable Trusts* (Cmd. 8710), 1952, Par. 44. Hereafter this document will be cited simply as *Nathan Report*, 1952.

[9] PEP, *Report on the British Social Services* (London, 1937), p. 49.

for social welfare," from which emerged the Nathan Committee and ultimately the Charities Act of 1960, Lord Pakenham for the Labour Government acknowledged in unstinting terms the public's indebtedness to the voluntary services.[10]

Until the decisive extension of the welfare services at the close of the Second World War, the State's action had been by no means precipitate. Very likely the critical steps, in principle, were those taken by the Liberal Government in the years 1906–11, for, in spite of their modest character, these established a solid precedent for further and more conclusive measures. Over the years, more often than not, public intervention has taken place in three stages.[11] At the outset the service is entirely voluntary; it is privately supported and administered, the response of a group of individuals to an observed social evil or social need. If the service appears to justify itself (and if suitable pressure can be applied at the proper points), the State may assist with a grant-in-aid on a temporary, experimental basis. Management and much of the financing remain in private hands, but the public now holds a stake in the venture and thus a measure of control. Finally (with the possibility of a number of intermediate stages and types of public-private collaboration) the State may take over the service and operate it as a public enterprise, with or without voluntary assistance.

This process has been repeated time and again — though sometimes it ends not in a full-dress state service but in one of the rather bewildering public-private co-operative agencies that are characteristic of the British Welfare State. But whatever the degree of intervention, those in charge for the State will be conscious of their debt to the individual Englishmen, past and present, who first pointed to a need, created organizations to meet it, and often continue to serve as auxiliaries of the state service that now occupies the field once held by the voluntary forces. Whatever the long-run future of philanthropy may turn out to be, none can deny the contributions to the welfare society of generations of public-spirited citizens who by giving of their substance and by their personal efforts laid the foundations on which the state services have been built.

[10] 5 *Parl. Deb.* (Lords), 163:119ff.
[11] As pointed out by a reviewer in *The Times Literary Supplement*, 20 Oct. 1961.

PART ONE

PHILANTHROPY IN THE AGE OF BENEVOLENCE
(1660's–1780's)

"For no sermon or admonition [on charity] is of so much avail as a deep-rooted custom."
— St. John Chrysostom

"Few institutions are more ticklish than those of charity."
— Lord Kames

WHATEVER uneasiness eighteenth-century Englishmen may have felt as they contemplated their society, thoughtful critics among them could discover at least one conspicuous merit. Their age, they liked to point out, was exhibiting a new sensitiveness to human need and was developing fresh instruments for dealing with it. "Charity," observed Henry Fielding as chief magistrate for Westminster to a grand jury in 1749, "is the very characteristic virture at this time. I believe we may challenge the whole world to parallel the examples which we have of late given of this sensible, this noble, this Christian virtue."[1] The familiar tags — "benevolence," "sensibility," "humanitarianism," and the rest — which we apply to the eighteenth-century ethos, like most conventions of the kind, distort but do not entirely misrepresent the complex reality. Whether or not the century created "modern philanthropy" (the notion of modernity is, of course, purely relative), at least it added new interests, new impulses, and new techniques to the charitable enterprise of Tudor and early Stuart times.[2]

By common consent the late seventeenth century marked a turning point of more than ordinary consequence in the history of British politics and society. The age that it inaugurated was to be one not only of compromise, of growing tolerance, of lessening acerbity in public life, but also of conspicuous material advance, of overseas expansion, of philosophical and scientific inquiry, which, in a greater or less degree, altered the temper and outlook of British upper- and middle-class society. And along with these came innovations in the practice of philanthropy that were recognizably modern. These developments were perhaps most apparent on the side of organization, where the philanthropic association arose to supplement and in part to supplant the efforts of the individual doer of good works. Henceforth, although the individual philanthropist would be as indispensable as ever, he would increasingly find his outlet by aiding, passively through his contributions, actively through his labor, or both, an organization dedicated to a cause which he wished to further. Rich men continued, of course, to carry on their own benevolences, but charity became less a person-to-person affair — almsgiving in the classic sense, though this persisted on a large scale — and more of a collective effort. In the future the hallmark of the philanthropist was to be not merely generous giving but also his support of worthy organizations.

[1] *Works*, X, 79, quoted in C. J. Abbey, *The English Church and Its Bishops, 1700–1800*, 2 vols. (London, 1887), I, 338.
[2] See Jordan, *Philanthropy in England, 1480–1660*, chaps. III, IV, VI.

Clearly the emergence of the new methods can be ascribed to no single influence. No doubt philanthropists learned something from the joint-stock boom of the 1690's, which sired a bewildering assortment of companies, honest and knavish, and even more from the Era of the Bubble. If commercial activity could be financed by drawing small amounts from numbers of individuals, perhaps a similar plan could be usefully employed in good works. Sometimes, indeed, as in the notorious Charitable Corporation, the joint-stock principle was applied with perverse and calamitous results. A version of the Continental *mons pietatis* and originally created to make loans to the industrious poor at low rates of interest, the company raised some £600,000 for the purpose, but presently discovered speculative finance to be more rewarding. Fraudulent management and, in the final stage, an absconding cashier, brought about the collapse of the Corporation amid the recriminations of outraged and ruined shareholders.[3] On a more reputable level, clerical propagandists for charity schools could discover a spiritual significance in joint-stock companies and could note that money invested would bring "a dividend in the improved happiness and morality of the poor."[4] As in a company, where shareholders and directors performed different functions, so in the charity of the future subscribers would furnish pounds and shillings, but the more active work would be left to other hands. Subscription lists were to become as vital to philanthropy as lists of shareholders were to a joint-stock company.

Contemporaries did not fail to take note of the new departure in charitable techniques. The network of charity schools and the new hospitals, some of the more outstanding established by group effort rather than by a single donor, offered a dramatic demonstration of what could be accomplished by associated action. All this, in fact, encouraged the hope (a perennial theme of charity strategists from that day to this) of broadening the financial base on which philanthropy rested. In 1758 a writer in the *Idler* found compensation for the disappearance of great benefactors, those who "in ancient times . . . possessed counties or provinces," in a growing charitable interest throughout British society. For "no sooner is a new species of misery brought to view, and a design of relieving it professed, than every hand is open to contribute something, every tongue is busied in solicitation, and every art of pleasure is employed for a time in the interest of virtue."[5]

This associated philanthropy was, in a large measure, middle class in its support and Puritan in temper. Early in the century Richard Steele deplored the fact that "only the middle kind of people" seemed to be concerned with teaching the

---

[3] A good deal of documentation, most of it denouncing or defending the management, resulted from the Charitable Corporation affair, but its bizarre story belongs more legitimately to the history of finance than to that of philanthropy. Brief accounts appear in Gray, *A History of English Philanthropy,* and W. R. Scott, *The Constitution and Finance of English, Scottish, and Irish Joint-Stock Companies to 1720,* 3 vols. (Cambridge, 1910–12), III, 380.

[4] W. K. Lowther Clarke, *A History of the S.P.C.K.* (London, 1959), p. 23. Kirkman Gray's pioneer study lays great stress on the idea and techniques of associated philanthropy.

[5] *Idler,* 6 May 1758.

young, providing for the aged, or restraining the wicked.[6] The hundreds of charity schools established during the first half-century, by all odds its greatest accomplishment in the realm of good works, were financed predominantly "by the modest benefactions of 'middling-class' philanthropists."[7] Though the great aristocratic donor by no means disappeared, most of the memorable philanthropists of the period were of middle-class origins. Benefactions might be modest or, in such instances as those of Thomas Guy or Sir John Morden, substantial, but donors came overwhelmingly from trade and commerce rather than from the great families.[8]

To recall the Puritan spirit that informed much of early eighteenth-century charity is to raise the question of motive. What special appeal did benevolence hold for sections of the middle class, and what persuaded them to devote money and effort to the relief of distress and the improvement of their social inferiors? Behind the bewildering miscellany of charitable movements and institutions created between the Restoration and the 1770's one can, perhaps, distinguish three main impulses, confused and intertwined, each with its particular variants. In the decades around the turn of the century philanthropy was closely related to the Puritan ideal, but Puritan in an ethical rather than a doctrinal sense. This was the philanthropy of an austere and practical piety common to High Churchman, Low Churchman, and Dissenter. Many would have endorsed Tillotson's reproof to Beveridge, "Doctor, Doctor, Charity is above rubrics."[9] Underneath their dogmatic and political differences, sincere and dedicated men of all communions shared an outlook that was fundamentally Puritan. "Conduct, not dogma," says Miss Gwladys Jones, "stamped the puritan of the eighteenth century."[10]

Disapproval of making money, providing it were put to good uses, had never formed a part of the Puritan ethic. On the contrary, the genuinely devout man would exhibit diligence in accumulating and prudence in spending — all to the greater glory of God. Robert Nelson, who, though a non-juring High Churchman, almost perfectly embodies this Puritan strain, pictures charity as "a Sort of Restoring that Proportion of Wealth, which doth not belong to You." If, in fact, "You do not do Good with Your Riches, You use them contrary to the Intention of GOD, who is the absolute Master of them."[11] Such notions of stewardship,

---

[6] *Guardian*, No. 79, 1713.

[7] M. Gwladys Jones, *The Charity School Movement* (Cambridge, 1938), p. 6.

[8] As in Tudor-Stuart times. (For a brief statement of W. K. Jordan's conclusions, see his article "The English Background of Modern Philanthropy," *American Historical Review*, 66:402–3 [January 1961].) Thomas Guy was, of course, the founder of the famous hospital, and Morden, a Levant merchant who established Morden College, Blackheath, "for twelve decayed merchants," a number later increased to forty.

[9] Quoted in C. J. Abbey and J. H. Overton, *The English Church in the Eighteenth Century* (rev. and abridged, London, 1887), p. 43.

[10] Jones, *Charity School Movement*, p. 6. I am indebted to Miss Jones's study for her suggestive analysis (pp. 3–14) of eighteenth-century puritanism.

[11] *Address to Persons of Quality and Estate* (London, 1715), pp. 220–21, 228.

though they tended to lose some of their force in the mid-century, emerged later in the philanthropic rationale of the Evangelicals. Henry Thornton, William Wilberforce, and Hannah More leave little to be desired as exemplars of the Puritan philanthropist.

The flowering of charitable effort, especially in the middle and latter part of the century, owed something to a vaguer, yet more pervasive, impulse than the Puritan ethic. Modern humanitarianism took its rise in the course of the century, and the benevolence and sensibility associated with it, though sometimes no more than emotions which it was fashionable to display, had a good deal to do with forming the social temper of the time. Often, no doubt, giving to charity and listening to charity sermons offered an escape from some of the unpleasant realities of the eighteenth-century world — its poverty, insecurity, and suffering. The practice of benevolence assured one of surpassingly agreeable sensations, "the most lasting, valuable and exquisite Pleasure." [12]

But there was more to it than this. To write off eighteenth-century humanitarianism as sentimental escape, as a half-involuntary search for pleasurable sensations, would do less than justice. Obviously some such motives — and others even less exalted — accounted for the columns of names on charity subscription lists. Yet it is impossible to miss the compassion with which certain members of the middle and upper classes could view the misfortunes of the lower or to suspect the disinterestedness of their efforts to mitigate them. Captain Coram and Jonas Hanway, though their subconscious drives may have been as complex as human nature itself, were first of all humanitarians, men who were impelled to relieve distress and, according to their lights, to right wrongs. Nowhere was the characteristic eighteenth-century hopefulness about mankind and the improvability of society more splendidly embodied than in such transparently sincere philanthropists.

There was, in short, a philanthropy of benevolence, genuinely humanitarian and even sacrificial at the center but shading off toward the circumference into the increasingly sentimental and self-regarding. With benevolence and Puritan piety, however, was associated a more plainly utilitarian thread, sometimes so tightly interwoven with the others as to be hardly distinguishable. Yet the political inspiration of some of the century's philanthropic schemes is unmistakable. Properly administered charities can almost be thought of as instruments of mercantilist policy, insofar as they tended to safeguard national power. To take one example, statesmen of the seventeenth and early eighteenth centuries were haunted by the specter of a declining population, and, in the absence of a census, the way was opened for the wildest conjectures and most futile debates. Uneasiness about depopulation thus joined with humanitarianism in some of the more popular philanthropic enterprises of the century — the Foundling Hospital, the Marine

[12] *Gentleman's Magazine,* II (August 1732), quoted in Betsy Rodgers, *Cloak of Charity* (London, 1949), p. 8.

Society, the various medical charities, and the Royal Humane Society (1774) for the resuscitation of victims from drowning, a venture which neatly combined philanthropic and scientific with mercantilist values.

Other charitable and quasi-charitable efforts had mercantilist overtones. Schemes for putting the poor to work reflected familiar mercantilist notions of getting the most out of the laboring force of the nation, and certain writers, Mr. Wilson has observed, could even support what amounted to an economy of high wages.[13] Jonas Hanway put the point with admirable succinctness: "As the true foundation of riches and power is the number of working poor, every rational proposal for the augmentation of them merits our regard." [14] Likewise the manpower requirements of Britain's maritime interest were never far in the background when charities for waifs and orphans were projected. Captain Coram, himself a former sea captain who had caught the vision of a great overseas empire, saw his Foundling Hospital as a potential source of artisans for the colonies, and Mr. Justice Hooke pictured charity schools as nurseries of seamen.[15] The Marine Society, founded in 1756 by Jonas Hanway and a group of friends, was explicitly designed to serve as a charitable recruiting agency for the fleet and merchant shipping, and such endowed institutions as Neale's Mathematical School in Hatton Garden taught navigation to boys from charity schools and elsewhere.[16] In such enterprises as these the twin impulses of relieving distress and contributing, in mercantilist terms, to the well-being of the nation were comfortably blended.

Puritan piety, a benevolently humanitarian outlook, and concern for the national interest all contributed to the complex of eighteenth-century philanthropy. But there were other influences, significant though less readily definable. Even a casual glance at the new endowments established during the century, especially in the country districts, suggests that benefactors were acting from force of social habit, almost social inertia. If in Tudor-Stuart times charity begot charity by example, and individual philanthropists and even parishes might engage in what were almost tournaments of competitive benevolence, by the eighteenth century — indeed, well before that — the practice of charitable giving had become a recognized element in the pattern of English life. More successfully than with most

[13] Charles Wilson, "The Other Face of Mercantilism," *Trans. Royal Hist. Soc.*, 5th ser. 9:84–87 (1959).

[14] Quoted in Rodgers, *Cloak of Charity*, p. 38. *The London Evening Post* (25–27 Feb. 1755) held widespread poverty and idleness to be "a *Burthen* on the *Industry* of *others*. In point of *Interest* this must affect the NATION deeply; and therefore how *rude* soever it might be to importune *People* of *Fashion* to think of the *Poor*, yet, as STATESMEN, they deserve their Notice." (Quoted by W. S. Lewis and R. M. Williams, *Private Charity in England, 1747–1757* [New Haven, 1938], p. 3.)

[15] R. H. Nichols and F. A. Wray, *The History of the Foundling Hospital* (London, 1935), pp. 14–15; Clarke, *S.P.C.K.*, p. 51.

[16] Established by will of Joseph Neale dated 1705. (*1st Report of the Commissioners on the Education of the Poor*, 1819, X-A, 174.) Even Lord Kames, whose view of many voluntary charities was as unenthusiastic as his opinion of the English Poor Laws, had only praise for the marine societies. (*Sketches of the History of Man*, 2 vols. [Edinburgh, 1774], II, 48.)

societies, the English had managed to graft onto the tradition of *noblesse oblige* a notion, however rudimentary, of *richesse oblige,* and among both upper and upper-middle classes there were those who accepted its responsibilities. When the Wiltshire gentleman settled a rent charge for the poor of his parish and the London merchant endowed a charity school in his home village in Shropshire, they not only were following their own charitable impulses, but were doing what their age appeared to expect of them.

CHAPTER I

THE PHILANTHROPY OF
EIGHTEENTH-CENTURY PIETY

I N T H E years before and just after 1700 the energies that went into philanthropy were connected, more or less directly, with the practice of religion. Numbers of Englishmen labored for the needy and distressed in the conviction that "it is Your Saviour Himself You assist in the persons of the Poor." [1] To identify this "Philanthropy of Piety" with the Anglican Revival of the turn of the century would be correct enough but less than adequate, for its emphases were pietistic and moral rather than ecclesiastical. Though the three representative philanthropists of the age were practicing Anglicans, they covered a wide spectrum of theological belief — from Thomas Firmin, unitarian in his views, through Thomas Bray, a middle-of-the-road Churchman, to Robert Nelson, the Non-juror. [2] But among the three there was no hesitation about co-operating in good works.

Naturally the force of the religious dynamic varied markedly from one philanthropist to another. With Robert Nelson, clearly, it was primary. It would not have occurred to the High Church pietist to think of his charitable labors as other than an expression of his religious commitment. But Thomas Firmin, though his indefatigable activity owed something to "a sound knowledge and a sincere love and obedience to God," [3] seems much more the quintessential philanthropist, for whom human distress is itself a sufficiently compelling argument. Although, according to his partner, Firmin might have accumulated an estate of £20,000, he rejoiced in the prospect of leaving only £3000. Beyond doubt he was the outstanding English philanthropist of the latter seventeenth century.

Firmin's frequently noted projects for putting the poor to work at flax-spinning have tended to obscure the range of his charitable interests. Actually his horizons comprehended a vast expanse of social terrain. The poor and unemployed, debtor prisoners, Continental and Irish refugees, Christ's Hospital, St. Thomas's Hospital, sufferers from assorted disasters, all benefited not only from his generous financial support but also from his untiring personal efforts. During the last twenty years of his life Firmin was virtually a full-time philanthropist.

[1] Robert Nelson, *Address to Persons of Quality and Estate*, p. 266.
[2] Certain other individuals with some claim to being considered representative (e.g., Thomas Guy) will be noticed in Chapters II and III.
[3] Tillotson, *Sermons*, XX, quoted in C. J. Abbey, *English Church and Its Bishops*, I, 338.

Thomas Firmin was one of those "middle kind of people" by whom the early philanthropic community was largely populated. Born in Ipswich of middle-class Puritan parents, to whom God had given "the wish of Solomon, neither poverty nor riches," [4] he prospered as a girdler and mercer in London, meanwhile abandoning his natal Calvinism for a less austere religious outlook. Notwithstanding his less than orthodox views, he developed a wide acquaintance with distinguished clerics of various shades of opinion, all of whom were welcomed to his Lombard Street house. What first put Firmin into the business of philanthropy was the Plague of 1665, when, with the departure from London of the better-to-do families, many of the poor were left without means of livelihood. His plan of providing them with raw materials for continuing their usual occupations, surprisingly enough, achieved a modest success, and he proceeded to experiment with stockpiling corn and coal to be sold to the poor at cost when hard times returned.

The projects "for the Imploying of the Poor," by which Firmin is best known to history, were launched in the mid-'70's, apparently at the time he abandoned his own business and took up the profession of philanthropy. To review the record of this undertaking would carry us down a bypath, for interesting as it was, the plan vanished with its founder. Yet it is worth recalling that this was an operation of considerable magnitude, with some sixteen or seventeen hundred spinners, in addition to flax-dressers, weavers, and others, and an annual investment of between £2000 and £4000. Firmin conceived of his enterprise as thrifty philanthropy rather than as an ordinary business, and he could look upon a loss of twopence in the shilling as money well spent. But obviously there was little future in it unless the public authorities could be persuaded to give their support. This they showed no eagerness to do, and Firmin's workshops must be put down as an imaginative but isolated experiment rather than as significant social pioneering.

Of more direct concern to the historian of philanthropy are some of Firmin's other charitable interests or, more accurately, his services as a kind of agent-general for good works. He was clearly one of those individuals for whom raising and disbursing money for worthy causes yielded enormous satisfaction. His assets were a warm heart, a wide acquaintance among the well-to-do, and enthusiasm tempered by a shrewd business sense — in short, an ability to enlist others in charitable projects and to command their confidence. For a number of years he collected from friends and acquaintances several hundred pounds annually for the poor. Charitable individuals developed the habit of using Firmin as almoner, for his knowledge of the poor was unexcelled and his methods of giving out relief prudent and discriminating. He had acquired a wholesome suspicion of ordinary almsgiving and a habit of investigating alleged distress before moving to relieve it. For one philanthropist he is said to have distributed over

---

[4] *The Life of Mr. Thomas Firmin, Late Citizen of London,* 2d ed. (London, 1791), p. 3. Save where otherwise noted, material on Firmin is taken from the *Life.* I have given specific references only for direct quotations.

£5000 in the course of two decades. As a governor of St. Thomas's, he was partly responsible for raising £4000 for rebuilding and repairs, and for Christ's Hospital he carried out a series of improvements, among them a sick ward and a school at Hertford, at a cost of not less than £3000.

When in the 1680's numbers of French Huguenots sought refuge in England, it was "our elemosinary general" who took the lead in arranging for temporary accommodations and who raised and disbursed in 1681–82 alone nearly £2500 for their relief. The Protestant refugees who fled from Ireland in large numbers in 1688–89 were dependent on English charity, and two successive briefs[5] were granted to them, with Firmin as one of the commissioners. From all over the country clergy and churchwardens transmitted their collections to him. In the course of it all, he handled over £56,500, besides the smaller sums that he solicited and distributed privately. When one recalls, in addition, the numbers of debtors he released from prison, the special winter collections for the poor he supervised, and the boys whom he put to apprenticeships, it is natural enough to think of Firmin as a kind of one-man council of social service or director of a common good fund for late seventeenth-century London. Not only his own investment in good works but his extensive services as middleman between benefactor and beneficiary give him an unassailable claim to the title bestowed by his contemporary biographer, "almoner general for the poor."[6]

Firmin was not indifferent to religion as a sanction for charitable action, and he was a sincere, if somewhat unorthodox, Christian. He was an early member of the Society for the Reformation of Manners, and he delighted to collect for his charities from those who were at once profane and affluent. He also contributed to the printing charity (the Welsh Trust) of his Nonconformist friend, the Reverend Thomas Gouge, whose output included an edition of the Bible and other religious works in Welsh. Firmin himself had printed ten thousand copies of a Scripture catechism for his spinners and their children. Yet his religious convictions, genuine as they may have been, were altogether less fundamental to his charitable work than were those, say, of "Pious Robert Nelson." If Nelson was conscientiously carrying out a Divine injunction, Firmin — "Devout without Bigotry, Ill-Nature, or Affectation"[7] — was drawn to good works more by his own restless and warm sympathy for the needy.

2

It was, however, to the religious philanthropists that the early eighteenth century chiefly belonged, and the most noteworthy organizations for philanthropic purposes were expressions of the religious impulse. This "Philanthropy of Piety"

---

[5] A brief was a semiofficial method of collecting charitable contributions and was used chiefly in connection with such disasters as fires. An undertaker received authorization from the Sovereign to make a collection through parish officials, ministers, and others, and was entitled to a percentage for his work.

[6] *Life;* p. 41.

[7] *The Charitable Samaritan or a Short Account of Mr. Thomas Firmin* (London, 1698), p. 2.

was a product of the Anglican Revival in one of its aspects, an emphasis on a fervent personal religion and commitment to the service of others. Churchmen who exemplified these tendencies preached and practiced to excellent purpose the new associated philanthropy. Not all of their organized efforts — the Society for the Propagation of the Gospel, for example — have a valid claim to inclusion in a study of philanthropy. The line between religion-in-action and philanthropy is, of course, difficult to draw, and no attempt is made in this book to establish a logical and consistent basis of distinction. In general, the approach here will be, in American constitutional terms, that of the "strict constructionist." Partly for reasons of space, Church and Chapel and their charitable activities will be largely passed over in favor of philanthropies without a specifically religious emphasis.

One body whose purposes were primarily religious it is impossible to ignore. For the historian of philanthropy the importance of the Society for Promoting Christian Knowledge does not lie in the mass of improving tracts that bore its imprint — Dr. Woodward's *Kind Caution to Profane Swearers, Serious Exhortations to Housekeepers,* and the rest — but rather in the Society's sponsorship of the most impressive social experiment of the age, the charity school movement. Not only was this a gallant attempt to meet the challenge of ignorance and moral delinquency among the children of the poor, but as an organized effort it offered a striking example of the new associated philanthropy in action.

The Society for Promoting Christian Knowledge took form in a relatively congenial social climate, for there was ample, if somewhat spotty, evidence of a deeper Christian dedication among numbers of Englishmen. The emergence of the Religious Societies, groups of young Churchmen who met together for devotional exercises and to "Reprove, Exhort, and Edifie one another," [8] seemed to reveal a new concern for the spiritual life on the part of the laity. The essential aims of these groups were spiritual but they were not without influence on more explicitly charitable activities. For one thing, they gave an instructive demonstration of what could be accomplished by groups of individuals voluntarily banded together, and they seemed to suggest that analogous organizations might be effectively employed for purposes less directly religious. Then too the Religious Societies presently discovered that love of God could not be separated from service to man. As their contemporary historian reports, "they visited the poor at their houses and relieved them, fixed some in the way of trade, set prisoners at liberty, furthered poor scholars in their subsistence at the University," and they provided something of a pool of teachers for the new charity schools.[9]

The Societies for the Reformation of Manners, established about two decades after the first of the Religious Societies, had only a tenuous connection with philanthropy as here conceived. No doubt the motive that inspired them was, as

---

[8] Josiah Woodward, *An Account of the Societies for the Reformation of Manners* (London, 1699), p. 15.

[9] Quoted in J. H. Overton, *Life in the English Church, 1660–1714* (London, 1885), p. 211; Jones, *Charity School Movement,* p. 99.

their historian suggests, "a puritanic and militant philanthropy." [10] If so, this was a philanthropic impulse that misfired. The Societies purposed to raise the tone of public morals by directing against offenders (turned in by Society informers armed with sheaves of warrants) the force of the criminal law. Statistics of prosecutions — about 3300 in 1708 [11] — tell a fearsome story of well-intentioned zeal. Not surprisingly, the Societies encountered a good deal of public resistance, active and passive, and Defoe could condemn the whole notion of thinking "to effect a reformation by punishing the poor, while the rich enjoy a charter for wickedness." [12] Yet one must remember that the foremost philanthropists of the age were warm supporters of the crusade. Robert Nelson could exult that "by the Blessing of GOD upon the Endeavours of this Society many Thousands of lewd and disorderly Persons have been brought to Legal Punishment." [13] What spelled failure for this unsavory campaign was, as much as anything, the gradual improvement of public enforcement agencies in the course of the century. Though one may appreciate some of the motives that inspired them, it is hard to view the Societies as other than aberrant examples of associated philanthropy.

The Society for Promoting Christian Knowledge, an expression of forces similar to those that had produced the earlier Societies, prescribed a different remedy for the evils that had distressed them. If the reform of morals and manners could not be accomplished through the sanctions of the law, Christian schooling might serve to stem "that Inundation of Profaneness and Immorality which we find of late broke in upon us." [14] Conceivably the faults complained of in the English poor — their immorality, improvidence, and irreligion — were the fruits of an undisciplined youth. Rather than schemes for reforming the behavior of adults, what was needed, perhaps, was a mechanism which would subject the children of the poor to discipline, train them in habits of industry, and inculcate in them moral attitudes and the teachings of the Protestant religion. In the charity school the early eighteenth century hopefully saw itself fashioning such a mechanism.[15]

The S.P.C.K., whose early fortunes were closely bound up with the charity schools, was the creation of the Reverend Thomas Bray — an admirable exemplar of philanthropic piety — and a group of friends. Like most of his kind, Bray, too, represented the middle orders of society, in his case rural society, for his family for generations had tilled a Shropshire farm. What launched him on his career as a philanthropist and provided him with one of the chief interests of his philanthropic career was an appointment as Commissary for Maryland, with which went the responsibility for maintaining an acceptable clergy in the colony. In trying

[10] G. V. Portus, *Caritas Anglicana* (London, 1912), p. 49.

[11] *Ibid.*, p. 77.

[12] *The Poor Man's Plea*, quoted in Gray, *English Philanthropy*, p. 90.

[13] Nelson, *Address*, p. 151.

[14] W. O. B. Allen and Edmund McClure, *Two Hundred Years: the History of the Society for Promoting Christian Knowledge, 1698–1898* (London, 1898), p. 10.

[15] For comment on the social philosophy embodied in the charity schools see R. H. Tawney's review of Miss Jones's book in the *Economic History Review*, 9:201–4 (1939).

to work his way through this problem the learned and devoted Bray became a precursor of the library movement. For it was obvious that such clergymen as could be persuaded to make the crossing would have to be provided with books. From this necessity developed his plans for parochial libraries. In his volume *Bibliotheca Parochialis* (1697) Bray explained his project in elaborate detail, with a formidable list of books suitable for clerical reading and study arranged under a series of subheadings. It was, to say the least, an impressive demonstration of learning and industry.[16]

Before he went to Maryland in 1699, Bray invested about £1775 of the nearly £2500 he had raised in more than seventy colonial libraries, forty-four receiving more than a minimal amount.[17] These were not simply professional libraries for the clergy but included works on history and travel, mathematics, biographies, the Latin classics, and an occasional volume of poetry.[18] Although it was the colonies, with their desperate intellectual poverty, that benefited most conspicuously from Bray's library projects, the homeland was not neglected. At the end of the century Bray and a committee of the S.P.C.K. took the lead in a movement to supply rural parishes and market towns with collections of books. He himself was enough convinced of the value of the plan to leave his personal library to any market town — it turned out to be Maidstone — which would add £50 for setting up a lending library. The committee, on which appeared, among others, the names of Robert Nelson and Henry Hoare, the banker, showed more than a little resourcefulness, raising about £1750 for the purpose in the years 1706–10 and inspiring an Act of Parliament (1708) "for the better preserving of parochial libraries."[19] Nearly seventy parochial libraries appear to have been founded during Bray's lifetime, and after his death the Associates of the Reverend Dr. Bray continued the estimable work.[20]

As established in the spring of 1699, the S.P.C.K. was a less imposing agency than Bray had hoped to found. His original plan had contemplated an Anglican body comparable to the Roman *Congregatio pro Propaganda Fide,* and the organizational model was to have been the Sons of the Clergy Corporation, which had been chartered by Charles II and had grown into a popular and increasingly well-

[16] The section on Bray is based largely on H. P. Thompson, *Thomas Bray* (London, 1954), which in turn makes extensive use of a number of articles by Professor S. C. McCulloch. For Bray's preparatory labors, see McCulloch, "Dr. Thomas Bray's Commissary Work in London, 1696–1699," *William and Mary Quarterly,* ser. 3, 2:333–48 (1945).

[17] Thompson, *Thomas Bray,* p. 29. Contributions were received not only from individuals but from religious societies and corporate bodies. Altogether, during these years, Bray spent nearly £3000 on his projects, leaving a deficit of nearly £500 to be made good by himself. (These figures do not agree precisely with those in McCulloch's article cited above.)

[18] S. C. McCulloch, "The Importance of Dr. Thomas Bray's *Bibliotheca Parochialis,*" *Historical Magazine of the P. E. Church,* 15:58 (1946).

[19] 7 Anne, c. 14.

[20] On this subject, see *The Parochial Libraries of the Church of England* (London, 1959), a report by a committee of the Central Council for the Care of Churches. Of the 253 parochial libraries listed in the report, only a minority were the direct result of the activity of Bray and the S.P.C.K., but from the numbers of libraries established in the same period there is reason to believe that their appeals may have aroused the interest of other benefactors.

supported charity. Contributions and bequests, in addition to the Corporation's annual festivals, were swelling its resources.[21] But there was reason to doubt whether the time was propitious for launching such an official body. Bray therefore fell back on the expedient of an informal society composed, at the outset, of himself and four friends who covenanted together to "promote Christian knowledge" as an antidote to the vice and immorality which they attributed to "gross ignorance of the principles of the Christian religion."[22] In its early days the S.P.C.K. was hardly more than a voluntary association, small in numbers but devoted and enthusiastic, for carrying out Bray's program. With the exception of Bray himself, all of the original members were laymen, and, as the group slowly expanded, it continued to be an effective fusion of bishops, lower clergy, and laity, while contriving to avoid any marked theological or political coloration. Indeed, S.P.C.K. leaders were tinged with every shade of opinion from non-juring to latitudinarian, including both extremes.[23]

3

The major achievement of the Society for Promoting Christian Knowledge, as far as this study is concerned, was its sponsorship of the charity school movement. The cause of the charity schools enlisted the personal efforts and financial support of thousands of English, Welsh, and Scots, who in the first half of the century established a far-ranging system of free schools for the children of the poor, which stood, in the view of Richard Steele, as "the greatest instances of public spirit the age had produced."[24] The raw figures alone offer a convincing demonstration of the force that could be mobilized through the association of numbers of individuals in a common philanthropic endeavor. In 1729, for example, 1419 schools are said to have been in operation in England with 22,503 pupils (5225 in London and Westminster) enrolled.[25] The movement in Wales, which reached its peak somewhat later than in England and took on a rather different character, could claim nearly 3500 schools, with more than 150,000 pupils, founded between 1737 and 1761.[26]

[21] In 1714, for example, the Corporation, as residuary legatee of Dr. Thomas Turner, President of Corpus Christi College, Oxford, became the richer by £18,000. At the turn of the century clerical widows and children were receiving over £500 a year. (E. H. Pearce, *The Sons of the Clergy, 1655–1904* [London, 1928], pp. 118, 155.)

[22] From the declaration to be signed by all members of the Society. (Thompson, *Bray,* p. 38.) See also S. C. McCulloch, "The Foundation and Early Work of the Society for Promoting Christian Knowledge," *Historical Magazine of the P. E. Church,* 18:3–22 (1949).

[23] It ought perhaps to be noted in passing that the S.P.C.K. sired the other great Church organization of the time, the Society for the Propagation of the Gospel in Foreign Parts. A visit to Maryland had convinced Bray that to support and organize missionary work in the colonies lay beyond the capacities of the S.P.C.K. and that the crisis demanded a Church auxiliary created specifically for the purpose. In due course King William granted his petition for a charter. (H. P. Thompson, *Into All Lands* [London, 1951], pp. 15–19.)

[24] Quoted in Jones, *Charity School Movement,* p. 59.

[25] *Ibid.,* p. 72. The discussion of charity schools that follows is based, in a large measure, on Miss Jones's admirable study. As a rule, I have given page references only for direct quotations and for statistical material.

[26] *Welch Piety* (anon.), London, 1761, p. 49.

The S.P.C.K. is not, of course, entitled to exclusive credit for the movement. A good many charity schools (in the sense of nonclassical schools for the children of the poor) had been endowed earlier in the century, and in 1685 two London clergymen had countered the challenge of a Jesuit charity school by setting up two Anglican establishments.[27] Among the charitable middle classes the extraordinary popularity of such schools owed a good deal to their assumed effectiveness in protecting the poor (and hence their betters) against the dangers that threatened. If the children of the poor could be at once immunized against the contagion of Popery, which was insidiously working to corrupt the faith of individuals and destroy the Protestant Succession, and drilled in habits of industry and sobriety, the gain in social stability would more than justify the comparatively modest financial outlay. Religious training was the prescription, and the charity school the instrument. The easy and certain way, the Bishop of Chester could proclaim in a charity sermon, "to Reform the Lives of a Class of Mankind, which, to the utmost Degree, needed Reformation . . . is, by beginning early with Children, before any evil Habit has taken Possession of them." [28]

Before the founding of the S.P.C.K., the approaches to the problem had been isolated and tentative. What the Society did, in Miss Jones's words, was to weld "together the separate and occasional charity of the benevolent into an organised movement for the education of the poor." [29] A model was at hand in Hermann Francke's school and orphanage at Halle, a pietist institution where the modicum of ordinary education provided was purely incidental to the main purpose of religious discipline. That a degree of public interest already existed is indicated by the immediate and generous response to the Society's initial appeal for support. Within a few months the directing committee had an operating fund of £450 and was carrying on an active correspondence with the clergy throughout the country, exhorting, advising, and strengthening the hands of local leaders. For the S.P.C.K., rather than attempting to create its own system of schools, was content to serve as a central bureau. In the "Rules and Orders" in its *Account of Charity Schools* of 1704 the Society established the standard form of organization, and it stood ready to assist local leaders by counseling on curriculum, supplying the names of possible teachers, and advising on financial problems. As financial counselor the central organization was able to give publicity to the method of financing-by-subscription, which permitted sympathizers of modest means to share in the work.[30]

The schools themselves were local enterprises, and their degree of success de-

[27] Dr. Symon Patrick, Dean of Peterborough, established one in St. Margaret's, Westminster; and Dr. Tenison, then Rector of St. Martin's-in-the-Fields, another in St. James's, Westminster.

[28] William Dawes, *The Excellency of the Charity of the Charity Schools,* St. Sepulchre, 1713, pp. 16–17.

[29] Jones, *Charity School Movement,* p. 38.

[30] Clarke, *S.P.C.K.,* p. 24. From his study of the minutes, Clarke concludes (p. 22) that the schools were a less important component of the total S.P.C.K. effort than one would gather from Miss Jones's account.

pended, in a large measure, on the interest and ability of the local people who could be enlisted in the cause. Endowed schools — over six hundred of these were founded during the first three decades of the century[31] — were, of course, less vulnerable than subscription schools, but even these could be made or ruined by their trustees. It was the subscription schools, financed as they were on a hand-to-mouth basis by local contributions and managed by the subscribers, that offered a stiffer test for the initiative and organizing talent of local middle-class leaders. For, although the wealthy and well-born might still establish schools by endowment, the day-to-day work of carrying on the subscription schools rested solidly on the backs of the "middling folk" of the community. In London and some of the other urban centers, tradesmen and their friends, inspired and guided by the S.P.C.K., carried their responsibilities with much credit to themselves and the Society. Five years after the launching of the S.P.C.K., there were fifty-four schools in London and Westminster, with annual subscriptions amounting to £2164, one of them receiving nearly £200. The total gifts to another came to nearly £1100.[32]

Obviously London had special advantages. Teachers were in moderately good supply, as were distinguished clergymen to preach the charity sermons on which the schools depended for a part of their income; the London labor market could readily absorb boys and girls trained in charity schools; and most important of all, the large middle-class stratum in the London population would support the schools for reasons of civic pride as well as conviction. The schools of the Metropolis, some of which accumulated substantial endowments in the course of the century, attained a much higher standard and greater degree of permanence than those in the provinces.

Two City institutions can stand as representative of the relatively solid and long-lived London schools. The older of these, the Redcross Street School of St. Giles's, Cripplegate, antedated by several years the S.P.C.K. itself. In 1690 some interested members of the parish formed a charity school society, and two years later, aided by a sermon by the Bishop of Gloucester, opened a school of sorts. A £200 legacy from a City merchant encouraged the managers to buy land in Redcross Street, and £550 raised from 160 contributors made possible the erection of a school building for a hundred boys.[33] At the same time, a bequest from Lady Eleanor Holles, daughter of the Earl of Clare, financed the opening of a school for fifty girls in a wing of the new building.

Both schools had reasonably prosperous histories, in spite of the untoward circumstances that tend to plague such ventures. One of these, incidentally, is called to mind by the list, almost a casualty list, of the fifteen masters who served the boys' school during the quarter-century 1710–35. Of these, six resigned, four died, three

[31] Jones, *Charity School Movement*, App. I.
[32] *Ibid.*, p. 57.
[33] Guildhall Library MS 75; William Denton, *Records of St. Giles' Cripplegate* (London, 1883), pp. 148–49.

were dismissed, one ran away, and the fate of the other is not known. But the Redcross Street institutions were relatively well supported. Owing to legacies and the rise in property values, they became increasingly independent of subscriptions, charity sermons, and *ad hoc* collections. In 1735, for example, interest and rent provided the boys' school with more than a third of its income, and by the early nineteenth century the balance had shifted, with more than 90 per cent of the revenue being drawn from these sources.[34] This proved adequate for educating and clothing 102 boys and apprenticing about ten each year. The girls' school, with its larger endowment, had even less trouble in making ends meet and in the course of the century was able to double its enrollment.[35]

St. Anne's, Blackfriars, got its school with less expenditure of effort than had been demanded of St. Giles's. In 1704 Peter Joye offered to found a school on land to be supplied by the parish, and as compared with similar institutions, he made fairly handsome provision for its support. But the resources of Joye's School increased less strikingly than did those of many City schools, probably because they were invested chiefly in farm land. After a century and a half the income of the School had grown from £161 to only £244.[36] A few items culled from the four minute books, which carry from 1707 to 1872, will recall some of the human problems with which these early educational philanthropists were forced to wrestle:[37]

7 October 1710. "Ordered that for the future if any Parent shall insult or abuse the Master or Mistress of the School in the Discharge of their Duty by way of Correction, their Child shall be excluded from the School ipso facto."

5 October 1720. "Mrs. Knight apply'd for her Son Henry Knight's Clothes but they being worn not above two Months she was Ordered to Return them and he his Bible was given him [on leaving school]."

29 June 1725. "Agreed that the Master and Mistress be ordered to keep the Clothes of such Children in their respective Schools as they suspect will abuse or imbezzel them and oblige all such to dress at school every Sunday morning and undress there in the Evening."

28 March 1765. The Master having complained against the mother of James Collins "for suffering her said Boy to go from Place to Place as Errand-boy instead of keeping him at School, the same was examined into; and it appearing that poverty and a large Family was the occasion for her so doing, and that the boy had learned as much as he could, the Gentlemen present allowed her to continue

[34] In 1735 the boys' school received £71 out of a total income of £175 from interest and rent, with only £14 6s. from subscriptions, the balance being made up by sermons, lectures, and a contribution from the Ironmongers' Company. (Guildhall Library MS 75; *2d Report of the Commissioners on the Education of the Poor,* 1819, X-B, 63–65.)

[35] *2d Report,* pp. 65–66. In the mid-nineteenth century the enrollment stood at 150, with an income from rent of £761 and from interest of £571. Twenty years later the income exceeded £1465. (Reports by Thomas Hare, 11 Dec. 1855 and 9 May 1871, *R. C. on the City Parochial Charities* [C. 2522], 1880, III, App. III, pp. 176, 187.)

[36] Report by Thomas Hare, 24 Nov. 1854, *ibid.,* pp. 48–50; Guildhall Library MS 9192–1.

[37] Guildhall Library MSS 1706, 9192.

him in the said capacity, till he shall come of Age to be put Apprentice, upon her Promise of sending him to School whenever he should be out of place."

Outside of London a few cities, notably Bristol and Newcastle-on-Tyne, were conspicuous for the number and quality of their charity schools. In the country districts, however, the movement encountered almost insuperable obstacles. The methods of associated philanthropy — which had built the London system — were not adapted to the countryside. Hostility of farmers, shortage of teachers, lack of middle-class leadership, these difficulties plagued the S.P.C.K. for as long as its interest in charity schools continued. There were exceptions, of course, most conspicuously in dioceses where the bishop himself was prepared to champion the movement; and in some neighborhoods the gentry supported or endowed schools as a private philanthropy. But the accomplishments of the charity school movement in the provinces were incomparably less than in London.

4

To understand the arid and meager curriculum of the English charity schools, one must recall their aim. They were not intended to be centers for mental training but "pious nurseries" for godly discipline. In these the children of the poor would receive religious instruction and social conditioning, from which they would emerge as industrious, sober, and docile members of a society which saw them as future hewers of wood and drawers of water. Submission and gratitude to their benefactors, these were the qualities which the teaching was designed to inculcate. "Make me dutiful and obedient to my benefactors . . . Make me temperate and chaste, meek and patient, true in all my dealings and industrious in my station," ran the opening prayer at a girls' charity school in the latter half of the century.[38] In schools where clothing was supplied to the children, managers went to some lengths to make sure that the uniform would be so dull and somber as to discourage vanity in the wearers.[39] But their anxiety to avoid any suggestion of educating the children beyond their station did not save them from frequent and bitter charges of doing precisely that. Later in the century Lord Kames could dismiss charity schools as "more hurtful than beneficial: young persons who continue there so long as to read and write fluently become too delicate for hard labour and too proud for ordinary labour."[40] Charity school children did, in fact, show something of a tendency to leave the ranks of unskilled labor and make their way as apprentices into counting-houses and retail establishments.

[38] *Poor Girls' Primer* (Sheffield Girls' Charity School), 1789, quoted in Jones, *Charity School Movement*, p. 75.

[39] Even so, clothes were no minor item in a charity school budget, and whether, on leaving school, children were entitled to keep them became a perennial source of contention between school and parents. By the 1730's the expenses of clothing at Peter Joye's School ran to £50–£60 a year out of a total annual expenditure of under £200. At the same period the Redcross School paid about £175 for clothing a hundred boys. (Guildhall Library MSS 75, 9192.)

[40] Lord Kames, *Sketches*, II, 50.

In a large measure the charity school curriculum consisted of religious instruction, as prescribed in *The Christian Schoolmaster,* a manual supplied by the S.P.C.K. Beyond this, most schools professed to offer the three R's, though without the high-minded purposefulness that informed their religious and moral teaching. About reading there could be no argument, for it was a means of access to the Catechism, the Book of Common Prayer, and the Bible. Writing, too, could be appropriately learned by more advanced pupils. But only after they had proved their ability to read and write, and then only in boys' schools, was there training in arithmetic. Although at one time some sentiment developed for grafting onto the so-called "literary curriculum" a plan of setting the school children to work, thus "inuring them to labour," this came to little. In girls' schools, to be sure, where the children were being prepared for domestic service, vocational training bulked large. Here the "literary curriculum" came to an end with a modicum of proficiency in reading, and in place of the other two R's, they were taught sewing and knitting. On the whole, however, the working charity schools failed to make a place for themselves, and their failure very likely cost the movement some of the public goodwill it had previously enjoyed.[41]

More disastrous in their effect on the charity school enterprise were the politico-religious struggles of the early century. Although the S.P.C.K. had striven with a good deal of success for comprehension in its membership, this did not save it from attack. The original purpose of the schools, that of countering Roman Catholic influence, assured the support of Dissenters, which in turn invited the assaults of the High Church Right. Both sides saw the schools as powerful weapons in the hands of whichever party could gain control of them. In the end, victory lay with Whiggery, Low Churchmanship, and the Protestant Succession, but at the cost of alienating supporters on both wings. The High Church attacks permanently estranged the Dissenters, and the S.P.C.K., alarmed at the bitterness of the factional conflict, gradually shifted some of its emphasis from schools to less controversial areas, notably missionary and publishing work.[42]

Elsewhere in the United Kingdom the course followed by the charity school movement was markedly different from that of the English philanthropy. Across St. George's Channel the project of transmuting Catholic Irishmen into Protestant Englishmen through charity school education achieved the meager success that, with the wisdom of hindsight, one might have predicted. In Edinburgh a Scottish S.P.C.K. attempted to introduce the civilizing influence of education into the Highlands and to check the progress of Popery. Unlike its English analogue, the Scottish Society closely supervised the schools it sponsored, handling their financial affairs, arranging curricula, appointing teachers, and deciding when they were to move to new locations — for these were itinerant institutions which might be shifted, after two or three years, to neighborhoods of greater need. By the mid-

[41] See Clarke, *S.P.C.K.,* pp. 44ff.
[42] The political controversy over the schools is discussed by Miss Jones in some detail in *Charity School Movement,* chap. IV.

century, the Edinburgh S.P.C.K. was claiming 150 schools with an attendance of over 6000.[43]

Wales offered what was, in many respects, a refreshing contrast; for the Principality, to quote Miss Jones, "was the scene of the most successful and sustained movement for the education of the poor in the eighteenth century."[44] About the Welsh schools there was little of the ulterior social and political motivation, only partly conscious, that colored the movement in other parts of the Kingdom. Charity schools in Wales were not designed as mechanisms for drilling the lower classes in the attitudes and responses most agreeable to their betters, and they operated without apparent class bias, the achievement of a society that still had about it a good deal of rough egalitarianism.[45] What bothered Welsh reformers was the simple indifference to religion of the bulk of their fellow countrymen — for no one would have associated an addiction to Bible-reading and hymn-singing with the Welshman of 1700.

The S.P.C.K. accepted the challenge presented by the backwardness of Wales and, with the active support of some of the Welsh gentry and clergy,[46] set about to improve the situation. The ground had been prepared in the 1670's by the Welsh Trust of Firmin's friend, the Reverend Thomas Gouge, which, as noted earlier in the chapter, issued devotional works in the vernacular (the Welsh Bible appeared in 1677–78) and established a number of schools for the children of the poor. In Wales the S.P.C.K. departed from the policy it had followed in England and itself founded numbers of schools, nearly a hundred in the first four decades of the century.

The most spectacular expansion of Welsh charity schools, however, took place in the mid-century and was connected with the name of Griffith Jones, rector of Llandowror, Carmarthenshire. It was Jones who was responsible for the new departure of itinerant schools and who organized and managed the spaciously conceived scheme. This was, in the best sense, a revolutionary plan, and it produced revolutionary results. During the years of Jones's leadership (1737–61), nearly 3500 schools were set up, and in 1761, the year of his death, 210 were in actual operation.[47] The whole enterprise was carried on at an absurdly low cost, which was borne in part by the Welsh poor and near-poor themselves and in part by well-to-do supporters, the most notable being the wealthy and pious widow Bridget Bevan. For fourteen years she underwrote the itinerant schools movement, but when she died in 1779, disaster came swiftly. The £10,000 trust that she established for the work was contested, and the bequest remained in Chancery for more than three decades.

Though the movement met an untimely end, its impact on Welsh society was

[43] *Ibid.*, pp. 179–83.

[44] *Ibid.*, p. 277.

[45] Tawney stresses this point in his review (previously cited, n. 15 above), p. 204.

[46] Notably Sir John Philipps of Picton Castle, Pembrokeshire.

[47] By its nature the itinerant school was an ephemeral institution. The figure 3500 evidently covers all of the places where masters opened schools for shorter or longer periods.

decisive. The introduction of Welshmen to the Bible and to a variety of improving
works in their own language had a great deal to do with forming a new national
character, with converting a gay and happy-go-lucky race into a people with an
almost intemperate concern for religion and politics.[48] In both Scotland and Ireland the charity schools followed models that were predominantly English, but
those in the Principality were, in a special degree, Welsh. Reading material was
printed in the native tongue and instruction given in the vernacular. This was
both a matter of choice on the part of the leaders and necessity, since for vast
numbers of Welsh children English was a foreign language. The charity schools
were thus no negligible factor in promoting the national revival of the nineteenth
century, both the literary-linguistic renaissance and, less directly, a new sense of
political distinctiveness.

To strike a balance sheet for the charity school movement as a whole would
be to do little more than to restate Miss Jones's conclusions. The schools varied
enormously in quality and effectiveness. Among them were the feeble and transient, the well established and relatively permanent. The survival record of those
with substantial endowments, such as some of the London and Westminster institutions, was naturally better than those which depended on annual subscriptions.
In the early nineteenth century, the Brougham inquiries[49] found many of the
endowments to be inadequate and maladministered, but some of the schools were
carrying on with a fair measure of success. Such foundations, under the pressure
of Charity Commissioners and educational reformers, were gradually adapted to
new needs. Some introduced the monitorial system of instruction and affiliated
with the National Society, and numbers were put through the same kind of
reorganization that other endowments received at the hands of the Charity
Commissioners and the Endowed Schools Commissioners. Plainly the legacies
and capital gifts to charity schools substantially increased the resources of the
country for elementary education, and this outpouring, as Miss Jones suggests,
had something to do with implanting in Englishmen the conviction that education was a field for voluntary action rather than a public responsibility.

The subscription schools fared less well. Many of them had only a brief and
troubled existence, and, as the rosier illusions of the pioneering days were shattered
and as the interest of the S.P.C.K. shifted, the mortality rate mounted. How many
of these managed to last after the mid-century is beyond the realm even of conjecture. But under the twin impulses of the Evangelical Revival and of an industry
which demanded regular labor of masses of children, the tradition of the subscription charity school re-emerged late in the century to produce the Sunday School.

The charity school movement also placed its stamp on British philanthropic
methods. Despite its manifest shortcomings, this first large-scale venture in associated philanthropy offered a convincing demonstration of what could be accomplished by the pooling of individual effort. Not only that but, more specifically,

[48] Jones, *Charity School Movement*, p. 321.
[49] Described in Chapter VII.

the pattern of a central committee guiding the work of numbers of local committees became a commonplace in organizing good works on a national scale. In dozens of other causes the same technique was employed, and, in some degree, the charity school movement supplied the model which was unconsciously followed by subsequent reforming and philanthropic enterprises.

The S.P.C.K. and its allies showed no little skill in dramatizing their work and thus commending it to the support of the charitable. The special charity service, to which the school children would "march two and two, in good order, all whole and tight in the same clothes," [50] had a tremendous appeal and would very likely pack the church. To see the objects of one's benevolence so neatly turned out and so well behaved was a heartening experience, and those who enjoyed the complacent emotion would probably contribute generously, especially if the preacher were a well-known figure. There was, in fact, a good deal of competition among charity schools for the assistance of the more distinguished and eloquent members of the hierarchy. These special services, held annually, semiannually, or quarterly, early became a chief financial resource, and they could bring in surprising amounts. One sermon at St. Margaret's, Westminster, yielded nearly £165, while St. Dunstan's-in-the-West received about £62 from two sermons preached on February 22, 1788 — but St. Dunstan's was fortunate in having two generous bankers, Henry Hoare and Francis Child, as interested parishioners.[51] In any case, the charity sermon, popularized in the service of the charity school movement, became an accepted method of raising money for philanthropic causes.

The annual assembly of the London charity schools, held each year from 1704 to 1877, proved an inspired stratagem for drawing public attention. The idea originated with the S.P.C.K., but management early passed into the hands of a Society of Patrons of the Anniversary of Charity Schools, which continued to work closely with the older body.[52] Until 1781, the assemblies were held chiefly in St. Sepulchre's, Snow Hill, and Christ Church, Newgate Street, and from 1782 in St. Paul's. Even in the Cathedral, the crowds — averaging 4500 children and 7500 others[53] — far exceeded the capacity of the great church, and wooden galleries had to be erected each year. For this was one of the sights of London, to delight tourists and give natives a pardonable thrill of self-satisfaction:

> O what a multitude they seem'd, these flowers of London town!
> Seated in companies they sit with radiance all their own.
> The hum of multitudes was there, but multitudes of lambs,
> Thousands of little boys and girls raising their innocent hands.[54]

Like a local charity service multiplied many times over, the army of well-scrubbed children marching by parishes, each school in its distinctive garb, seemed a dra-

[50] Jones, p. 58.
[51] Clarke, *S.P.C.K.*, p. 35; Guildhall Library MS 3004–1.
[52] Allen and McClure, *Two Hundred Years*, p. 150.
[53] *Ibid.*, p. 149.
[54] William Blake, "Holy Thursday."

matic proof of the reality of British charity and an irrefutable argument for associated benevolence. The schools might be summoned in force for occasions of national thanksgiving — the accession of George I, the recovery of George III, or the
ending of a war. When the coming of peace was celebrated in 1713, some four
thousand charity children viewed the spectacle from eight rows of elevated benches
running six hundred feet along the Strand, "where they saluted the two Houses of
Parliament and the great officers of state, with hymns sung in unison." [55] Though
no doubt innocent of such pecuniary motives, the charity school trustees who
financed the gathering could justifiably have charged the cost to publicity.

5

Like other innovations in the charity world, the charity school assemblies were
chiefly the handiwork of Robert Nelson, who can stand as the representative
philanthropist of the early century and was admired by the age as the special
embodiment of Christian charity. The son of a wealthy Turkey merchant, in his
origins Nelson conformed closely to the pattern of the eighteenth-century philanthropist. Though solidly High Church and Tory in his views — for twenty years
after 1689 he obstinately held to his non-juring position — he was too much the
philanthropist to be the bigot. Although they had drifted apart in middle life,
Archbishop Tillotson, whose conception of the Church was at the opposite pole
from Nelson's, is said to have died in his arms, [56] and he was on easy terms with
Thomas Firmin.

Nelson was not a theologian but a devout Christian who sought holiness and
who found it, in part, in the practice of his religion. Not even in the ranks of
professed Nonconformists would one discover a more perfect expression of the
Puritan spirit or a more satisfying exemplar of the philanthropy of eighteenth-
century piety. Nelson's mission, as he conceived it, was to call the upper and
middle classes to repentance and to lay upon their aroused Christian conscience
a responsibility for the poor and ignorant. To persons of quality he commends
the Religious Societies, and he sees in the Society for the Reformation of Manners
a mechanism, blessed by God, for "Rescuing Souls from everlasting Destruction." [57] Much of his energy was, in fact, devoted to specifically religious interests,
though in his case it is uncommonly difficult to separate religion from philanthropy, for he saw them as indissolubly joined. He was the author of a series of
devotional and homiletic works, of which his *Companion for the Festivals and
Fasts of the Church of England* (1704) went through some twenty-eight editions
in the course of the century. [58] Among the more ardent Churchfolk this nontechnical introduction to Anglican theology came to be regarded as the ideal
gift book.

[55] J. P. Malcolm, *Anecdotes of the Manners and Customs of London during the Eighteenth Century,*
2d ed., 2 vols. (London, 1810), I, 19.
[56] C. F. Secretan, *Memoirs of the Life and Work of Pious Robert Nelson* (London, 1860), p. 47.
[57] Nelson, *Address,* p. 154.
[58] Secretan, *Memoirs of Robert Nelson,* p. 166.

In the realm of action, Nelson's exertions were limited only by his time and strength. Especially during the last two or three decades of his life (1656–1715), he apparently gave himself exclusively to the work of furthering his religious and charitable interests. He was an early, though not a charter, member of both the S.P.C.K. and the S.P.G., his omission from the list of S.P.G. founders being very likely the result of his non-juring views, which he took no pains to conceal. As a leader in the S.P.C.K., Nelson had a finger in many (or most) of the Society's pies. At various times we discover him as a member of a committee to establish lending libraries in Wales, reporting a gift from the Earl of Berkeley for the relief of French confessors in the galleys, attempting unsuccessfully to get reprieved prisoners moved out of Newgate, and waiting upon Sir Christopher Wren with a proposal to hold charity school anniversaries in St. Paul's.[59]

But it was in the charity school movement that Nelson found his fullest and most satisfying outlet. He undertook to advise the local sponsors of schools at York, Nayland in Suffolk, Beverley, Leicester, Wootton-under-Edge, Cirencester, Tring, and Bray. For the new school at Bath he managed to find a master who made of it one of the three or four most effective provincial schools, and he performed a similar service for St. Anne's, Soho. At home, he was a trustee of St. Andrew's School, Holborn, and promoter of the school of St. George's, Queen Square. From *The Whole Duty of Man,* an anonymous work which enjoyed esteem second only to the Bible and the Prayer Book, he compiled a catechism for use in the schools. As the most active of the Patrons of the Anniversary of Charity Schools, upon Nelson fell the major responsibility for these annual festivals. He had to make arrangements for preachers and financial support, to handle details of the procession and seating, and even to take steps to insure reasonable behavior on the part of the four thousand children being exhibited. On one occasion, the S.P.C.K. instructed him to get word, through the local trustees, to masters and mistresses "strictly to charge the children under their care to observe a due decorum . . . and to keep silence when the service requires it." [60]

It is hardly possible even to note the other religious-philanthropic interests of this prodigy of good works — his support of Bray's parochial library projects, for example, and his services as one of the commissioners appointed in 1710 to arrange for the building of fifty new churches in the Metropolis.[61] What is more to the point is to recall Nelson as a shrewd and knowledgeable observer of his society, who, in spite of the Puritan spectacles through which he viewed the life around him, canvassed the social needs of his time and outlined a considered program of philanthropic giving for his well-to-do contemporaries. Naturally enough his suggestions reflect his own prepossessions and those of the age, but, viewed in its own context, Nelson's *Address to Persons of Quality and Estate,* of which his

---

[59] *Ibid.,* pp. 107–31.

[60] *Ibid.,* p. 131.

[61] The Commission made little specific progress until after Nelson's death, and then only a fraction of the projected buildings were completed.

"Ways and Methods of Doing Good" forms a part, must be put down as a remarkably prescient document.

Nelson's purpose was to appeal to the Christian beliefs and humanitarian sensibilities of the upper classes and to indicate in a systematic fashion the particular areas where their charitable energies and contributions could be most usefully employed. For even when the hearts of those in plentiful circumstances are ready to assist the poor, "they may be at a Loss for fit and proper Objects to exercise their Charity upon." [62] In his exhortation to those of superior station, Nelson's premises are, of course, those of a Christianity which enjoins charity on those who profess to follow it and of a Divine Law which has imposed on the rich the duty of looking after the poor. But those who give to the poor and feed the hungry are not merely obeying God's command; they are also following a natural impulse, responding to that "compassionate Sense of the Misfortunes of others deeply rooted in our natures." [63] Resting as it does on an innate sympathy, the practice of charity can also be the source of exquisite pleasure to the philanthropist himself. And, he reminds his readers a bit ominously, there is always the Day of Judgment, and the great "Stress . . . laid on CHARITY, without which we shall certainly perish among the Reprobate." [64]

Much of Nelson's general appeal was commonplace enough, the stock content of charity sermons. Of greater significance is the section of more than a hundred pages entitled "Ways and Methods of Doing Good." Here he surveys the charitable activities in progress and then notices some of the sore spots in British society which invite the attention of the philanthropist. Many of the enterprises that he commends, especially those dealt with under the rubric "Wants relating to the Souls of Men," are precisely what one would anticipate. They are, on the whole, the causes for which he labored most single-mindedly — the S.P.C.K., the S.P.G., charity schools, and the rest. In considering the "Wants relating to the Bodies of Men," he allows his imagination greater play. In his examination he not only covers the chief areas of charitable effort of his day but also notes, sometimes with an amazingly prophetic eye, evils in English life which the hand of the philanthropist might ameliorate.

Some of these were already drawing support: the Corporation of the Sons of the Clergy was beginning to attract substantial gifts, and Nelson could cite a few examples of "poor distressed Housekeepers" and their families tided over periods of unemployment, and "decay'd Tradesmen" enabled to continue in business through a bad season. He professed a warm interest in projects for educating the poor in industry, which, he had no doubt, was a better remedy for crime "than all the Gibbets and Whipping-Posts in the Kingdom." [65] The plight of prisoners had also begun to impress humane souls, who were distressed by the unjust

[62] Nelson, *Address*, p. 101.
[63] *Ibid.*, p. 102.
[64] *Ibid.*, p. 239.
[65] *Ibid.*, p. 179.

sufferings of those in English gaols for small debts and more deeply and roman-
tically moved by Britons held captive by the Turks or immured in a prison of
the Inquisition. Certainly to discharge debtors was a useful act of Christian charity
and a "Method of Doing Good [which, Nelson pointed out] may be made more
extensive than is easily apprehended at first." [66]

It was when Nelson passed from work in progress to "wants" that he became
most suggestive. The great schools, hospitals, and other charities of London, he
eloquently concluded, may turn out to be "but a Reproach to the Present" unless
British philanthropy pushes ahead to meet new wants. One of the most critical
gaps had to do with medical charities, where Nelson discovered a need for better
provision for the incurable and a series of institutions for special diseases — for
such afflictions, perhaps, as diseases of the eye, gout, stone, dropsy, asthma, rheumatism, and consumption. Two classes of unfortunates, exposed infants and penitents, had drawn his sympathetic eye, and his call for refuges for them was to be
answered before too many decades by Captain Coram and Jonas Hanway.[67] The
human refuse of the streets, the children "called the *Black-Guard*," should be
provided with schools or hospitals (refuges), an interesting forecast of the nineteenth-century Ragged School. To modern eyes some of his other "wants," such
as a college for receiving converts from Popery, will appear less urgent than they
did to the devoutly Protestant Nelson. But precisely because he was so much a
man of his age, Nelson's "Ways and Methods of Doing Good" seems the more
remarkable both as a survey of the charitable activities of the day and as a preview
of the philanthropy of the century.

[66] *Ibid.*, p. 195.
[67] A hospital for penitents had been proposed by Thomas Bray in 1698 in *A General Plan of a
Penitential Hospital for Employing and Reforming Lewd Women.* (S. C. McCulloch, "Dr. Thomas
Bray's Commissary Work in London," previously cited, n. 16.)

CHAPTER II

THE PHILANTHROPY OF EIGHTEENTH-CENTURY HUMANITARIANISM

T O C L A S S I F Y men's charitable acts into neat categories according to the impulses assumed to have prompted them would be dangerous and absurd. Human behavior rarely exhibits such helpful singleness of motive. Still, if one takes the two most noteworthy philanthropic achievements of the eighteenth century, the charity schools and the hospital movement, it is clear that, with the former, religious purposes predominated, while the latter must be ascribed to other and more complex motives, social, scientific, humanitarian. Both groups of institutions, incidentally, instance the conviction of the eighteenth (and nineteenth) century that education and medical care, insofar as the individual was unable to manage for himself, might be properly left to the associated effort of private philanthropists. It took many decades before Englishmen concluded, first for elementary education and later for medical care, that these interests were too vital to be left to the hit-or-miss operation of private charity.

In the realm of secular philanthropy the eighteenth century accomplished nothing of more ultimate importance than to lay the foundation of the voluntary hospital system. Before 1700 there were only the Royal Hospitals of St. Bartholomew and St. Thomas, and one or two special institutions in London and the provinces.[1] Between 1719 and 1750, five new general hospitals were founded in the Metropolis, along with nine in the country, a figure which reached thirty-one by 1800.[2] These were in addition to a number of special hospitals and a small multitude of dispensaries which appeared in force in the last three decades of the century.

It would be idle to speculate on the magnitude of charitable investment represented by these enterprises, but individual balance sheets indicate that, from the beginning, the hospital held a strong appeal for the philanthropic and was likely to become a powerful competitor — in the latter nineteenth century, the dominant competitor — for the pounds and shillings of charity. The London Hospital, for

---

[1] Such as Bethlem, also a Royal Hospital, and Bellott's Mineral Water Hospital (1610) at Bath.
[2] See the list in M. C. Buer, *Health, Wealth, and Population in the Early Days of the Industrial Revolution* (London, 1926), p. 257.

example, in the twelve years 1742–43 to 1753–54, had a total income of £51,245, or an annual average of nearly £4300.[3] In its first year (1734), St. George's received over £4100, while Westminster's receipts in 1738–39, two decades after its establishment, exceeded £2025.[4] One provincial hospital — the Durham, Newcastle-on-Tyne, and Northumberland Infirmary — during its first five years averaged better that £2300 in subscriptions and donations.[5] The early eighteenth century, in short, marks the beginning of that productive alliance between medical care and science on the one hand and private philanthropy on the other which has contributed so strikingly to modern social advance.

The century did not, of course, invent hospitals for the care of the sick, but the period saw decisive changes in the nature of these institutions. The typical medieval hospital was a refuge for the poor and infirm, travelers and unfortunates, "an ecclesiastical, not a medical, institution . . . for care rather than cure . . . preeminently for the refreshment of the soul." [6] For such houses the term "hospital" was used interchangeably with "almshouse," "Maison Dieu," and "bedehouse." [7] The notion of the hospital as a specialized institution for the care of the sick did not come easily. Although the transformation had begun in Tudor times, some of the institutions founded in the early eighteenth century were obliged to proclaim their purpose in specific terms, sometimes to use the word "infirmary" along with or in place of "hospital," lest they be confused with almshouses. Thus the London Hospital (1740) was launched as "The London Hospital, or Infirmary, for the relief of sick and diseased persons, especially Manufacturers and Seamen in Merchant-Service." In the provinces, founders tended to be even more explicit, as with "The Infirmary for the Sick and Lame Poor of Durham, Newcastle-upon-Tyne, and Northumberland." [8] As late as 1771, John Aikin thought it necessary to stress the notion of a hospital as "a place designed for the cure of the sick and not an almshouse for the support of the indigent and decrepit," [9] and nearly a half-century later when Anthony Highmore issued his *Pietas Londinensis* (1810), he did not hesitate to list under "hospitals" such nonmedical institutions as Emanuel Hospital, St. Katherine's Hospital, Whitgift's Hospital, and the French House of Charity ("the Soup").

One can only hint at the apparently unrelated sources from which the modern hospital movement emerged. Obviously, if institutional care for the sick poor was thought desirable, then the facilities of the growing Metropolis were gravely inadequate. Of general hospitals, there were only St. Bartholomew's and St.

---

[3] Thomas Secker, *A Sermon Preached before the Governors of the London Hospital*, 1754, with an "Account of the Hospital," p. 34.

[4] Malcolm, *Manners and Customs of London*, I, 44–45; Isaac Maddox, *A Sermon Preached before the Trustees of the Public Infirmary in James Street, Westminster* (Westminster Hospital), 1739.

[5] Edmund Tew, *Frugality the Support of Charity* (a sermon for the Durham, Newcastle-on-Tyne, and Northumberland Infirmary), 1756, p. 27.

[6] R. M. Clay, *The Mediaeval Hospitals of England* (London, 1909), pp. xvii–xviii.

[7] *Ibid.*, p. 15.

[8] Newton Hyslop, "London Hospitals in the Eighteenth Century," p. iv, a MS thesis for the A.B. with Honors, in the Harvard College Library. I must here acknowledge my indebtedness to this useful study.

[9] *Thoughts on Hospitals* (London, 1771), p. 52.

Thomas's, which had been re-established after the Dissolution and which, in a large measure, had made the transition from the medieval to the modern conception of a hospital. They had carried over with them, however, and were to transmit to the new hospital world the view that the concern of the hospital was with the sick poor rather than with the generality of sick persons. Henceforth English hospitals were committed to the treatment of curable (or what was assumed to be curable) disease, but they were equally charities for the poor. To qualify for admission, applicants must be both sick and poor.

The few hundred beds maintained by the two ancient London foundations made a feeble enough showing against the precipitate growth of a population which may have nearly trebled in the course of the seventeenth century.[10] London was the magnet which attracted immigrants from all over the Kingdom, drawing them in such numbers that, in spite of its high death rate, the eighteenth-century Metropolis expanded from decade to decade. Only a quarter of the cases at the Westminster General Dispensary between 1774 and 1781 were native Londoners; about four-sevenths of the total were from other English and Welsh counties, the balance being chiefly Scotsmen and Irishmen.[11] It was this almost catastrophic growth, with its concomitant evils — epidemics, food and work shortages, and pervasive filth and squalor — that forced the plight of the sick on the attention of humanitarians and others. In the increasing congestion of metropolitan London it was hard to shut one's eyes to the reality of destitution and disease. As the future Archbishop of Canterbury put it in a charity sermon, "Religion, Humanity, common Prudence, loudly require us to rescue" the sick poor.[12] In fact, all of these considerations affected the hospital movement, together with a further, and in some instances a commanding, motive, that of advancing medical knowledge.

What Bishop Secker called "common Prudence" had an obvious influence on promoters of hospitals. The mercantilist was alarmed at the effect of a high death rate on the labor force of the nation and, when he considered it, uneasy over the loss of working time through illness. John Bellers, the Quaker philanthropist, could estimate the death of every industrious laborer capable of having children as causing a "Two Hundred Pound Loss to the *Kingdom*."[13] The "Improvement of Physick" — meaning hospitals, state support of medicine, and endowment of research, among other things — was, he urged, a necessary "Branch of Politicks" and essential to the well-being of all ranks and classes.

A more important factor in the hospital movement was the instinctive response of the humanitarian to the suffering of others. Such an impulse could, of course, draw ample justification from ideas in the eighteenth-century air — the belief,

---

[10] Clapham's estimate (*Concise Economic History*, p. 189) of an increase from 150,000 to over 400,000 covers not only the City, Southwark, and Westminster, but London "as a more or less continuous town."

[11] M. D. George, *London Life in the XVIIIth Century* (London, 1925), p. 111.

[12] Secker, *London Hospital Sermon*, 1754, p. 3.

[13] *Essay towards the Improvement of Physick*, reprinted in A. R. Fry, *John Bellers* (London, 1935), p. 111.

for example, in a common humanity and in the uniformity of human nature. From the pulpit repeated charity sermons asserted that "In Minds not inhumanly deprav'd, a strong and powerful Sympathy prevails; one common Sense and Feeling: Nor can Men, without doing Violence to their own Nature, be insensible and untouch'd at the Distress and Misery of their Fellow-Creatures." [14] Such sentiments may have impelled some listeners to concern themselves with possible remedies for suffering, but a more powerful influence must have been contact with the reality itself. As the distinguished surgeon and mildly eccentric (he is said to have insisted on appearing in full court dress when receiving corpses from the hangman) Sir William Blizard put it in the 1790's, the London hospital had been created "chiefly by men moved by the distress that immediately presented itself, without foreseeing all the great benefits that could occur from their good works." [15]

Ordinary humanitarianism was probably the main impulse actuating those (other than medical men) who promoted the hospital movement. But humanitarians, certainly English humanitarians, more often than not were men of sincere and sometimes fervent religious beliefs. For them charity was a Christian duty, and in providing medical care for the poor they were carrying out the Divine injunction. One may, perhaps, discount the burden of charity sermons, which naturally put the case for hospitals in terms of the Christian message. Sometimes they were extolled as a convenient channel for religious instruction, which "Will guard and complete the cure, which the physic of charity hath wrought." [16] Sir William Blizard also pictures hospital wards as a strategic field for religious and moral training, which might be carried on by workers apparently combining the characters of evangelist and the future hospital almoner or, in American terms, medical social worker.[17]

More specifically, clergymen are often discovered taking an active, sometimes a leading, part in establishing new infirmaries, especially in provincial centers. Dr. Alured Clarke, prebendary of Winchester and Westminster, was the driving force in the movement to found a hospital at Winchester, and, after his promotion to be Dean of Exeter, he repeated his achievement with the Devon and Exeter Hospital, which was opened for patients on New Year's Day, 1743.[18] At Leicester the project of an infirmary was warmly supported in a letter addressed by the

[14] Maddox, *James Street Infirmary Sermon*, 1739, p. 9.

[15] *Suggestions for the Improvement of Hospitals and Other Charitable Institutions* (London, 1796), p. 3. Blizard, co-founder of the medical school at the London Hospital and twice president of the College of Surgeons, held views not only of hospitals but of philanthropic effort in general that placed him well ahead of his time. He had little patience with the charge that charities encouraged dependence and sapped the moral fiber of their beneficiaries. Charities, he asserted, "have been the *consequences,* and not the causes, of poverty and distress" (p. 102). Blizard stands as the champion of an organized and rational humanitarianism, preaching a well-articulated, cooperative attack by the entire charitable army on the distresses of the lower classes.

[16] Thomas Hayter, *A Sermon Preached before the Governors of the London Hospital*, 1759, pp. 25–26.

[17] *Suggestions for the Improvement of Hospitals*, p. 80.

[18] George Oliver, *The History of the City of Exeter* (Exeter, 1861), p. 162.

Bishop of Lincoln to the clergy of the county, and the list of subscriptions which appeared in the *Leicester Journal* in February 1767 was credited in part to the effectiveness of the episcopal appeal.[19] Very likely the plans for an infirmary at Norwich would have been realized sooner had not Bishop Hayter been translated to London.[20] Dissenting ministers could be equally helpful. The distinguished Nonconformist divine, Philip Doddridge, who had already established a charity school at Northampton, figures as one of the founders of its General Hospital. His sermon, preached in September 1743, and printed by the committee in a large edition, was considered to have been a decisive factor in bringing the new institution into being.[21]

Yet hospitals in the modern sense are institutions for the treatment of sickness, and in them the medical profession has a special and natural interest. For a sufficient explanation of the rise of hospitals in the eighteenth century it is hardly necessary to look beyond the advances made by the age in medical science. Medicine was emancipating itself from medieval traditions, and many practitioners were men of some scientific training who were eager to experiment and to add to the sum of medical knowledge. It would be as wrong to think of the eighteenth-century doctor as a modern medical scientist as to accept the satirists' picture of him as "a pompous ass in a large wig, sniffing a knobbed stick, while he tries to look wise and to conceal his ignorance under a flow of meaningless technical terms." [22] Still, there were numbers of individual physicians and surgeons who were men of inquiring minds and remarkable devotion to their calling. Such doctors were acutely aware of the limitations imposed on their work by inadequate hospital facilities. It was not merely the fact that patients might be more efficiently cared for in an institution designed for the purpose; in the case of the eighteenth-century hospital this did not necessarily follow. What disturbed the abler medical men was that only through a hospital would they have access to a supply of clinical material both for their own studies and for teaching purposes. Without it, however gifted they might be, their appeal to students would suffer and their own work would be handicapped. Bishop Secker must have been speaking for many of the more capable doctors when he pointed to hospitals as places in which "the Art of healing is improved . . . by frequent Occasions for able Professors to consult, and ingenious Candidates to learn from them, to the common Advantage of all Ranks of Men." [23] Hospitals, in short, were thought of as demonstration laboratories for medical educators and as incubators of medical progress.

It was natural, therefore, that medical men should be in the forefront of hospital projects. Unquestionably the major force in establishing the London Hospital (1740) was John Harrison, its first surgeon. While, with only a hundred guineas

[19] James Thompson, *The History of Leicestershire in the Eighteenth Century* (Leicester, 1871), pp. 131–32.
[20] Sir Peter Eade, *Norfolk and the Norwich Hospital* (London, 1900), p. 35.
[21] *Victoria County History* (hereafter *VCH*), *Northampton,* III, 39.
[22] Buer, *Health, Wealth, and Population,* p. 113.
[23] *London Hospital Sermon,* 1754, p. 5.

guaranteed, other interested leaders were wondering what was to be done, Harrison marched into the meeting with an additional ten guineas and the news that the Duke of Richmond had become a subscriber.[24] Few would question his right to the distinction of "principal founder" with which the bust in the Hospital's committee room credited him.[25] The secession from the Westminster Hospital which resulted in the founding of St. George's was the result, in part, of the discontent of some of the leading doctors with their situation in the older institution. In the provinces one need only to call the roll of eighteenth-century hospitals to confirm the interest of the medical profession in better accommodations for the sick. At Birmingham, for example, the General Hospital was, in a large measure, a monument to the activity of Dr. John Ash; in Northampton the initiative came originally from Dr. Stonehouse; and in Cambridge it was a bequest by Dr. John Addenbrooke that led, after some decades, to the establishment of Addenbrooke's Hospital. The new ferment in their profession aroused medical men to the importance of institutions for treating the sick and studying disease, and they were quick to recognize and, in some degree, to guide the humanitarian sensibilities of their age.

2

There could be little doubt that, for the growing Metropolis, existing hospital accommodations were gravely inadequate. The two Royal Hospitals strove valiantly to meet the need, but the pressure on their wards was more than they could cope with, especially when both had finished the previous century in a less than flourishing condition. Though its own fabric had not suffered in the Great Fire, St. Bartholomew's had lost heavily in damage to its income-producing property, and in the mid-1690's the governors were deploring the fact that "the certain income of this hospital doth amount to very little more than a moiety of its necessary payments." [26] During these years, therefore, the decisions of the governors often seem like attempts to adjust their policy to two contradictory pressures, the need for retrenchment and the demand for expanded accommodations. Various expedients were employed to get more space, while at one time or another operations in the outlying branches were suspended and outpatients at the Hospital itself were limited.

After the turn of the century the financial situation eased somewhat, and the governors began to take tentative steps toward expansion. But it was not until 1723 that they were brought to contemplate a drastic rebuilding program. James Gibbs, the distinguished architect, supplied the comprehensive plan, and voluntary contributions financed the erection, in a series of stages covering three decades, of a new hospital with 420 beds. This was a building operation of considerable

[24] E. W. Morris, *A History of the London Hospital* (London, 1910), p. 48. I was not able to see A. E. Clark-Kennedy, *The London: A Study in the Voluntary Hospital System,* 2 vols. (London, 1962–64), until after this chapter was in revised draft.

[25] Anthony Highmore, *Pietas Londinensis* (London, 1810), p. 157.

[26] Sir Norman Moore, *The History of St. Bartholomew's Hospital,* 2 vols. (London, 1918), II, 348.

magnitude, which made a powerful appeal to the civic pride as well as the charitable impulses of City men. Between 1745 and 1752 alone, contributions came to nearly £14,500.[27]

St. Thomas's, the other Royal Hospital, which stood at the Southwark end of London Bridge, reached its decision to expand earlier and with less hesitation. Like St. Bartholomew's it had escaped direct damage in the Great Fire, as well as in serious fires in Southwark in the 1670's and '80's, but its revenues had suffered. Apparently these near-disasters turned the attention of the governors to the dilapidated condition of the building, and in 1693 they launched a building program. During the first three years, the fund reached £6000 and in the end came to a total of about £38,000, contributed by about 450 individuals. Included in this figure were three wards built by Thomas Guy in 1707 and three by another governor. In this appeal the Hospital is said to have profited from the shrewdness or good luck of certain individuals who managed to unload their South Sea shares before the collapse. The outcome of all this was an approximately doubled capacity. At the turn of the century, St. Thomas's could handle something over two hundred patients; when John Howard visited it in September 1788, 440 in-patients were on the books, a figure somewhat below maximum capacity.[28]

The increased capacity of the Royal Hospitals, substantial as it was, was not enough. Those most closely associated with them were aware that the pressure was still excessive and that relief could be obtained only through the founding of new institutions. The lead might be taken by doctors, clergy, or public-spirited citizens — or these might be aroused to action by a bequest such as Addenbrooke's in Cambridge or Lord Feversham's in Wiltshire, which set off the movement that led to the General Infirmary at Salisbury.[29] But whatever the source of the initiative, the method was predominantly that of philanthropic association. Of the five new general hospitals established in London, only one — Thomas Guy's foundation — was the gift of an individual. The other four were the result of combined effort, as was true of the bulk of the new special and provincial institutions. The techniques of associated philanthropy, the Bishop of St. Asaph reminded the governors of the Westminster Hospital, were not only expedient but

[27] D'Arcy Power, "Rebuilding the Hospital in the Eighteenth Century," p. 31, *St. Bartholomew's Hospital Reports*, 1926.

[28] Benjamin Golding, *An Historical Account of St. Thomas's Hospital, Southwark* (London, 1819), pp. 88, 96–109, 140; John Howard, *An Account of the Principal Lazarettos in Europe*, 2d ed. (London, 1791), p. 135. Shortly after he began his investigations of prisons, John Howard (1726?–90) became interested in the condition of other public institutions, and especially in their problems of health and disease. In the course of his visits to prisons, he had occasionally inspected lazarettos, and he had been struck by how vulnerable to "that most destructive of all contagious distempers, *the Plague*," were the great trading nations. In an effort to get at the facts, Howard undertook an extensive survey (1785–87) of lazarettos on the Continent. His *Account*, first published in 1789, included "*further* observations on some foreign prisons and hospitals; and additional remarks on the present state of those in Great Britain and Ireland." (John Aikin, *A View of the Character and Public Services of the Late John Howard, Esq.* [London, 1792], pp. 128ff, 151ff; Leona Baumgartner, "John Howard [1726–1790], Hospital and Prison Reformer: A Bibliography," *Bulletin of the History of Medicine*, 7:521 [May and June 1939].)

[29] *VCH, Wiltshire*, V, 340.

scriptural, for as *"Members one of another* . . . we are plainly directed to form an Alliance against Misery, and accomplish deliverance by united Assistance, which no single Endeavours could procure." [30]

The five new general hospitals in the Metropolis were all founded within a span of less than three decades, between 1719 and 1746. The Westminster, the earliest of the voluntary hospitals, was the creation of a group of Londoners, among whom a leading spirit was Henry Hoare, a member of the banking family, who was also a pillar of the St. Dunstan's-in-the-West Charity School. It was the purpose of these "several charitable and well-disposed persons" to arrange for assistance to the sick and needy, and they eventually decided on an infirmary in St. Margaret's Parish, Westminster, "there being nothing of that Sort within the populous City and Liberties of Westminster." [31] They took a house in Petty France and began to receive patients in May 1720 — at a rate which before long taxed their modest facilities and strained their resources.

The second great voluntary hospital, St. George's, was born of strains within the Westminster Charitable Society. The secession of the group that established the new institution resulted in part from a controversy within the board of governors over a new site. One faction wished to stay in the original neighborhood, while the other was attracted by Lanesborough House at Hyde Park Corner, which had recently become available. But this was not the whole of the story. The Westminster plan of organization was too democratic for some of the Hospital's richer sponsors, since all subscribers, even those of little means, were considered governors and were entitled to vote at the meetings of the board. In its new constitution, the founders of St. George's protected themselves adequately from being swamped by small subscribers by setting an annual subscription of five guineas as the qualification for governors. Among the voluntary hospitals, St. George's had the most aristocratic sponsorship, and its growth seems to have been accomplished with less pain than the others. During the first year, subscriptions approached £2300 and donations exceeded £1850.[32] The first president of St. George's was the Bishop of Winchester, who was followed by the Prince of Wales and a succession of members of the Royal Family, and the initial subscription list contained at least 150 five-guinea subscribers, among whom appeared bishops in ample supply, dukes, Lord Chesterfield, Lord Burlington, Lord Bathurst, Sir Robert Walpole, Garrick, and other notables.[33]

The London Hospital had humbler origins. Like the others, its creation was a response to the "number of those unhappy objects that daily offered themselves more than could be received by the hospitals then in being." [34] Although their financial support at the outset was fairly shaky — the first year's receipts were

[30] Maddox, *James Street Infirmary Sermon,* 1739, pp. 9–10.
[31] *Ibid.,* App.
[32] Malcolm, *Manners and Customs,* I, 44–45.
[33] Gray, *English Philanthropy,* p. 130; J. Blomfield, *St. George's Hospital, 1733–1933* (London, 1933) p. 13.
[34] *Gentleman's Magazine,* 17:564 (December 1747).

under £300 — the founders went ahead, and in less than twenty years after its foundation (1740), the Hospital had already outgrown its two earlier locations.[35] By the late 1750's, it was established in a new building on Whitechapel Road, which, however, because of financial stringency, contained only half as many beds as had been originally planned.[36] But from this time on it was the distinction of the London to be the one large general hospital ministering to the congested parishes of the East End. The governors might have to assure potential subscribers that, even though they could not give it their personal oversight because of its remoteness, this was a responsible and well-run charity.[37] The London was, in fact, reasonably well supported, and, like so many institutions of the kind, interest in it became hereditary in certain families. The names of Buxton, Barclay, Charrington, and Hanbury, for example, figure prominently in the annals of the Hospital.[38]

Of the eighteenth-century voluntary hospitals the Middlesex had the heaviest uphill battle. Founded in 1745 as the Middlesex Infirmary in two small houses in Windmill Street, it experienced financial troubles from the start. By the mid-1750's, led by the Earl of Northumberland who served as president for thirty years, the governors were planning a permanent building in Marylebone. Their building program, in fact, kept the Hospital in perilous condition during the latter half of the century, so much so that its efficiency was gravely affected. When John Howard paid his visit in 1788, he could find little good to say of the institution and the care given to its seventy patients.[39] It was not until the end of the century that the financial tide turned, partly as a result of paying patients in the form of French emigré clergy.[40] In one respect, however, the Middlesex stands out as an important pioneer in hospital practice. Alone among the early general hospitals, special provision was made for lying-in women. Indeed, well before the move from Windmill Street had taken place, the governors established a maternity ward and appointed William Hunter, the distinguished anatomist, as surgeon-accoucheur.

In the circumstances of its origin, the fifth metropolitan hospital stands apart from the other four, the creation of a single great philanthropist rather than of a group. "Founded at the sole costs and charges of Thomas Guy, Esquire," the Hospital in Southwark was the crowning monument to the Englishman whose benefactions were probably more extensive (in a financial sense) than those of any other man of his time.[41] Born in London, he was taken to Tamworth at the

---

[35] Secker, *London Hospital Sermon*, 1754, "Account," p. 34. The first site of the Hospital was in Featherstone Street, but within a few months it was moved to Prescot Street, Goodman's Fields.

[36] Morris, *London Hospital*, pp. 81, 87.

[37] *Gentleman's Magazine*, 17:564 (December 1747).

[38] Morris, *London Hospital*, pp. 53–54.

[39] *Lazarettos*, p. 133.

[40] H. St. G. Saunders, *The Middlesex Hospital, 1745–1948* (London, 1949), pp. 14–18.

[41] The following paragraphs are based chiefly on William Maitland, *The History and Survey of London from Its Foundation to the Present Time*, 2 vols. (1760 ed.), II, 1305–1309; Sir Samuel Wilks and G. T. Bettany, *A Biographical History of Guy's Hospital* (London, 1892); Bettany's article on Guy in *DNB*; William Roberts, *The Earlier History of English Bookselling* (London, 1889); H. C. Cameron, *Mr. Guy's Hospital, 1726–1948* (London, 1954).

age of eight by his widowed mother, and it was there that he received the elements of an education, presumably at the Tamworth Grammar School. The foundation of his fortune lay in the bookselling business which he carried on in his shop at the corner of Lombard Street and Cornhill, but more particularly in his activities as an importer of Dutch-printed copies of the English Bible, in which he infringed on the monopoly enjoyed by the Universities, the King's Printer, and the Company of Stationers. For a time, in fact, Oxford retired from the struggle and authorized Guy to print on its behalf, in competition with the King's Printer, and Guy turned out a number of well-printed Bibles and other books while at the University.

Guy's publishing business, along with certain speculative operations which he carried on, was sufficiently profitable to launch him on his career as a philanthropist. He established almshouses in Tamworth, his boyhood home, and built a town hall; he made provision for poor relations and contributed to the relief of insolvent debtors, distressed families, and refugees from the Palatinate. Possibly Guy found giving his money away an agreeable diversion. Himself unmarried, his habits of life seem to have been excessively frugal, almost miserly, and, as far as one can learn, he had no pleasures other than making money and disposing of it.

What changed the well-to-do business man into a personage of vast wealth was his judgment in knowing when to sell South Sea shares, an insight shared by few of his contemporaries. By disposing of his £100 shares, for which he may have paid no more than £50 or £60 each, at prices from £300 to £600, he was able to multiply his original investment several times over. Between April and June 1720, Guy sold £54,000 South Sea shares for nearly £235,000.[42] With such resources he could now proceed to develop the philanthropic interests which appealed to him most strongly. Since 1704, Guy had been a governor of St. Thomas's, apparently one of the more active of the board, and he had already built and presented three new wards to the Hospital. It was his original intention to place the new institution which he purposed to found under the administration of the St. Thomas governors, and he took a 999-year lease of land belonging to the older hospital. But while the building (whose completion in 1725 places it chronologically between Westminster and St. George's), was still in course of construction, he changed his mind and determined on an independent establishment, though his early governors were also governors of St. Thomas's.[43]

Guy lived to see the completion of only a part of his magnificent plant, but he provided handsomely for the Hospital as residuary legatee of an estate valued at some £335,000. After distant relatives were taken care of and legacies for the benefit of Christ's Hospital, poor debtors, apprentice fees, and other conventional eighteenth-century charities had been duly honored, "Mr. Guy's Hospital" found itself with an endowment of over £220,000. A substantial fraction of this capital, following the intentions expressed by Guy in his will, was invested in agricultural

[42] Cameron, *Mr. Guy's Hospital*, p. 29n.
[43] For Guy's original idea of founding an institution to supplement St. Thomas's, see *ibid.*, pp. 40–41.

land in Lincolnshire, Essex, and Herefordshire — a decision that meant relative penury for the Hospital during the depression of the late nineteenth century. But whatever adversities the future might hold, the new institution, with its four hundred beds, made an imposing addition to metropolitan facilities for the care of the sick. The heavy endowment supported an exceptionally large staff and allowed the Hospital to carry an annual salary charge of £1350.[44] Beside the struggles for survival of some of the voluntary hospitals, the situation of Guy's in the early days seems almost idyllic.

A movement for establishing hospitals in the provinces paralleled the advances made in London. Some of these were designed as county institutions, others simply as local infirmaries for provincial centers. It would be dangerous, as well as profitless, to place the stamp of primacy on any of the four or five claimants. Addenbrooke's at Cambridge, for which the date 1719 is often given, is clearly disqualified, since nothing much was done to carry out the benefactor's wishes until the 1760's.[45] Edinburgh (to look north of the Border, where significant advances in medical education were taking place) and Winchester opened houses for receiving patients in 1729 and 1736. But as a regularly established institution with a building constructed for the purpose, the Bristol Infirmary can probably claim priority, at least by a few months, over Winchester, its closest English competitor.[46] The group whose efforts founded the Bristol Infirmary represented an interesting combination of medical men with well-to-do Quakers and others, among them John Elbridge, the wealthy, Massachusetts-born Collector of Customs who on his death bequeathed the hospital £5000. During its early years, the income of the Infirmary ran in the neighborhood of £1000 with about two hundred subscribers, and by the mid-'50's exceeded £3000.[47] After Bristol and Winchester came, more or less in order of foundation, York County, Exeter, Northampton, Salop, Liverpool, and Worcester, which, with Aberdeen in Scotland, Cork and three establishments in Dublin, completed the roster of British institutions established before 1750.

All of these hospitals, metropolitan and provincial, followed similar patterns in organization and operation. They drew their support at the outset chiefly from annual subscriptions or lump payments from life governors. After the Westminster Hospital's early experiment with democratic government, most London institutions required a minimum annual subscription of five guineas or a single payment of thirty before the donor was entitled as a governor to vote in meetings of the board. This was not wholly a matter of philanthropy or even of status on the part of subscribers. For a subscription carried with it the perquisite of recommending to the hospital a stated number of patients a year, a figure that might vary with the size of the subscription. In fact, the normal way — and for some hospitals

[44] *Ibid.*, pp. 60–62.
[45] *VCH, Cambridge*, III, 106.
[46] G. Munro Smith, *A History of the Bristol Royal Infirmary* (Bristol, 1917), p. 9; *Annual Account of the Bristol Infirmary*, 1744.
[47] Smith, *Bristol Royal Infirmary*, pp. 44, 57, 72.

the only way save for emergency cases — of gaining admission was to obtain from a governor a letter of recommendation, which would entitle the bearer to treatment, unless the admitting committee found good reason for turning him away.

All this not only gave to the patron an agreeable feeling of benevolence, but, where the patient was a dependent, may have resulted in some small saving to him. For these were, broadly speaking, free institutions, in which only incidental charges were imposed. But such items as the fees collected by nurses, porters, and others, and burial deposits, refunded if the patients were fortunate enough to leave the institution alive, could be serious burdens for the poor. St. Bartholomew's, for example, collected 19s. 6d. on admission; St. Thomas's and Guy's had similar dues. The system was less highly developed at the voluntary hospitals. Westminster and London denied charging fees.[48] But the deplorable practice, as familiar in the provinces as in the Metropolis, continued to a greater or less degree, and it was in protest against it that in 1828 Dr. Marsden founded the Royal Free Hospital.[49]

3

To attempt an estimate of the eighteenth-century hospital as a facility for the treatment of disease would go beyond the scope of this study. On the whole, it has had a fairly bad press from historians, no doubt deservedly in more instances than not. What is more important here is to notice the hospital as an eighteenth-century philanthropic interest. It is, of course, impossible even to guess at the total financial support which the reconstructed Royal Hospitals and the newly established voluntary hospitals drew from the community, but one can point to certain pieces of evidence which suggest a widespread enthusiasm for these institutions. The considerable sums collected for the renovation of St. Thomas's and the rebuilding of St. Bartholomew's have already been noted. In 1754 the London Hospital could list about six hundred life governors (at thirty guineas each) and 170 annual governors (at five guineas a year). In the same year the treasurer reported total receipts of over £7500, about £2500 of which was earmarked for the building fund.[50] The following shows the income of a representative group of voluntary hospitals in typical years in mid-century:[51]

Westminster (1738–39)	£2087
London (1750–51)	5447
Middlesex (1749–50)	992
Bristol (1757)	3197
Newcastle-on-Tyne (1751–52)	2643

[48] Howard, Lazarettos, pp. 131, 136.
[49] John Aikin, Thoughts on Hospitals (London, 1771), p. 55; Sir D'Arcy Power, "Medicine," Johnson's England (Oxford, 1933), II, 283–84.
[50] Secker, London Hospital Sermon, 1754, "Account," p. 34.
[51] The figures are taken from the hospital reports published with the sermons and from Smith, Bristol Royal Infirmary, p. 72.

Of these amounts, subscriptions would probably account, on the average, for half to two thirds. For the rest the hospital would have to depend on legacies (which might be funded or, more likely if no trust provisions were attached, used for current expenses), donations, and special collections. The anniversary sermon was a staple item on the money-raising program of hospitals, as of charity schools, but here it was coupled with a dinner, where "conviviality and charity . . . coalesced." It was reassuring to remember, observed Malcolm, that "dinners and collections after dinners, when the mind generously dilates, have relieved thousands from the deepest misery." [52] The annual dinner, with its assault on the pockets of more or less befuddled diners, became an essential feature of charity economy. With the London Hospital, for example, the annual festival began not long after its foundation. The sermon in one of the City churches was followed by a procession to the hall of a City Company or to a tavern for dinner. Although diners were required to buy tickets, the feast itself was provided by the festival stewards at the cost of twenty or twenty-five guineas each, receipts from the ticket sales going to the Hospital itself. At least the stewards could take comfort in the tradition that exempted them from paying for what was drunk after midnight (the dinner began at five). At the first dinner, £36 14s. was collected, and at the second £82. A little more than a century later, in 1856, the diners gave up the record sum of £26,000! [53]

There were smaller, incidental sources of income. The poor box would produce a few pounds each year, and occasionally a theatrical or other benefit performance might come to the rescue. As the invested funds and landed property of the institution increased, dividends and rent became significant elements in hospital receipts. In each of the three years 1782–84, these two items, amounting to about £1000 annually, accounted for roughly a third of the London Hospital's income.[54] When the affairs of a hospital reached a really critical state or a building program was contemplated, a special appeal would have to be organized, and support solicited from as wide a public as possible. Building beyond their resources was a not uncommon failing of eighteenth-century hospitals, for governors felt keenly the pressure for accommodations and sometimes expanded imprudently in an effort to meet it. For new buildings they were often assisted by gifts of land from wealthy owners or from public bodies. At Liverpool and Newcastle the hospitals were built on land given or supplied at a nominal rent by the Corporation, and when the London Hospital came to put up its new building in Whitechapel, it was on land leased from the City at a low figure.[55] Sometimes private landowners stepped in, as when a friend of Dean Clarke gave the site for the Devon and Exeter Hospital, and Lord Grosvenor aided the expansion of St. George's with a ninety-

---

[52] *Manners and Customs,* I, 56–57.

[53] Morris, *London Hospital,* pp. 73–77; Clark-Kennedy (*The London,* I, 51–53) gives an interesting account of the festival of 1744.

[54] "Report by F. O. Martin," *Corr. between the Treasury, Home Office, Charity Commissioners,* 1865, p. 236.

[55] Thomas Baines, *History of the Commerce and Town of Liverpool* (London, 1852), p. 412; S. Middlebrooke, *Newcastle upon Tyne* (Newcastle, 1950), p. 122; Morris, *London Hospital,* pp. 81–82.

eight-year lease of two acres at a peppercorn rent.[56] But eighteenth-century hospitals, like those of later periods, had grave difficulties both in meeting operating expenses and in financing additions to their physical plant.

These difficulties seemed to multiply during the latter half of the century, when the general hospital movement in the Metropolis tended to bog down. It is, perhaps, significant that no new general hospital was founded between the Middlesex in the mid-1740's, and Charing Cross in 1818, and some of those that had been launched with apparent success barely managed to keep afloat. Certain institutions had overextended themselves in building programs, and others had been the victims of bad luck or bad management, as when a collector of subscriptions for the Middlesex Hospital embezzled £400 of the Hospital's funds.[57] Some of them, one gathers from John Howard, had been allowed to get into shocking condition, even by eighteenth-century sanitary standards. And Dr. John Aikin, who agreed that in the abstract a hospital should have been immensely preferable to the squalid and filthy dwellings of the poor, was not reassured when he faced the fetid reality of a crowded hospital ward, where the sick perished "by mutual contagion."[58]

Apparently hospitals had lost some of the appeal that they had held for charitable donors earlier in the century. Possibly the dispensary movement had diverted some of their former support, as John Howard and certain boards of governors suspected.[59] Or it may have been that general hospitals no longer caught the imagination of the well-to-do, as they had done in the past. In any case, for voluntary hospitals in London this was a half-century of financial stringency and sporadic retrenchment, in which new buildings, put up in the exuberance of the 1750's and '60's, were being operated at much less than capacity. The 1780's give a dismal picture of wards closed down, comprising, in some cases, up to 75 per cent of the total number of beds. When the new London Hospital building in Whitechapel opened its doors in 1757, it contained only 161 beds instead of the 350 originally planned, and by 1785 financial pressure was such that six wards with sixty-five beds had to be closed.[60] On the occasion of John Howard's visit in September 1788, there were only 120 patients in the wards. It was about this time that the committee of governors, in a panic over the state of the Hospital's finances, passed an amazing rule to limit annual expenditures to £2500 and new in-patients in any one week to twenty.[61] St. George's had fifty of its two hundred beds unoccupied, and in 1810 Highmore speaks of the closing down of several wards at the Westminster Hospital and only sixty-six patients (plus fourteen incurables) in the institution.[62]

The Middlesex had a conspicuously rough time. To finance the new building

[56] Oliver, *City of Exeter*, p. 162; Stephen Paget, *John Hunter* (London, 1897), p. 196.
[57] Sir Erasmus Wilson, *The History of the Middlesex Hospital* (London, 1845), p. 39.
[58] *Thoughts on Hospitals*, pp. 8–9.
[59] Wilson, *Middlesex Hospital*, p. 50; Howard, *Lazarettos*, p. 140.
[60] "Report by F. O. Martin," *Corr. between the Treasury* . . . , 1865, p. 236.
[61] Morris, *London Hospital*, pp. 87, 100–101; Howard, *Lazarettos*, p. 131.
[62] *Lazarettos*, pp. 136–37; Highmore, *Pietas Londinensis*, p. 313.

in the '50's, the governors persuaded David Garrick to give two benefit perform-ances of *Much Ado About Nothing,* while Thomas Arne, composer of "Rule Britannia," offered an oratorio, and the proprietors of Ranelagh Gardens also did their bit. But new wings completed in 1766 and 1780 remained closed for lack of funds, for by the early '80's the income of the Hospital had shrunk to £1264 and the number of subscribers to 442. Heavily in debt to tradesmen, the governors anxiously canvassed possible sources of revenue, such as musical performances in Westminster Abbey similar to those which were said to have enriched St. George's and the Westminster Hospitals by as much as £4000. Although hospital concerts in the Abbey were suspended for a time (owing to the illness of their patron, the King), they were finally resumed — and the Middlesex governors named one of their wards "Handel" in gratitude.[63] It is little wonder that Sir William Blizard proposed a house-to-house solicitation of the metropolitan area on behalf of the undernourished voluntary hospitals, whose financial situation stood in shocking contrast to the relative affluence of the two Royal Hospitals and Guy's. At the time of John Howard's visit, these institutions, in fact, were treating nearly three times as many patients as all of the voluntary hospitals combined.[64]

Conceivably some of the support which might have gone to general hospitals was being diverted to a group of specialized institutions founded in the middle third of the century. The most significant, and indeed the most successful, of these were maternity hospitals, whose record, on the whole, was rather better than that of the general hospitals. Although it trailed Edinburgh in the early century, during the middle years London emerged as the leading obstetrical center not only of the Kingdom but possibly of Europe. The years 1749–65 saw the founding of a surprising number of lying-in hospitals in the Metropolis: the British Lying-In (1749),[65] the City of London Lying-In (1750), Queen Charlotte's as it later became (1752), the Westminster Lying-In (1765), and the General Lying-In (1765) in Lambeth — these in addition to the Lying-In Charity, later the Royal Maternity Charity, established in 1757 for assisting women in their homes.

The maternity hospitals, all relatively small institutions, reached rather higher standards of cleanliness than did other voluntary hospitals, perhaps because "this was one class of hospital in which, at this time, women took an important part in the management." [66] In any case, their record of successful deliveries was highly creditable. During its first twenty-one years, the British Lying-In delivered 9108 mothers with a loss of 196, or one in about 46½. By the 1790's the proportion had declined, Highmore asserts, to one in 288, a ratio that seems incredible, especially when one recalls that such an institution would get an exceptional number of abnormal and complicated cases.[67] For their size the lying-in hospitals enlisted

[63] Wilson, *Middlesex Hospital,* pp. 36–50; Saunders, *Middlesex Hospital,* p. 16.
[64] Blizard, *Improvement of Hospitals,* pp. 95–101. The Royal Hospitals and Guy's handled 1172 patients against 4255 in the voluntary institutions.
[65] Originally simply "The Lying-In Hospital," to which "British" was prefixed in 1756.
[66] Buer, *Health, Wealth, and Population,* p. 129.
[67] *Account of the British Lying-in Hospital, 1749–70* (London, 1771), p. 17; Highmore, *Pietas,* pp. 191–92.

relatively strong support. During its first twenty-one years, the total receipts of the British Lying-In came to nearly £27,000, including about £8300 in legacies from forty individuals. In 1770 the Lying-In could publish a list of more than eighty life governors (at thirty guineas), headed by the Duke of Portland, the patron of the Hospital, and well over two hundred annual governors (at three guineas).[68]

Though admirable institutions, the maternity hospitals, whose total beds did not much exceed two hundred, could handle only a small fraction of the births among the London poor. Very likely their greatest contribution, aside from adding to the sum of obstetrical knowledge, was their utility as training centers for midwives. A more realistic approach to the maternity care of the poor was probably the various schemes, notably the Lying-In Charity (1757), for sending midwives to assist in delivering women at home. Whereas the British Lying-In Hospital annually delivered between four and five hundred women, the Lying-In Charity averaged ten times that figure. In 1774–75 deliveries by Lying-In midwives totaled 5428, a figure equal to nearly a third of the total baptisms in the Bills of Mortality, and during the first half-century of its operation the Charity assisted nearly 180,000 women. Not only that, but the free training of midwives carried on by the Lying-In had something to do with improving the technical competence of the profession.[69]

It is impossible to do more than to note the other areas where doctor and philanthropist collaborated. Some of these were determined by the policies followed by the general hospitals of limiting the types of case they would accept. Such conditions as smallpox, venereal disease, consumption, cancer when thought to be incurable, and acute mental disturbance were unwelcome. On the whole, the general hospitals existed for patients with noninfectious, presumably curable afflictions and especially for emergency and accident cases, which some intelligent observers regarded as their special province.[70] Among the institutions designed to take up some of the slack left by the general hospitals was a modest building for smallpox patients on Windmill Street, which opened in July 1746 as the Middlesex County Hospital for Small-pox.[71] Other units were presently established until something of a chain of institutions had been created for treating the disease and inoculating against it. The success of the effort was doubtful. Among other things, the fact that patients under the age of seven were excluded denied assistance to those in greatest need. But effective or not, this was a fairly well-supported charity, as evidenced by the new building in St. Pancras erected in 1766–67 at a cost of about £9000 and intended to house three hundred inoculation patients.[72]

It would perhaps be as well to avert one's eyes from the treatment of mental

[68] Lying-in Hospital, 1749–70, pp. 24–29.

[69] Buer, Health, Wealth, and Population, pp. 143–44.

[70] Aikin, Thoughts on Hospitals, pp. 23ff; Blizard, Improvement of Hospitals, p. 33.

[71] Gray (English Philanthropy, pp. 130–31) confuses this institution with the Middlesex Hospital.

[72] Highmore, Pietas, p. 289. An inoculation patient was required to spend three or four weeks in the Hospital.

disease in the eighteenth century. Bethlem, one of the Royal Hospitals, appears to have been everything that such an institution ought not to be. Some improvements were introduced in the course of the century; the admission of sightseers and visitors (which had yielded a tidy £400 a year) was stopped in 1770 as contrary to "the great design of recovery by tranquillity," a condition never particularly identified with Bethlem. But at the end of the century John Howard could find little good to say of the institution.[73]

In 1750 a group of benevolent Londoners determined to establish a hospital for lunatics, many of whom, they imagined, might be saved to society if their maladies were dealt with promptly. Not only were they concerned over the lack of facilities for treating the mentally disturbed, but they apparently had some hope of interesting medical men in the study of "one of the most important branches of physic." [74] The result of their efforts was St. Luke's Hospital for Lunatics, which opened its doors in the following year to receive patients. A half-century later to the year, the Hospital moved from near Finsbury Square to a new building in Old Street planned to accommodate three hundred patients, an establishment characterized by John Howard as a "noble hospital . . . neat and clean." [75] From the beginning St. Luke's was an exceptionally well-supported philanthropy, enjoying a heavy and reasonably regular flow of legacies. During the first thirty years over 150 benefactors left legacies totaling about £66,000, so that by the turn of the century the resources of St. Luke's exceeded £131,000 in addition to the building.[76]

4

The mid-century became aware of other social problems of a medical and quasi-medical nature, among them the evils of prostitution and illegitimacy, and created mechanisms of a sort for dealing with them.[77] Of these the Lock Hospital, founded in 1746, for the relief and rehabilitation of venereal disease patients can be mentioned only incidentally. It was an undertaking that had to contend against prejudice and hostility, and its sponsors were driven to emphasize as a *raison d'être* the "many innocent women of irreproachable character themselves [who] have received infection from the profligacy of their husbands." [78] The staggering record of cures claimed by the Lock — over 30,200 for its first half-century — is even more suspect than most eighteenth-century statistics of the kind, especially for a hospital with only about sixty-five beds. But at least this was a courageous

[73] *Ibid.*, p. 19; Howard, *Lazarettos*, p. 139. See also Kathleen Jones, *Lunacy, Law, and Conscience, 1744–1845* (London, 1955), pp. 11ff.

[74] Highmore, *Pietas*, p. 173.

[75] *Lazarettos*, p. 140.

[76] *Reasons for Establishing St. Luke's Hospital* (London, 1780), pp. 32–36; Highmore, *Pietas*, pp. 181–82. See also the centennial volume of *Reasons for St. Luke's* (1851), pp. 40–62, for a complete list of donations and legacies during the hundred years.

[77] The dispensary movement belongs in the late eighteenth and early nineteenth centuries and will be noticed in Chapter IV.

[78] Highmore, *Pietas*, p. 143.

attempt on the part of mid-century philanthropists to grapple with one of the more noisome evils of their time.

Of a quite different order of magnitude was the Foundling Hospital, the most imposing single monument erected by eighteenth-century benevolence. The story of the Foundling, so perfectly designed to appeal to the sensibility of the age and to enlist the aid of its artists and musicians — Hogarth, Reynolds, and Handel — has often been told. Here we can do little more than to notice some of the main threads in the Foundling's first half century and some of its claims to a special place in the history of British charities. This was a capital example of eighteenth-century humanitarianism in action, allied, in the thinking of some of its friends, with characteristic mercantilist solicitude for a flourishing population and anxiety over any intimation of decline. Unlike the charity schools and unlike nineteenth-century societies for reclaiming children, there was little religious inspiration, other than of a formal sort, among the builders of the Foundling, and they had none of the characteristic evangelical concern for the souls of their charges. In the large, the Foundling can stand as representative of the open-handed, uncalculating benevolence, which, though easy to exaggerate, profoundly affected the eighteenth-century outlook.

Thomas Coram, the retired sea captain who had settled at Rotherhithe, had some of the sensitive feeling for children not uncommon with childless men. What spurred him into action was apparently the shocking sights he had witnessed on his way to and from the City — babies, alive or dead, left by the roadside, and in one instance, so the story goes, a girl in the act of deserting her child. Coram became a man with a mission, one which took up the next seventeen years of his life. He was ruthlessly single-minded in pressing his idea, until, as a friend remarked, "even people of rank began to be ashamed to see a man's hair become grey in the course of a solicitation by which he could get nothing." [79] In the end persistence conquered, and he was able to rally notable support in the world "of Quality and Distinction" for his project of an institution for foundlings. It was a memorable occasion when in November 1739, before a gathering at Somerset House headed by six dukes, eleven earls, City magnates, and professional men, including William Hogarth and Richard Mead, probably the most distinguished physician of his day, Coram received a charter of incorporation and presented it to the Duke of Bedford, who served as president of the Foundling for more than thirty years.

The committee got the work under way with amazing smoothness and dispatch, profiting, perhaps, from the preliminary thinking that had already taken place. For the notion of such an institution was familiar enough to humanitarians and mercantilists alike. A quarter century before, in No. CV of the *Guardian,*

[79] Dr. John Brocklesby, quoted by Nichols and Wray, *Foundling Hospital,* p. 15. Except where otherwise noted, my treatment of the Hospital is based on this work. A more careful study of the Foundling records, whose opening to scholars was announced a few years back, no doubt will make possible a more solidly based estimate of the work of this institution as well as illuminate other aspects of eighteenth-century social history.

Addison had denounced the exposure of infants, both as inhumane and as robbing "the commonwealth of its full number of citizens," and had anticipated some of the procedures later followed by the Foundling.[80] Temporary premises in Hatton Garden were leased, and two groups of thirty children admitted. But rapidly as matters moved, progress seemed slow to the enthusiastic Coram, who, noting in September 1740 between £5000 and £6000 cash paid in, 526 annual subscriptions (at a minimum of £2), and legacies of £2300 in sight, deplored the failure of the governors to push their building plans more aggressively.[81]

The old sea captain was presently to quarrel with his fellow-governors and sever his official connection with the institution. Still, he had piloted the project through the preliminary stages, and he had been the target of bigoted critics, who had charged him with encouraging vice and illegitimacy and had made him the butt of their ribald humor. Before he withdrew, he had seen plans for a new building well launched. The site was to be fifty-six acres near Lamb's Conduit Street for which the Earl of Salisbury was asking £7000. When the committee declined to go above £6500, the Earl solved the problem neatly and philanthropically by himself contributing the £500 difference. Acquiring such an estate turned out to have been one of the more inspired early decisions of the Foundling committee. The famous plant, of which the original building was begun in 1742, was finally completed a decade later at a total cost of a little over £28,000.[82]

But the Hospital was beset with a variety of medical and administrative problems that were only gradually and partially solved. During the first year, instead of the intended sixty, some 136 infants were admitted, of whom fifty-six died. As a result, the committee decided to board children up to the age of three with foster-mothers in country districts. Though the mortality rate continued at (to twentieth-century eyes) a shockingly high level, the prospects of survival for a child in the Hospital were still markedly better than those of a Poor Law child in the Bills of Mortality.[83] It is true, also, that many children entered the Hospital in exceedingly bad shape, some half-dead and with little prospect of survival.

During the first two or three years, in fact, there was no systematic admission policy. The riotous scenes staged by mothers who stormed the doors of the Hospital led the governors to introduce a plan of admission by drawing lots, a white ball assuring immediate admission, a black ball meaning rejection, and a red ball

[80] 11 July 1713. The Harvard College Library contains a pamphlet, apparently dating from the late 1720's and attributed to Dr. Bray, urging support for "the worthy Capt. C———m" in his proposals for "an Orphanatrophy or Hospital for the Reception of Poor Cast-off Children or Foundlings." This copy is marked as "The Gift of Mr. Coram."

[81] Nichols and Wray, *Foundling Hospital*, p. 21.

[82] An authoritative and handsomely illustrated account of the building is given by Walter H. Godfrey and W. McB. Marcham, *King's Cross Neighbourhood* (St. Pancras, Part IV), *L.C.C. Survey of London*, XXIV (London, 1952), chap. 2 (Plates 15–41).

[83] From 1741 to 1756, when the admission policy changed sharply, the Hospital lost 37 per cent (511 out of 1384) of its children under two years, while among workhouse children in the Bills of Mortality (1728–50) the casualty rate was nearly 59 per cent. These figures for Hospital deaths vary somewhat from those given by Jonas Hanway in *A Candid Historical Account of the Hospital* (London, 1759). My 37 per cent is based on the table in Nichols and Wray (p. 62) which in turn is taken from the Foundling Hospital Register begun in January 1767.

giving an alternate's position. Among the curious and unforeseen administrative complications of the work were those resulting from the rule which provided for the baptizing of children on the Sunday following their admission. To supply such a legion of foundlings with suitable names called for a measure of ingenuity. Naming children after themselves or their friends produced some embarrassing consequences for the governors, when in later years their namesakes sometimes claimed a blood relationship or demanded their full perquisites as godchildren. Many were named for historical figures and for characters in contemporary novels. Charles Allworthy, Clarissa Harlowe, and Tom Jones mingle with John Milton, Peter Paul Rubens, and Michaelangelo. But later, as admissions mounted, such categories ran dry, and even birds and beasts, handicrafts and trades, were exhausted. Finally, the secretary prepared a list of acceptable names by which the little foundlings could be baptized.

During the first fifteen years of its life, the Hospital had its ups and downs. What was most disturbing to its supporters was their growing suspicion that their efforts were not, in any significant fashion, improving the lot of the deserted children of the Metropolis. The hundred foundlings admitted each year comprised a hardly perceptible fraction of "the thousands who are still drooping and dying in the hands of parish nurses." [84] Perhaps there were ways of extending the benefits of the Hospital, while relieving the institution of some of its more pressing financial difficulties. An obvious expedient was to appeal to Parliament, for clearly the State was directly interested in the problem with which the Hospital was wrestling. Neither philanthropists nor public authorities accepted the view which to the nineteenth century seemed axiomatic, that private charity and the State each had their proper spheres and the less mixing of the two, the better for both. When in 1756 Parliament responded with a grant of £10,000, it was on two conditions, both of them ruinous — that the Hospital establish a series of branches throughout the country, and, even more disastrous, agree to accept all applicants below a given age, set first at two months, then six, and finally a year.[85] The decision was taken at a time when Parliament was uneasy over losses suffered in the war with the French and, Sir Frederick Eden suspected, may have looked toward "recruiting the nation, then engaged in an expensive and depopulating contest." [86]

To say the least, the following years do not offer an encouraging example of cooperation between a voluntary body and statutory authorities. Obviously no one had the slightest notion of what would happen when the doors of the Foundling were thrown open to all comers. On the first day, 117 children were deposited in the basket hung on the gate of the Hospital in Guilford Street, and the first month brought 425 infants, all presumably under two months. From all over the country they streamed into London, nearly 1800 in the first six months, and conveying un-

---

[84] Nichols and Wray, p. 46.
[85] Ibid., pp. 48–49.
[86] State of the Poor, quoted by Rodgers, Cloak of Charity, p. 31.

wanted infants to the Foundling became something of a country-wide industry.[87] The Hospital had made no preparations for such a flood, and the mortality figures are a fair measure of its unpreparedness. It is amazing that the officers were able to carry on as well as they did, given the mountain of clerical work, which they apparently handled with exemplary care, and even during the period of indiscriminate admission, the death rate was not notably higher than at other institutions of the time. Still, the statistics were sufficiently grisly: during the forty-six months of unrestricted admission, 68.3 per cent of the nearly 15,000 children taken in failed to survive, and of these over 5500 died before reaching the age of six months.[88] Nor was the scheme inexpensive for the public purse. The original grant of £10,000 was only the thin edge of the wedge, and in the end the Treasury paid out nearly £550,000.[89] When in February 1760 Parliament decided to call the experiment off, the Hospital was carrying on its books, in London and the provinces, nearly 6300 children, whose maintenance per capita was estimated to average £6 a year. For these dependents the Government continued to make grants for another eleven years but with growing restiveness and with increasing pressure on the Hospital to apprentice the children with as little delay as possible.

The governors of the Foundling emerged from the partnership with the Government poorer, sadder, and probably wiser. They had been obliged to expand their plant, especially in the country branches, while, with so much money coming from public sources, subscriptions declined. The withdrawal of the Government left the Hospital so impoverished that rigid economy, including a drastic reduction in the numbers of children admitted, was the only way out. What restored the Foundling to financial health was the therapy that benefited many another urban charity. When the Earl of Salisbury insisted on the Hospital's buying the fifty-six acres of his Lamb's Conduit Fields property, rather than the thirty-four they had wished, he was doing the governors the greatest possible favor. And finally, in their financial stringency in the late 1780's, they decided to develop their estate. The details are laid out in Messrs. Nichols' and Wray's *History*. Here, it is enough to recall that, having made improvements in their property, such as opening up the four new streets into Southampton Row — Tavistock, Great Coram, Bernard, and Guilford Streets — the governors granted extensive leases

[87] Nichols and Wray, pp. 52–53. Although the Hospital was in process of establishing the branches called for by the Commons resolution, the intention was to make the London institution the sole reception center, from which children would be sent to the rural units.

[88] *Ibid.*, p. 62. The figures are:

Living	4,103
Apprenticed	484
Claimed	143
Dead	10,204
	14,934

Hanway's figures (*Candid Historical Account,* pp. 77–78) are somewhat more favorable but appear to have been distorted by his failure to allow for deaths among children of over two years of age.

[89] Nichols and Wray, p. 80. This total includes a considerable sum paid by the Government after indiscriminate admission had ceased for the support of children admitted while the policy was still in force.

for building. It was not easily managed, but by the end of the century the rent exceeded £3000. In 1836 the property was bringing more than £5350, and, to look ahead, in 1908 the rental from the Foundling property in Lamb's Conduit Fields amounted to £25,000.[90]

In spite of its late-century troubles, the Foundling remains the representative charity of the Age of Benevolence. Not only was it the largest single agency of its kind, but an astonishing number of the great of the eighteenth-century world were enlisted in its support. The register of governors at the time of the charter included numbers of dukes and earls, Sir Robert and Horace Walpole, Henry Pelham, William Hogarth, and a phalanx of distinguished medical men. It was Hogarth who was responsible for the plan of decorating the walls of the new building with works of art and who persuaded a group of artists to contribute to the cause, with the result that the fame of the Hospital as an art gallery almost exceeded its prestige as an orphanage. The Foundling chapel was the special interest of George Frederick Handel, who donated the organ and on May 1, 1750, gave a performance of the "Messiah," which realized £728. His presentations of the oratorio were said to have brought in, over the years, a total of £7000, and on his death he bequeathed "a fair copy of the score and all parts" to the Hospital.[91] In its achievements and failures alike the Foundling could provide future philanthropists with helpful object lessons.

5

The experience of the Lock and the Foundling Hospitals inevitably raised questions about the unfortunate women themselves. In a letter to the *Rambler,* "Amicus" pictured himself as wandering "wrapped up in thought [when] my eyes were struck with the hospital for the reception of deserted infants, till by a natural train of sentiment, I began to reflect on the fate of the mothers. For to what shelter can they fly?"[92] Testimony from the Lock seemed to suggest that, when discharged, its female patients had little alternative but to return to their former life. Nothing else could be expected unless some scheme were devised which would restore them to a measure of self-respect and supply them with means of earning an honest living.

The chief founder of the Magdalen Hospital was Robert Dingley, whose pamphlet, *Proposals for Establishing a Public Place of Reception for Penitent Prostitutes* (1758), set off the movement. Dingley, a merchant in the Russian trade in whose firm Jonas Hanway had been a partner, was a man of some imagination, a member of the Dilettanti Society of artists and patrons, a friend of Sir Joshua Reynolds, and from 1748 a member of the Royal Society.[93] The original com-

[90] *Ibid.,* pp. 283–84.
[91] *Ibid.,* p. 205.
[92] No. 107, 26 March 1751.
[93] H. F. B. Compston, *The Magdalen Hospital* (London, 1917), p. 26. Betsy Rodgers (*Cloak of Charity*) gives an excellent account of the founding of the Magdalen, but, perhaps because her principal theme is Hanway, ascribes more credit to him, as against Dingley, than the official historian of the institution would endorse. (Compston, *Magdalen Hospital,* p. 148.)

mittee of eight, which included the names of Hanway, major benefactor of the new institution, and John Thornton, pioneer Evangelical, appears to have been a more than moderately prosperous group, for seven gave £50 and the eighth, £30.[94] The Magdalen took over premises recently vacated by the London Hospital and prepared with some apprehensiveness to receive fifty penitents. For, although the plight of the prostitute struck a peculiarly tender chord in eighteenth-century sensibilities, the notion that great numbers wanted to be rehabilitated might turn out to be only wishful thinking. But a group appeared at once, from which six were admitted, a number being rejected as diseased and one for lack of professional qualifications, "being no prostitute." [95]

Notwithstanding the touch of sentimentality with which the age viewed such projects, the Magdalen appears to have been administered with a good deal of common sense and understanding. Dingley himself preached "the utmost Care and Delicacy, Humanity and Tenderness: so that this Establishment may be coveted, and not thought an House of Correction, but an happy Asylum." [96] His hopes seem to have been realized, for there was no lack of applicants. By March of 1761, nearly three hundred had been admitted, and during its first half century (1758–1807), the Hospital had 3865 inmates.[97] The instruments of rehabilitation were religious and moral instruction on the one hand and training in a useful trade or craft on the other. How effectively the institution fulfilled its primary purpose must remain in doubt. There was no lack of critics to charge that treating common prostitutes with such "singular humanity" was merely to reward and encourage vice. A study of the 246 inmates discharged in the years 1786–90, however, indicated that about two-thirds (157) were conducting themselves acceptably, while seventy-four were reported as "behaving ill." [98]

As eighteenth-century charities went, the Magdalen enjoyed good financial support. During the first eighteen months receipts exceeded £8100, and in a little over ten years the governors had laid the cornerstone for a new building in St. George's Fields, Southwark. In the early years, legacies came in at an average annual rate of nearly £1500.[99] A significant item in the Hospital's income was that of chapel collections, for Sunday services at the Magdalen attracted fashionable crowds more in search of sensation than of spiritual consolation.[100] Not only that, but the lurid eloquence characteristic of the chapel was admirably calculated to draw tears from the eyes and money from the pockets of such congregations.

[94] *Ibid.*, pp. 37, 39.

[95] *Ibid.*, p. 46. It was decided not to provide in the scheme for girls deserted by their parents, as had been at first contemplated. In consequence, Sir John Fielding started the Asylum for Female Orphans.

[96] Quoted by Rodgers, *Cloak of Charity*, p. 51.

[97] *Ibid.*; Highmore, *Pietas*, p. 221; Lord Kames, *Sketches*, II, 46.

[98] Highmore, *Pietas*, pp. 221–22.

[99] "Report by Walter Skirrow," *Corr. between the Treasury* . . . , 1865, p. 113. From the founding date to 1782, the figure was about £27,500, and from 1783 to 1802, about £19,500.

[100] Figures from 1758–95 apparently have not survived, but in the period 1796–1828 collections amounted to about £57,750.

It was the first chaplain of the Hospital, the ill-starred Reverend William Dodd, who set the pattern and from whose highly charged sermons the treasury unquestionably did handsomely, though in the end he brought grave discredit to the institution. Dodd's was, in fact, a tragic case of excessive ambition, extravagance in money matters, and lack of moral fiber, which drew him deeper and deeper into debt. In the end, he forged Lord Chesterfield's name to a bond, was tried and convicted, and was executed at Tyburn in June of 1777. This was not the kind of record ordinarily associated with chaplains of charitable institutions, and the Magdalen suffered temporarily from the unhappy affair. But presently the Dodd tragedy receded, and his successors, employing the same style of pulpit oratory, were hardly less skillful in dissolving a susceptible congregation into a state of lachrymose benevolence.

Some of the same charitable hands that established the Magdalen had been involved, two years before, in founding the Marine Society, an organization intended to cope with the twin problems of naval recruitment and destitute boys. The active agent was Jonas Hanway, whose philanthropic career was among the more memorable of the century. He had spent some years in Russia in charge of Dingley's St. Petersburg factory, where his most dramatic exploit was his taking a boatload of English cloth down the Volga and across the Caspian in an attempt to establish direct trade relations with Persia, at the time in a state of semi-anarchy. Returning to London in 1750, he retired from business and devoted the thirty-six years remaining to him to the theory and practice of philanthropy. Hanway was the principal founder of the Marine Society, one of the major figures in the Magdalen, and for fifteen years in the 1770's and '80's, he was vice-president of the Foundling, some of whose policies he sharply criticized.[101] What disturbed this vigorous, independent, mildly eccentric reformer was not the high death-rate as such but his conviction that the Hospital was only nibbling at the edges of the problem of neglected children. Presently he turned his critical eye also on the appalling waste of life in the parish workhouses of the Metropolis. His best-known efforts, which unhappily achieved no definitive success during his lifetime, were his heroic exertions to relieve the tragic lot of the climbing boys.

The Marine Society involved a conscious fusing of charity and patriotism. "British benevolence," Hanway foresaw, "being thus united with *native British fire,* will diffuse the *genuine* spirit of patriotism through these realms; and we may soon hope to see such *improvements* in maritime affairs, as posterity looking back, will view with *equal gratitude* and *applause*." [102] To man the fleet adequately against the French had put a heavy strain on ordinary methods of recruiting and was challenging patriotic ingenuity. Sir John Fielding, whose magistrate's bench offered an incomparable vantage point from which to study the criminal classes of the Metropolis, was gravely disturbed about the problem of

---

[101] *Candid Historical Account of the Hospital* (London, 1759) and *The Genuine Sentiments of an English Country Gentleman* (London 1759).
[102] *Account of the Marine Society,* 6th ed. (London, 1759), p. 13.

deserted children and had already developed a plan for sending such boys to sea.[103] Jonas Hanway, troubled by the same situation, got together a group of shipowners and merchants who in 1756 formed a Society to supply men and boys for the sea service and to equip them with the proper gear. During the war years 1756–63, some 10,625 men and boys were fitted out for sea duty at a cost of about £23,500.[104]

At the close of the War, however, the activities of the Marine Society lapsed, apparently waiting until the demand for seamen should revive and until a legacy of £22,000 left by an English merchant in Hamburg should be realized. In 1769 the bequest was cleared by the courts and the Society (richer by about £18,000 rather than the £22,000 originally left) returned to action. Now its schemes were directed chiefly toward discovering destitute or deserted boys, fitting them out, and apprenticing them in the merchant service. In 1786, the Society acquired a ship, where 150 to 200 boys would be "separated from their evil companions, cleansed from their rags and filthiness, softened into habits of subordination and obedience, inured to gentle discipline." [105] In terms of numbers affected and money involved, the Marine Society developed into one of the more imposing eighteenth-century charities. During its first half century (from 1756 to 1808), over 27,500 boys were equipped for service at sea and more than 36,000 landsmen volunteers were clothed as seamen for His Majesty's ships. Receipts came to nearly £246,000.[106]

To return to the medical and quasi-medical undertakings of the century, one cannot pass over the Royal Humane Society, though moderns may be more than a little mystified by the enthusiasm which it evoked. Its purpose was to encourage the resuscitation of apparent victims of drowning and to spread familiarity with the techniques of "the Godlike Art of Resuscitation," [107] which were evidently unknown at the time or, at any rate, rarely practiced. The Society thus managed to arouse interest not only by its humanitarian purpose but by the ingenious (and sometimes absurd) semi-scientific gadgetry it recommended. This was a combination that the latter eighteenth century, the England of the Society of Arts, found immensely appealing. The immediate inspiration came from Holland, where the ease of falling into canals and the large numbers of resulting fatalities had led to the formation of a society for reviving drowned persons. A memorandum of the Dutch society, translated by Dr. Thomas Cogan, so impressed William Hawes, an apothecary and later a physician, that he launched what was virtually a one-man rescue movement, offering to pay out of his own pocket those who brought to him, within a given time, the bodies of immersion victims. It was apparently Cogan who pointed out to him the absurdity of so taxing himself and suggested that others be enlisted to share the burden.[108]

[103] Highmore, *Pietas*, p. 788.
[104] *Ibid.*, p. 794.
[105] *Ibid.*, p. 813.
[106] *Ibid.*, pp. 815–16.
[107] *Brief Statement of the Royal Humane Society* (London, 1801), p. 73.
[108] J. Johnston Abrahams, *Lettsom* (London, 1933), p. 141.

The consequence was the formation in the spring of 1774 of a society for "the Recovery of Persons who are supposed Dead of Drowning" or other forms of suffocation — including "the fatal effects of a most heinous crime, said by FOREIGNERS, to be almost peculiar to this country — SUICIDE." [109] Some of the methods recommended by the Society were moderately hair-raising, such as the prescription of insufflating the large intestine with tobacco smoke, but other suggestions were less bizarre and, in fact, sound enough in principle, such as some of those for artificial respiration. But the Society showed a good deal of skill and imagination in dramatizing its activities. There were medals for those who had done distinguished work for the cause and prizes for essay writers. At annual meetings, those who in the course of the year had been reclaimed from death were exhibited to the governors, who could not help but feel a thrill of satisfaction as they contemplated the living fruits of their benevolence.[110] The Society established numerous stations in London and elsewhere in the Kingdom, and even such farflung points as Jamaica, Prague, St. Petersburg, and Boston, Massachusetts, joined in the movement. During its first twenty-seven years the Society boasted of having been responsible for saving nearly twenty-six hundred lives for a relatively modest (though unspecified) expenditure. Its list of more than six hundred subscribers, a fair number of them life governors at ten guineas, establishes the regard in which it was held by the charitable public.[111]

6

The movement for prison reform as a whole lies outside, or at least on the periphery, of philanthropy as understood in this study. Nor can the story of the debtor prisoners, more directly relevant since thousands were relieved by the action of charitable individuals and groups, be recalled in detail. It is enough to note that debtors' prisons were populated by men held for relatively trivial sums, with many of whom legal and jail fees far exceeded their original debt. The extortionate fees collected by jailers and the impositions of attorneys, bailiffs, and an army of hangers-on often made the debtor a semipermanent prisoner. A Commons Committee in 1792 reported such absurdities as costs of £28 superimposed on a debt of £12, and £6 6s. 10d. on 14s., and discovered one prisoner who had spent eight or nine years in the Fleet for a debt of £4 10s., and another who had been imprisoned twenty-four years for £35.[112]

Dismal as conditions appeared to the Commons Committee, there had, in fact, been some advance in the course of the century. The assertion of a reformer in 1716 that sixty thousand debtors were languishing in prison may not, Mrs. George

---

[109] *Trans. Royal Humane Society, 1774–84*, p. xvii.

[110] Malcolm, *Manners and Customs*, I, 83.

[111] *Brief Statement of the Royal Humane Society*, pp. 8–9, 77, 79. I have seen no financial statements of the Society for a sequence of years in the eighteenth century. Such reports as I have examined consist largely of accounts of successful cases and material designed to arouse interest in the work rather than figures on receipts and expenditures. For 1800, however, the income was about £1525, a sum that is probably typical enough of the annual receipts.

[112] *Commons Journals*, 47:647 (2 April 1792).

suggests, have been such a fantastic conjecture, if dependents living with them were included.[113] Whatever the total, there can be no doubt that in the early century the debtor prisoner population was of staggering dimensions. Over the decades some improvement in the situation of the debtors and other prisoners resulted from the action both of the Legislature and of private individuals, though neither was sufficiently sweeping to have a decisive impact on the problem.[114] A project for reforming Newgate and other prisons appeared early on the agenda of the S.P.C.K., and got as far as representations to members of the Society in Parliament.[115] Some prison visiting was carried on by the S.P.C.K. and by Wesley and the early Methodists, though the primary aim with both seems to have been the reform of prisoners rather than prisons.[116] It was James Oglethorpe who, bursting with indignation over the death of an acquaintance through maltreatment in the Fleet, obtained the appointment of a Committee "to inquire into the State of the Gaols of this Kingdom" and thus made prison reform, if only for a time, something of a public question.[117] A direct consequence of the Oglethorpe Report, with its melancholy revelation of a prison administration rotten from top to bottom, was an "Act for the Relief of Debtors," [118] which, whatever its shortcomings, made possible the release of several hundred of these unfortunates.

It was the unhappy situation and bleak prospects of this mass of liberated debtors that drew Oglethorpe into his quasi-philanthropic colonial project. Why not make it possible for such men to get a fresh start in the New World? The funds came from curious and disparate sources. Some £5000 was drawn from an estate of £15,000 left for charitable purposes. The estate got into litigation, and for Oglethorpe's services in handling the case the executors contributed £5000 to his project. A substantial sum was received from the Associates of Dr. Bray, who had banded together to perpetuate Bray's benevolences and to administer a bequest from D'Allone, secretary to Queen Mary in the years 1689–94. Yet £11,000, the figure the fund had now reached, was far too little for launching such an enterprise as Oglethorpe envisioned, and he and his friends found themselves carrying on a vigorous and uncommonly well-publicized campaign for subscriptions. For the original plan of settling a hundred debtors had burgeoned into a scheme for planting a new colony. Once the charter had been granted, City sources were successfully tapped, with the East India Company subscribing £600 and the Bank of England £300, while the Government, sensing a possible means of coping with the widespread vagrancy of the day, provided a grant of £10,000.

Although Oglethorpe's efforts established a new British settlement in North America, they offered no simple method of handling freed debtors or, indeed, of

---

[113] George, *London Life*, p. 307.

[114] J. L. Hammond, "Poverty, Crime, and Philanthropy," *Johnson's England*, I, 326; S. and B. Webb, *English Prisons under Local Government* (London, 1922), pp. 40–41.

[115] Allen and McClure, *Two Hundred Years*, pp. 54–57; McCulloch, "The Foundation of the S.P.C.K.," *Historical Magazine of the P. E. Church*, 18:14–15 (1949).

[116] Eric McC: North, *Early Methodist Philanthropy* (New York, 1914), p. 52.

[117] For the Oglethorpe Report, see *Commons Journals*, 21: 274ff, 376ff, 576ff.

[118] 3 Geo. II, c. 27.

British poor in general. During the first eight years, 915 British emigrants went to Georgia, not all, by any means, worthy souls who lacked only a fair chance to become self-maintaining.[119] And however philanthropic Oglethorpe's intentions may have been, from the beginning this was far more a public enterprise than a privately supported charity. Between 1733 and 1740, the colony received £94,000 in grants from Parliament, while collecting £18,000 in benefactions.[120] The source of the Georgia settlement lay in a philanthropic imagination, but its fulfillment would have been out of the question without the aid of the State.

Even before Oglethorpe's exposure of conditions in the Fleet and the Marshalsea, the plight of poor debtors had engaged the efforts of certain charitable souls, who, in general, were satisfied to relieve individual sufferers without denouncing the system itself. In August 1717, for example, an anonymous benefactor was said to have released thirty persons from Whitechapel Prison, clothed them, given them a dinner, and supplied each with 2s. 6d. and to have repeated his intervention six months later. Malcolm reports that, within three years, some eleven hundred small debtors (the number is difficult to credit) had been discharged from the Marshalsea by contributions from Roman Catholics. The impulse to do something for these unfortunates affected the most exalted circles. George I gave £1000, and his valet, a Turk named Mahomet, was said to have discharged nearly three hundred prisoners held for small sums.[121] There were, moreover, a number of charitable endowments, most of them small, which were added to in the course of the century, for releasing prisoners or for providing them with food and money.[122]

What could be accomplished by individual charity was obviously limited, but it was not until the early 1770's that the techniques of associated philanthropy were applied to imprisonment for debt. Here the driving force was James Neild, a prosperous London jeweler, who in his apprentice days had been shocked by a visit to a fellow apprentice held in the King's Bench for debt. In the 1760's he managed to spend a good deal of his leisure time as an investigator of prison conditions. But it was apparently a sermon preached in February 1772 by the bizarre "macaroni parson," the unfortunate William Dodd, in the Charlotte Chapel, Pimlico, that impelled Neild to invite the formal collaboration of others in the cause.[123] The collection, which came to £81, permitted Neild and a small committee to release thirty-four prisoners. The initial step seemed so reassuring that in May 1773 they constituted themselves a Society for the Discharge and Relief of Persons Imprisoned for Small Debts.

This was, on the whole, a well and prudently managed philanthropy, which could assert, with some justice, "that no charitable establishment hath met with

---

[119] *An Account Shewing the Progress of the Colony of Georgia,* 1741 *(Force's Tracts,* I, 30).

[120] *Ibid., passim;* L. F. Church, *Oglethorpe* (London, 1932), p. 252.

[121] Malcolm, *Manners and Customs,* I, 23–24, 27. For examples of the discharge of debtors by members of the nobility and gentry, see Lewis and Williams, *Private Charity in England, 1747–1757,* pp. 15ff.

[122] *S. C. on King's Bench, Fleet . . . ,* 1814–15, App. 29–30.

[123] The official *Account of the Society* discreetly omits naming the preacher.

a more universal concurrence, than that in which they have so warmly engaged." [124] The Society would act only where the debt was no more than £10
(or, rather, where the creditor could be satisfied for that sum) but the average
cost of releasing a prisoner came to somewhat less than £2 11s., including overhead. The policy was never to pay the whole debt but to require full clearance
from the creditor. Officials of the Society were at a good deal of pains to select
worthy cases, men with families who looked as though, if released free of debt,
they might be able to carry on adequately. From its foundation to the end of
the century, the Society was responsible for discharging 16,405 prisoners, or about
six hundred a year, at a total expenditure of £41,748. [125]

More than most charities, the Thatched House Society, as it was called, seems
to have caught the imagination of all sorts and conditions of benefactor. It was
aided, also, by the income from certain trust funds bequeathed in times past for
the discharge of debtors and now turned over to the Society. [126] The list of benefactors (from the date of foundation) takes up seventy-five pages in the 1799 edition of the *Account of the Society,* and includes the proceeds of charity sermons,
gifts from business firms, legacies, hackney coach fines, wagers, dining clubs, as
well as individuals. Such items as these will give the flavor of the Society's accounts:

	£	s.	d.
The Trustees of Bishop Andrews's Charity, fourteen Benefactions	1600	0	0
The Overplus of a Tavern-reckoning	0	12	9
A Wager concerning the fate of Mr. Wilkes's Election to the Mayoralty, intended to have been spent at a Tavern	3	13	6
Fines from nine Hackney Coachmen	3	8	0
The Provost of Eton	5	5	0
Sir Robert Herries, and Co., twenty-three Benefactions	84	5	0

It would be a mistake to think of the Thatched House Society as occupied
solely with freeing individuals from prison. Although no other purpose was
specified in its "Rules and Orders," the leaders never accepted imprisonment for
debt as just or tolerable, and they directed a continuous stream of propaganda
against it. The Annual Reports regularly began with denunciations of "Imprisonment for small Sums [as] unjust, impolitic, inhuman, and injurious to Society,"
and with a reasoned argument for its abolition. Indeed, one of the signal services
of the Society was precisely that of exposing the iniquitous treatment of small
debtors and the ghastly conditions in the country's penal institutions. James
Neild, an investigator of prisons standing as the legitimate successor to John

---

[124] [J. Neild] *An Account of the Society for the Discharge and Relief of Persons Imprisoned for
Small Debts* (1799 ed., London), p. 27.
[125] *Ibid.,* end paper.
[126] *Ibid.,* pp. 27–28.

Howard, may claim his share of credit for the gradual improvement of English prisons. His correspondence with Dr. Lettsom, published in the *Gentleman's Magazine* between 1803 and 1813, with its vivid details of prisons and prisoners, and his other accounts of his inquiries, culminating in his *State of the Prisons* (1812), assure him a conspicuous place in the line of penal reformers.

A category of prisoner other than those in English jails merits a passing reference, for few appeals were more certain of a favorable response than those on behalf of Christian captives confined or enslaved in Muslim states. In this study, trusts for ransoming such captives will figure chiefly as transcendent examples of the obsolete charity, whose income rose as its beneficiaries vanished, providing Chancery and Chancery lawyers with much complicated and profitable work.[127] It is worth recalling, however, that in the eighteenth century ransoms *were* being paid to the Barbary states for the release of Christian captives and that these releases were financed by direct contributions, as well as by income from bequests in trust. After a treaty with Morocco in 1721, when 280 persons were returned to England, their repatriation was made the occasion for something of a charitable carnival. "Clad in the Moorish habit," they went in procession to St. Paul's, where the crush was so great as to interfere with the collection, so that the "benevolent intentions of many charitable persons were frustrated" and only £100 was realized. At St. James's the King inspected them and gave them £500, after which they proceeded to Leicester House, where the Prince of Wales bestowed £250.[128] Again in 1734, 135 Britons, nine of them ship captains, recently freed from Barbary captivity, were received by the King, given suitable cash presents, and tendered a dinner at the Ironmongers' Hall.[129] How negotiations were handled and financed is obscure. Nor is it possible to estimate the volume of British charitable expenditure which was drawn into the patriotic and pious cause. But for some Englishmen, the plight of Christian slaves possessed a powerful and romantic appeal, vaguely related, perhaps, to the attraction which foreign missions in remote and exotic lands held for later generations.

The persecution of Protestants in Central Europe aroused comparable emotions among Englishmen. After harrying the Protestant residents of his province for some years, in 1731 the Archbishop of Salzburg finally drove them into exile, and thousands of families sought new homes in other German states and in Lithuania. When news of their afflictions reached London, a relief fund was at once launched which realized a total of about £33,000. At St. Margaret's, Westminster, for example, the Salzburgers benefited from four charity sermons and a house-to-house collection.[130] In fact, mass distress at home or abroad would often set off an

[127] Well-known foundations of this kind were the bequest of Thomas Betton (1723) who left half of his residuary estate for the purpose and the earlier bequest of Henry Smith (1627). The Smith bequest was a relatively minor item in what Jordan calls "the most important and certainly the most interesting" of the charitable trusts created in the 180 years covered by his study. (*The Charities of London, 1480–1660* [London and New York, 1960], p. 122.)

[128] Malcolm, *Manners and Customs*, I, 26.

[129] *Ibid.*, I, 42. Also see Lewis and Williams, *Private Charity*, pp. 68–70.

[130] Church, *Oglethorpe*, pp. 141–44; Malcolm, *Manners and Customs*, I, 29.

emergency fund. Large-scale fires invariably brought generous aid, and severe winters usually stimulated special relief collections, as in 1767–68, when Earl Percy contributed £400 and some £200 was collected at Almack's.[131] A wave of bad trade and unemployment, if sufficiently sharp, might arouse the charitable to open a subscription. To such appeals the response of eighteenth-century England may have been a bit erratic, but ordinarily, when any striking emergency arose, a group of well-placed individuals would sponsor a subscription list and would succeed in collecting a goodly sum for the cause. Associated philanthropy of an informal sort was an important element, along with organized societies, in the eighteenth-century charity complex.

A final category of social need which engaged the efforts of the charitable had to do with gaps in the Poor Law system. For the Law of Settlement, which defined eligibility for parish relief, disqualified such groups as Continental refugees, French prisoners-of-war, German Palatines en route to America, as well as Scots, Irish, and English without legal settlements. In the early century, the situation of the Huguenots in England excited a measure of compassion on the part of their fellow-Protestants and resulted in a series of institutions for their relief. Best known is the Hospital for Poor French Protestants (1718), part almshouse and part hospital (in the modern sense), which by the end of the century had space for "200 poor who are either very aged, or disordered in body or mind."[132] Other Frenchmen came to England as prisoners during the Seven Years War. When insufficient clothing, cold weather, and unsanitary quarters brought suffering and death to numbers of them, about £1800 was collected by subscription for their relief and a benefit staged at the Drury Lane of which the tone was set by the prologue:

> Cowards to cruelty are still inclin'd
> But generous pity fills each Briton's mind.
> Bounteous as brave; and though their hearts are steel'd
> With native intrepidity, they yield
> To Charity's soft impulse: this their praise,
> The proud to humble, and th'oppress'd to raise . . .
> All, who want it, your protection find;
> For Britons are the friends of all mankind."[133]

Germans as well as French were aided by the readiness with which Englishmen responded to a humanitarian appeal. On more than one occasion German Palatines were enticed to England by promoters who promised to ship them to America and then deserted. In 1764, for example, six hundred poor Palatines were abandoned by the (German) promoter and left to starve in the fields in the neighborhood of Bow, in addition to another two hundred still held on board ship for nonpayment of their passage from Germany. The pastor of the German Lutheran

---

[131] Malcolm, *Manners and Customs,* I, 74.
[132] Highmore, *Pietas,* p. 255.
[133] Malcolm, *Manners and Customs,* I, 52–53.

Church in Goodman's Fields took the initiative in opening a subscription list. The patrons of Batson's Coffee House provided £800, the King sent £300, and the Government supplied tents and other necessaries. Before the Palatines departed for Carolina, however, they were unhappily exposed to another side of eighteenth-century London when four tents filled with clothing were looted on Sunday morning during divine service, the children left to guard it having been decoyed by an offer of halfpence for cakes.[134]

One pervasive source of distress was the ineligibility of certain classes of citizens for public relief. In all of the larger cities, numbers of the poor, being without a legal settlement, had no claim on the parish authorities. Some of these were given a helping hand by more prosperous fellow-countrymen resident in the city. The Scottish Corporation of London had been chartered by Charles II in 1665 for the relief of "poor Natives of North-Britain, who are not entitled to any parochial Relief in England."[135] As the "Most Honourable and Loyal Society of Ancient Britons," Welsh residents of London established a successful charity school for children of their unfortunate countrymen, first in a single room near Hatton Garden, later at Clerkenwell Green, and finally in Gray's Inn Road, where facilities were provided for 150 pupils.[136] Some of the counties, of which Hereford (1710) was the earliest, founded associations for the assistance of needy compatriots in the Metropolis.

The most cosmic impulses were embodied in a late-century organization whose name, almost aggressively eighteenth-century, was the Society of Universal Good Will. Its origin lay in Norwich with the Scots Society, an agency for relieving Scotsmen not entitled to parochial relief, which in 1784 expanded its sphere almost to the dimensions implied by its new name, the Society of Universal Good Will. Scots continued to have first claim on its resources, then Englishmen, and finally foreigners, of whom a goodly number were assisted. Within a decade, over a thousand individuals from at least eighteen countries shared in the universal goodwill.[137] Although the Society itself failed to take root in London, the Strangers' Friends Societies, metropolitan and provincial, served a comparable purpose. It was the early Methodist visiting societies, with their design of "Visiting and Relieving Sick and Distressed Strangers and other Poor, at their respective Habitations,"[138] that here supplied the pattern. This was, in fact, one of the few areas in which the Wesleyan movement directly influenced philanthropy in the Age of Benevolence.[139]

[134] Ibid., I, 17, 64–72.
[135] A List of Charitable Institutions in Great Britain (York, 1794).
[136] A Brief Account of the . . . Society of Ancient Britons for Supporting the Charity School (London, 1827).
[137] Articles and Regulations Proposed for the Society of Universal Good Will (1789); Gray, English Philanthropy, pp. 169–70.
[138] From the title of the Benevolent, or Strangers' Friend Society founded in 1785 by London Methodists, quoted by Ford K. Brown, Fathers of the Victorians (Cambridge, 1961), p. 238.
[139] North, Methodist Philanthropy, pp. 46–52. For an example of a provincial Strangers' Friend Society organized by Methodists see Margaret B. Simey, Charitable Effort in Liverpool in the Nineteenth Century (Liverpool, 1951), p. 21.

Like other humane and informed observers of the eighteenth-century world, John Wesley had no doubt that its philanthropic activities represented a huge credit item. However gloomy he might be about the morals and manners of the age, he still had to grant it a new sensitiveness to human suffering. "While luxury and profaneness have been increasing on one hand," he conceded toward the end of his life, "on the other, benevolence and compassion toward all forms of human woe have increased in a manner not known before, from the earliest ages of the world. In proof of this we see more hospitals, infirmaries, and other places of public charity have been created, at least in or near London, within this century, than in five hundred years before." [140] The historian would be little inclined to reverse Wesley's judgment.

[140] Quoted by North, *Early Methodist Philanthropy,* p. 118.

CHAPTER III

THE EIGHTEENTH-CENTURY DONOR
AND THE CHARITABLE TRUST

THUS FAR the focus of this study has been on new agencies and institutions — notably on hospitals and charity schools, the most sriking innovations in the welfare pattern — established in the course of the century. More often than not, these were the handiwork of voluntary associations formed for the purpose, and the British middle- and upper-class community discovered in subscriptions to such societies an acceptable substitute for, or adjunct to, direct almsgiving. Still, the philanthropist whose benefactions ranged far beyond the subscription lists remained a decisive force in the world of charity. In the pages that follow the point of view will therefore shift from beneficiary to benefactor, from agencies to donors, especially to those whose resources were as substantial as their inclinations were charitable.

It would be hardly rewarding to speculate at length on the motives which inspired them to donate or bequeath sizable sums for public purposes. As with the support of voluntary organizations, piety, humanitarian concern, and patriotism might, in varying degrees, play a part, not to forget such less exalted but undeniably operative considerations as hope of public (or local) esteem, zeal to perpetuate one's name, and even antipathy to relatives, an unappealing but by no means unknown auxiliary of good works. It must suffice merely to note some of the trends characteristic of eighteenth-century charitable giving — the directions it took and the objects it favored, certain of its representative practitioners, and the legal arrangements governing the activities of benefactors.

At the outset it will be useful to recall that charities, in the view of the law, fall into two wholly distinct categories — voluntary and endowed. Although these may perform similar functions, in a legal sense they are quite unrelated. A children's home maintained by voluntary subscriptions operates on an entirely different basis in law from an orphanage supported by income from funds in trust. In the former the law is relatively uninterested, making few demands and offering few concessions, but around the charitable trust, the charitable benefaction in perpetuity, has grown up one of the more demanding and complicated (as well as lucrative) branches of equity practice. The law of charities is, of course, an immensely involved subject, and to attempt even a sketch of its development

would lie beyond the scope of this study and the capabilities of the writer.[1] Even
so, since charitable endowments will figure heavily in the chapters that follow,
some nontechnical paragraphs of explanation appear unavoidable.

Although the obvious take-off point is the Elizabethan Statute of Charitable
Uses of 1601,[2] the charitable trust was already a familiar enough device. Originally
a method of making charitable dispositions for religious purposes, it had developed under the patronage of the ecclesiastical courts, and had gradually been
extended to include secular uses.[3] That is, a donor or testator might now convey
in trust to another person or persons property to be used for purposes held in law
to be charitable, and the Court of Chancery, which inherited the work of the
ecclesiastical courts and was generally presided over by Churchmen, showed itself
favorably inclined toward such dispositions. If the objects of a trust were charitable,
the Court would not only accept it in perpetuity, waiving the ordinary rule of
law limiting the duration of a trust, but should the original purpose fail, would
specify new ones as near as possible (*cy-près*) to the testator's original intention.
For it had been assumed that the aim of the testator was "to benefit his own soul
by charitable works," and it would thus have been unthinkable that his intention
should be disappointed merely because the particular mode designated had proved
impracticable.[4] In short, as summarized by the Nathan Committee, charitable
trusts enjoyed three special privileges: "the privilege of exemption from the rule
against perpetuities; the privilege of being a valid or 'good' trust even if the testamentary disposition to charity was in imprecise terms (in which case precise terms
would be laid down by the Court); and the privilege of obtaining fresh objects
if those laid down by the founder were at the outset, or became, incapable of
execution."[5]

What the great Elizabethan Statute did was not so much to create a concept
of charitable uses as, in Jordan's words, to codify "a body of law badly wanting
classical statement" and to stimulate charitable giving by promising solid legal
protection to donors.[6] This epochal document proclaimed unmistakably that
charity had ceased to be exclusively a religious exercise and had now become an
instrument of social construction. A primary purpose of the Elizabethan Law was
to correct and prevent abuses in the administration of charities, and procedures
(to be noticed later in the chapter) were outlined for assuring reasonably honest
management of the nation's treasure in trust. There was also something of a
propaganda content in the Statute, a bid to other donors to follow the example
set by Sovereigns and "sondrie other well disposed persons." For them this

---

[1] A recent, not excessively technical, discussion by an acknowledged authority is George W. Keeton,
The Modern Law of Charities (London, 1962).

[2] 43 Eliz., c. 4.

[3] For a discussion of the background and significance of 43 Eliz. see Jordan, *Philanthropy in England*, pp. 109–17; for a summary account see Lord Nathan, *The Charities Act, 1960* (London, 1962),
pp. 2–4.

[4] *Nathan Report*, Par. 71, quoting *Tudor on Charities*, 5th ed. (1929), pp. 142–43.

[5] *Ibid.*, Par. 70.

[6] Jordan, *Philanthropy in England*, p. 112.

Elizabethan Parliament not only enumerated in the preamble of the Act, almost as an *aide-mémoire,* a wide variety of uses considered charitable, but also offered specially favored treatment to benefactions left for such purposes.

No doubt, by clarifying the legal status of dispositions to charity and by stressing the benevolent interest of the public authorities, 43 Elizabeth had something to do with the amazing outpouring of wealth for public purposes that marked the first four decades of the century. More than that, the old enactment, and specifically the preamble, with its apparently casual enumeration of charitable uses, became the foundation on which, during the following three and a half centuries, was erected a massive, elaborate, and (some equity lawyers have been inclined to urge) wobbly structure of charity law. From that day to this the preamble has remained the ultimate authority in determining a charitable use, even though it provides no definition, merely a somewhat random list of objects deemed charitable centuries ago. Yet, though at various times sentiment has seemed to be gathering in favor of a more precise definition, in the end the decision has always gone against attempting to reduce the concept to a legal formula.

To reach satisfying quantitative conclusions about the volume and direction of eighteenth-century giving would require statistical analysis comparable to Professor Jordan's of Tudor-Stuart philanthropy. New charitable dispositions and bequests tended, by and large, to follow paths already explored and made familiar by donors of an earlier age. Save for medical institutions (admittedly an important qualification) and, less significantly, charity schools, the age saw few departures of consequence in the objects for which philanthropists bequeathed their resources. With a good many exceptions — Thomas Guy's majestic foundation is perhaps the most memorable — new eighteenth-century endowments lack the imaginative sweep that Professor Jordan finds in those of the two previous centuries, when Englishmen were seeking to translate "their bold aspirations into social reality by prodigal outlays of their own substance." [7]

Yet to conclude that eighteenth-century philanthropy had gone into a drastic decline would be to miss the significance of the new mechanisms through which charitable giving was carried on. The most commanding accomplishments of the century, to repeat, were not those of individuals establishing perpetual trusts for public purposes but of societies and associations, and these wrought a profound change in philanthropic procedures. A charitable impulse that in the past might have found expression in a perpetual rent charge on property now might take the form of subscriptions to an established institution or society. The founding of the Lunatic Asylum at York in the 1770's, for example, was accomplished through a subscription list of about three hundred names, which included a number of amounts as high as £500 and many of £100. [8] The new general and special

---

[7] *Ibid.,* p. 322.
[8] *Abstract of the* [Gilbert] *Returns of Charitable Donations, 1786–88,* repr. 1816, pp. 1440ff.

hospitals, as a whole, were made possible by such bodies of subscribers, and their successful operation depended on a continuous flow of benefactions.

This was only part of the change. The existence of responsible voluntary institutions appealing regularly for support led to alterations in the habits of testators — how generally it is hazardous to guess. Certainly perpetual trusts did not figure as heavily in charitable bequests as had been the case, on Jordan's evidence, in the earlier period.[9] Benefactors, more often than not, left legacies with no strings attached to agencies which, suffering from the penury native to the charity world, tended to regard them as current income. Such benefactions were not added to the charitable endowments of the country and therefore find no place in official charity inventories (the Gilbert Returns and the Reports of the Brougham Commissioners). Save for legacies to the more famous institutions, with their annual reports and other published materials, they have dropped out of the historical record and for practical purposes are irrecoverable.

Still one can point to such figures as the £27,500 received by the Magdalen Hospital in legacies during its first sixteen years, the bulk of it without specific trust provisions, and the same applies to the £8300 which went to the British Lying-In between 1750 and 1770. In the years 1751–91 St. Luke's Hospital for Lunatics was left more than £80,000 in legacies (including £30,000 from a Master of the Rolls, Sir Thomas Clarke). What fraction came in trust is not clear, but most of it seems to have been treated as capital by the charity. As early as 1780 the dividend income of this institution exceeded £3000.[10] The London Hospital took a rather daring step two years after its foundation in 1740 when the committee decided to form a capital stock and to consider legacies as belonging to this fund — from which one may infer that a substantial number came as free money.[11] All this is to suggest that no study of eighteenth-century endowments, however exhaustive, would provide an adequate measure of philanthropic giving. To a degree unknown in Tudor-Stuart times the stream of charity flowed outside channels marked by the law of charitable trusts.

Even with the volume of giving that took the form of subscriptions and cash legacies, the value of Britain's charitable endowments increased enormously in the course of the century. It would be impossible to fill in a statistical picture of this growth, which, of course, resulted both from the rise in value of older endowments and the founding of new. All that can be done is, by means of a few, almost random, samples, to give some indication of the trend.

It is obvious that the growth in income from older endowments reflected chiefly the increased value of land, urban and agricultural. For land provided better than three-quarters of Britain's charitable income.[12] Trustees, to be sure,

[9] Jordan, *Philanthropy in England*, p. 118.

[10] *Corr. between the Treasury, Home Office, and the Charity Commission*, 1865, p. 113; *Account . . . of the British Lying-In Hospital* (1771), pp. 26–29; *Reasons for Establishing St. Luke's* (1780); *Reasons for the Establishing and Further Encouragement of St. Luke's* (1851).

[11] *Corr. between the Treasury . . . .*, 1865, p. 235.

[12] Although this proportion is based on the highly incomplete Gilbert Returns, it gives what is

often failed to get full benefit from the general rise in values, owing to their addiction to excessively long leases, sometimes on over-generous terms, and to the practice of reletting at the old rental with only a fine to represent the increase in value. A case in point is the Girls' Hospital at Norwich, where, the Brougham Commissioners discovered, of about twenty leases only one was for less than ninety-nine and one for 202 years, with the average about 125. The property, the Commissioners noted disapprovingly, was let "for terms of much longer duration than is usually prescribed by a court of equity, even for building leases, and the rents in general fall far short of the value of the demised premises."[13]

Though charity property may have been handled less efficiently than ordinary land, it shared in the beneficent effects of urban growth and agricultural improvements. Receipts from the Holborn estate of St. Clement Danes, for example, nearly doubled in the course of the century.[14] The Elephant and Castle charity property was rented originally (1673) for £5 a year; by 1797 it was returning £190 and, by 1818, £623.[15] The Coventry property belonging to the Free Grammar School showed the following gratifying increases in income:[16]

1743	£155	14s.	0d.
1763	202		
1780	223	4	
1801	284	8	
1820	486	5	

During the first half of the century the endowed income of the Somerset Hospital at Froxfield, Wilts., grew from £226 to £500, while a farm of forty-one acres, left in trust to the Feltmakers' Company in 1692, by the early nineteenth century was yielding three times its original rental.[17] It would be easy to cite more spectacular increases. Even though the most dramatic rise in land values was a nineteenth-century phenomenon, clearly British charities were profiting from the expansion of the economy that took place between the Restoration and the Revolutionary Wars.

But as regards new endowments the eighteenth century was by no means a sterile period. Even though these were established, on the whole, for fairly conventional purposes, their number was great and their total value considerable. As a means, admittedly crude, of gauging the volume of new endowments, about a thousand (973) trusts were tabulated with their dates of foundation. These benefactions, taken from the Gilbert Returns and the Brougham Reports, represent

probably a fair enough picture. The Gilbert totals are about £210,450 from land as against about £48,250 from invested funds. (*Abstract of the [Gilbert] Returns, 1786–88,* repr. 1816, p. iii.)

[13] *27th Report of the [Brougham] Commissioners,* 1834, p. 552.

[14] R. J. Pooley, "History of the St. Clement Danes Holborn Estate Grammar School, 1552–1952" (unpubl.), pp. 31, 43.

[15] *16th Brougham Report,* 1826–27, p. 380.

[16] *28th Brougham Report,* 1834, p. 127. By 1832 the property was yielding nearly £900.

[17] *R. C. on the London Livery Companies* (C. 4073), 1884, III, 378, 421.

a half-dozen scattered counties and include both urban and rural areas. Of the total, a little less than 40 per cent (39.47) antedated 1688, another 35 per cent (35.66) were established in the years 1689–1740, and about 25 per cent (24.87) between 1740 and 1788. That is, over 60 per cent of the endowments noted dated from the century 1689–1788. There was, of course, a good deal of variation from district to district. In ten City of London parishes, the preponderance of early foundations was predictably heavy, some 80 per cent antedating 1688; the records of St. Dunstan's-in-the-West show all but three of its thirty-two trusts to have been established before 1688. In other areas — parts of South Lancashire and the High Peak of Derbyshire, for example — the balance was nearly as great on the side of later foundations. Such raw and meager data are, of course, no more than indicative, and they lead to no very solid conclusions.[18] They do suggest, however, that the habit of remembering charity in one's will, which produced so many of the Tudor-Stuart foundations of all sizes, continued to influence eighteenth-century testators. More conclusive, at least for one important branch of charitable concern, are the figures, shown in the table, on the foundation of almshouses and charities for the aged as reported by the Rowntree Committee. These reveal the early eighteenth century as a conspicuously productive era for such trusts:[19]

	CHARITIES WITH RESIDENT ACCOMMODATION	WITHOUT ACCOMMODATION
1496–1595	55	13
1596–1645	121	24
1646–1695	99	44
1696–1745	116	47
1746–1795	34	47

In its record of establishing almshouses the eighteenth century failed to maintain the standard set by its predecessor (150 to 220) but was far ahead in nonresidential charities for the aged (94 to 68). Even though, to repeat, much of eighteenth-century giving took place other than through charitable trusts and though these tended to be rather traditional in their objects, still the number of new foundations was formidable.

Neither in establishing new trusts nor in ordinary cash bequests did eighteenth-century testators show much inclination to branch out into new fields of philanthropy. An examination (with no attempt at statistical exactitude) of the Brough-

---

[18] These figures, it will be noted, have to do only with the *numbers* of trusts and not their *value*. To reach a satisfying estimate of the latter would require more effort than seems justified in a work of this kind, and a higher degree of statistical sophistication than the writer possesses. See also the analysis of Charles Wilson ("The Other Face of Mercantilism," *Trans. Royal Hist. Soc.,* 5th ser., 9:93–94 [1959]), whose concern is chiefly with the half-century after 1660.

[19] B. S. Rowntree, Chairman, *Old People: Report of a [Nuffield Foundation] Survey Committee* (Oxford, 1947), p. 117. The charities in this table are those that were "restricted by residence of beneficiaries." In unrestricted endowments, few in number, the eighteenth century surpassed the sixteenth and seventeenth.

am Commissioners' material on a half-dozen scattered provincial communities gives a reasonably accurate impression of the range of eighteenth-century endowed charities. The largest number of new trusts, often trivial in amount, were for doles for the poor — or, as sometimes expressed, "for the benefit of the poor generally." Probably doles in money or kind would represent something like half of the total number of new trusts founded. Behind doles would follow trusts for educational purposes, smaller in number but larger in individual amounts. In some cities religious and almshouse foundations were of consequence. Beyond these objects there was a scattering of benefactions for miscellaneous purposes, such as apprenticeship fees, loans to tradesmen, marriage portions, or land for general public purposes. Up to the end of the eighteenth century, medical charities figure occasionally, but their legacies were likely to come without trust provisions.

A glance at eighteenth-century endowments in a number of the older provincial cities tends to confirm what has already been suggested. Major foundations most commonly date from Tudor or Stuart times, and eighteenth-century donors directed their flow of benevolence to those established institutions or to the familiar charities for the poor. Scrutiny of eighteenth-century trusts at Exeter, for example, reveals no considerable change in the objects of charity. In 1800 bequests were being left for about the same purposes as in 1660. There is, to be sure, some tendency to remember charity schools, but the majority of legacies are for the classic charitable objects — bread, clothing, or money for the poor, maintaining the poor in an almshouse or boys and girls in one of the "hospitals," or relief for poor tradesmen or artisans. Benefactors were as various as beneficiaries. There were merchants, often members of one of the Companies, remembering the poor of their own Mysteries; there were professional men, physicians or clergymen, two of whom left funds for the support of local boys at the universities; and there was an occasional country gentleman.

Norwich conforms in general to the pattern of Exeter and other old and prosperous provincial cities. Here again the chief charitable establishments date, in the main, from the sixteenth or seventeenth century, but their resources were markedly increased by the benevolence of the eighteenth. If one compares the charity landscape of 1700 with that of 1800, the difference seems to be one of degree rather than of kind. The Great Hospital, for example, established originally by a grant of Edward VI, was so generously remembered by testators and profited so handsomely from the rise in land values that by the time of the Brougham survey in the early nineteenth century its annual income was nearly £6000.[20] Other old foundations experienced similar growth, but the basic charity situation remained little changed. Norwich, however, was the site of one institution which looked, however uncertainly, toward the future. This was a hospital, one of the earliest in the country, for the care and treatment of the insane. The founder, Mrs. Mary Chapman, a clergyman's widow, first built and in 1717 endowed Bethel Hospital "for the convenient reception and habitation of lunaticks, and not for natural-born

[20] *27th Brougham Report*, 1834, p. 519.

fools or ideots." [21] The Hospital promptly became a favorite philanthropy for charitably inclined Norwich testators, receiving in the course of the century some thirty-five legacies totaling nearly £8000. [22]

Rural and village charities, as might be expected, tended to be smaller and even more traditional in character than those of urban localities. A random sequence of trusts established in rural Cheshire includes the following bequests: £400 for apprenticing poor children (1732); £200 to the poor of the parish (1737); £50 for bread for the poor (1786); £1 4s. annually to buy books for children (1719); £10, the interest to provide bread for widows and orphans at Christmas (1789); £150 left by a London merchant for the poor of two villages (1721). [23] Such a list is adequately representative of rural charities throughout the country, and suggests both the dimensions and the scope of the run-of-the-mine bequest. [24]

Not infrequently a local boy who had made his fortune in London might leave a substantial bequest to his native village. This was, in fact, a familiar pattern. Such benefactions, especially if they involved London real estate, sometimes provided charity resources far beyond the needs of a village population and even became engines of demoralization. Or a local gentleman, perhaps for reasons which did him little credit, might leave his entire estate to village charities. Of such was the notorious Jarvis bequest (1793) in Herefordshire, by which George Jarvis, apparently piqued over the marriage of his daughter, left a fortune of about £100,000 to the poor of three parishes, whose total population was under nine hundred. This fantastic trust, though reformed by a special Act of Parliament in 1852, continued to plague the Charity Commissioners, who, as late as 1946, were holding a public inquiry into its administration. [25] Clearly the Jarvis endowment merits its inclusion in Lord Beveridge's "Charities' Chamber of Horrors." [26]

Metropolitan testators appear somewhat more aware of new opportunities for philanthropy than those in provincial cities and villages. The larger wills not infrequently remember, along with the classic objects — doles for the poor, trusts for apprenticeship fees, and the rest — one or more of the recently established agencies. If one examines the obituaries in the *Gentleman's Magazine* for a typical year (1750 in this case) he will find a series of bequests predominantly traditional in their objects but with occasional recognition of newer interests. Mrs. Mary Parker of Clapham, to take a fair example, left a series of bequests totaling £1500 and divided as follows: £100 to the London Infirmary; £300 for the relief of the sick; £300 to bind poor children; £300 for the relief of poor widows; £200 for the relief of poor men; £300 for the discharge of poor prisoners for debt.

In the same year, Mrs. Dash, reported to have died "immensely rich," left £500

[21] Anon., *The History of the City and County of Norwich* (Norwich, 1768), pp. 495–96.
[22] *27th Brougham Report,* 1834, p. 597.
[23] *31st Brougham Report,* 1837–38, pp. 461ff.
[24] Dole charities, as the records of the Charity Commission show, have by no means gone completely out of fashion. See, for example, the list of trusts founded between June and October 1951, as printed in the *Nathan Report,* App. H.
[25] Memorandum by the Charity Commissioners to the Nathan Committee, d. 25 May 1950.
[26] *Voluntary Action* (London, 1948), p. 366.

for building and endowing an almshouse in Isleworth, where she was buried in the grand manner. Mrs. Ducasse left £2500 to the poor of the French Church. John Locke, a City merchant, enriched the Foundling Hospital and St. Thomas's by £500 each, and one Willis, a stationer, left £500 to the poor of St. Margaret's, Westminster, £500 to the Westminster Infirmary, and — this introduced something of a novel note — £600 to "the farmers about Tothill fields, who had suffered by the cow distemper." [27]

3

Perhaps the sweep and variety of eighteenth-century philanthropy can best be suggested by noticing a half-dozen additional donors. These will make up an oddly mixed bag, for the century produced the same diversity as other ages. One finds mingled in variable proportions the impulses of religion, humanitarianism, vanity, social responsibility, malice, determined (and often bigoted) convictions on some special question, or the simple puzzlement of testators who lacked close relatives. But this was an age which took pride in its charitable activities and was inclined to honor the testator who did not forget to remember good works when making his will — so much so, in fact, that the fashion of philanthropy occasionally evoked ironic protests. A newspaper in 1748 could report that "Last week died Dr. Brown, a Physician of great eminence in Bedford: and has left his fortunes which were considerable, to a very great number of relations, notwithstanding the current vanity of this age to leave a fortune to some public body which might give him a name and overlook his own kindred." [28]

A London philanthropist at once conventional and eccentric was Samuel Wright, who died in 1735, leaving to charity some £21,000. His benevolence has been commemorated in a pamphlet entitled somewhat equivocally *London's Wonder: Or the Chaste Old Batchelor.*[29] Wright had inherited a fortune of over £40,000 from his father, a master wire-drawer, who apparently had done handsomely from sales of gold and silver lace during the Restoration. Although Samuel's religious affiliation was Nonconformist, he included both Church and Dissent in his charitable bequests. These, however, followed the familiar pattern — large amounts for twelve clergymen (six Church of England and six Nonconformist), for forty poor families, forty widows, forty maids, and twenty boys. Also profiting were the Society for the Reformation of Manners, the S.P.G., St. Thomas's, St. Bartholomew's, Bethlem, prisoners in four London prisons, and the poor of five parishes. Indeed, the most original thing in Samuel Wright's last will was his vehement denial of emotional interest in womankind: "I do hereby under my own Hand, and in the presence of Almighty God, and his Holy Angels, before whom I am going to appear, declare to all the world that I never carnally knew any Woman whatsoever, as a Man does his Wife nor [was] ever under any Contract or En-

[27] *Gentleman's Magazine*, 20:139, 188, 429, 479 (1750).
[28] *General Advertiser*, 18 July 1748, quoted by W. J. P. Wright, "Humanitarian London from 1688 to 1750," *Edinburgh Review*, 246:295 (October 1927).
[29] London, 1737.

gagement with any Woman directly or Indirectly, upon any Account whatsoever."
Samuel Wright's philanthropy appears to have been a function equally of piety
and misogyny.

Bristol offers two curiously contrasting types of eighteenth-century philanthropist, one from the early and the other from the latter part of the century. Although
religion bulked heavily in the charitable activities of both, the two embodied such
contrary conceptions of duty to God and one's neighbor as to raise doubts about
the usefulness of such a category as "religious motivation." Edward Colston
(b. 1636), whose name is perpetuated in present-day Bristol by a series of foundations, as well as by streets and buildings, was in most of his qualities a man of the
previous century, and his charitable preoccupations were those of the Anglican-
Tory Revival, with all of the narrow bigotry of which the movement was capable.
The pattern of his life was typical of many shrewd and ambitious provincial
youths who preferred to compete for high stakes in the Metropolis rather than
enjoy the certainty of a good livelihood at home. And like others of his contemporaries who prospered, especially those who remained celibate, Colston lavished large sums, perhaps in the neighborhood of £80,000, on his native city.[30]

It is hardly surprising that Colston's philanthropies reflected his violent religious
prejudices. For his political and religious attitudes had been molded during the
Commonwealth and Restoration, and all of his charities had on them the stamp
of his fanatical High Anglicanism, his hatred of Whiggery and Dissent, and an
unembarrassed determination to impose his own convictions on his beneficiaries.
Within two decades (1690–1710), he built and presented to Bristol the almshouse
on St. Michael's Hill and a school (Colston's) to accommodate a hundred boys;
he contributed to the rebuilding and enlarging of the Merchants' Almshouses and
supplied the building for a charity school (Temple Colston) which had formerly
been supported by voluntary contributions;[31] he founded a series of Lenten lectures, himself prescribing the subjects, and provided funds for beautifying and
adorning four or five Bristol churches and the Cathedral itself.[32] But Colston's
charitable activities, in which are mingled the strains of civic pride and politico-
religious emotions of a violent sort, were lacking in the kind of human sympathy
that we associate with a genuinely philanthropic outlook. His gifts were hedged
about with rigid political and religious restrictions — such as those barring the
admission of non-Anglicans to Colston's School and prohibiting the apprenticing
to Dissenters of boys from the School or from Temple Colston. His schools, in
fact, were designed less as vehicles for education than as instruments for indoc-
trinating Bristol youth with the true faith, political and religious. Colston's path
as a philanthropist followed a narrowly sectarian groove.

Edward Colston and Richard Reynolds, the Quaker philanthropist, had little
in common beyond a pronounced talent for making money and a certain addiction

[30] Bryan Little, *The City and County of Bristol* (London, 1954), p. 183.
[31] John Wade, *An Account of Public Charities in England and Wales* (London, 1828), p. 90.
[32] Little, *The City and County of Bristol*, p. 184.

to giving it away. Between them lay decades of social change, and they are marked off spiritually by at least the hundred years that separated their birth dates. The passions of the era of Sacheverell and the Schism Act which had animated Colston were long since spent, and the philanthropy, even the religious philanthropy, of the late century was less closely allied with sectarian exclusiveness. The religious impulses which inspired Reynolds, one of the great line of Quaker philanthropists, were, of course, of wholly different texture from Colston's. To Reynolds, as to his associates in the Society of Friends, property was a trust held of God, and as stewards they were accountable for their stewardship. The requirements of charity could not, therefore, be met merely by giving away a surplus that could be readily spared or leaving a bequest as a memorial to oneself. Reynolds had little use for what he called *post-mortuary* charities and included no such legacies in his will.[33] For him charity was virtually a way of life, made possible not only by a large fortune but by a scale of living so frugal and unostentatious as to be almost austere.

Reynolds has the distinction of being one of the earliest philanthropists who owed their resources to the new industrialism. The son of an iron merchant, he became the partner and then the son-in-law of Abraham Darby II, whose iron works in the Severn Valley were the scene of the country's most revolutionary advance in iron production. During the bulk of his working life, he was in charge of the furnace at Ketley, which was operated as an autonomous undertaking,[34] but for several years in the 1760's, after the death of his father-in-law, he managed the parent works at Coalbrookdale. Throughout his life Reynolds was engaged in the practice of charity, the charity both of personal service and shared wealth, but his retirement from business in his mid-fifties (1789) enabled him to concentrate more exclusively on well-doing. He had already contributed generously to schools both at the sites of the Darby furnaces and in other parts of the country. Now, during his retirement, first at Coalbrookdale and even more after his move to Bristol in 1804, philanthropy became, along with his Quakerism, the consuming preoccupation of his life.

The bulk of his benevolences it is impossible to trace, for he adhered to the Scriptural teaching. Reynolds' alms were not done before men to be seen of them but, in what must have been a great number of instances, were bestowed anonymously. One of his favorite expedients was, after having made his regular contribution, to forward a larger gift with no name attached. He was also accustomed to place large sums at the disposal of poorer Friends who were themselves unable to give much. As a Bristol philanthropist he was concerned with aiding both institutions and individuals. In the former category it was such charities as the Strangers' Friend, the Orphan Asylum, and the Alms-Houses that enlisted his greatest interest. In 1808 he established a trust with capital of £10,500 (invested by

---

[33] Hannah M. Rathbone, *Letters of Richard Reynolds with a Memoir of His Life* (London, 1852), p. 243.

[34] T. S. Ashton, *Iron and Steel in the Industrial Revolution* (Manchester, 1924), pp. 42–43.

trustees in lands in Monmouthshire) for the benefit of seven such agencies, and he
was always ready to come to their rescue in special crises. On various occasions,
for example, he contributed £4000 to the Trinity Alms-Houses, £2600 to the
Bristol Infirmary, and £1260 to the Strangers' Friend. With time and energy
Reynolds was as generous as with money. To such philanthropic activities he
brought some of the shrewdness that had made him a successful businessman — as
when he refused a check for £500 from a man of wealth, who then promptly
substituted one for twice the amount.[35] Nor was Reynolds' range of interest confined to Bristol. He maintained agents in London, to one of whom he remitted
some £20,000 during the distress of 1795.[36] In both his local and his more distant
charities he combined the compassionate sympathy of the pious Quaker with the
insistence of the Quaker businessman on methodical procedures. Although it
would not do even to guess at the volume of Reynolds' benevolences, by eighteenth-
century standards they must have been enormous — at one time he was said to
be regularly distributing £8000 a year — and they offer a suggestive index of the
magnitude of the fortune that an astute and enterprising manufacturer might
accumulate.[37]

   More typical of the race of sizable provincial philanthropists was Richard Taunton (1694–1752), leading wine merchant and mayor of Southampton, whose legacies enriched the charities of his district by some £13,000. Taunton's career
followed, in essentials, a familiar enough eighteenth-century curve — the rise to
wealth through trade and with it social acceptance and political influence. This
is not to imply that Taunton's ascent began on the lowest rung of the ladder. His
father and grandfather had been prosperous maltsters in the town, and there were
already intimations of future local eminence.[38] Richard himself turned from the
malthouse to the wine trade, at the time the most active commerce of the port,
and presently found himself the leading wine merchant of the town. With his
growing wealth he moved first into local real estate and then into local politics
and society, passing through the conventional stages to the mayoralty in 1734 (and
again in 1743) and a coat of arms in 1735. A second marriage had already paved
the way to his acquiring an estate near Andover and establishing himself as lord
of the manor. Even his involvement in two notoriously corrupt parliamentary
elections, one of which was investigated and the outcome reversed by the Commons, left Taunton's prestige in Southampton undimmed. This was, after all, the
Age of Walpole and the Pelhams.

   One suspects that Taunton's philanthropies were principally those of the local
patriot who was inspired by a desire to benefit his city and, presumably, to gain
recognition from contemporaries and posterity as a benefactor of the community.

---

[35] Rathbone, *Letters of Richard Reynolds,* pp. 70–74, 299.

[36] *Ibid.,* p. 73.

[37] Arthur Raistrick, *Quakers in Science and Industry* (London, 1950), pp. 144–45.

[38] Taunton's sister Mary was married to John Bampton, future Canon of Salisbury and founder of
the Bampton Lectures at Oxford, and an aunt, the wife of Isaac Watts, Sr., was the mother of the
hymn-writer

Of his lifetime charities we know little save that he was one of the earliest subscribers to the Winchester County Hospital, a pioneer among provincial medical
institutions. Presumably the fact that Taunton had no direct heirs accounted in
a large measure for his leaving to charity what might otherwise have gone into
launching a county family. Specifically he bequeathed £5000 to the Winchester
County Hospital to erect a new building, £100 to St. Luke's Hospital for Lunatics
in London, £1400 to the Southampton Corporation to pay the minister of Holy
Rood for reading public prayers twice daily and "for the relief of decayed Alder-
men" or their widows, and £200 for bread for the poor.

It was also Taunton's intention that his entire estate, after the payment of
specific legacies, should benefit "my dear town of Southampton aforesaid, by the
employment and maintenance of poor people there and bringing up their children
in work and industry fitting them for the sea." [39] But a Chancery suit brought
by the heirs at law under the Mortmain Act of 1736 invalidated the bequest as far
as the real property was concerned, and resulted in a loss to the trustees of some
£300 a year. [40] In the end a Chancery scheme (1760) authorized a school where
not more than twenty Southampton boys should be taught reading, writing, arithmetic, and navigation to fit them for service at sea. Though losing its distinctive
maritime character in the mid-nineteenth century, Taunton's School continued
to emphasize practical training and to fulfill the purposes which its founder had
envisioned. Eighteenth-century practitioners of charity were, to say the least, a
varied group, and it would, perhaps, be excessive to speak of any as "representative." Still, the benefactions of Richard Taunton proclaimed in highly characteristic
terms the aspirations of the provincial mercantile philanthropist whose civic loy-
alty and robust belief in improvement blended with a natural desire to leave a
fitting memorial to his name.

If Taunton's philanthropies were reasonably orthodox, those of the Reverend
William Hanbury of Church Langton, Leicestershire, were imaginative to the
point of fantasy. It would be hard to find a more utopian cluster of charitable
schemes than those projected in the 1750's by the exuberant and eccentric rector,
who proposed, through the magic instrumentality of compound interest, to equip
his village with an amazing array of cultural and religious institutions. The basis
of the parson's sanguine plan was his own enthusiasm for horticulture and his
conviction that it could be made an instrument of social regeneration. [41] He laid
in a supply of plants and seeds, importing quantities from North America, and

[39] Taunton's will. Through the kindness of Mr. John Bowle, information on Richard Taunton and
his benefactions was supplied to me by the Headmaster of Taunton's School.
[40] E. R. Aubrey, ed., *Speed's History of Southampton* (Southampton, 1909), p. 80. The Mortmain
Act and its significance will be considered later in this chapter.
[41] On the Hanbury project see William Hanbury, *An Essay on Planting and a Scheme for Making
it Conducive to the Glory of God and the Advantage of Society* (Oxford, 1758), and his *History of the
Rise and Progress of the Charitable Foundations at Church Langton* (London, 1767); *32d Brougham
Report,* Part V, 1839, pp. 246ff; John Nichols, *History and Antiquities of the County of Leicester,*
4 vols. (London, 1795–1815), II, 685–92; Guy Paget and L. Irvine, *Leicestershire* (London, 1950),
pp. 220–23; *VCH, Leicestershire,* I, 395–96; II, 242.

covered fifty acres with nearly twenty thousand trees. Unfortunately the rector
was a better hand with trees than with trustees, and the history of the project
was a chronicle of dissension between the headstrong founder and those in whom
he had vested legal responsibility for the venture. Hanbury's earlier proposals,
though certainly out of the ordinary, showed little trace of the megalomania that
later pervaded them. They called for the sale of trees from the nursery, with the
interest from the proceeds (when these reached £1500) to be used for improvements in the parish church and for establishing a school. As the returns increased,
other projects would be added, and when the resources of the charity amounted
to £10,000, its beneficent operations might be extended to other parishes.

Yet Hanbury was not the kind of man to be satisfied with modest success or
reconciled to moderate failure. During the first eight or nine years, in spite of his
feuds with trustees, the project still had some relation to reality. But in 1767, on
the strength of success that was by no means spectacular, he cut loose with a series
of deeds of trust, which take up more than half of his 450-page book on the
Church Langton charities. These singular documents, suggesting a touch of
paranoia, seem almost designed as blueprints for a fountain of eternal wealth
and welfare. Conceivably the rector had persuaded himself of the truth of such
paeans as the verses written in his honor by the poet and satirist Charles
Churchill:

> Borne on the wings of endless fame,
> To distant climes shall Hanbury's name
>   With wonder be conveyed;
> While future sons, with wild surprise,
> On those bleak hills see cedars rise,
>   And roses form a shade.
>
> Wrapt into future times, I see
> (O glorious aid of Prophecy!)
>   Aspiring columns rise!
> See from this charitable plan,
> The youth by learning form'd to man,
>   And fitted to the skies.[42]

These deeds, more than a dozen of them, made over to trustees a part of the
nursery and projected an assortment of charitable institutions — beef charities, a
public library, picture gallery, printing office, and six professorships. Hanbury's
method of financing his battery of good works is explained in a "Final, or Explanatory Deed," which can justly claim a place among the classics of utopian
philanthropy.[43] The rector, it appears, shared the current faith in the miraculous
powers of compound interest, and he proposed to start on his major improvements
only after it had demonstrated its beneficence. Nothing, in short, would be done
until the resources of the charities were large enough to yield £10,000, and even

[42] Hanbury, *History*, p. 131.
[43] *Ibid.*, pp. 442ff.

then, he enjoined his trustees with what must seem excessive caution, they were to begin spending only after the income had reached £12,000. To say the least, Langtonians could not complain that their rector was a man of limited vision.

It seems almost cruel to note the disparity between Hanbury's well-intentioned air-castles and the meager reality. Sixty years later, when a Brougham Commissioner visited Church Langton, he found the total income of the trusts to be £574, and the only part of the plan in actual operation was the beef charity for the poor.[44] Still, this was not negligible, save when measured against the grandiose schemes of the founder, and by the late 1860's the 345 acres deeded by Hanbury were yielding nearly £900 annually.[45] From the Hanbury trust had already come a free school for Church Langton, considerable sums for restoring parish churches, and a series of smaller miscellaneous benefactions.[46] Eccentricity has often taken less productive forms than in the case of the hopeful Leicestershire clergyman.

Two of the more original foundations of the century were created by dissenting clergymen, both named Williams. Daniel Williams (1643?–1716), a childless minister and one of the leading figures in the Presbyterian community, left to charitable uses an estate of perhaps £50,000. He provided specifically for two Presbyterian chapels, St. Thomas's Hospital, Glasgow University, Harvard College, and other institutions, leaving the residue to trustees for two thousand years. Among the various clauses of his will was the requirement that an appropriate building be bought or built for his books and a librarian installed. Williams' own collection, together with another that he had purchased for £500, formed the nucleus of Dr. Williams' Library, an institution which for more than two centuries filled an important place in the Nonconformist community. Over the years, other collections have been acquired, as well as source materials on the history of Dissent. One of the most useful functions of the institution was to serve as a lending library for Nonconformist ministers, especially those in villages and small towns where books are difficult to come by. Altogether, Dr. Williams was conferring future benefits on his co-religionists and others on a scale that he could hardly have foreseen.[47]

David Williams (1738–1816) lived and died almost precisely a century after his fellow-Dissenter. One can, of course, speak of "fellow-Dissenter" only with qualifications. For, although David Williams was an ordained Dissenting Minister and had served a number of congregations, his religious views were so innocent of dogmatic basis as to have inspired Benjamin Franklin to bestow on him the nickname, "Orpheus, Priest of Nature." [48] It was, in fact, as an educational pioneer, a political radical, and a preacher of tolerance that Williams is most memorable. Conceivably his own meagerly rewarded work as a writer had directed his atten-

[44] *32d Brougham Report*, Part V, 1839, pp. 272–73.
[45] *General Digest of Endowed Charities*, 1877, *Leicestershire* (1867–68).
[46] Paget and Irvine, *Leicestershire*, p. 223.
[47] *Short Account of the Charity and Library . . . of the Late Rev. Daniel Williams, D.D.* (London, 1917), p. 31ff; *DNB*, XXI, 385–89.
[48] Nicholas Hans, *New Trends in Education in the Eighteenth Century* (London, 1951), p. 164.

tion to the plight of distressed authors. In any case, in 1788 he drew up a constitution for a Literary Fund, a favorite project of his, which in the spring of 1790 attained formal existence through a general meeting and election of officers. This was not at the outset an endowed charity but one that maintained itself through subscriptions. Yet it was the kind of enterprise that appealed to the imagination of the time, and throughout its history the Fund has enjoyed a special kind of prestige in the charity world. After its incorporation in 1818 the Fund gradually acquired an endowment until, after a century of existence, half of its income of £4000 was drawn from investments. During its first hundred years the charity granted some £119,000 to nearly 440 distressed authors.[49]

4

The growth in the nation's charitable resources, impressive as it may have been, was accompanied by no comparable development in state policy. It is not surprising that the age was little interested in such humdrum administrative matters as giving adequate supervision to these thousands of endowments, new and old. As in other areas of government, the century brought a palpable slackening of the controls exerted by Westminster over the provinces and a noticeably greater disposition to leave individuals and local authorities to their own devices.

Even governmental support of charitable collections became more fitful, as indicated by the decline in the use of charity briefs, the standard Tudor-Stuart device for raising funds under official sponsorship for sufferers from fire, flood, or plague, or for rebuilding or repairing churches. A local authority might appeal to King or Parliament, and, if approval were granted, the Sovereign issued Letters Patent authorizing a collection by parish officials.[50] What led finally to the abolition of the charity brief, which had been increasingly restricted to the ecclesiastical sphere, was the spread of the methods of associated philanthropy, specifically the formation in 1818 of the Church Building Society, composed of twenty-guinea life members and two-guinea annual subscribers. A decade later an Act of Parliament gave the new association corporate status and brought to an end the issuance of charity briefs.[51]

For the supervision of charitable trusts the eighteenth century not only failed to develop effective new techniques but allowed the older machinery devised by Elizabethan statesmen to fall into disuse. The Elizabethan Statute had proposed to prevent the misapplication of trust funds by means of special commissioners empowered to "make Enquiry by the Oaths of twelve Men or more" into possible abuses and to take the necessary measures to return the charity to the intention of the donor. For more than a century the mechanism of the special commission, cumbersome as it now seems, was liberally employed. In 1818, in urging the

[49] *Charity Record,* 19 April 1884.
[50] L. G. Ping, "Raising Funds for 'Good Causes' in Reformation Times," *Hibbert Journal,* 35:54 (1936).
[51] 9 Geo. IV, c. 42. For a list of briefs issued in the period 1642–1827 see W. A. Bewes, *Church Briefs* (London, 1896), pp. 269–361.

appointment of his commission of inquiry, Brougham stressed the decline of the institution. Because of the destruction of the docket books in the Crown office it is difficult to estimate the degree of activity up to 1643, but for the next century the figures, as given by Brougham, are precise enough:[52]

1643–1660	295
1660–1678	344
1678–1700	197
1700–1746	125

From the mid-seventeenth to the mid-eighteenth century, then, 961 special commissions were created under the Statute of Charitable Uses. But at that point, for reasons not entirely clear, the special commission as an investigatory device fell into disfavor. In the years 1746–60 only three commissions were issued, and, if Brougham's assertion is correct, only six in the seventy-five years before 1818 and none in the twenty years before. Obviously the old method of enforcement had become unworkable.

Not only was the device itself sufficiently clumsy, but, as Brougham warned, "it leads him who pursues it sooner or later into the court of Chancery" — and that was no prospect to be lightly contemplated. On this point the history of the last commission, issued in 1787, is instructive. The commission was not fully executed until 1803, and in the following year Chancery was petitioned to confirm the commissioners' decree. But exceptions were taken, learned counsel debated lengthily, and it required another four years before the case was ready for a decision. Then for a decade it awaited the Lord Chancellor's (Eldon's) judgment, for the last four years occupying the place of honor at the top of his list of cases to be decided. In a word, if an order of the commissioners met with less than unanimous approval on the part of those affected, the case might be thrown into Chancery, with its interminable delays and probably disastrous consequences for the resources of the charity. Whatever one's view of Chancery as a font of equity law, it clearly left much to be desired as an agency for handling matters that were at least semi-administrative in character.

If the procedure established by the Elizabethan Statute had become a dead letter, the common law offered a remedy only slightly more practicable. Here the mechanism was an information filed by the Attorney-General, who usually acted on the relation of an individual willing to state that the charity had been abused. Yet possible relators, if men of ordinary prudence, would hesitate to become involved, for unless the action were successful, they would find themselves liable for the costs of long-drawn-out court proceedings.

There was little apparent inclination in official quarters to simplify these procedures or to bring charitable endowments under more direct public supervision. Only one development of consequence took place during the century, and this

---

[52] *1 Hansard*, 38:606–7. He pointed out, however, that in the year after the passing of 43 Eliz. some forty-five commissions had been issued.

was of significance chiefly as the first link in a chain of events that led, more than a half-century later, to the establishment of the Charity Commission. Yet the inquiry that was undertaken in the 1780's, incomplete and faulty as were its results, did imply a useful curiosity about the extent of the country's endowments and some question as to whether they were being effectively employed. As the great survey of the 1820's and '30's derived from Brougham's concern for education, so its primitive precursor reflected Thomas Gilbert's commitment to Poor Law reform. His Act[53] requiring ministers and churchwardens to furnish data on charities for the benefit of the poor was designed to supplement another Act, passed shortly before, which called upon overseers to report statistics on Poor Law expenditures for the years 1783–85.[54] Clearly both poor rates and charitable income must figure in a calculation of the nation's resources for the care of the poor. Parishes were not expected to supply detailed information — merely to indicate "by whom, when, and in what Manner, and for what particular Purpose" each benefaction had been made, to distinguish between those in land and in money, and to specify the annual produce of each.

In terms of numbers the response from English parishes was surprisingly complete. Out of thirteen thousand, only fourteen, it is said, failed to make a return, and the totals showed the annual income of charities for the poor to be nearly £260,000. The congratulatory tone with which the returns were first greeted, however, became more critical as they were examined, and it presently appeared that for many localities the information was absurdly incomplete and imprecise. Even if its accuracy had been beyond reproach, the Gilbert Returns would have given nothing like a complete picture of English charitable endowments, for it had been explicitly restricted to funds for the "Use and Benefit of Poor Persons," a definition which would rule out large categories of charitable trusts. Even within the limits prescribed by 26 Geo. III, the data left much to be desired, as a Select Committee discovered in 1787 when attempting to make an abstract of the material. The consequence was a follow-up circular sent to over four thousand parishes, about four-fifths of which replied.[55] And when the Returns were printed, red ink was used to indicate the supplementary information. At some points the corrections and additions are so numerous as to give to the page a certain artistic elegance.

Still, Gilbert's efforts were by no means valueless. Not only did his attempt to take an inventory of English charities arouse some slight interest in endowments as a national asset and public problem, but his evidence proved enormously useful to charity reformers. The two large volumes served as something of an armory from which Brougham and his associates could always draw a suitable weapon — perhaps some abuse, picturesque or merely sordid — with which to emphasize their

[53] 26 Geo. III, c. 58.
[54] 26 Geo. III, c. 56; S. and B. Webb, *English Poor Law History: The Old Poor Law* (London, 1927), p. 153.
[55] *Abstract of the [Gilbert] Returns, 1786–88*, repr. 1816, p. iii. *The Returns* were reissued in 1810 and again in 1816,

demand for change. One can think, fairly enough, of the Gilbert Returns as the first step toward a more rational and responsible attitude on the part of the State.

On only one occasion in the course of the century did the Legislature intervene to regulate charitable donations. This enactment, the so-called Mortmain Act of 1736,[56] was not one of Parliament's more inspired decisions in the charity field, nor, for that matter, one of the more readily intelligible. It seemed to mark a reversal of the traditionally indulgent attitude shown by the law toward charitable dispositions. Conceivably, Courtney Kenny has suggested, Thomas Guy's magnificent bequest had given rise to so much loose talk and so many malicious rumors about disinherited kinfolk (the governors of the Hospital thought it prudent to print and circulate his will in order to scotch the gossip) as to raise the specter of legal heirs sacrificed to a rich man's vanity.[57]

For our purpose it is enough to note that the sponsors of the Bill apparently had two objects in view, neither especially reasonable. One was to prevent the large-scale accumulation of land in the hands of corporations, notably Queen Anne's Bounty, whose land-buying operations seem at the time to have excited an exaggerated fear.[58] Certainly a current of apprehension about the Corporation and its powers runs through the debates. The other motive behind the Mortmain Act was the more general one of protecting the rights of legal heirs, though there is no reason to suspect that these had been losing out to charity in any exceptional degree. Both in and out of Parliament the Bill was interpreted as an instrument for preventing "the mistaken Charity of men, who, in such Circumstances are apt to hope to compound for the Faults of their past Life, by a Fine to be paid by their Heirs to some use which they call a Religious one." [59]

Hitherto some technical limitations on gifts of land to a corporation had been in force, but the new Statute was much more drastic. Such gifts and settlements of land were henceforth illegal, save as these were made by deed a year before the death of the donor and were enrolled in Chancery within six months. They were, moreover, unconditional and irrevocable; benefactors were not entitled to second thoughts about the business. Bequests of land to corporations remained, as before, illegal, save in the case of certain bodies specifically exempted, notably the universities and public schools.

This is not the place to consider the subsequent history of the Mortmain Act. How gravely it may have handicapped the generality of charitable bodies is impossible to judge, though some groups, notably the Roman Catholics,[60] felt it to

---

[56] 9 Geo. II, c. 36.

[57] *Cobbett's Parliamentary History*, IX, 1126: Courtney Kenny, *The True Principles of Legislation . . . for Charitable and Other Public Uses* (London, 1880), pp. 56ff, contains an excellent discussion of the Mortmain Act. For more recent treatments, especially on the Act as it related to Queen Anne's Bounty, see Alan Savidge, *The Foundation and Early Years of Queen Anne's Bounty* (London, 1955), pp. 100–4, and G. F. A. Best, *Temporal Pillars* (Cambridge, 1964), pp. 104–10.

[58] See the *Gentleman's Magazine*, 6:204 (1736). Kenny (*True Principles of Legislation . . .* , p. 65) estimates that the Corporation had already spent between £700,000 and £800,000 in purchasing land.

[59] *Gentleman's Magazine*, 6:204 (1736), quoting the *Old Whig*.

[60] For reasons to be indicated in Chapter XII.

be especially oppressive. The difficulty lay not merely in the terms of the Act itself but in the extraordinarily rigid construction placed upon it by the courts. We have it on the authority of a late-Victorian Lord Chancellor that the Statute led to an "enormous amount of litigation, and to distinctions being drawn which I do not think anybody could call other than absurd." [61] But silly or sensible, the Mortmain Act remained intact for more than a century and a half, long after nineteenth-century reformers had wiped out other anachronisms in the body of charity law. And although late-century legislation moderated the severity of the earlier Statute, it required the comprehensive Charities Act of 1960 to liquidate the law of mortmain.

[61] Lord Herschell. (*3 Hansard* 354:714.)

PART TWO

PHILANTHROPY IN THE AGE OF IMPROVEMENT
1780's–1860's

"They have a wonderful heat in the pursuit of a public aim."
— Ralph Waldo Emerson

"We are just now overrun with philanthropy, and God knows where it will stop, or whither it will lead us."

— Charles Greville

I T W A S the lot of late-century philanthropists to carry on their beneficent labors in a world undergoing rapid, even revolutionary, change.[1] Along with this went a less obvious but no less real change in the ideas by which contemporaries explained and defended their charitable efforts. No doubt it is easy to exaggerate the contrasts. The tone of eighteenth-century philanthropy was not suddenly altered in the 1780's or even after 1789. Yet there were differences, and these had their significance. The forces that were creating a new material environment and influencing its social values were inevitably to affect the aims and methods of its charitable undertakings.

The most obvious of these pressures was clearly the complex of changes that we call the Industrial Revolution. Whatever qualifications one wishes to apply, a "new civilization," in the Hammonds' expression, *was* growing up, and it was a society which posed problems for philanthropists different in degree and kind from those they had faced in the past. From this time forward British philanthropy was to be shaped in a large degree by the demands of industrial society.[2] For the present purpose the aspect of economic and social change that matters most was the staggering growth of the British population in general and of the urban population in particular. In the newer industrial centers, especially in the textile districts, as well as in London, the increase had effects that verged on the cataclysmic. We need only recall that in the early nineteenth century certain industrial cities were growing at the rate of 30 to 40 per cent and even more in some decades. In the years 1821–31, for example, the population of Manchester and Salford rose by nearly 45 per cent, Liverpool by slightly over 45 per cent, and Leeds by more than 47 per cent.

We need not labor the point. If Englishmen increasingly were to live their lives in congested cities rather than in small towns and villages, the social pattern would be decisively altered, and the problems of the common life gravely accentuated. It would be out of the question to translate to an urban environment the network of relationships, personal and institutional, that made rural England an ordered society. Thus those who sought to improve the lot of their fellows

[1] The caption of this section I owe, of course, to Asa Briggs's *The Age of Improvement* (London, 1959).

[2] Notwithstanding the fact that some of the well-known efforts around the turn of the century, notably Sir Thomas Bernard's Society for Bettering the Condition of the Poor, had what was still a rural orientation.

faced a situation in which some of their traditional methods came to seem grossly inadequate, if not actually mischievous. Direct almsgiving and neighborhood charity, which in a village could be carried on without fear of being unduly imposed upon, now served to encourage the professional mendicant. In any case it was out of the question for the philanthropist, however well disposed, to seek out for himself the cases of greatest need and to become familiar with them. The consequence was, of course, to stimulate the growth of charitable societies serving as intermediaries between individual philanthropist and beneficiary. Although it was no new phenomenon, the nineteenth century saw the charitable organization come to full, indeed almost rankly luxuriant, bloom.

Evils which had not disturbed the rural philanthropist now thrust themselves on the attention of his urban counterpart. Such matters as health and housing, for example, took on a new significance, and the care of neglected children — waifs, orphans, and what would today be termed juvenile delinquents — under urban conditions seemed to have little connection with problem as it appeared in the country village, as little connection, in fact, as the army of metropolitan beggars or industrial unemployed had with the shiftless village good-for-nothing.

Education too responded to new pressures. Training that had served well enough in a peasant milieu was clearly inadequate for an industrial society. Tim Bobbin the Lancashire operative was a different character from Hodge the agricultural laborer, and an education which aimed only at a command of letters sufficient to read the Bible was plainly unsuitable. Here, more than in some areas, secular philanthropy (loosely speaking, of the Whig-Utilitarian school) joined with religious humanitarianism to supply the dynamic. In a large degree it was Henry Brougham's belief in the critical importance of schooling and his notion, ill-founded as it proved to be, that the country's endowments might furnish the basis for an educational structure that made him a charity reformer. From his agitation emerged a series of parliamentary inquiries into educational endowments and finally to the grand survey of the nation's charitable trusts which led ultimately to the creation of the Charity Commission.

In the domain of voluntary action both Churchmen and Nonconformists organized their separate agencies to grapple with the problem of education. Mrs. Trimmer, to be sure, could still caution against giving prizes for "excelling in *penmanship* or *reading,* which are very inferior things in comparison with upright conduct,"[3] and Hannah More would put up with no nonsense in her Mendip schools (which were, however, located in a remote and backward district): "My plan for instructing the poor is very limited and strict. They learn of week-days such coarse works as may fit them for servants. I allow no writing."[4] As will appear presently, these ladies and their allies were on the losing side. Sir Thomas Bernard, perhaps the representative English philanthropist of the Age

---

[3] *The Oeconomy of Charity* (1801 ed., London), I, 122–23.

[4] M. Gwladys Jones, *Hannah More* (Cambridge, 1952), p. 152. For a rather elaborate statement of this characteristic eighteenth-century point of view, see John M'Farlan, *Inquiries concerning the Poor* (Edinburgh, 1782), pp. 235ff, a volume dedicated to Lord Kames.

of the French Revolution, denounced as preposterous "the prejudices that *have* existed against extending the common and general benefits of education to the poor, and the extraordinary supposition that an uneducated and neglected boy will produce a mature age of industry and virtue." [5] Gradually the view spread, first among reformers and then more generally, that an ignorant, illiterate working class was incompatible with the well-being of the nation. It was private philanthropy that first accepted the challenge and attempted, with less than complete success, to fashion appropriate weapons for dealing with it.

An influence of another sort was exerted by the evangelical movement. So unwearied in well-doing were certain groups of Bible Christians that in the public mind the word "philanthropist" became all but synonymous with "evangelical," and "philanthropy" was applied to the good works that appealed most to evangelical tastes.[6] The evangelical social conscience is a large and complex subject, and we can make no pretense of weighing its virtues and limitations. Nor can we speculate upon the contradictory emotions that the evangelicals managed to arouse, both among contemporaries and latter-day critics. Which, after all, was the authentic expression of their social conscience, the Society for the Suppression of Vice or the Anti-Slavery Society? Which most characteristically represented their aims, Michael Sadler's Factory Bill or Sir Andrew Agnew's Sunday Observance Bill, termed by G. M. Young "the most rigorous piece of moral — and, indeed, class — legislation since the Long Parliament?" [7]

These are futile questions, for, whatever their blind-spots, the Saints were anything but one-cause reformers, and their zeal knew few bounds, geographical or topical. Their capacity for personal sacrifice was remarkable enough. Though the Evangelical credentials of all of them may not, perhaps, be as unimpeachable as he assumes, Professor Ford Brown's roll of about eighty philanthropists, each of whom subscribed to more than fifteen societies, makes an impressive exhibit. Wilberforce, who regularly gave away a quarter of his income, subscribed to some seventy organizations, while three of the Grant family accounted for 51 subscriptions, six Hoares for 220, and four Thorntons for 173.[8] In fact, John Thornton is said to have disposed of £150,000 on good causes in the course of his life. His son Henry, City Banker and pillar of the Clapham group, was obliged by his marriage to reduce his benevolences from six-sevenths to two-thirds of his income![9]

[5] *Report of the Society for Bettering the Condition of the Poor,* 1799, quoted by George, *London Life,* p. 252.
[6] The word "evangelical" is here used in a comprehensive sense to include the entire community of English Bible Christians and not merely those within the Church of England. Where the latter group is meant I have used the capitalized form "Evangelical."
[7] *Victorian England: Portrait of an Age* (London, 1936), p. 50. Though Agnew's measure failed to pass, it obtained the support of 128 members of the Commons with Lord Ashley at their head.
[8] Ford K. Brown, *Fathers of the Victorians* (Cambridge, 1961), pp. 71, 354–58; Charles I. Foster, *An Errand of Mercy* (Chapel Hill, 1960), p. 36. Chapter 9 of Brown's book, "Ten Thousand Compassions," is an exceeding interesting and exhaustive discussion of the Evangelical involvement in philanthropy, with a good deal of information on organizations, individuals, and Evangelical strategy and tactics.
[9] John Venn, *The Life and . . . Letters of . . . Henry Venn* (New York, 1855), p. 365; E. M.

Apart from their activity in specific causes, the signal achievement of the evangelicals was to reforge the link between philanthropy and religion. Though never wholly broken, it had worn a bit thin during the middle decades when charity tended to reflect a benevolence not directly related to the promptings of religion. Now it was not only explicitly religious ventures that felt a new and vigorous impulse, but a good deal of secular philanthropy became infused with the spirit of evangelical Christianity. One may have reservations about certain details of Professor Brown's picture of evangelical operations, but it is impossible to deny the vast expansion in philanthropic projects that coincided with the emergence of the evangelical community. Not only that, but older institutions and organizations in some instances found themselves falling under evangelical influences.[10] Philanthropy, as championed by evangelical groups, became something of a fashion, and in 1813 Mrs. Barbauld could write, "There is certainly at present a great deal of zeal in almost every persuasion . . . Bible societies, missionary schemes, lectures, schools for the poor set afoot and spread, not so much from a sense of duty as being the real taste of the times." [11] The philanthropic efforts of the early century, and indeed of the whole Victorian Age, took much of their color from the evangelical outlook.

Clearly the primary commitment of the evangelicals was not to philanthropy or social reform. They were, first of all, devout Christians whose essential concern was witnessing for Christ before the world and sharing with others their Christian experience. Their most vigorous efforts, broadly speaking, were directed to causes immediately relevant to their religious interests — foreign missions, Bible societies, the antislavery movement, Sunday schools. But within the larger community were groups of strategically placed evangelicals consciously seeking to reform the manners and morals of the nation,[12] sometimes by methods that are fairly unappealing to twentieth-century tastes. Very likely, too much has been made of these crusades, in which evangelical attitudes appear in a less than kindly light. One would not look for advanced reformers in such a group. Their stupendous achievement in demolishing slavery atoned handsomely for the myopia with which they sometimes viewed other public issues.

Yet evangelical philanthropy, especially as it had to do with the poor, exhibited traits that made it easy game for such critics as Cobbett and Sydney

---

Howse, *Saints in Politics* (London, 1952), pp. 126–27, who apparently takes the fractions from G. W. E. Russell, *The Household of Faith* (London, 1902), p. 227. Other authorities put the figures a bit lower, but all agree that Thornton's giving reached a sacrificial level. In 1793, for example, he gave away over £6000: (E. M. Forster, *Marianne Thornton, 1797–1887* [London, 1956], p. 13.)

[10] The imposing list assembled by Brown, pp. 329–40, gives a notion of the rate at which philanthropic organizations were being hatched during these years. Whether the relation between this phenomenon and evangelical action was as direct as he implies may be arguable. His demonstration, which relies heavily on the analysis of individuals, groups, and their interconnections, is immensely suggestive and convincing up to a point. Certainly it is true that "the 'mushroom growth' came after the French Revolution when Wilberforce and his associates set to work," but presumably Professor Brown would agree that other important influences also were operating.

[11] Quoted by Maurice J. Quinlan, *Victorian Prelude* (New York, 1941), p. 121.

[12] The thesis of Brown's book.

Smith and, more recently, for the Hammonds and others. Evangelicals shared with their contemporaries a conception of class relationships that accepted the existing order of society as divinely ordained and more or less immutable. Rich were rich and poor were poor. God had called them to their particular stations, and both were to show gratitude — the rich to God, and the poor to their well-to-do benefactors, as well as to God. Not only that but along with other Englishmen, the evangelicals had absorbed the notion — identified with Malthus, Ricardo, and lesser thinkers — that poverty was an inexorable fact of life. But what from Malthus might seem brutally realistic, from certain evangelical spokesmen appeared merely sanctimonious. It was one thing to announce to the poor that their prospects were exceedingly bleak but another to preach uncomplaining submission as an injunction of Divine law.

To condemn the evangelical position as hypocrisy is simply to misinterpret evangelical values. Temporal welfare was an important but distinctly secondary good. If evangelicals were "concerned that the poor should be comfortable . . . they were more concerned that the poor should be pious." [13] It was this conviction that conditioned their work as philanthropists and accounted for the increasing emergence of the strictly moral and religious element in some of their charitable projects. A case in point was the Clapham branch of the Society for Bettering the Condition of the Poor, where virtue and piety rather than need were prerequisite for assistance.[14] The critical issue, Hannah More's biographer observes, was not "the incidence of wealth and poverty but . . . the overriding importance of sin and redemption." [15] What must be emphasized here, however, is that British philanthropy, like Victorian society as a whole, became tinctured with the evangelical spirit.

Evangelical sectarianism, to note an influence of a more specific sort, also had something to do with the amazing proliferation of charitable societies that went on in the nineteenth century. For, although some groups, notably the "Clapham Sect," cooperated readily with other men of goodwill, more commonly each denomination or splinter sect demanded its full complement of auxiliary organizations. Obviously other factors, such as the tendency to extreme specialization on the part of charitable societies, encouraged that fecundity of organizations which so disturbed those who turned an even mildly critical eye on the world of philanthropy. Each category of need seems to have required its own agency, sometimes an array of them. Sir James Stephen was not exaggerating when, concluding his essay on the Clapham group, he wrote in the familiar passage: "Ours is the age of societies . . . For the cure of every sorrow by which our land or our race can be visited, there are patrons, vice-presidents, and secretaries. For the diffusion of every blessing of which mankind can partake in common, there is a committee." [16]

[13] Howse, *Saints in Politics,* p. 129.

[14] Quinlan, *Victorian Prelude,* p. 134. The extracts from the Report of the Clapham Society printed by Mrs. Trimmer in her *Oeconomy of Charity,* II, 60–78, leave no doubt on the point.

[15] Jones, *Hannah More,* p. 236.

[16] *Essays in Ecclesiastical Biography,* 4th ed. (London, 1860), p. 581.

For this development evangelicals would have been not only willing but eager to accept a large measure of responsibility.

The growth of an industrial-urban society enormously magnified and altered the problems of the common life, and these called forth gallant, often sacrificial, effort on the part of individuals and groups of Englishmen. As new evils were identified, voluntary agencies emerged to deal with them; subscription lists multiplied in number and amount; and in some of its branches organized philanthropy was accumulating a fund of experience, the harvest both of success and failure, that would later be drawn upon by the larger community through its statutory agencies. At the same time, the demands of the new civilization turned the attention of reformers to the social resource embodied in the nation's endowed charities and to the possibility that with some reorganization and central supervision, these might be made to contribute more constructively to the common welfare.

But in spite of the determined optimism of annual charity reports and the reassuring promises which accompanied appeals for subscriptions, there were uneasy doubts. Champions of charitable effort, especially those who looked beyond their individual agencies, had reason to be discouraged over the modest advances made by private philanthropy against the mass of ignorance, disease, and destitution of the early Victorian city. Although the full extent and complexity of the problem were mercifully concealed until the latter decades of the new century, the obvious disparity between the magnitude of the evil and the resources available for dealing with it raised questions in the minds of certain observers who were more tough-minded than their contemporaries.

Yet, however great their skepticism, no other alternative was possible. Poverty — even widespread destitution — was probably unavoidable, given the staggering growth of population and the means available for its support. In these circumstances poverty could be mitigated only through a redistribution of wealth of sorts, a solution that, of course, made little appeal to the rich. Want was to be taken as inevitable and the poor schooled in the more serviceable traits of character, those that would encourage sturdy self-reliance or would enable them to bear their lot with resignation. Preaching the virtues of independence — industry, frugality, temperance — and practicing private charity, an indispensable resource in the Victorian Age, exhausted the acceptable solutions. In some areas these early Victorian philanthropists attained notable triumphs, but in others, conspicuously in those connected with urban destitution, they gravely misconceived the nature of the problem and underestimated its dimensions. Only when a more favorable ratio between production and population had been established — that is, when the transition to industrialism had been fully accomplished — could a powerful and better articulated attack on poverty be carried out.[17]

[17] Some of these points are made to good effect by Calvin Woodard, "Reality and Social Reform: The Transition from Laissez-faire to the Welfare State," *Yale Law Journal*, 72:286–328 (December 1962).

CHAPTER IV

CHARITABLE ENTERPRISE IN EARLY INDUSTRIAL SOCIETY

IN THE later decades of the century the practice of philanthropy took on a character rather different from the open-handed, slightly careless benevolence that one associates with such ventures as the Foundling Hospital. The late-century approach was more calculating, more concerned with consequences, and at least certain philanthropists were taking a harder look at the tasks before them. The exuberant optimism that informed the activities of some of their predecessors seemed badly out of key. Philanthropists around the turn of the century were a gloomier lot, disillusioned about the easy and inexpensive successes that had been envisioned, and they were, in fact, faced with growing difficulty in financing their own projects.[1] The road was plainly going to be longer and rockier than the Age of Benevolence had suspected.

It is not clear how much this less hopeful temper owed to the shock of the French Revolution. Certainly the shadow of Jacobinism was partly responsible for the chilling atmosphere that surrounded some of the philanthropic ventures of the period. These became, to a degree, insurance against revolution, a means of keeping the populace, if not contented, at least reasonably submissive. Yet the worst of the anti-Jacobin hysteria had passed by the mid-1790's, and it is questionable whether philanthropic undertakings, as distinguished from reform and radical movements, suffered unduly. There is some suggestion of a greater sensitiveness on the part of the upper classes to distress among the poor which might lead to disturbances. Thus the bad year 1796 produced a chain of soup kitchens in London at about the time Sir Thomas Bernard was launching his Society for Bettering the Condition of the Poor. The stagnation of trade in 1811 led a group of philanthropists to organize an Association for the Relief of the Manufacturing and Labouring Poor and to raise during their first year something over £15,000.[2] In such activities as these, fear of unrest, evangelical piety, and genuine humanitarianism were often present in varying proportions.

Whatever the explanation, during these years philanthropy, even in the hands of those whose intentions were above reproach, seemed to take on a cautious and calculating, almost harsh, tone. Charitable effort was suffused with a mood of

[1] Gray, *History of English Philanthropy*, pp. 270–73.
[2] *Report of the Society for Bettering the Condition of the Poor*, 1813, p. 11.

pessimism and imbued with an emotion, unadmitted and only partly conscious, akin to fear of the poor, who were imagined to be a dangerous force which must be propitiated or forcibly restrained. How much of this outlook can be charged to the Revolution itself is arguable. It is worth recalling that Wilberforce's Proclamation Society, often cited as a symptom of the late-century reaction,[3] was founded in 1787. This association, formed to enforce the Proclamation against Vice and Immorality which Wilberforce had persuaded George III to issue, was one of the less admirable Evangelical schemes for reforming the behavior of the lower classes and re-creating them in the image of their respectable betters. The anti-Jacobin panic no doubt left its mark on the record of the Proclamation Society, as in its vindictive prosecution of an obscure bookseller for publishing Paine's *Age of Reason,* but its founding antedated the Revolution by two years.

The more wary approach to human distress, in part the consequence of fears induced by the Revolution, was sanctified by the prevailing social philosophy. If charity was a response to human need, it was also an instrument for inculcating approved social attitudes. The new philanthropist frowned on almsgiving, without careful investigation, and tended to judge charitable efforts by their success in encouraging recipients to stand on their own feet.[4] Properly conceived, charity should be limited to the "deserving," that vaguely defined class of unfortunates which figures so heavily in nineteenth-century writing on the subject.

Here the views of Malthus are instructive and were undeniably influential. His proposal for the gradual abolition of statutory provision for the poor assumed a substantial flow of private charity for their relief. Surely, he urged, it would be absurd "to characterize as harsh and severe any propositions which may leave them to be provided for by voluntary charity — by those feelings which Providence seems to have implanted in our breasts for that express purpose," and he asserted "the moral obligation of private, active, and discriminate charity."[5]

In the *Essay on Population* the stress was on the necessity for discrimination.[6] The impulse to benevolence and the sexual impulse, he observes, are both "natural passions excited by their appropriate objects." Though the latter is ultimately more dangerous, both can produce dreadful consequences unless controlled by reason and the lessons of experience and utility. Malthus' prescription for charity, indeed, almost offers a preview of the Charity Organisation Society, when he urges the benevolent to get thoroughly acquainted with those whom they are to relieve, checking "the hopes of clamorous and obtrusive poverty with no other recommendation but rags" and encouraging "the silent and retiring sufferer laboring under unmerited difficulties." Indiscriminate charity only increases the sum of poverty and misery, and must therefore be considered contrary to the laws of nature. The proper sphere of charity is in relieving those suffering from "un-

---

[3] Perhaps not with entire justice. See Howse, *Saints in Politics,* pp. 119–20.

[4] See William Allen, ed., *The Philanthropist* (London, 1811–19), VI, 313ff.

[5] "A Letter to Samuel Whitbread" (1807), in D. V. Glass, ed., *Introduction to Malthus* (London, 1953), pp. 188, 190.

[6] Fifth ed. (London, 1817), Book IV, chap. X.

merited calamities" and unforeseen misfortunes. And if Scriptural support were needed, one could always balance against Christ's commendation of the Good Samaritan, St. Paul's warning, "If a man will not work, neither shall he eat."

2

The uneasy temper of British society during these decades — the furor over population, the mounting poor rates, and the erratic behavior of the economy — raised questions about the actual condition of the poor and prompted speculation as to the proper scope and methods of private charity. The evangelical conviction that the rich were accountable to God for their stewardship added a certain moral urgency to these issues. As a whole, the statements that emerged contained little systematic thought and offered no considered rationale for philanthropic effort. With most of the writers, as with Malthus, the impulse to aid one's less fortunate fellows was taken as an axiom, as innate in civilized human beings and certainly in Christian Englishmen. But how this instinct could be most productively expressed was not so easily decided.

Philanthropists articulate enough to put their ideas on paper made up in variety what they lacked in number and included such contrasting types as the kindly and indefatigable Mrs. Trimmer (who in life could hardly have been as smugly pious as in her writing) and the pioneer social economist Patrick Colquhoun. Mrs. Trimmer's *Oeconomy of Charity,* designed to interest ladies in charitable work and written "with a particular view to the cultivation of religious principles, among the lower orders of people," [7] is largely descriptive of charity schools and other enterprises. But sections on household servants and the laboring poor ("useful members of the state, for their services are essential in the greatest degree, to the comfort and convenience of the higher orders of society") explain the social utility of charitable effort. Indeed, the resources of charity may be "considered as a kind of *National Bank* replete with benefits, on which those who are reduced by misfortune or casualty, to extreme distress, may freely draw," a view in substantial agreement with that of Malthus. Beyond the giving of money, Christian charity also enjoins a personal interest in the lower orders; visiting them in their cottages, even though they may seem "little better than savages and barbarians, with whom any familiar intercourse would be degrading . . . if not dangerous," might nurture in the poor a sense of gratitude to their superiors. But Mrs. Trimmer could reprove as well as exhort the rich. She was especially distressed that they could permit such numbers of the common people to "live in extreme indigence, while the plenty and riches of the land enable the higher ranks to indulge in all the conveniences and luxuries of life." [8] Hers, to say the least, was no rigorously logical mind. Even the most virtuous of purposes could hardly compensate for the ineffably patronizing tone that informed so much of what she wrote.

Although Mrs. Trimmer and her kind left a sinister stamp on nineteenth-

[7] From the title page.
[8] The quotations in this paragraph are from *The Oeconomy of Charity* (1801 ed.), II, 45–60.

century charity which was only gradually obliterated, they were doing hardly more than enunciating the conventional views of their class and time sicklied o'er with a pale cast of piety. Systematic thinking about poverty and its treatment owed more to the work of two social investigators, Sir Frederick Morton Eden and Patrick Colquhoun. Eden was impelled, he tells us, to undertake his survey of the poor "from motives both of benevolence and personal curiosity" with regard to the distress of the year 1794–95, and his *State of the Poor,* published in 1797 when its author was thirty-one years of age, added a new dimension to discussions of the condition of the lower classes.[9]

All that can be noticed here is his ideas on voluntary charity and on the relative merits of public and private systems of poor relief. Though unhappy with some features of the Poor Laws, Eden was convinced that public provision for the poor could not be equitable dispensed with. He urged, in reply to Lord Kames, that "to leave the Poor to voluntary charity, whatever advantages it might produce in other respects, would necessarily take the burthen from the shoulders of the hard-hearted, and unfeeling . . . and throw it entirely on the considerate and benevolent," an argument which even Mrs. Trimmer had not hesitated to use.[10] The danger arose from philanthropy which was too "unbounded and indiscriminate" and which, by causing, in Lord Kames's phrase, " 'an overflow of charity in the good people of England,' " promoted idleness and pauperism.[11]

What place, then, should be assigned to private charity in the British social economy? Plainly the existence of the Poor Law had not obviated the need for large expenditures on the part of the well-to-do — on Eden's rather exuberant estimate, well above £6 million annually and considerably in excess of the cost of public provision for the poor.[12] An ample field remained for the exercise of the greatest of the Christian virtues, for the nation in its collective capacity was committed only to "the removal of extreme wants in cases of urgent necessity," and not "to educate the orphan, feed the ancient and impotent, and provide employment for the industrious." The State thus acts only within narrowly prescribed limits, "leaving the rest to the faithful trusts of the sentiments of our minds, the feelings of our hearts, the compunctions of our consciences" as friends of the poor.[13] Voluntary charity, in short, taking up where the Poor Law left off, was indispensable to the smooth functioning of England's social mechanism.

Patrick Colquhoun, Glasgow merchant turned London police magistrate, asked more searching questions than did Eden and offered more original answers.[14] What apparently turned his interest toward social improvement was his exposure

[9] *The State of the Poor,* 3 vols. (London, 1797), I, i.

[10] *Ibid.,* I, 358.

[11] *Ibid.,* I, 359, 458.

[12] *Ibid.,* I, 465. Eden regarded this estimate as erring on the side of caution.

[13] *Ibid.,* I, 486–87.

[14] The best account of Colquhoun and his work is that of L. Radzinowicz, *A History of English Criminal Law and Its Administration from 1750,* 3 vols. (London, 1848–56), III, 211ff, but a more extensive treatment is badly needed.

to life in the Metropolis when he became London representative of Glasgow mercantile interests and more particularly when in 1792 he was made one of the new police magistrates. For a man of Colquhoun's active curiosity and speculative intelligence, Bow Street offered an admirable vantage point. Some of his notions, especially his proposals for a more constructive state social policy, had about them more than a hint of modernity, so much so that a recent writer can characterize him as "An Eighteenth Century Beveridge Planner." [15]

But in spite of some advanced ideas, such as that of a central agency generally responsible for what might be termed social welfare, Colquhoun was no John the Baptist of the Welfare State. The most favorable setting, he suggested, for his social experiments might be the court of a benevolent despot, perhaps one like that of the Elector of Bavaria, where Count Rumford had accomplished some of his most important work. His reforms, in short, were to come from the top. Instruction given to the children of the poor was to include nothing "that shall pass the bounds of their condition in society . . . To exceed that point would be utopian, impolitic, and dangerous, since it would confound the ranks of society, upon which the general happiness of the lower orders, no less than that of those in more elevated stations, depends." [16] From one point of view, Colquhoun can be considered almost mercantilist in his ideas, perhaps the last of the political arithmeticians.

His writings encourage little optimism over the potentialities of private benevolence. In popular education he notes the meager achievements of a century of charitable effort and concludes flatly that "the object is too gigantic for the efforts of private benevolence." [17] Nor is he sanguine about the efficacy of private philanthropy in improving the life of the poor and preventing indigence. For to Colquhoun, poverty, the normal state of those who must labor for subsistence, is different from indigence (or destitution), "which implies *want, misery,* and *distress.*" Since only a shaky barrier separates the one from the other, it is imperative that society "prop up poverty by judicious arrangements at those critical periods when it is in danger of descending into indigence." [18]

What had charity accomplished by way of preventing indigence? Here Colquhoun's tough-minded conclusion seemed to dash with cold water the rosy claims of charity prospectus writers and sponsors. The annual aggregate of public and private charities in England and Wales (including income from endowments) he estimates at something under £4 million, an outpouring which "exceeds perhaps *tenfold* what is manifested in any other civilized nation in the world of the same number of inhabitants." But how unproductive it all had been! "The indigent have been clothed and fed; but few, very few, have recovered their former useful station of *independent poverty,*" to the grave injury of the country, which is not

[15] Oscar Sherwin, *American Historical Review,* 52:281–90 (1947).
[16] *Treatise on Indigence* (London, 1806), p. 148
[17] *Ibid.,* p. 143.
[18] *Ibid.,* pp. 8–9.

only put to the expense of maintaining them but also suffers the loss of their labor.[19]

This is hardly more than a generalized statement of the conclusion that Colquhoun had already reached with regard to London. In his *Treatise on the Police of the Metropolis,* first published in 1796, he sadly contrasts the magnificent facilities for promoting the welfare of the lower classes with the misery and wretchedness that persisted. With some £585,000 (exclusive of poor rates)[20] being spent on behalf of the metropolitan poor, their miseries "do not appear to be alleviated, and their morals grow worse." What is important to notice here is how sharply Colquhoun's views, formed as they were from his experience as police magistrate and his own charitable activities, differed from the hopeful fantasies of the Age of Benevolence. To Colquhoun and his contemporaries a prodigious outlay for charity had produced only trivial benefits. Beyond a doubt the London police magistrate, with his realistic outlook and his collection of data, was a force in destroying some of the illusions of eighteenth-century philanthropists and inducing in them a social pessimism which would be content with more modest accomplishments.[21]

Notwithstanding marked differences among them, most of those who reflected on the principles and methods of charity would have admitted to a large area of agreement.[22] Few of them, pious or secular, were particularly sanguine about the prospects of British society, whose regeneration no longer seemed within the resources of private benevolence. Even the *Philanthropist,* which William Allen issued in the years 1811–19 and which served as something of a mouthpiece for the Quaker-Evangelical-abolitionist interests, revealed some of the same cautious, empirical spirit. Allen himself was not unduly parochial in his philanthropic concerns. In 1813, along with Jeremy Bentham and a group of Quakers, with what now seems like guileless innocence, he put up the capital for the purchase of the New Lanark Mills by Robert Owen, whose religious opinions, however, presently became too strong medicine for his partner. But Allen, too, in his first article "On the Duty and Pleasure of Cultivating Benevolent Dispositions," strikes some of the familiar chords. All classes, even the poorest, may assist in the good work. As for the well-to-do, it is their responsibility not merely to give money, but "to discriminate between the idle and profligate, and the industrious and deserving, to inquire into their condition, and to see that what we bestow is properly applied."[23] Allen the Quaker, Malthus the economist, Colquhoun the restlessly inquisitive police magistrate, and even Mrs. Trimmer's notions, when we can cut through the genteel luxuriance of her prose, are not out of accord.

[19] *Ibid.,* pp. 60–62.

[20] But including income from endowed charities. (*Treatise,* p. 382.)

[21] George, *London Life,* p. 322.

[22] I am referring here to what may be defined as "general charity" — that is, undertakings having to do directly with the relief and training of the poor. Such philanthropies as foreign missions and medical charities offer something of a special case.

[23] *Philanthropist,* I, 4.

A certain uneasiness about what is taking place in the British social order pervades the writings of all of them, a fear that it was being menaced within and without. They were aware, in a greater or less degree, of an economy and society in revolutionary change, but (most of them were from the South of England) they had not adjusted their thinking to the fact. All pictured their social world as a hierarchy made up of classes, each with its special duties and responsibilities, and highly interdependent. Distinctions between social classes, scripturally sanctioned and inevitable because of differences in individual talents, were part of the Great Design. To be industrious and tractable was, of course, the obligation of the poor. Not everyone would have discovered in a near-famine, as did Hannah More, the plan of "an all-wise and gracious Providence to *unite* all ranks of people *together* and show the *poor* how immediately they are dependent upon the *rich*."[24] Yet the deference owed by the poor to the rich was a ubiquitous theme in the charity literature of the time. They were to understand that their welfare was more adequately "promoted by the gradations of wealth and rank, than it ever could be by a perfect equality of condition; even if that equality had not been in its nature chimerical and impracticable."[25]

The upper classes also had their responsibilities, and these derived both from the injunctions of Christianity and from their superior position in society. "Rank, power, wealth, influence," cautioned Sir Thomas Bernard, "constitute no exception from activity or attention to duty; but lay a weight of accumulated responsibility on the possessor."[26] An anonymous work published at Bath in 1815 reminds the well-to-do that, if class distinctions are recognized throughout the Bible, it is also true that the rich are repeatedly exhorted to give alms. "That conduct which the order of nature suggests, the Gospel solemnly sanctions and commands."[27] This was not merely a moral obligation. As William Allen did not hesitate to warn, the practice of charity was no more than the exercise of simple self-interest, for the security of the rich, "in the enjoyment of their possessions, may be materially affected by the degree of virtue which exists in the great mass of the people."[28] Philanthropy, in a word, was scriptural, socially admirable, and self-protective for the upper classes.

But — again there is general agreement — for the rich to give their money was not enough. "The wand of charity divides the rock of avarice with a touch, and wealth flows forth like a torrent,"[29] too often to no good purpose. The times called not for impulsive charity but for care and discrimination, for greater personal interest on the part of donors, who only in this way could separate the deserving from the impostors and the idle. Members of the upper classes who undertook

[24] "And to show both *rich* and *poor* that they are all dependent on Himself." (Quoted by Jones, *Hannah More*, p. 158.
[25] J. B. Baker, *The Life of Sir Thomas Bernard Baronet*, (London, 1819), p. 7.
[26] *Ibid.*, p. 8.
[27] *Collections on Charity* (Bath, 1815), p. 6.
[28] *Philanthropist*, I, 7.
[29] *Collections on Charity*, p. 9.

personal service on behalf of the poor not only gave a demonstration of Christian virtue in action but also helped to reinforce a social fabric that showed evidence of strain.

To emphasize the note of class superiority that ran through virtually the whole body of writing on charity would be to criticize the period for not conforming to twentieth-century notions of social democracy. Even the most devoted and self-sacrificing of those who served the poor never dealt with them on terms of equality, nor did it occur to them to do so. The author of the Bath *Collections,* after sensibly reminding his upper-class readers that the poor, though crude in manners, were shrewd enough to see through fancy rhetoric and affectation, cautions them that nothing "should ever be even remotely suggested or uttered before them, or expressed by gesture, which may excite discontent with a state which cannot be amended." [30] To even the most high-minded of philanthropists, not unnaturally, the charitable work most deserving of support was that which nourished in the poor qualities especially esteemed by their social superiors, preeminently projects which encouraged them to rely on their own exertions. [31]

In spite of all the ferment over philanthropy, little of the thinking was of a systematic sort. Most of the formulations were the work of publicists who were disturbed by the insistent problem of the poor, or philanthropists whose charitable purposes were more notable than their capacity for analytical thought. Virtually all of the writers, some with reluctance, conceded the necessity for public provision for the poor. None shared Lord Kames's Scottish notion that voluntary contributions collected by a parish committee would be preferable to the English plan, [32] and none saw private charity as an adequate substitute for public provision. But from it all emerged no memorable theory of charity. By far the most elaborate and influential rationale was that of the Scottish Church leader Thomas Chalmers, whose *Christian and Civic Economy of Large Towns,* prehistoric as most of his assumptions seem today, was at least a considered attempt to develop a theory of charity. South of the border, however, Chalmers' views had little practical effect until the latter half of the century when, as we shall see, [33] they supplied the dogmatic basis for the London Charity Organisation Society.

3

In the late eighteenth century the word "charity" connoted, more than anything else, the relief of distress. Indigence, hunger, helpless childhood, these seemed appropriate fields for charitable endeavor. In an earlier period such needs would have been met by personal almsgiving or aid supplied through the Church, but now they were thought of increasingly as lying beyond the reach of individual charity and requiring the intervention of an organized group. Broadly speaking,

---

[30] *Ibid.,* p. 200.
[31] "Proposal for a Society for the Poor," *The Philanthropist,* VII, 313ff.
[32] *Sketches of the History of Man,* II, 58–59.
[33] In Chapter VIII below.

poverty as such did not come within the scope of this associated philanthropy, though such bodies as the Society for Bettering the Condition of the Poor did not hesitate to give their clients helpful advice about ordering and improving their domestic economy. Even when poverty, in Colquhoun's expression, descended into indigence, it was assumed that the sufferers would rely on parish relief, doles from endowed charities, or casual almsgiving. Only if poverty were complicated by other factors — a bad winter, crop failure, or an epidemic — was it thought to lie within the proper sphere of associated philanthropy.

The war years fulfilled some of these conditions. During the latter 1790's bad harvests and rising prices combined to cause a drastic fall in real wages, an effect that was particularly marked in 1795-96 and in 1799-1800.[34] Altogether there was a good deal about the social situation to raise questions in the minds of the upper classes, as with Sir Frederick Eden, and to lead them to consider the plight of the poor. Presumably Thomas Bernard (1750-1816), perhaps the most notable British man-about-good-works of these years, was aware of the social crisis when he decided to form his Society for Bettering the Condition of the Poor. Bernard himself offers a capital example of the philanthropic impulse in a singularly pure form. For, although he himself was a devout Churchman and warmly advocated the founding of free chapels "for the instruction and conversion of our neglected fellow creatures, THE PAGAN INHABITANTS IN THE CENTRE OF LONDON,"[35] the texture of his charity was not that of the typical Evangelical philanthropist.

It would be too easy, possibly, simply to describe Bernard as one who got pleasure and satisfaction from working to improve the condition of his fellow men. As he explains his entrance into the world of philanthropy: "When I thought I had acquired in my Profession such a competence as satisfied my desires, I determined to quit the Law, & try what useful Occupation I could find that was not likely to increase *l'embarras des richesses*. The Endeavour to meliorate the domestic habits of the labouring Class, was the first amusement that occurred."[36] For Bernard philanthropy added the satisfaction of constructive achievement to the thrill "of the gaming Table without its Horrors."[37] It is true, he recalled a little ruefully, that one sometimes loses his stake in philanthropy as in other games of chance, but more commonly, he concluded a few months before his death, his gambles had paid off.

The son of the last Royal Governor of Massachusetts, Thomas (later Sir Thomas) returned to England on the recall of his father in 1769. A remunerative marriage and a successful career as a conveyancer allowed him to retire after fifteen years of practice to become what was virtually a full-time philanthropist. Like other well-disposed persons, notably Jeremy Bentham, Bernard put a good

[34] A. D. Gayer, W. W. Rostow, A. J. Schwartz, *The Growth and Fluctuation of the British Economy, 1790–1850*, 2 vols. (Oxford, 1955), I, 9.

[35] Quoted by Baker, *Bernard*, pp. 62–63.

[36] Sir Thomas Bernard, *Pleasure and Pain, 1780–1818* (London, 1930), p. 49.

[37] *Ibid.*, p. 55.

deal of faith in the power of applied science — ingenious contrivances and more efficient methods — as an instrument of social improvement, and he was much taken with Count Rumford's demonstrations of the utility of mechanical inventions in ordinary domestic life, especially in promoting economy of fuel and food. One of his first steps when he became treasurer of the Foundling Hospital in 1785 was to re-equip the kitchen and fireplaces under the Count's supervision, a reform which, we are told, cut the consumption of coal in the kitchen by more than two-thirds.[38]

Bernard was bursting with plans for spreading Rumford's ideas, and a number of specific experiments were tried. He failed, however, to persuade the committee of the Marylebone Workhouse to introduce the Count's methods, even though, along with Wilberforce and others, he had raised a sum with which to finance the test. This rebuff by the Marylebone authorities led to the decision to form a Society for Bettering the Condition and Increasing the Comforts of the Poor. Among its leaders the Evangelical element was strongly represented in the persons of Wilberforce, Zachary Macaulay, and a number of Clapham figures, but one can picture the "Bettering Society" as an Evangelical agency only with grave qualifications. Among other things, the leading spirit and heaviest initial contributor (£52 10s.) was Thomas Bernard, whose Evangelical credentials cannot be accepted without question. Although far from a one-cause philanthropist, it was the Bettering Society that engaged his principal energies, so much so that in some of its activities the Society was hardly more than Bernard under another name.

As originally conceived by the founding group, the Society was to serve (in the modern idiom) as a "clearing-house" for information about the condition of the poor and for helpful ideas for improving it — "*useful* and *practical* information derived from EXPERIENCE, and stated *briefly* and *plainly*."[39] Here was an attempt to apply to the problem of poverty the empirical methods which Bernard considered typical of his age, to have done with vague benevolence and "deal with *facts*."[40] On the whole, the *Reports* of the Society, which were reprinted in a cheap edition for wider circulation, carried out this design. They were full of accounts of plans, usually based on experience, for bettering the lot of the poor — friendly societies, cottage gardens, parish mills for corn, village kitchens and soup shops, dietary economies and similar projects.

From the beginning the Society evinced a lively, sometimes almost morbid, interest in the dietary problems of the poor, born in part of hopes aroused by Count Rumford's methods. In the *Reports* there was no lack of recipes which were presumed to be cheap and palatable, though some — such as the item submitted by a Derbyshire lady, "Of the Manner and Expence of Making Stewed Ox's Head for the Poor,"[41] — strike the twentieth-century eye as verging on the

[38] Baker, *Bernard*, pp. 11–12.
[39] *Reports of the S.B.C.P.*, I, App., p. 3.
[40] Bernard's preface to the 1800 edition of the *Reports*.
[41] *Reports*, I, 81–85.

grotesque. During the grave food shortage of 1800–1801, the Society raised among its members some £4000 for supplying fish to the Metropolis and kept *au courant* with similar efforts in other districts. Meanwhile, Bernard explained to the poor that His Majesty was doing all "that a kind parent can do to diminish the pressure of the times," and had set an example by curtailing the use of bread in his own household in favor of potatoes or rice.[42]

Apart from the publication of the *Reports,* the Society sired an assortment of projects. An account of the Asylum for the Blind at Liverpool written by Bernard and printed in the *Reports* led to the founding of a school for the indigent blind in London. The Society's contributions to the care of the sick were the Cancer Institution and the Fever Institution, the latter modeled on the House of Recovery in Manchester, whose founding marked an important step in the development of isolation hospitals.[43] During the earlier years, Count Rumford's influence was pronounced, but as the pile of *Reports* mounted, the Society found itself countenancing a wide variety of proposals, some of them well ahead of the time. A case in point was a plan for old-age pensions to be drawn from a fund to which employers would contribute a stated fraction of their wage bill and occupiers of land a percentage of its value.[44] Bernard, in a word, seems to have conceived of the Society as a facility for the exchange of ideas and something like a holding company for certain specialized activities affecting the welfare of the lower classes.

Perhaps because of its unquestioning acceptance of prevailing notions of class relationships, the Society's activities have aroused little interest among latter-day social historians. It is true that few daring ideas found their way into the *Reports*. One is impressed how largely, in spite of their concern for the poor of the Metropolis, the leaders were still thinking in terms of a rural environment. Many of their most enthusiastic prescriptions had to do with village charities, and there were frequent complaints over factories, which were bringing ruin to the old cottage industries. Bernard could congratulate the laborer on his good fortune, though lacking comforts "which *we* are habituated to consider as *essential ingredients* in the cup of life," in that "*his Duty* is as limited as his *enjoyment*." Yet in the same letter he could also remind his well-to-do readers that "the inhabitant of the spacious and airy mansion can have *no conception* of the sufferings which [from contagious fever] the poor undergo in their close and crowded apartments." [45]

On some issues the Society could take a more positive stand. In 1800, for example, Bernard attempted to found an institution for the protection of climbing boys. He discovered, however, that with the exception of a few of the better ones, the master sweeps were highly uncooperative, and the plan accomplished nothing.[46] The Society also showed some interest in the cause of parish ap-

[42] *Ibid.,* III, 66.
[43] Baker, *Bernard,* pp. 49–50, 69–76.
[44] Countess of Jersey, "Charity a Hundred Years Ago," *Nineteenth Century,* 57:656 (April 1905).
[45] Introduction by Bernard, d. 15 Feb. 1803, *Reports,* IV, 21–24.
[46] Bernard, *Pleasure and Pain,* p. 61. On the movement to protect climbing boys, see J. L. and B. Hammond, *The Town Labourer, 1760–1832* (1928 ed., London), pp. 176–95.

prentices in Lancashire cotton mills. A gift of £1000 from Sir Robert Peel the Elder, a vice-president of the Society,[47] was originally earmarked for this purpose, and when mill-owners at Burley, near Otley, protested against the clause in Peel's Factory Act of 1802 prohibiting night work for children, the Society replied vigorously enough. To their credit, Bernard and his group refused to concede anything to the argument of the master spinners — that free labor could be obtained for night shifts only on unfavorable terms — noting drily that this was less than adequate justification for forcing orphans and foundlings to do work which free laborers refused.[48] Yet one cannot wax lyrical over the record of the Society in factory reform. Incredible as it seems, Bernard doubted whether the condition of the factory children held out "sufficient demand" for the Peel fund, and it was therefore diverted to promoting education in various parts of the Kingdom.[49]

During the war years a good deal of energy was expanded by the Society and philanthropic individuals on soup kitchens and other cheap-food charities. These were intended not only to mitigate the suffering caused by wartime shortages but also to school the poor in the habits of thrift. With bread, the staple of working-class diet, scarce and dear, a good deal of ingenuity went into contriving tasty dishes of which potatoes or rice formed the basis. "Indeed," advised Dr. Lettsom, "a well-boiled or roasted mealy potatoe is at once a little loaf, and forms the cheapest substitute for that of wheat."[50] Both London and the provinces broke out into something of a rash of food charities, most conspicuously after the bad years of the mid-nineties and again in 1799–1800.[51] In London, where Patrick Colquhoun was a leading spirit in the movement, the committee got under way in early 1797 and at once found itself managing a flourishing business, feeding some ten thousand individuals twice a week at a penny a meal or less. Three years later soup was being issued from twenty-two different establishments in the Metropolis, for which in 1799–1800 London philanthropists contributed over £10,000.[52] The committee was able to extract about a third of the total from twenty-three commercial and corporate bodies, with 540 individuals supplying the remainder. In late 1799, when famine seemed to menace, the Lords of Trade interested themselves in soup kitchens and distributed throughout the country a series of suggestions drawn up by Colquhoun.[53]

Not all of the motives that went into the soup shops were humanitarian. Mrs.

[47] The elder Peel was also president of the House of Recovery in Manchester, governor of Christ's Hospital, and vice-president of David Williams' Literary Fund. (Norman Gash, *Mr. Secretary Peel* [London, 1961], pp. 26–27.)

[48] *Reports,* IV, App. 1, p. 3; Countess of Jersey, "Charity a Hundred Years Ago," (n. 44), pp. 664–65.

[49] Bernard, *Pleasure and Pain,* p. 62.

[50] J. C. Lettsom, *Hints Designed to Promote Beneficence* . . . , 3 vols. (London, 1801), I, 37.

[51] Apparently the pioneer experiment was Rumford's kitchen on the Foundling Hospital estate, which had been designed to provide low-cost meals for three hundred persons. (Bernard, *Pleasure and Pain,* p. 52).

[52] A Magistrate (Colquhoun), *An Account of a Meat and Soup Charity* (London, 1797); *General Report of the Committee of Subscribers* (London, 1800).

[53] Lettsom, *Hints,* I, 95. Lettsom devotes over 165 pages in one of his volumes to soup kitchens and dietary suggestions.

Trimmer saw in them a possible lure with which to attract the poor to the new free chapels.[54] At the other extreme, food charities offered an irresistible temptation to those who would exploit the innocence or good nature of their social betters. There was, for example, the Laudable Institution, which started off in 1800 with an address to the public carrying the names of five dukes, six marquesses, and assorted peers and peeresses. Its professed purpose was to supply the poor with good meat and vegetables at low prices. But presently the Laudable Institution (its promoter must have had a sardonic sense of humor) turned out to be a complete swindle, the inspiration of a well-known Bow Street character.[55] Though the soup kitchen became a more or less permanent feature of London slum life, as an agency of social betterment it never justified the hopes of Bernard, Colquhoun, and its other sponsors. Before long enthusiasm had turned to skepticism and hostility, and the more "scientific" philanthropists came to regard such charities as a baneful influence in the life of the poor.

4

To the ordinary upper-class city-dweller perhaps the most obtrusive evidence of social malaise was the army of mendicants subsisting on the good nature or feeble resistance of the public. Naturally no figures on such a phenomenon are wholly trustworthy, but the most responsible estimates put the total for the Metropolis at slightly over fifteen thousand, of whom possibly a third were Irish immigrants. Many of these were, of course, professionals, but considerable numbers were unemployed laborers or strangers from the provinces who had failed to find work.[56] One cannot even guess at the size of the armies of beggars and vagrants said to be swarming over such resorts as Bath and Buxton. Evidence collected by the Mendicity Committee in 1815–16 pictures mendicancy in St. Giles, for example, as a highly organized business, with beggars divided into companies, and companies subdivided into "walks," each with its assigned territory and time.[57] A refinement of specialization was the begging-letter writer, the "two-penny post beggar," often a person of some education, perhaps a schoolmaster, who would write letters of appeal for a fee of twopence each.[58]

The movement which led to a ventilation of the mendicity situation in the Metropolis was largely the work of Matthew Martin, a businessman whose avocations were natural history and philanthropy. He combined a humanitarian outlook with some of Colquhoun's zest for social investigation. In its early stages his inquiry into London mendicancy was a private venture of his own, by which he hoped to convince himself that not all beggars were hopelessly depraved or irreclaimable. He enlisted the cooperation of the Society for Bettering the Condition of the Poor, and for a time served as its secretary. When it appeared that the

[54] *Oeconomy of Charity*, II, 241.
[55] *S. C. on Mendicity*, 1815, pp. 69–71.
[56] Matthew Martin and Patrick Colquhoun, *ibid.*, pp. 5ff, 54ff.
[57] *Ibid.*, pp. 48ff.
[58] *S. C. on Mendicity*, 1816, p. 8.

job was too great for one individual, he appealed to the Duke of Portland for official support, and with £500 from the public funds (later augmented by another £500), he set up an office, engaged a staff, and began his systematic inquiries. As a bait to attract beggars and paupers for interviews, he distributed tickets which would entitle the bearer, after he had told his story, to some small assistance. In a matter of seven months he examined about two thousand beggars, together with some six hundred paupers.[59]

Martin, who brought to his task a measure of sympathetic understanding, soon satisfied himself that beggary was often a matter of misfortune rather than of choice and that there was little basis for the comfortable illusion which held all beggars, by definition, to be shiftless rogues. This earlier inquiry, which occupied the years 1800–1803, produced no significant change in methods of relieving poverty or reducing mendicity.[60] But during the trade depression of 1811, the Society for Bettering the Condition of the Poor persuaded the Home Secretary to revive the Martin inquiry. During the years 1811–15, he examined about forty-five hundred cases and during the worst of the distress raised a fund with which to provide employment for some of the more necessitous.[61]

During the same crisis the leaders of the Society and others sought to relieve some of the pressure by establishing a nation-wide cheap food charity. This Association for the Relief and Benefit of the Manufacturing and Labouring Poor hit upon fish as the answer to the diet problem of the poor, and not only exhorted them to satisfy their hunger with mackerel and salt cod but itself sold quantities of fish at low prices — on a single day as many as seventeen thousand mackerel at a penny each. This was to be a national organization, with a central committee and local associations, the latter, in many instances, stimulated to activity by grants from the national body. During the first year about £4000 was issued in fifty-four grants, some running as high as £200 to £300. In 1813–14 the Association spent over £21,000, about £12,000 going for the purchase of fish and salt![62]

For our purpose the most significant consequence of the alarm over mendicity was the determination of a group of individuals to do something about the problem. This, of course, followed the recognized procedures of an age when citizens looked less to remedial action by public agencies than to the voluntary efforts of groups of individuals. The London anti-mendicity organization was not first in the field. For some years similar bodies had been carrying on at Bath, Edinburgh, and, less notably, at other places. Bath, as the natural hunting-ground of the professional mendicant, was almost predestined to be the site of an anti-

---

[59] Matthew Martin, *Letter to the Rt. Hon. Lord Pelham on the State of Mendicity in the Metropolis* (London, 1803); *S. C. on Mendicity*, 1815, App. IV.

[60] Martin had proposed more centralized methods of dealing with the metropolitan poor, especially the out-of-parish poor, and various measures designed to prevent street-begging (*Letter to Pelham*, pp. 20ff).

[61] *S. C. on Mendicity*, 1815, p. 5; Martin, *Appeal to Public Benevolence for the Relief of Beggars* (London, 1812).

[62] *Reports of the Association*, 1813–14; *The Philanthropist*, II, 229–39; III, 374–78.

mendicity campaign. The "Bath beggar" represented the ultimate in importunate and skillful mendicancy. As its name suggests, the Bath Society for the Suppression of Common Vagrants and Impostors, Relief of Occasional Distress, and Encouragement of Industry was dedicated primarily to getting rid of beggars who during the season made the streets of the city noisome and even dangerous. The Society itself employed an officer to apprehend professional beggars. But even at the beginning the members recognized that genuine distress did in fact exist, and the committee found itself running a casework agency of sorts. Members took turns in the office, receiving and investigating applications, and granting relief, usually by food tickets. Gradually the more negative side receded, and the Bath Society developed into an interesting pioneer charity, with a permanent pension fund, loan funds for small businessmen (during the decade 1820–30 loans were being granted at the rate of over £600 a year with losses of only about 1½ per cent), and with relief arrangements for the needy and unemployed. In 1817, for example, the Society spent £1200 in providing work of various kinds, and its representatives visited 1850 cases.[63]

The initiative in London came from an advertisement in *The Times* and *Chronicle* signed "Philanthropos," who turned out to be W. H. Bodkin later celebrated by Thomas Hood in his ode:[64]

> Hail, King of Shreds and Patches, hail,
>   Disperser of the Poor!
> Thou Dog in office, set to bark
>   All beggars from the door!
>
> . . . . . .
>
> Doubtless thou are what Hamlet meant—
>   To wretches the last friend:
> What ills can mortals have, they can't
>   With a bare *Bodkin* end?

As it took form, the Mendicity Society boasted the usual complement of noble patrons, but on the board of management appeared the names of David Ricardo, Patrick Colquhoun, William Allen, and Joseph Hume. It was Hume, in fact, who made the motion that set up and named the Society.[65] The problem of mendicancy was to be approached, as at Bath, both punitively and constructively. The repressive activities of the Society were carried on largely by constables, at the outset eight in number, who roamed the streets in pairs to apprehend beggars and bring them to the Society's office in Red Lion Square or turn them over to the magistrates. The constables seem to have pursued their unattractive calling with a good

---

[63] The story of the Bath Society is told by P. V. Turner, *History of the Monmouth Street Society* (Bath, n.d.).

[64] "Ode to H. Bodkin, Esq." (1825). Bodkin was later called to the Bar, served as Recorder of Dover, assistant judge of the Middlesex Sessions, and M. P. for Rochester. In 1859 he received a knighthood.

[65] Mendicity Society Minute Book, 8 Jan. 1818.

deal of vigor, for during the first fourteen years of the Society's history, its agents apprehended over 9500 vagrants, of whom nearly 4800 were convicted.[66]

The leaders of the Society, however, thought of themselves as philanthropists as well as quasi-policemen, and they were aware that some relief would have to be provided for cases of genuine distress. But to make certain that assistance would be confined to legitimate cases, the Society set out to break the public of its ancient habit of giving money to beggars.[67] If instead of alms the beggar received a ticket entitling him to apply at the Red Lion Square office, his bona fides could be carefully examined. Subscribers were entitled to an unlimited number of tickets, while others could purchase five for a shilling.

The new system did not work flawlessly. Among other things, the beggars themselves, at least English-born beggars, put up a good deal of resistance to the Society's tickets (though Irish paupers accepted them with alacrity), and subscribers could find little satisfaction in offering aid that was certain to be refused, particularly, the managers conceded, as the rejection is "frequently accompanied by abuse." [68] During periods of greatest hardship, the ticket scheme broke down completely, and the Society took on the aspect of an ordinary relief agency. In the severe winter of 1819 so many of the legitimately unemployed took to the streets that the Society had to stop harrying beggars and use its entire staff in relief work.[69] Again, one reads of the mobs of poor, apparently consisting of Irish laborers ineligible for parish relief (during the early years nearly a third of the Society's applicants were Irish) [70] who in bad years would surround the Red Lion Square headquarters. Very early in their work the managers concluded that tickets and investigation were not enough, and they introduced a labor test. At first this consisted of stone-breaking, the classic proof of good faith and hunger on the part of the poor, but later the Society acquired a mill and put its clients to grinding and preparing corn for the bread distributed as relief.[71]

Whatever its shortcomings, the statistics of the early years of the Mendicity Society comprise an impressive record. During its first year, for example, it handled nearly 3300 cases, of whom over 550 were ordered to be prosecuted, over 1220 referred to London parishes, and others relieved in various ways (or judged not to be in serious need). In the second year, the office of the Society registered nearly 4700 cases and gave over 33,000 meals, and up to 1831 dealt with nearly 27,000 cases and distributed over a half-million meals.[72] By this time the annual expenditure ran to £5400 a year, drawn from about 3000 subscribers and contributors. Not the least useful service of the Mendicity Society, in the view of its members, was the begging-letter department, which in a little more than ten

---

[66] *14th Rept.*, 1831.
[67] As announced in the *1st Rept.*, 1818.
[68] *9th Rept.*, 1826.
[69] *2d Rept.*, 1819.
[70] *1st Rept.*, 1818; *11th Rept.*, 1828.
[71] *11th Rept.*, 1828.
[72] *2d Rept.*, 1819; *14th Rept*, 1831.

years investigated some 28,000 letters.[73] The Society tried in all sincerity to deal charitably with the unfortunate and severely with the rascally, convinced, as the managers reminded themselves, that "whilst Benevolence *stimulates,* Prudence must *restrain*." [74]

5

The various mendicity societies pointed more or less directly to the social case-work of the later nineteenth century. It is hard to discover any such prophetic element in the popular schemes for providing the children of the poor with suitable training. Whatever their individual emphases, the education movements of the 1780's and '90's were, more than ordinarily, creatures of their time. The menace of Jacobinism and infidelity made it even more urgent than before that the lower orders should be instructed in the duties of the Christian religion, and the tremendous increase in the numbers of infant poor in the cities, whose "temper and disposition and manner can scarce be said to differ from the brute creation," [75] challenged the Evangelical-Nonconformist conscience. The Sunday School itself was the product of industrialism in the sense that factories could spare the children only on the Sabbath. But Sunday Schools, charity schools, and schools of industry, all were less interested in developing the intellectual aptitudes of the children than in setting up, in Miss Jones's words, "a shield and defence against the specific religious, political and social perils of the age." [76]

At the end of the century, three types of charitable undertaking were offering education of a sort to the children of the poor. Numbers of the older charity schools were, of course, still in existence, the better established of them on the way to becoming "the aristocracy of schools for the lower orders." [77] It was, in part, the loss of momentum of the charity school movement that created the opening for the Sunday School, an institution which revived on a one-day-a-week basis the aims and methods of the charity school. The Sunday School was no more committed to education in the twentieth-century sense than was its full-time prototype; it was to be an agency for reforming the behavior of the lower orders and implanting in them a becoming reverence for the Christian religion and their social superiors. Of necessity it functioned on the only day of the week when employed children could attend — and when they might otherwise run the streets and make the Sabbath hideous for others.[78]

There was little that was novel about the idea of instructing poor children on Sunday, but it required the writings and personal advocacy of Robert Raikes, the Gloucester newspaper publisher, to create a national movement out of what had

---

[73] *14th Rept.,* 1831.
[74] *2d Rept.,* 1819.
[75] Letter by Robert Raikes, quoted by Jones in *Charity School Movement* p. 146.
[76] *Ibid.,* p. 343.
[77] R. K. Webb, *The British Working Class Reader, 1790–1848* (London, 1955), p. 16.
[78] This section on Sunday Schools and that on schools of industry is based, save where otherwise noted, on Miss Jones's *Charity School Movement,* chap. IV.

been purely local efforts. To the propaganda carried on by Raikes, the Mendip schools of the More sisters, some of them of the Sunday variety, and Mrs. Trimmer's schools at Brentford added the evidence of practical demonstration, as well as persuasive advertising, for both Hannah More and Sarah Trimmer were accomplished in the arts of pious publicity. What must be emphasized here, however, is that behind Raikes and the Sunday School movement stood an active and organized body of philanthropists. The Sunday School Society never reached the dimensions of the British and Foreign Bible Society or the great missionary societies, but it showed a good deal of the same vigor and tactical shrewdness that marked the other Evangelical-Nonconformist ventures.

The initiative that led to its foundation came chiefly from a well-to-do Baptist merchant and philanthropist, William Fox, who had already founded a free day school at Clapton, where he was lord of the manor. He had been canvassing the possibility of a national system of education, and he discovered in Raikes's plan the basis for such a system. The Society, which eventually emerged out of a meeting called by Fox in August 1785, was formed to promote Sunday Schools and thus to rescue the children of the poor "from low habits of vice and idleness, and to initiate them into a moral and religious course of life." [79] The primary medium of reformation was assumed to be the Bible. Hence the overpowering emphasis on reading instruction, with the Bible, the Book of Common Prayer, and the Catechism as the chief vehicles, and acceptance by the Society of responsibility for providing these and other textbooks. The founders were determined to submerge sectarian differences. Evangelicals had no prejudice against working with Nonconformists, and the Sunday School Society offers an admirable instance of that cooperation. The managing committee of twenty-four was to be equally divided between Church and Chapel, and both were represented by names distinguished in the annals of philanthropy. In 1813, for example, such names as Hoare, Thornton, Buxton, Gurney, Wilberforce, Grant, and William Allen are conspicuous.[80]

The launching of the Sunday Schools appears to have been exceptionally well timed. Large numbers of the poorer classes, in contrast to their behavior earlier in the century, now exhibited the greatest eagerness to acquire the rudiments of an education, especially if this could be managed without interfering with their regular work. What lay behind this extraordinary burst of zeal for learning is not wholly clear. The Methodist Revival (with its stress on Bible-reading), the spread of radical ideas among the working classes, and the expansion of knowledge, scientific and economic, which took place during the latter part of the century may have had something to do with the passion for self-improvement. Obviously, also, literacy was an asset to the industrial worker, especially to one who would improve his position.[81] Whatever the explanation, the statistics issued by the Sunday

---

[79] *Plan of a Society for . . . Sunday Schools* (1810), pp. 8–9.
[80] *Plan of a Society* (1813), p. 13.
[81] As suggested by Jones, p. 149; see also Webb, *Working Class Reader*, p. 15.

School Society, inflated and overoptimistic as they may have been, give a picture of almost fantastic growth. One may dismiss some of Raikes's claims as preposterous, but as early as 1787 the Society was in contact with 201 affiliated schools attended by 10,200 scholars. During the next decade these figures were multiplied more than fivefold and at the end of its first quarter-century, the Society could point to 3350 schools established and 275,000 "scholars educated." [82] These figures presumably represent no more than a fraction of the aggregate of Sunday School activity, for most of the schools were started through local initiative, were financed locally, and owed little to the Society. Financially, as compared with some of the other great voluntary associations, the Sunday School Society remained a small operation, with annual expenditures rarely exceeding £1800.

The confident hopes that Sunday Schools aroused in their supporters seem in retrospect unbelievably naive. Yet, however lamentable their instruction and however false their premise that schooling was something that could be fitted in at odd moments, the Sunday School experiment helped to put the issue of popular education into a new perspective. Although they still conceived of education of the poor as missionary work on behalf of a neglected class, the leaders of the movement sensed that the growth of the urban working population was altering the terms of the problem. Whatever the defects of their prescription, they saw popular education as a national question and sought to deal with it on a national scale. And their work served to make the schooling of the masses into something of a public question.

No such claim can be fairly made for the third type of charity school. In spite of the devoted efforts of Mrs. Trimmer and the propaganda of the Bettering Society, the schools of industry left no permanent legacies. Whereas Sunday Schools would take care of employed children, industrial schools were designed, as Mrs. Trimmer put it, to rescue the others "from the dangers to which idleness exposes every human being." [83] In retrospect they hardly justified the effort, not to mention the printer's ink, expended on them. Nor is it clear in what degree they were philanthropic undertakings in the pecuniary sense. The school at Lewisham, one of the older and more successful, depended on a parish allowance and profit from the manufactory for 90 per cent of its budget.[84]

The schools of industry, as a whole ineffective and ephemeral, rested on a series of misapprehensions about the currents that were revolutionizing British life. Of these the Bettering Society and the other advocates of industrial schools were only dimly aware. A barrister who thought of himself as something of an authority on the poor could still (1808) deny that a legitimate demand for training in writing

[82] *Plan of a Society* (1810), p. 46. The Society could also report the distribution of 285,000 spelling books, over 62,000 Testaments, and over 7700 Bibles.

[83] *Oeconomy of Charity*, I, 195. For an account of Mrs. Trimmer and her work, see Betsy Rodgers, *Cloak of Charity*, pp. 125ff, and W. K. Lowther Clarke, *Eighteenth Century Piety* (London, 1944), pp. 118–25, both of whom view her more sympathetically than I have been able to do.

[84] *Education of the Poor* (selections from the Bettering Society's reports on education, London, 1809), p. 186.

and arithmetic existed among the lower orders, for business and industry were already adequately supplied with these skills. To imagine "any large proportion of the population rising in life by such means, it is too ridiculous . . . to deserve a serious answer." [85] The school of industry, to a degree representing similar views, soon proved itself an anachronism in an increasingly industrial society. The straw-platting and hand-spinning, which were the staples of the work-school curriculum, were productive neither economically nor educationally — despite Mrs. Trimmer's confidence in the schools as media for the moral training of children of the poor.

By the late century the base of the movement for popular education had become noticeably broader. While in an earlier period the leaders had been impelled by motives of piety, philanthropy, and social discipline, other elements now appeared, among them philosophical radicals and a small but growing group of working-class representatives, whose interest in education was more broadly social. With such rising enthusiasm for education, one might have expected a public system to develop. But the outcome was quite the contrary; the voluntary principle emerged more strongly than ever. What preserved and reinvigorated it was, more than anything, the support evoked by two new voluntary organizations. The astonishing success achieved by the National (Bell) and the British and Foreign School (Lancasterian) Societies seemed to reconfirm the validity of the voluntary principle and to re-establish education as a branch of philanthropy. Elementary education, the evidence was thought to indicate, could be better left to private benevolence than handed over to a bureaucracy which might blight the flourishing growth of British charity.[86]

Either of the two great voluntary societies would provide an instructive example of an early-century philanthropic association. The National Society, a lineal descendant of the S.P.C.K., was more handsomely financed. During its first four years (1809–13), its leaders managed to raise £60,000 for "promoting the Education of the Poor in the Principles of the Established Church." [87] But in most respects the National Society was a less representative philanthropic effort than was the rival body, for in a large degree it functioned as a Church of England auxiliary. The British and Foreign School Society, with fewer theological preoccupations, and leaders who at various times covered a spectrum from devout Nonconformity and Evangelical Anglicanism to semimilitant secularism, in general stands as a more typical example of the voluntary association.

The origin of the British and Foreign School Society lay in the Borough Road School of Joseph Lancaster, a man whose sense of mission as an educational reformer was as authentic as was his talent for accumulating debts. At Borough Road he exhibited the monitorial system (that is, the use of pupils, themselves coached by the master, to teach other pupils and to carry on the routine adminis-

---

[85] John Weyland, Jun., *Letter to a Country Gentleman on the Education of the Lower Orders* . . . (London, 1808), p. 50.
[86] See Jones, *Charity School Movement,* chap. IX, pt. I, "Triumph of the Voluntary Principle."
[87] H. B. Binns, *A Century of Education* . . . *1808–1908* (London, 1908), p. 81.

tration of the school) at its best, for he had the teaching gift in generous measure, and he showed a good deal of ingenuity in drilling and supervising his pupil-teachers. Indeed, Lancaster's achievement at Borough Road was responsible, both at the time and subsequently, for overemphasis on the monitorial system as the distinctive feature of the new schools and for an unseemly and barren controversy among the disciples of Lancaster and Dr. Bell as to which was the discoverer of the magic technique (though in reality it was no novelty).[88] A generation which explained its own economic progress as a triumph of labor-saving machinery could readily believe that an analogous method would accomplish similar wonders in spreading popular enlightenment. "The man who first made a practical use of the division of labour . . . did not do more essential service to *mechanical*," exulted Sir Thomas Bernard, "than Dr. Bell has done to *intellectual* operations . . . The principle in manufactories, and in schools is the same." [89]

Extraordinary success at Borough Road was not sufficient for Lancaster. His restless imagination could always discover new directions in which to expand the work, and that, combined with his uninhibited personal extravagance, kept the Lancasterian enterprises in constant hot water. Obviously these could not be continued as a one-man affair. The first two who in 1808 associated themselves with Lancaster as a committee, William Corston the Moravian hat-maker and Joseph Fox the well-to-do Baptist dentist, were able, at enormous sacrifice to themselves, to settle with some of the creditors and to hold the others temporarily at bay. It was not until the committee was expanded to include the two Quakers William Allen and Joseph Foster that a degree of prudence and realism entered the undertaking.[90] Allen, the manufacturing chemist of multifarious charitable interests, discovered a congenial cause in the Lancasterian system, whose virtues he warmly praised in his publication, the *Philanthropist*. A plan of raising capital by selling interest-bearing shares in the philanthropy (for there was the possibility that Lancaster's printing-office for schoolbooks might be made to pay) failed to restore the schools to solvency, and their director continued to behave as though expense were a matter of indifference. By 1810 his operations had accumulated a deficit of over £8000.

To broaden the base of financial support was an obvious step, for the Lancaster system had been widely acclaimed as the answer to Britain's problem. Originally the sponsoring group had been largely Nonconformist and Evangelical, but this committee proved unable to curb Lancaster's financial irresponsibility. An enlarged and more representative committee might act with greater effect, and when the

[88] J. W. Adamson, *English Education, 1789–1902* (Cambridge, 1930), p. 24; Chester W. New, *The Life of Henry Brougham to 1830* (Oxford, 1961), pp. 200–201.

[89] *Education of the Poor*, pp. 35–36. The exterior of the Borough Road school is pictured in the L. C. C. *Survey of London, St. George's Fields*, XXV (1955), Plate 7.

[90] *Life of William Allen*, 2 vols. (Philadelphia, 1847), I, 72–73; Binns, *Century of Education*, pp. 32ff. Save where otherwise noted, my discussion of Lancaster and the British Society is based on Binns's volume.

new finance committee of forty-seven members was formed, it included not only the familiar Evangelical and Quaker names but also those of Brougham, Francis Horner, James Mill, and Samuel Romilly. This was a critical step. The movement was now passing from the hands of Lancaster's friends and co-religionists into those of a public philanthropic association. The new management was able to better the financial situation in some degree, aided by the decision of a number of holders of £100 shares who, perhaps recognizing the inevitable, converted them into gifts, but the outlook remained bleak. What forced a further change was a counteroffensive of the partisans of Dr. Bell, who considered popular education to be a function of the Established Church and regarded Lancaster, in Mrs. Trimmer's classic tag, as the "Goliath of schismatics." The formation of the National Society made it only a matter of time until the Lancasterians should respond in kind.

The circumstances, some of them painful enough, which set the stage for the British and Foreign School Society, need not be reviewed. It is enough to say that the break between the committee and Lancaster was complete, and the Society formed in the spring of 1814 was dedicated to spreading the Lancaster system without the cooperation of Lancaster or his name. This marked a further step in the secularization of the movement, for additional Whigs and Radicals now took their places on the committee, some as vice-presidents — Whitbread, Lord Byron, Sir James Mackintosh, Francis Place, and David Ricardo.[91] During these critical years, free-thinking radicals had more than a little to do with formulating policy.

It would be out of the question to trace the subsequent history of the British and Foreign Society or, for that matter, of its Anglican rival. The word "Foreign" was purposely included in the Society's name, and the committee was much occupied with plans for introducing the British system not only into Western Europe and the colonies but into such unlikely areas as Russia, Spanish America, and Madagascar. At home the record of the two societies was statistically impressive, qualitatively less so. A recent authority attributes to Bell and Lancaster the responsibility for the British elementary school of the nineteenth century, with "its mechanical methods, its low standards, its large classes and mass production, its emphasis on cheapness."[92] But there can be no doubt that the societies, even their quarrels, did something to make elementary education a live issue for the British public, and they were the means of giving a mass of children some smattering of schooling.[93]

Whether one views the work of the two societies with a sympathetic or critical eye, their success tended to reinforce the conventional view of education as a

[91] Binns, *Century of Education*, pp. 72–73.
[92] H. C. Barnard, *Short History of English Education, 1760–1914* (London, 1947), p. 68.
[93] Calculations of the numbers enrolled in the schools of the two societies show the widest discrepancies. See, for example, Frederic Hill, *National Education: Its Present State and Prospects*, 2 vols. (London, 1836), I, 65–66; Barnard, *English Education*, p. 67; G. Kitson Clark, *The Making of Victorian England* (Cambridge, Mass., 1962), p. 173, citing H. J. Burgess, *Enterprise in Education* (London, 1958), pp. 210ff.

branch of private philanthropy. Obviously their activity and the "denominational" rivalry which they represented had a good deal to do with delaying the intervention of the State. The voluntary societies raised considerable sums from their charitable constituencies, as indicated in the accompanying table, which covers the period from their foundation through 1859.[94]

	£000's
National Society	725
British and Foreign Society	157
Catholic Poor School Committee	72
Home and Colonial Society	116
Church Education Society	10
Wesleyan Education Committee	88
Congregational Board of Education	174
London Ragged School Association	58

Not only did the school societies draw successfully on British philanthropists, large and small, but they also formed the channel by which the State, with extreme timidity, entered the field of popular education. When in 1833 the Government voted its first educational grant, £20,000 for school buildings, "in aid of Private Subscriptions," the money went to the two pioneer societies, with other bodies gradually added. In elementary education, in fine, the private philanthropist not only was the pioneer but it was he who, in a large measure, determined the conditions on which the State intervened. Slowly the pattern of relationships emerged. The State was not to displace private agencies in education, but was to become a partner, its junior and supervisory status expanding over the years until the balance had conclusively shifted to the public side.

If the turn of the century marked a growing recognition of the problem of educating the masses, it also saw the beginning of special training for some categories of the handicapped. In work for the blind, as in other philanthropic ventures, Liverpool led the way with its School for the Indigent Blind, established in 1790. The idea of a specialized charity for the blind is credited to Edward Rushton, who himself had been blinded by malignant ophthalmia while treating afflicted slaves on a ship bound for Dominica. What Rushton and his associates contemplated was not so much another asylum as a training school which would equip the blind to contribute to their own support. In addition to spinning, basket-making, and the familiar staples, musical pursuits were regarded as especially suitable for those with sufficient talent. Perhaps, lest the School seem to encourage more blind fiddlers to take to the streets, the original appeal for funds announced that "violins are excluded." [95] When Thomas Bernard visited the Liverpool institution in the summer of 1798, he returned full of enthusiasm for planting

[94] R. C. on Popular Education (C.2794), 1861, I, 575.

[95] Simey, Charitable Effort in Liverpool, pp. 19–20. Mrs. Simey notes that there is some question about Rushton's part in the founding of this charity.

such schools up and down the land. Edinburgh and Bristol joined the movement, and in London Bernard's report inspired the founding of an institution for the blind in St. George's Fields. The charity was an immediate success. Within a few years, the School was training over fifty blind persons, had accumulated a funded capital of about £9000, and was clearing (1808) from sales and subscriptions more than £3100.[96] Not unnaturally, philanthropies for the blind always held a special appeal.

The deaf and dumb also became objects of concern. Indeed, the first institution for their training, the Asylum for the Deaf and Dumb Children of the Poor in Bermondsey, antedated the London School for the Indigent Blind by seven years. Although something was known about teaching the deaf and dumb to communicate, the notion that they merited special sympathy and understanding developed slowly. The first organized effort on their behalf was the joint project of an Independent minister, John Townsend, and the rector of Bermondsey, Henry Cox Mason, with assistance from Henry Thornton and others. At the outset the promoters had to contend against the ingrained belief that nothing much could be done for the deaf and dumb, but the list of subscribers grew and what had been intended as a local Bermondsey institution became established as an important national charity with applications far exceeding its capacity.[97]

The conscience of the late-century philanthropist was moved by youthful victims of physical misfortune. It is impossible to say whether it was his sympathetic or prudential nervous system that reacted to the plight of children whose backgrounds apparently predestined them to careers of crime. Certainly a mixture of motives entered into the Philanthropic Society, which was established in 1788 to reform the nation's criminal poor by rehabilitating the children. Admittedly this was a project to "unite the purposes of *charity* with those of industry and police," an institution for the prevention of crime which would appeal alike to the benevolence and the self-interest of the community.[98] The clients of the Society were thus to be, in modern parlance, juvenile delinquents or those whose parentage and environment made them likely candidates for delinquency.

The Philanthropic turned out to be something more than another voluntary charity. Almost from the beginning it took on a semiofficial status, as magistrates and judges committed certain juvenile offenders to the Society for discipline and training in useful trades, the boys to work as apprentices under the supervision of master workmen.[99] Later it became a regular procedure for children sentenced to long terms of imprisonment and pardoned under the Parkhurst Act to be

[96] Thomas Bernard, "Account of the School of Instruction for the Blind," ext. in Lettsom, *Hints,* II, 121ff.

[97] *Ibid.,* II, 105–6.

[98] *Address to the Public from the Philanthropic Society* (1791 ed., London). On the committee appear the names of Jeremiah [*sic*] Bentham and Dr. Lettsom.

[99] Lettsom, *Hints,* III, 162ff; Sydney Turner, "Early History of the Reformatory and Industrial Schools," *Report of a Departmental [Home Office] Committee on Reformatory and Industrial Schools* (C. 8204), 1896, App. I, p. 176; S. C. on Criminal and Destitute Children, 1852, Q. 223ff.

placed in custody of the Philanthropic.[100] This pioneer reformatory school, in short, offers an interesting early example of a voluntary organization receiving government support for performing what were essentially public police functions. As will appear later, this pattern persisted and was developed in the course of the nineteenth century not only with the Philanthropic but with other reformatory schools as they were founded.

From the beginning the demands on the Society exceeded its resources, though it presently became a reasonably well-supported charity. By the turn of the century nearly five hundred young persons had passed through its hands, most of them the products of the grisliest of environments.[101] Starting with a few houses at Cambridge Heath, within a few years the Philanthropic transferred its principal center to St. George's Fields. For the benefit of genuine delinquents the Society kept a House in Bermondsey known as the Philanthropic Reform, where rehabilitation was begun with intensive instruction in morals and religion supplemented by regular shifts of oakum picking, lest the inmates be confirmed in idle habits. When their reformation reached a satisfactory point, they might move to the manufactory, where they enjoyed some slight degree of freedom. In an adjoining building the girls were trained for domestic service.[102] A measure of the Society's growth and utility is its income, which at the end of the second decade had risen to nearly £6150. Two years before, the committee had ventured to build a chapel at the cost of over £6000, financing it partly by the sale of interest-bearing shares and partly by donations.[103] The Philanthropic Society played a notable part in the story of Victorian charity not merely for its own achievements but because it provided a take-off point for other attacks on the problem of delinquency.

6

To shift from morals to matter, turn-of-the-century philanthropy was responsible for two innovations of consequence in the care of the sick. These were the years in which the dispensary movement flourished, in some degree at the expense of the general hospitals, and isolation hospitals first appeared. Both were the work of physicians with a sense of social responsibility who were supported by groups of philanthropists. It was, in fact, one of the distinctions of eighteenth-century medicine that for the first time there appeared physicians who sought to use their skills for the benefit of the masses. The institutional expression of this new tendency was the dispensary, to which the poor could come for free medical advice and treatment. Dispensary doctors would also make house calls on patients confined to their homes. In the course of their work, such physicians not only relieved much suffering but themselves received something of an education in the sociology of disease, especially disease associated with poverty and dirt. To inter-

[100] 1 & 2 Vict., c. 82.
[101] Lettsom, *Hints*, III, 152–61, 171–73; Highmore, *Pietas Londinensis*, p. 861.
[102] *Ibid.*, pp. 866–68.
[103] *Ibid.*, pp. 869–71; *Philanthropic Society—List of Subscribers* (1850).

ested contemporaries, dispensaries seemed to be one of the more productive types of charity, and with the poor they acquired an almost embarrassing popularity. Governors with the right to recommend patients sometimes found themselves almost swamped with applications. It was predictable that the movement would spread rapidly both in London and the provinces.

For dispensaries, at least in London, the big period of growth was probably the late 1770's and '80's, but the pioneer experiment was the General Dispensary in Aldersgate founded in 1770. Although in the previous year Dr. George Armstrong had started his establishment in Red Lion Square for the Relief of the Infant Poor,[104] it was Dr. Hulme's General Dispensary that set the pattern. One ought not, perhaps, to take the statistics of the early dispensary and its claims of cure at their face value. The General Dispensary, for example, professed to have treated about 140,000 patients in thirty-eight years, and the London Dispensary nearly 100,000 in a little over twenty.[105] Dr. Lettsom, who was associated with Hulme in the General Dispensary and was one of the more enthusiastic champions of the cause, estimated that in the Metropolis 50,000 poor annually received treatment through dispensaries, at least a third of them in their own homes, at a cost of £5000.[106] It is impossible to be precise about the number of dispensaries founded, but by 1820 at least twenty-five were operating with greater or less effectiveness in the Metropolis and perhaps thirty-five in the provinces, some of which would evolve into general hospitals.[107]

A second departure in the care of the sick had to do with the control of contagious diseases, especially typhus or gaol fever. For our purpose the principal interest centers in houses of recovery (as fever hospitals were often termed with more than a dash of euphemism). Here the provinces led the Metropolis, for both Chester and Manchester were in the field before London established its institution. Although there had been some experiments with fever wards in general hospitals in Dumfries and Edinburgh, the pioneer in the treatment of fever by isolation was Dr. John Haygarth of Chester. Whereas in the past only those who contracted the disease in the hospital had been admitted to fever wards, Haygarth not only opened them to patients from outside but carried on something of a campaign for his method of treatment by isolation. Manchester followed in 1796 with a small house of recovery and in 1805 opened a larger institution for which subscribers contributed some £5000.[108] In London it was the typhus epidemic of 1800-01 that underlined the efforts of such philanthropists as Thomas Bernard and pushed doctors and public into action. The result was the House of Recovery in Gray's Inn Road, which admitted 785 patients in the nine years after its opening in 1802

---

[104] G. F. McCleary, *The Early History of the Infant Welfare Movement* (London, 1933), pp. 17–18; Malcolm, *Manners and Customs*, I, 74–77.

[105] Highmore, *Pietas,* pp. 376, 378.

[106] Lettsom, *Hints,* III, 185–86.

[107] For a list of these dispensaries, see Buer, *Health, Wealth, and Population,* p. 258.

[108] An account of the movement is given in Buer, chap. XV.

and discharged 696 as cured, a substantial reduction from the usual mortality rate.[109]

Fever hospitals operated on the periphery of private philanthropy. Not even the most convinced disciple of political economy could view a fever epidemic as a crisis to be met through voluntary effort. In Liverpool the House of Recovery was supported entirely out of the rates, and Manchester's was founded by a group of doctors assisted by prosperous merchants and factory-owners. In London voluntary support proved disappointing and the hospital was increasingly dependent on allowances from parish authorities (sometimes at the rate of two guineas per patient) and at least one large grant from Parliament.[110] Fever hospitals held no great attraction for the ordinary run of subscribers, for, among other things, they offered no such inducements as voting charities provided. After all, an institution could hardly require an applicant afflicted with typhus fever to equip himself with a recommendation from one of the governors.

A by-product of improved medical care was the gradual recognition that a patient's discharge from the hospital might be merely a stage in restoring him to full health. There were, as the Reverend Dr. Glasse noted in his account of the Samaritan Society, many poor patients "who had received the benefit of the Hospital, but, upon being discharged, had no service or employment ready for them, or if there had been such, were not sufficiently recovered in point of health and strength, to resume their places of employment." [111] The hospital referred to was the London Hospital in Whitechapel, where in 1791 a group of governors formed a society to assist patients after their discharge. Some lacked clothing or had families in distress; others might be helped to return to their homes in the country or could be given a week or two at the seashore. The Sea-Bathing Infirmary at Margate, in whose founding the Quaker Dr. Lettsom, philanthropist and publicist, was a principal agent, was opened in 1796 at a cost of over £2000 and added its evidence to the growing conviction that therapy was more complicated than had been assumed.[112] Yet organized work for convalescents was fairly slow in getting under way. Other hospitals created their Samaritan Societies, but only in the latter half of the nineteenth century did the convalescent home become well established as an object of philanthropy.

Chronic and disabling afflictions also attracted the notice of the charitable public. A case in point was the prevalence — estimated at over 10 per cent[113] — of hernia among the working population of London, and medical philanthropists mobilized to provide the relief recommended by medical authorities. The National Truss Society (1786), the Rupture Society (1796), and the City of London Truss Society

[109] Bernard, "Account of the Proposed Institution [for] Contagious Fever," in Lettsom, *Hints*, I, 312ff; George, *London Life*, p. 54.
[110] Buer, *Health, Wealth, and Population*, p. 207.
[111] Lettsom, *Hints*, II, 5.
[112] Raistrick, *Quakers in Science and Industry*, p. 311.
[113] George, *London Life*, p. 203.

(1807) appeared successively on the charity scene. The last became an especially popular and (however improbable) a rather fashionable charity, with a socially distinguished sponsorship and considerable sums to spend on its work.[114]

Methods of handling mentally disturbed patients took a slight turn for the better — or, more accurately, at the end of the century patients in at least one institution were receiving relatively enlightened treatment. The Retreat at York had a marked influence on techniques of dealing with mental patients, especially after the appearance in 1813 of Samuel Tuke's widely circulated *Description of the Retreat.* Curiously enough, it was the appalling condition of another local institution, itself a charitable enterprise, that led to the founding of the Retreat. The York Asylum, established in the 1770's as a subscription charity, had fallen on evil days and by the early '90's, far from offering superior treatment, had deteriorated to the point where its standards were no better than the most abandoned institutions of the period. There was every reason why in 1815 the York Asylum should have figured heavily and unfavorably in the proceedings of the Select Committee on Madhouses.[115]

What is important here, however, is that the malpractice of the asylum led members of the Society of Friends to found a new and progressive institution. The death of a member of the Society confined in the asylum aroused the suspicions of her co-religionists, and the upshot was a movement, with William Tuke at the head, to start a refuge for disturbed "persons of all ranks."[116] "The Quakers," remarked Sydney Smith, "as usual succeeded (for they never fail),"[117] and their retreat became something of a milestone in the treatment of the insane. In 1797, after a year of operation, the Retreat could claim nearly £6000 in property, and was drawing annual support from the entire English community of Friends. Figures published in 1812 showed all but six English counties represented in the £8700 of donations and £2900 of annuities contributed by the various Meetings — and incidentally credited the Retreat with assets worth £11,500.[118]

7

From this survey of late-century philanthropy, long as it has turned out to be, there is still lacking a category of activity which many could cite as preeminent among the good works of the age. Certainly, if the evangelicals were the leading philanthropists of the day, they would have pointed to the antislavery crusade and foreign missions as their crowning achievements. It is impossible to make even a reasonable guess as to how many shillings and pence from each philanthropic

---

[114] In 1881, £4510. (*Charity Record,* 2 Feb. 1882).
[115] *S. C. for the Better Regulation of Madhouses,* 1814–15, pp. 1–10.
[116] D. H. Tuke, *Chapters in the History of the Insane* (London, 1882), p. 113.
[117] *Edinburgh Review,* 28:433 (August 1817).
[118] Samuel Tuke, *Description of the Retreat . . . for Insane Persons* (Philadelphia, 1813), pp. 53–54. Kathleen Jones (*Law, Lunacy, and Conscience, 1744–1845,* pp. 57ff) recalls that the Retreat was not a general charity but a facility maintained by a body with restricted membership for its own constituency. In general, patients were charged (at various rates) for accommodations.

pound went to these causes, but the fraction cannot have been negligible. By the mid-century (1860) the leading missionary societies were being credited with annual receipts exceeding £450,000:[119]

	£000's
Society for the Propagation of the Gospel	90
Church Missionary Society	146
Baptist Missionary Society	30
London Missionary Society	93
Wesleyan Missionary Society	107

Yet important as they are, the antislavery and foreign missionary movements lie on the fringe of the main story of philanthropy as conceived by this study. Granted that the line between humanitarian-reform and philanthropic movements is anything but precise, and even hazier when the motivation is explicitly religious; still, if the support of churches at home is not to be included in this survey of philanthropic giving — and however justifiable in principle, it would be both impracticable and distorting to do so — one can hardly deal at length with their overseas work or with their home missionary activities. Rather than attempt a considered account of the missionary movement as such, we shall merely notice it briefly, in what is perhaps a secular perspective, as an element in the British philanthropic complex.

The flowering of missionary effort around the turn of the century was, of course, a by-product of the Evangelical Revival, and its most notable expressions, all (in a loose sense) the result of evangelical initiative, were the London Missionary Society, the Church Missionary Society, and the British and Foreign Bible Society. But these bodies were anticipated by the Baptists, whose organization was, in a large degree, the personal achievement of William Carey, who went to India in the summer of 1793. The Baptist Society conformed to the familiar pattern of charitable organizations save that voting memberships were set at a lower figure than in more fashionable voluntary bodies.[120] For our purpose the significance of the Carey mission lies chiefly in his influence on the larger Protestant missionary effort. For it was a letter from Carey which focused on the problem of founding a missionary society the vague interest already existing among certain groups of "Evangelical Dissenters who practise Infant Baptism." [121]

The Missionary (later the London Missionary) Society which was finally formed in late 1795 after a series of preliminary steps was intended to be nonsectarian

---

[119] Sampson Low, *The Charities of London in 1861* (London, 1862), pp. 256–57.

[120] H. Newcomb, *Cyclopedia of Missions* (New York, 1854), pp. 170–71. During the first two decades of its history the income of the Baptist Society averaged only about £2700 a year, but the next twelve years saw the annual average rise to approximately £10,000.

[121] Richard Lovett, *The History of the London Missionary Society, 1795–1895*, 2 vols. (London, 1899), I, 5. The quotation is from the title of a paper published by the Reverend David Bogue in the *Evangelical Magazine*.

and to enlist not only Dissenters and Methodists but Anglicans with Evangelical sympathies. Yet the Society was, in fact, strongly inclined toward Independency and tended more and more to become an Independent (Congregational) agency. The committee which drafted the scheme of organization was aware that missionary work of the scope that they envisioned would be costly, and they provided for various categories of membership, with the minimum set at a guinea subscription and with additional privileges attached to larger gifts.[122] This was not, to repeat, intended as a charity in the ordinary sense of the word. As the plan of organization put it, "the sole object is to spread the knowledge of Christ among heathen" and to rescue that "melancholy proportion of the inhabitants of the globe [who] still remain in the shadow of death!"[123] It would oversimplify the matter to imply that the early missionaries were occupied merely with "saving souls," but clearly the activities that we ordinarily think of as "philanthropic" — educational, medical, social — were for a long time considered to be distinctly secondary to the essential religious and theological objective. Whether or not missions were philanthropic in essence, at least the support which they enlisted offers an indication of the extent to which Englishmen, especially middle-class Englishmen, would give of their substance to benefit fellow human beings in remote lands.

In the early years the London Society made its share of mistakes and suffered its share of bad luck. At the outset the selection of missionaries left something to be desired, and some of the earlier financial inspirations of the committee — such as the plan of making the Society self-supporting by importing salable goods on returning missionary ships — were moderately bizarre. A French privateer, by capturing the ship *Duff* with thirty missionaries aboard, was responsible for loss estimated at £10,000.[124] Yet after the initial period of trial (and error), the management of the Society showed itself intelligent and statesmanlike, exhibiting an idealism tempered with shrewd business sense. It was not for nothing that the guiding hand in financial matters during the first two decades was a transplanted Yorkshireman and City merchant, Joseph Hardcastle.

After enjoying enormous success in raising money at the outset, the directors became convinced that pennies were as vital to their work as guineas, and they developed a plan of "auxiliary societies," local missionary groups, to which members would contribute small sums regularly. Although the effects of the new departure were not immediately reflected in the Society's income, which for a dozen or more years remained well below the first year's receipts, in the long run these local bodies became the most fruitful sources of revenue. From 1813 on, income rose steadily and strikingly to £15,000, £20,000, £40,000 (1825), with a

[122] *Ibid.*, I, 30–32.
[123] The phrase quoted is from "An Address to the serious and zealous Professors of the Gospel" by the Reverend George Burder, *ibid.*, p. 19.
[124] *Ibid.*, pp. 62-63. The figure of £10,000 was clearly an overstatement of the actual loss, but apparently the missionaries, by no means a carefully chosen group, who returned to England were demanding compensation from the Society.

substantial return from legacies and investments. During its first century the Society raised over £5,600,000 for spreading the Gospel abroad.[125]

For a time the London Society commanded the support of certain Church of England Evangelicals, but it was not long before these launched their own organization. To Churchmen of the Clapham school, the London Missionary Society, with its congregational principle, was not acceptable; and the existing Church agencies, the S.P.G. and the S.P.C.K. were impossible, for, other questions aside, they were notoriously resistant to active Evangelical influence.[126] Gradually sentiment crystallized in favor of a missionary effort which would be Anglican in affiliation and Evangelical in outlook. The immediate source of the decision to organize a missionary society "on the church principle; but not on the High Church principle," was a speech by Henry Venn in March 1799, before the Eclectic Society, a group of Evangelical clergymen.[127] Clapham philanthropists were conspicuous among the leaders of the Society that developed. Wilberforce declined the presidency, but he and Charles Grant became vice-presidents. Inevitably Henry Thornton was elected treasurer, and the chairman of the committee was the Rev. John Venn.

In point of revenue, the Church Missionary Society got off to a slow start.[128] Only as the committee followed the lead of its Nonconformist forerunner, the London Society, could an adequate financial basis be laid. Obviously the whole Evangelical wing of the Church must be persuaded to adopt the new Society; the widow's mite must be drawn upon to reinforce the philanthropist's talent. To educate the Evangelical constituency, the Society sent some of its leaders on tour in "deputations," in whose wake appeared numbers of local missionary associations. Almost immediately these became the main support of the Society. In 1812–13, for example, the total income was only about £3000, but in the following year, when local societies were being formed on a large scale, receipts jumped to over £13,000. By 1819–20 they had risen to £30,000, a tenfold increase in seven years, and in fact so far exceeded expenditures that considerable sums were invested in government securities. This unlikely situation, of course, did not last long, and the Society sometimes found itself with the kind of deficit regarded as normal for philanthropic agencies. During the 1830's and '40's, contributions from local associations accounted for at least four-fifths of the Society's revenue, with not more than a twentieth drawn from legacies. In their money-raising activities, missionary societies, one suspects, belong among the more democratic of philanthropies. The C.M.S., the L.M.S., and the other recently formed societies relied on

[125] *Ibid.*, I, 88.
[126] Eugene Stock, *The History of the Church Missionary Society*, 4 vols. (London, 1899–1916), I, 64–66.
[127] Howse, *Saints in Politics*, p. 76.
[128] Probably the most signal achievement of the early years was the pressure successfully applied to open India to missionary work. The critical decision was embodied in the East India Company's Charter of 1813, which legalized the teaching of Christianity. To gain this victory the Society had carried on a large-scale campaign, supporting Wilberforce's appeal in Parliament by nearly 850 petitions containing over a half-million signatures.

the small gifts of numbers of devoted individuals rather than on the large benefactions of a few London philanthropists.[129]

Naturally enough (some would say, by concerted design) there was a conspicuous degree of overlapping in the leadership of evangelical philanthropies. The
same names figure on committee after committee, almost as a series of interlocking
directorates. The groups responsible for the London and the Church Missionary
Societies joined forces in two well-known causes, the British and Foreign Bible
Society and the crusade against the slave trade and then slavery itself. Although
its status as a "philanthropy" is even more questionable than that of the regular
missionary societies, the Bible Society offers a significant index of the labor and
sacrifice of which British evangelicals were capable on behalf of causes which, in
their terms, involved questions of morality or religion. Both in the magnitude of
its operations and in its financial support, the British and Foreign Bible Society
was a huge undertaking. Other Bible societies, some of a more specialized nature,
were already carrying on, but the organization that was founded in early 1804
took as its object the "circulation of the Holy Scriptures without note or comment" throughout the world. Among the thirty-six members of the first committee, almost a *Who's Who* of evangelical philanthropy, both Church of England
Evangelicals and Dissenters were well represented. It is fair to say, however, that
the former was the dominant voice, and this was presently reinforced by the
adhesion of two bishops, Porteus of London and Shute Barrington of Durham.

The Bible Society enjoyed a prosperity that was extraordinary for such agencies.
William Wilberforce doubted whether the annual income would ever go above
£10,000, but in its fourth year it was more than £12,000, and at the end of the
first decade it exceeded £70,000.[130] One key to this amazing growth lay in the
numbers of widely scattered auxiliary societies that grew up, sometimes through
local initiative, sometimes with the encouragement of the central office. The better
organized auxiliaries handled their money-raising activities in a systematic fashion,
ordinarily transmitting half of their receipts to London for the general work of
the Society and retaining the balance for local evangelism. In any case, this
decentralized financing produced astonishing results. By 1814–15, five years after
their first appearance on the Society's balance sheet, the auxiliaries were providing
£62,000, or nearly 90 per cent of the total, and were a primary factor in making
the Bible Society one of the best supported philanthropies of the early century.[131]
In a little over two decades (1802–25), the Society, with its 859 English auxiliaries,
spent £1,165,000 and distributed 4½ million Bibles, printed in a variety of tongues.
One is tempted to agree with the verdict that this was indeed "the greatest single
agency of moral reform under the Christian dispensation that the world has
seen." [132]

[129] The financial data come from Stock, C.M.S., chap. XXI. For an account of C.M.S. local auxiliaries,
see Ford Brown, *Fathers of the Victorians*, pp. 270ff.
[130] William Canton, *A History of the British and Foreign Bible Society*, 5 vols. (London, 1904–10),
I, 13–14, 50–51.
[131] *Ibid.*, pp. 48–51; Foster, *An Errand of Mercy*, pp. 87ff.
[132] Brown, *Fathers of the Victorians*, pp. 246–50.

If the foreign missionary movement seems to fall in the rather vague border country between religious and philanthropic effort, the antislavery crusade raises questions about the boundary between philanthropy and politico-social reform. Since the aims of Wilberforce and his friends could be achieved only as they mobilized public opinion of a sort and brought it to bear on Parliament, their campaign was more an exercise in reform agitation than an example of the voluntary effort that we customarily think of as philanthropic. Yet the victorious fight to free the black man was the supreme accomplishment of the evangelical reform forces and their allies. In this cause the Clapham men, the "brotherhood of Christian politicians," were reinforced not only by Dissenters — men of the London Missionary Society, Baptists, Wesleyans, and most signally Quakers — but later by secular reformers untouched by the Evangelical Revival. The group that in the summer of 1787 formed itself into a Committee for the Abolition of the Slave Trade was composed predominantly of Church of England Evangelicals and Quakers (who for some years had had their own smaller committee). Granville Sharp, a Claphamite, though not, strictly speaking, an Evangelical, who fifteen years before in the Somerset case had established the illegality of slavery in England, became the first chairman, with Samuel Hoare, the Quaker banker and "serene philanthropist," [133] as treasurer.

Even with all that has been written, it is still not easy to get a coherent picture of the activities of the antislave brotherhood, especially of such grubby aspects as organization and finance.[134] Like subsequent reform movements, the Abolition Committee discovered that appealing to the reason and benevolence of Parliament would accomplish little and that, however reluctant Wilberforce might be to engage in a large-scale agitation, it must attempt to mobilize public opinion. One of the first steps was to collect data on the slave trade — since this was to be an assault on the traffic rather than on the institution of slavery — and the indefatigable Thomas Clarkson was despatched on a fact-finding trip to Liverpool, Bristol, Lancaster, and other centers. Techniques of agitation developed as the magnitude of the task became more evident. Five hundred circular letters sent at the outset produced a goodly number of favorable replies, among them, incongruously enough, letters from John Wesley and Brissot de Warville, and the Committee presently had its network of correspondents, each of whom was supposed to serve as a local center of agitation.[135]

There was novelty in some of the devices employed. Cowper's poem, "The Negro's Complaint," not one of the loftier expressions of his muse, was undeniably effective as propaganda, especially when set to music as a popular ballad:

[133] The phrase is that of his descendant, Lord Templewood, in *The Unbroken Thread* (New York, 1950), p. 47.

[134] The earlier phases of the movement are described by Howse (*Saints in Politics*). There are also the older accounts by Klingberg, Mathieson, and Coupland, as well as the familiar sources: Clarkson, *History of the . . . Abolition of the African Slave Trade*, 2 vols. (Philadelphia, 1808); Prince Hoare, *Memoirs of Granville Sharp*, 2 vols. (London, 1828); and the five-volume *Life of Wilberforce* (London, 1838) by his sons. Reginald Coupland's admirable *Wilberforce* (Oxford, 1923) is, of course, largely concerned with the movement.

[135] Clarkson, *Abolition*, I, 353, 356ff, 392–96.

> Fleecy locks and black complexion
> Cannot forfeit Nature's claim;
> Skins may differ, but affection
> Dwells in black and white the same.

Josiah Wedgwood, added to the Committee not long after its formation, designed a seal portraying a kneeling Negro, which as a cameo on snuffboxes and bracelets, became something of a rage. And, for direct action, some of the more eager abolitionists organized a boycott of slave-grown sugar in which, Clarkson asserted far too optimistically, some three hundred thousand people took part.[136] In a little over a year in 1787–88 the Committee printed and distributed over fifty thousand pamphlets and books, in addition to more than twenty-six thousand reports of debates in Parliament, and the like.[137] The practical consequence was 519 petitions on the table of the House when, in the spring of 1792, Wilberforce was ready to make his motion for the abolition of the trade.

One chapter in the story brings us closer to genuine philanthropic action (as construed in this volume), though not to resounding triumph, for not even Clapham enthusiasm, labor, faith, and obstinacy could cope effectively with the difficulties inherent in the Sierra Leone project. The settlement was, of course, intended to provide for the fourteen thousand ex-slaves freed by Lord Mansfield's decision in the Somerset case. It was out of the question that these freedmen should be supported indefinitely by Sharp or the Committee for Relieving the Black Poor, as the group formed in 1786 called itself. The solution was to resettle these Negroes in Africa, the Government agreeing to provide the cost of transportation and weekly allowances for the settlers.[138] The new colony encountered the trials that are almost standard for such undertakings, especially when idealism is accepted as a substitute for experience. Half of the nearly five hundred settlers died during the first year, and the others were saved by the arrival of a ship which Sharp had sent out at his own expense. Indeed, before the little colony had reached its first birthday, the generous and by no means wealthy Sharp found himself about £1750 out of pocket.[139] What appeared to be the final curtain was rung down when a neighboring chief, after due warning, burned the settlement in revenge for the destruction of his own village by British slave traders.

Yet Sharp was undismayed. The obvious step, he concluded, was to establish the venture as the collective responsibility of abolitionists in general and of his Clapham friends in particular, and the Sierra Leone Company, incorporated in 1791, combined elements of a private philanthropy, a business corporation, and a government-sponsored colonial project.[140] Sharp continued, along with Wilberforce, Charles Grant, and Lord Teignmouth, as one of the directors. But it was

---

[136] Coupland, *Wilberforce*, pp. 154–56; Howse, *Saints in Politics*, pp. 40–41.

[137] Clarkson, *Abolition*, I, 454.

[138] Coupland, *Wilberforce*, p. 276.

[139] Hoare, *Granville Sharp*, II, 87.

[140] It had been organized in 1790 as the St. George's Bay Association "for opening and establishing a trade in the natural productions of Africa."

Henry Thornton, the businessman, on whom as chairman the chief responsibility fell. Thornton's, writes J. C. Colquhoun, "was the directing mind . . . In every difficulty the appeal was to him." [141] In soliciting capital the directors took pains to stress the philanthropic side of the undertaking, for there was, they conceded, "the uncertainty of its turning out a profitable concern." [142] What was at stake in their view was abolishing the slave trade and bringing civilization to Africa. It was not too difficult to raise a large capital fund, especially after the decision to settle (at government expense) in Sierra Leone a thousand Negroes who had been marooned in Nova Scotia when the British armies were demobilized after the American War and whose plight made a strong appeal to British subscribers. In the end, the Company's funds approached £250,000, and the fortunes of the colony seemed to have taken a turn for the better.

But the Four Horsemen have rarely enjoyed a lusher pasture than early Sierra Leone. Malaria, swarms of ants, intractable colonists, and near-destruction by a French naval squadron — these were some of the hazards of the first decade. The young Zachary Macaulay, in whom Thornton had found the answer to the problem of the governorship, had acted with incredible energy and devotion, and when in 1799 he had returned to England, he left a community of twelve hundred colonists and three hundred houses which at least was no longer on the verge of disaster. But some of the virtues of Sierra Leone, it turned out, were little more than fantasies of its sponsors. Macaulay's scheme of apprenticeships for ransomed slaves had led, young Perronet Thompson discovered when he came out in 1808, to restoring slavery *de facto*.[143] And the white settlers composed anything but a godly, sober community. Though Thompson was the first royal governor (Thornton had negotiated the transfer of the colony to the Government), he found that the Company still exercised enormous and, in his view, not always salutary, influence. The colony never became self-supporting, and Henry Thornton himself lost between £2000 and £3000, as well as years of effort. Yet neither he nor his colleagues considered their experiment a total failure. This was a loss for which he could have no undue regret, for he agreed with his friends that the Company was "really a great Missionary Society." [144]

Like most agitations, the antislavery movement proceeded fitfully, now lapsing into quiescence, now bursting forth into vigorous activity. This was not a case of steadily mounting pressure against a steadily weakening resistance, even after the organization of the Anti-Slavery Society in 1823 had inaugurated the final stage of the campaign.[145] This association, of which Zachary Macaulay was the principal

[141] Quoted by Howse, *Saints in Politics,* p. 47.
[142] Quoted by Coupland, *Wilberforce,* p. 277.
[143] L. G. Johnson, *General T. Perronet Thompson* (London, 1957), p. 40. This volume takes a relatively unenthusiastic view of the Evangelical achievement in Sierra Leone, as does the recent historian of the colony (Christopher Fyfe, *A History of Sierra Leone* [London, 1962], e.g., pp. 46–47).
[144] Quoted by Howse, *Saints in Politics,* p. 50.
[145] W. L. Burn, *Emancipation and Apprenticeship in the British West Indies* (London, 1937), p. 83. The abolitionists had gravely underestimated the difficulty of enforcing the prohibition against the trade, and the African Institution which they hopefully created to civilize Africa had to focus its major efforts on the perennial fight to stamp out the trade itself.

architect, announced to the world that the new goal of these philanthropic agitators was to be the abolition of slavery itself. In the large, the leadership was Evangelical, but it is worth recalling that in the inner circle, as a member of the antislavery cabinet, was the indubitably non-Evangelical figure of Henry Brougham.[146] The new drive, skillfully managed by Macaulay, was more systematic than the earlier attack on the trade. Thomas Clarkson, back in the saddle again, took off on a journey through the country in the course of which he formed nearly two hundred local committees.[147] Local associations, in fact, carried a good deal of the burden. The *Anti-Slavery Reporter,* founded, edited, and mostly written by Macaulay, occasionally published lists of subscribers and donors. In November and December 1830, for example, the Society received nearly £300, of which only £60 came from individuals directly, the balance from local associations. Typical benefactions were £35 from the Liverpool Ladies Association, £21 12s. from the Edinburgh Association, and £22 10s. from the Coalbrookedale Association.[148] The activities of local bodies were not, of course, limited to donations. At critical junctures in the campaign, they promoted public meetings on a grand scale, passed resolutions, and flooded Parliament with petitions.

If pecuniary sacrifice and sensitiveness to human suffering are earmarks of a philanthropic movement, then the antislavery crusade clearly meets the test. It is impossible even to guess at the total contributed to improve the lot of the slaves and then to free them, the bulk of it presumably from donors who were not themselves wealthy. From the *Anti-Slavery Reporter* one gets the impression of a movement supported chiefly, at least in its later stages, by large numbers of people in moderate or modest circumstances. For some, notably Zachary Macaulay, their devotion to the cause meant virtual penury. Macaulay's fortune, at one time in the neighborhood of £100,000, melted away in the warm sun of his benevolence toward Negroes.[149]

Like most philanthropists around the turn of the century, evangelicals had their favorite evils and seemed relatively indifferent to others. They shared and even magnified the prevailing fear of Jacobinism and irreligion, and they half accepted the current social philosophy, with its Malthusian fatalism, which often seemed to paralyze the hand, and certainly the imagination of the charitable. If the Saints, to recall Ford Brown's argument, planned to conquer Britain for morality and religion (as they conceived these) by converting the great of the world, by organizing charitable and reforming societies, and by infiltrating and taking over those already in existence,[150] their success was no more than partial. Yet, however misdirected certain of their activities have seemed to latter-day

[146] E. L. Griggs, *Thomas Clarkson* (London, 1936) p. 162.
[147] New, *Brougham,* p. 297. The other members were Lushington, Macaulay, and Fowell Buxton.
[148] *Anti-Slavery Reporter,* IV, 76.
[149] Howse, *Saints in Politics,* p. 126.
[150] Among other tactics (as summarized by Brown, *Fathers of the Victorians,* p. 5). See also David Spring, "The Clapham Sect: Some Social and Political Aspects," *Victorian Studies,* 5:35–48 (September 1961).

critics, the humanitarians of the age were able to smooth some of the rougher places on the road to an industrialized society. At the least, their work served to remind suffering human beings, at home and abroad, that among the English middle and upper classes there was a measure of sympathy, if not always understanding.

CHAPTER V

THE CHALLENGE OF
URBAN POVERTY
1820–1860

D URING the Regency and the early Victorian Age, the issues of philanthropy tended to define themselves in terms of the working population, or at least the poor, of the cities. The alarming and inescapable fact that large segments of the new industrial cities, as well as the metropolis, were inhabited by populations living the most marginal, and indeed subhuman, kind of existence haunted contemporary observers, tough and tender alike. For London, of course, this was no new phenomenon, but by the latter decades of the eighteenth century other centers had begun to feel the pinch of large numbers of industrial poor, who at best were at the mercy of the season and the trade cycle and at worst on the way to becoming perennial derelicts. In 1752, when the founders of the Manchester Infirmary appealed for continuous support from residents of the community, they pointed out that the hospital would meet a permanent need of the city, "which by reasons of the Numbers employ'd in our Manufactures must always be burthen'd with a great Number of the Sick Poor." [1]

In the first half of the nineteenth century, the industrial-urban poor became what was perhaps the most striking feature of the social landscape in South Lancashire, the West Riding, and in sections of the Midlands, the Tyneside, and Lanarkshire. The industrial cities continued to grow at a terrifying pace, until the Census of 1851 could picture a country half of whose population was urban. Local authorities and private citizens looked out on this social revolution with a fearful pride mixed with bafflement. Vigorous and dynamic, yes, but was it compatible with stability and the ordered progress that formed the bourgeois, and increasingly the English, ideal?

Broadly speaking, this was a new class of poor, called into existence by the economic revolution. In the mid-eighteenth century only London, and possibly such centers as Bristol and Norwich, whose populations at the time of Queen Anne may have approached thirty thousand, gave any intimation of the problems

---

[1] Quoted by Leon S. Marshall, *The Development of Public Opinion in Manchester, 1780–1820* (Syracuse, 1946), p. 45.

that urbanization would create. In the larger cities the poor were a race as un-familiar as foreigners, at the lowest level almost a race of savages, whom nobody knew and who lived in sections which nobody visited. In his *Condition of the Working Classes in 1844*, Friedrich Engels drew a memorable picture, not wholly accurate yet terrifying in its implications, of the social isolation of the Manchester poor,[2] and Matthew Davenport Hill, Recorder of Birmingham, pointed to the growth of cities as a major factor in crime. In large towns, he observed, "an inhabi-tant of the humbler classes is unknown to a majority of the inhabitants, whereas in a smaller place a natural police system operates which keeps each individual under the public eye. Moreover, the separation of classes in cities, where everyone who could afford it, [as Engels noted] lived away from the center, had produced a sharp chasm between classes."[3] Many well-to-do residents of Manchester must have been far more familiar with London and even Paris than with the squalid working-class courts that lay behind the shopfronts.

As a final commentary on the conditions of life in the new cities, it is enough simply to recall the disparity in urban and rural mortality rates. In the agricultural districts of Yorkshire, Durham, Northumberland, Cumberland, and Westmore-land, 204 out of every 1000 inhabitants reached the age of 70, while in London it was 104, in Birmingham, 81, and in Liverpool and Manchester 63.[4] During the first two decades of the century, the towns were able to hold the death rate at bay, but by the 1830's population growth had made obsolete the old municipal machin-ery and its sanitary facilities, and industrial England experienced a sharply rising death rate. For five major cities the average increase during the decade was from 21 to 31 per thousand, with the Birmingham rate nearly doubling (14.6 to 27.2) and Liverpool's rising from 21 to 34.8.[5] It is not necessary to romanticize the state of well-being in rural England to appreciate the contrast between the life of the countryman and that of the poor in the frantically expanding industrial cities. This was something new, and it raised issues for local authorities and for every Englishman who was concerned with social stability and with reintegrating these uprooted masses into the English community — in short, with reuniting the Two Nations.

The situation, of course, produced a multitude of counselors and a variety of counsel. For not until the century was nearly over was there anything like an adequate understanding of the nature of poverty in an industrial society. In the earlier decades much of the discussion focused on the Poor Laws, their maladmin-istration and possible revision. Although the question bears on our theme only indirectly, public policy with regard to poor relief obviously had a good deal to do with establishing the area to be occupied by private charity. Whatever the

[2] W. H. Chaloner and W. O. Henderson, ed., *The Condition of the Working Class in England* (New York, 1958), pp. 53ff.

[3] *S. C. on Criminal and Destitute Juveniles*, 1852, Q. 386.

[4] *First Report of the Registrar-General*, 1839, p. 15.

[5] G. Talbot Griffith, *Population Problems of the Age of Malthus* (Cambridge, 1926), pp. 186–87; S. E. Finer, *The Life and Times of Sir Edwin Chadwick* (London, 1952), p. 213.

claims of its sponsors, they saw the Poor Law of 1834, in reality, as an antidote to pauperism among the agricultural laborers of the South, not as a social policy for the growing industrial society. Conceiving of poor relief in punitive and deterrent terms, the framers of the new law were prepared to offer only the barest minimum, assuming that more constructive assistance would be provided by voluntary charity. It was one of the unhappy consequences of this view that philanthropy was left with the obligation of laboring not merely to relieve unfortunate individuals (which it might do with some effectiveness), but also to alleviate the distress that was endemic among considerable sections of the working population.[6] Charity, it was taken for granted, would carry the main burden of working-class welfare, insofar as this was not handled by workers' self-help organizations. Those whose needs could not be met through self-help, mutual aid, or charity must be prepared to face the rigors of the workhouse.

Not all of those who subscribed to the punitive philosophy of the new Poor Law could accept charitable effort even as a mechanism for easing the lot of the poor. In its essentials the interpretation of poverty championed later in the century by the Charity Organisation Society was familiar enough to the earlier decades. The early Victorians were inclined to define their social problem in moral terms, and to carry over into the new urban-industrial environment answers that had been formulated in the pre-industrial age. To them the critical social evil was not mass poverty but pauperism, and this they ascribed largely to individual weakness. Unless the working classes could acquire the essential virtues of thrift, temperance, industry, and family responsibility there was little hope for British society.[7]

Harriet Martineau, to take a conspicuous example, was convinced that poverty, for the most part, resulted from failure of individual character — or from the operation of the inexorable laws of nature. There was every reason, she wrote while the Royal Commission on the Poor Laws was sitting, to substitute for the old hit-or-miss arrangements a new scheme which would impose harsh penalties on pauperism and encourage the poor to stand on their own feet. But what benefit would there be in such a system if soft-hearted philanthropists persisted in bestowing alms or otherwise aiding those who should be compelled to rely on their own efforts? Most charities she would unhesitatingly liquidate. Which ones might still be tolerated? Only those which neither lessened the fund of capital nor tended to increase the population. This meant chiefly schools (though these should drop any provision for lodging or feeding pupils), casualty hospitals, and institutions for the blind and deaf, whose unproductive consumption of capital was so small as to be imperceptible. Almshouses, of course, were evil institutions, for they allowed young people to evade the responsibility of looking after their helpless parents, whereas "it should be as universal a rule that working men should support their

[6] As Mrs. Simey points out in her *Charitable Effort in Liverpool*, p. 23.

[7] As developed by Dr. Calvin Woodard in his suggestive (unpublished) Cambridge University doctoral thesis, "The Charity Organisation Society and the Rise of the Welfare State" (1961), pp. 174, 179.

parents, as that they should support their children. If this rule were allowed, we might see some revival of that genial spirit of charity and social duty among the poor, whose extinction we are apt to mourn." [8]

To score points off Harriet Martineau would be too easy. One must remember that these tales were exercises in popular education, almost popular journalism, and that they were written under great pressure and at enormous speed. Furthermore, they reflected Miss Martineau's early infatuation with the Dismal Science, and her conviction that an understanding of its principles was the first step to social improvement. Her mature views were considerably more sophisticated than one might gather from the *Illustrations*. Yet the "Summary of Principles" which she appends to her tale of "Cousin Marshall" is worth reading as an application, breathtaking in its guilelessness, of classical theory (or Miss Martineau's version of it) to social welfare. The practice of charity, she proclaims, involves an arbitrary and unproductive distribution of the subsistence fund, and all such "arbitrary distribution of the necessaries of life is injurious to society, whether in the form of private almsgiving, public charitable institutions, or a legal pauper-system." [9]

Not all observers found the solution as embarrassingly simple as did Miss Martineau. In the *Edinburgh Review*, William Empson, a colleague of Malthus' at Haileybury, was appalled at her summary way with private charity,[10] and indeed early Victorians as a race, including the architects of the new system of poor relief, had little stomach for such drastic solutions, however appealing these may have been in theory. They continued to think of the public system as supplementing, in the more extreme cases, "the active exercise of private charity, and the philanthropic efforts of individuals." [11] By attempting rigidly to circumscribe the field in which public relief would operate, the British State left a tremendous social expanse to be occupied by private benevolence.

Yet implicit in the arguments for a more rigorous public policy was a criticism of the lax ways, the undiscriminating procedures, of the practitioners of private charity. The Commissioners of Inquiry were little more enthusiastic about the slack methods of charity than about the old Poor Law itself. The baneful consequences of hit-or-miss benevolence form a continuous theme in Victorian reflections on the state of the poor, and some of the more obvious shortcomings of early Victorian charitable practice will be noted in the following chapter and later. Here it is enough to recall one piece of evidence included in Edwin Chadwick's report on London and Berkshire which excited a good deal of comment. This was an account of Spitalfields charities, endowed and voluntary, by the Reverend

[8] Harriet Martineau, *Illustrations of Political Economy*, 9 vols. (London, 1832–34), No. VIII, pp. 40–42.

[9] *Ibid.*, p. 130. On Harriet Martineau and political economy see the illuminating discussion in R. K. Webb, *Harriet Martineau: A Radical Victorian* (New York, 1960), chap. IV.

[10] "It is a great fault to overstate a case," he remonstrates, "and to go on tightening an argument until its cord inevitably snaps." (*Edinburgh Review*, 57:31 [April 1833].)

[11] Samuel Laing, Jun., *National Distress: Its Causes and Remedies* (London, 1844), p. 137 — an interesting and temperate commentary.

William Stone, who gave to the Commissioners a discouraging picture of their demoralizing effects. During the previous year, he noted, he had been connected with the distribution of over £8000 in Spitalfields, about half of it in food from the Soup Society, and over £2000 in tickets for bread, coal, and other supplies, through visitors of the Spitalfields Association. Such charities, according to this rather flinty clergyman, merely created the distress they were intended to relieve and failed to relieve the distress they created. The existence of such a lavish relief mechanism, he charged, served as a magnet for paupers from other parishes, for voluntary workers issued medical and food tickets with little attempt to distinguish between worthy and undeserving applicants. Stone's social outlook can be gathered from his inability to discover a single instance of severe distress that was not due to improvidence of some kind, "the great improvidence being marriage." Plainly he was not suffering from a surfeit of charity, Christian or otherwise.[12]

This picture of Spitalfields charities did not go unchallenged. Not only were the cases from which Stone generalized relatively few in number, but, more important, he had ignored the tragic decline of the Spitalfields silk manufacture, with its train of low wages and unemployment. Spitalfields was clearly something of a special case. But whether the attack was more or less valid — and it was not entirely without foundation — such critics helped to fortify the Commissioners' decision to apply a firm hand to the poor. Public relief and private charity were complementary services, the public operating in a limited, closely defined sphere, the province of charity less precise. In the view of the Commissioners and others, the faults of private benevolence, unorganized and undiscriminating as it was, to a degree paralleled those of the old Poor Law, and called for some of the same rationalizing treatment that the public system was about to receive.

2

If the crucial problems of British philanthropy during these years were presented by the new urban masses, the first step was to establish contact with them and to discover means of restoring them to the British community. The procedures inevitably had to be those of trial and error. To translate the person-to-person charity from the village or the small town to an urban slum seemed, and indeed was, an impossible hope. The major contribution of the early Victorians to the problem was the various plans of district visiting, under which representatives of a religious body or other charitable organization called on the poor in their own homes.[13] Such visits were intended not to be Lady Bountiful expeditions but to serve specific purposes, anticipating in some degree the methods and aims of modern family casework. For the Victorians the family was the foundation stone on which their entire social structure rested. Whatever tended to maintain it was, by definition, good, and what tended to weaken it was bad.

[12] *Extracts from the Information Received by the Commissioners* (London, 1833), pp. 283ff.
[13] For an interesting brief account, see E. C. P. Lascelles, "Charity," in *Early Victorian England*, II, 337–38.

District visitors above all were concerned with situations, emergency or continuing, which threatened the stability of the poor family. They would get to know a particular group of slum-dwellers, their special condition of life, their needs, and their weaknesses, so that, unlike random almsgiving and the casual benevolence of some charitable organizations, relief given through visitors would meet the requirements of the particular case. They would withhold, as well as extend, material assistance, for they were to be friends and counselors as well as almoners. Although the full impact of Dr. Chalmers' achievement in organizing one of the more squalid sections of Glasgow was not felt until later in the century, his writings and his evidence before the Select Committee on the Irish Poor Law (1830) aroused interest south of the Border. One did not have to share his inveterate hostility to public relief in any form or to think of his system, as he did, as a complete alternative, to find promise in it.[14] Perhaps, some dared to imagine, a bridge which followed the blueprints of the Scottish leader might join the Two Nations.

The agencies which showed the greatest initiative in trying to make contact with the urban poor worked under religious auspices. Visiting societies might represent a single communion or might be inter- or nondenominational, but the religious conviction of their leaders is generally apparent. Their objectives were likely to include, more or less explicitly, the religious instruction and moral reformation of the poor. Visiting the poor as a Christian duty had, of course, a long and honorable history, enjoined as it was by Scripture and practiced by the deacons of the Early Church. The Anglican Religious Societies had engaged in visiting as a secondary activity related to their essential devotional purpose, and the Wesleyans, as we have noted, made much of visiting as a regular mechanism of church organization. In their Strangers' Friend and other visiting societies they expanded their charitable efforts beyond the Methodist community to needy poor generally, especially to those who, lacking a legal settlement in the town, were barred from parish relief.[15]

Specifically religious aims might or might not predominate in any particular society. In general, however, the purpose of regular visiting was to befriend the poor, to gain some familiarity with their conditions of life, and to provide relief where it was merited. For many middle-class visitors this was an enlightening and astringent experience. As early as the 1790's in Liverpool, "an earnest and rather shocked band of voluntary visitors [of the Strangers' Friend Society] met weekly to discuss their cases and allot relief." [16] They strove nobly to reconcile their more sympathetic human emotions with the obvious need for principle and regularity of procedure. This was never an easy conflict to resolve, and critics did not hesitate to condemn the laxness of visitors who issued medical and food coupons with

---

[14] A case in point is the anonymous *Essays on the Principles of Charitable Institutions* (London, 1836), pp. 142–43, the author of which was familiar with Chalmers' views.
[15] North, *Early Methodist Philanthropy*, pp. 49–52.
[16] Simey, *Charitable Effort in Liverpool*, p. 21.

little investigation and who might even announce in a semipublic fashion that they had tickets to give away. Much more admirable, in the view of the don't-pauperize-them school, were the aims of such groups as the District Visiting Society of Brighton, whose primary purpose was "to call forth the energies of the poor themselves," with gratuitous relief "only a subsidiary object." [17]

This was a movement of substantial proportions, mobilizing large numbers of volunteer visitors. At one time in London alone some two thousand visitors were calling on forty thousand families, inquiring about their religious affiliation, the education of their children, their financial resources, and their possible need of medical treatment.[18] If relief were given, presumably this would not be in cash but in tickets entitling the holder to the help of a more specialized agency. No doubt many of these relatively untrained volunteers made inefficient caseworkers. Sometimes their intrusions were warmly resented, not always in as emphatic terms as the brick-maker's ultimatum to Mrs. Pardiggle: "I want a end of these liberties took with my place. I wants a end of being drawed like a badger." The Mrs. Pardiggles were rare among visitors; a more common fault was probably an excess of sympathy and a tendency to view their clients in a sentimental light. Yet undue condescension or immoderate nosiness would produce sullen uncommunicativeness on the part of the hosts, or perhaps even locked doors. The visitor was therefore warned that the poor would think his attentions only officious and meddlesome "if he deem it unnecessary to treat them with the same respect and delicacy which he would observe towards his equals in rank . . . Let it never be forgotten that the lower classes are extremely sensitive to the *spirit* in which they are treated, and that the moral influence of charity depends infinitely more upon the manner of the donor than upon the value of his gift." [19]

During the 1820's and '30's visiting societies expanded rapidly in both the Metropolis and the provinces, with all of the larger communions active in the work. The agencies might be local or district societies or they might be more comprehensive organizations operating through local committees. In 1828, for example, a number of Evangelical-sponsored bodies joined together in a General Society for Promoting District Visiting, and three years later some 573 visitors "regularly employed" by the Society were making nearly 165,000 calls.[20] Fifteen years later the London diocese officially entered the field with an organization conceived on broader and more statesmanlike lines. Even though it will not be typical, we may take the Metropolitan Visiting and Relief Association, an over-all federation of parish visiting societies, as illustrating the movement as a whole.

The Association emerged directly out of the bad winter of 1843, when reports of desperate want in the poorer districts prompted something of an investigation

---

[17] Anon., *Essays on . . . Charitable Institutions*, pp. 208–9.
[18] A. F. Young and E. T. Ashton, *British Social Work in the Nineteenth Century* (London, 1956), p. 88.
[19] Anon., *Essays on . . . Charitable Institutions*, pp. 210–11.
[20] Brown, *Fathers of the Victorians*, p. 241.

by clergy and laymen. It was not, they concluded, merely the result of a season of depressed trade, but a deeper malaise. In short, they discovered the abject poverty in which sections of London's working class existed, a poverty, they concluded, that was deepening. Many families, they noted, which had been doing well enough through their honest industry had been reduced to extreme indigence.[21] This unhealthy situation called for a dual attack, relief of destitution combined with an honest attempt to improve the social and religious condition of the poor. The proper agency appeared to be a diocese-wide organization, with a central committee allocating among poorer parishes the contributions of the more prosperous. For however logical the parish might be as an administrative unit, it was out of the question to handle relief on a parochial basis, given the fantastic disparities in wealth. A good many parishes already had visiting societies of their own, but those in poorer districts, where the need was most conspicuous, were badly handicapped by lack of funds.

The Metropolitan Visiting and Relief Association[22] was brought into existence in December 1843. Its immediate purpose was to channel relief to the most necessitous poor through district visiting societies, "after due inquiry into the circumstances of each particular case," but there were broader objectives   to remove "the moral causes which create or aggravate want; to encourage prudence, industry, and cleanliness . . . and to promote kindly feelings between those classes of society which are kept so far asunder by the difference of their worldly conditions." [23] These were humane aims, if a bit suggestive of middle-class values to be imposed on the poor, and the leaders — the dynamic Bishop Blomfield and others — were actuated by the most praiseworthy of motives in their eagerness not only to relieve distress but to promote better class relations. No doubt they were disturbed by the apparent indifference of the poor to the Church, but the Association was not intended merely, nor even chiefly, to serve institutional ends.

As metropolitan charities in the 1840's went, this was a large-scale, handsomely financed venture, with an affluent and distinguished sponsorship. On the central committee were such outstanding City figures as Thomas Baring and George Carr Glynn, along with the usual representation from the clergy and the peerage, including the ubiquitous Lord Ashley. The initial subscription list contained a good many donations of £100 and £200, with £300, the largest single gift, contributed by the Marquess of Westminster. A number of business houses — for example, the Royal Exchange Assurance Corporation, with £200 — appear among the contributors. During the first year, receipts exceeded £20,000. The main responsibilities of the central committee were those of raising and disbursing funds in grants to individual parish societies. With its control of the purse, the committee was enabled to apply certain standards to local societies and to require them to

[21] M.V.R.A., *1st Ann. Rept.*, 1844, p. 1.
[22] Officially "The Metropolitan Association for Promoting the Relief of Destitution and for Improving the Condition of the Poor, by Means of Parochial and District Visiting."
[23] Constitution of the M.V.R.A.

accept a measure of supervision. During the first year parochial groups received £8125 from the treasury of the Association.[24]

To view with a skeptical eye the claims made in the annual reports of charitable organizations is the beginning of wisdom for the historian as for the donor. Since such documents are intended to serve not merely as records of the year's work but as appeals for support, the achievements of a society rarely suffer in the telling. Yet, making all allowances, the M.V.R.A.'s early record was impressive. During its first five years, more than £30,000 was voted to the various parishes, this in addition to funds raised locally for the work of individual societies.[25] It was, in fact, the policy of the central committee to reward with larger grants parishes that had exerted themselves to finance their own work and to penalize the laggards.[26] In times of special emergency, the Association could always expand its resources, as during the cholera epidemic in 1849, when nearly £12,000 came in.[27]

One of the more characteristic policies of the M.V.R.A. was to encourage thrift on the part of the poor by offering pecuniary inducements. Some parishes were already operating savings funds, but the central committee's proposal to make grants for establishing and maintaining parochial provident societies led to a modest expansion in systematic working-class saving. In 1850, for example, the Association assisted thirty-six provident societies with 28,550 depositors and £13,356 in deposits.[28] It was a sign of the times and an augury of the future, unrecognized though it was, when in 1880 the Association abandoned its grants to provident societies because of the superior facilities of the Post Office for investing savings. Though only a minor instance of private philanthropy yielding to a public agency, it was at least a straw in the wind.

In the 1840's and '50's, between seventy and eighty societies, with a thousand to twelve hundred visitors, were affiliated with the Association. On the ability and diligence of these depended the whole venture, and, like most volunteer forces, they were a variegated lot. Some visitors showed little skill in dealing with people so different in background and status from themselves. Others simply faded out when their initial enthusiasm was exhausted. It is a hazard to which volunteer charities are perpetually exposed. Yet after a few years the Association could hail with some justice the apparent willingness of "the higher classes of society to mingle with, and take an active part in the improvement of the London poor," and could point to numbers of workers whose previous doubts about the utility of visiting the urban poor, with their "too frequent exhibitions of vice," had been successfully allayed.[29]

One may well discount the more extreme claims about the accomplishments of

---

[24] *1st Ann. Rept.*, p. 35.

[25] *5th Ann. Rept.*, 1848, p. 7; *14th*, 1857–58, p. 16.

[26] *4th Ann. Rept.*, 1847, pp. 11–12, 22. For a table of grants made to individual societies in the two years 1859–60, see John Hollingshead, *Ragged London in 1861* (London, 1861), pp. 260–62.

[27] *6th Ann. Rept.*, 1849, p. 14.

[28] *12th Ann. Rept.*, 1855. For the provident societies assisted, their deposits and depositors, see Hollingshead, *Ragged London*, p. 265.

[29] *7th Ann. Rept.*, 1850, p. 21.

the visiting societies and their influence in promoting class understanding. In the middle 1860's even the M.V.R.A. was deploring the constantly growing chasm between rich and poor, created in part by the movement of the upper classes away from the city.[30] Yet on its own terms the Association was not ineffective. A good many middle-class Anglicans had been brought into firsthand contact with the destitute, and poor families not only were assisted with food, coal, or clothing but were sometimes put into touch with other agencies which could provide more specialized aid. In the early 1850's the Association could boast (how reasonably it is impossible to say) that the most shocking cases of distress now occurred in districts outside its range of operation, and that, on the most primitive level of social welfare, its efforts had checked deaths from starvation, "a fearful evil which a few years since had become so common" that it made little impression on the public.[31] In sum, the large-scale experiment in volunteer casework conducted by the M.V.R.A. proved by no means unproductive. Though the walls of class isolation were not perceptibly shaken, some of the principles and methods of the Association anticipated those of later casework bodies, notably the Charity Organization Society. Yet in its approach there was, perhaps, a more genuine humanity, and certainly the Association was innocent of the abrasive social doctrines that marred the activities of the C.O.S.

3

To visit the poor in their homes was an admirable project — but only for those who had homes. In the growing cities, there was a class of poor, varying with the season and year, who lacked any regular place of residence. Though the houseless poor were not, of course, a novel phenomenon, in an urban environment the problem was so much more acute as to be different in kind as well as in degree. The new city homeless were composed not only of vagrants and floaters, but unemployed artisans, seasonal workers, and victims of a whole train of misfortunes. Especially if the winter brought heavy snowfalls and freezing temperatures, suffering would be widespread and severe. It is easy to forget how much at the mercy of the weather were the marginal classes in the cities and how sharply a bitter winter increased the pressure on relief agencies.

It was such a winter, that of 1819–20, which set off the first significant attempt to offer the city's houseless population some sort of temporary accommodations. The movement to provide shelter for "the nightly outcast," it is not unfair to recall, owed something to motives of prudence. Peterloo had taken place the previous August, the Six Acts had been passed in November and December, and the Cato Street Conspiracy was being hatched for February. In this tense atmosphere it was easy to discover something providential *"even in the rigour of the season,* which, by calling forth the most unprecedented exertions for the relief of the poor, effectually recalled them to a knowledge of their real benefactors" —

[30] *20th Ann. Rept.,* 1865, p. 6.
[31] *9th Ann. Rept.,* 1852, pp. 10–11.

this in the face of efforts "to spread disaffection and discontent among the lower orders (who had been in too many instances deluded into a belief that the rich were their oppressors)."[32] A glance at the subscription list of 3500 names suggests motives other than those of disinterested philanthropy. Among those giving £10 or more appear several members of the Government, including Liverpool, Eldon, Peel, Castlereagh, with another ten guineas from Lady Castlereagh.[33]

The Committee for Nightly Shelter for the Houseless Poor (which was to become the Society for Relieving the Houseless Poor) got into action with exemplary speed. A philanthropic proprietor offered some premises at London Wall, and, six hours after a subscription list had been started, the Houseless Poor Asylum began to receive inmates — an average of over two hundred a night. The Government assisted with clothing, the London Gas Company contributed light and heat, the New River Company gratuitously supplied water, and metropolitan theaters helped out with benefit performances. The Committee tried to keep their refuge from becoming a mere charitable flophouse. Daytime work for some of the residents was provided, and, on occasion, the committee did not hesitate to advance small sums or to supply clothes or tools to men who might thus become self-supporting again. The Seaman's Society also assisted by arranging berths for sailors, who represented the largest single occupational group being served.

This was purely a winter charity. For some years the committee operated on an *ad hoc* basis, making arrangements for premises in the fall and then standing by to see whether the season would be mild or severe. In 1830–31, for example, the Society ran three refuges and handled nearly 55,000 admissions (over 6500 different individuals) and issued 135,000 rations.[34] Such success was reassuring enough, but it also raised questions. Were the asylums being imposed upon? At the outset the Society had been so generously financed, ending its second year with assets of nearly £10,000, that it could be free and easy in its hospitality. But presently it appeared that whole families were moving into the refuges merely for the sake of the free meals, and reports of the largesse were attracting guests from the country. There was nothing to do but to adopt more rigorous practices, cutting down the ration, making sure that the sleeping accommodations were not too comfortable, and scrutinizing the applicants with greater care.[35]

To practitioners of "scientific charity" the ways of the night refuges always seemed more than doubtful. They could never investigate each case adequately, and they were regularly victimized by the vagrant, the drunk, the impostor, and the minor criminal. The Mendicity Society was convinced that they diminished the willingness of the "idle and profligate" to look for work and that certainty of having a place to sleep encouraged them to spend the day in public houses rather

---

[32] *Report of the Houseless Poor Society,* 1819–20.
[33] *Ibid.;* see also John Sard, *S. C. on District Asylums,* 1846, Q. 4581, Q. 4653. For an enthusiastic view of the nightly shelter movement, see "The Unseen Charities of London," *Fraser's Magazine,* 39:639–47 (June 1849).
[34] *Report of the Houseless Poor Society,* 1830–31.
[35] *Reports,* 1826–27, 1829–30.

than at work. In a later decade the Charity Organisation Society took an equally unenthusiastic view.[36] At least during their early days, legitimate charitable refuges acquired something of a bad odor by being confused with shelters which, operating behind a charitable façade, with sponsoring committees of gentlemen, were largely private promotions of a manager.[37] Although in some instances these refuges later achieved respectability, the proprietary or semiproprietary shelter was no ornament to early Victorian philanthropy.

Yet the charitable night refuge did provide a cushion of sorts for the casualties of the growing city. Following the lead of the Society for Relieving the Houseless Poor, other shelters were established in London and elsewhere. The Liverpool Night Asylum for the Houseless Poor opened its permanent shelter in 1830, having taken over and virtually rebuilt a large double house in the slums.[38] As for the London Society, in the mid-1840's its three Houseless Poor Asylums were furnishing accommodations for 1200, and the organization could boast of having supplied about 1,500,000 night lodgings and over 3,500,000 rations of bread.[39]

4

Among the social tragedies which most terrified humane Victorians and challenged their sympathies was that of the grievously neglected child, the juvenile outcast of urban life, Oliver Twist and Joe the crossing-sweeper. These were, in Mary Carpenter's phrase, the children of the "perishing and dangerous classes," meaning those ("the perishing") who, unless they were rescued, would be drawn inexorably to a criminal career, and those ("the dangerous") who were already living by thievery and were well on the road to prison.[40] Admittedly, juvenile crime had reached alarming dimensions, and was apparently increasing more rapidly than law-breaking in general. Thus in 1834 criminals between the ages of ten and twenty who were committed to prison amounted to 1 in 449 of the population, while in 1844 they represented 1 in 304.[41] Before the Lords Committee of 1847, Serjeant Adams, who incidentally identified the problem of juvenile crime chiefly with cities, testified that of the hundred prisoners whom he tried each fortnight, between sixteen and forty would be boys, and Matthew Davenport Hill reported that about 25 per cent of those tried at the Birmingham Sessions were sixteen or under.[42] Not only that, but recommittals were considerably more frequent with juveniles than with adults.[43]

[36] S. C. on District Asylums, 1846, p. xx; The Houseless Poor of London, 1891 (C.O.S.).

[37] G. Guyerette, Q. 2060ff, and S. Hughes, Q. 1732ff, S. C. on District Asylums, 1846.

[38] Simey, Charitable Effort in Liverpool, p. 27.

[39] S. C. on District Asylums, 1846, Q. 4617; William Tuckniss, "Agencies for the Suppression of Vice and Crime," in Henry Mayhew, London Labour and the London Poor, 4 vols. (1861–62 ed., London), IV, xxviii.

[40] Mary Carpenter, Reformatory Schools for the Children of the Perishing and Dangerous Classes (London, 1851), p. 2.

[41] S. C. (Lords) on the Execution of the Criminal Law, 1847, 1st Rept., Q. 2927.

[42] Q. 90, 279.

[43] In Liverpool, an inspector of prisons reported in 1840, about two-thirds of the male juveniles con-

Few of those who wrung their hands over juvenile criminality saw the absurdity of a criminal law that made a child of seven capable of committing a felony (though until he reached fourteen there was a presumption against felonious intent).[44] Lord Harrowby wrote to the Birmingham Conference of 1851, "Only last week we had in our county gaol two children of six and a half and seven years of age." [45] Children with records of five convictions and one or two sentences of transportation commuted to imprisonment were not unknown. The squalid rookeries, the "Tom-all-Alone's" of *Bleak House,* where even the police hesitated to intrude, inevitably produced, in Dr. Guthrie's words, "Arabs of the city . . . wild as those of the desert." [46] To such social depths none of the existing agencies, the voluntary schools or the visiting societies, pretended to penetrate. These children, delinquents or incipient delinquents, were not merely the children of the poor, nor even of paupers; they were the human refuse of the Victorian city.

On the problem of outcast children, early Victorian philanthropists made a three-pronged attack. Voluntary societies, spurred on as always by enthusiastic individual leaders, established three main categories of institution. Ragged Schools (day or evening), industrial schools, and reformatory schools differed in methods and clientele and were designed for different degrees of misfortune or depravity; but they all formed parts of a movement on behalf of the child outcast.

Although some of the leaders were chiefly occupied with a single phase, as Lord Ashley and the Ragged School Union, others saw the problem in a somewhat broader perspective. Mary Carpenter, the heart and soul of the movement, who as a Unitarian lacked Ashley's strong Evangelical prepossessions, was determined to remodel the whole treatment of juvenile delinquency and to change official policies as well as to enlist the support of private philanthropists. Among the rooms full of filthy young savages in her St. James's Back Ragged School in Bristol, she took special interest in the more hardened cases, those who were well on the way to a criminal career, if, indeed, they had not already embarked on it. She had no use for the kind of retributive punishment meted out to young offenders in the courts, a view shared by some of the more enlightened judges, notably Matthew Davenport Hill, Recorder of Birmingham, with whom she became associated in her crusade. Miss Carpenter's first book, *Reformatory Schools for the Children of the Perishing and Dangerous Classes and for Juvenile Offenders* (1851) not only was a plea for special residential institutions for youthful offenders but also offered a persuasive rationale for other schools dedicated to the civilizing of Victorian waifdom.[47] There was a desperate need, she liked to reiterate, for schools

---

victed were repeaters, while only 36 per cent of the adults had previously done time. With respect to juveniles convicted, however, Liverpool was well above the national average. (*Ibid.,* Q. 1613.)

[44] Between the ages of seven and fourteen the child was presumed *doli incapax,* but that could be, and often was, rebutted by the evidence of the prosecution. (*S. C. on Criminal and Destitute Juveniles,* 1852, Q. 1822; see also Radzinowicz, *English Criminal Law,* I, 12.)

[45] Mary Carpenter, *S. C. on Criminal and Destitute Juveniles,* 1852, Q. 940.

[46] *Seed-Time and Harvest of Ragged Schools; or a Third Plea* (Edinburgh, 1860), p. 25.

[47] A new biography of Mary Carpenter would be a useful contribution to Victorian social history. The old one by her nephew, J. Estlin Carpenter (*The Life and Work of Mary Carpenter* [London, 1879]), is inadequate. A brief account appears in Young and Ashton, *British Social Work,* pp. 163–72.

which would serve children who were "*beyond the pale* of the [regular] educational institutions of our country." Of such were (1) those willing to come and receive education free; (2) those whose wild habits had made them "street Arabs"; and (3) those already in the hands of the law.[48]

Best publicized and enrolling by far the largest number of children were the Ragged Schools, which were attended by the first and, to some extent, by the second class of slum children. To single out any one individual as the founder of the Ragged School would misrepresent the reality. There was so little distinctive about the idea that some such response was natural enough for any humanitarian distressed over the ignorance and barbarity of the children of the poor. Some Sunday Schools focused their efforts chiefly on slum children, and John Pounds, a crippled shoemaker, was accustomed to round up child outcasts in Portsmouth, some five hundred in the course of thirty years, and to train them up in virtue and knowledge — probably more of the former, since Pounds himself was a man of little education. Yet he was, as Dr. Guthrie noted, "a genius in his way," and he had an instinctive gift for dealing with the kind of urchin who was drawn to his shop.[49]

In London the Ragged Schools were closely identified with evangelical effort, and in their virtues and limitations alike they owed a good deal to the evangelical outlook. The London City Mission, organized to bring the Gospel to the poor in their own homes, was a principal pioneer agency in setting up Ragged Schools, but what transformed these half-dozen or so struggling and straggling schools into a philanthropic movement was the accession of powerful allies in the persons of Lord Ashley and, secondarily, Charles Dickens.[50] To Ashley the Ragged School offered a weapon for attacking an evil that had been increasingly haunting him, the condition of London's waifs. And when, in February 1843, he saw in *The Times* an appeal for aid for a Ragged School in a singularly unsavory district to the north of Holborn Hill known as "Jack Ketch's Warren," he responded with enthusiasm.

The Field Lane School had been carrying on for two years under the auspices of the London City Mission, holding sessions on Sunday and Thursday evenings.[51] That such an institution had been able to operate at all was testimony to the heroism and devotion of its evangelical teachers. "An awful sight it is," Dickens reported to Angela Burdett-Coutts. "I blush to quote Oliver Twist for an authority, but it stands on that ground, and is precisely such a place as the Jew lived in . . . The children in the Jails are almost as common sights to me as my own, but these are worse, for they have not arrived there yet, but are as plainly and certainly

---

[48] Carpenter, *The Claims of the Ragged Schools to Pecuniary Educational Aid*, a pamphlet (London, 1859), p. 2.

[49] D. K. and C. J. Guthrie, *Autobiography of Thomas Guthrie and Memoir by His Sons*, 2 vols. (London, 1874–75), II, 112–13.

[50] *S. C. on Criminal and Destitute Juveniles*, 1852, Q. 3282; C. J. Montague, *Sixty Years in Waifdom* (London 1904), pp. 34–35.

[51] Edwin Hodder, *The Life and Work of the Seventh Earl of Shaftesbury*, 3 vols. (London, 1887), I, 481.

traveling there, as they are to their graves." [52] Unpromising as it appeared, this was precisely what Ashley had been looking for, and he took up the cause with all the ardor of the Christian crusader. He gave himself an intensive course in squalor, and, his biographer remarks, "became almost as familiar with the district of Field Lane as with the neighbourhood of Grosvenor Square." [53] The Ragged Schools were to become his favorite philanthropy, and they could hardly have made a more providential conquest. Ashley's cachet at once made them a worthy charity and gave them a wholly new status in the eyes of donors and others.

Later in the same year Dickens visited the Field Lane School as unofficial almoner to Angela Burdett-Coutts, to whom the secretary had appealed. This would be something of a gamble, he concluded after investigation, but the genuinely humane person ought to accept it. The ghastly filth of Field Lane was not a cause to attract that delicate philanthropy "which is not at all shocked by the existence of such things, but is excessively shocked to know of them." [54] It was through Dickens' mediation that Miss Coutts became one of the large and regular benefactors of the Ragged School movement. Theologically the novelist had little in common with the evangelicals who were its guiding spirits. But his love of children was as deep as theirs and more disinterested, and he hated cruelty and brutality with a furious intensity. It was this that made him an eloquent champion of the Ragged Schools, in spite of occasional reservations about the teachers ("so narrow-minded and odd") and some of the arrangements ("such a scramble").[55]

The Ragged School Union, formed in 1844 by a small group of London teachers, made possible a measure of central control and financing. Ashley, who took over the presidency at once and held it for over forty years, in a sense *was* the Ragged School Union. It was formed largely in his image, its policies reflected his ideas and biases, and to the public he stood as the incarnation of the movement. In the mid-century, measured by attendance and financial support, the London Ragged School Union was one of the more flourishing of Victorian philanthropies. In 1861, for example, the Union could claim 176 schools with about twenty-five thousand as an average day attendance, and an annual income, including that of individual schools, of over £35,000.[56] At the completion of a quarter-century some 424 paid teachers were serving in schools affiliated with the Union in addition to 3500 volunteer workers.[57]

Among the 176 Ragged Schools were sixteen overnight refuges which the Union had reluctantly started. This development ran counter to a major premise of the Ragged School effort and indeed of Victorian social work, the fundamental

---

[52] Edgar Johnson, ed., *Letters from Charles Dickens to Angela Burdett-Coutts, 1841–1865* (London, 1853), pp. 50–51.

[53] Hodder, *Shaftesbury*, I, 484.

[54] *Letters from Charles Dickens*, p. 54.

[55] *Ibid.*, p. 173.

[56] *S. C. on the Education of Destitute Children*, 1861, Q. 5, 186. Of this amount between £5000 and £6000 represented the receipts of the Union itself.

[57] *Report of the Conference on the Ragged Schools*, Exeter Hall, 11 April 1863, p. 24.

importance of home and family life. So basic was this in the Ragged School *credo* that in schools of the Union, children were even sent home for their meals, for, among other things, it was assumed that improvement in the child would be transmitted to the home itself. Unhappily it presently became clear that the influence might act in the opposite direction and that a child who had been in school for a few hours could be hopelessly corrupted by spending the rest of the twenty-four in a vicious environment. Not only that, but, as the sponsors of one school discovered when they turned the boys loose at nine o'clock, some of them had no home to return to. Starting with a few hammocks in the Old Pye Street schoolroom, the movement expanded until sixteen refuges were in operation.[58]

Not every advocate of Ragged Schools would have endorsed completely the philosophy of the London Union, dominated as it was by Ashley and his Evangelical outlook. All Ragged Schools, of course, sought to reach children who were too poor and (literally) too ragged to attend ordinary pay schools, but in the London Schools the religious and missionary element bulked more heavily than in some of the provincial and especially the Scottish institutions. The secretary of the Union could refer to its Schools as "Great Gospel Machines." The evangelicals conceived the Ragged School movement as a branch of the home missionary enterprise. When they looked for a key to the prevalence of crime and the threat of disorder, they usually found it in irreligion, particularly in lack of religious training, and when they attributed the aberrations of the lower classes to ignorance, what they meant was lack of religious knowledge — inability to repeat the Lord's Prayer, for example.[59] Consequently the main emphases of the Ragged School Union were, first, on imposing a degree of discipline on the children of costermongers, dockworkers, brickmakers, rag dealers, and the rest, and secondly, on inculcating some of the more elementary truths of religion. For religious instruction the Bible served as the chief vehicle, supplemented by *Pilgrim's Progress* and other writings of an improving character. As for the rest, a smattering of arithmetic and training in reading such volumes as Samuel Smiles's *Self-Help,* which, when it appeared in 1859, was at once installed as a basic text — these must suffice.[60]

No one could find much distinction in the education offered by the Ragged Schools. Their problem, as they and some of their critics saw it, was not that of achieving scholastic excellence. It was rather to resist the temptation to social-climbing that has been more or less characteristic of educational institutions. "Stick to the gutter," Shaftesbury exhorted them, and on the whole the Ragged Schools kept the faith. When children seemed to be rising above the most primitive educational or social level, they were encouraged to transfer to a pay school or to enter some such trade as shoeblacking.[61] Nothing must be allowed to interfere with the missionary and religious purpose of the Union Schools, not even educa-

[58] *S. C. on the Education of Destitute Children,* 1861, Q. 402, 403.
[59] Carpenter, *Reformatory Schools,* pp. 21–23.
[60] Montague, *Sixty Years in Waifdom,* p. 311.
[61] *S. C. on the Education of Destitute Children,* 1861, Q. 91.

tion, as Shaftesbury repeatedly stressed. This was Christian indoctrination of an elementary sort, and it was, in Shaftesbury's view, far preferable to secular learning. In 1870, while the Education Bill was passing through Parliament, he lamented that "the godless, non-Bible system is at hand; and the Ragged Schools, with all their Divine polity, with all their burning and fruitful love for the poor, with all their prayers and harvest for the temporal and eternal welfare of forsaken, heathenish, destitute, sorrowful, and yet innocent children, must perish under this all-conquering march of intellectual power." [62] Conscience of the Victorian Age that he was, friend of the outcast and the downtrodden, Shaftesbury's humanitarianism was unmarred by any democratic taint. He could appreciate the misery of the poor more sympathetically than their aspirations.

The London Union did not have the field to itself. Not only were there schools in nearly every town of consequence but some of these operated on principles rather different from those of the Metropolis.[63] In 1861, Liverpool, with a Union of its own, was said to have had 64 schools; and Manchester, 17, with average attendances of 7500 and 3500 respectively.[64] Mary Carpenter's five schools in Bristol were famous nationally. Although she stressed moral and religious training, her approach was less heavily evangelical than that of the London schools. But the most striking contrast in method was offered by the Scottish schools which owed, in their origins, little to English models. The pioneer here was Sheriff Watson of Aberdeen, who in 1841 started a school as a means of coping with juvenile delinquency so serious as to give the police much concern. His would be an "Industrial Feeding School," which children would be encouraged to attend by police pressure and bribed into remaining by three meals a day. They would receive instruction in religion, morals, habits of industry, as well as in the three R's.

The Aberdeen experiment took root in Dundee, Dumfries, and most conspicuously in Edinburgh, where Dr. Thomas Guthrie, friend of Watson and a distinguished preacher of the Free Kirk, launched three schools on the Aberdeen pattern. In Edinburgh, as elsewhere, juvenile crime was causing alarm, and the background of the children who during the first year attended the new schools seems to justify the dismay with which the "city Arabs" were viewed. Of 742 children, 120 were part orphans whose surviving parents were drunkards; 199 were known or thought to be children of thieves; 232 had been beggars; and 69 had been in jail or in a police office.[65] The Edinburgh schools were feeding schools, a fact which presumably had something to do with their exceptional attendance record, and they were industrial schools, with a program of work designed both to

---

[62] Hodder, *Shaftesbury*, III, 266.

[63] It should be said, however, that the Union remained a rather loose federation, as Shaftesbury preferred it to be. He was opposed to dictation from the center. For a list of towns with Ragged Schools in 1851, see *S. C. on Criminal and Destitute Juveniles*, 1852, Q. 3396.

[64] *S. C. on the Education of Destitute Children*, 1861, Q. 324. The number 64 seems excessive. Another witness gives 20, a more reasonable figure.

[65] Guthrie, *Seed-Time and Harvest*, pp. 65–66.

train the child and to reduce the cost of the institution.[66] In the London Union only a few of the schools were industrial, though a number had industrial classes, but in Scotland industrial training was a basic principle. Again unlike the situation in London, where the schools remained entirely voluntary institutions, in Scotland there was cooperation with the city authorities. Naturally the Scottish movement never reached the dimensions of the English, but in some respects it was guided by a sounder social realism than were the schools of the Metropolis.

In the annals of education the Ragged School movement can claim only a relatively minor place. The more memorable contributions of the Schools were made in the social sphere. Not only did they bring a touch of civilization to their unpromising human material, so that Taine could speak of them as instruments of "moral disinfection," [67] but under their patronage sprang up a variety of welfare efforts. There were clothing clubs and penny banks (boasting, in 1861, twenty-eight thousand depositors and £19,000 in deposits), "Ragged Churches" for the parents, and fresh-air holidays in the country.[68] Aided by a temporary grant from the Government, the London Union's emigration fund enabled a number of boys each year to seek their fortunes overseas, while at home in some years as many as two thousand children were placed out. Most colorful of all the Ragged School offshoots was the Shoeblack Brigade, organized in 1851 by John Macgregor ("Rob Roy") to serve the crowds at the Crystal Palace. In the course of the Exhibition, some twenty-five or thirty boys cleaned 101,000 shoes at a cost to the public of £500![69]

When the Act of 1870 destroyed its educational *raison d'être,* the Ragged School movement, after a period of uncertainty, made the necessary adjustment. The schools became "missions," with their chief activities religious and social.[70] But the Ragged School movement may fairly claim to have been a seminal influence in social work for underprivileged children. By confronting sympathetic members of the upper and middle classes with the young victims of urban destitution, the Ragged Schools made certain that other agencies would be created and other needs met. In Ragged School annals appear the names of Quintin Hogg, Dr. Barnardo, Tom Hughes, General Gordon, and Professor Leone Levi. The Barnardo Homes grew directly out of the Ragged School movement, as did Quintin Hogg's Polytechnic Institute.[71] This was neither the first nor the last charity whose by-products turned out to be of more lasting significance than were its more consciously sought results.

[66] *Ibid.,* pp. 80–81.
[67] *Notes on England* (1958 ed., New York), p. 171.
[68] *S. C. on the Education of Destitute Children, 1861,* Q. 181.
[69] Hodder, *Shaftesbury,* II, 342. John Macgregor gives details of the organization in his evidence before the S. C. on Criminal and Destitute Juveniles, 1852, and also in "Rob Roy," *Ten Thousand Street Folk* (London, 1872).
[70] In 1893 the Union was incorporated as the Ragged School Union and Shaftesbury Society. Twenty years later it became the Shaftesbury Society and Ragged School Union. Today it is simply the Shaftesbury Society.
[71] A brief account of this undertaking will be given in Chapter IX.

5

Mary Carpenter's well-known call to action, *Reformatory Schools,* had to do not only with "the children of the perishing and dangerous classes" but also with juvenile offenders actually in the hands of the law, the most clearly defined category of delinquent. It would be redundant to note once more the absurdities of mid-century criminal law as applied to youthful prisoners. Before the Commons Committee of 1852 a judge recalled having had to try a child of seven and to face another charged with the theft of a penny tart.[72] Five years earlier an inspector of prisons reminded the Lords Committee that transportation might still be inflicted on the very young: "I conversed this morning with one [child] under Sentence of Transportation who is only Nine Years of Age . . . I have written the Secretary of State this morning to request him to send back a Child Nine Years old from the Transport Depot, as being utterly unfit, under any Circumstances for Transportation." [73]

Uneasiness about juvenile crime and the procedures of criminal justice was not a novel worry on the part of the humane and public-spirited. The Philanthropic Society, as we have seen, dated from the late 1780's, and at the time of the furor over mendicity in the Metropolis a Society for the Improvement of Prison Discipline and for the Reformation of Juvenile Offenders undertook to study the causes and possible cure of delinquency. The committee, which included the familiar names of William Allen, David Ricardo, T. F. Buxton, Samuel Hoare, and James Mill, learned a good deal about the organization of juvenile crime and concluded that, among other things, the severity of the criminal code and the system of prison discipline were mechanisms which produced juvenile offenders.[74] There were a few experiments in homes for delinquents, but, save for these and the work of the Philanthropic Society, the early century accomplished little of constructive significance.[75]

During the 1840's, however, as statistics on juvenile crime continued to alarm, the issue took on greater urgency. Their experience in the Ragged Schools aroused in the minds of some of the managers and teachers, most notably Mary Carpenter, a serious and combative interest in the treatment of the juvenile criminal. Matthew Davenport Hill, conspicuous for his social conscience both as barrister and jurist, was increasingly unhappy with the criminal law as he had to apply it to youthful offenders. His *Report upon the Principles of Punishment,* drafted in 1846 for the Law Amendment Society, took its stand upon the premise of reformatory rather than deterrent punishment.[76] The *Report* had something to do with inspiring the

---

[72] Serjeant Adams, *S. C. on Criminal and Destitute Juveniles,* 1852, Q. 1819–20.

[73] Rev. W. Russell, *S. C. (Lords) on the Execution of the Criminal Law,* 1847, *1st Rept.,* Q. 674.

[74] *Philanthropist,* 6:199ff (1816); see also Radzinowicz, *English Criminal Law, 1750–1833,* p. 597.

[75] In 1818 the Warwickshire Magistrates, as private individuals, founded a small asylum at Stretton-upon-Dunmore for juvenile delinquents, an institution that survived until 1854, when it was obliged to close for lack of funds. (M. D. Hill, *S. C. on Criminal and Destitute Juveniles,* 1852, Q. 420; Rosamond and Florence Davenport Hill, *The Recorder of Birmingham* [London, 1878], p. 156.)

[76] See *S. C. (Lords) on the Execution of the Criminal Law,* 1847, Q. 415.

appointment of a Select Committee of the Lords under the chairmanship of Brougham, whose conclusions, although mildly on the side of the angels, marked no very substantial advance.[77]

Meanwhile, rumors of an exciting and successful experiment across the Channel gave something of a fillip to the movement, if such it could be called, for a more rational handling of the juvenile offender. The agricultural colony for young offenders which M. De Metz, a criminal judge, opened in 1840 on an estate near Tours, made a deep impression on Englishmen who visited it and convinced them that he had hit upon a creative method of dealing with delinquents. The heart of the plan was the cottage or house system, an attempt to maintain, even in a correctional institution, a semblance of the family group. The principal reformatory device was the close personal relationship between the individual boy and the masters in his house, who had received special training for their duties. Work in the fields took up most of the day, though there was also a formal education of sorts, in which music figured heavily. It was De Metz's canny notion that the boys should be so constantly occupied as to be thoroughly tired at the end of the day.[78]

As echoes of De Metz's achievement reached England, a visit to Mettray became almost a routine expedition for Englishmen concerned with juvenile delinquency. Some, such as Matthew Davenport Hill, who undertook his first trip hesitantly, verged on the rhapsodic. "No Mahommedan," he avowed, "believes more devoutly in the efficacy of a pilgrimage to Mecca, than I do in one to Mettray." [79] As for the Reverend Sydney Turner, chaplain of the Philanthropic Society and later Inspector of Reformatories under the Home Office, who had been the first of the English visitors, he returned to persuade the Philanthropic to leave St. George's Fields and move to the country. With the founding in 1848 of the Society's farm school at Redhill in Surrey and the adoption of Mettray methods, the reformatory movement in England, Turner implies with some justice, entered the modern era.[80]

At the time of the shift, the Philanthropic had completed six decades of useful activity and was by far the most securely established agency of its kind. In the mid-century its subscription list contained about twelve hundred names, among them the Bank of England from which was received £2125. It had acquired legacies of nearly £105,000, and the annual cost of its establishment at Redhill was in the neighborhood of £3000 for about a hundred boys.[81] Roughly half the

[77] The *Lords Report* also appears in the *Commons Papers* for 1847.

[78] *S. C. on Criminal and Destitute Juveniles*, 1852, Q. 431, 433. Although Dr. Wichern, the German Evangelical who opened the Rauhe Haus in 1833, anticipated the Mettray experiment, it seems to have been the latter that influenced English practice most profoundly. (Kathleen Heasman, *Evangelicals in Action* [London, 1962], p. 184.)

[79] Hill, *Recorder of Birmingham*, pp. 158, 160.

[80] Turner, "Early History of the Reformatory and Industrial School Movement," *Departmental Committee on Reformatory and Industrial Schools* (C. 8204), 1896, App. I, p. 176.

[81] Philanthropic Society, *List of Subscribers and Contributors*, d. March, 1850; S. Turner, *S. C. on Criminal and Destitute Juveniles*, 1852, Q. 303.

inmates were voluntary, the other half consisting of young prisoners under sentence of transportation who had received conditional pardons and boys placed in the school by relatives or friends who paid for their keep. The Redhill farm of 150 acres was to be operated on Mettray principles, and, with Sydney Turner as the guiding spirit, these were introduced as rapidly and completely as possible. The limiting factor, it presently appeared, was the shortage of competent masters, and for a few years Redhill had to abandon the family system. In spite of the initial difficulties, the farm school was an intelligent and well-considered approach to the rehabilitation of juvenile delinquents — this, notwithstanding some complaint about excessive cost and the objection of the Director of H. M. Convict Prisons that the family system involved too great familiarity between officers and inmates. "With us," he declared, "the distinction of classes is a national characteristic. There may be considerable kindness between classes, but there is no cordiality" [82] — which was, of course, precisely what disturbed some of his more sensitive contemporaries.

Before reformatory schools could be widely established, the question of their relation to the State's penal system had to be resolved. The treatment of juvenile delinquency, in fact, offers an instructive modification in practice of the Victorian doctrine which sharply distinguished between the spheres of voluntary effort and public authority. Where in assigning responsibility for young delinquents ought the line to be drawn? If reformatory institutions were to be set up, should not these be public institutions in the full sense of the word? The more thoughtful reformers suspected that such agencies would turn out to be virtual prisons for juveniles, but privately managed asylums had two grave defects which could be remedied only by state intervention. On the one hand, their financial underpinning was feeble and precarious, and on the other, they lacked coercive power. Magistrates must be given authority to send offenders to reformatory schools instead of to prison, and schools the right to detain them. Perhaps a fusion of public and private effort might be managed on such a basis.

Probably most of the reformers would have subscribed to some such notions as these. In any case, the conference held in Birmingham in December 1851 reached substantially these conclusions. This gathering, in which Mary Carpenter and Matthew Davenport Hill were the guiding spirits, marked something of a turning point in the British approach to juvenile crime. In essentials, the conclusions of the conference had been forecast by Miss Carpenter's book which had appeared earlier in the year and by the circular of invitation, drafted presumably by the same hand. These proposed, to repeat, three types of school — the free day (ragged) school, the industrial feeding school (with compulsory attendance), and the reformatory school for young convicts. All three were seen as "best conducted by individual bodies, with close and rigid inspection by the State as to their effective working" and, of course, with public support. In short, the ideal envisioned by Mary Carpenter and her group was a series of institutions for

---

[82] Capt. D. O'Brien, *S. C. on Criminal and Destitute Children*, 1852–53, Q. 881.

neglected and delinquent children managed by voluntary bodies and financed by private contributions, payments from parents, and grants from the State. This would be a quasi-official system, with the public authorities providing legal sanction, financial aid, and a measure of supervision.[83]

The Birmingham Conference succeeded not only in making juvenile delinquency into a minor public question but in inspiring the reformers themselves to practical activity. The early 1850's saw the founding of a series of reformatory schools in widely separated sections of the country — Barwick Baker's at Hardwicke in Gloucestershire, Joseph Sturge's at Stoke Farm (near Bromsgrove), Captain O'Brien's at Newcastle-on-Tyne, and others. Probably the best known were Mary Carpenter's Kingswood Reformatory and her Red Lodge Girls' Reformatory in Bristol and the school at Saltley in which C. B. Adderley (Lord Norton) established that untutored but gifted genius in handling wild boys, Cobbler Ellis, who had been carrying on a small institution in Birmingham. All of these reformatories sought to vary the Redhill formula, for this was considered by many to be too costly and rather artificial (and perhaps unEnglish!), and to develop their own simpler and more economical methods.[84]

The Youthful Offenders Act of 1854, drafted by Adderley and carried by Palmerston — "the Magna Charta of the neglected child," Hill called it — authorized the establishment of reformatory schools by private groups.[85] To such certified institutions courts or justices might send prisoners under sixteen, who could be held from two to five years (their stay in the school to be prefaced by a brief taste of regular imprisonment). For offenders thus committed the Treasury paid, during most of the century, at the weekly rate of six or seven shillings a child.[86] This was a mutually profitable and prophetic meshing of public authority and private philanthropic initiative, and, as a glance at the twentieth-century Welfare State will demonstrate, it established a pattern of a sort for statutory-voluntary relations.[87]

It would be unrewarding to look closely at the details of this dual system. What is important is to emphasize that the schools, though supervised and as a group largely supported by the State, retained their essential character as independent, semiphilanthropic institutions. In 1861 the Newcastle Commission reported forty-seven certified reformatories (two of them ships) in England and Wales, which

[83] The circular of invitation to the Birmingham Conference and the resolutions passed are reprinted in Mary Carpenter, *Juvenile Delinquents* (London, 1853), pp. 330–33.

[84] A brief history of these institutions appears in Turner, "Early History of the Reformatory and Industrial School Movement"; see also W. S. Childe-Pemberton, *Life of Lord Norton, 1814–1885* (London, 1909), p. 128. A useful summary of the "history, principles, and working" of Mary Carpenter's *Red Lodge Girls' Reformatory School* was published by the School (Bristol, 1875) on completion of its first two decades.

[85] 17 & 18 Vict., c. 86. A bill introduced by Adderley in the previous year had failed because of the lateness of the session. The Act of 1853 was followed by a series of amending Statutes and finally in 1866 by a consolidating Act, 29 & 30 Vict., c. 117.

[86] *Inter-Departmental Committee on the Provision of Funds for Reformatory and Industrial Schools* (Cd. 3145), 1906, p. 1.

[87] This will be described in Chapter XIX.

received more than two-thirds of their income from the Treasury.[88] This compromise, Victorian Englishmen were convinced, was preferable to a state-administered system. Thus *The Times* could find in the success of the schools a solid justification for its belief in voluntary association rather than state action as an agent of social betterment.[89]

The situation of the industrial schools was more complicated than that of the reformatories, for their purpose was to handle the rather ill-defined middle group of young delinquents. They were to furnish "a finer sieve than the Reformatory," to catch "the children either before they have committed crime at all, or at so tender an age as would make the infliction of imprisonment revolting."[90] With the Youthful Offenders Act well launched, in 1857 Adderley carried a bill applying the same certification procedure to industrial schools and enabling magistrates to commit to them children convicted of vagrancy.[91] Industrial schools could now receive grants on the same basis as ordinary day schools. To a much greater degree than the reformatory schools, they remained voluntary institutions, supported by private benevolence and attended chiefly by children free of legal compulsion. At the time of the Newcastle Commission's inquiry (1858–61), there were in England eighteen certified industrial schools with nearly twelve hundred pupils, but only about a seventh of these were committed by magistrates, the great majority to three institutions. Grants from the State accounted for only 15 to 20 per cent of the receipts of industrial schools.[92]

On the question of state aid to ordinary Ragged Schools those who were concerned with the "perishing and dangerous classes" sang in less harmonious chorus, and public policy itself was anything but clear. A sharp difference of opinion arose between the provincial schools and the London Ragged School Union, which, led by Shaftesbury, vigorously opposed state aid, since this would presumably affect the religious and missionary character of the schools. Mary Carpenter, as heartily in favor as Shaftesbury was opposed, implied a bit acidly that the Union, being fairly well financed, could afford the luxury of its principles.[93] For her part she asserted that all Ragged Schools would be the better for government inspection and that their case for assistance was conclusive, especially if they offered industrial training as an important part of their work.

In the end the Government declined to accept Miss Carpenter's argument. The Select Committee on the Education of Destitute Children and the Newcastle Commission agreed that subsidizing Ragged Schools would be a doubtful use of public resources, and they were inclined to regard the schools, as did the Com-

---

[88] *R. C. on Popular Education,* 1861, Part I, p. 406. The 47 reformatories had about 2600 inmates. In 1858 they received about £52,000 from the Treasury and £16,000 from subscriptions and legacies.
[89] *The Times,* 8 Aug. 1856.
[90] Hill, *Recorder of Birmingham,* p. 173.
[91] 20 & 21 Vict., c. 48.
[92] *R. C. on Popular Education,* 1861, Part I, pp. 399–400. In an income of £20,000, Government grants amounted to a little less than £3000. The previous year (1859) these had totalled about £4250. Only a minority of industrial schools applied for certification.
[93] *S. C. on the Education of Destitute Children,* 1861, Q. 2172, 2379.

mittee of Council, as "provisional institutions," whose utility would be no more than temporary.[94] This judgment was presently vindicated by the Education Act of 1870 which radically altered the elementary school situation. The Newcastle Commission had foreseen some such outcome and, while praising the incomparable sacrifice of Ragged School teachers and managers, had already written an epitaph for the movement: "The time may come when their generous and charitable efforts may advantageously be replaced by a general system, but the fact that they first directed public attention to the subject, and that their labours showed the extent and urgency of the evil to be met . . . ought never to be forgotten." [95]

6

If voluntary day schools for neglected children were about to become redundant, other institutions — refuges, asylums, orphanages — could look forward to long and useful careers. By the late 1930's voluntary societies were managing something over a thousand homes and probably caring for as many children as the public assistance institutions, which in 1938 sheltered about 35,500.[96] The nineteenth century created orphanages with a lavish hand and in an infinite variety as regards size, auspices, and policies. Some served a limited constituency; others were relatively open-handed in their hospitality. Many of them, especially those founded in the latter half of the century, were more selective and were intended for children of more respectable backgrounds than the refuges which extended a welcoming hand to the poorest of the poor. One of the earliest, for example, the Royal Asylum of St. Anne, a product of the High Church resurgence, was founded in 1702 for children whose parents had seen better days. The nineteenth-century orphanage often had special qualifications for admission, such as father's work (Bank Clerk's Orphanage, Metropolitan and City Police Orphanage, Merchant Seamen's Orphan Asylum, Railway Servants' Orphanage); social status ("for destitute children . . . of middle-class parents");[97] or very commonly, religious affiliation.

The largest and most remarkable of the early-century orphanages were evangelical[98] in inspiration, and, indeed, throughout the Victorian Age much of the work for children was quasi-missionary in character and was so conceived by those who directed it. Dr. Barnardo's Homes, the greatest agency of their kind in the Kingdom, were the single-handed creation of a man who, influenced by Hudson Taylor, founder of the China Inland Mission, had volunteered for medical missionary work and had been diverted to the service of slum children

---

[94] Circular of 30 Jan. 1958, quoted by the *R. C. on Popular Education*, 1861, Part I, p. 394.

[95] *Ibid.*, p. 404.

[96] R. M. Wrong, "Some Voluntary Organizations for the Welfare of Children," in A. F. C. Bourdillon, ed., *Voluntary Social Services*, p. 31.

[97] The British Orphan Asylum (1827).

[98] By "evangelical" I mean, of course, to include the entire body, Nonconformist and Anglican, of those who thought of themselves as "Bible Christians."

by his experiences while training in the East End. For some years he called his enterprise the East End Juvenile Mission, and he thought of it as an evangelistic, as well as a welfare, agency. This was philanthropy of a different texture from that which had built the Foundling Hospital or the Orphan's Working School (1758).

Children's homes, though indubitably religious in purpose, were not, especially in the earlier decades, denominational in their orientation. In its period of greatest vigor evangelicalism did not stress sectarian boundaries but tended, at least for the purpose of good works, to regard all Bible Christians as fellow soldiers in the war against evil. But later in the century orphanages were planted more exclusively in denominational vineyards.[99] It would be a curious denomination which did not have a home planned primarily for orphans of its own communicants. The "Waifs and Strays" took care of Church of England orphans; the National Children's Home and Orphanage, the Wesleyan; and, on another scale, the New Orphanage, the Swedenborgian.

The most conspicuous figures in the work of founding homes for the fatherless were two evangelical ministers, Dr. Andrew Reed and the Reverend George Müller, the latter an extreme evangelical in his views. Their differences were nearly as great as their similarities, Reed the practitioner of a relatively orthodox philanthropy, while Müller's methods were highly unconventional. But the institutions that they founded were the largest of the century until Dr. Barnardo created his amazing chain of children's refuges.

Andrew Reed was the driving force behind a half-dozen of the more estimable charities of the Metropolis, three of them for the care of orphans. For a full half-century (1811–61) he held the pulpit of the Congregational Chapel in New Road, St. George's-in-the-East, and throughout his East End ministry he actively pursued the avocation of a philanthropist, or, perhaps more accurately, of a philanthropic entrepreneur, though his own benefactions were substantial. What apparently turned his attention to the plight of poor orphans was the exploitation of them practised by a certain individual who regularly accepted children as young as five for long-term apprenticeships. To work such children for long hours in a Wapping spinning establishment and then to promote them at twelve to a shoe factory on Tower Hill seemed to Reed inconsistent with the employer's claim of carrying on a philanthropic undertaking, and in 1813 he began to agitate, in and out of the pulpit, for a genuine refuge, to be called the "East London Orphan Asylum and Working School." It was slow going. His first appeal yielded only £66, but Reed took a house, nearly stripped his own home for furniture, and admitted a few orphans.

The struggling charity was turned into a relatively flourishing one when Reed, following the formula for successful philanthropy, managed to enlist a Royal patron. With the Duke of Kent presiding at a public dinner for the Asylum, the respectability of the venture was attested, and prospects took a turn for the better. Reed, an aggressive canvasser, now found it less difficult to wrest subscrip-

[99] R. M. Wrong in Bourdillon, ed., *Voluntary Social Services*, p. 37.

tions from City men, and he proceeded to make plans for a new building. This London Orphan Asylum at Clapton, opened in 1825, cost about £25,000 to build, most of it raised by Reed himself, and housed three, and later four, hundred orphans.[100] But, as often occurred in the annals of philanthropy, progress toward meeting one need served to expose others. It presently appeared that the London Asylum was not equipped to handle very young children. The answer was to be not a new wing but a separate institution. Again, with solid Royal patronage, a movement was launched which, by the early 1840's, had established the Infant Orphan Asylum at Wanstead in a large building accommodating six hundred children under seven.[101]

In one respect, as he discovered, Dr. Reed's sponsorship was too impeccable. Little of the sectarian himself, he opposed the introduction of denominational teaching or observances. His committee disagreed and insisted that the orphans be taught the Church of England Catechism, which, in effect, excluded the children of Reed's co-religionists. One suspects that other questions may have been at issue, for, like many dynamic individuals, he was not the easiest of associates. The upshot was that he cut his connection with the two institutions and determined to found a new and undenominational home. The Asylum for Fatherless Children went through the same series of moves from small to larger quarters as had Reed's other ventures — Richmond, Hackney Road, Stamford Hill — but finally in the late '50's achieved a permanent building near Croydon on an estate whose name was changed to Reedham in honor of the doctor.[102] It was an eminently deserved memorial, for in the course of fifty years he had been the most important single agent in providing shelter and training for over thirteen hundred fatherless children in institutions whose annual income is now of the order of £60,000.[103]

Two other interests of Reed's must be noted here, though they do not belong under the rubric of "neglected children." How he developed his concern for the mentally deficient and the incurably sick is not clear. Obviously his benevolence was not of the passive sort, and he restlessly searched out areas of distress into which charity might move to good effect. One of these he discovered in the lack of adequate institutions for the care of the mentally deficient whose families were unable to pay for their maintenance.[104] Reed began in 1847 to raise money for the project which, with the outlay of about £30,000, grew into the Asylum for Idiots at Earlswood (now the Royal Earlswood Institution for Mental Defectives) with a branch for younger patients at Colchester. The situation of the indigent incurables also drew Reed's sympathetic attention, for these, in general, were not welcomed by the regular hospitals. The result of his efforts was the

[100] Andrew and Charles Reed, eds., *Memoirs of . . . Andrew Reed,* 2d ed. (London, 1863), p. 101.
[101] Now the Royal Wanstead School.
[102] The institution is now known as the Reedham School.
[103] Beveridge, *Voluntary Action,* p. 167.
[104] Although Shaftesbury's Lunacy Act had been passed in 1845, there had been insufficient time for it to have much effect.

Royal Hospital for Incurables at Putney, which has grown into one of the great London medical charities, with receipts currently of well over £100,000.[105]

Reed was singularly gifted as a charity promoter. Plainly he felt deeply about the unfortunate; his own donations to the causes he was championing are said to have reached £5000, a generous fraction of £130,000, the approximate total raised.[106] Not only could he be eloquent in pressing the claims of the distressed, but his arguments generally had a solid factual basis. Reed was anything but the impulsive and sentimental charity evangelist. Before he launched his campaign for the Asylum for Mental Defectives, he visited institutions on the Continent and corresponded with interested individuals in America, which he had visited in 1834 as a member of a Congregational deputation. And when he was ready to make a public appeal, he had grounded himself thoroughly in his subject. Yet in Reed's charities, successful as they were, one finds no inclination toward innovation in matters of organization and administration. With all three of the orphan asylums, admission was by vote of the subscribers or by purchase (meaning a lump payment on behalf of the child).[107] As voting charities they almost perfectly exemplified the faults that charity reformers in the 1870's and '80's objected to. The Royal Hospital for Incurables supplied some of the more noisome examples of the hardships imposed by the voting charity, and it was, in fact, a protest by a subscriber to the Incurables that helped to precipitate the attack on the system conducted by Sir Charles Trevelyan and the Charity Organisation Society.[108]

The Reverend George Müller, founder of what were perhaps the most remarkable of the pre-Barnardo children's homes of the century, represented evangelical philanthropy in its most extreme Biblical simplicity. The orphan houses on Ashley Down, near Bristol, which at the end of thirty-five years of service could house over two thousand orphans and which had required a building fund of about £100,000, were financed entirely by spontaneous donations, without, as Müller often reiterated, "any one having been personally applied to for anything by me." [109] This institution, for which a total of over £370,000 was received during the thirty-five year period, stands as a capital example of faith-and-prayer philanthropy.

Müller himself had come to England from Prussia in 1829 to train for service as a missionary to the Jews. Before long, however, he convinced himself that it was unscriptural to serve under a missionary society, and likewise to receive a stated salary. His Scriptural Knowledge Institution, which sponsored the work for orphans, as well as a variety of other activities, was itself a projection of Müller's interpretation of the New Testament. The Institution neither incurred debts nor appealed for funds. Prayer and faith, he had no doubt, were sufficient,

---

[105] In 1953–54 the figure was £111,000 (*Annual Charities Register and Digest,* 1955, p. 58.
[106] Emma R. Pitman, *George Müller and Andrew Reed* (London, 1885), p. 121.
[107] In 1904, for example, a payment of £100 to £145 was required to gain admission for a child of from seven to eleven years of age. (*Annual Charities Register and Digest,* 1904, pp. 263–64.)
[108] As will be described in Chapter XVII.
[109] George Müller, *The Life of Trust* (1873 ed., Boston), p. 475.

and on the evidence of total receipts during the first half-century of more than
£1 million, it would be hard to say his confidence was misapplied.

Müller was persuaded to do something for destitute orphans for reasons that
most humanitarians, whose concern for their fellows was less theological, would
find faintly perverse. Though clearly he wished to succor the fatherless, his homes
were founded principally to magnify the power and goodness of God and to
vindicate the power of faith. The corollary was that to go into debt exhibited a
lack of faith, and it was an immutable principle of all Müller's enterprises to
make no financial commitments without cash actually in hand. In consequence,
their growth at times seemed slow and uncertain, their history punctuated by crises
of greater or less gravity. The annals of the Scriptural Knowledge Institution are
full of miraculous answers to prayer, as when, in October 1838, the Infant Orphan
House was down to two pence, but "the Lord most manifestly again answered
prayer by sending four pounds three shillings and one penny." [110] To one of less
simple faith Müller's methods would have been nerve-racking. Yet, measured by
results, they were undeniably effective. Starting in Bristol in 1836 with a few
orphans in a single house and resources which at the end of the year totaled £800,
his establishment grew within a decade to four houses, and 125 to 150 orphans
maintained at an annual cost of about £1500. [111] After ten years in Bristol, he
made the decision to move to Ashley Down and began to pray for the necessary
funds. Within two years about £11,000 had come in, and two years after that
the institution could offer accommodations to more than two thousand children.

Although Müller's Christian faith and his belief in prayer guided all of his
actions, this was not enough to explain his success. He was obviously a splendid
promoter and an able administrator. Merely as a receiving and disbursing operation, his orphan houses formed a substantial business. In 1871–72, for example, the
balance sheet of the Scriptural Knowledge Institution showed donations of about
£19,000 (in addition to a balance on hand of nearly £15,000) for the orphans alone,
and over £14,000 for the other projects of the Institution. During that year the cost
of carrying on the orphans' work exceeded £23,000. [112] He was scrupulous in accounting for every penny, as well as for every article donated (not all of the income came in cash, and the nonmonetary receipts included some fairly bizarre
items), [113] for sale in the shop that he established.

He had a way of taking donors and potential donors into his confidence and of
making them feel themselves partners in a noble enterprise. His *Life of Trust*
gives a candid and detailed picture of the growth of the Müller philanthropies.
That and the other Müller publications, circulating in the evangelical community and noted in the evangelical press, must have proved an effective auxiliary
to the power of prayer. Müller's decisions, which he agonized over before God,

---

[110] *Ibid.*, p. 163.
[111] *Ibid.*, p. 304.
[112] *Ibid.*, p. 479.
[113] As the list of articles received in 1872 (*ibid.*, pp. 476–78) will suggest.

were sometimes daring but they were never impulsive. Invariably they emerged from a long process of balancing pros and cons. Like most successful philanthropies in which religion was the dominant factor, the architect of the Müller enterprises was one in whom the wisdom of the children of light was admirably and fortunately blended with that of the children of this world.

During the four decades 1820–60 British society felt the full impact of uncontrolled urban growth, and humanitarians were appalled by the consequences. Private charity did what it could — sentimentally, wisely, or foolishly — to mitigate some of the worst of them. Organizations which were formed to deal with this or that category of distress or class of unfortunates, as will be emphasized in the next chapter, multiplied recklessly. Charitable agencies were able to help individual sufferers over rough places and to make life less intolerable; they could give shelter to some of the fatherless and salvage a few of the incipient juvenile delinquents. Individuals and voluntary groups were responsible for an occasional public amenity, as when Joseph Strutt presented the Arboretum to Derby at a cost of £10,000, and when Manchester raised some £30,000 for public parks.[114] Yet when the philanthropist could bring himself to look critically at the accomplishments of urban charity he could scarcely exult.

As measured against the problem, voluntary effort was performing no miracle. It had not succeeded in bridging the gap between rich and poor, if, indeed, this had been a serious aim, nor had it taken more than a tentative step or two toward civilizing the brutish masses or improving their material environment. Still less had it been able to modify the basic fact of urban destitution. As long as poverty was thought of as the result of moral failure (or exceptional misfortune), there was little to be done save to encourage and assist in individual reformation. Taken all in all, however hesitant and muddled their work may have been, public authorities did more to improve city life than did private charity. Mrs. Simey's conclusion for Liverpool applies with equal force to the Metropolis and other cities, that "in the field of public administration immense strides were made, [but] in charitable work the characteristic note was one of bafflement." [115]

[114] J. L. and B. Hammond, *The Age of the Chartists, 1832–1854* (London, 1930), pp. 345–46.
[115] Simey, *Charitable Effort in Liverpool,* p. 61.

CHAPTER VI

THE CONTOURS OF EARLY
VICTORIAN BENEVOLENCE

HE MOST exciting opportunities offered to early Victorian philanthropists had to do, more or less directly, with the growing pains of an urban society. The mass of destitution, the congestion of slum-living, and the apparent depravity of slum-dwellers posed for charitable Englishmen a disheartening complex of problems for which they were unable to find a convincing solution. Within the world of philanthropy there was chaos and confusion — uncertainty as to the job to be done and the tools to be employed — and there seemed little reason to modify the hardheaded judgment passed by Patrick Colquhoun at the turn of the century.[1] In spite of the admirably constructive labors of some of the more specialized voluntary organizations, private charity had failed to make an appreciable dent in the mountain of urban misery.

Yet, whatever reservations one may have about the achievements of mid-century charity, there can be little complaint about its rate of growth. The resources of charitable agencies multiplied handsomely, as did the separate agencies by which the flow of benevolence reached the recipients. Organizations and institutions flowered more luxuriantly than ever, overspecialized, repetitive, and often persisting, according to some mysterious law of charity inertia (sometimes not unrelated to endowments that had been acquired) after the need which called them into existence had vanished. The period was marked not only by the emergence of new needs, which evoked a variety of attempts, well-considered or fatuous, to relieve them, but also by the extension and proliferation of agencies launched in an earlier era. A parent idea or institution might generate, by fission or emulation, a bewildering number of variants, not all of indubitable utility. It was the boast of the modern historian of the Magdalen Hospital that over four hundred charities more or less similar to that institution had been established. In any case, by the 1850's London's fallen women, in their several degrees of abandonment, might seek rehabilitation at no less than twenty-five or thirty penitential homes.[2]

---

[1] Colquhoun, it was pointed out in Chapter IV, doubted whether the heavy charitable expenditure on behalf of the poor had produced constructive results.

[2] Compston, *Magdalen Hospital*, p. 16. One may note, as examples, the Guardian Society Asylum, the London Female Penitentiary, the Home for Penitent Females (Female Aid Society), the London Female Dormitory and Industrial Institution, the nine Homes and six Houses of Refuge (not all in London)

At least one category of metropolitan needy, whose claims always exerted a singular pull on Victorian sensibilities, was adequately, if not redundantly, provided for.

Although the condition of the charity world aroused critical comment in some quarters, for most Englishmen the hundreds of charitable institutions represented one of the glories of the British tradition and stood as a monument to the superiority of voluntary action over state intervention. They were warmed by an instinctive glow of pride as they contemplated the magnitude of British resources dedicated to the improvement of British life. And they would have been inclined to praise Taine for his shrewd understanding of the British ethos when, after noting the "swarms of societies engaged in good works," he went on to observe that "an Englishman rarely stands aside from public business. . . . He does not live withdrawn; on the contrary he feels himself under an obligation to contribute, in one way or another to the common good." [3]

To try to explain why so many upper- and middle-class Victorians devoted so much of their time to charitable endeavors would raise all sorts of unanswerable questions. Obviously the promptings of religion, especially, to repeat, of an evangelical humanitarian ethos, accounted for advances along some of the philanthropic fronts. It is impossible to miss the frequency with which such names as Gurney, Hoare, Buxton, and Thornton, not to mention the omnipresent Lord Ashley, appear among the officers of charitable organizations. There was a good deal of interlocking among the directorates of London charities; one would hardly venture a guess at the number of organizations for which Samuel Gurney or John Gurney Hoare — or, for that matter, John Labouchere — served as treasurer. Numbers of institutions were, of course, sponsored semiofficially by the Established Church or one of its diocesan organizations or by a Nonconformist communion. Hospitals, especially those for the treatment of specific diseases, were often the creation of physicians interested in better clinical facilities who were able to enlist sufficient support among friends and other well-wishers to found a new institution. For some charitable donors, also, civic pride was a powerful incentive. Old communities, such as the City of London, had long traditions of philanthropy, while newer cities strove, in their civic patriotism, to emulate and even surpass the more ancient centers. Perhaps it is enough to say that associated philanthropy was a valid expression of the social temper of the nineteenth century. For, with all of its blind spots and its social sins of omission and commission, this was a humanitarian age. Men believed that both individuals and the common life could be improved, and they discovered in the human lot a promise which other ages would have denied.

It would not do to imply that this outlook was universal, even among the more

---

of the Church Penitentiary Association, the Female Temporary Home, the St. Marylebone Female Protection Society, the South London Institution for the Protection of Young Females, the London Female Preventive and Reformatory Institution (four Homes), the Society for the Rescue of Young Women and Children (five houses for "those who have fallen"), Trinity Home, the London Diocesan Penitentiary, St. James's and St. George's Home, not to exhaust the possibilities.

[3] *Notes on England,* trans. E. Hyams, p. 168.

enlightened. For some charity served as a kind of moral or emotional tonic. The generous Richard Potter, Beatrice Webb's father, found the practice of philanthropy rewarding, most of all, to himself: "'What luxury it is to do good!,' he thought, as he put £5 rather than a few coins in the collection for the poor and walked away to 'feel good' for the rest of the day." [4] Sometimes charity might provide compensation for a loosening of faith in religious or, for that matter, political verities. Such benevolence easily degenerated into sentimentality, in Fitzjames Stephen's words, a "kind of vapid philanthropic sentiment . . . a creed of maudlin benevolence from which all the deeper and sterner elements of religious belief have been carefully purged away." [5] Dickens' gospel of social betterment was hardly more than a hymn to kind hearts and warm human sensibilities. Certain more austere souls were fearful lest, in all the welter of benevolence, serving on charity committees should be regarded as an acceptable equivalent of the moral life. This, Carlyle thundered, was "a blind loquacious pruriency of indiscriminate Philanthropism substituting itself, with much self-laudation, for the silent divinely awful sense of Right and Wrong; — testifying too clearly that here is no longer a divine sense of Right and Wrong." [6]

The Victorians, though caring as much about right and wrong as most human societies, turned a deaf ear to such warnings, and continued to interest themselves, often to excess, in philanthropic undertakings. Some recognition of the obligation at least to subscribe to charity, from whatever motives, was so widespread among the upper and upper-middle classes that philanthropy became a social imperative, a convention observed by those who were, or wished to be, anybody. At its most vulgar, of course, this was a form of Victorian snobbism, with the comfortably off following the lead of the rich, and the rich taking their cue from the aristocratic and conforming to the tradition of paternal benevolence toward the poor and distressed.

It would be unfortunate to overemphasize the notion of Victorian charity as a ladder for social climbing, though certainly those who wished to rise in the world of society had best exhibit a decent interest in good works. What is more to the point is that Victorian charities in their organization were a fairly faithful mirror of the social hierarchy, and one of the conditions of success was sponsorship by royalty or by representatives of the higher branches of the peerage, some of whom, incidentally, worked diligently and unselfishly for their favorite philanthropies. Naturally the most coveted name was that of the Queen herself. When in 1835 the Princess Victoria and the Duchess of Kent agreed to become patrons of the Society for the Prevention of Cruelty to Animals, in the view of its promoters, "from that moment the continued existence of the Society was assured." [7] The Royal National Life-boat Institution, with its powerful patriotic appeal, had the good fortune to start out under the patronage of George IV, and the vice-

[4] Georgina Meinertzhagen, *From Ploughshare to Parliament* (London, 1908), p. 170.

[5] Quoted in Walter E. Houghton, *The Victorian Frame of Mind, 1830–1870* (New Haven, 1957), p. 275.

[6] *Ibid.*, p. 276.

[7] F. G. Fairholme and W. Paine, *A Century of Work for Animals* (New York, 1924), p. 72.

patronage of five royal dukes, with the two archbishops and a covey of bishops listed as vice-presidents, and Lord Liverpool, Prime Minister at the time, as president.[8]

This is not to say that nothing was needed beyond distinguished patronage. On the leadership of the president, noble or untitled, a good deal depended, for, among other things, he stood as the representative of the charity before the world of potential subscribers. The man-of-all-work about the institution was usually the secretary, honorary or paid, whose initiative and judgment might be critical for the well-being of the charity. With the larger agencies this might be a full time post, a heavy responsibility often carried by a man of private means who found pleasure and satisfaction in the work.

Yet certainly the number of high-born names attached to a charity made a difference to Victorian subscribers. The Duke of Cambridge, youngest and least disreputable of the "wicked uncles," turned out to be a valuable auxiliary for an amazing number of philanthropies. Not only did he lend them his vociferous oral support, but he also contributed his guineas to a substantial amount. These, his cynical contemporaries intimated, were like the china eggs planted in a nest to encourage the hen to lay.[9] No doubt the promoters of the various charities looked forward to precisely this result, but, to be fair to the Duke, he seems to have had a genuine, if not particularly discriminating, interest in a variety of philanthropies. The dukes, especially Cambridge, were in great request as chairmen of the now-traditional charity dinners, where, a French visitor remarked, the English managed to combine the pleasure of doing good with that of getting drunk with the rich.[10] As the eighteenth century had noted that at charity sermons the size of the collection was not unconnected with the popularity and standing of the preacher, so at dinners a distinguished chairman and speaker could lure from the mellowed gathering far more generous contributions than could a mediocre team. *The Times* charged, in its jocular fashion, that Lord Ashley's dashing about "to meeting-rooms and taverns, making speeches and eating dinners on behalf of every scheme that is nominally devoted to charitable purposes" was encroaching on the preserve of the royal dukes, whose "good nature and garrulity" fitted them admirably for presiding at charity dinners. The Duke of Cambridge, *The Times* insisted, was entitled to more consideration from the Evangelical peer, for "his heart and his mouth are always open to the call of charity." [11]

2

Early Victorians, then, interested themselves in philanthropy for a variety of reasons: sympathy and compassion for their fellows, the promptings of religion (and in some instances, perhaps, to compensate for a shaky faith), concern for the

[8] A. J. Dawson, *Britain's Life-Boats* (London, 1923), p. 50.
[9] Roger Fulford, *The Wicked Uncles* (New York, 1933), p. 306.
[10] A. J. B. Defauconpret, *Six mois à Londres en 1816* (Paris, 1817), p. 69, who also remarked on the part played by "l'ostentation et la vanité . . . dans tous ces actes de bienfaisance."
[11] *The Times,* 15 July 1845.

stability of their society, the social pressures brought to bear on them, or their own special ambitions. But whatever motives, conscious or unconscious, may have actuated them, there can be no doubt that charity held a place of some importance in the Victorian world. Although Mrs. Beeton's *Complete Letter-Writer* included some fairly special items — such as how to write an affirmative answer to the marriage proposal of a clergyman going to Africa as a missionary — it is not without significance that among her models was a letter "from a lady inviting another to aid a charity." [12] To a great many Englishmen, one can be sure, the volume of charitable giving and the myriad of charitable organizations offered convincing evidence that they were living in a progressive and humane age.

Certain more skeptical Victorians hesitated to join in the paeans of self-congratulation with which others hailed the philanthropy of the time. Throughout the century, and indeed carrying over from the previous century, there was an undercurrent of doubt and even hostility toward the good works about which their fellows busied themselves. The critics found much to cause uneasiness as they contemplated the confusing universe of Victorian charity. Among the various doubters it ran all the way from the dismay of those who turned a cool eye on the jungle of duplicating, conflicting, proliferating agencies of the Metropolis to more fundamental queries about the social utility of it all. Such ventures as education, housing experiments, and medical charities, they were inclined to endorse, though with substantial reservations, but other branches of the charitable effort they regarded not only as sterile but as actively harmful. The charity woods, they insisted, were full of small, inefficient, redundant agencies, which had yielded no benefits proportional to their number and to the pounds, shillings, and pence collected for them. As a correspondent in *The Times* charged, metropolitan charity flowed "in so many and partial channels that few of these have power to reach the objects designed; many are utterly dried up in their course." [13] Such complaints, by no means peculiar to our period, form a continuous counter-theme in charity history, and, in the course of a few years, when developed more circumstantially, they would generate the charity organization movement.

Critics were not concerned merely with the mechanical defects of the charity system. Throughout the age there echoed the lamentations of those who deplored charitable giving as encouraging the poor to depend on others rather than on their own efforts. Such misgivings, familiar enough in essentials, changed in detail from decade to decade, but on the whole the doubters conceived most forms of philanthropy to be questionable, an impulsive and ill-considered response which, on balance, would be more productive of evil than good. In a kind of plaintively Malthusian soliloquy, Walter Bagehot remarked, "Great good, no doubt, philanthropy does, but then it also does great evil. It augments so much vice, it multiplies so much suffering, it brings to life such great populations to suffer and be vicious, that it is open to argument whether it be or be not an evil to the world, and this

[12] Quoted in James Laver, *Victorian Vista* (London, 1954), p. 69.
[13] *The Times,* 4 Dec. 1850.

is entirely because excellent people fancy that they can do much by rapid action
— that they will most benefit the world when they most relieve their own feelings,
that as soon as an evil is seen 'something' ought to be done to stay and prevent
it." [14]

The editor and translator of Faucher's *Manchester in 1844* — a local man —
could speak of "the number and extent of our charitable institutions, and the
large amount of indiscriminate relief afforded [as] a growing evil . . . If habits
of self-respect, and an honest pride of independence, are the safeguard of the
working classes, and a barrier against the inroads of pauperism, it will follow that
any public institutions which lead them, directly or indirectly, to depend upon
the bounty of others in times of poverty or sickness, and which tend to encourage
idleness and improvidence . . . are not public charities, but public evils." [15] Such
apprehensions received statistical documentation in 1850 with the publication of
the first edition of Sampson Low's directory of London charities.[16] Commenting
on the manual under the caption "Charity, Noxious and Beneficent," a *Westminster* reviewer pictured his age as "foolishly soft, weakly tender, irrationally maudlin, unwisely and mischievously charitable. Under the specious mask of mercy to
the criminal and benevolence to the wretched, we spare our own feelings at the
cost of the most obvious principles of morality, the plainest dictates of prudence,
the dearest interests of our country. We are kind to every one except society." [17]
There was nothing novel about the indictment. It was the standard attack on
thoughtless charity, "benevolent error," which was content simply to relieve misery
but shrank from the harder task of teaching "suffering and destitution to prevent
themselves" by following sound principles of social science, meaning, of course,
precepts similar to those which later guided the Charity Organisation Society. "It
is as dangerous," the *Westminster* reviewer asserted, "to practise charity, as to
practise physic without a diploma."

But was the country oversupplied with charitable agencies? Clearly English
charities "in extent, variety, and amount, are something perfectly stupendous,"
providing for every contingency in the lives of the poor. "From the cradle to the
grave, they are surrounded with importunate benevolence." The reviewer recalls
the picture of Spitalfields charities sketched for the Poor Law Commissioners by
the Reverend William Stone who had graphically illustrated the situation in terms
of a hypothetical young weaver, his wife, and child. This family elected to take
advantage of all the opportunities for free attention, with disastrous results to the
child, whose life was converted into an exercise in mendicancy. "He was *born for
nothing — nursed for nothing — clothed for nothing — educated for nothing; —*
he has been *put out apprentice for nothing — he has had medicine and medical
attendance for nothing; —* he has had his children *also born, nursed, clothed, fed,*

---

[14] *Physics and Politics*, Mrs. Russell Barrington, ed. (London, 1915), *Works*, VIII, 122.
[15] Quoted in Norman McCord, *The Anti-Corn Law League, 1838–1846* (London, 1958), p. 27.
[16] Sampson Low, Jun., *The Charities of London* (London, 1850). Charles Knight, ed., *London*,
6 vols: (London, 1841–44), VI, 337–52, offers a readable survey of London charities in the early 1840's.
[17] *Westminster Review*, 59:62–88 (January 1853).

educated, established, and physicked for nothing. There is but one good office more for which he can stand indebted to society, — and that is his *burial*. He dies a parish pauper; and, at the expense of the parish, he is provided with shroud, coffin, pall, and burial-ground."

What bothered the *Westminster* reviewer, as it had disturbed Patrick Colquhoun a half century before, was the apparent paradox between charitable expenditure and social improvement. It was comforting to believe, as the reviewer professed to hold, that destitution and charity were temporary evils, which would disappear as wiser benevolence restored society to sanity and soundness. Once charitable giving was brought under rational control, everything would come into reasonably satisfactory balance. Plainly such critics were gravely overestimating the country's charitable resources against the job to be done, or, more accurately, were underestimating the task and assuming that, in a large measure, it would take care of itself.

3

To reach quantitative conclusions about the country's charitable organizations and their finances would be out of the question. It would be difficult for endowed charities and impossible for voluntary societies, to say nothing of the mass of unorganized charity, the individual almsgiving and the *ad hoc* subscription lists. From 1850 on, however, our information for the Metropolis becomes richer with the publication of the first issue of Sampson Low's *Charities of London,* followed by a second edition eleven years later. From these pages, even allowing for inaccuracies and incompleteness, emerges an extraordinary picture of the variety and multiplicity of London's agencies. Although professedly restricted to the Metropolis, Low's survey is, in fact, somewhat less limited, for it includes numbers of national philanthropies, such as the R.S.P.C.A. and the Sons of the Clergy Corporation, whose offices were in London but whose scope was nation-wide. On the other hand it lists a good many agencies whose status as philanthropies (for the purpose of this study) is questionable.[18] Whatever Low's shortcomings, to page through his volume is a liberal education in the infinitely diverse expressions, almost aberrations, of the humanitarian impulse.

Low's grand totals of income and agencies are relatively meaningless, for his roster of charities includes so many doubtful categories.[19] What is of consequence is information on particular types of charity and their growth, and, indeed, on the rate of expansion of the charitable effort as a whole. A letter to *The Times* in 1850 deplored the fact that every year saw the addition of fifteen or twenty more benevolent institutions, a claim that was confirmed for the 1850's by the 1861 edition of Low, which listed 144 new agencies established during the decade,

---

[18] Of such are the 25 foreign missionary societies and at least some of the 56 Bible and home missionary societies.

[19] For what it is worth, Low's 1861 edition puts the aggregate income of 640 London charitable agencies at nearly £2½ million, of which about £1,600,000 was drawn from voluntary contributions and nearly £850,000 from rent, dividends, and trade.

an increase, that is, of 25 per cent.[20] During the same period, charitable income among the institutions covered rose by more than a third, from about £1.75 to nearly £2.5 million. One can be even less precise about the decades before Low's first edition, but a rough check of dates of founding confirms the impression that the period saw a striking increase in institutions devoted to the myriad purposes of charity. Only in orphanages and institutions for the aged was the rate of expansion less than dramatic. In such areas as medical relief, aid for the physically handicapped, relief of destitution and helplessness, the treatment of delinquency, the years 1820–60 saw the energies of the philanthropist reach a high, almost a frenetic, pitch.

Measured by their resources, the most spectacular growth among secular philanthropies took place in the medical sector. Here the humanitarian concern of the Victorians and their confidence in science as an agent of human progress joined in beneficent alliance. Granted that early Victorian hospitals were not all that they might have been and that some of them may have killed as many as they cured, in the long run such philanthropies turned out to be as constructive as most of the causes to which charitable Englishmen chose to give their money. At the end of our period Londoners were contributing about £155,000 a year to their hospitals and dispensaries, in addition to the £210,000 that these drew from invested funds and real estate.[21] In the provinces, as well as in London, the increase in numbers of institutions was conspicuous. Although no more than a crude approximation is possible, it appears that outside the Metropolis the number of medical institutions established in 1820–60 was about four times the number founded during the previous forty years.[22]

The chronology of metropolitan general hospitals is erratic. After the founding of Guy's, Westminster, and the rest in the first half of the eighteenth century over seventy years intervened before another was established. From the foundation of the Middlesex Hospital in 1745 no new major hospitals appeared in London until 1818, when the launching of the West London Infirmary (Charing Cross Hospital) inaugurated a new period of hospital-building. The Charing Cross grew out of the charity practice of Benjamin Golding, a distinguished physician, who became convinced of the need for a medical charity in the Charing Cross district. In the movement which established the new institution, Golding and his friends were able to raise over £6000, and early in the 1830's they put up a building at the cost of about £20,000.[23] Like other institutions in the charitable world, the Charing Cross was heavily buttressed with royal and noble patrons, but the committees of management relied to a great degree on solid London burghers.

Neither the University College nor the King's College Hospital, opened in 1833

---

[20] *The Times*, 4 Dec. 1850.

[21] *Low's Charities of London in 1861*, p. vii.

[22] Based on the dates of founding given in *Burdett's Hospitals of the World* (1906 ed.). Scotland and Ireland are not included.

[23] Benjamin Golding, *The Origin, Plan, and Operations of the Charing Cross Hospital* (London, 1867), pp. 36, 41.

and 1839 respectively, was intended as a charitable facility. Their primary purpose was to provide clinical material for medical students. Although the founders of the new college on Gower Street planned a medical course less exclusively clinical and empirical than had been conventional for British physicians, hospital facilities were still essential.[24] At one time it was hoped that a plan of cooperation with the Middlesex Hospital might solve the problem, but in 1833 the University College Council determined to take the plunge, financing the venture by mortgaging the Gower Street property and soliciting subscriptions. In a burst of optimism the Council assumed that, once built, the Hospital would be self-sustaining, but, like the other general hospitals in London, it was always heavily dependent on voluntary contributions.[25]

Like its Bloomsbury relative, King's College decided reluctantly to found its own hospital. Alterations to the old St. Clement Danes workhouse in Portugal Street, which the College took over, proved costly, and, although a fund of about £10,000 had been raised within a few months, the new institution started life with meager capital. Financial crisis, indeed, was a more or less chronic condition for the Hospital. Building funds could be, and continued to be, raised with some success, but running expenses and annual deficits, which regularly resulted, were another matter. Not only that, but the demands of the Hospital sometimes had serious repercussions on the finances of the College itself. For, although the Hospital had its own committee elected by the governors (£3 3s. subscribers), ultimate responsibility rested with the College, since the essential purpose of the Hospital was to serve its medical school.[26]

The most distinctive development in the field of medical institutions, however, was not the general but the special hospital. The earlier period had seen the founding of establishments for the treatment of specific conditions, notably venereal disease, fever, and maternity cases, but during the mid-century new facilities were founded, in considerable number, to treat other diseases. Between 1820 and 1860, three times as many special hospitals (over forty) were opened in the Metropolis as in the previous four decades, and they now interested themselves in such diseases as consumption — the most characteristic of Victorian afflictions — heart conditions, eye and ear complaints, children's diseases, and orthopedic deformities. By 1860, the sixty-six special hospitals, according to Low's figures, were enjoying an income of nearly £755,000 in subscriptions and donations and about £80,000 from investments and property.[27]

The motives that created these establishments were, of course, mixed and not necessarily philanthropic in essence. Probably the most powerful factor was simply the desire of medical specialists to have hospitals of their own or perhaps to

[24] H. H. Bellot, *University College, London, 1826–1926* (London, 1929), pp. 54–55.
[25] For the sources of the Hospital's income in the early period, see Newton H. Nixon, *North London or University College Hospital* (London, 1882), p. 12.
[26] F. J. C. Hearnshaw, *The Centenary History of King's College, London, 1828–1928* (London, 1929), pp. 142–46, 229–30.
[27] *Low's Charities of London in 1861*, p. vii.

transform themselves into specialists by virtue of setting up a hospital, and some of these institutions, in spite of the conventional front of patrons and committee, were hardly more than one-man affairs. Both as philanthropies and as medical institutions the special hospitals were a variegated lot. The better ones, however, formed a splendid addition to the health agencies not only of the Metropolis but of the country, for London hospitals were, in some degree, national institutions.

If the early Victorian decades marked the rise of the special hospital, they also saw a tapering off in the dispensary movement in London, though not in the provinces. The late eighteenth century had been disposed to see the dispensary as the answer to the problem of medical care for the poor, and money that might have gone into the financing of hospitals was diverted to dispensaries. Although these continued to be founded in the Metropolis, the pace slackened appreciably. In the provinces, on the other hand, dispensaries continued to flower in the greatest luxuriance. About half of those operating at the turn of the twentieth century were founded between 1820 and 1860. Not only that, but numbers of provincial hospitals had started life as dispensaries and had later attained full hospital status. It was a natural evolutionary pattern.

The real revolution in nursing and nurses' training was just beginning in the early 1860's. Florence Nightingale's school at St. Thomas's Hospital opened in 1860, and in Liverpool at the same time William Rathbone was embarking on his investigations that were to lead to the district-nursing movement.[28] Yet philanthropy had made some tentative moves, apparently inspired by Continental nursing orders, Catholic and Protestant. The eighty to one hundred nurses of the Institution of Nursing Sisters, in whose founding in 1840 Quaker ladies took a prominent part, gave aid gratuitously to the poor when unable to pay and to others at moderate cost.[29] Nine years later a similar organization under Church of England auspices was started at St. John's House, Norfolk Street, whose nurses were divided between King's College Hospital and cases in private homes. Ten years after its foundation St. John's House had annual receipts of roughly £5500, about half from subscriptions and donations. These were, of course, meritorious undertakings, but, to repeat, such pioneering ventures only pointed the way to decisive changes that took place in the later decades.

In the area of quasi-medical charities one may recall those in aid of the various categories of the physically handicapped, notably the blind and the deaf. Immemorially, blindness has excited the compassion of the charitable, and those so afflicted have always seemed to have a special claim on the sympathy and alms of their less unfortunate brethren. Some of the funds for their relief, such as the pensions administered by City Companies, might be of considerable antiquity. But, as we have seen, institutional care and training of the blind was introduced

[28] Cecil Woodham-Smith, *Florence Nightingale, 1820–1910* (London, 1950), p. 346. Rathbone's work is discussed in Chapter XVI below.

[29] "The Unseen Charities of London," *Fraser's Magazine,* 39:640–41 (June 1849); *Low's Charities of London in 1861,* pp. 35–36.

only in the 1790's, first in Liverpool and then in Bristol, Edinburgh, and London. The early Victorians not only added to the institutions benefiting the blind but also developed new methods of aiding them. Of such, for example, were the London Society for Teaching the Blind to Read (1839), the Home Teaching Society for the Blind (1855), and the Association for Promoting the General Welfare of the Blind (1856), this last an agency to assist the blind in supporting themselves.

Although the most handsome enlargement of the country's resources for the blind came only in the 1880's with the Gardner bequest of £300,000, the earlier decades registered a genuine advance. In the 1830's, for example, they profited from a legacy of £100,000 left by Charles Day of the City firm Day & Martin for those who, like himself, had been deprived of their sight. The Court of Chancery, however, elected to employ the income not very productively in small pensions. In 1861 Low can list sixteen metropolitan agencies and funds for the welfare of the blind and the deaf, all of them save the older pension funds, the School for the Indigent Blind at St. George's Fields, and the Asylum for Deaf and Dumb Children (1792) postdating 1820. These various efforts accounted for an annual income of about £45,000, of which nearly a third represented voluntary contributions. The provincial story was similar, with something like forty charities for the blind and the deaf dating from the 1820–60 period.[30]

Among the causes whose appeal, as we have seen, benevolent Victorians found most irresistible, were those having to do with the preservation of female virtue or the rehabilitation of those who had lost it.[31] The large number of institutions launched during the period represented a high degree of specialization and included not only refuges of various types but more militant agencies working for the legal protection of women, the suppression of brothels, and the punishment of procurers. What fraction of London's charitable income may have gone into this work it is hardly possible even to guess. We can only note Low's 1861 estimate of nearly £95,000 in revenue, of which £43,000 was in benefactions and nearly £52,000 in dividends, rents, and receipts from work done by inmates.

4

Low's guide devotes a considerable number of pages to pension funds established for the benefit of persons of standing who had been the victims of untoward circumstances. Such charities were thought by the Victorians to be especially worthy, for they served a class of unfortunates who, critics of charitable practice charged, were often neglected while benevolence was showered on the more clamant but less worthy destitute. It is hard to classify such arrangements, for in many instances, especially those benefiting particular trades or professions, they were as much provident funds as charities. The Licensed Victuallers Fund (1794),

---

[30] Based on the dates of founding as given in the *Annual Charities Register and Digest.*
[31] See above, n. 2.

a case in point, paid out over £375,000 in its sixty-five years, but to qualify for benefits one had to pay an admission fee of three guineas and to subscribe to the *Morning Advertiser* (the victuallers' newspaper, whose profits contributed heavily to the fund) while in business and upon retiring to pay 22s. a year in lieu of a subscription.[32] Some were closer to mutual insurance companies or friendly societies than charities, while others depended heavily on voluntary contributions from nonmembers or, as with the City Companies and some of the more affluent trade associations, on subsidies from the general funds of the organization. Low was able to discover seventy-two such professional funds, with an annual income of £173,000, of which £55,500 was put down to voluntary contributions. This figure does not include twenty pension funds for clergymen or Dissenting ministers, which accounted for another £50,000. Low estimates that about £250,000 was received and, after allowing for heavy overhead costs, was distributed to perhaps twelve thousand individuals.[33]

The less restrictive pension arrangements covered a good deal of charitable ground. Gentlewomen, governesses, and others came in for assistance from the Governesses' Benevolent Institution, the Establishment for Gentlewomen during Temporary Illness, the Friendly Female Society, and the Home for Gentlewomen (in reduced circumstances), not to mention the Ladies' Institution for Females of Weak Intellect at Chiswick. A number of agencies, such as the National Benevolent Institution, the Royal General Annuity Society, the British Beneficent Institution, and the City of London General Pension Society, were dedicated to providing pensions for decayed business and professional men and their survivors. Of these the most notable was the National Benevolent Institution, established in 1812 largely through the efforts of Peter Hervé, the painter of miniatures. From the beginning this was a relatively select charity and, once on its feet, a well-supported one. During its first half century the National Benevolent granted £183,000 to over a thousand pensioners, chiefly indigent gentlemen and members of the professions, and as early as 1836 its annual expenditure was exceeding £5600.[34] It was not long before the Institution began to attract legacies from those who were touched by the plight of members of their own social stratum. In 1860, for example, of an income of £11,500, about £4000 came from annual subscriptions and the rest from legacies and dividends.[35]

In Low's roll call of London charities is included a category which, though heterogeneous and hard to define, seemed especially deserving to Victorian philanthropists. This appeared under the rubric of organizations "for aiding the industrious," and it comprehended such ill-assorted agencies as institutions for training and aiding servants and for assisting needlewomen and milliners, and a series of day nurseries for the infant children of working mothers. Here also Low lists the

---

[32] *Low's Charities of London in 1861*, p. 146.
[33] *Ibid.*, p. 120.
[34] E. Evelyn Barron, *The National Benevolent Institution, 1812–1936* (London, 1936), p. 34.
[35] *Low's Charities of London in 1861*, p. 121.

county societies, which had been formed on the model of the original Hereford Society (1710) and which, among their other activities, financed the apprenticing of children from their respective counties. The income of this entire group of twenty-one agencies is estimated at about £8500, three-quarters of it from benefactions.

This catalogue does not begin to exhaust the six-hundred-plus institutions listed by Low. Some of these are noticed elsewhere, the housing projects in a later section and certain agencies called forth by urban conditions in the preceding chapter. Such institutions in the London area — that is, reformatories, industrial schools, and miscellaneous agencies for the relief of street destitution — numbered forty-five, and, according to Low's estimate, enjoyed an annual income of not less than £100,000. Other distinctively urban charities might also have been recalled, as, for example, the attempt to combat the lack of sanitary facilities by providing baths and washhouses. The committee to promote the cause throughout the country dated from the mid-'40's, and the first establishment was set up in Liverpool. Within fifteen years the bathhouses of the Metropolis were credited with the awesome total of two million baths a year. Although it required the initiative of philanthropists to launch the movement, baths and washhouses presently became self-supporting from the small fees paid by their patrons. The need for free drinking fountains for thirsty city dwellers, who might otherwise be tempted to allay their thirst in less wholesome fashion, resulted in the forming of the Metropolitan Free Drinking Fountain Association (Samuel Gurney, treasurer) in 1859. In this movement Liverpool had been in the van, but the Metropolitan Association carried on an active campaign both to raise money for its own fountains and to persuade possible donors to proceed on their own account. Two years later London could claim more than eighty fountains, some presumably antedating the Association, built at a cost of about £20,000.[36]

Aggregate statistics for charitable giving almost inevitably understate the reality. Even apart from the individual almsgiving which leaves no record, a large volume of benevolence was comprehended in *ad hoc* collections, both local and nationwide. Only the latter — the various patriotic funds and the collection in 1861 for Indian famine sufferers — have achieved much of a place in the annals of Victorian philanthropy. The kind of generosity which responded to appeals in *The Times,* as when in the winter of 1859 the Reverend H. Douglas raised £15,000 for his starving parishioners in the Victoria Dock district, does not figure in the totals.[37]

The "poor-boxes" in metropolitan police courts offer another case in point. These boxes, intended originally for the relief of cases of conspicuous destitution or misfortune coming before the magistrates, were so generously patronized as to become an embarrassment. Police magistrates had neither the time nor training to serve as public almoners. The Southwark Police Court, to take a single instance,

[36] *Ibid.,* pp. 49–51.
[37] *Ibid.,* p. 80.

was hard-pressed to know what to do with £1371 received in the winter of 1860, especially when nearly £300 additional had been carried over from the previous year, and had to call on the aid of clergy, lady visitors, city missionaries, and others. The magistrates of the Metropolis were obliged to discourage contributions beyond the amount necessary to relieve the deserving cases which they encountered in line of duty.[38]

Emergencies and disasters could always be depended upon to arouse the public-spirited to action. London, according to Low's estimate, raised an average of £100,000 a year for such purposes.[39] Even to begin to recall these various efforts would be out of the question. Sometimes, as in the case of Lloyd's Patriotic Fund, set on foot in 1803 for the relief of the survivors of British soldiers and sailors, and of the Patriotic Fund, which dates from the Crimean War, such collections evolved into charitable foundations which continued or extended their activities beyond the original purpose.

Certainly the most imposing of these efforts was that carried on by the Royal Commission of the National Patriotic Fund which in the years 1854–57 raised over £1.5 million and in the course of it so gravely overestimated the claim of war widows and orphans as to leave a substantial balance. The Commissioners therefore broadened their operations, founding the Royal Victorian Patriotic Asylum (now the Royal Victoria Patriotic School) for war orphans and maintaining numbers of children at other institutions. Ultimately the Commissioners became a quasi-official relief agency which administered a series of patriotic emergency funds.[40] The Indian Mutiny Relief Fund, for which about £475,000 was raised in three years, gave further evidence of the immediate and lavish response evoked by distress resulting from service to the nation. The promoters of such efforts were neither the first nor last to discover how much more readily pockets are turned inside out for a dramatic emergency or national crisis than for the year-by-year requirements of constructive philanthropy.

5

The years 1820–60 also saw the launching of a number of national organizations, which, though not easily classifiable, stand out as among the most imposing and characteristic of British charitable undertakings. Pre-eminent among these were the Royal National Life-boat Institution and the Royal Society for the Prevention

[38] *Ibid.*, pp. 8off. The embarrassment caused by the large poor box fund collected by the Thames Police Office during the winter of 1860–61 is described by two magistrates, E. Yardley and H. S. Selfe before the *S. C. on Poor Relief* (England), 1861, Q. 2177ff and 3911ff.

[39] *Ibid.*, p. 163. This amount clearly represented more than the benevolence of Londoners. The headquarters of emergency funds were ordinarily in the Metropolis, but they received contributions from all over the Kingdom. The National Patriotic Fund is not, of course, included in Low's estimate of £100,000 a year in emergency funds.

[40] By the late century the Fund approached the million mark, and the accumulated surplus of income presented a problem. A Select Committee recommended that the Commissioners be given greater discretionary power in dealing with surplus funds. (*S. C. on the Royal National Patriotic Fund*, 1895, 1896.)

of Cruelty to Animals, both of which managed to link philanthropy with other interests close to the British heart.

To Americans it is something of a paradox that in semi-socialized Britain an essential service, which in the United States from the early days was handled by the Coast Guard, is left to a private charitable agency. Like many other things that foreigners find mysterious in British life, this is the result of historical circumstance, almost of historical accident. During most of its career the R.N.L.I. carried out its duties so satisfactorily and with so little expense to the public purse, and over the decades became so solidly entrenched that the twentieth-century social revolution left its position unshaken. Founded in 1824, the Institution owed its existence to the joint efforts of Sir William Hillary, who, while a resident of the Isle of Man, had witnessed a series of appalling shipwrecks, and Thomas Wilson, M.P. for the City of London.[41] Although the patronage of George IV and initial receipts of nearly £10,000 seemed to forecast a prosperous life for the new philanthropy, decline set in at once. During the 1830's contributions fell from a high of £1714 to a low of £254, and throughout the 1840's failed to reach £800.[42]

What began to change the fortunes of the Institution was the tragic disaster at South Shields in December 1849, which cost the lives of twenty of a lifeboat crew of twenty-four. The renewed interest in the neglected service was effectively capitalized by the Institution, and when in the early '50's the Duke of Northumberland became president, its fortunes took a sharp turn for the better. As the table indicates, receipts mounted strikingly.[43] From the 1850's on, the position of the R.N.L.I. was markedly strengthened by legacies and special gifts until in the

YEARS	ANNUAL AVERAGE
1851–60	£ 6,400
1861–70	33,000
1871–80	50,500
1881–90	71,700

decade 1887–96, there were some 225 of these, the largest a bequest of £50,000 for twenty lifeboats and carriages, with maintenance.[44]

The Institution became one of the more genuinely national of British charities. It was hard, after all, to resist the appeal of an agency that could claim to have saved nearly forty thousand lives in seventy years.[45] The committee showed more than a little astuteness, after the reorganization of the early '50's, in encouraging donors to finance lifeboats as memorials for departed relatives or thank-offerings for escapes from drowning, with the privilege of naming the craft. Individual benefactors were followed by cities, towns, corporate bodies, clubs, and other

[41] The following account, save where otherwise noted, is based on Patrick Howarth, *The Life-Boat Story* (London, 1957), and Dawson, *Britain's Life-Boats*.

[42] R.N.L.I., *10th Ann. Rept.*, 1839; *S. C. on the R.N.L.I.*, 1897, App. 7.

[43] Sir E. Birkbeck, *S. C. on the R.N.L.I.*, 1897, Q. 2; App. 7.

[44] *Ibid.*, Q. 21; App. 29.

[45] *Ibid.*, Q. 2.

groups, who provided specific pieces of equipment. In fact, the Institution suffered from the affliction, chronic among certain charities, of an adequate supply of material equipment but a shortage of funds for maintenance and miscellaneous needs.

Even with the large income on which the R.N.L.I. could count, in some years the committee had to draw heavily on capital — in 1890, for more than £33,000.[46] During the 1880's, to look beyond the chronological limits of this chapter, there was uneasiness over the relatively narrow base on which the finances of the Institution rested. Roughly two-thirds of the regular income was provided by about a hundred individuals.[47] The solution, introduced at Manchester in 1891 by Charles (later Sir Charles) Macara, who took a leaf out of the book of voluntary-hospital financing, was the Lifeboat Saturday Fund, which spread to the larger cities and towns through the Kingdom and added thousands of pounds to the income of the Institution. In 1896, for example, it accounted for over £16,000, about 14 per cent of the total revenue of over £117,000:[48]

£39,673	subscriptions and donations
16,367	Saturday Fund
17,548	dividends and interest
43,449	legacies

The Institution has never been in imminent danger of nationalization, and, save for some small payments from the Board of Trade in 1854-69, it has carried on without financial assistance from the State. Not only that, but at the Grosvenor Gardens headquarters one senses a determination, born of a long and honorable tradition, to continue as an independent service, neither subsidized nor controlled by public agencies.[49] For the Institution the closest call came in the mid-1890's, when charges in a number of periodical articles led to the appointment of a Select Committee to examine the allegations and canvass the case for nationalization.[50] Most of the charges were dismissed as groundless, including that of having issued misleading financial statements, though it appeared that the Institution's form of accounts left something to be desired. On the larger question, the Committee came out solidly against nationalization of the lifeboat service, "so long as it is maintained as efficiently and successfully as at present by public benevolence."[51]

The year 1824, which gave birth to the R.N.L.I., also marked the official founding of the Royal Society for the Prevention of Cruelty to Animals. The formal organization, however, was preceded by a period of some uneasiness and mild agitation. Eighteenth-century humanitarians had protested on occasion against

[46] Charles Macara, *ibid.,* Q. 10,638.
[47] *Ibid.*
[48] *Ibid.,* p. v.
[49] See Howarth, *Life-Boat Story,* pp. 64ff.
[50] The principal attack, "Nationalising the Lifeboat Service" by E. H. Bayley, appeared in the *Westminster Review,* 147:120-27 (February 1897).
[51] *S. C. on the R.N.L.I.,* 1897, pp. vi-ix.

brutal treatment of animals, and, after the turn of the century, there were a number of moves to establish a degree of legal protection for them. Lord Erskine, when Lord Chancellor, sponsored such a proposal, and at least one society "for the Suppression of Wanton Cruelty to Animals" enjoyed a fleeting existence.[52] The first decisive step was taken when Richard "Humanity" Martin, a warm-hearted, peppery, slightly eccentric Irish M.P., succeeded in getting on the statute book a fairly comprehensive, if not very precise, measure intended to assure for horses, cattle, and sheep a minimum of protection.[53]

If Martin was the forerunner, the founder of the Society was the Reverend Arthur Broome of St. Mary's, Bromley-by-Bow, who resigned his living to give undivided attention to the work. After some false starts, he succeeded in June 1824 in launching an organization whose two chief committees included a number of names notable in early-century philanthropy, T. F. Buxton, Wilberforce, Samuel Gurney, and Sir James Mackintosh. Like many associations whose aims cannot be reduced to a single simple reform, the Society was faced at the outset with the issue of tactics. Should it set up as a prosecuting society, with paid agents, or should it take a more irenic path of public education and propaganda? As is often the case, the tactical question was settled by compromise. The Society was to seek to change public sentiment toward the treatment of animals, "to spread amongst the lower orders of people . . . a degree of moral feeling which would compel them to think and act like those of a superior class." [54] Yet it was not to shrink from legal action. During its first year, in fact, the Society carried out 149 successful prosecutions.[55]

The early years of the S.P.C.A. formed no record of unbroken triumph. Activities exceeded financial resources. Broome was held legally responsible for the Society's debts and thrown into prison, while his successor, Lewis Gompertz, fell foul of the sectarian biases of the committee, which would accept nothing less than a solidly Christian organization. During the 1830's, however, some progress seemed visible: public opinion appeared a little more sympathetic, and some legislative successes were recorded. In 1840, when the young Queen in renewing her patronage allowed the Society to use the prefix "Royal," it was clear that the work would survive — on what scale was still to be established.

What Charles Loch was to the Charity Organisation Society, John Colam was to the R.S.P.C.A., and his forty-five years (1860–1905) as secretary roughly paralleled Loch's reign over the C.O.S. During his tenure, to look ahead, the Society's inspectors increased from six or seven to 157, and its branches from almost none to over 425. Of the growth in R.S.P.C.A. resources it is difficult to speak, since the centenary history is reticent about such matters. By the turn of the century, however, the annual income of the Society (including its branches) had

[52] This was a Liverpool organization. (Fairholme and Paine, *Century of Work for Animals*, p. 23.)

[53] 3 Geo. IV, c. 71.

[54] Speech of the chairman, T. F. Buxton. (Fairholme and Paine, p. 55.)

[55] *Ibid.*, p. 59.

reached £40,000, and it had become one of the standard charities remembered by British maiden ladies and others when making their wills.[56] In special crises, particularly those where patriotism and British affection for animals coincided, the R.S.P.C.A. could raise funds of astonishing dimensions. A case in point is the £200,000 collected and spent for the welfare of Army animals during the First World War.[57]

Animal-lovers tend to be people of pronounced views, at least where their pets are concerned, sometimes verging on the cranky. The R.S.P.C.A. has had its share of difficulties with a membership which ranges from militant vegetarians to those broadly opposed to inflicting wanton cruelty on animals. On vivisection, a perennially hot issue in R.S.P.C.A. circles, the only possible position was to refuse to take one, and the Society declined to commit itself, as an organization, on the issue. The coming of the motor age has, of course, altered the situation and policies of the Society, for the horse was perhaps the greatest beneficiary of its concern. Yet well before this revolution, the Victorian public had absorbed the message of the R.S.P.C.A., and had become convinced that the mass maltreatment of animals was not to be tolerated.

6

One of the major categories in Low's survey consists of foreign and home missionary societies and other agencies whose essential aims were religious. Such organizations, in much of their work, lie beyond the scope of this study, but we may at least note that few, if any, branches of philanthropy showed a more striking gain in resources. To look at the figures for a sample group of foreign missionary societies is to realize that, whatever might be happening to the wicked, the virtuous were flourishing like the green bay tree. In 1861, five of the larger societies had an aggregate income exceeding £450,000:[58]

Church Missionary Society	£145,000
Methodist Missionary Society	107,000
London Missionary Society	95,000
Society for the propagation of the Gospel	90,000
Baptist Missionary Society	30,000

The whole body of twenty-five foreign missionary funds and societies had a total income of over £570,000 in voluntary contributions and another £66,000 in dividends and interest.[59]

It is impossible to deal with the home missionary effort in even these far from precise terms. What is called home missionary work embraces such a variety of activities, religious and semisecular, that any totals must be regarded as arbitrary.

[56] *Ibid.*, p. 288; *Annual Charities Register and Digest,* 1904, p. 513.
[57] Fairholme and Paine, p. 213.
[58] *Low's Charities of London in 1861*, pp. 256–57.
[59] *Ibid.*, p. xi.

Low's figures for fifty-six heterogeneous enterprises operating outside the regular church organization are worth noticing simply as another element in the complicated structure of Victorian giving. In 1860 these organizations received in voluntary contributions over £332,500 and nearly £36,000 in interest and dividends.[60]

Such a casual survey of early Victorian philanthropy must inevitably be misleading. Even for London, much has been left out — causes on which charitable Britons spent a greater or less amounts of money — and it has taken only incidental account of provincial giving. But to be more inclusive would be difficult and unrewarding. No one could possibly cover, or would wish to cover, the vast numbers of small, sometimes ephemeral, societies for every conceivable purpose. During the mid-century associative philanthropy ran riot, and those who complained about the multiplicity of organizations, as did practically everyone familiar with the charity world, were only too justified. No doubt there are all sorts of explanations: the demand of each communion to have its full panoply of auxiliary societies; the notorious readiness of the Anglo-Saxon to create a society whenever convinced of a job to be done; the fission of older agencies; bequests in trust around which organizations grew; and, to be fair, the emergence of new social needs. Of the vast numbers of charities, sensible and silly, trivial and significant, there can be no doubt, nor of the fact that their receipts were far in excess of Low's estimates.

Still, one may note once more, the pride which the Victorians took in their philanthropy was tinged with uncertainty and disappointment. Was charitable work accomplishing what it had set out to do? Was there the kind of improvement in the poor that the charity promoters had forecast so hopefully? With all the talk about getting at causes, was philanthropy acting to prevent or merely to palliate, and even in some instances to aggravate? Although hospitals, schools, housing projects, and provident societies were generally acclaimed, thoughtful Victorians could still doubt whether the expansion of charitable effort had brought a commensurate decline in destitution or an improvement in the condition of the lower classes. It is now a commonplace that the Victorians' picture of social distress was sadly out of focus, and that, to repeat, in conceiving of poverty as an individual moral failure rather than a social disease, they laid on private charity a burden that far exceeded its strength, with whatever degree of efficiency this might be organized and applied. For, although to the Victorians the ultimate salvation of the poor might lie with themselves, in the meantime philanthropy was left with heavier responsibilities than it could possibly discharge.

[60] *Ibid.*, p. x.

CHAPTER VII

THE "DOMESDAY BOOK" AND
THE CHARITY COMMISSION

EIGHTEENTH-CENTURY BRITAIN, to repeat a historical commonplace, was little interested in matters of administrative improvement, and it was natural that the country's charitable endowments should share in the official indifference. Yet the Gilbert Return of 1786, inadequate and inaccurate as it was, brought to the notice of British statesmen the charitable resources of the Kingdom and started the chain of events that led ultimately to a more positive policy. The Return, reprinted in 1810 and again in 1816, gave some suggestion of the extent and value of the nation's charitable trusts, and more than a suggestion that these stood in grave need of better administrative supervision. Conceivably the country was not getting full return from its endowments.

The radical charity reformer of mid-Victorian times would urge that the whole jungle of trusts, some of them obsolescent, archaic, and socially harmful, was due for drastic reorganization. The early century, however, was less demanding. The immediate problem was not how to revise obsolescent trusts or how to alter the expressed wishes of the founder, even when he had wished absurdly, but to correct some of the more flagrant abuses in administration. At the outset there was little thought of a permanent supervisory body; what was needed were more summary remedies for certain abuses and more summary methods of revising obsolete trusts. Remedy, it will be recalled, could be had only through the tortuous proceedings of Chancery. These were not only involved and expensive, but hazardous to the instigator. For the wheels of Chancery could be set turning only by the Attorney-General, who acted on information supplied by an individual, public-spirited to the point of sacrifice, who might have to pay heavily for his concern.[1] It is not surprising that the army of relators was by no means legion. A more summary way of dealing with administrative malpractice was plainly called for.

The first attempts at solution accomplished little beyond demonstrating the good intentions of their sponsors. The Charitable Donations Registration Act of 1812, which required the central listing of endowments with a view to preventing their

---

[1] *1 Hansard,* 19:515–16; *Memoirs of the Life of Sir Samuel Romilly, Written by Himself,* 3 vols. (London, 1840), II, 385.

possible loss, was honored more in the breach than the observance.[2] Likewise Sir Samuel Romilly's proposal to expedite and reduce the cost of Chancery proceedings advanced the cause only slightly.[3] Though the Charities Procedure Act (1812) was intended to provide a summary remedy, " 'summary'," a mid-century Attorney-General drily remarked, "must be interpreted according to the glossary of the Court of Chancery."[4] Not much progress was possible as long as even minor cases could be settled only through the intervention of Chancery.

The movement that led to a more positive policy, specifically to the creation of the Charity Commission, grew out of the grand inquiry into the country's endowments identified with the name of Henry Brougham. And it drew on the current of reform that can be called, not to be too precise about it, Scottish-Whig-Utilitarian. About these advocates of charity reform there was little of the humanitarian compassion and pity that drove such eighteenth-century philanthropists as Captain Coram or of the evangelical compulsions that inspired the activities of a Wilberforce or a Buxton. Rather were they men who were rightly convinced that the British legal and political system was full of outmoded elements. They sensed that a changing economic environment and shifts in the distribution of power among social classes demanded institutional adjustments. Whether conscious followers of Bentham or not — most of them were not — they were still utilitarians with a small *u*, and they tended to measure British institutions by criteria that the commercial and industrial middle classes understood and appreciated.

Among their specific reform demands, a more adequate system of education held a conspicuous place. For it was an individualistic and competitive, though orderly, society that they envisaged, one in which a selective process would operate equitably. Success should crown the efforts of those whose brains and character had brought them to the top in a competition open to all and in which none would be unduly handicapped. This ideal implied better educational facilities, both as a mechanism for screening out abler members of the lower middle and working classes and for furnishing the kind of minimal school training that an expanding urban society required.

The reformers, heavily Scottish themselves, could point to the North British arrangements as much superior to the English. In Scotland education was accepted as a public responsibility, and the provision of suitable schools formed an integral part of the parish system. The parish schools, which were public enterprises, though not free, were supplemented by private schools, and the two were presumed to work together sufficiently well to form a national system. Of the Scottish educational idea, the major prophet in England, at least the most articulate in the political sphere, was Henry Brougham.[5] Himself a product of the system, he

[2] 52 Geo. III, c. 102; Romilly, *Memoirs*, III, 20; *Journals of the House of Commons*, 20 March 1812; *1 Hansard*, 22:1119–20.

[3] 52 Geo. III, c. 101.

[4] Sir Frederick Thesiger (later Lord Chelmsford), *3 Hansard*, 120:21.

[5] New, *Brougham*, p. 199; see also L. J. Saunders, *Scottish Democracy, 1815–1840* (Edinburgh, 1950), pp. 241ff.

not unnaturally discovered a good deal of merit in it. In his public behavior Brougham sometimes laid himself open to ridicule; demagoguery came readily to him. Still, when the accounts are cast up, British liberal reform will emerge heavily in his debt. Whatever suspicions his championship of certain causes may have aroused, he had two entirely genuine reform interests in addition to his commitment to the antislavery crusade, law and education, and in the field of endowed charities the two came together. As a lawyer, Brougham was appalled by the laxity with which charitable trusts were being handled; as an educational enthusiast, he suspected that if these myriad endowments were properly administered, they would go a long way toward providing the country with a civilized educational system. And, one may add, as a quasi-Benthamite, he could look forward without terror to steps which might introduce a measure of rational order into the jumble of educational trusts. In short, the primary motive behind Brougham's demands for an inquiry into charitable endowments was his hope of putting many of them to effective educational use.

He directed his initial attack toward limited goals. His first proposals, moreover, were so manifestly unobjectionable as to raise no possible opposition. Those who agreed so readily to his motion in May 1816 for a Select Committee on the Education of the Poor in the Metropolis could hardly foresee that this modest project would burgeon out into a great survey which would cover nearly the whole field of English endowed charities, would occupy more than two decades, and would fill about forty volumes. The Committee, with Brougham as chairman and Romilly, Wilberforce, Mackintosh, and Thomas Babington among its members, not only conducted a whirlwind investigation into the various categories of schools specifically for the poor but also moved onto a higher rung and examined such foundations as Christ's Hospital, St. Paul's, and Charterhouse, whose class affiliations by this time were less definite. Brougham never hesitated to press such advantage as he enjoyed, and he was not reluctant to poke his investigating finger into ancient and dignified endowments. It was, in his view, unfortunate that London schools so often used their resources to board and clothe a small number of pupils rather than to provide education for a larger number.[6]

While the scrutiny of London charities was in progress (the Committee was reappointed in 1817), the chairman's alert nose sniffed an even more noisome reservoir of abuses in educational endowments outside the Metropolis, and he began to press for an inquiry of broader scope. What was indicated, he urged, was a commission, which, enjoying more latitude than a select committee, could go from place to place and take evidence on the spot. Parliament agreed to extend the range of Brougham's Committee to cover the entire Island, but his proposal to set up a commission was less hospitably received. Brougham had attempted to protect the bill from excessive revision by clearing it in advance with the Tory ministers. His original intention had been that the inquiry should include all endowed charities, but, as a result of ministerial objections, he agreed (with mental

---

[6] *1 Hansard*, 34:1230ff; New, *Brougham*, p. 211.

reservations) that, for the immediate future, its scope should be limited to education.[7]

Notwithstanding Brougham's precautions, the bill encountered heavy weather in Parliament. Old Harrovians Peel and Robinson were pained that the list of foundations to be exempted from the commission's attentions stopped with Oxford, Cambridge, Eton, Winchester, and Westminster. Others opposed even these exceptions, or threatened to add Rugby, Shrewsbury, and the free schools of Norwich, if Harrow were placed on the special list.[8] Brougham would have preferred no exemptions whatever, but the omission of Eton, Winchester, and Westminster could be plausibly defended on the ground that the Select Committee had already dealt with them. They and their statutes had been given something of a going-over by the Committee, which suspected that with the passage of time these foundations had been diverted from their original purpose of educating the poor. It was not a profitable controversy. An inordinate amount of zeal and erudition was spent, in and out of Parliament, on such questions as the precise meaning of *scholares pauperes et indigentes,* the class for which some of the foundations had been intended.

Of more critical importance was the question of scope. Brougham had agreed to limit the inquiry to certain educational charities, but he was not without hope that the House might extend the terms of reference. Even the casual inquiry of the Select Committee on Education had shown that charity abuses were by no means peculiar to educational foundations. Quantities of charity land appeared to have been let at rentals far below their market value, sometimes by trustees to themselves or their friends. An estate of 650 acres near Lincoln belonging to Meer Hospital was let for 10s. 6d. an acre, from which the poor Brethren received only £24, the balance apparently being appropriated by the Warden and his lessees.[9] This, no doubt, was exceptional, since the estate was a branch of the patronage system of the notorious Bishop Tomline. Less scandalous but hardly less baneful was the common practice of granting excessively long leases, thus sacrificing the advantage of rising land values, and of reletting merely for fines, with no advance in rent.

There was also the general problem of slipshod administration. Some charities, the Committee had reason to believe, had already been lost and others were in imminent danger.[10] More immediately relevant, however, was the simple fact that it would be frequently impossible for Commissioners to separate educational from noneducational endowments, so intermixed were they. A body of trustees in Yeovil, for example, watched over estates benefiting four different charities,

[7] *1 Hansard,* 36:822–23; 37:815ff, 1297–98; Henry Brougham, *A Letter to Sir Samuel Romilly . . . upon the Abuse of Charities* (London, 1818), p. 3.
[8] *1 Hansard,* 38:614–16.
[9] Brougham, *Letter to Romilly,* p. 13; *S. C. on the Education of the Lower Orders, 3d Rept.,* 1818, pp. 173ff.
[10] The Gilbert Returns had already supplied evidence. In Berkshire, for example, nearly £2000 in charity funds admittedly had been lost. (Francis Charles Parry, *An Account of Charitable Donations to Places within the County of Berkshire* [London, 1818], pp. 130ff.)

only one of which was a school. Yet the Commissioners, as Brougham put it, could "inspect the deeds and accounts relating to school revenue, but they must suddenly shut the book when they perceive any mention of other charities."[11]

Though the Commons finally agreed to his bill,[12] Brougham's premonitions of more determined opposition in the Lords were amply justified. Other things aside, the formidable presence of the Lord Chancellor was sufficient earnest of trouble ahead. For Eldon, though he might sometimes express disgust over the lax ways of trustees, was not going to be a party to this kind of intervention or to any implication that the remedies offered by the Court of Chancery were less than adequate. The passage, often quoted by reformers as evidence from an unwilling witness, implies a Lord Chancellor who might not be hostile to change: "It should be perfectly understood, that Charity Estates all over the Kingdom are dealt with in a manner grossly improvident; amounting to the most direct Breach of Trust."[13]

No impression could have been more illusory. In Eldon's eyes, it was a vexatious and needless interference that Brougham was proposing, not the less vexatious, of course, because Brougham was the proposer. The Lord Chancellor must have been stung by Brougham's attack in the Commons on the snail-like tempo of his Court. The only commission issued under Elizabeth 43 since 1787, we have seen, was still in 1818 awaiting final settlement. Although ripe for decision in 1808, the case had been becalmed in Chancery for a decade.[14] Yet in one respect the Tory Lord Chancellor had a firmer grasp on reality than did the exuberant Brougham when he pointed to the absurdity of allowing only £4000 for the expenses of the inquiry. This, he correctly charged, would not cover even a fortieth of the necessary work[15] Eldon may have considered forty times £4000 a fantastic sum, but, as it turned out, even his intentionally wild estimate was far too modest. When the bill was finally added up, the inquiry had cost more than £250,000.[16]

During its passage through the upper House, the Lords saddled the bill with amendments that Brougham regarded as crippling. The scope of the inquiry, expanded by the Commons, was contracted by the Lords. The Commissioners were now to confine themselves to educational charities, and they were also restricted in their power to require the attendance of witnesses and the production of documents. To the list of exempted institutions were added not only Harrow and Rugby but, more unhappily, all charities which were under the care of special visitors. These latter, in fact, included some of the more rancid situations unearthed by the Select Committee, such as that of the Pocklington School in Yorkshire, an ancient foundation which had visitors from St. John's College, Cambridge. By the nineteenth century this substantial endowment supported only one pupil,

---

[11] Brougham, *Letter to Romilly*, p. 15.
[12] *Public Bills*, 1818, I, 503 (d. 8 May 1818).
[13] *Attornely-General* v. *Griffith*, 13 Ves. Jun. 580.
[14] *1 Hansard*, 38:608.
[15] *Ibid.*, pp. 975–77.
[16] *Statement of the Expenses Incurred by the Commissioners* (*Parl. Pap.*, 1846).

and the school had been converted into a sawpit or lumber-room.[17] Brougham and his friends were naturally indignant over the manhandling the Lords had given their bill. For them Castlereagh's pledge to reconsider the business in the following session offered fairly cold comfort.[18]

Brougham was even more distressed when the personnel of the new Commission was announced and it turned out that only two of the names suggested by his Select Committee on Education had been appointed.[19] Presumably some of Brougham's pique resulted from the rejection "with silent contempt, by the eminent head of the Home Department [Castlereagh]," [20] of his own offer to serve as a Commissioner. But it was also his fear that nominees of the Tory Government, one of whom was supposed to have suggested that "a great anxiety for the welfare of the poor is symptomatic of Jacobinism," [21] would be more concerned to defend and justify than to expose.

The weeks following the debate in Parliament and the appointment of the Commissioners produced a barrage of charges and countercharges. Brougham's attack was embodied in his *Letter to Romilly,* which went through at least eleven editions.[22] The counterclaims of the Government appeared in a *Letter to the Rt. Hon. Sir William Scott,* one of the Commissioners against whose appointment Brougham had protested.[23] The author could find little virtue in Brougham or in his notions "that the principles of Adam Smith or the Scotch economists are to supersede the established maxims of the law of the land and of the constitution." [24] It all looked suspiciously like a Dissenting plot to get control of educational endowments and divert them to Lancasterian schools.

Neither side lacked literary support, nor did champions of individual foundations hesitate to defend them against Brougham's allegations.[25] The *Edinburgh Review,* of course, struck out on behalf of its leading political writer. Three articles on charity abuses, the Education Committee, and the new Commission, written on the basis of material supplied by Brougham,[26] appeared between March 1819 and January 1820. The most weighty assault, however, had already been mounted by the *Quarterly.* The seventy-seven-page article, written by the Regius Professor at Cambridge, James Henry Monk, but with substantial assistance from

[17] *S. C. on the Education of the Lower Orders, 3d Rept.,* 1818, pp. 144ff; Brougham, *Letter to Romilly,* p. 17.
[18] *1 Hansard,* 38:1212ff.
[19] Brougham, *Letter to Romilly,* p. 34.
[20] *Ibid.,* p. 40.
[21] *Ibid.,* pp. 35–36.
[22] The number listed in the British Museum Catalogue.
[23] The Catalogue notes five editions of this pamphlet.
[24] *Letter to Scott* (London, 1818), p. 59. The B. M. Catalogue attributes the pamphlet to Dean Ireland of Westminster, author of the *Letter* on the Croydon charities (n. 25 below).
[25] For example, W. L. Bowles, *Vindiciae Wykehamicae* (London, 1818); Liscombe Clarke, *A Letter to H. Brougham, Esq. . . . on Winchester College* (London, 1818); John Ireland, *A Letter to Henry Brougham . . .* (London, 1818). This last, by the Dean of Westminster, had to do with the charities of Croydon, which had come in for unfavorable mention.
[26] New, *Brougham,* p. 223.

Messrs. Gifford, Croker, and Canning, was marked predictably by a violent animus against Brougham, and it scored some telling points against his management of the undertaking. But the quality of the author's social understanding emerged in his startling conclusion from the evidence of the Committee on Education "that the profanation of the Sabbath is the almost universal cause from which the profligacy of the lower orders originates."[27] Here was the voice of Church and State Toryism denouncing the attack on "the frame of our Ecclesiastical polity." Interference with charitable endowments would be intolerable save as it served to return them to the original purpose of their founders. The *Quarterly* wanted no part of an inquiry which might bring them into the hands of the State and parcel "them out anew according to the lights of modern refinement."[28] To such Tory opinion Brougham's "march of mind" was anything but an inspiring procession.

2

The inquiry was thus to be carried on initially under restricted terms of reference and on a provisional basis. The Commissioners were not to venture outside the field of educational charities, and within the prescribed area they were barred from the two universities and their colleges, six public schools,[29] institutions having special visitors or overseers, cathedrals or collegiate churches, and Jewish or Quaker schools. Of the maximum fourteen Commissioners, only eight were to be paid, and, since it required a quorum of three to conduct an examination, progress would inevitably be slow. While this restriction obtained, there were only two teams of Commissioners on the road, though, with the help of an honorary Commissioner, another was formed to sit in London.[30]

Their first two reports, however, allayed some of the fears aroused by their appointment, and Brougham's *Letter to Romilly* had turned out to be effective propaganda for his cause.[31] In the spring of 1819, therefore, Castlereagh made good his commitment and moved to extend the terms of reference to include noneducational charities, though still, to Brougham's regret, exempting those with special visitors, an immunity which lasted until 1831.[32] He proposed also to increase the size of the Commission as a means of expediting its work. Henceforth there were to be twenty Commissioners, ten of them stipendiary and any two empowered to act as a board.[33] The Commission was thus given the form and vested with the powers that were to govern its work for more than a decade.

During this period the inquiry progressed steadily enough, but slowly and with

[27] *Quarterly Review*, 19:50 (January 1818). On the question of authorship see Hill Shine and Helen Chadwick Shine, *The Quarterly Review under Gifford* (Chapel Hill, 1949), p. 64.
[28] *Quarterly Review*, 19:567.
[29] Eton, Winchester, Westminster, Harrow, Rugby, and Charterhouse.
[30] W. Grant, *S. C. on Public Charities*, 1835, Q. 115.
[31] New, *Brougham*, p. 220.
[32] *S. C. on Public Charities*, 1835, Q. 23.
[33] *1 Hansard*, 40:660, 1154ff; 59 Geo. III, c. 81.

a disturbing lack of system. All of the Commissioners were barristers, some of them with active practices, who continued to carry on their professional pursuits, so that, more often than not, they could give only half or two-thirds of their time to the inquiry.[34] Nor was the survey proceeding according to any discoverable plan. Material on the charities of a city or county might be scattered through a half dozen or more volumes of reports. As the Select Committee of 1835 remarked critically, the charities of Bristol were dealt with in six volumes and Bedford in five, while for the County of York the student would have to examine more than twenty volumes. Some of this disjointed character resulted from the requirement that the Commissioners submit semiannual reports, and some from the fact that they were occasionally called upon to handle emergency situations in different parts of the country, but in a large degree the confusion reflected the casual direction of the undertaking. Individual Commissioners were allowed a good deal of leeway in arranging their schedules, and a central plan was conspicuously lacking.[35]

The typical investigating team was composed of two Commissioners and a clerk. On arriving at a new place, they first attempted to take an accurate inventory of the charities to be studied, and then issued summonses to those who were presumably best able to supply the necessary information. In this routine the Commissioners were beset by a variety of difficulties, one of the most puzzling that of a simple lack of information. As Dr. Folliott remarked, when informed by the Commissioners of their mission to inquire into the public charities of his village: "The state of the public charities, sir, is exceedingly simple. There are none. The charities here are all private, and so private, that I for one know nothing of them."[36] Although notices of the visit were regularly inserted in the county paper, few local people seem to have appeared without specific invitation.[37] The Commissioners were convinced that there was no substitute for investigation on the spot, where oral testimony could be taken and deeds and other documents scrutinized. It did not follow, however, that a personal visit would necessarily make the task an easy one. The Commissioners were constantly learning of lost records or of records alleged by their custodians to have been lost, and occasionally were met by a flat refusal to produce documents, as when the Dean and Chapter of Lincoln barred a Commissioner from materials relating to the scandalous conditions at the Meer Hospital. The Dean's claim that this disreputable charity belonged among the exempt institutions did not prevent the Commissioners from certifying it to the Attorney-General.[38]

During most of the 1820's the Commissioners pursued their labors without intervention by Parliament, and by the end of the decade had issued twenty-four

---

[34] S. C. on Public Charities, 1835, Q. 26, 50ff.
[35] Ibid., Q. 310ff.
[36] Thomas Love Peacock, Crotchet Castle, chap. VIII, "Science and Charity."
[37] S. C. on Public Charities, 1835, Q. 101, 108ff.
[38] 32d Rept. of the [Brougham] Commissioners, Part IV, 1839, pp. 394–99.

reports covering charities having a total annual income of over £500,000.[39] This was essentially a fact-finding enterprise, an inventory of the nation's charitable endowments rather than a procedure for correcting their abuses. There was little that the Commissioners could do unless the maladministration were so gross as to justify their reporting it to the Attorney-General so that he might start up the ponderous machinery of Chancery. Short of this, their only remedial action lay in the salutary influence of their published reports on careless or inefficient trustees. It was either all or next to nothing.

In the late '20's the Commission acquired a Parliamentary gadfly in the person of Daniel Whittle Harvey, economy-minded radical and newspaper publisher. Between 1828 and 1835, sometimes in collaboration with Joseph Hume, he introduced a series of motions critical of the work of the Commission, its slowness, its cost, and the meager number of suits instituted to correct abuses.[40] More knowledgeable men, notably Peel (who had opposed the Commission originally but had now discovered merit in it) and Brougham, undertook to set him right. They stressed the importance of the main achievement of the Commissioners, an accurate, detailed record of every charitable endowment in the country, and they insisted that the simple fact of investigation had itself abated evils in charity administration and, in many instances, had made it unnecessary to start proceedings.[41]

The earlier Commission expired in July 1830, and it was not until sixteen months later that a new Act[42] set the wheels in motion again, to turn, it was hoped, at an accelerated rate. When this Commission came to an end in late 1834, the great bulk of English charities, some 26,751 of them, had been dealt with, though about half of Wales and six English counties remained wholly untouched, as well as several others only partly finished.[43] Daniel Whittle Harvey, who had now worked himself into a more constructive attitude toward the Commission, was not alone in his feeling that, unless something was done, this might develop into an inquiry in perpetuity. His motion for a Select Committee to examine the evidence of the Commissioners and to consider measures for completing the inquiry empowered the Committee also to deal with the larger question of the proper administration of charity funds. No fair-minded observer could regard the filing of information with the Attorney-General as even an approach to a solution. It was only necessary to note the scandals unearthed by the Commissioners to which no corrective treatment had been applied, mired, as were the cases, in Chancery proceedings. Neither for the first nor last time, Parliament was reminded that ordinary equity procedures were ill-adapted to most charity cases and that

[39] *S. C. on Public Charities*, 1835, p. v.

[40] *3 Hansard*, 18:981–85; 21:1756–57.

[41] *Ibid.*, 21:1759.

[42] 1 & 2 Will. IV, c. 34. For the succession of Acts renewing the Commission see *Tudor on Charities*, 4th ed. (1906), pp. 21–22. For the present purpose this edition is more useful than the later (1929) revision.

[43] *S. C. on Public Charities*, 1835, p. vi.

what was needed was an easy, prompt, and inexpensive method of dealing with such questions.[44]

The Select Committee on Public Charities was a better than average group, with Harvey himself as chairman and with Russell, Peel, Goulburn, and Hume among its members. There was no doubt in the Committee that the inquiry, which had already cost something over £200,000, must be brought to an early conclusion, and the obvious method was to increase drastically the number of Commissioners and to permit them to act individually rather than only in pairs. These improvements, the Committee held, should enable the inquiry to meet the deadline of 1 March 1837. Beyond this, however, was the more basic question, termed by the Committee a matter of "national concern," that of ensuring a reasonably efficient management of endowments yielding about a million annually. How could these be adequately supervised? Here the Committee did not hesitate to prescribe what must have seemed to some a moderately heroic treatment, though the notion of a central supervisory agency was familiar enough. The Poor Law Commission had just been brought into existence and had not yet acquired the full measure of odium that it was later to achieve, and the Ecclesiastical Commission was about to be created. For the overseeing of endowed charities the Committee's remedy was roughly that which Parliament was persuaded to adopt two decades later, a board of three Commissioners. They would superintend the sale and exchange of charity property, scrutinize charity accounts, appoint and remove trustees in certain circumstances, remove, where necessary, masters and ushers of endowed schools, and suggest schemes for the government of charities and the correction of abuses in their constitution and administration.[45] Such proposals were hardly revolutionary, and, especially when one recalls their impeccable sponsorship, it seems odd that they should have been left dangling for nearly twenty years.

3

Stimulated by the increase in staff and the more efficient procedure recommended by the Committee, the grand inquest was pushed to completion. The final report, the thirty-second, appeared in six parts between 1837 and 1840. It is difficult, perhaps hardly worth while, to do more than hint at the contents of the huge "Domesday Book." County by county, parish by parish, though in a rather unsystematic fashion, the Commissioners had covered the country, attempting to elicit and record the main facts about the nearly thirty thousand endowments. They drew their information from trustees and other local informants, from indentures, wills, and such legal documents as might be available, and from miscellaneous parish artifacts — tablets in churches and the like. The result of their labors, staggering in bulk and impressive in its detail, forms an indispensable work of reference for students of endowed charities, ancient or modern, and it

---

[44] 3 Hansard, 28:675ff.
[45] S. C. on Public Charities, 1835, pp. viii–ix.

remains perhaps the most frequently consulted work in the office of the Charity Commissioners.

The usefulness of the reports was considerably enhanced by the Analytical Digest, compiled in 1840 and issued a few years later, which sets forth in tabular form the essential data on each charity, together with a precise reference to the full Report.[46] From the summary one can obtain an admirable panorama view of the British charities in their financial aspect. Their capital resources were as follows:[47]

Land acreage	442,915
Funds, Bank and India Stock	£5,656,746
Mortgages and other Personalty	£1,001,782

In their holdings of charity land, English counties ran all the way from Norfolk with more than 28,000 acres and Durham with more than 22,000 to Cumberland's 1380 and Cornwall's 1249. As would be expected, the Welsh counties were most meagerly supplied, only five of them with more than 1000 acres and two (Cardigan and Carmarthen) with less than 250. The charities of London were, of course, the most liberally endowed of all, with more than 47,000 acres scattered throughout the Kingdom, of which the Royal Hospitals accounted for nearly 34,000. In charity investments in the funds, stocks, and mortgages, the more heavily urbanized counties naturally made the strongest showing. Middlesex with nearly £370,000 and Kent with nearly £310,000 head the list, while the poorest of the English counties were Cornwall, Bedford (though Bedford did well enough in total charity resources), and Huntingdon, with only about £10,500, and so down to Cardigan which had only about £2500. London again must be regarded as a special case, with charity investments exceeding £1,825,000, of which about £865,000 was in the hands of the Royal Hospitals, nearly £750,000 in those of the City Companies, and over £220,000 in parochial charities.

More significant, however, was the matter of income, and here the Commissioners reported on endowments having a total annual yield of £1,209,397, comprising:[48]

Rent	£874,314
Rent-charge	79,930
Interest	255,151

In income the most prosperous counties (exclusive of London, whose charity revenue, owing chiefly to the Royal Hospitals and the Livery Companies, exceeded £250,000) turned out to be the West Riding (about £53,000), Kent (about £40,000), and Surrey (about £38,000), and the poorest were Huntingdon (£3650), Cumberland (£3400), and Cornwall (£3250). Once more Cardigan

---

[46] The *Digest* appears in the *Parliamentary Papers* for 1843, XVI, XVII.

[47] *Digest*, II, 826–27.

[48] *Ibid.* This tabulation undervalues the total of endowment income, for, as later transpired, the Commissioners missed a considerable number of charities — something like four thousand of them.

brought up the rear, with only £371 of charity income. What was especially striking about the income figures was the vast number of minute endowments. Of
the 28,880 charities listed by the Commissioners, nearly half (13,331) yielded less
than £5 a year, and only 1749 returned more than £100.[49] Obviously any agency
set up to supervise charitable trusts would find itself handling a considerable
volume of petty detail.

The Brougham Commissioners attempted no functional breakdown of the
charity income of the Kingdom, beyond reporting the total for educational purposes as about £312,500.[50] But there is no reason to suspect that the proportions
devoted to the various charitable purposes would have shifted drastically between
the time of the Brougham inquiry and the 1860's and '70's, when the Charity
Commissioners issued a new Digest. This included, as its largest component, the
charities covered by the earlier Report, but it also took into account those established after and those omitted, for one reason or another, from that tabulation.
The later Digest showed education holding first place and comprising about 30
per cent of the total, as compared with the 26 per cent shown in the Brougham
figures. This was followed by almshouses and pensions, doles in money or kind
(vast in numbers but generally of small amounts) and endowments for the general
uses of the poor, and medical charities. Beyond these one moves into the minor
but familiar categories of apprenticeship funds, endowments for lectures and
sermons, and trusts for public purposes.[51]

All in all, the achievement of the Brougham Commissioners was an imposing
one. The mass of accumulated benevolence which their Report exposed justified
an outburst of self-congratulation on the part of Parliamentary orators and
others. Here, indeed, was a social phenomenon unique in history and a reservoir
of public resources which, as patriotic spirits liked to note, constituted one of the
glories of the British way of life.[52] This was true in spite of the frequent examples
of ineptitude, mismanagement, and occasionally worse, that the inquiry revealed.
For there was this other side, and the Commissioners were concerned to bring
it to light. In the course of their labors they certified about four hundred charities
to the Attorney-General, who filed informations against a large share.[53] Their
primary assignment was that of surveying and reporting, and this they carried

[49] The various categories (as given by the R. C. for Inquiring into Cases Reported but not Certified
[1849], 1st Rept., 1850, p. 3) were as follows:

Under £5	13,331	£50 to £100	1,540
£5 to £10	4,641	£100 to £500	1,417
£10 to £20	3,908	£500 to £1000	209
£20 to £30	1,866	£1000 to £2000	73
£30 to £50	1,799	Over £2000	50

The total of these figures, incidentally, comes to about 35 less than the 28,880 reported by the
Brougham Commissioners.
[50] In 1843 they also listed the dole charities for the poor but without attempting to give their
total value. This summary is printed in the Parliamentary Papers, 1843, XVIII.
[51] General Digest (Parl. Pap., 1877, LXVI), pp. 16–19.
[52] Nicholas Carlisle, An Historical Account of the Origin of the Commission (London, 1828), p. 3.
[53] R. C. for Inquiring into Cases Reported but not Certified (1849) 1st Rept., 1850, p. 3.

out with scrupulous objectivity. Yet they also looked forward to laying the ground-work for a more rational charity policy. To their final factual Report they there-fore appended a brief summary of their observations and a series of recommenda-tions for the future.

Of such gross abuses as outright peculation and breach of trust the Commis-sioners found gratifyingly few examples. What was more disturbing was the bur-densome legal arrangements which, in many instances, made the efficient manage-ment of charities almost impossible. The essential weakness was the lack of a jurisdiction more summary than that of the equity courts, for, above all, some authority was needed which could act promptly and inexpensively to make what were often fairly minor decisions. Such an issue was that of appointing trustees in cases, perhaps, where no trustees had been legally invested by the donor or where their appointment had not been renewed. Sometimes aged or incompetent trustees had to be replaced by those who would carry on their duties properly. There was, for example, the case of Sir John Glanville's Gift at Tavistock, a seventeenth-century charity providing for a scholarship at the local grammar school and at the university. The charity had had no legal trustee since 1796, though the son of the next-to-last trusteee so regarded himself and was accustomed to receive the rents.[54] Obviously, the Commissioners concluded, a suitable person ought to be appointed trustee, and this should be possible without resort to any equity court.

The Commissioners also discovered charities to be unduly hampered with re-gard to the sale or exchange of their property. Authority for sanctioning sales was almost nonexistent, and the method of effecting exchanges under existing law[55] was so cumbersome as to be quite out of the question for smaller charities. Trustees, moreover, required some supervision over their investments. In rare instances their complaisance might go to excessive lengths, as when they made loans to individuals on their personal security or leased charity lands on generous terms to themselves or their friends.[56] The Huntingdon Corporation did so hand-somely by its burgesses at the expense of the charity estates that an information was filed with the Attorney-General.[57] As charity trustees, in fact, municipal cor-porations had a spotty record. The Municipal Corporation Commissioners could discover evidence of mismanagement on a significant scale, citing as bad examples, Exeter, Truro, Coventry, Newark, Ipswich, and Cambridge.[58]

Even when no venality was involved, some of the common procedures of charity trusteees, especially in their management of land, were disastrous. Of such was the custom, already mentioned, of letting for fines — that is, re-leasing

---

[54] *5th [Brougham] Rept.*, 1821, pp. 332ff.

[55] 1 & 2 Geo. IV, c. 92.

[56] J. (later Lord) Wrottesley, *S. C. on Public Charities*, 1835, Q. 450–51.

[57] *S. C. on the Education of the Lower Orders, 3d Rept.*, 1818, pp. 213–18.

[58] For the charity holdings of municipal corporations see the detailed *Return of Corporation Charity Funds (Parl. Pap.,* 1834). The municipal reform of the 1830's did something to straighten out the situation but by no means cleared it up completely.

land at the old rate and merely charging the lessee a fine as token of the increased value of his land. This failure to take advantage of rising land values obviously cost British charities thousands of pounds a year. The Commissioners noted that a splendid Oxfordshire property of over 4500 acres brought to the Almshouse at Ewelme an average annual return of only £725, or a little more than 3s. 2d. an acre.[59] At Truro, where charity property was let for a fine and a nominal rent, the Corporation applied the rent to the charity and appropriated the fine for its own purposes.[60] It was hard sometimes to judge whether letting for fines should be put down to sharp practice or merely lack of imagination and inertia on the part of charity trustees.

There were abuses not only in the management of charity capital but also in the spending of the income. Although as long as trustees were observing the terms of their trust the Commissioners could not object, however useless or even vicious they may have considered the charity, sometimes the provisions of a trust were stretched beyond the limits of legality. Parishes, for example, occasionally followed a tradition of applying to the local poor rate charity income which had been earmarked by trusts, vaguely drawn, for the benefit of the poor. The custom, not widespread, was sometimes to be encountered in districts, such as the City of London, where charity income was increasing more rapidly than the objects to which it could normally be applied. Beyond that, charity mismanagement was largely a matter of loose administration, sometimes growing out of ill-defined trusts, and often sanctified by custom. Where the amounts involved were large, the Commissioners usually certified the case to the Attorney-General; otherwise they relied on remonstrance and publicity.[61]

An instance which the Brougham Commissioners did not certify was that of the town lands of South Lopham, Norfolk. Here the Wortham Estate, bequeathed in 1486, was to be used "especially for taxes, taliages and other charges happening to the said parish and parishioners, and for the support of the poor inhabitants of the parish for the time being." By the nineteenth century, and no doubt for some time previously, the £130 income was being spent, in a completely haphazard fashion, for doles to the poor, the support of schools, and, insofar as there was a surplus, to relieve the poor rate. Commissioners appointed in 1850 to scrutinize a number of cases which the Brougham Commissioners had decided not to certify, discovered no deliberate maladministration but thought such random application of charity receipts so indefensible that they reported it officially to the Attorney-General.[62] They were prepared to be exceedingly firm with parishes which employed trusts left "for the benefit of the poor" to lighten their own burdens.[63]

In such a comprehensive survey as the Brougham Commissioners carried out,

<hr/>

[59] R. C. for Inquiring into Cases (1849), 1st Rept., 1850, pp. 6–7.
[60] 1st Rept. of the Municipal Corporation Commissioners, 1835, p. 47.
[61] Final [Brougham] Rept., 1837–38 (in the 32d Rept., Part I, pp. 3–6).
[62] R. C. for Inquiring into Cases (1849), 2d Rept., 1851, p. 12.
[63] W. Grant, S. C. on Public Charities, 1835, Q. 237.

it would have been impossible to miss the anachronisms that dotted the charity landscape.[64] Among the most obvious were some of the ancient hospitals established before the Reformation to maintain religious or "superstitious" observances and to provide homes for small numbers of poor persons. These were now thoroughly out of tune with the times, and even with some, where no question of illegal action was raised, reform was long overdue. At the Hospital of Archbishop Holgate in York, a Reformation (1555) foundation, the brethren and sisters were so few and the yield of the endowment so handsome that each received an annual increment of £94, "an income unnecessarily and mischievously large for persons in that station of life." [65]

A more famous case, involving the appropriation of charity receipts by a nobleman in orders, was that of St. Cross, Winchester. It was this episode that supplied Trollope with some of the material for his account of Hiram's Hospital.[66] Here, it appeared, the Earl of Guilford, who owed his post as Master of St. Cross to his father, the Bishop of Winchester, was profiting personally by about £1200 annually, though evidently doing well enough by the inmates and keeping the premises in good order. Actually the Hospital had had a long and at times extraordinarily inglorious history of misappropriation of revenue by its Masters, and the clergyman-peer was by no means the worst offender. In the autumn of 1849, however, the Attorney-General instituted proceedings, and four years later judgment, accompanied by a stiff penalty, was given against the Master.[67]

When they came to the question of trusts that were in their judgment useless or harmful, though not necessarily unworkable, the Commissioners grasped the nettle rather gingerly but at least they grasped it. They held a low opinion of doles, as did their more enlightened contemporaries, and they regarded such benefactions as sheer waste or worse.[68] They had been struck by their experience in such districts as the large parish in London where £200 was given away on certain fixed days in amounts of 1s. or 1s. 6d. a person. These doles, they reported, found their way without delay to neighboring gin shops which regularly employed extra help for these bonanza days. In the North, they conceded, such funds had less disastrous results than in the South, for these were ordinarily distributed in larger amounts and with more careful scrutiny of the applicants.[69] The mass of dole charities, in the view of the Commissioners, formed a substantial charity resource that was going to waste. Why should not these endowments be diverted

[64] One of the most complicated problems had to do with the decayed grammar schools, where, as the Commissioners noted, instruction was "limited to the dead language, or extended to other branches only on terms, which exclude such children as were the immediate objects of the foundation." The question of the endowed schools and their reform will be examined in Chapter IX.
[65] R. C. for Inquiring into Cases (1849), 2d Rept., 1851, pp. 5–6.
[66] On the other ingredients in Hiram's Hospital, see G. F. A. Best, "The Road to Hiram's Hospital," *Victorian Studies*, 5:135–50 (December 1961).
[67] *Proceedings in Equity Relating to Charities*, 1852, p. 16; *30th [Brougham] Rept.*, 1837, p. 843; *Attorney-General* v. *St. Cross Hospital*, 17 Beav. 435–69.
[68] *Digest of Dole Charities*, 1843, p. vi.
[69] W. Grant, *S. C. on Public Charities*, 1835, Q. 230–31.

to education or some other purpose of genuine benefit to the poor? This was, of course, a congenial theme for Commissioners appointed through the initiative of Brougham, whose original motive had been his concern for better schools. It would be an advantage, they intimated, if there were a competent authority which could order such new uses — and by "competent authority" they were not referring to an equity court.

What the Commissioners were doing, obviously, was to echo and emphasize the recommendation of the Select Committee of 1835 for a permanent board armed with supervisory powers over the nation's charitable endowments. Before the Committee, in fact, one of their number had sketched such a scheme in detail.[70] But the Commissioners went a surprising distance, further perhaps than they realized, when they called for a "competent jurisdiction . . . to vary the directions of the founder, when a strict conformity therewith is impracticable or unsuitable to the altered state of society."[71] Presumably they meant nothing revolutionary by their last phrase. They may have had chiefly in mind such unmistakable anachronisms as Lady Mico's or Betton's huge charities for the redemption of Christian slaves — though they would probably have been willing to leave large endowments of this kind in the care of Chancery. There were, however, masses of smaller charities, of whose unsuitability "to the altered state of society" the Commissioners were thoroughly persuaded — certain ancient hospitals, some of the endowed grammar schools, and the bulk of the dole charities. Their proposal of a permanent board of supervision, essentially administrative in character but exercising some of the quasi-judicial functions of Chancery, offered a promising approach to reform. But the way proved longer than anyone would have imagined.

4

Though often complaining of the time and money consumed by the Brougham inquiry, Parliament showed no headlong haste to carry out the recommendations of the Commissioners. Fifteen years were to pass before a bill, timid as it was, finally reached the statute book, as Lord John Russell drily remarked, "the usual period required by improvements in this country in order to arrive at maturity."[72] The delay was especially curious since few denied the need for legislative intervention, mild or drastic. Yet proposals to regulate charities never managed to enlist the support of Governments in the 1840's, not, at least, to the extent of applying the necessary pressure to overpower special and local interests. Bills were presented in dreary succession, but for one reason or another — special interests, party advantage, more pressing legislative business, or simply indifference and inertia — nothing was accomplished until 1853 and then only after another Royal Commission had done its prodding.

The aim of the reformers was to prevent the wasting of the country's charitable

[70] J. Wrottesley, *ibid.*, Q. 466ff.
[71] *Final Rept.*, p. 4.
[72] *The Times*, 4 Aug. 1853.

substance by maladministration or its being swallowed up by legal costs. As a minimum, the State must create machinery to provide for some of the more basic requirements of charitable trusts without their having to resort to the hideously expensive and slow equity remedies or having to bear the cost of a private bill in Parliament. Such an agency would offer a simple and economical method of appointing new trustees, of obtaining authority to sell or exchange charity land, and of varying the terms of trusts that had become unworkable. About this last there was naturally a greater difference of opinion, but few equity lawyers could regard Chancery procedure as other than absurd when applied to smaller charities. For provincial cases, four sets of solicitors were required, and, since the Court sat only in the Metropolis, either the entire body of evidence must be written or the witnesses must go to London and wait until their testimony was called for.

One does not have to push far into the Brougham Reports to find in the world of charity litigation cases nearly as hair-raising as *Jarndyce* v. *Jarndyce*. Endowments entirely devoured by the costs of Chancery proceedings or incomes committed for a long period, in one instance for a matter of twenty-five years,[73] were not unknown. There was the case of the charity property valued at £3000, whose annual yield of about £150 had been misapplied toward the poor and church rates. In the course of prolonged Chancery proceedings, which were financed by the sale of parts of the property, its value was reduced to £105, but there still remained unsatisfied court costs of £2000. That sum was raised by a mortgage at 4½ per cent, so that the charity was left with about £15, or a tenth of its original income.[74] For a charity of less than £30 annual income, a writer in the *Edinburgh Review* asserted, to go to law was simply to commit suicide. One of £60 would be reduced by a half, and one of £100 by a third.[75]

This, of course, was only half the case against Chancery and probably the least debatable part. Beyond questions of expense there was the fact that the action of Chancery was purely legal and judicial. The Court could not move without a formal complaint, and it could rectify only technical abuses — that is, the employment of charity property in ways other than those intended by the founder — or, in the case of failure of a trust, prescribe new uses *cy-près*. What was required was a procedure to take care of the administrative needs of charities, apart from the contentious jurisdiction of the Court. Although some might argue that the proper solution lay in a reform of Chancery procedures, there were good reasons for regarding this as an exceedingly feeble reed. The situation called for a jurisdiction more summary than that which could be provided even by a reformed Chancery.

No legislation would be of much use which failed to include these minima. The more eager reformers wished to go a good deal further and to apply a firm hand to

---

[73] Wilks's Almshouses, Leighton Buzzard. (*12th* [*Brougham*] *Rept.*, 1825, pp. 24ff.)

[74] *Edinburgh Review*, 83:476 (April 1846). For other examples see Courtney Kenny, *The True Principles of Legislation with regard to . . . Charitable . . . Uses*, pp. 148–49, and Standish G. Grady, *Gross Abuses of Public Charities*, 2d ed. (London, 1853), pp. 11–12.

[75] *Edinburgh Review*, 83:477.

trusts that were obsolete and, in their view, baneful. They were little inclined, for example, to defer to the founder's wishes when these prevented the reapplication of dole charities to the service of education or when they limited grammar schools to Latin and Greek in places where there was little demand for a classical curriculum. The reformers could cite the artlessly revolutionary proposal of the Select Committee of 1835 that, once a supervisory agency was established, one of its functions "in cases in which that [the founder's] object is useless or unattainable, to suggest such other appropriation as may appear desirable." [76] The notion of revising an "unattainable" trust would bother nobody. That, after all, was the purpose of the *cy-près* formula, but to speak of revising "useless" trusts was to raise issues of a different order.

To look forward to an agency authorized to revise trusts when these had proved impracticable or unsuitable "to the altered state of society" might do well enough as a long-range hope. Indeed, the debate continued throughout the nineteenth century, and the question was by no means dead when the Nathan Committee reviewed charity law in 1950-52. Yet it was chimerical to imagine that early Victorian Englishmen would countenance any general revision of "useless" trusts or would interfere with the management of charities beyond an unavoidable minimum. They would do a good deal to see that charitable resources were conserved and to prevent dishonesty in their management, but they had no stomach for interfering with private property. Nor could they regard the wishes of a departed founder, though in some instances admittedly fantastic and even malicious, as other than sacrosanct. Trusts, in their view, should be altered only in cases of direct necessity and in a manner as consonant as possible with the founder's (sometimes absurd) will.

During the 1840's and early '50's, the question of carrying into effect the recommendations of the Brougham Commissioners came before one or both Houses something like ten times. Sir Robert Peel's Government (1841–46) showed more than a perfunctory interest in the issue, especially through Lord Lyndhurst, the Lord Chancellor, who in three successive years (1844–46) brought forward legislative proposals in the Lords. The second bill, based on the report of the Select Committee of 1835, passed the Lords but died in the Commons. [77] Lyndhurst made his final and most determined attempt in 1846, when his bill would certainly have passed the Lords, had it not been caught up in the political antipathies and factiousness of the Corn Law struggle.

In introducing the second reading the Lord Chancellor made one of the classic and most frequently quoted arguments for charity regulation. It was a brilliant performance, cogent, trenchant, and superbly ironic at points. Once more the Lord Chancellor stressed the inadequacy of his Court in dealing with small charities and regaled the House with a new series of examples of ruinous Chancery

[76] *S. C. on Public Charities*, 1835, p. ix.

[77] *3 Hansard*, 80:766ff. Among the features of Lyndhurst's proposal which outraged some of the wealthier and more influential charities was his suggestion of a 1 per cent tax on charity incomes as a means of financing the work of a board of commissioners.

costs. Regretfully he admitted that irresistible pressure had persuaded him to exempt certain categories of charity, notably the universities, schools of royal foundation, the great hospitals, voluntary (nonendowed) charities, and sectarian religious philanthropies. But to the City Companies, who had mobilized to oppose the bill, he refused any concessions. Indeed, it was for the guilds that he reserved his most astringent irony, noting that nineteen informations had been filed against the eleven Companies which had petitioned against the bill. Their claim to exemption, he implied, would be better if their record as charity administrators were on a par with their professions. He pointed a derisive finger at the Trinity Monday junket of a delegation from the Mercers' Company to Greenwich, nominally to visit Lord Northampton's Charity. The founder had allowed £5 for the annual inspection, but the expenses for the 1833 trip had swelled to £89 10s. 5d., with breakfast, luncheon, and a handsome dinner generously provided out of the funds of the charity. This, Lyndhurst noted wryly, was the Mercers' Company, "which claim to be exempted from the operation of the Bill on account of the strict and faithful manner in which they have hitherto discharged their duties, and are likely to discharge them again." [78]

Ample opposition had developed among some of the more powerful charity interests affected. The Royal Hospitals, the Foundling Hospital, the S.P.G., the charities of Coventry, and others petitioned against the bill, while the City Companies had their case for exemption brought to the floor of the House.[79] What wrecked Lyndhurst's effort, however, was the inability of the Whig peers to resist the lure of party politics. They saw in the blind rage of the Tory Protectionists against Peel an opportunity to seal the ultimate doom of his Government. The Corn Law bill had not yet reached the Lords, but when the Protectionists, headed by the Duke of Richmond, proposed a coalition with the Whigs to throw out the charities bill, "We, alas! had not the virtue to withstand temptation," a penitent Lord Campbell later admitted. As a result of the alliance, the bill went down to defeat by two votes, "and I must with shame confess very factiously . . . The argument was against us, but the Protectionists were with us." [80] It was the beginning of the end for Peel, and a defeat for charity regulation which would put off action for another seven years. "The voice of a single peer decided against the Chancellor's proposed inquisition," *The Times* lamented, "and secured to trustees and corporations a little longer lease of irresponsibility and immunity." [81]

Although Lord John Russell's Whig Government introduced charitable trusts bills almost annually, these made remarkably little difference. Sometimes they were introduced too late in the session to stand a chance of passing, and sometimes their support was no more than perfunctory. No one challenged the need for regulatory action, but the opposition was never at a loss to find weaknesses in

[78] *3 Hansard*, 86:747.
[79] *Ibid.*, 85:149.
[80] Lord Campbell, *The Lives of the Lord Chancellors*, 8 vols., 2d ed. (London, 1846–69), VIII (1869), 160, 542.
[81] *The Times*, 20 May 1846.

every proposal. Equity lawyers could extol the advantages of a reformed Chancery, and other opponents could plead for exemption for their pet charities. The same old demands for exemption by Christ's Hospital, the Royal Hospitals, and other metropolitan institutions were presented, and Sir Robert Inglis could press the claims of the Royal Literary Fund for the relief of authors in distress, urging that it would humiliate such beneficiaries, who, "from the nature of their minds and occupations, were peculiarly sensitive and susceptible [to] have their distress known as publicly as those who entered the union workhouse." [82]

Meanwhile, in 1850–51, additional pressure had been applied by a new Royal Commission. This body, appointed to inquire into cases of charity malpractice which the Brougham Commission had not certified to the Attorney-General, took occasion to nudge the Government and to call once more for "some public and permanent authority, who should be charged with the duty of supervising the administration of all these charitable trusts." [83] In the end it fell to Lord Cranworth, Aberdeen's Lord Chancellor, to introduce the bill that was finally to pass into law. Although by this time it was impossible for anyone to claim an original approach to the problem, Cranworth's proposals were not unadventurous. In addition to their more routine duties, the Charity Commissioners would have enjoyed a good deal of freedom in dealing with obsolete or vicious endowments. In cases where the object of a trust had failed or where it had "tended to the encouragement of pauperism or immorality" [84] (elastic words in the Victorian vocabulary), the Commissioners might authorize a different use of the endowment. In this and in certain other respects Cranworth's draft went farther than any bill yet introduced and well beyond the rules and precedents on which Chancery acted.

Predictably enough the Lords declined to vest such authority in a Commission, and the bill that was sent to the other House called for a supervisory agency with drastically reduced powers. In the Commons the debate had to do chiefly with subordinate issues, since there was little disposition to quarrel on essentials. What occupied the Commons was Lord John Russell's amendment to exempt Roman Catholic charities (an obvious reflection of the hue and cry over "Papal Aggression"). The Government was plainly reluctant to raise as an issue the questionable legality of a large body of Roman Catholic charities. Since many of them had, in fact, been established to provide masses for the dead, they could never have stood scrutiny under the Law of Superstitious Uses, and many had therefore failed to enroll under the provisions of the Mortmain Act of 1736. In other words, the legal position of Catholic charities was so shaky that, until the law was amended, it would be ruinous to place them under the jurisdiction of the Charity Commissioners. [85]

---

[82] *3 Hansard*, 120:228.
[83] *R. C. for Inquiring into Cases* (1849), *1st Rept.*, 1850, p. 4.
[84] *3 Hansard*, 126:1017.
[85] *Ibid.*, 129:1158.

5

The Charitable Trusts Act of 1853,[86] as it finally reached the statute book, turned out to be a moderate, almost tentative prescription for the ills of endowed charities and less drastic than that recommended by the Select Committee of 1835 or the Royal Commission of 1850–51. The enthusiasm of *The Times* was excessive: "We have never seen a more complete or efficient measure," though there was, of course, some ground for adding, "never one more urgently called for — never one framed on fuller and riper deliberation." [87] The new Commissioners, three of them to be paid and two of these to be barristers of at least twelve years' standing, were given fairly generous powers of investigation into endowed charities. Indeed, their principal powers were inquisitorial. They could examine, through their inspectors, trustees under oath, and they could require the production of documents. Trustees were to submit annual accounts to the Commission. Obviously it was the hope of Parliament that abuses in charity administration could be handled through inquiry and exposure and without tampering with the essentials of charity law.

One of the more far-sighted provisions of the Act had to do with the custody of charity funds, whose slipshod management had appalled the Brougham Commissioners. The Secretary of the new Commission was to serve as Treasurer of Public Charities (later the Official Trustee of Charity Lands), a legal corporation, in which might be vested charity property. More important, there were also created the Official Trustees of Charitable Funds, into whose care, at no cost to themselves, trustees might give over their funds for safekeeping and investment. The income would be remitted to them to be applied in the usual fashion. The office of the Official Trustees turned out to be an immensely useful piece of machinery, as its steadily increasing volume of business testified.

Cranworth's Act set up a Charity Commission which could curb certain varieties of administrative malpractice, but it left unimpaired the commanding position of the equity courts.[88] The Commissioners, for example, lacked authority even to appoint new trusteees without recourse to Chancery, and the problem of obsolete trusts and their revision remained about where it had been before 1853. Where the Commissioners discovered a trust requiring alteration, they must appeal to other bodies. If it could be dealt with in terms of *cy-près,* they would apply to Chancery through the Attorney-General. If *cy-près* would not suffice and a more sweeping reorganization were necessary, they could only frame a scheme embodying their plan and present it to Parliament for enactment. In the one case, they would have to reconcile themselves to the familiar delays, expense, and limited scope of

---

[86] 16 & 17 Vict., c. 137.

[87] *The Times,* 22 July 1853.

[88] The Master of the Rolls and the Vice-Chancellor were empowered to deal with charities whose income exceeded £30, and the new County Courts and the District Courts of Bankruptcy with the smaller ones.

Chancery jurisdiction. The alternative, they soon discovered, led to even greater frustration.

The personnel of the new Commission did not evoke universal acclaim. *The Times,* its information not altogether accurate, doubted whether the Commissioners were "sufficiently qualified by their eminence in any pursuit." [89] The Chief Commissioner was to be Peter Erle, brother of the Lord Chief Justice of Common Pleas and a conveyancer of great technical skill. Such a background, *The Times* suspected, might not be ideal training for a post where vigor and originality were demanded, though conceivably he might rise above the biases of his order. In the two decades that Erle served as Chief Commissioner, he was the guiding hand of the Board, and he was at least partly responsible for its heavily judicial and legal — in the eyes of some of its more recent critics, legalistic — approach to charity problems. Yet it would be unjust to charge him with lack of vigor or courage.

His associates were to be a barrister, James Hill, and a clergyman, the Reverend Richard Jones, neither of whom impressed *The Times* favorably. But here the editor was firing wide of the mark. Not only was Hill the author of a useful work on trustees and a member of the Royal Commission of 1850–51, but, according to a fellow barrister, in appointing him the Government had resisted a good deal of political pressure.[90] There is some reason to believe that Hill was a principal author of the Charitable Trusts Bill as introduced by Cranworth.[91] Nor was Jones without qualifications. He had been professor of political economy at King's College, London, and at Haileybury, and had served as secretary to one important government commission. The fourth (and unpaid) Commissioner was Sir George Grey, who was about to become Colonial Secretary and who, aside from representing the Board in the House, would be able to give little time to charity matters.

Of the two Inspectors associated with the Commission, one was a man of outstanding talents. Thomas Hare, remembered today chiefly as the originator of proportional representation, made a conspicuous contribution to the better management of English charities. In his activities as Inspector and Assistant Commissioner, he combined the qualifications of sound legal training, industry, and judgment with a much rarer speculative gift. He could dig out and arrange the facts on a group of charities as ably as any other investigator, but that was never the end. Hare was always as much interested in the "why" as the "what," and he was no slave to his own legal training. His masterly series of reports on the parochial charities of the City of London supplied the factual basis for the Royal Commission of 1880 and led to the amalgamation of these endowments in the City Parochial Foundation.[92] Unlike others whose profession is inquiry, Hare did

[89] *The Times,* 26 Oct. 1853.

[90] *Ibid.,* 31 Oct. 1853. Two of the Commissioners were to be permanent, the third (Jones) to be temporary, but by the Act of 1855, after the death of Jones, all three Commissionerships became permanent.

[91] *Ibid.,* 12 July 1854.

[92] As described in Chapter X below.

not hesitate to criticize and generalize. His addresses before the Social Science Association and elsewhere, usually well considered, sometimes a bit overimaginative, but always stimulating, reflect a commitment to thorough, almost extreme, charity reform, similar to that championed in the 1870's by Sir Arthur Hobhouse. In Hare the Commission acquired a marvelously capable and acute investigator.

It was only gradually that the Commissioners came to sense the weakness of their position, especially their lack of the powers necessary to carry out significant reforms. From the beginning they proved useful to local charity officials, especially in furnishing assistance and advice of a routine sort. Their correspondence, in fact, proved so heavy as to preclude much progress on more comprehensive projects. At the end of the first year, the Commissioners reported some eleven hundred special applications from trustees for aid and advice on a variety of questions. Although they had hopefully looked forward to receiving accounts from forty thousand charities,[93] the first-year total was a disappointing ten thousand. How charities were to be persuaded to submit regular accounts turned out to be one of the problems that the Commissioners never succeeded in solving and one which, a century later, disturbed the Nathan Committee. The Inspectors, with what seems extraordinary activity, were able to look into some eight hundred endowments, including several large individual foundations, and the charity structure of certain cities, notably Coventry, Warwick, and the City of London, all of which were conspicuously well equipped with ancient and, in many instances, badly employed endowments.

The Commissioners were, however, discovering that their direct remedial powers were gravely circumscribed, and they were beginning to chafe under the restrictions. The method set up for appointing new trustees through applications authorized by the Commissioners to Chancery or a County Court was still complicated and costly enough to discourage small charities. Especially irksome were the controls governing the transfer of charity funds to the Official Trustees, for the Commissioners themselves had no power to authorize it. This admittedly beneficial machinery could be set in motion only on a court order. Likewise, the Commissioners were dissatisfied with their limited powers of inquiry, since it was only from trustees, and not from third parties, that they could demand information. Altogether, as long as the Act of 1853 governed the activities of the Commission, any revolution in the charity world was likely to be on an exceedingly small scale.

By the summer of 1854, *The Times* was disillusioned not only with the Commission but with the Act itself, which twelve months before it had hailed as the perfect solution. The editor had finally discovered that the Act was largely permissive in its operation and had been drawn on the curious premise that trustees who are devouring and misappropriating the assets committed to them

---

[93] The number of endowments had, of course, increased markedly since the Brougham inquiry. Though these new trusts were chiefly responsible for the larger figure, those which the Brougham Commissioners failed to discover also contributed to the total.

"desire nothing more than an opportunity of redressing their own misdeeds."[94] Such complaints were occasionally echoed in the House of Commons, where in 1854 in the debate on supply the younger Ellice deplored the great care which was taken "to avoid giving [the Commissioners] the least power beyond the power of inquiry, which power was not so very essential, inasmuch as full inquiry had been made by the old Charity [Brougham] Commissioners."[95] If the Commissioners were to have only such limited authority, there ought to be a frank admission that, in effect, nothing had been altered by the Brougham inquiry or the Charitable Trusts Act.

The amending Act of 1855 shored up the Commissioners' position only in minor respects.[96] The most useful of its provisions was that which elaborated the powers and responsibilities of the Official Trustees and permitted charities to transfer funds to them without recourse to a court. Other provisions, equally desirable, vanished as the bill passed through the Commons.[97] Such a diffident prescription as the amending Act could hardly put off, to say nothing of obviating the need for, a more sweeping measure, and, indeed, no one pretended to regard it as final. While the bill was still in Parliament, *The Times* was appealing for an Act which would vest in the Commissioners the primary jurisdiction, as regards charity matters, of the equity courts, "subject to summary appeal to those courts."[98]

What was most frustrating of all to the Commissioners was the immovable roadblock set up in Parliament against most of their schemes for individual foundations. The Act of 1853 had provided that charities whose trusts could not be revised *cy-près* might be reorganized by schemes framed by the Commissioners and put through Parliament in the usual way. It appeared at once, however, that the Commissioners could hope for nothing from this source, save in the few cases where their proposals offended no local interests or opinions. They were finally driven to conclude that it was futile even to present controversial schemes and that their best course was to tone down their proposals to the point where they could be handled *cy-près* in Chancery.[99]

The case of Christ's Hospital at Sherburn, near Durham, afforded them an instructive and sobering experience. Here was a foundation whose dire need for reorganization was indisputable, but the Commissioners' scheme encountered such opposition, clerical and lay, that they could only abandon their attempt at thorough revision. The Hospital, established in the twelfth century for the relief of persons afflicted with leprosy, now provided for a Master, appointed by the Bishop of Durham, and thirty brethren, half of whom were resident. The property of the Hospital, largely in land, mines and minerals, and tithes, had increased handsomely

[94] *The Times,* 12 July 1854.
[95] *3 Hansard,* 134:1310–12.
[96] 18 & 19 Vict., c. 124.
[97] *3 Hansard,* 139:1875–93.
[98] *The Times,* 19 April 1855.
[99] *6th Annual Report of the Charity Commissioners,* 1858, p. 5.

and by mid-century the income approached £4700. It was a thoroughly Trol-
lopean situation, for the surplus over running expenses came to about £3000. This
accrued to the Master without, the Commissioners observed, "the obligation to
perform any duty of importance." [100] His enormous profit was slightly offset by
sums which the Master contributed toward the maintenance of schools in the
neighborhood, augmentation of vicarages in the patronage of the Hospital, and
improvement of the buildings. Still, the Mastership remained an incredibly lush
clerical sinecure.

The death of the Master gave the Commissioners their chance to propose a
more constructive application of the endowment. Far from flouting the will of
the founder, they proposed to revert to his original intention by re-establishing the
charity as an institution for the relief of chronic diseases, the modern analogues
of leprosy. In addition, their scheme provided for permanent augmentations of
the vicarages of the Hospital and for certain contributions to local institutions for
the benefit of the poor, as well as annual contributions to the Durham County
Hospital. They proposed also to liquidate the clerical Mastership and to set up
a form of management better adapted to the new functions of the institution. It
had been impossible, the Commissioners innocently remarked, to broaden the
uses of the endowment and at the same time to preserve for the Master "the
large pecuniary advantages hitherto enjoyed with the office." [101]

The scheme was rational enough, but the Commissioners had contrived to step
on both clerical and lay toes. Their proposal to discontinue a clerical Master outraged the Bishop of Durham. Contributions to the County Hospital were opposed
on the ground that such was an improper use of charity funds and, contrariwise,
that the grant should be extended to other hospitals. When the bill came to the
upper House, their Lordships mangled it so disastrously that the Commissioners
could only give up the battle.[102] Yet with the charity virtually in abeyance and its
income piling up at an alarming rate, action of some sort was forced on the Commissioners. They had no alternative but to salvage what they could by applying
to Chancery for a *cy-près* scheme. The Court would not prescribe the treatment
that, in their view, the Sherburn Hospital merited, but there was no likelihood
of persuading the House of Lords, with its bench of bishops, to take a more indulgent attitude.

The Sherburn case was no isolated instance. Some of the Commissioners'
schemes, such as that for St. Mary Magdalen at Newcastle, were thrown out,
others saddled with crippling amendments, and still others simply allowed to
languish. They made little progress in their plans for reorganizing the mélange
of foundations in Coventry and Bristol, and, although certain schemes which
aroused no opposition were accepted, the Commissioners could feel little optimism

[100] *2d Ann. C. C. Rept.*, 1854, *Suppl. Rept.*, App., p. 6.
[101] *3d Ann. C. C. Rept.*, 1855, App., p. 16.
[102] *4th Ann. C. C. Rept.*, 1856 (d. 1857), p. 5; *Corr. between the Bishop of Durham and the Charity Commrs.* (Parl. Pap., 1856, LIX).

about gaining Parliamentary sanction on any adequate scale. During their first fifteen years, on the testimony of W. E. Forster, they were able to carry only eighteen bills.[103] At an early stage they were obliged to reconcile themselves, at least until their powers should be increased, to working through Chancery within the limits of *cy-près*.[104] Meanwhile they looked forward to a change in the law which would not only confer on their Board summary jurisdiction comparable to that exercised by Chancery but which might even authorize, under some circumstances, a departure from strict adherence to the founder's instructions, though "without any substantial violation of the founder's principal intention." [105]

Although the Charitable Trusts Act of 1860 fulfilled only half of the hopes of the Commissioners, it was this Statute that really established the Board and armed it with powers beyond those of inquiry. The debate in both Houses was curiously thin, for, as was now apparent, there were strong arguments either for extending the authority of the Commission or abolishing it. The Lord Chancellor conceded that the earlier bill had left smaller charities without a satisfactory remedy, since an application to Chancery would still cost them an average of £50.[106] The essential aim was to create, in matters administrative rather than judicial, an inexpensive substitute for Chancery. The vital clause therefore empowered the Commissioners "to make Orders such as may now be made by any Judge of the Court of Chancery sitting at Chambers, or by any County Court or District Court of Bankruptcy" — orders for establishing schemes and appointing or removing trustees, as well as authorizing financial transactions of various sorts.[107]

The action of the Commissioners was, however, limited in two significant respects. In the first place, their scheme-making powers were applicable only to charities with an annual income of £50 or less; for others they must have the consent of a majority of the trustees. Thus an overwhelming proportion of English endowments, over 80 per cent of them, were brought under the Board's jurisdiction, but only a small fraction of the total charity property. For, as the Chief Commissioner testified in the mid-1880's, 10 per cent of the endowments accounted for 85 per cent of the charity income.[108] The £50 ceiling was not to the Commissioners' liking, and it became less and less so as the years passed. As long as this obtained, they could establish new schemes for larger charities, however badly needed, only by invitation of the trustees.

[103] 3 *Hansard*, 194:1370. On the difficulties of getting a scheme through Parliament see the evidence of Sir Arthur Hobhouse, *S. C. on the Charitable Trusts Acts*, 1884, Q. 2880.

[104] See the evidence of Henry Longley, *ibid.*, Q. 149; also Robert Lowe, *Schools Inquiry [Taunton] Commission* (C. 3288), 1867–68, IV, Q. 6547.

[105] *7th Ann. C. C. Rept.*, 1859, p. 6.

[106] 3 *Hansard*, 159:1188. I am at a loss to explain the statement by the Select Committee of 1884 (p. iv) that a more radical bill was introduced by Robert Lowe based on the recommendations of the Select Committee of 1835 but that it was drastically amended by the House. The bill that Lowe introduced came down from the Lords, and significant amendments were made in neither House. Lowe's speech makes no reference to any other bill or to clauses more drastic than those included in the final Act.

[107] 23 & 24 Vict., c. 136, s. 2.

[108] Henry Longley, *S. C. on the Charitable Trust Acts*, 1884, Q. 185, 189, 190.

The second limitation was of a different sort. With regard to the smaller charities, the Act described the Commission's administrative powers as those of a "Chancery Judge sitting at Chambers," an exceedingly imprecise definition. The Commissioners could refer to no Act of Parliament, for the powers of Chancery had never been so regulated. In short, they soon became aware of a certain vagueness in their authority, because, as the Chief Commissioner put it some years later, "unlike the jurisdiction of most administrative bodies, it is not found within the corners of any document, but only in such books as Tudor on the Law of Charitable Trusts." [109] The cautionary Section V, which warned them against intervening in contentious cases that belonged properly to a judicial tribunal did not add to their sense of security.

Nevertheless, the Act of 1860 established the Commission as a much more useful and responsible body. Once scheme-making powers had been granted, the business of the office grew rapidly at the expense not only of the Chancery Judges but also of the County and District Courts. The Commissioners could offer the modestly endowed charity, at virtually no cost, all that these other bodies could provide. Indeed, through the years the Board has thought of itself, above all, as a kind of poor charity's Chancery, whose administrative jurisdiction offered most of the advantages, with few of the defects, of the Court itself. [110]

[109] *Ibid.,* Q. 156.

[110] Readers familiar with the work of Oliver MacDonagh will not miss the fact that charity reform follows rather closely the "model" set up by him in his article "The Nineteenth-Century Revolution in Government: A Reappraisal," *The Historical Journal,* I (1958), no. 1, esp. 57–61.

PART THREE

PRIVATE PHILANTHROPY
AND PUBLIC RESPONSIBILITY
1860's–1914

"Time makes ancient good uncouth."
— James Russell Lowell

"For they have no conception of the duty of government who wish to limit it to the settling of disputes over
money or to the punishment of criminals. On the contrary,
it is much more important for the magistrates to devote
their energy to the producing of good citizens."
— Juan-Luis Vivès (1526)

THE HALF CENTURY bounded by the 1860's and the out-
break of the first World War brought about something of a revolution,
by no means complete in 1914, in Englishmen's ideas about the relative
domains of private charity and public action. To a degree this reflected a more
fundamental change in their notions of poverty and its treatment in an industrial
society. A good deal of nineteenth-century thinking about social distress and its
remedies had little to do with nineteenth-century realities but was carried over
from the pre-industrial world. Broadly speaking, the Victorian ethos ascribed
such evils as poverty, destitute old age, and even much of the suffering from unemployment to individual inadequacies rather than to any more general failure
of the social mechanism. These were thought of, in short, as exceptional and
personal, not as a disease endemic in British society. As long as one conceived of
the Victorian social problem in a moral framework, in terms of the shortcomings
of individuals, there was little reason to question the Victorian solution.

This involved a well-understood, if tacit, agreement between private charity
and statutory authorities as to the sphere in which each properly operated. An
age that takes for granted large-scale public social services can appreciate only with
difficulty the distinctive role assigned by the Victorians to charity. Certainly
throughout the nineteenth century and into the twentieth the main responsibility
for social welfare lay with voluntary agencies. The function of the State was
largely supplementary, to fill such urgent gaps as might be left by the network
of private agencies and to carry out its traditional obligation of relieving the
genuinely destitute.

That the mid-Victorians managed to be satisfied, even exultant, as they contemplated this division of responsibilities suggests how limited was their conception of the social problem. They suffered from the twin defects of lack of social
knowledge and want of social imagination. The amazing expansion of British
economy during the high Victorian era and the annually improving fortunes of
the middle and artisan classes made it easy to miss, if not to deny, the existence
of what it later became fashionable to call the "submerged tenth." Even such
revelations as Henry Mayhew's in his *London Labour and the London Poor* had
little apparent effect on the social thinking of his contemporaries. His volumes
appeared in the early 1860's, but at the close of the decade the newly founded
Charity Organisation Society could embody in institutional form the conventional
assumptions which guided Victorian social action.

The history of the C.O.S. is not without its ironic elements. When the Society was formed, most enlightened Victorians would have accepted its platform, at least its essential philosophy, with little question. But the C.O.S. turned out to be a monument to a dying faith, or one which, within two or three decades, was mortally ailing.[1] Increasingly from the middle 1880's the validity of the mid-Victorian formula was called into question, and the late Victorians were driven to explore other solutions. The factors in this changing social outlook have been often analyzed, and we need not recall them in detail.[2] The bad years of the mid-'80's underscored the reality of unemployment in industrial society and led to a new awareness of the extent and depth of social distress, in part the outcome of a series of explorations, both scientific and sensational, into the life of the lower strata of the British population. Conceivably voluntarism was not in itself the answer. The community, as represented by the State, might have an obligation to deal with distress and want if these were as widespread as the data of Charles Booth and others seemed to imply. Not only that but, with the maturing of British industrialism, society's resources had vastly increased, and these could now be applied to the problem of welfare with some hope of success.

The new solution was not to be readily accepted, for plainly it ran counter to some of the most self-evident "truths" of the Victorian credo. Here the late Victorians were brought face to face with what has been called "the most urgent moral dilemma" of their age, "namely, the reconciliation of collective action designed to remedy social abuses, and promote the well-being of the individual, with the maintenance and encouragement of personal responsibility and initiative."[3] The specific issues on which the debate centered were twofold, pensions for the aged and unemployment relief, and on these the contending forces met head-on. It was a bitter enough controversy, but by 1914 the balance was clearly shifting. Henceforth the main welfare burden would rest on the State, and increasingly the role of private philanthropy would be that of supplementing the growing system of statutory services.

In this period, as at other times, the State drew heavily on the experience of charitable agencies. There was point to the faintly Podsnappian hymn to voluntary effort sung by *The Times* in the mid-'50's:

It is this spontaneity of action which distinguishes our social, as it distinguishes our legislative, proceedings . . . The individual eye sees, the individual hand indicates, the social malady. Individual charity finds the remedy. If the experiment succeed, Parliament and the Government follow in the wake . . . But it rarely, very rarely, happens that in England any great scheme of comprehensive benevolence is initiated

[1] Calvin Woodard in his Cambridge doctoral thesis (unpublished), "The Charity Organisation Society and the Rise of the Welfare State," offers an interesting interpretation of the changes which so rapidly made obsolete the principles on which the Society had been built.

[2] For example, Helen M. Lynd, *England in the Eighteen-Eighties* (New York, 1945); Gertrude Williams, *The State and the Standard of Living* (London, 1936), chap. I; Charles Loch Mowat, *The Charity Organisation Society* (London, 1961), pp. 114–20; Beatrice Webb, *My Apprenticeship* (London, 1926), chap. IV.

[3] T. S. and M. B. Simey, *Charles Booth* (Oxford, 1960), p. 5.

by the Government, which is only too happy to await the results of private enterprise and private experience.[4]

In practice the Government might enter at various stages and by various routes, and the degree of involvement might vary from service to service. But the process was repeated time and again — in education, housing, medical care, juvenile delinquency, and, after a fashion, in old-age assistance and unemployment relief. Henceforth, in matters of social welfare, government policy would be in an ever-increasing degree the controlling factor.

In such efforts individual benefactors of substance, as well as organized groups, figured heavily. The harvest of Victorian prosperity had been so abundant that manufacturers, merchants, and financiers, if disposed to concern themselves with the needs of the community, were able to engage in philanthropy on a generous scale. It is unnecessary here to list individuals or mention specific gifts. We need only note the new hospitals established and the old ones periodically rescued from bankruptcy; the institutions of higher education — the redbrick universities — that were founded; the medical and scientific research financed; the cultural and recreational facilities — libraries, museums, art galleries, and public parks — given or bequeathed by wealthy citizens; and the urban housing experiments and industrial villages that were launched. At least some small fraction of the profits of the Victorian economy were now being applied to the Victorian welfare account.

The reconstructed and progressively more democratic government of Victorian England was also brought to reform some of the more obvious anachronisms in the world of endowed charities. Among charitable endowments of ancient lineage, two groups above all called for drastic treatment — the mass of obsolescent parochial charities in the City of London and the chaotic accumulation of endowments for educational purposes, especially secondary education. To adapt these to modern needs the Government was obliged to proceed in an almost revolutionary fashion, vesting extraordinary powers in commissioners charged with the work of reorganization. These two operations (Chapters IX–X) marked the extreme limit to which the State pushed its authority over charitable trusts and the only major instances in which it explicitly cast aside *cy-près* as the basis for revision.[5] On the other hand, after three or four decades of vigorous activity the energy of the Charity Commission itself palpably waned, and its policies tended increasingly to follow conventional paths. The Commissioners were never able to obtain from Parliament the powers they sought, and in the years before 1914 (and after) their performance, as compared with their earlier initiative, seems unadventurous and routine.

In the course of the half century, then, the British State showed a growing inclination to grapple with the problems of the common life. The advance of political democracy made inevitable a greater concern for social politics, and some of the barriers, ideological and economic, that in the past had inhibited public

---

[4] *The Times,* 8 Aug. 1956.

[5] The courts and the Charity Commissioners, it will be recalled, were bound to apply the *cy-près* formula, though it could, of course, be disregarded in parliamentary schemes.

action were gradually being worn away. The new and disturbing analysis of poverty which emerged from Booth's elaborate survey made almost inevitable a more positive social policy, and it underscored the suspicion, rapidly becoming a certainty in some quarters, that charity was not enough. However vital for effective state action may have been the fund of experience accumulated by voluntary organizations, the essential task, as twentieth-century Englishmen were now seeing it, clearly lay beyond them.

CHAPTER VIII

"SCIENTIFIC CHARITY": THE CHARITY ORGANISATION SOCIETY

THE CHARITY organization movement stands as perhaps the most representative current, certainly the most characteristic innovation, in the philanthropic practice of the mid-to-late Victorian Age. Few bodies can have made more sweeping claims for their own answer to the social question than did the London Society for Organising Charitable Relief and Repressing Mendicity or, indeed, set goals loftier than those established for the Society by its more high-minded apologists. Few have evoked greater devotion, especially during the years when its influence was most pervasive, and few have inspired more cordial antipathy.

The charity organizers were aware of their less than universal appeal. One of the pioneers of the Society, in putting his own case to be considered the chief founder, felt obliged to explain why "three gentlemen should think it worth contending for, to which of them is due the invention of the most unpopular and misunderstood society in the metropolis." [1] There was a suspicion in some quarters — and not merely among those whose interests, selfish or charitable, had suffered — that the "scientific charity" preached by the Society was impersonal, grudging, and wrapped in red tape and that its homilies against indiscriminate and thoughtless charity too often meant no charity at all. As a High Church clergyman who was a leader in the Christian Social Union put it, "Theories which, on the lips of Canon Barnett, are spiritual, if mistaken; and from the pen of Mr. Loch are able, though fallacious, become in the practice of meaner men merely the gospel of the buttoned pocket." And he suggested as the proper motto for the Society the lines from George Herbert:

> Only a sweet and virtuous soul
> Like seasoned timber — never gives.[2]

Christians who persisted in regarding the act of almsgiving as itself the practice of a Christian virtue enjoined by Scripture could find little enthusiasm for the

[1] W. M. Wilkinson, *The Invention of the C.O.S., Charity Reform Papers,* No. 10.
[2] Charles L. Marson, *Charity Organization and Jesus Christ* (London, 1897), p. 33.

tenets and procedures of the Society. Even among men and women who had dedicated themselves to the service of the poor, there were growing doubts whether private charity, however responsibly administered, held the answer and whether exhortations to thrift, sobriety, and decorum, still less merely the suppression of indiscriminate almsgiving, would much affect the mass of wretchedness.

The Charity Organisation Society was little inclined to discover merit in criticisms of its philosophy or methods. Its own apologists tended to regard critics as either featherbrained or selfishly interested in perpetuating unsound philanthropy, and those who resisted the light as perversely wrong-headed. Indeed, to view the record of the Society objectively is difficult, still more to appreciate the prestige that it enjoyed and the emotions that it aroused.[3] The social philosophy that informed its procedures and tactics seems unbelievably dated and, in retrospect, so contrary to the direction in which the British community was to move that sympathetic understanding does not come readily. It was the misfortune of the C.O.S. to be founded near the close of an era and on postulates which at the time commanded widespread acceptance but which were presently to seem outmoded and irrelevant to increasing numbers of Englishmen.

Still, as articulated by its more high-minded champions, there was genuine nobility in the Society's proclaimed ideal of charity as personal service as well as pecuniary aid, of involvement beyond mere almsgiving. No one can discount the claim of the Society to a pre-eminent position among the pioneers of modern social casework. Yet the notion of neighborly service sometimes seemed to accord strangely with the tough-minded professionalism of its procedures and the condescension that accompanied them. The Society never came within measurable distance of its announced ends, save perhaps those of a negative sort. It never succeeded in rationalizing charitable relief in London nor establishing itself as a kind of superclearing-house for metropolitan charities. Neither voluntary organizations nor the Poor Law authorities, who in C.O.S. theory were assigned a particular role, followed the C.O.S. script. As the years passed, the Society's grasp of social and political realities became more and more tenuous, until it developed, in the Webbs' words, into "the most exclusive of sects."[4]

A variety of ingredients went into the curious amalgam that became the Charity Organisation Society, some of them idealistic, some merely prudential, so much so that it is often difficult to decide what was the authentic C.O.S. message. The social factor most immediately concerned was the apparent increase in pauperism in the 1860's. Though Local Government Board statistics do not entirely support this presumption, the prevailing view was that pauperism was on the rise and

---

[3] Professor Charles Loch Mowat's valuable study (*The Charity Organisation Society, 1869–1913* [London, 1961]) appeared after this chapter was in draft. My purpose and perspectives are somewhat different from his, and, although I have altered some details, I have made no substantial changes on the basis of his volume. I have, however, drawn heavily at points on his earlier article, "Charity and Casework in Late Victorian London: The Work of the Charity Organisation Society," *Social Service Review,* 31:258–70 (September 1957).

[4] Sidney and Beatrice Webb, *English Poor Law History: The Last Hundred Years* (London, 1929), p. 456.

at a shocking rate, and there was no lack of figures that seemed conclusive.[5] As for the country as a whole, both numbers of paupers and the cost (per capita of population) were indubitably increasing.[6]

However grave or trivial may have been the increase in pauperism, the explanation assumed by the fathers of the C.O.S. — that of a lax and captious Poor Law combined with indiscriminate almsgiving — was altogether too easy. Beatrice Webb recalls the belief, almost "an obsession," widely accepted in the 1860's, "that the mass-misery of great cities arose mainly, if not entirely, from spasmodic, indiscriminate, and unconditional doles, whether in the form of alms or in that of Poor Law relief."[7] Those who adopted this view seemed unaware not only of the jumpy behavior of British economy during the decade — the financial crisis of 1866 and the poor harvests — but also of the fact that the 1860's were a period of upheaval in the life of London's lower classes, especially those of the City and adjoining areas. Large numbers who were displaced by the Metropolitan Railway, the cutting through of new streets, and other "improvements" re-established themselves with difficulty and, no doubt in many instances, were reduced to dependence on charity or the rates.[8]

But it is also true that on the chaos and looseness of Poor Law administration can be fairly visited some of the responsibility for the situation. The system had completely failed to realize the systematized regularity contemplated by the Act of 1834, and local Boards of Guardians enjoyed a wide degree of latitude. Throughout the mid-century, practices grew less rather than more uniform, and the number of Unions to which the Outdoor Relief Prohibitory Order was applied steadily declined. In other words, the rigid principles enunciated by the Poor Law Commissioners in 1834 not only had never been fully put into effect but from year to year were being progressively eroded.[9]

Those who were disturbed about the increase in pauperism could find little to reassure them in the methods of voluntary charity. One does not have to accept the whole force of the C.O.S. indictment to suspect that the charitable public was getting by no means full value for its pounds and shillings laid out in philanthropy.

[5] Professor Mowat (*Charity Organisation Society*, p. 5) notes, on the basis of Local Government Board figures that during the 1860's the rate of pauperism in the Metropolis was actually declining. But statistics widely accepted by the founders of the Society seemed to show the contrary — that in the decade 1858–68, for example, the ratio rose from 2.9 to 5.09 per cent. (J. H. Stallard, *Pauperism, Charity and the Poor Laws* [London, 1869]; Thomas Hawksley, M.D., *The Charities of London* [London, 1869], p. 8; E. L. O'Malley, "Charity Organisation," *Trans. Social Science Assn.*, 1873, p. 589.)

[6] Mowat, *Charity Organisation Society*, p. 5. During the decade the number of paupers rose from 844,000 to 1,032,000, and their cost from £5,454,000 to £7,673,000. (O'Malley, "Charity Organisation," n. 5.)

[7] Beatrice Webb, *My Apprenticeship* (London, 1926), p. 200.

[8] The consequences of urban "improvements" will be noted at several other points, especially in connection with the problem of charities in a depopulated City of London and with housing projects. Here one may cite the opinion of Edward Denison, the forerunner of the C.O.S. itself, who attributed to metropolitan improvements most of the increase in London pauperism. (Sir Baldwyn Leighton, ed., *Letters and Other Writings of the Late Edward Denison* [London, 1872], p. 130; M.V.R.A., *20th Ann. Rept.*, 1865, pp. 6–7.)

[9] The Webbs, *English Poor Law History*, pp. 204–5.

The charity expenditure of the Metropolis in the late '60's may have run between £5½ and £7 million annually.[10] This outflow did a good deal to mitigate the weight of misery borne by the poor of London, but in the unsystematic and indiscriminate way in which much of it was dribbled out, it also did something to fasten on them the habit of dependence on charity, considering it, in fact, as no more than their due. Many of the institutions dedicated to charity were correctly regarded by the enlightened as useless, even pernicious, but still more demoralizing was the wholesale distribution of doles in cash or tickets for food or coal, with little distinction as to need or merit. The Barnetts' early years at St. Jude's were made hideous by perpetual demands for money or tickets, backed by intimidation and threats. If the person appealed to dared to refuse, a full-dress mob scene might be enacted. It was after a mob laid siege to their vicarage that the Barnetts had a door cut from the vicarage into the church, through which the vicar could slip out to summon the police.[11] William Whiteley, the "universal provider," regularly walked from his home in Kildare Terrace to his store in Westbourne Grove, "running the gauntlet of hundreds of beggars, whose importunity, he once estimated, cost him nearly tenfold what he would have spent if he had traversed the distance by cab." [12]

No rational person could doubt that much of London's benevolence, though it may have given donors an agreeable feeling of virtue, failed to be socially constructive and that it implanted in the recipient precisely those habits of shiftless dependence and irresponsibility which it should have been designed to correct. Such criticisms of charitable practices were commonplace enough. We have encountered them before and will do so again. The C.O.S. was entitled to be disturbed over pauperism and the pauperizing tendencies of certain charitable activities. If its concern for mass poverty had amounted to even a fraction of its alarm over pauperism, one would look back on the Society as one of the more prophetic voices of the late century.

It would be unprofitable to try to isolate the source of the charity organization idea. Nor would it be useful to identify any one individual as founder of the Charity Organisation Society, still less to follow the rather unedifying controversy that later developed as to who deserved principal credit.[13] Not only did a number

---

[10] Hawksley, *Charities of London*, p. 6.

[11] Henrietta O. Barnett, *Canon Barnett, His Life, Work and Friends*, 2 vols. (New York, 1919), I, 84. The Reverend J. R. Green reported a similar state of affairs in his East End parish. (See Karl de Schweinitz, *England's Road to Social Security* [Philadelphia, 1943], pp. 141–42.)

[12] R. S. Lambert, *The Universal Provider* (London, 1938), p. 133.

[13] The most objective and credible account is that of E. C. Price, "The Origin of the London C.O.S.," *Charity Organisation Review*, 8:355–72 (October–November 1892). In the Family Welfare Association (C.O.S.) Library is a volume of pamphlets and clippings on the controversy, including C. B. P. Bosanquet, *The History and Mode of Operation of the Charity Organisation Society* (1874); Thomas Hawksley, *Objections to "The History"* (n.d.); W. M. Wilkinson, *A Contribution Towards the History of the Origins of the Charity Organisation Society* (1875); G. M. Hicks, *A Contribution Towards the History of the Origin* (1875?); Sartor Minor (presumably Hawksley), *Philanthropic Tailoring and Historic Cobbling* (1875). Also relevant are Wilkinson, *The Invention of the C.O.S.* (Charity Reform Papers, No. 10) and *Lord Lichfield and the Origin of the C.O.S.* (No. 11); W. A.

of individuals make specific contributions, but, in a broader sense, something like the Charity Organisation Society had been in the air for some years. In Liverpool, William Rathbone's determination to replace muddle by method resulted in 1863 in the amalgamation of three relief agencies into the Central Relief Society, and in Scotland the Edinburgh Society for Improving the Condition of the Poor (1867) anticipated some features of the London organization. On a different level, many of the methods of the C.O.S., it has been suggested, were already in use by Evangelical bodies and what the Society did was to make these techniques more general.[14]

The most direct forerunner, however, was the Society for the Relief of Distress, established, to quote its initial report, by "a few gentlemen, taking into consideration the deficient harvest and the high price of provisions in the autumn of 1860, the distress revealed in the proceedings of the police courts, and the occurrences of death from starvation."[15] Not only in some of its methods did the S.R.D. look toward the Charity Organisation Society, but there was also some duplication of personnel among the leaders of the two bodies. The earlier Society recruited a sizable body of volunteer almoners who were assigned districts (too large, as it turned out) in the needier sections of London.

Edward Denison, the John the Baptist of the C.O.S., obtained his first acquaintance with East End poverty while serving as an S.R.D. almoner in Stepney. Convinced that relief through doles was self-defeating, he resolved to share the experience of the poor in a fashion impossible for a part-time almoner. Taking up residence in Stepney, he became virtually a one-man settlement house.[16] The experiment lasted less than a year, for a successful campaign for a seat in Parliament and other interests drew him away from the East End, and he died in 1870, only about two years after he had gone to Stepney to see for himself. Denison's approach to poverty, in his essential economic orthodoxy and his belief in a more rigorous Poor Law, foreshadowed some of the C.O.S. doctrine, and he was convinced of the disastrous consequences of uncoordinated charitable efforts. Occasionally he seems to look beyond the rigid ideology of the C.O.S., but on the whole there is little reason to question Denison's credentials as the forerunner of the Society.

Its more immediate architects were several, though their specific contributions are difficult to untangle and for the present purpose of little consequence. As an almoner for the S.R.D., G. M. Hicks became dissatisfied with its methods and

Bailward, "The Charity Organisation Society: A New Historical Sketch," *Quarterly Review*, 206:55–76 (January 1907). Mowat (*Charity Organisation Society*, p. 18) lists other and more recent accounts.

[14] Simey, *Charitable Effort in Liverpool*, chap. VI; Heasman, *Evangelicals in Action*, p. 290.

[15] Quoted in the *37th Ann. Rept.*, 1897. The principal founder was William Bromley Davenport, a young country gentleman, who, in London during the bad winter of 1860–61, had been horrified by the distress that he heard of and witnessed. Davenport was given a bad time by the Select Committee on Poor Relief when his evidence, imprecise and unbuttressed by statistics, was made to look incredibly naive, however justified his suspicions may have been. (*S. C. on Poor Relief* [England], 1861, Q. 1597ff; W. L. Burn, *The Age of Equipoise* [London, 1964], pp. 121–23.)

[16] Leighton, ed., *Letters of Edward Denison*, pp. vii–ix.

outlined a series of improvements which in some respects looked toward the C.O.S. plan, notably greater use of local offices for receiving and investigating applications.[17] It was also Hicks who compiled and published in *The Times* a fascinating table of London charities with their incomes and drew from the editor three leading articles.[18] But more immediately, the Charity Organisation Society grew out of an earlier body, with large and undifferentiated aims, which called itself the London Association for the Prevention of Pauperism and Crime. Urged on by that indefatigable champion of reform and enlightenment, the Reverend Henry Solly, the Association started out bravely enough, with the Bishop of London as President and a prospectus drafted by John Ruskin.[19] But the organization contained within itself the seeds of its own imminent dissolution. It was made up of incompatible elements. At the outset a group whose special concern was unemployment found itself contending against another which was determined to enlist the Association in the cause of charity organization. Whatever the relative merits of the two causes, the program of the latter group appeared more practicable, and the Association immediately took steps to establish contact with the mass of London charities. This new organization would not be another relief agency but a body which would advise charities and seek to coordinate their work. With the almost Candide-like optimism that characterized the earlier activities of the C.O.S. group, some 1250 invitations to a general conference were sent out, from which fewer than 400 acceptances were received. (A few weeks later 1700 copies of a circular to charities produced only two responses.)[20] The conference accomplished little save to register in unmistakable terms the reluctance of London charities to submit to "organization."

In the course of it all, however, the outlines of the new body began to emerge. The essential feature of its structure was to be decentralization — that is, the plan of district offices where applications would be received, applicants investigated, and worthy ones referred to proper charitable agencies.[21] It was vital, moreover, that in dealing with the poor a sharp distinction be maintained between relief and charity; neither might properly be used to supplement the other, though for obvious reasons they ought to work in close concert. Charity was for the "deserving," while public relief should be the lot of the others. On these two basic elements, district offices and a clear differentiation of charity from poor relief, was grafted a plan for discouraging beggars, a system of mendicity tickets similar to that developed by a clergyman at Blackheath.[22]

---

[17] *Charity Organisation Review*, 8:357–59 (1892).

[18] *The Times*, 11–13 Feb. 1869.

[19] Ruskin to Solly, 29 Oct. 1868, Solly Papers (London School of Economics). Incidentally, Ruskin's name appeared for years among the vice-presidents of the C.O.S.

[20] *Charity Organisation Review*, 8:370 (1892).

[21] As suggested by Dr. Hawksley in the paper read at a meeting of the Society of Arts and later published as *The Charities of London*.

[22] The Reverend Martyn Hart. W. M. Wilkinson, who put forward his own claims as the founder of the Society, apparently was the author of a plan embodying various features which had been proposed and debated back and forth. See Mowat, *Charity Organisation Society*, p. 17.

This program gradually commended itself to the leaders, most of whom had turned against the more cosmic purposes which animated some of the original group. The primary object of the Association was to be that of securing cooperation among charitable agencies. During these early days the most influential voice was that of Lord Lichfield, who served as chairman of the C.O.S. Council from 1869 to 1877. He not only established the new organization in rooms on Buckingham Street, where it remained until the building of Denison House on Vauxhall Bridge Road some thirty-five years later, but he installed his own private secretary, Ribton-Turner, as secretary of the organization. More than to anyone else, it fell to Lichfield to pick up the pieces when the paid secretary absconded with £42 of the Society's meager resources, having also forged a check on its bankers.[23] And he presided over the decision, taken in late April 1869, to change the name of the Association for the Prevention of Pauperism and Crime to the Society for Organising Charitable Relief and Repressing Mendicity.

2

The new agency, conceived its major purpose to be, as the first annual report put it, that of providing "machinery for systematizing, without unduly controlling, the benevolence of the public." [24] During the earlier years especially, the negative and quasi-punitive elements in the C.O.S. philosophy emerge strongly. Secure in the fashionable thesis that ill-considered and unsystematic philanthropy was the chief source of pauperism, the Society pushed its crusade against mendicity, indiscriminate almsgiving, and laxity in Poor Law administration with enormous zeal. One of its immediate objects was a working understanding with the Poor Law authorities which would mark off from each other the respective spheres of public relief and private charity. Not only was charity to deal only with "deserving" cases — a category later altered to "helpable" by a generation which discovered that often nothing could be done even for patently worthy cases — but it was taken for granted that the "deserving" were readily identifiable.[25] Though certain more realistic Organisers suspected that only a shadowy line might separate undeserving Poor Law cases from deserving charity cases, the work proceeded on the comfortable assumption that such a line could be drawn without too much difficulty.

At this point the Society discovered an ally in George Goschen, President of the Poor Law Board in the Gladstone Government, whose Minute of 20 November 1869 emphatically supported the C.O.S. stand.[26] Though it would be natural to infer C.O.S. influence behind the Goschen statement, evidence is lacking.[27] In

[23] Helen Dendy Bosanquet, *Social Work in London, 1869–1912* (London, 1914), p. 26.

[24] *1st Ann. Rept.,* 1869, p. 6.

[25] O'Malley, "Charity Organisation," *Trans. Social Science Assn.,* 1873, pp. 592–93; Beatrice Webb, *My Apprenticeship,* pp. 201–2.

[26] Poor Law Board, *22d Ann. Rept.,* 1870, pp. 9–12; also, W. Chance, *The Better Administration of the Poor Law* (London, 1895), pp. 232–35.

[27] Calvin Woodard, "The Charity Organisation Society and the Rise of the Welfare State," unpubl. diss., Cambridge University, p. 110.

any event, the Board subscribed unequivocally to the fundamentals of C.O.S. doctrine: the separate and distinctive responsibilities of private and public relief agencies and the utility of district offices with registers containing particulars of those receiving relief, charitable or parochial. By thus denying assistance to those who were already Poor Law clients, voluntary agencies would cease to encourage pauperism.

Throughout its history the Charity Organisation Society carried the scars of the panic that led to its creation, and it could never shake off an almost pathological fear that pauperism might get out of control. The real problem, as suggested by a not unfriendly critic, should have been "how to relieve poverty without pauperizing, but the Society misconceived it as . . . how to prevent dependence upon public funds and stop giving relief." [28] The essential aim of C.O.S. policy was therefore to establish a clearly marked boundary between public and private relief and to insure appropriately rigorous procedures on the part of public agencies. As missionaries of this gospel, leaders of the Society took office as Poor Law Guardians and sought to reform local relief practices. The main point of their attack was, of course, on outdoor relief, and they demanded a virtual return to the principles of 1834. In three East End Unions — St. George's-in-the-East, Whitechapel, and Stepney — the Guardians and the voluntary societies reached an agreement under which the former were to abolish outdoor relief and the latter were to deal with paupers thought to be redeemable.

It would be hard to draw significant conclusions from the results. When outdoor relief was withdrawn, the numbers assisted naturally decreased, and such C.O.S. stalwarts as the philanthropic and devoted A. C. Crowder in St. George's continued to view the experiment with satisfaction. What was not emphasized, and perhaps not wholly realized, was that, as public relief went down, the outlay of voluntary organizations increased. Even though the C.O.S. might hold the line against indiscriminate relief, other bodies, such as the Salvation Army and the Church Army, were by no means so uncompromising. In the end, the Society's campaign against a lax Poor Law accomplished little. Humane and thoughtful Englishmen would presently begin to explore approaches to the problem of urban poverty more promising than the punitive C.O.S. formula.

The bases of the Society's activities were established at the start. Its operations were to center in a series of district committees, each intended to be roughly coterminous with a Poor Law Union. The C.O.S., in fact, conceived of itself as a federation of district committees united by a common philosophy of charity and standing for common policies of relief. The Council itself was designed to represent the views of local committees. In official theory these should not serve as relief agencies, though, as it turned out, they inevitably tended to become such. Their intended function was rather that of bringing together the applicant (whose need had been established by proper investigation) and the voluntary agency best

[28] U. M. Cormack, "Developments in Case-Work," in A. F. C. Bourdillon, ed., *Voluntary Social Services* (London, 1945), p. 94.

equipped to assist him. As the second annual report put it, "The Committees clear the way for private charity, by obtaining information which individuals can often not obtain for themselves, and they then most gladly leave the applicant to any charitable individual who is willing and able to assist him." [29] Yet the Council had to leave the way open for committees "in the last resort" to provide relief, but preferably only in cases where temporary assistance was likely to be of permanent benefit.

What success the committees attained in carrying out these policies is indicated by the annual totals. Of the 12,656 cases dealt with in 1874, for example, by the thirty-five district committees, 4738 were dismissed as ineligible, undeserving, or not needing relief. Of the remaining 7918 cases, 3163 were referred to other agencies, but 4755 were assisted by the committees themslves through grants, loans, employment, or letters to hospitals.[30] In spite of exhortations to local committees by the central office, the dilemma remained, and by the early '80's the annual reports are no longer distinguishing between cases referred to other agencies and those assisted directly. Even though it was the proclaimed intention of the Society "not to become the great relief agency of London, but to make itself the servant of all other agencies," this distinction did not come easily to district committees, most of which continued to dispense relief in substantial volume.[31]

Local districts had established their committees with an alacrity that was almost embarrassing, so that a year after the founding of the Society some nineteen were in existence.[32] It was natural that the lead should be taken by sections where rich and poor lived in closest proximity to each other, where the need for charity was most obvious and the appeals most importunate. Marylebone, the district of Lord Lichfield and Octavia Hill, was first in the field, followed by St. George's Hanover Square, Paddington, and Kensington. The poorer districts of the East, Shoreditch, Bethnal Green, Whitechapel, and the rest, presented more of a problem, for leaders and workers were in short supply, and the Council, loyal to its own self-help philosophy, hesitated to offer subsidies until everything possible had been done locally.[33] Inevitably there was an enormous disparity in the resources of the thirty-five district committees (which had been brought into existence by 1873), and the Council was looking for means of channeling to the poorer areas some of the funds which could be readily raised in the more affluent sections. During the first year of the Society's life, St. George's Hanover Square assisted St. Giles and the needier districts of Westminster, and presently made available £1000 for the District Committee's Aid Fund, a sum that was supplemented by smaller amounts from other local committees and individual donors.[34] But the Council never managed to persuade local committees to follow uniform policies.

[29] 2d Ann. Rept., 1870, pp. 5–6.
[30] 6th Ann. Rept., 1874, pp. 2–3.
[31] Ibid., pp. 3–4; 11th Ann. Rept., 1879, pp. 13–14.
[32] 2d Ann. Rept., 1870, p. 2.
[33] 4th Ann. Rept., 1872, pp. 3–4.
[34] Bosanquet, Social Work in London, p. 39.

A high degree of local autonomy, after all, was a major premise of the Society, and committees continued to vary enormously in the efficiency with which they operated.

3

It took only about a year to demonstrate that a group of honorary secretaries could not supply the executive leadership that was called for. In mid-1870 the Council appointed as paid secretary Charles B. P. Bosanquet, whose volume *London, Its Growth, Charitable Agencies and Wants* (1868) had pointed in the direction of some such organization as the Society.[35] When in 1875 he retired to his Yorkshire estates, the Council was faced with the choice of a successor. Rarely has a selection committee been gifted with greater prescience, or perhaps enjoyed more signal good luck, than the C.O.S. Council when out of two score of candidates it chose a young man of twenty-six.

It would be excessive to imply, as did the *Oxford Magazine* in 1905 when the University awarded him a D.C.L., that the real history of the Society began with the coming of Charles Stewart Loch as secretary. The main lines of development had, in fact, been laid down during the earlier years, but certainly Loch, only a few years out of Balliol, added not only organizing drive and administrative grasp, but also an element of positive idealism that was not apparent, or at least not articulate in the initial period. For nearly forty years the history of the Society and the biography of C. S. Loch were almost identical, so much so that to many outsiders he *was* the C.O.S. In the words of the *Oxford Magazine,* he "formulated a principle and created a type," though its further judgment that under Loch the Society became "the repository of wise counsels concerning the relief of the poor" would not have been unanimously endorsed.[36] Still, the world of late Victorian philanthropy knew no voice more influential than that of C. S. Loch. By his articles and books, his letters to *The Times,* his service on a series of royal commissions, he achieved a position of almost unique authority on matters of social policy affecting the poor.

In Loch executive talent of a high order was combined with a rich human sympathy which was never entirely buried under his rigidly individualistic social philosophy. Such a body as the C.O.S., he reflected shortly after taking office, demanded of its leader "the heart of a Dickens and the head and will of a Bismarck," and within Loch's nature there were more than traces of both.[37] Within the limits set by his ideology, his policies and procedures were those of a statesman, and, more than most of his C.O.S. associates, he could bring to the immediate

[35] When Charles Bosanquet took over as secretary, Ribton-Turner became organizing secretary. It was largely the result of his efforts that local committees were established so promptly.

[36] Quoted by Beatrice Webb, *My Apprenticeship,* p. 196. An excellent biographical sketch of Loch will be found in chap. IV of Mowat's volume and an admirably balanced discussion of Loch and his influence in Kathleen Woodroofe, *From Charity to Social Work in England and the United States* (London, 1962), pp. 28ff.

[37] MS diary (Family Welfare Association Library), 17 Sept. 1877.

task a perspective and a degree of scholarly detachment. His social outlook had been shaped less by the thinking of T. H. Green, his tutor during part of his time at Balliol, than by the writings of his fellow-countryman Thomas Chalmers, whose rediscovery Loch regarded as the most significant development in the charity world during the latter part of the century.[38] To reconstruct the C.O.S. on the Chalmers pattern and to infuse it with his particular brand of social idealism was Loch's conscious purpose.[39]

Thomas Chalmers (1780–1847) figures in the annals of the nineteenth century chiefly as leader in the secession from the Kirk which produced the Free Church of Scotland. But in his thinking and writing he ranged widely. The problems of British economy, especially in their social aspects, held a continuing fascination for him, and his theories, as presented in his evidence before the Select Committee on an Irish Poor Law and in the weighty *The Christian and Civic Economy of Large Towns,* commanded influence well beyond the limits of his Scottish milieu. His vigorous repudiation of poor relief as a proper field for governmental action struck a responsive chord in a generation alarmed by mounting poor rates and suspicious of centralization. His formula for mitigating distress by the simple expedient of compelling pauperized city populations to stand on their own feet harmonized with the self-help convictions of his audience. The social values of the country village, he argued plausibly, might be restored to large urban communities if these were divided into smaller units and the poor given the kind of neighborly supervision and assistance that would develop in them the qualities of self-reliance and independence. A twelve-year ministry in rural Fifeshire, where Scottish peasants, unspoiled by an English Poor Law, maintained themselves in "industry and virtuous independence," had convinced Chalmers that, to yield beneficial results, charity must proceed on the basis of close personal knowledge and human understanding.[40]

To Chalmers the ultimate source of social distress lay not in external conditions but in the individual character. Human weakness, not the organization of society, was at fault, and he unhesitatingly accepted the social arrangements of his age, the class structure and the categories of "rich" and "poor." If, as he urged, social advance hinged upon the strengthening of individual character, the first condition was to have done with the Poor Law, with all of its inducement to indolence and dependence. When the Poor Law had ceased to demoralize, then self-help, mutual aid, and charity, in beneficent cooperation, would take over. For reasons which a later age finds obscure, Chalmers and his spiritual heirs in the Charity Organisation Society saw in private charity, administered, to be sure, with care and sympathy, "so beautiful a part of man's relations with man" and fiercely resented

[38] C. S. Loch, *Charity and Social Life* (London, 1910), p. 345.
[39] MS diary, 17 Sept. 1876.
[40] N. Masterman, ed., *Chalmers on Charity* (London, 1900), p. 264ff. A thoughtful and judicious account of Chalmers and his work is given by Saunders, *Scottish Democracy, 1815–1840,* chap. 4; see also de Schweinitz, *England's Road to Social Security,* chap. XI.

the notion of public assistance partly because it would do violence to this sacred rapport.

The appeal of Chalmers' theories did not rest exclusively on the eloquence with which they were set forth or the spiritual aura which he threw around schemes that, in a more cynical (and certainly unfair) view, might be thought to have as much to do with saving public money as with inculcating public virtue. He had, in fact, put his ideas to the test of experience and had demonstrated to his own satisfaction and to that of some of his contemporaries that they were not only workable but were indispensable to social well-being. During the four years of his ministry at Tron, Glasgow, a parish of over eleven thousand population in which habits of pauperism had become deeply ingrained, Chalmers, whose energy seemed inexhaustible, managed to visit every family. The survey, which confirmed his already gloomy suspicions, seemed to reveal widespread indifference to religion and a distressing willingness to live on relief, public or private.

On the strength of these results Chalmers persuaded the Glasgow Town Council to set up a new parish, St. John's, in an abysmally poor and squalid section of the city, which would provide a social laboratory of sorts for its gifted and vigorous minister. In his four years at St. John's Chalmers achieved a stunning success in organizing an urban community. This was undeniable, whether or not one sub-scribed to the broader inferences that he drew from the experience. There was more than a little point to Carlyle's observation — hotly denied by later Charity Organisers since it seemed to attribute Chalmers' accomplishments to his personal talents rather than to his grasp of the "true principles" of charitable work — that "with a Chalmers in every British parish much might be possible."[41] His objective was to reproduce in his large amorphous city parish something of the character of a smaller rural community, or rather a series of small communities, and he began by setting up some twenty-five divisions, each under a deacon charged with the oversight of about fifty families. It was the duty of the deacons to investigate applications for aid and, whenever remotely possible, to meet them by encouraging the applicant to greater industry and economy and his relatives and working-class neighbors to join in helping him.[42] Only as a last resort would they draw on Chalmers' relief fund, which was purposely kept at a relatively low figure.

Chalmers had no doubt that his four-year (1819–23) experiment at St. John's had not only justified itself locally but pointed the way to a better method of dealing with the nation's poor. Answers returned by the deacons to Chalmers' questionnaire at the time he left to take the chair of moral philosophy at St. An-drew's indicated that only about five applications a year were reaching each deacon, and that less than one person in each division was receiving relief.[43] For us such evidence may suggest different conclusions from those drawn by Chalmers and his

---

[41] Quoted by Masterman, *Chalmers on Charity*, p. 323.
[42] *Ibid.*, p. 299ff.
[43] *Ibid.*, p. 309.

followers. Certainly it does not show that a state of social well-being had been established in St. John's parish. Obviously if relief were impossible or extremely difficult to get, applicants would prefer to run their chances with resistant relatives and neighbors. There is no satisfactory evidence, moreover, that the plan produced closer and more sympathetic relations between rich and poor. What Chalmers did demonstrate, of course, was the value of systematic voluntary work based on thorough knowledge of the individual situation. In stressing this approach he was not solving the social problem, nor even indicating the direction in which a solution would lie, but he was laying the foundations for what came to be known as social casework.

There is a touch of irony in the fact that Chalmers' theories made less of an impression in his own day than in the later century, when the tide of social policy was about to turn in a direction that he would have deplored. To find mid-century attempts to establish a Chalmers system one would have to look across the North Sea to Elberfeld, in the Rhineland, where a plan more or less approximating his ideal was introduced. In some degree it is fair to say that the Chalmers message reached England by way of Germany. Yet certainly his rehabilitation owed a good deal to the C.O.S. group, especially to Charles Loch. For these men and women he provided not only an example and a set of principles but also a spiritual and philosophical rationale for an approach to which some of them were already pretty well committed. There can be no doubt of Chalmers' influence on such leaders as Octavia Hill and C. S. Loch. His stress on charity as an almost sacred relationship between two individuals; his precept that a thorough understanding of the applicant's situation was indispensable for effective relief; his conviction that casual almsgiving was an unmitigated evil — these were taken over as axioms by the Charity Organisers.

In Chalmers' thinking, also, there were some of the ambivalences that appeared in the attitudes of the C.O.S. group. All agreed that the individual held the key to the social problem and that ultimately social improvement depended on persuading, encouraging, and coercing him into standing on his own feet. True charity therefore implied sympathy and understanding on the part of the donor and was fulfilled not in a single act but in a continuing relationship. Among charity organization leaders, however, much talk about — and, indeed, a genuine belief in — neighborliness as the essence of charity, was combined with a patronage and arrogance, no less real because largely unconscious, which accorded ill with their professions. One need only cite Octavia Hill's attitude toward her tenants to realize how completely this was a patron-client relationship and how easily it was assumed that the superior virtue of the rich entitled them to regulate the lives of the poor. Henrietta Barnett recalls that at the Hill "At Homes" for old tenants they "entered shyly by the back door." [44] It is possible to think of Chalmers' conception of properly administered charity as, in one sense, quasi-organic,

---

[44] Quoted by Beatrice Webb, *My Apprenticeship*, p. 206; also see the Webbs, *English Poor Law History*, p. 456.

since it would provide links from person to person and class to class and thus tend to make them members one of another. But neither Chalmers nor the C.O.S. leaders who professed his philosophy of charity were seriously tempted to deviate from their severely individualistic line.

The truth is that Loch adopted not only Chalmers' theories of charity but also a good deal of his early nineteenth-century social ideology. In the C.O.S. leader, the poet and the pastor, important ingredients in his make-up, were often elbowed aside by the political economist of the most rigidly orthodox views. Throughout his life Loch moved only slightly, if at all, from his bitter hostility to any state action which might encroach on the area assigned by the Society to voluntary charity or which might abate the responsibility of individuals to make their own way or parents to provide for their children. His whole career and that of the agency which he dominated rested on the thesis that pauperism (and to a considerable extent, poverty) was the result of moral weakness on the part of the individual. When, therefore, the Charity Organisers talked, as they frequently did, of getting at "causes" rather than mere "symptoms," they were not thinking of what a later generation might consider causes, but simply of the individual, his family situation, his habits, and other personal factors. With all his great abilities, Loch's outlook on certain larger social issues was extraordinarily myopic, and as it became clear that Britain was not going to be satisfied with the C.O.S. answers, he began to look increasingly like a twentieth-century Mrs. Partington vainly trying to sweep back the wave of collectivist innovation.

Though Loch's coming meant no drastic change in the Society's outlook, a more positive note was sounded in its message. One senses this in reading Loch's annual reports, many of them brilliant expositions of C.O.S. philosophy and obviously designed to educate membership and public. He was adroit in changing the form from year to year, sometimes emphasizing one aspect, sometimes another, but always plugging away at the C.O.S. case. One year, for example, he started his report with *anti* and *pro* columns in which were enumerated respectively the common criticisms of the Society and the answers to them; on another occasion he would take off from a summary and analysis of a decade's developments in the world of charity and on still another from a historical survey of charity — medieval, Tudor, and modern — with a pause now and then to lash out at those "red-hot reformers [who] despise us as hide-bound and antiquated . . . and give us the go-by as they hurry on to make all things new." [45] Loch had some of the gifts of the skillful university lecturer. He knew the tricks of organization and emphasis that make a lecture effective, and he could put his case, even when arguable, in a fresh and arresting fashion.

The four decades of Loch's consulship saw the C.O.S. reach the apogee of its influence and enter upon its decline. Even before his retirement it was clear that the Society had passed its prime. Its rationale of charity seemed oddly out of tune with a social temper increasingly inclined to regard poverty as a public respon-

[45] *23d Ann. Rept.*, 1891, p. 1; see also the *32d*, 1899–1900, and the *33d*, 1900–1901.

sibility. Pronouncements of the C.O.S. became hardly more than whistles to keep up the courage of a diminishing membership, and its dogmas appeared, as a Fabian critic put it, almost grotesquely out of accord with the facts of everyday experience.[46] In its broader claims, though certainly not in its more limited case-work activities, the Charity Organisation Society seemed to many thoughtful Edwardians to be an echo out of the past rather than a wave of the future.

4

That the Society deserved credit for certain achievements would have been generally admitted. Its leaders declared war on charity malpractice and vowed no quarter on mendicity, the fly-by-night charity, and the begging-letter writer, a familiar feature of the London charity world. In 1874 the Society came into possession of some thirty-four directories used by a gang of begging-letter impostors, with check-marks indicating the status as prospects of about three thousand London residents.[47] In their assault on fraudulent charities, the efforts of the Organisers were handicapped by a law so porous as to let all but the most flagrantly dishonest enterprises slip through. One character, for example, who specialized in relief societies for firemen, operated with a good deal of success throughout the 1870's and '80's. He employed a large staff of collectors and raised sizable sums of money, contriving to make his successive swindles sound as though they had a connection with the Metropolitan Fire Brigade.[48] The Society was able to gain a few convictions, but against dubious charities its most useful weapon was the widely distributed Cautionary List containing the names of such organizations, a device which the courts declined to regard as libelous.[49]

On other fronts the C.O.S. vigorously pushed its attack against what it held to be unsound charity practices, even though short of overt fraud. Such well-intentioned efforts as metropolitan soup kitchens engaged the Society's critical attention, for virtually all were operated below cost and made no attempt to distinguish between worthy and undeserving applicants.[50] Nor, as we shall see in a later chapter, did the Council, with Sir Charles Trevelyan leading the charge, hesitate to align itself against the traditional procedures of the "voting charity." [51] The Society's attitude was amply justified, but it would have been hard to imagine a technique better calculated to arouse the suspicion and hostility of some of the older and wealthier London agencies. Whatever the weaknesses of the Charity

[46] Emily C. Townshend, *The Case against the Charity Organisation Society* (Fabian Tract 158, 1911), p. 5.
[47] J. Hornsby Wright, *Thoughts and Experiences of a Charity Organisationist* (London, 1878), p. 34.
[48] *19th Ann. Rept.*, 1887, pp. 17ff.
[49] Bosanquet, *Social Work in London*, pp. 130–31. For other examples of C.O.S. proceedings against fraudulent charities, see Mowat, *Charity Organisation Society*, p. 48.
[50] *Report on the Metropolitan Charities Known as Soup-Kitchens and Dinner-Tables*, 1871; *2d Ann. Rept.*, 1870, pp. 12ff; *3d Ann. Rept.*, 1871, pp. 11–12.
[51] *5th Ann. Rept.*, 1873, pp. 6–7.

Organisation Society, nobody could charge it with seeking popularity at the expense of principle.

In some instances zeal exceeded discretion. A case in point was the charges against Dr. Barnardo's Homes, one of the more appealing and rapidly growing charities of the Metropolis, in which the Society managed to get involved. Like George Müller, Barnardo had been diverted from an intended career as a foreign missionary by the needs of neglected children at home, which, as superintendent of a Ragged School, he had seen at close range. Starting in 1867 with an "East End Juvenile Mission for Care of Friendless and Destitute Children" and a boys' home at Stepney Causeway, Dr. Barnardo's Homes grew at a phenomenal rate, with receipts which rose from £215 in 1867–68 to £30,000 in 1876–77.[52] Yet this warm-hearted, enthusiastic, almost aggressively nonscientific charity had its disquieting features. The unedifying controversy was set off by a pamphlet written by a Baptist minister in Stepney which made a series of allegations against Barnardo and his Homes, the most serious of which had to do with his use of the funds collected.[53] At this point the Society came on the scene and appointed a special committee to investigate, an offer that was promptly declined by Barnardo's trustees on the ground that they had already arranged for a board of arbitration.

In the proceedings that followed, the Society took what in some quarters was regarded as an unbecomingly prominent part, so much so as to arouse the suspicion that the real initiative behind the attack was C.O.S. Although at the hearings Barnardo made matters difficult by refusing to submit to cross-examination, the board cleared him of the gravest charge, that of misappropriating funds. Yet the inquiry raised questions that had not been satisfactorily answered, and the arbitrators had to state part of their decision in qualified terms. What had emerged was the fact that both Barnardo and his Homes constituted something of a special case. Notwithstanding his group of trustees, Barnardo's enterprise was a one-man affair, and more than due for the reorganization that it was presently to receive; his own medical degree from Giessen was shown to be of the mail order variety, though in the preceding year he had, in fact, taken his final examinations and qualified for the Diploma of Licentiate of the Royal College of Surgeons, Edinburgh; the finances of the homes were wholly in the hands of Barnardo himself, who each year received and disbursed large sums of money without benefit of a rational accounting system. This was, in short, a highly personal, somewhat irresponsible agency, managed by one who was both a reckless promoter and an authentic genius, whose flair for publicity was extraordinary but whose love for children was deep and understanding.

The Society might better have let the matter drop. At the beginning of the trouble, the Homes had been placed on the Cautionary List, and now the committee issued a circular pointing out that, because of Barnardo's attitude, certain

[52] J. Wesley Bready, *Doctor Barnardo* (London, 1930), p. 105. The best, though probably overenthusiastic, biography of Barnardo is A. E. Williams, *Barnardo of Stepney* (London, 1943).

[53] George Reynolds, *Dr. Barnardo's Homes: Startling Revelations* (London, 1877).

vital facts had never reached the arbitrators. To concede justice in some of the Society's accusations is not to agree that its actions were well advised. Barnardo may have been taught a useful lesson; an immediate and beneficial consequence of the inquiry was the appointing of a committee "to assist" the director, as the board had recommended. But the affair also helped to fasten on the C.O.S. its reputation as a charity kill-joy more interested in checking inefficient philanthropy than in promoting positive efforts.[54]

In the more constructive phases of its program, the Society's progress must have been disappointing. It made no measurable progress toward coordinating charitable work. Even in the campaign against begging and fraudulent charities, there was never more than a paper cooperation with the Mendicity Society, though on three occasions the C.O.S. proposed merging. With the Society for the Relief of Distress its relations were more cordial, though without inspiring any enthusiasm for organic union.[55] Nor were any substantial triumphs scored for the Society in persuading charities to avoid duplicating activities or even to establish an efficient common register in which would be recorded the names and circumstances of applicants for assistance and particulars of the aid received. It was almost as though charitable agencies were driven by some elemental law of institutional life to struggle to maintain their own identities, often against arguments of efficiency and common sense.

One area in which the Society invested much time and energy with meager results was the chaotic world of London hospitals. This is not the place to survey the policies and problems of the medical institutions of the Metropolis, their determined individualism, their hand-to-mouth financing, and their perennial deficits. The concern of the C.O.S. was really twofold. For one thing, there was a conviction that out-patient departments were being widely abused by those who could well afford to pay for treatment. But beyond this the Society had reason to believe that hospital administration, in a number of its branches, was sloppy and wasteful.

Although Sir Charles Trevelyan was the most articulate critic of out-patient departments, his views were shared by the leadership of the Society. In 1875, for example, a C.O.S. committee, studying the out-patients of the Royal Free Hospital, concluded that out of a random sample of 641 who had applied for treatment nearly 250 could have afforded either to go to a private practitioner or to subscribe to a provident dispensary. Of the others only 169 were regarded as proper cases.[56] Four years before, in its first report, the Society's medical committee had

---

[54] *The Charity Organisation Society and the Reynolds Barnardo Arbitration* (London, 1878) gives an account of the affair, with documents.

[55] *5th Ann. Rept.,* 1873, p. 6; *12th Ann. Rept.,* 1883, p. 21; Report of a Committee of the Mendicity Society, 1 July 1872, and a letter to the Mendicity Society from the C.O.S., February 1879 (Family Welfare Association Library).

[56] *Report by the Administrative Committee of the C.O.S. on an Inquiry into the Out-Patients of the Royal Free Hospital,* 1895. Patients not regarded as proper cases comprised those who gave false addresses (103), those about whom no adequate information was available, and those for whom the parish should have taken the responsibility.

viewed with alarm the nearly 550,000 out-patients credited by Low's *Charities of London* to the sixteen general hospitals and had pictured medical charities as almost bidding against each other for the patronage of the lower classes. Numbers of applicants, the committee warned, were no measure of the good being done by an institution — even though hospitals had discovered that this kind of statistic carried an appeal to donors.[57] What bothered the Society was not merely the encouragement to "medical pauperism" on a gigantic scale but, more legitimately, the overcrowding of out-patient departments so gravely as to interfere with proper individual treatment.

Against the abuses of the free out-patient departments the Society set the virtues of the provident dispensary. These institutions, a C.O.S. publication lamented, seemed to be making heavy weather in London, possibly because of the large number of "improvident dispensaries," but they were flourishing in provincial cities.[58] The movement attained some success but hardly justified the high hopes with which it had been launched or the energy expended in promoting it. In 1889 the hostile *Charity Record* could note, accurately enough, that the dispensaries still depended on benefactions and could predict that without such support the movement would promptly collapse.[59] Not only that, the Metropolitan Provident Dispensaries Association had finally conceded that in some districts dispensaries could never be made self-supporting.[60]

In the 1880's and '90's the Society's point of attack shifted, in part, from out-patient departments to a broader sector. In the hit-or-miss administrative procedures of London hospitals and their lack of uniform policies the medical committee discovered an area that seemed to call for charity organization on a grand scale. And it was, in a large degree, through C.O.S. initiative that a Select Committee of the House of Lords (1890–92) studied the condition of the metropolitan hospitals.[61] In some critical quarters, in fact, it was pictured as the instrument by which the Charity Commissioners and the C.O.S. hoped to gain control of the country's medical institutions. The sponsorship of the Society, the editor of the *Charity Record* implied, amounted to a kiss of death for any institution and was a capital way to discourage donors — such was the unpopularity with which the C.O.S. was credited.[62] Although C.O.S. representatives appeared before the Committee to urge, among other things, the establishment of a central board with some authority over hospital policies and practices,[63] the final recommendations

---

[57] *Report of the C.O.S. Medical Committee*, 30 Oct. 1871.

[58] *On Selecting a Charity* (*Charity Reform Papers*, No. 5).

[59] *Charity Record*, 19 June 1889.

[60] *Philanthropist*, Christmas 1889.

[61] *15th Ann. Rept.*, 1883, p. 56; *S. C. of the House of Lords on Metropolitan Hospitals*, 1890–92. For a number of years the hands of the medical committee were strengthened by an anonymous donor who provided for the salary of a secretary, Colonel Emanuel Montefiore. He carried on a series of studies and propagandized with a good deal of energy.

[62] *Charity Record*, 19 April 1891. This comment probably ought not to be taken at face value, for the *Record* was almost a house organ of the London voluntary hospitals.

[63] *S. C. (Lords) on Metropolitan Hospitals*, 1890–91, Q. 222–228; 26,166.

were less than revolutionary — pallid enough, in fact, to satisfy most of those who wished little interference.

The Society continued to agitate but without visible result. In the long run what forced a greater degree of uniformity was not so much the exhortations of the Charity Organisation Society as the growing financial difficulties faced by the medical institutions of the Metropolis. As will appear in a later chapter, the Hospital Sunday and the Prince of Wales's (King Edward's) Funds did not hesitate to attach conditions of sorts to their aid, and this introduced some degree of order. In the long run, however, it appeared that only grants from public funds could keep London hospitals at a decent level of efficiency and, in some instances, in business at all. Even this expedient failed to solve the problem, and the final solution was, of course, the taking over of voluntary hospitals by the State. It was one of the more paradoxical chapters in the Charity Organisation Society's curious history that the goal it sought could be attained only through means that ran counter to its deepest convictions.

In one significant, if relatively unspectacular, respect, the Society left its mark on British hospital practice. If in its broader activities the most permanent and distinctive C.O.S. contribution was its casework methods, the conclusion also applied to the medical field. Studies of patients treated in the great metropolitan hospitals had convinced the medical committee that what was wanted was more careful inquiry not only into the financial status of applicants but into their whole background. Many were clearly less in need of specific medical treatment than of assistance in ways that might be only vaguely connected with physical disabilities. Before the Lords' Committee in 1890–91 Loch outlined the functions of the hospital almoner and emphasized the importance of hospital casework.[64] Four years later the Society cooperated with the Royal Free Hospital in installing and maintaining an almoner, one of the C.O.S. secretaries. In spite of some initial misunderstanding with hospital authorities, who tended to think of the almoner as a detective charged with the task of scenting out fraud and determining the real financial status of patients, the more constructive side took over and the profession of hospital almoner was created. For over a decade the main responsibility for discovering and training these caseworkers rested with a special C.O.S. committee, until in 1907 it was transferred to a composite body, the Hospital Almoners' Council.[65]

If the Charity Organisation Society encountered insuperable obstacles when it tried to bring order into the confused world of metropolitan charities, it faced some of the same problems with its own constituent bodies, the district committees. Its essential machinery consisted of the forty-odd (at the peak) grass-roots committees (if one may use the term of metropolitan London), where the actual work of investigating and dealing with applicants proceeded. These local com-

[64] Ibid., Q. 26,125.
[65] Young and Ashton, British Social Work in the Nineteenth Century, pp. 108–9.

mittees varied widely in resources and energy. Some were amazingly efficient, with paid secretaries, diligent volunteers, and adequate funds. Others were struggling and marginal, unable or unwilling to carry out policies assumed by the central office to be axioms of Charity Organisation. Where the divergence was most critical was at one of the key points in C.O.S. philosophy. Although from the beginning a cardinal assumption had been that this was not another relief agency, to persuade local societies to act accordingly proved out of the question. No doubt things were not the same at the center as they were on the periphery. To proclaim a policy was one thing; to apply it in local districts, with committees often undermanned and underfinanced and with pressure from applicants for immediate relief, was a different matter. And the issue between "relief" and "organisation" remained unresolved throughout the history of the Society.[66]

Such disparities as those within the London C.O.S. were even more conspicuous among provincial societies. From the early 1870's the charity organization movement expanded rapidly, and in his report for 1891 Loch could list about seventy-five bodies in England in correspondence with the London Society, together with two in Ireland and nine in Scotland. To assist these new societies and to school them in C.O.S. doctrines seemed urgent to the London group. There was reason to believe that some of these new societies were employing methods that deviated markedly from the C.O.S. norm.[67] A common approach to questions of relief seemed essential if Charity Organisation as a movement was to have any meaning. One step was to re-establish the annual conferences of provincial societies, and from 1890 these met regularly. Another device was to create a subcommittee whose particular care was the extra-metropolitan societies. This group, led by one of the more consecrated of the C.O.S. circle, collected information, took responsibility for the annual conferences, and arranged for regular visiting of the outlying societies by members of the London body — in short, attempted to encourage local groups in every way possible and dissuade them from straying too far from the ideological path of the C.O.S.

For, although the movement was more inclusive than the London Society, the metropolitan group was the fountainhead of orthodoxy for the Kingdom.[68] Provincial units looked to the London Society for guidance and counsel, and the London Society was not unmindful of its obligation. From its officers and committees issued a stream of pamphlets explaining, advising, and warning — describing the Society's procedures and expounding its philosophy, as in the *Charity Organisation Papers* and *Occasional Papers*. The organ of the Society, first called the *Charity Organisation Reporter* (a weekly), and after 1885, the *Charity Organisation Review* (issued monthly), reached a much larger constituency than the metropolitan area, and in his annual reports Loch made a special point of including material from the provinces. In 1882 he began the annual publication of the

---

[66] See, for example, the *11th Ann. Rept.*, 1879, pp. 13–14, and the *14th*, 1882, pp. 21–23.
[67] Bosanquet, *Social Work in London*, p. 394.
[68] And its overseas influence, especially in the United States, was significant.

immensely useful *Charities Register and Digest,* one of the most permanent of the movement's contributions to the cause of charity organization.. In these stout volumes — up to 1914 they approached a thousand pages — he undertook to list, classify, and describe the charitable agencies of the Metropolis, and did it in a more detailed and authoritative fashion than the various commercially sponsored directories. To each annual edition, also, he contributed a long introduction reviewing the year's developments in the charity world, criticizing or applauding government decisions, and elaborating the C.O.S. point of view. Like most of the other activities of the C.O.S. (or, as it is now, the Family Welfare Association) the *Annual Charities Register* has been considerably curtailed, but it remains an invaluable handbook for anyone, social worker or student, interested in British charities.

5

In the multifold activities of the Charity Organisation Society during the four decades of its ascendancy, two categories of achievement stand out as of special significance. Most generally recognized and probably of greatest permanent benefit was its pioneering in social casework. But also through its special investigating committees the Society did an important service in educating Londoners and others in the problems of the community, in drawing issues, and in proposing solutions that at least could be usefully discussed. These special fact-finding reports were amazingly miscellaneous in their subject matter and naturally varied widely in quality.[69] Some had a perceptible effect on public opinion and even on public policy. Not surprisingly, one of the first inquiries was focused on the congenial topic of vagrancy, which was investigated by a formidable committee of eighty-one, which included eleven peers and forty M.P.'s. Another early report had to do with dormitories and night refuges for the homeless, on which the Organisers turned a moderately stony eye. An interesting investigation in the '70's exposed the importation of Italian children by *padroni* and inaugurated a campaign for the suppression of the cruel and infamous traffic. The report of the special committee on working-class housing had something to do with bringing about Cross's Artisans' Dwelling Act of 1875, and a subsequent report in the early '80's presumably influenced the parliamentary inquiries which followed.[70]

One of the more fruitful series of special reports had to do with the socially handicapped — the blind, the deaf, and the mentally defective. Here the committees not only represented the most advanced views of their own day but pointed the way to further improvement in the treatment of the handicapped. One committee discovered grave faults in the handling of the blind. Some of the principal agencies for their assistance were spectacularly inefficient, dribbling their

[69] For a summary of these, see Bailward, "The Charity Organisation Society," *Quarterly Review,* 206:58ff (January 1907). Mowat (*Charity Organisation Society,* pp. 73ff) gives details of the procedures followed by these committees.

[70] For a list of special reports, see Mowat, p. 179.

resources out in cash relief rather than training these unfortunates in methods of self-support. With all the money poured out for the assistance of the blind, a C.O.S. publication asserted, not two per cent of them could earn their own living.[71]

The Society was also concerned about the treatment of mental defectives — or "improvable idiots," as they were infelicitously known. Sir Charles Trevelyan, who took the problem as one of his special interests, saw clearly that these unfortunates merited training different from that given to imbeciles and lunatics. Since it was obvious that voluntary bodies could not provide the facilities necessary, the Society admitted public intervention to be appropriate, and the committee did not hesitate to urge specific steps on the Government, such as a series of rate-supported training schools throughout the country. It was a long pull before the State could be brought to consider a program even approaching that urged by the Society, but the C.O.S. continued to pound away with reports, resolutions, and deputations. Certainly the careful work of these special committees proved of genuine value, partly for the measures they advocated and the material they assembled, but perhaps more for their success in directing public attention to certain social problems. To say of the Society, as the Hammonds remarked of Edwin Chadwick, that he was "a bad beacon [but] an admirable searchlight"[72] would be both more and less than the truth, yet it would not miss the mark entirely.

In the long run, however, the importance of the Charity Organisation Society did not lie in its social inquiries, creditable and useful as many of them were, still less in its pretentious — and in our latter-day view, rather preposterous — ideology. The supreme contribution of the Society grew out of its conviction that the indispensable condition for social progress was steady, self-reliant individuals and families and that to deal with the problems of individuals and families was both a science and an art. Here in a sense the limitations of the C.O.S. social vision were an asset. For it was precisely because its doctrine excluded the possibility of social advance save through individual improvement that the Society laid so much stress on sound casework methods. In a word, the permanent legacy of the Society, as of the charity organization movement as a whole, was its success in developing the techniques of casework and establishing social work as a recognized profession.

To describe the methods employed lies beyond the scope of this study.[73] Here the services of the Society were probably less those of creator than of systematizer, since casework of a sort had been carried on extensively by visiting societies and

---

[71] *On Selecting a Charity* (*Charity Reform Papers,* No. 5). The large Gardner Trust for the blind, which was strongly influenced by C.O.S. ideas, will be noted in Chapter XVII below.

[72] J. L. and B. Hammond, *The Age of the Chartists, 1832–1854* (London, 1930), p. 60.

[73] For this aspect of the subject, see Mowat, "Charity and Casework," *Social Service Review,* 31: 258–70 (September 1957); Mowat, *Charity Organisation Society,* chap. II; Kathleen Woodroofe, *From Charity to Social Work,* chap. II; Young and Ashton, *British Social Work in the Nineteenth Century,* pp. 102ff.

other bodies. The essence of the C.O.S. procedure was thorough investigation of every case, and the district committee, as we have seen, provided the machinery for screening and deciding upon applications. So committed was the C.O.S. to the principle of careful investigation that unfriendly critics could discover in the Society's policies a greater interest in preventing unsound charity practices than in relieving distress, and clerical supporters might feel obliged to explain that the cautious procedures of the Society were by no means at odds with the Christian spirit of tenderness.[74] Yet a group that could introduce its warning against alms-giving to beggars and children with the caption "A PENNY GIVEN AND A CHILD RUINED" could not fairly complain that its essentially humane purposes had been misinterpreted.[75] More objective critics, even some who rejected C.O.S. social belief, could find merit in its casework methods. Lord Snell, for example, who as a young man had a not entirely pleasant experience as a worker for the Woolwich C.O.S., concluded that, "taken as a whole, the case work . . . was not only well done, but was on the right lines." [76] To the familiar complaints of delay, red tape, and failure to assist when most needed Snell gave little credence.

The district committees, to repeat, provided the machinery for processing applications. By the late '70's and '80's they were handling well over twenty thousand cases a year — in 1886–87, for example, about 25,500 — of which over half were reported as "assisted." Applicants might be rejected for a variety of reasons, substantial or technical. They might be disqualified on the ground that they were already receiving relief through the Poor Law, or they might land in that obscure but inclusive category of "undeserving," altered in 1886 to "not likely to benefit." Two years later even that tag was abandoned, and C.O.S. statistics distinguished merely between "assisted" and "not assisted." Obviously the "deserving-undeserving" classification had created dilemmas, both logical and practical, for the Organisers. Was it not possible, for instance, that the "undeserving" might be those most desperately in need of help?[77]

Although the formal categories were altered, there was little disposition to grant aid to those considered undeserving. Some applicants proved to be outright impostors; others had already solved their problem and were no longer in need; with still others, investigation revealed a history of drunkenness or bad behavior which was held to disqualify them. Some of the strict constructionists of the early days were even inclined to deny assistance to the wives and children of the undeserving. The *Charity Organisation Reporter* told of the death from starvation of a child, whose father, it was stated at the inquest, "had lost several opportunities for earning a livelihood through love of drink." The Hon. Secretary of the East London (C.O.S.) Enquiry Committee concluded that "neither charitable agency

[74] Samuel A. Barnett, "Christianity and the C.O.S.," *Economic Review*, 4:184–94 (April 1894).
[75] "C.O.S. Leaflet" for April 1883.
[76] Lord Snell, *Men, Movements, and Myself* (London, 1936), p. 71. Beatrice Webb passes judgment, by no means entirely unfavorable, on the Society's work, in *My Apprenticeship*, pp. 194ff.
[77] Mowat, *Charity Organisation Society*, p. 37.

nor Poor Law could prevent a child being starved under these circumstances. It was a type of many so called 'starvation' cases." [78]

A more agreeable category of case was the "assisted." It was a canon of C.O.S. work that relief should be adequate, that is, should be both sufficient and adapted to the needs of the individual situation. When a committee had decided to give assistance, its first aim was to persuade relatives or friends to help out and, failing that, to put the applicant into contact with the appropriate agency, perhaps a rest home or a society specializing in surgical aids. There was an inevitable residue of cases which could not be passed along but which still had a legitimate claim to aid. To relieve even such worthy applicants from the Society's own limited resources was thought undesirable, but, as an alternative, committees were encouraged to raise funds specifically for individual cases. The *Review* regularly carried appeals for needy individuals and families, with detailed accounts of their circumstances. If a committee could find a donor willing to provide a needy widow with a sewing machine or a costermonger with a donkey, not only might it restore them to independence, but this would be an activity consistent with the original aims of the Society. The district committee, as the channel by which relief flowed to the recipient, would be applying the principles of charity organization to the benevolence of individuals.[79] Yet such dependence on other agencies and individual benefactors proved unsatisfactory, and as younger and less orthodox leaders emerged in the districts, local committees increasingly conceived their chief function to be the administering of relief. The trend was so general, in fact, that at the end of the 1880's a C.O.S. stalwart could query in the *Review,* "Is the Administration of Relief the Only Function of the Charity Organisation Society?" [80]

Originally the Society had assumed the volunteer to be the proper agent for the practice of charity, and, particularly in the earlier decades, it managed to enlist numbers of the more fortunate classes in regular work on behalf of "the poor." In the beginning, indeed, there was more than a touch of prejudice against the professional and a robust confidence in the trained amateur. To employ paid workers seemed contrary to the neighborly spirit that the Society, in the Chalmers tradition, held to be the essence of charity. A paid secretary was, of course, indispensable in the central office, but for some time the management of the district committees was wholly in the hands of volunteers, supplemented, to be sure, by a meagerly paid individual called an agent, collector, or enquirer, who would certainly not qualify as a trained professional.[81] From the late '70's, paid secretaries appeared in one district office after another, until by the turn of the century more than half of them were so administered. This did not mean that the Society had lost faith in the volunteer worker. On the contrary, a common justification of the paid

[78] *Charity Organisation Reporter,* 6 March 1872.
[79] *23d Ann. Rept.* 1890–91, pp. 3–4.
[80] *Charity Organisation Review,* 5:24–32 (January 1889).
[81] Mowat, "Charity and Casework," *Social Service Review,* 31:265 (September 1957).

secretary was that he would free the volunteer for more important labors outside the office.

Of one thing the Society was rightly convinced. Something more than an eager and willing spirit was needed if charitable work was to be effective. This was a craft in which the worker had to be schooled, as in any other. Conferences, lectures and discussions, practical experience under supervision in a district office, these were some of the techniques by which new volunteers were trained in casework and grounded in C.O.S. philosophy.[82] Novices were encouraged to study the neighborhood in which they were to work, its institutions and problems, to learn something of working-class attitudes and outlook. Altogether, whether the Society realized it or not, a new profession was emerging (even though some of its finest practitioners remained technically amateurs). Professor Mowat's summary of this side of the C.O.S. achievement puts the point well enough: "Partly from good sense, partly from imperfectly conceived ideas, partly from luck, the COS stumbled into casework, refined it, and gave it form." [83]

6

The remaining chapters of the C.O.S. story, in twentieth-century perspective, are less happy. Certainly from the mid-1880's the leaders misapprehended the forces working in British society, and, when they recognized these currents, dismissed them as temporary aberrations which would soon exhaust themselves. The converse of the Society's stress on the self-reliant individual and family as the keys to social well-being was an implacable hostility to most proposals looking to action by the State to mitigate poverty. In his 1889–90 report Loch discovered two tendencies in late-century social thought: "The one would wish to move the class, as if it were living on a floating island, and could be towed into a new social state. The other would work from the *terra firma* of our social past, and would build out of the materials which lie ready to hand the better structure which new generations require. The one would impose a general social discipline. The other would trust rather to that self-imposed discipline which life teaches and charity inspires." [84] Authoritative C.O.S. doctrine continued to dismiss as superficial and self-defeating any approach to social reform other than through the rehabilitation of individuals.

It is impossible to explain fully why C.O.S. philosophy remained frozen in what was virtually its original form and why it was so doggedly resistant to the changing social climate.[85] In an England that was looking increasingly to the State as an engine of social improvement, the Society continued to proclaim that,

[82] Young and Ashton, *British Social Work in the Nineteenth Century,* pp. 105–6.

[83] Mowat, "Charity and Casework," p. 269.

[84] *22d Ann. Rept.,* 1889–90, p. 1. The most extreme statement of the individualist position is probably that of Mrs. Bosanquet in *The Strength of the People* (London, 1902), a robust defense of personal character and self-reliance as ingredients in success.

[85] Acknowledgment should be made once more of Calvin Woodard's unpublished Cambridge dissertation and the suggestive conclusions that he reaches on this point.

almost by definition, public action demoralized but private charity, properly administered, offered redemption. It was almost as though the C.O.S. claimed a
vested interest in the poor and felt entitled to dismiss proposals from other sources
as infringing on its beneficent monopoly. No doubt the dominating influence of
C. S. Loch was partly responsible for the steadfastness with which the Society
clung to the eternal verities. He had infused into C.O.S. thinking an idealistic,
almost evangelical, element which owed something to the Chalmers tradition and
had invested it with quasi-theological authority.[86] Occasionally a note of uneasiness creeps into his annual reports, but his doubts were never more than
momentary.

Loch was naturally disturbed by the defection of some of the earlier pillars of
the Society, notably Canon and Mrs. Barnett. Year by year they had been growing more restless as members of a group which they now believed to be "out
of sympathy with the forces that are shaping our times." [87] Their work in the
slums had proved highly instructive, and they had discovered a whole complex of
evils against which "scientific" charity would be only slightly more effective than
indiscriminate almsgiving. They were no longer appalled at the prospect of an
active state social policy. As early as 1883, the year before he became Warden of
Toynbee Hall, Barnett had come out for a "Practicable Socialism," which
amounted to public initiative in providing housing, education, medical treatment,
and old-age pensions.[88] In the following year (in a leaflet issued by the C.O.S.
itself) Mrs. Barnett took occasion to reprove the Society for its apparent lack of
interest in social reform of the broader sort.[89]

Through the '80's Barnett's social ideas developed along with his East End
experience, and his alienation from the Society became more marked. In 1895 he
spoke before the Council, offering what he called, probably without intentional
irony, "A Friendly Criticism of the C.O.S." [90] Actually it turned out to be a
fairly sweeping indictment of the Society, its doctrines, policies and practices. Not
only, he implied, had the C.O.S. failed to grapple with the vital issues of poverty
and welfare, but it had bitterly and blindly opposed any attempts, public or
private, that deviated from its own rigid orthodoxy. A state pension, in his view,
was not necessarily more demoralizing than one from a Society, and he thought
it nonsense to equate "state-supported" with "pauperized." Why should the
C.O.S. hosts be seized with panic at the mere mention of socialism? In a word,
what had been launched as a movement to reform British charitable practice had
"become the expounder of a certain way of charity" and had lost contact with the
living currents of philanthropy.

[86] Mowat (*Charity Organisation Society*, pp. 72–73) points out that Bernard Bosanquet, an intimate
friend of Loch, supplied a philosophical justification, in the form of "a sort of right-wing Hegelianism,"
of Loch's social and political outlook.
[87] Henrietta O. Barnett, *Canon Barnett*, II, 267.
[88] *Practicable Socialism* (London, 1888). The chapter entitled "'Practicable Socialism'" appeared in
the *Nineteenth Century* for April 1883.
[89] "What has the Charity Organisation Society to do with Social Reform?"
[90] Barnett, *Canon Barnett*, II, 266ff.

To Loch the criticism was shocking, almost blasphemous, and he replied with a rancorous personal attack on Barnett. But the charity organization movement was, in fact, losing momentum. After 1906 there were rumblings within the Society itself over the uncompromising hostility of the central office toward the Liberal reform legislation. Leaders complained that young volunteer workers were not coming forward as in the past but were rallying to the State, which "offers them not voluntary service, but a short way out of all social evils." [91] Loch's final report (1911–12) furnishes an admirable illustration of both the clarity and the myopia of the C.O.S. social vision: "When the gusts of State philanthropy . . . have passed by, what do we now find but that the people with whom it was difficult to deal are still what they were — and still difficult . . . Thoughtful officials are not satisfied. The public for the moment is satisfied. It has not learned the truth. And if public interest wanes — and most of us can tell of its rising and falling — there is no way left for those who have given their lives, or much of their lives, to the quest, but to return to the simplicities of personal and social endeavour, adequate aid, and self-maintenance." [92]

More revealing, perhaps, than the rigidity of the Society's theory was its attitude toward specific proposals intended to mitigate social misery through public action. The C.O.S. was never less appealing than in its bitter resistance to schemes for providing needy school children with free dinners. The earliest experiments in feeding school children, carried on in the 1860's, were humanitarian schemes, pure and simple, and were intended to benefit such children as those in the Ragged Schools.[93] The problem became much more insistent in the '70's when the new elementary schools brought together large numbers of working-class and slum children and disclosed their shocking condition. There was, it appeared, a connection between health and ability to absorb an education. Throughout the 1870's and '80's school children's dinners, whether supplied gratis or for a penny, were assumed to be the responsibility of voluntary agencies. But these operated in close cooperation with the school boards and their visitors. To all such projects save perhaps those that were self-supporting, the C.O.S. was uncompromisingly hostile. What seemed especially pernicious to Loch and his group was "relieving" such children outside of the home and without thorough investigation. This was not only, in effect, promiscuous almsgiving to children but also encouraging parents to neglect their responsibilities. It would be possible, he speculated, for parents to refuse a child morning and evening meals if he were getting a good noon meal. This would amount to increasing the earnings of the parents and would give them an unfair advantage in the competition for employment, since they could afford to work for less! [94]

The official position of the Society was laid down in a pamphlet, "The Feeding of School Children," issued in 1889, when a subcommittee of the London School

[91] *44th Ann. Rept.*, 1911–12, p. 2; *41st Ann. Rept.*, 1908–1909, pp. 5–6.
[92] *44th Ann. Rept.*, p. 4.
[93] See M. E. Bulkley, *The Feeding of School Children* (London, 1914), chap. I.
[94] *16th Ann. Rept.*, 1883–84, p. 32.

Board was also considering the question.[95] Children in a chronic state of destitution belonged to the Poor Law authorities, and those whose parents were ill required family relief. The third category of hungry children, those with improvident, negligent, or vicious parents aroused all the smug rectitude of which the C.O.S. temper was sometimes capable. "To feed their children for them is to debase the moral standard . . . by practically inviting parents . . . to spend in idleness or drink the time and money which should have been given to making provision for their family." Anyway, it was hard to tell who needed aid and who did not. Children, it was reassuring to believe, who look "too respectable to have a penny given them need it the most."

Like most of the doctrinal pillars of the C.O.S. temple, this one suffered little erosion over the years. While the Education (Provision of Meals) Act was making its way through Parliament in 1906, Helen Dendy Bosanquet, the most relentless individualist of the group, was denouncing the iniquity of it all in the introduction to the *Annual Charities Register*. It was this Act which, by empowering local school authorities to arrange for meals, made the provision of them a quasi-public function. All this the Society found unwise and unnecessary — for the more the need and condition of the children were investigated, the less justification for feeding them would emerge.

On the question of unemployment, as on other social issues, the Society resolutely refused to turn the corner into the twentieth century. Only with the greatest reluctance and then in qualified terms would the C.O.S. — that is, the central office — admit unemployment to be a fact. In his annual reports Loch habitually put the word *unemployed* in quotation marks, and he devoted much of his attention to criticizing the efforts of others to deal with the problem. It was partly that he regarded unemployment, where it was a fact, as lying outside the province of charitable activity (and, practically speaking, beyond the reach of any remedy but the classic one of adjustment of labor supply to demand). Anyway, he said, "the want of employment is in truth but a small part of the distress that goes by that name . . . Out of work cases are very frequently want-to-thrift cases." [96]

Not all the district committees could follow the narrow path laid down by the central office, and there were, in fact, marked differences in procedure from one section to another. The Society altered its official policy sufficiently to admit the possibility of starting relief works, if the unemployment were the result of some special factor and was due to be of limited duration. But a C.O.S. Committee on the Relief of Exceptional Distress, reporting in the exceedingly bad year 1886, was confident that the resources of voluntary organizations were fully equal to dealing with the emergency, providing there were adequate machinery for investigating the cases to be relieved. Time and again Loch came back to the ultimate social

---

[95] *C.O.S. Occasional Papers*, 1st ser., no. 14, 1889.

[96] *19th Ann. Rept.*, 1886–87, pp. 32–33. See also Loch's evidence before the *R. C. on Labour* (C. 7063–I), 1893, Q. 5802ff.

truth that, in helping those out of work, the only sound method was "by personal influence on the individual case. Nothing short of helping a man to balance his accounts, to live thriftily, to lay by what he can, is of any real value." [97]

The C.O.S. leaders felt only scorn for such expedients as the Mansion House Funds and General Booth's "Darkest England" plan. There was, as will be indicated in a later chapter, good reason for viewing with uneasiness the huge fund (nearly £80,000) raised by Cardinal Manning's Mansion House committee in 1885–86.[98] Still, the critical letter which Loch wrote to *The Times* excited some concern even in his own council, where one member was said to have denounced it as "not only untimely and ungenerous, but unwise." [99]

Leaders of the Society were equally outraged by the scheme propounded by General Booth of the Salvation Army in his *Darkest England,* sensing in the widespread interest aroused by Booth's pretentious plan — it divided the reading public into the Boothite and anti-Boothite camps[100] — a threat to their own principles and position. From the beginning the Society had detested the Salvation Army, whose open-handed, undiscriminating charity, in Mrs. Bosanquet's words, "cut at the root of all the teachings and endeavours of twenty years." [101] In C.O.S. terms the Army's approach was hopelessly sentimental, and its direction irresponsible and autocratic. But the organization, then as now, carried a remarkable public appeal, and the C.O.S. viewed with alarm the wasting (and worse) of such charity resources. In December 1890 the Society went on record when Loch denounced "General Booth's Social Scheme" in a letter to *The Times*. In the following year the attack was renewed when the letter, in expanded form, appeared as a book, along with papers by Bernard Bosanquet and Canon Dwyer.[102] Although Loch was thoroughly justified in some of his objections to the Army's formula for unemployment, his own answer was no more satisfying. It was absurd to insist, as he did, that existing agencies would be sufficient to meet the crisis if they were only properly organized and coordinated.[103]

The C.O.S. continued to be a bit uneasy, but less about the validity of its own solution than about the tendency of public authorities and others to favor lamentably indulgent policies. In 1904 a committee composed chiefly of a C.O.S. in-group (though including also George Lansbury, who wrote a dissenting paragraph to the report) studied unemployment relief. Some of the specific suggestions had merit, but there was little about the committee's conclusions that marked them off from any other hymn to prudence, foresight, and self-reliance composed under

[97] *19th Ann. Rept.,* 1886–87, pp. 55–56.
[98] Cf. the *Report of the Mansion House Relief Fund,* 1886.
[99] *Charity Record,* 6 May 1886.
[100] As pointed out by Herman Ausubel, "General Booth's Scheme of Social Salvation," *American Historical Review,* 56:519–25 (April 1951). The scheme is described in Chapter XVII below.
[101] Bosanquet, *Social Work in London,* p. 341.
[102] C. S. Loch, Bernard Bosanquet, and Philip Dwyer, *Criticisms of "General" Booth's Social Scheme* (London, 1891).
[103] See H. Greenwood, *General Booth and His Critics* (London, 1891).

C.O.S. inspiration.[104] Even when the balance of qualified opinion was turning toward regular and systematic protection against the hazard of unemployment, the Society was still urging its traditional prescription — that the thriftless and idle be given the deterrent Poor Law treatment and that voluntary charity take care of the steady and respectable, without recourse to relief works or public funds.[105] To the C.O.S. leaders, the National Insurance Act of 1911 naturally stood as the ultimate aberration in social policy, and the editor of the *Annual Charities Register,* no longer C. S. Loch, grew furious as he contemplated the adoption of a measure "opposed in every possible way to English traditions of individual liberty and of voluntary cooperation." [106]

C.O.S. officials took a gloomy view of most of the social legislation of the period. "While careful treatment prevents dependence, new Acts," Loch warned, "are passed which create it on a large scale." [107] For some time the Society had been uneasy about proposals for state pensions for the aged. Not only was this held to be a capital example of indiscriminate mass benevolence but it would also cut across the pension activities which some of the district committees had developed. From the early '80's the policy of the Society had been against paying pensions from its own resources, but various local committees had been able to raise funds (in 1895, something over £12,000) from relatives, friends, and former employers. Even the convinced Charity Organisers, however, suspected that such sources might not be sufficient, and in 1895 Loch was urging that more dole endowments be converted into pensions.[108]

As a member of the Aberdare Commission on the Aged Poor (1893–94), Loch left little doubt that, in his view, Charles Booth's plan of noncontributory state pensions was sheer quackery. The year before he had gone on record against it and in 1899 he joined with a group of C.O.S. leaders to form a Committee on [against] Old Age Pensions "to arrange for bringing influence to bear upon Members of Parliament . . . with a view to the prevention of legislation of a pauperising nature." [109] In the same year the editor of the annual volume compiled from the reports of provincial Societies professed to be shocked at the way the old man "occupies the popular imagination, having supplanted those former favourites the 'unemployed' and the 'submerged.' " [110] It was a curious, almost mystical argument that Loch invoked against state action on behalf of the aged. Grants from the State were by definition impersonal and therefore lacking in charity. "Now charity, rightly understood, strengthens social obligations . . . but grants without charity weaken them. And only such grants can be made by the

---

[104] C.O.S. Special Committee, *The Relief of Distress Due to Want of Employment,* 1904.
[105] *37th Ann. Rept.,* 1904–1905, pp. 9–11.
[106] 1912 ed., p. cccxxxi.
[107] *40th Ann. Rept.,* 1907–1908, p. 2.
[108] *27th Ann. Rept.,* 1894–95, p. 13; *C.O.S. Occasional Papers,* 2d ser., no. 3.
[109] Mowat, *Charity Organisation Society,* p. 142; papers in the Family Welfare Association Library collected by the committee; see also *Old-Age Pensions: The Case against Old-Age Pension Schemes* issued in 1903 by the committee.
[110] N. Masterman, ed., *Introductions* (London, 1899), pp. 14–15.

State."[111] Yet Englishmen who were concerned about social welfare found this train of argument increasingly unconvincing, and the Act of 1908, cautious as it was, established the principle of noncontributory pensions. To the official spokesmen of the Society, this simply marked the revival of state almsgiving on a gigantic scale, "not unlike the assured dole of the old endowed charity,"[112] with the Legislature wantonly encouraging dependence on the part of the aged.

7

Throughout these early years of the new century the Society expended so much energy in deploring and resisting the collectivist trend that it gave little thought to the more vital question of readjusting its own activities. Certain qualms occasionally appear in Loch's annual reports, and there were clearly some differences of opinion within the C.O.S. organization.[113] The Majority Report of the Poor Law Commission, on which the Society staked so much, did in fact reveal a perceptible relaxation in C.O.S. orthodoxy. Yet to such innovations as national insurance and old-age pensions the response was largely negative. Until 1914 and even beyond, it was the fashion in C.O.S. circles to dismiss them as not much more than temporary deviations. The British public would soon come to its senses and have done with schemes so destructive alike of individual character and of the helpful, friendly relations between individuals, which, the Society was convinced, informed its own work.

By this time Loch was an old man and in frail health, and he had come to maturity in a world very different from that in which Edwardian Liberalism flourished. To the Victorians rich were rich and poor were poor. It was the duty of the rich to assist the poor to become self-reliant and respectable. For the poor to aspire to too much was not to be recommended. In the course of a rather acid introduction on the current reform tendencies, Loch could quote with approval from *Felix Holt*: "If there is anything our people want convincing of, it is, that there's some happiness and dignity for a man other than changing his station."[114] Able and intelligent, even sensitive, as was the Society's master builder, he completely failed to understand the new England that had risen in the course of the half century. To his Edwardian contemporaries the neighborly helpfulness professed by the C.O.S. seemed often to be hardly more than the patronage of a social superior, the more striking because so basically innocent.

The years after the first World War found the Society still unreconciled to the newer tendencies.[115] To any group less convinced of its own special revelation, the new social services would have seemed more than a passing phase. Loch was no longer at the helm, but his successor was singularly lacking in the feeling

[111] *27th Ann. Rept.*, 1894–95, p. 15.
[112] *40th Ann. Rept.*, 1907–1908, p. 2.
[113] As is implied in the *41st Ann. Rept.*, 1908–1909, pp. 5–6.
[114] *30th Ann. Rept.*, 1897–98, pp. 1–2.
[115] In 1920, for example, W. A. Bailward, a C.O.S. leader of many years' standing, published a volume (whose purport is obvious from the title), *The Slippery Slope*.

for reality that might have freed the Society from its mid-Victorian illusions. It seems incredible that a leader in British social work could write, as did the Reverend J. C. Pringle in his annual report for 1930–31: " 'Farewell, Miss Julie Logan' . . . Collectivism was a phantasm in our England, bewitching in its way. Like Miss Julie Logan, it has vanished." [116] Not until the mid-'30's, with the coming of B. E. Astbury as secretary, was the Society brought to face the fact of a Britain becoming increasingly collectivist. Obviously the question was not whether the trend could be reversed, but rather whether the experience and special skills of the Society would be superfluous in a semi-social-service state. To that the answer was unmistakable. However elaborate the statutory welfare machinery might become, there would still be a place for the expert in individual and family problems working under the auspices of a voluntary agency. Lord Beveridge put the point well enough at the Seventy-Fifth Jubilee Annual Meeting in 1944 when he asserted that "whatever the State does, since that must be the same for all citizens, there will always remain the scope for personal help, individual care of those who for whatever reason need something more or different." [117]

This, then, was to be the Society's future sphere of action, immensely important though less ambitious than the one originally staked out. The new orientation was reflected in the decision to abandon the old name, around which were associated the traditions of three-quarters of a century, as well as strong emotions for and against, in favor of one which would more precisely describe the chief concern of the agency, that of family casework. When in 1946 the Charity Organisation Society became the Family Welfare Association, the break in one sense marked the end of an era in social work. More accurately, the new label merely registered what had in fact taken place years before but had been concealed by the Society's reluctance to reconsider its role in a semicollectivist society.

---

[116] *63d Ann. Rept.*, 1930–31, p. 19. The reference is, of course, to Sir James Barrie's "Wintry Tale," which was first published in 1931 as a supplement to *The Times.*

[117] *76th Ann. Rept.*, 1943–44, p. 1.

CHAPTER IX

REMODELING ANCIENT TRUSTS:
THE ENDOWED SCHOOLS

O F ALL the branches of philanthropy, in some respects the most formidable for the historian is education. It is hard enough, especially for the non-Briton, to keep one's bearings in the maze of the English educational system, to understand its terminology, untangle the intricacies of organization, and appreciate the rancorous emotions aroused by the conflicting interests of Church and Chapel. More specifically there is the almost impossible problem of defining and isolating the philanthropic component in the English school structure, for here, perhaps more than elsewhere, charity, self-help, and state action mingled and interacted in a confusing fashion. In the early century, when Brougham first interested himself in the question, no one would have urged education as a legitimate charge on public resources. The almost unanimous assumption was that the upper and middle classes would pay for their schooling, save where endowments had been established for their benefit, while private benevolence — generally considered in the context of "charitable relief" rather than of public obligation — would provide the poor with training suitable to their station. It was the achievement of the nineteenth century to bring about a shift in the balance. Gradually and hesitantly Britain came to accept education as a public responsibility, and the State emerged as the chief partner in the enterprise.

This chapter is focused, perhaps arbitrarily, on one phase of the process, that in which the Charity Commission was most heavily involved. The 1870's and '80's saw a significant attempt to reorganize the nation's endowments for secondary education in such a way as to provide the basis for a national system. The Newcastle Commission (1861) had reported on the education of the lower classes, and the Clarendon Commission (1864) on that of the upper classes in general and on the nine public schools in particular.[1] Between these two extremes lay a vast and relatively unexplored educational terrain, which, it was assumed, was to be occupied by the middle classes.

The Brougham inquiry had established the existence of a mass of endowments for what would be loosely called secondary schools, institutions occupying a

---

[1] *Report of the Commissioners Appointed to Inquire into the State of Popular Education* (C. 2794), 6 vols., 1861; *Report of H. M. Commissioners on . . . Certain Schools and Colleges* (C. 3288), 4 vols., 1864.

middle ground between elementary schools and universities. The term "secondary school" was anything but precise, but it usually referred to the endowed grammar schools, foundations which dated, in the main, from the sixteenth or seventeenth century.[2] The considerable variety in size of endowment and quality of education among grammar schools as originally established had become infinitely greater by the time of the Brougham survey. The passing decades had left their mark, so that not only were individual foundations overdue for reform or extinction, but the whole complex of endowed schools seemed singularly ill-adapted to the needs of the century. Their location naturally owed more to local patriotism and the special attachments of their founders than to a consideration of the country's educational requirements. From the point of view of population, there was an almost spectacular maldistribution, with numbers of villages boasting large endowments while populous centers were meagerly provided for. The fact was that, by the time of the Brougham inquiry, it was difficult to distinguish, in the quality of their education, many grammar school foundations from elementary schools and even to decide whether an endowment had been intended for elementary or secondary education.[3]

If anything were needed to hasten the process of atrophy in secondary schools, Lord Eldon's decision in the Leeds Grammar School case (1805) was admirably fashioned for the purpose.[4] The question arose when the governing body of the School proposed to use its endowment to teach arithmetic, writing, and modern languages, in addition to the classics. The Court of Chancery granted the petition, but was overruled on appeal by the Lord Chancellor. Eldon's reasoning was not convincing to everyone at the time or subsequently. S. T. Coleridge, suggesting that the Lord Chancellor was insufficiently familiar with sixteenth-century history and literature, recalled that "Ben Jonson uses the term 'grammar' without any reference to the learned languages," and a Victorian Lord Chancellor pointed out that some of the grammar schools dated from a period when Greek was not a subject of instruction.[5] But Eldon's analysis, if historically shaky, was not lacking in assurance. The Leeds Grammar School had been founded "for the free teaching of all young scholars, youths, and children, who should resort to it." Since "free" was equivalent to free grammar school and a grammar school, according to Samuel Johnson, was one intended for the teaching of the learned

---

[2] The eighteenth century contributed few grammar schools, and, indeed, virtually none were established after the accession of George I. (A. F. Leach, "On the History of Endowed Schools," *R. C. on Secondary Education* [C. 7862–iv], 1895, V, 59.)

[3] For the unfavorable impression made on the Brougham Commissioners see the evidence of William Grant, *S. C. on Public Charities*, 1835, Q. 141ff.

[4] *Attorney-General* v. *Whiteley*, 11 Ves. Jun. 241.

[5] *Table Talk*, quoted by J. P. Fearon, *The Endowed Charities* (London, 1855), p. 58; Lord Westbury, *Report of Commissioners . . . on Certain Schools not Comprised in H. M. Two Recent Commissions* (Schools Inquiry Commission) (C. 3966), 21 vols., 1867–68, Part IV, Q. 16,625; for the opinions of other equity lawyers see the evidence of Sir W. P. Wood (later Lord Hatherley), *ibid.*, Q. 12,802; Lord Romilly, *ibid.*, Q. 13,453; Sir Roundell Palmer (Lord Selborne), *ibid.*, Q. 14,219. Sir Horace Davey also dealt with the point before the *S. C. on the Endowed Schools Acts*, 1886, Q. 5141.

languages, it followed that the Leeds foundation was intended to support instruction in the classics and nothing else.[6] For the governors to introduce other subjects would be to commit a breach of trust.[7]

Though hardly a primary cause of the sad state of the grammar schools discovered by the Brougham Commissioners, the Eldonian straitjacket became more irksome as the century advanced. Small endowments, quite insufficient to support a master equipped to teach Latin and Greek, could not legally be applied to humbler uses, such as providing the elements of an ordinary English education, and were thus left without function. In the commercial and industrial towns, on the other hand, there was little demand among the middle classes for a classical education but a great deal for a form of training more appropriate to their adult life and work. This did not necessarily imply a "commercial" education, but certainly the classics would yield place to mathematics, English literature, and modern foreign languages.[8]

Attempts to lift the yoke of the Leeds decision achieved little. Sir Eardley Wilmot's Act (1840) was framed to give the governing bodies of grammar schools a freer hand with regard not only to the curriculum but also to other restrictive trust provisions when these handicapped the work of the school — and thus to accomplish "a substantial Fulfilment of the Intentions of the Founders."[9] But, although the Act formally authorized courts of equity to make drastic changes in the administration and curriculum of endowed schools, their power of initiative was gravely circumscribed. They could intervene only "if it shall be found necessary from the Insufficiency of the Revenues." This meant that only the most destitute of foundations could profit from the new law, for no court would intervene save in an exceptionally glaring instance.[10]

Nor was the situation of the endowed schools much affected by the establishment of the Charity Commission. Although school endowments came under their authority in the same degree as other trusts, they had no authority to undertake a major reform. They could frame schemes *cy-près* for schools as for other charities, but ordinarily they would expect to do so only in the most desperate cases. Neither the Commissioners nor Chancery could deal with schools in relation to each other, as parts of a larger structure; they must be approached as discrete institutions. Hence even to think of recasting the secondary school system was to indulge in fantasy. In spite of memorable advances made by some of the endowed schools, especially the more prosperous, better-established foundations, with the great bulk the record was otherwise. By the 1850's the untidy mass of educational endowments seemed ripe for administrative rationalization and curricular reform.

[6] For the decision and some subsequent judgments on the issue, see *Tudor on Charities* (4th ed.), pp. 631–32.

[7] Brian Simon, *Studies in the History of Education, 1780–1870* (London, 1960), pp. 105–8, has an interesting discussion of the case and some of its repercussions.

[8] Sir W. P. Wood, n. 5 above.

[9] Preamble of 3 & 4 Vict., c. 77.

[10] Lord Romilly, *Schools Inquiry Commission*, 1867–68, Part IV, Q. 13,452; see also J. P. Fearon, *ibid.*, Q. 13,281.

Perhaps they could be remodeled so as to fill a significant place in the national educational system toward which Victorian England was groping.

Of the three great mid-century inquiries into the state of education in Britain, that dealing with the endowed schools was the last to be launched. Initiative came from the Social Science Association, which successfully appealed to the Government to extend its studies to middle-class education.[11] (It was taken for granted that secondary education was to serve the middle classes.) When the roll of the Schools Inquiry Commission was completed, it included Lord Taunton (Henry Labouchere) as chairman, and its most active members turned out to be Dr. Frederick Temple, Headmaster of Rugby and future Archbishop of Canterbury; Lord Lyttelton, who, as Chief Endowed Schools Commissioner, was later to be even more intimately identified with the work of renovating English secondary schools; Sir Thomas Acland; and W. E. Forster.[12] Robert Lowe declined to serve, expressing in a characteristically vinegary note his lack of confidence in those who would have been his colleagues.[13]

After three years of sitting, with some one hundred and fifteen separate meetings, the Commission submitted its report. Resting on more exhaustive investigations than those of the Newcastle Commission and more penetrating in its analysis, the Taunton Report is rightly regarded as one of the most impressive public documents of the century. Apparently the Commission was able to carry on without serious disagreement, at least on fundamentals, and certainly without the sharp cleavages that had impaired the work of the Popular Education Commission. Furthermore, the Schools Inquiry Commission proved to have been either inspired or fortunate in its choice of the Assistant Commissioners who carried on its field studies at home and abroad. The names of Matthew Arnold, James Bryce, T. H. Green, Joshua Fitch, and James (later Bishop) Fraser, among others, guaranteed that the evidence would be not only responsibly gathered but brilliantly marshaled and presented.

It is impossible to summarize adequately the Report itself, which occupies a stout volume, still less the evidence, which takes up twenty additional volumes. Of the roughly 3000 endowed schools, about 800 — all but 70 or 80 of them grammar schools — were of direct concern to the Commission as offering education beyond the elementary level.[14] These schools enrolled nearly 37,000 boys, a quarter of them boarders, and enjoyed an aggregate net income of nearly £200,000 (£335,000 gross) plus nearly £15,000 in exhibitions. Within this mass of foundations, of which 500 were more than two centuries old, there was the greatest diversity in resources, quality of training, and organization. They ran all the way from Christ's Hospital, with an income of £42,000 in addition to its site and buildings, to pitiful little establishments with less than £10 a year. The bulk of

[11] *Trans. Social Science Assn.*, 1863, p. 351; E. G. Sandford, ed., *Memoirs of Archbishop Temple*, 2 vols. (London, 1906), I, 133 (chap. by H. J. Roby).

[12] A. H. D. Acland, *Memoir and Letters of Sir Thomas Dyke Acland* (London, 1902), pp. 244ff.

[13] Lord Edmond Fitzmaurice, *The Life of Earl Granville, 1815–1891*, 2 vols. (London, 1905), I, 433.

[14] *Schools Inquiry Commission*, 1867–68, Part I, p. 108.

them were by no means affluent; far fewer than half could claim an annual
income as great as £100:[15]

£2000 or over	9
£1000 to £2000	13
£ 500 to £1000	55
£ 100 to £ 500	222
	299

The Commission was also disturbed by the erratic distribution of foundations
for secondary education. In most of the counties, secondary endowments yielded
between £1000 and £4000. The income of Cornish grammar schools, however,
did not exceed £400, while Lincolnshire accounted for £7000 and Lancashire for
nearly £9000. Of towns with over 2000 population, 304 had secondary endowments and 208 were without. Often the size of the trust bore no relation to the
needs of the community. The largest foundation in Yorkshire was at Rishworth
(near Halifax), which was not counted as a town. With a gross income of £3000,
the school maintained and educated 55 boys and 15 girls. Admission to the school
was by nomination of the trustees, who, like the governors of Christ's Hospital,
enjoyed a valuable piece of patronage.[16]

Alhough most of the eight hundred secondary institutions were nominally
grammar schools, Lord Eldon would have been appalled to learn that 43 per cent
taught neither Latin nor Greek, and only 27 per cent could be considered classical
schools.[17] In some instances the endowments could not support a classical curriculum; in others, parents were interested neither in a classical training for their
sons nor in paying for tuition in other subjects. The Commission noted with
marked distaste the gratuitous education specified by most founders, especially
when the endowments were inadequate for the purpose. Only three schools, the
Report concluded — King Edward VI School (Birmingham), the Bedford Grammar School, and the Manchester Grammar School offered training that was both
gratuitous and superior. Equally to be deplored was the practice of indiscriminate
admission from a particular locality (often required by the trust) or admission
on nomination by a trustee. Indiscriminate admission and higher education, the
Report asserted, were quite incompatible, for grammar schools were crowded
with pupils fitted only for elementary training. If further evidence were needed,
there was the poor record of endowed schools in preparing boys for the universities. Fewer than forty sent as many as three students a year to Oxford and
Cambridge, even though grammar schools, as a whole, were thought to have
as their main function that of preparing for the universities.

In the large, the Commissioners pictured a group of schools, which, with a good

---

[15] *Ibid.*, pp. 109–10. The income of Christ's Hospital is given elsewhere in the *Report* (p. 473)
as £48,000 applied to education.
[16] *Ibid.*, pp. 110, 404.
[17] *Ibid.*, p. 131.

many distinguished exceptions, were dangerously near moribund, governed by obsolete statutes, administered by trustees often unable or unwilling to give the necessary attention and masters who were frequently inexperienced and incompetent. Most of them neither gave a sound classical education nor had they been able (or perhaps willing) to develop instruction in the modern subjects for which there was a greater demand. As one of the Assistant Commissioners put the point, the classical professions of a school sometimes furnish "the pretext for the neglect of all other useful learning," and the same official, Joshua Fitch, whose duties for the Commission took him to Durham and Yorkshire, concluded that four-fifths of the grammar schools were doing acceptable work in neither classical nor modern subjects.[18] In the end, the real aims of the founders had been frustrated through the literal fulfillment of an antiquated will or deed.

Two basic conditions must be met before the problem could be dealt with successfully. First, the wholly unwieldy mass of endowed schools must be considered as a whole, not simply as isolated units. The Commission urged strongly the *national* interest in these institutions. "Schools have been regarded as subjects of special trusts of a precisely limited character," the Report observed, "not as local contributions to the higher education of the country, which might be freely adjusted to change as they occurred . . . They now exhibit neither the will of the dead for their time nor the will of the living for our time." [19] What was called for was an authoritative agency which would approach secondary education from the angle of the nation's needs, adjusting the functions of individual schools to each other, preventing wasteful rivalry, and thus creating an opportunity for all to reach the highest possible level of education. Secondly, little could be accomplished, however, without a revision of charity law. Neither Chancery nor the Charity Commissioners provided a useful mechanism, since their action was confined to trusts that could not be carried out.[20] Only Parliament could make it possible to "*alter the trusts* of charity which *can* still be executed," a category which covered most of those in which the Commission was interested.[21]

These two principles accepted, the Commission could proceed to its specific prescriptions. The basis of these was to be a thorough recasting of secondary schools into a neatly articulated system, almost Gallic in its symmetry. Schools would be classified into three grades, each offering education appropriate to the length of time pupils would remain and, indeed, to a particular segment of the middle class. The Commission unhesitatingly accepted the notion of education as a function of social class. As Lord Harrowby put it in his evidence, "I should like to club the grammar schools with some relation to locality, and I should like to say, you shall be a good lower middle-class school; you shall be a middle middle-class school; you shall be a higher middle-class school, that which is now

[18] *Ibid.*, p. 133; J. G. Fitch, "Educational Endowments," *Fraser's Magazine,* 79:6 (January 1869).
[19] *Schools Inquiry Commission,* 1867–68, Part I, p. 115.
[20] *Ibid.*, pp. 463ff.
[21] *Ibid.*, p. 469.

called a grammar school." [22] In substance, the Commission's proposals followed this pattern. Schools of the top grade would enroll boys remaining to the ages of sixteen to eighteen and would offer a strong classical or semiclassical training, acceptable as preparation for the universities, while, at the other extreme, the third grade, designed for those leaving between twelve and fourteen, would give an education somewhat above the elementary level.

If Taunton and his colleagues were committed to providing training appropriate (in their view) to the several subsections of the middle class, they were no less convinced that the arrangements must be made decently flexible. The "ladder of education" on which a gifted boy could rise from a lower to a higher grade of school, by the same token, would enable him to rise in the social scale. To this end competitive scholarships and exhibitions in vastly greater numbers were indispensable, and as part of the sweeping reorganization of endowments contemplated by the Commissioners, they urged the conversion of the smallest school trusts into scholarships. They would do away also with gratuitous education, which they regarded as pernicious, but would reward talent, again, from a larger reservoir of scholarships. The ladder of education was an appealing concept, especially for an age inclined to deify competition, but the fact remained that the Commissioners, in apparent innocence, were advocating a plan of secondary education that took as its basic premise the mid-Victorian class structure.

The Taunton Commission concluded that a central agency, armed with substantial powers, was essential both for the initial regrouping operation and for later supervision. No one regarded the Charity Commission as ideally fitted for the purpose, but a court of law was clearly out of the question. Only an administrative body could handle the situation, and, on these terms, it seemed preferable to call on the Charity Commissioners rather than to create a new agency. Along with this central body, however, the Commission proposed provincial boards, which, among other duties, would submit schemes to the Charity Commissioners for schools in their district and would approve schemes framed by the Commissioners. This plan deserved more consideration than it received when the Government got ready to introduce its bill on the endowed schools. [23]

2

No one could have regarded the Taunton Report as a reckless or ill-considered document. More than any of the other members, Dr. Temple was responsible for its structure and was the author of two of the fundamental chapters. [24] The Commission had, however, gravely erred in its optimism about the willingness of Government and people to support drastic measures. It would have been expecting too much to imagine that a Government would follow such a revolu-

[22] *Ibid.*, pp. 578–79.
[23] *Ibid.*, pp. 637–44.
[24] Sandford, *Archbishop Temple*, I, 135. The chapters written by Temple were those weighing the claims of the various types of education and presenting the Commission's recommendations.

tionary prescription completely, and the bill which W. E. Forster introduced omitted two of the cardinal recommendations of the Commission. Instead of a permanent supervisory agency, Commissioners were to be appointed only for a three-year term. Again, the Government would have no truck, at least for the time being, with local boards through which the central authority proposed by the Taunton Commission would have functioned.[25]

Forster's bill was not received with unanimous acclaim in the House. There were the familiar complaints over the irresponsible powers of three government-appointed Commissioners, and protests, not unreasonable, from some of the better schools — Sherborne, Uppingham, Repton, and others — whose claims to public school status were considerable and who resented being placed under the jurisdiction of the Endowed Schools Commissioners. Churchmen were fearful lest the new plan prove a step toward the secularizing of endowments, and Nonconformists uneasy about the matter of religious teaching in the schools. The Commission's solution of this issue was the famous "conscience clause," which permitted Nonconformists in Church of England schools (the bulk of secondary endowments were held to be Anglican) to withdraw from religious instruction.

The bill escaped serious mutilation in Parliament and reached the statute book in about the form the Government had intended. The Endowed Schools Act[26] called for the appointment of three Commissioners with a secretary and suitable staff. In dealing with trusts their authority far exceeded that of the Charity Commissioners, for they could alter, add to, or consolidate educational endowments "in such manner as may render any educational endowment more conducive to the advancement of the education of boys and girls, or either of them."[27] Not only that, but initiative in reorganizing trusts would lie with the Commissioners, and unless trustees or others directly interested undertook proceedings against a scheme, it would go into effect as soon as approved by the Committee of Council on Education.[28]

The Act broke most sharply with precedent, perhaps, in Clause 30, which threw *cy-près* into the discard for certain types of endowment. With the consent of trustees, the Commissioners were empowered to take over for educational purposes trusts for doles, marriage portions, redemption of prisoners and captives, relief of poor prisoners in debt, and others, established before 1800, "which have failed altogether or have become insignificant in comparison with the magnitude of the endowment." Even though its effectiveness depended on the cooperation of local governing bodies, this clause was probably the most forceful blow struck against the Dead Hand in the course of the century.[29] Obviously the Government

---

[25] *3 Hansard*, 190:113, 1371–72.

[26] 32 & 33 Vict., c. 56.

[27] Section 9.

[28] Those opposed to a scheme might appeal to the Judicial Committee of the Privy Council or might demand that it be laid before Parliament. In the latter case, the burden of proof would be on the opponents, for, unless the House took adverse action within forty days, the scheme would go into effect.

[29] The only comparable powers were those granted in 1883 to Commissioners for reorganizing the parochial charities of the City of London, as described in Chapter X.

did not intend the Endowed School Commissioners to be merely a minor Court of Chancery.

Yet the later experience of the Commissioners leaves no doubt that, however badly needed, the Act left public opinion far behind. When the Government announced the names of the Commissioners-to-be, local apprehensions and sectarian fears deepened. The Chief Commissioner was Lord Lyttelton, husband of Mrs. Gladstone's sister, Mary Glynn, and a member of the Clarendon and Taunton Commissions. Lyttelton had first declined to serve on the reasonable ground that he had publicly committed himself to a radical approach to the problem, but he was promptly overpowered by his wife's masterful brother-in-law.[30] Only the previous year at the Birmingham meeting of the Social Science Association, in expounding the philosophy of the Schools Inquiry Commission, he had explicitly disclaimed an attitude of unquestioning deference toward founders' wills.[31] The appointment of Arthur Hobhouse was even less calculated to reassure the anxious. A brilliant lawyer and Q.C. who in 1866 had abandoned his career at the Bar to become a Charity Commissioner, Hobhouse was well known as an advocate of a firm hand and no nonsense in dealing with charitable endowments. Just after they had been designated as Commissioners but before the bill had passed the Lords, Hobhouse and Lyttelton had been indiscreet enough to take part in a joint meeting of the Social Science Association and the Society of Arts in London. Hobhouse read what was perhaps the ablest formulation of his case against the Dead Hand, "On the Disposition of Property to Public Uses." In commenting on his colleague's ideas, Lyttelton conceded that managers of endowed schools might have "some cause for complaint in being placed under men of such pronounced views as Hobhouse and himself." [32]

It would have been odd if no questions had been raised in the Lords, especially when Lyttelton was known to have been the author of the section of the Schools Inquiry Report dealing with eight large foundations. The list included Christ's Hospital, which never lacked influential friends, and these were determined themselves to handle the reforming of the Hospital if any was to be done. Lyttelton met the attack in straightforward fashion. Though he denied that his remarks had gone beyond the Report, he admitted — and had suggested to the Government — that a Commissioner of less decided convictions might have been preferable.[33] Hobhouse was in no position to defend himself directly, but two years later in another connection he vigorously repudiated the charge that his private views on charity reform prevented his administering existing law in a judicial manner. It was, he retorted, his purpose to "promote a *general reform of the*

[30] B.M. Add. Mss. 44,240, folios 97,99. An illuminating study of Lyttelton is that by Peter Stansky, "Lyttelton and Thring: A Study in Nineteenth Century Education," *Victorian Studies,* 5:205–23 (March 1962).

[31] *Trans. Social Science Assn.,* 1868, pp. 38ff.

[32] He insisted, however, that his own views were less extreme than those of Hobhouse (*Social Science,* 1868–69). The Hobhouse paper appears as chap. III in his volume, *The Dead Hand* (London, 1880).

[33] *3 Hansard,* 197:1866ff.

Law," but he could still apply "in (I think) the driest professional temper, the very law which so required alteration." [34] However thoroughly convinced of their own fair-mindedness, it required no great prescience to see trouble ahead for the Commissioners. Gradually the country became aware of the dynamite that had been planted in the Endowed Schools Act.[35]

The obvious procedure for the Commissioners was to concentrate first on the endowments of a pilot group of counties, and they chose to begin with the West Riding, Dorset, and Somerset. Predictably enough, it all went more slowly than they had estimated. Although they had expected to deal with foundations in groups and to effect combinations on a large scale, the Commissioners presently discovered that each trust was a special case and each required a special scheme. There were also specific factors which prevented them from proceeding method-ically from county to county. For one thing, their attention was constantly being diverted from their selected areas to more critical situations elsewhere. They were torn between their desire to move ahead systematically in the work of reorganiz-ing secondary education and their reluctance to delay action in the case of such important schools as the Bedford Grammar School, the King Edward VI School at Birmingham, Dulwich College, and other foundations, which required the Commissioners' intervention before they could function efficiently. The resulting policy was a compromise between the claims of a predetermined schedule and the appeal of special cases.[36]

Another and more annoying diversion was created by the problem of endowed elementary schools, to which from the beginning the relation of the Commis-sioners was ambiguous. Save for certain categories, these were included in their commission, but, as executors of the Taunton Report, they considered their major responsibility to be for secondary education. Yet it was never possible to draw a sharp line between elementary and secondary endowments, and one of the peren-nial dilemmas of the Commissioners was to decide in which class a trust legally belonged. Numbers of institutions founded as grammar schools had sunk to the elementary level. In many such instances the Commissioners sought to restore the endowment to the service of secondary education by converting it to scholar-ships and exhibitions tenable at a grammar school — to the considerable indigna-tion of local residents. Their alleged favoring of secondary as against elementary education was a standard charge directed against their work.

The Commissioners had hardly entered upon their duties when the Education Act of 1870 put the issue of elementary endowments into a new perspective. If it was now the statutory obligation of parishes to furnish elementary schooling, what use could properly be made of trusts formerly applied to that purpose? The Commissioners gave their answer promptly and in terms that formed one of the chief bones of contention between themselves and local authorities. They had

[34] L. T. Hobhouse and J. L. Hammond, *Lord Hobhouse, A Memoir* (London, 1905), pp. 38–39.
[35] Lord Colchester, "The Endowed Schools Inquiry," *National Review*, 9:216 (April 1887). The third Commissioner was to be Canon H. G. Robinson, a Broad Churchman in his outlook.
[36] D. C. Richmond, *S. C. on the Endowed Schools Acts*, 1886, Q. 65.

been embroiled in the problem at the outset by a specific clause in the Act. Since parishes were required to provide suitable elementary schools where there was a deficiency, parishes were naturally eager to demonstrate that no such deficiency existed. Trustees made haste to enlarge or improve their facilities, taking advantage of grants from the Education Department. To qualify for this assistance, however, a site or building must be assigned *by scheme* to elementary education. In consequence a flood of applications rained in on the Commissioners.

They handled the spate of applications as best they could, though at the cost of delaying their main work, but they also took occasion to issue a general statement of policy. Since elementary education had now become a public responsibility, it was questionable, "Paper S" cautioned, to use endowment income for the ordinary running expenses of a school. Such resources should be reserved for buildings, classroom equipment, scholarships to more advanced schools, and, in short, for needs above the bare educational minimum.[37] Such opinions naturally proved less than satisfying to many vestries and school boards. The Victorians found the notion of a school rate an extraordinarily bitter pill, and it was only by degrees that they accustomed themselves to the taste.

Whatever criticisms may be leveled against the Commissioners, no one could charge that they approached their task in a craven spirit. Tactical prudence might have counseled a start with foundations whose governors were aware of the need for reform and were begging for attention or with those too weak to offer effective opposition. Instead they unhesitatingly challenged powerful and influential corporations who were immensely hostile to interference and who could muster formidable support in Parliament. A case in point was that of the scheme for Emanuel Hospital, Westminster, whose rejection in 1871 by the House of Lords proved a grave blow to the Commissioners and helped to rally anti-reformers and vested interests outside as well as in London. Possibly the location of the Commission's office in Westminster had something to do with the decision to tackle this ancient foundation, for, as the Secretary recalled later, within a stone's throw were a number of large endowments which "seemed to me to invite large and early reform."[38] Hobhouse agreed, and the Commission went into action.

Emanuel Hospital, founded by Lady Dacre in the sixteenth century and administered by the Corporation of the City of London under a royal charter of Elizabeth, had been designed to accommodate twenty poor aged people and to maintain and educate twenty poor children. Since the income had increased handsomely, the twenty ancients in the almshouse and the children, now numbering sixty, were well taken care of. Nomination was a perquisite of members of the Corporation. Although no overt maladministration was alleged by the Commissioners, the system itself was the antithesis of that contemplated by the Schools Inquiry Commission in that it provided free board, lodging, and schooling at an elementary level for a group of children chosen by patronage. The Commissioners

---

[37] *Rept. of the Endowed Schools Commissioners* (C. 524), 1872, pp. 4–5, 27ff., App. 7.
[38] Hobhouse and Hammond, *Lord Hobhouse*, p. 49.

proposed to create a rational structure of secondary schools for Westminster by combining Emanuel with St. Margaret's Hospital, the Greycoat Hospital, and another foundation in such a way as to form two day schools and one suburban boarding school, each with an enrollment of three hundred. These were no longer to be free schools, though generous exhibitions were to be established, and they were to be managed by a new governing body of twenty, on which the Corporation would have three members. This was enough for the City Corporation. The City Solicitor sounded the alarm, issued statements, called meetings, and sought to mobilize opposition throughout the country.[39] When a petition from the Lord Mayor and Corporation reached the House of Lords, Lord Salisbury spoke as its principal advocate, supported, by way of comic relief, by Lord Buckhurst, a descendant of Lady Dacre, who on behalf of the foundress' family endorsed the Corporation's management.[40]

There were, in fact, two legitimate criticisms to be made of the Commissioners' schemes, neither of which had much to do with the City opposition. In attempting to expand these endowments to provide for nine hundred children, the Commissioners, as they often tended to do, were stretching an income farther than sound education would justify. So determined were they to deal sternly with waste, they sometimes seemed to judge the efficiency of a school by the ratio between pupils and income. In this precept they were echoing one of principal themes of the Taunton Commission. Again, there was force in the charge that by imposing even a small fee, they were in effect withdrawing some of the endowment from the service of the poor. This argument was pressed in a notably fair-minded speech by Lord Cairns, the former Conservative Lord Chancellor, who, however, privately disclaimed any "sympathy with the narrow and selfish views of the Corporation of London."[41] Lord Salisbury, appearing in the unlikely role of champion of the poor and enjoying the part hugely, made a good deal of the class bias of the Emanuel scheme. This was not the last time that the Commissioners (who, as Lyttelton reminded the House, were carrying out policies laid down by the Taunton Report and the Endowed Schools Act) were to be pilloried as despoilers of the poor for the benefit of the middle classes.

When the Lords rejected the Emanuel scheme, it became pointless, as well as impossible, to defend the parallel schemes for St. Margaret's and the Greycoat Hospitals. Two years later, in 1873, Gladstone was able to push through the Commons a revised scheme for Emanuel Hospital, showing in the course of a vigorous speech that the City Corporation had itself behaved cavalierly toward the wishes of the pious foundress for whom such veneration was professed.[42] But as far as the Commissioners were concerned, their prestige had been seriously shaken. The controversy had given hope to the disaffected and had shown them

---

[39] The Corporation also appealed to the Judicial Committee of the Privy Council, which sustained the Commissioners. (*S. C. on the Endowed Schools Acts,* 1873, Q. 178.)

[40] *3 Hansard,* 207:873–74.

[41] *Ibid.,* pp. 880–84; Hobhouse and Hammond, p. 43.

[42] *3 Hansard,* 215:1875–1960.

that the schemes of the Commissioners might be successfully opposed by anyone who could muster sufficient parliamentary influence. The lesson was learned, apparently with little delay, for in the following year three of the Commissioners' schemes were thrown out by the Lords.[43]

3

The report issued by the Commissioners during their third year in office was by no means a crow of triumph. Their summary of work completed and in progress showed with embarrassing clarity how optimistic had been the estimates of the time required to reorganize England's endowed schools. In the three years only twenty-four schemes had actually passed into law, with thirty-four framed and submitted to the Education Department for approval and eighty-four draft schemes published. Schemes were under discussion for another 214 schools. But there was a terrifying disparity between the 142 schemes and draft schemes actually completed and the nearly three thousand endowed schools, most of which were presumably to receive the same treatment.[44] If the rate of the first three years were maintained, completing the assignment would be a matter of decades.

The Commissioners did not attempt to hide a certain disillusionment with regard to their task, and they made no extravagant claims of success. Though this was hardly, as Beresford Hope ironically remarked, "an appeal to the merciful consideration of the House from a moribund Commission" setting forth "how persecuted it has been of gods and men," they made a good deal of the myriad difficulties that had beset them.[45] They reflected sadly on the frustrations of trying to work out in practice a reform that everybody (they asserted with a good deal of exaggeration) agreed to in the abstract. Very likely, at least one of the Commissioners suspected, the Act itself had been premature, and he doubted whether it would have passed originally, had not the attention of the public been focused on the Irish Church Act. Arthur Hobhouse, the principal draftsman of the Commissioners' report, was not sanguine about the success of their labors: "I always looked upon ourselves as missionaries sent to lighten the heathen, and to be persecuted and perish at their hands."[46] He could hardly have been surprised, therefore, at the recalcitrance of the unconverted. At the office of the Commission there would have been some disposition to endorse the *Times* verdict: "The Commissioners were in advance of their age. The Schoolmaster had not been abroad long enough for them."[47]

As long as the Gladstone Government survived, the position of the Endowed Schools Commissioners was secure enough. Early in 1872 their situation had been made slightly easier when Hobhouse, considered in some quarters to be an

[43] *S. C. on the Endowed Schools Acts*, 1873, Q. 102.
[44] *Rept. of the Endowed Schools Commissioners*, 1872, p. 12.
[45] *3 Hansard*, 215:1889.
[46] Hobhouse and Hammond, p. 46.
[47] *The Times*, 19 April 1872.

irritating element, was translated to India as Law Member of the Governor-General's Council.[48] In the following year the Commissioners appeared before a Select Committee presided over by W. E. Forster and controlled by their Liberal friends. Lyttelton and his colleagues succeeded, at least to the satisfaction of their friends, in justifying some of their controversial policies. In answer to the perennial charge of interfering with the "good" schools along with the "bad," he insisted that the fact of "goodness" was often precarious and accidental and that, unless their constitutions were altered, there was no assurance that such schools would continue to be "good." His fellow-Commissioner, H. J. Roby, who had been promoted from the secretaryship to succeed Hobhouse, recalled that Sherborne, an excellent school, had applied for a scheme and was wholly satisfied with the result.[49]

Lyttelton sought also to mollify those who were disturbed over the Commission's commitment to the principle of competition for admission and advancement. This, he suggested, did not necessarily imply that everything would hang on a competitive examination. The essential principle was that the prize should be given for "merit" — "for something which is in the boy himself, and not in the circumstances of his parents." This formula was unobjectionable, but its effect may have been vitiated when Lyttelton went out of his way to deny any claims to the special advantages of education to the poor man "who has chosen to become poorer still by marrying and having a dozen children without the means of bringing them up. I do not blame him; it is what many of us have done [Lyttelton himself was the father of twelve], and it may be a proper case for voluntary and private benevolence; but I do not consider that it gives that man any claim to educational advantages for his children." [50] Defensible, possibly, when stated in this tendentious fashion. Yet critics of the Commission believed that vast numbers of these educational endowments had been established specifically for the *poor*. No doubt competition was an admirable procedure as long as the competitors were drawn wholly from the ranks of the poor, but Lyttelton's explanation hardly satisfied those who suspected (correctly, as the system developed) that the advantage would lie inevitably with boys from the middle classes.

From the Forster Committee the Commissioners received a vote of confidence slightly qualified, but the Government's bill to renew their appointment for three years fell foul of the Tory Lords. Rather than see the extinction of the Commission, Gladstone had to accept a one-year term — which served notice of trouble ahead when the seals of office should pass to the Conservatives.[51] The bill introduced in the following year by the Disraeli Government was not only conceived in the Church of England's interest but was so unabashedly sectarian and so vaguely drawn as to make its passage doubtful, even with the heavy Conservative

---

[48] Hobhouse and Hammond, p. 59.
[49] *S. C. on the Endowed Schools Acts*, 1873, Q. 1242–43, 1165–66.
[50] *Ibid.*, Q. 1261.
[51] *Ibid.*, Q. 1248; *3 Hansard*, 217:1418.

majority. *The Times* regarded it as a preposterous document and denounced it almost daily in leading articles.[52]

The bill contemplated two principal changes. The first of these would liquidate the Endowed Schools Commission, along with its entire establishment and would transfer its duties to the Charity Commissioners, whose number would be augmented for the purpose. Here the Government was on strong technical ground in that the rearrangement could be presented as a reversion to the original proposal of the Schools Inquiry Commission. But obviously this was as much as anything an attempt to placate the country gentlemen, local trustees, and others who were crying for the heads of the Commissioners, especially Lyttelton's and that of Hobhouse's successor, Roby. It must have entertained the Charity Commissioners to hear their praises sung as tactful, sympathetic, experienced counselors in contrast to the Schools Commissioners with their penchant for riding roughshod over local interests and traditions. Had they realized that some of the unpopularity acquired by the Schools Commissioners would be visited on themselves, the Charity Commissioners might have been less willing to accept the added responsibilities. Although they had been made painfully aware that tact and caution were the first conditions of survival, these would not be sufficient to protect them from attack. In any case, there was no possibility of saving Lyttelton and his colleagues. If they could be praised for having acted *fortiter in re,* they had sometimes failed to behave *suaviter in modo,*[53] and they had to be sacrificed.

The other main provision of the Conservative bill had to do with the sticky question of denominational endowments. Since this section — a miracle of obscurity, *The Times* called it — was finally withdrawn, with the unsportsmanlike implication that the fault lay with the draftsman, there is no occasion for an analysis. Broadly speaking, whereas the Act of 1869 tended to create a presumption in favor of nondenominationalism, the Tory bill would have worked in the opposite direction, whatever its precise intentions. In the course of the typically long and acrid debate, so many of the more controversial provisions were abandoned that little was left save the transfer of the endowed schools undertaking to the office of the Charity Commission.

The shift ushered in a period of relative calm. The two Charity Commissioners for Endowed Schools were Canon Robinson, who was carried over from the old Commission, and Lord Clinton, former Under-Secretary of State for India and a member of the University Commission.[54] The peace which now descended on the endowed schools front was the result, in some degree, of a more conciliatory attitude on the part of the Commissioners. They recognized that a cardinal virtue was ability to tread softly, and they did not hesitate to concentrate on schools which would present relatively few problems and which might be kept out of

[52] *The Times,* 15, 21–24 July 1874.
[53] *3 Hansard,* 221:573–75.
[54] Meanwhile, the Charity Commission itself was strengthened by the appointment of Henry Longley, who, for the last quarter of the century, was to be the dominant voice in its affairs.

the arena of controversy. Also, the shift to the Charity Commission made for fewer administrative complications. Since every endowed school was also a charitable trust, it was an advantage to have both the educational and legal sides in the hands of the same agency. Sectarian bitterness, moreover, appeared to be moderating. It had been the misfortune of the Lyttelton Commissioners to begin their work at a time when relations between Church and Chapel were as inflamed as at any time during the century, with Nonconformists smarting over their defeat in the education controversy and Anglicans determined to stand on their rights.[55]

Perhaps most important of all was the gradual conversion of the public to the principles that the Commissioners represented. In spite of everything, the Lyttelton Commissioners had accomplished a good deal in educating opinion, and without their rather willful martyrdom the path of their successors would have been much more rugged. The new Commissioners, too, during the seven or eight years in which they were allowed to work quietly, accustomed trustees and others to the aims and methods of school reorganization. As the number of renovated foundations increased, they offered an instructive object lesson for the governing bodies of other schools, whose hostility, in some cases, turned to envy.[56] A measure of the easier relations between the Commissioners and local bodies was the few obstacles encountered in Parliament by the schemes. For a decade or more after the shift took place, none of the more than five hundred schemes framed by the Commissioners was rejected by the Legislature, though some produced discussion and one or two inspired hostile motions.[57]

4

It was nearly a decade before the Commissioners had to face another wave of opposition and criticism. This new attack was different in inspiration and content from that directed against the Lyttelton Commissioners. For, although the familiar vested charity interests were still involved, the main pressure came from men who had identified themselves with the democratic aspirations of the time. No doubt, like most periods, the 1880's were a time of contrary trends, currents and countercurrents. Yet, on balance, the British public was becoming increasingly responsive to appeals on behalf of social justice, and this greater sensitiveness was not unrelated to the movement for political democracy which had triumphed in the boroughs in 1867 and was to be extended to the counties in 1884–85.[58] It took no great astuteness on the part of the politician to foresee that social questions would occupy a prominent, perhaps pre-eminent, place among political issues.

For endowed charities the most relevant aspect of the democratic movement was the demand for the reform of local government, county and municipal. In

[55] *S. C. on the Endowed Schools Acts*, 1886, Q. 5884, 5887.
[56] *Ibid.*, Q. 5904.
[57] *Ibid.*, Q. 90–91.
[58] This theme will be discussed in more detail in Chapter XVIII.

Birmingham, Joseph Chamberlain, Harris, Schnadhorst and their group were building the model of a reformed municipal government committed to advanced social policies. Presumably the Birmingham achievement, with its special assets in the commanding personality of Chamberlain and the organizing talents of Schnadhorst, has tended to obscure the accomplishments of other cities which may have anticipated Birmingham. At all events, those who were guiding the democratic movement in county and city were prepared to claim a greater voice for the people in the management of charitable endowments. This naturally conditioned the work of the Commissioners. At this distance we cannot be sure whether, as Lord Colchester charged, the whole controversy was whipped up by Chamberlain and his henchman Jesse Collings.[59] It seems unlikely that, without the impulse from Birmingham, the criticisms would have assumed the dimensions of a campaign and would have figured so heavily in Parliament. However disinterested or otherwise the Birmingham men may seem as champions of the poor, plainly they provided a smokescreen for the much less disinterested objections of ratepayers, local trustees, and other special groups.

Section 30, the clause authorizing the Commissioners to disregard *cy-près* and to convert to education certain categories of endowment, caused remarkably little trouble. During their first sixteen years, they framed something over a hundred such schemes, many of them comprising several charities, with an aggregate income of nearly £16,000.[60] In general, the Commissioners proceeded on revisions of this kind only when no vigorous opposition seemed likely, but once or twice they dared to ignore local hostility, especially when they enjoyed local support.

They did not hesitate, for example, to intervene in the barely credible case of the Rochester Bridge Trust. Since the sole purpose of this ancient charity was to maintain the stone bridge over the Medway at Rochester, the latter nineteenth century found it with an absurdly swollen surplus. Repairs to the bridge took only about £700 out of an income of over £8000.[61] The bridge wardens themselves, in their embarrassment, proposed using £20,000 of the accumulated surplus for certain educational purposes in Rochester and Maidstone. This provoked a loud protest from sources outside the two cities, especially from certain Kent magistrates. The burden of their argument was that the surplus should be used to build bridges for other parishes along the river (the Commissioners had, in fact, explored that possibility and discovered that it could not be done *cy-près*),[62] but the real basis of the controversy was the jealousy with which some of the rural parishes viewed the good fortune of Rochester and Maidstone. Although the Trust had recently completed a bridge at the cost of some £200,000, the chairman of Quarter Sessions could still argue against alienating any of the surplus. What would happen, he asked portentously, "if that bridge was blown up by dynamite or

[59] *National Review*, 9:214 (1887).

[60] *S. C. on the Endowed Schools Acts*, 1886, App. 7.

[61] *Ibid.*, Q. 1649, 4661. For the earlier history of the bridge, see W. K. Jordan, *Social Institutions in Kent, 1480–1660* (*Archaeologia Cantiana*, 75:44, 62 [Ashford, 1961]).

[62] *S. C. on the Endowed Schools Acts*, 1886, Q. 4642.

destroyed by an enemy, and the funds of Rochester were alienated . . . ?"[63] Actually at the time of the protest, the Commissioners were considering a *cy-près* scheme to use some of the surplus for the repair of other Medway bridges. Little more was heard from the Kent justices, and the plans of the Commissioners were carried out with no serious change.

The shifting of endowments to educational purposes produced only minor outcries, though criticism on this score was later to increase, as British society gained a greater awareness of the insecurities of working-class existence.[64] Much more important in the 1880's was the issue of class bias with which the endowed schools undertaking had been bedeviled from the beginning. This was the most material of a cluster of grievances, real and imaginary, which received an airing before a Select Committee in 1886–87. Two years before, a Select Committee on the Charitable Trusts Acts had reported that the unpopularity of the Charity Commissioners was chiefly a consequence of their operations in the endowed schools field, a conclusion that seemed to point toward a further and more specific investigation. The new Committee was presided over by Sir Lyon Playfair and numbered among its members Courtney Kenny, a distinguished legal scholar and advocate of charity law reform.

The Committee listened to all the familiar criticisms, tediously reiterated, of the policies of the Commissioners — which, in some degree, were merely those recommended by the Taunton Commission and established by the Endowed Schools Acts. The attack was bitter and sometimes bigoted, and it covered both the secondary and elementary sectors of the endowed school front. As for the secondary schools, the most savage complaints had to do with the repudiation by the Commissioners of gratuitous schooling and their insistence that, if the poor were to enjoy the advantages of a secondary education, they must establish their right by merit. The critics had taken comfort from a decision of the Judicial Committee of the Privy Council which required the Commissioners when making schemes that abolished or modified the privileges or educational advantages of any particular class "to have due regard to the educational interest of such class of persons."[65]

For their part the Commissioners refused to accept the premises on which their opponents argued. They recalled that the Judicial Committee had also denied the necessity of giving a new educational advantage to a class where it had been thought wise to abolish the old. They rejected the view that grammar schools, in general, had been intended primarily for the benefit of the poor and that the term "free school" was synonymous with "gratuitous education" — a question that was discussed with great acerbity and some erudition before the

---

[63] *Ibid.*, Q. 4590.

[64] In 1951 the Nathan Committee received a memorandum from the National Association of Almshouses on the "Diversion of the Endowment of Almhouses for Educational Purposes." There were, of course, sporadic protests at the time, as witness three letters to *The Times*, 5 and 9 April 1888.

[65] The Wiggonby School case. (*26th Ann. C. C. Rept.*, 1879, p. 6.)

Committee.[66] Rather, they urged, grammar schools had been established to further education in particular localities for all who might be willing and able to learn, though admittedly founders often stipulated that no fees would be required of the poor or, in some instances, of anyone. The claims of the poor were, indeed, rather more persuasive when put forward, as by James Bryce, "not so much on the basis of any intention of the founder to benefit the poor as upon the fact that it is the duty of the community to help the poor." [67]

The elementary endowed schools raised problems of their own, even though large numbers of the smaller ones had been transferred to the Educational Department by the Act of 1873. Although many of these institutions had been established for the poor and had provided a gratuitous education, the Commissioners held that the Act of 1870 had made such arrangements obsolete. It was bad public policy to use such endowments to relieve ratepayers of their obligations, and they questioned whether it was the design "of the founders of these endowments 300 years ago to step in in relief of liabilities now imposed by law." That might be conceded, but to argue, as did one of the Commissioners with an amazing lack of discretion, that if the middle and upper classes were called upon to pay for the education of the poor, then they were entitled to the pecuniary benefits of the old endowments (for the poor) — this seemed to confirm the supicions of those who sensed on the part of the Commission a bias against the lower classes.[68] The Commissioners adhered to the policy announced fifteen years previously in "Paper S" that such endowments ought to be used to provide extra benefits, and, if sufficiently large, to make it possible for some pupils to move up a rung or two on the educational ladder. This decision of the Commissioners, which seemed so eminently rational to themselves, brought maledictions on their heads not only from ratepayers but also from groups among the poor who felt deprived of advantages that rightfully belonged to them.

The case of the Grammar School and Sandes Bluecoat School at Kendal, to take an example, was cited to the Committee of 1886–87 by Jesse Collings as a specimen of bureaucratic tyranny and oppression of the poor.[69] Formerly the Bluecoat School had educated and clothed about eighty-five children, a great boon, Collings alleged, to the poor of the town. The plan of the Commissioners to amalgamate the two institutions into a high school and to impose fees, assisting the poor through scholarships tenable at the Grammar School, was pictured as having aroused violent opposition among both the poorer and more prosperous inhabitants. In pointing an accusing finger at the Kendal scheme, Collings was

[66] Sir Horace Davey, *S. C. on the Endowed Schools Acts,* 1886, Q. 5265ff.
[67] *Ibid.,* Q. 5526.
[68] D. C. Richmond, *ibid.,* Q. 5459; S. C., 1887, Q. 6871.
[69] *S. C. on the Endowed Schools Acts,* 1887, Q. 7240ff. For other examples see Simon, *Studies in the History of Education,* pp. 329–32. Changes in the Manchester Grammar School caused a heated discussion at the 1879 meeting of the Social Science Association held in Manchester. (*Transactions,* 1879, pp. 161–68.)

badly advised, and the Commissioners had no difficulty in proving his version inaccurate and irresponsible.[70] Far from having been a well-administered school, the Bluecoat foundation had been a chaotically run establishment, to which the free boys were elected by a committee of subscribers, who, by subscribing something like £46 a year, enjoyed control of an annual income of over £500. The Bluecoat School, the Commissioners demonstrated, had been established originally as a secondary school and had declined to the status of a poor, uninspected elementary school. No one could doubt that in this instance, as in others, the Commissioners' plan of offering scholarships to the Grammar School gave the poor a better and fairer opportunity than existed under the system of patronage that it superseded.

The truth is that the Chamberlain-Collings accusations lifted the lid on a Pandora's box of grievances, most of which had little to do, at bottom, with protecting the poor from spoliation. A good deal of the opposition came down to such matters as the desire of a village to assure to itself the exclusive use of a large endowment, resistance to proposals to move a foundation to a more populous center, or reluctance of the inhabitants of a town to pay school fees or impose a school rate on themselves.

A case which involved a good many characteristic and confusing elements was the charity established by Alderman Dauntsey in 1542–43 to provide a grammar school and almshouse in the parish of West Lavington in Wiltshire.[71] To maintain the school Dauntsey left certain valuable pieces of property in the hands of the Mercers' Company. The Mercers faithfully discharged their specific obligations, and, indeed, did more than was legally required of them. They also pocketed a substantial surplus, to which presumably in law they were "beneficially entitled." The school deteriorated badly. There was no pretense of going beyond the elementary level, and the Schools Inquiry Commissioners considered it much inferior to the government-inspected elementary school for girls. The Mercers were eager to get rid of their vague responsibilities, and they offered a lump sum of £30,000 to be quit of them. The Commissioners, who regarded this as a handsome offer, proposed to devote £14,000 to West Lavington, a village with a scattered population of less than 1900. Part would go to the almshouses, part for the school and scholarships, and part for exhibitions to finance the further education of West Lavington boys. The balance of £16,000, regarded by the Commissioners as a freewill offered from the Mercers' Company and not subject to a specific trust, they planned to devote to "that kind of education which seems to have been contemplated by Alderman Dauntsey, namely, education of a kind higher than elementary" and not limited to West Lavington.[72] Such a sum, supplemented by other benefactions, might lay the foundation for a county school in Wiltshire, located probably at Devizes.

[70] D. R. Fearon, *S. C. on the Endowed Schools Acts*, 1887, Q. 8100ff.
[71] For the early history of the Dauntsey benefaction, see W. K. Jordan, *The Charities of London, 1480–1660* (London, 1960), pp. 139, 224.
[72] *S. C. on the Endowed Schools Acts*, 1886, Q. 1601.

The case developed an amazing number of complexities, including two wills by Dauntsey, which caused a long wrangle about the precise relation of the Mercers to the charity. In West Lavington itself there were sharp enough differences of opinion. Though none doubted that whatever might be realized belonged to West Lavington and should be used locally, some favored accepting the Mercers' offer, while an articulate group contended that the parish was entitled to the entire endowment and that the Mercers' Company was merely a trustee.[73] This latter faction sought to convict the Commissioners of defrauding the poor as well as of callous indifference to local sentiment in denying free education, "especially when property has been distinctly provided for that purpose." [74] Such spokesmen put the best face they could on the fact that the ratepayers and indirectly the landlord would share in the relief enjoyed by the poor. Basically, of course, those who opposed the Commissioners at West Lavington and elsewhere were contending neither for the poor nor the ratepayers. These were rather voices raised, half-instinctively, in defense of local privilege, selfish or not, and against comprehensive reform, centrally initiated. England, the Secretary of the Commission admitted, was a country "where men dislike extremely being overhauled." [75]

The Select Committee of 1886–87 was not disposed to be heavily critical of either the Acts themselves or the Commissioners' performance. Though their progress continued to be less spectacular than had been hoped, they had managed to reconstruct approximately eight hundred endowments, with a total income of about £400,000, and these schools now enrolled twice as many pupils as before their reorganization.[76] Another decade, one of the Commissioners estimated, might be necessary to complete the work.[77] The Committee accepted rather too readily the claim of the Commissioners that their system of scholarships and exhibitions provided adequately for the poor. There was good justification for the inclination of the Commissioners to favor secondary in preference to elementary education, since the latter was now a public responsibility, but almost inevitably their policy worked to the advantage of the middle classes. Yet working-class children, the Commissioners could reply, now enjoyed "that which they had never had before, an opportunity of obtaining higher education," and they adduced evidence in support of their claims.[78] Nettled by disparaging comments in the Commons, they had circularized between 200 and 300 schools whose schemes provided for scholarships and exhibitions. Returns from 101 representative schools showed that a considerable number of working-class children were, in fact, making use of their opportunities.[79] Figures for 1882, the so-called Fortescue Return, indicated that about 1150 of the nearly 3000 scholarships and exhibitions in secondary schools had been won by children from public elementary schools,

[73] *Ibid.*, Q. 2408, 2597, 5411ff.
[74] *Ibid.*, Q. 2390.
[75] *Ibid.*, Q. 5906.
[76] *Ibid.*, App. 2–3.
[77] Sir George Young, *ibid.*, Q. 687.
[78] J. G. Fitch, *ibid.*, Q. 1221.
[79] D. R. Fearon, *ibid.*, Q. 5812–17.

presumably working- or lower middle-class children.[80] A table of the exhibitioners at the United Westminster Schools also seemed to suggest that working-class children were doing well enough in the competition.[81]

Yet there remained in otherwise friendly, as well as in hostile, quarters doubts about the efficacy and fairness of the educational ladder. Courtney Kenny wondered whether the Commissioners' scholarships reached below the artisan class into the stratum of unskilled labor, and Bryce thought them of little use in districts of extreme poverty.[82] Despite its general approval, the Select Committee did not hesitate to add a cautionary word, reminding the Commissioners that, when endowments belonging to the poor were converted into scholarships and exhibitions, everything possible should be done to guard their "paramount interest." [83] This warning by no means disposed of the problem. Though the Commissioners can generally be exculpated from the cruder charges of applying endowments for the poor to the purposes of middle-class education, their competitive system naturally favored those with superior preparation, and presumably, therefore, those who had attended the better schools and whose family background was above the most primitive. The justification given originally by the Taunton Commission rather confirms one's suspicions that the terms of the competition were being unconsciously rigged: "Since the object is to select those who are to make education a means of rising, the best test of all is that the competitors should be pitted against other boys of the very class into which they are to make their way." [84]

It is apparently in the nature of educational institutions to rise above their station, to draw their students from a class higher than that for which they were founded. The endowed schools reform probably contributed to this social-climbing or, in the sociologist's phrase, this upward social mobility of schools. The Commissioners' vigorous rejection of gratuitous secondary training, their reliance on competitive scholarships (many of them drawn from funds left for the benefit of the poor), and their tendency to upgrade endowments to the secondary level, these policies, rightly or not, gave color to the suspicion that the education of the middle classes was being furthered at the expense of the poor.

5

In the late 1880's and early '90's the situation of the Schools Commissioners became even more uncertain and confusing. The new complications resulted

[80] *Ibid.*, App. 4. Whether or not this was a creditable showing is, of course, a matter of opinion. Simon (*Studies in the History of Education*, pp. 333–34) takes it as confirming his view that the "ladder" was exceedingly narrow.

[81] *S. C. on the Endowed Schools Acts*, 1886, App. 8, 10. James Bryce and others also pointed out that the Commissioners had aided the poor by introducing into the curricula of classical schools subjects of more use to them or, in some instances, converting the school into one teaching modern subjects. This had served to bring some schools into contact with the poor. (*Ibid.*, Q. 5510; Henry Longley, Q. 6261.)

[82] *Ibid.*, Q. 5511.

[83] *S. C. on the Endowed Schools Acts*, 1887, Par. 5.

[84] *Schools Inquiry Commission*, 1867–68, Part I, p. 596.

chiefly from a series of parliamentary decisions which pointed the way to an administrative revolution in English education. First of all, the Local Government (County Councils) Act of 1888, together with the Parish Councils Act of 1894, established local bodies in which could be vested some responsibility for education. Inevitably such democratically elected authorities would claim a larger voice in the administration of charity funds and of the school system. For the Charity Commissioners this reform in local government turned out to have both advantages and complications. During the 1880's they had been steadily introducing a representative element in their reorganized boards of trustees but had often been embarrassed by the lack of a body competent to choose such members. If the establishment of local councils solved that problem well enough, it also added another element to an already hopelessly chaotic web of administrative relationships. The Commissioners felt strongly the necessity of working in the closest kind of cooperation with the new County Councils, but, given the complexity of the administrative hierarchy, this proved impossible. They never managed it successfully, though they took some useful steps, such as altering their schemes for thirty-six London schools in order to give the London County Council representation on the governing bodies.[85]

The Technical Instruction Act (1889) also added to the troubles of the Commissioners. Not only were local authorities empowered to develop technical education but they were provided with resources for the purpose. This assistance came in the form of "whisky money," as it was popularly known, the proceeds of a tax on spirits and beer proposed by the Salisbury Government to compensate publicans whose licenses were not being renewed. Instead, as the result of violent opposition in Parliament, the Government accepted an amendment allocating the receipts to technical education. The term "technical education," however, came to be so broadly interpreted as to embrace almost any nonclassical subject. The consequence was that County Councils began to appeal to the Commissioners for schemes which would revive moribund grammar schools or other institutions which had languished for lack of endowment.[86]

These enactments, generally beneficial as they were, tended to make the duties of the Commissioners even more complex. To this situation the Intermediate Education Act (1899) for Wales, in part a by-product of the Welsh Home Rule movement, added another element of confusion, for it transferred the power of initiating schemes from the Commissioners to local bodies. Here, in short, was the kind of local responsibility and local control that the Schools Inquiry Commission had contemplated, but it increased the difficulties of the Commissioners, who were now obliged to follow one procedure in England and another in Wales.

There was little about any of these developments that would accelerate the laborious process of scheme-making, and when the Commissioners took stock of their position in the mid-1890's, they were not sanguine. They were now predict-

[85] *40th Ann. C. C. Rept.*, 1893, pp. 32–33.
[86] *R. C. on Secondary Education*, 1895, I, 12–13.

ing, as they had done eight years before, that the task of reorganizing secondary education might require another decade.[87] Nor had their special problems disappeared. They had found, for example, that the neat hierarchy of first-, second-, and third-grade secondary schools was impractical. Especially with the improvement of public elementary education and the disposition of some local school boards to push up to the secondary level, there seemed no useful place for the third-grade secondary school.[88] Again, determined local opposition was still being encountered, and there was a good deal to justify Sir Henry Longley's notion that much of the fine crusading ardor of the early days of educational reform had melted away.[89] It would be unfair to imply that the Commissioners' attack had bogged down, but certainly the administrative arrangements under which they worked were disheartening enough. The world of secondary education had become a chaotic wilderness, full of vague jurisdictions and overlapping functions, and the hand of the rationalizer was long overdue.[90]

The Rosebery Government threw the problem in the lap of a Royal Commission, which, under the chairmanship of James Bryce, carried on the last of the great nineteenth-century education inquiries. The Bryce study followed the familiar pattern, with assistant commissioners carrying studies in the field, circulars of questions to persons and institutions at home and abroad, and oral examination of witnesses. The Commission produced a substantial volume of report, together with eight volumes of evidence and appendices. To summarize its recommendations is neither possible nor necessary, but for the historian of philanthropy at least two of the conclusions are of significance.

In the first place, the Bryce Commission had no doubt of the vast improvement in the endowed grammar schools since the Taunton Commission. They were dealing with greater numbers of students and educating them more effectively. But that was not enough. The Commission was finally brought to accept the painful conclusion, which the Charity Commissioners themselves had been gradually reaching, that endowments could not possibly provide an adequate system of secondary education.[91] To a greater or less degree, educational reformers since the days of Brougham had been deluding themselves with the hope that the charities of past ages, if efficiently administered, could supply everything necessary beyond student fees. The Schools Inquiry Commission, in fact, had based its report on that assumption.[92]

By the 1890's this comforting doctrine had become untenable. For one thing, there were the grave discrepancies from county to county in the available endowments, a condition that was well known. Bedford, because of the magnificent

[87] D. R. Fearon, *ibid.*, Q. 10,840, 10,843.
[88] *42d Ann. C. C. Rept.*, 1895, pp. 38–39.
[89] *R. C. on Secondary Education*, 1895, Q. 11,416.
[90] On the late-century administrative confusion in British education, see J. W. Adamson, *English Education, 1789–1902* (Cambridge, 1930), chap. XVI.
[91] D. R. Fearon, *R. C. on Secondary Education*, 1895, Q. 10,857–58; Part I, p. 176.
[92] *Ibid.*, I, 94.

Harpur Foundation, could boast of 13.5 scholars per thousand of population, while the West Riding had only 1.95. In Lancashire the increase in population had so far outstripped the increase in endowments as to reduce the ratio to only 1.1 per thousand.[93] A Charity Commissioner had pointed to eleven large towns, seven of them county boroughs, which were entirely without secondary schools, and a distinguished legal witness went to the heart of the matter when he asserted that in large sections of the country endowments would not suffice to form even the "sub-stratum" for a system of public secondary education.[94] No intelligent person could longer hold to the illusion that British youth might reasonably depend for their secondary education on the charity of pious founders.

How then would they acquire secondary training, especially those of slender resources? The answer, of course, depended on one's conception of the place of secondary education in society, specifically of the size of the group that ought and would wish to attend secondary schools. Here, although it was clear that public authorities must assume greater responsibility, the Bryce Commission was not inclined to a drastic prescription.[95] The main obligation for supplementing existing institutions was to lie not with the central government but with local authorities. In short, secondary education was to follow, hesitantly and at some distance, the path that elementary education had already taken. This was by no means a "public system," but it would be impossible henceforth to think of secondary education in terms of "semi charitable relief," or as something that could be safely left to hit-or-miss private auspices.

More significant, in the second place, were the administrative recommendations of the Commission. It had been charged specifically with considering "the best methods of establishing a well-organised system of Secondary Education" from the muddle of overlapping and conflicting authorities. Although the appeal of a neatly articulated, centralized system must have been felt, the Commissioners chose the more cautious approach. Their supervisory structure would balance local against central agencies, each supporting and limiting the other. Each county and county borough would have its education authority, which would be armed with substantial powers. To the student of charity history, however, the critical reforms were those affecting the central administration. For here the Commission had to face the issue of the Charity Commissioners and their authority over educational endowments. The powers that they had exercised since 1874 combined supervision (and reconstruction by scheme) of the endowments themselves with functions more directly connected with school administration and instruction. The first of these required legal qualifications, the second educational, and the Charity Commission was equipped to handle only the former.

Yet in practice it would be awkward to separate the two aspects. Clearly a central authority was to be set up to supervise elementary and secondary educa-

[93] Ibid., I, 48, 424.
[94] D. R. Fearon, ibid., Q. 11,006; Lord Davey, Q. 15,351.
[95] Ibid., I, 182–83, 314–15.

tion, including smaller elementary endowments.[96] A school, after all, had to be considered as a single entity, not as a readily divisible combination of legal-financial with educational elements. Not only that, but, although the Charity Commissioners had dealt efficiently enough with individual foundations, this had been done on a piecemeal basis rather than on the comprehensive lines pictured by the Taunton Commission. The Charity Commission was in no position to formulate or carry out a national educational policy.

The Bryce Commission considered several possible solutions. Sir Henry Longley, Chief Charity Commissioner, agreed that the more distinctly educational responsibilities must be transferred to the new central body but favored retaining the legal and financial work.[97] Others favored shifting the whole secondary school enterprise, even though that would separate educational from other endowments and might further damage the prestige of the Charity Commissioners. For if their proceedings under the Endowed Schools Acts explained a good deal of the "honourable odium" visited upon them, it is no less true that these accounted for nearly a quarter of their budget.[98] What seemed beyond question was that the problem of secondary education must be dealt with in its totality. With the increasing pressure for secondary schooling, it was more than ever vital that the older schools should be correlated with the new and the whole system be made to function in accordance with a considered and comprehensive policy. In the end, the Bryce Commission recommended, as the least objectionable solution, transferring the whole endowed schools department of the Charity Commission to the new central authority.

The logic of their position should have led the Bryce Commissioners to propose a full-dress ministry of education, but instead they chose a compromise course.[99] The central authority that they recommended was to be no new ministry but rather an extension of the old Education Department, which would absorb the Science and Art Department and the endowed schools work of the Charity Commission. The bill introduced by the Conservative Government — "a very little Bill," Bryce called it[100] — ignored his recommendation with regard to local authorities and had to do merely with the issue of a unified authority at the center. Here the solution was to be a Board of Education, comparable to the Board of Agriculture and presided over by a Minister. To the question of transferring to the new Board the educational duties of the Charity Commission the Government chose a tentative approach. Instead of providing explicitly for the shift, the Act merely authorized the transfer in suitable stages through the use of Orders in Council.[101]

[96] The new agency would, of course, take over the responsibilities of the Department of Science and Art for technical education and those of the Education Department for elementary.

[97] *R. C. on Secondary Education*, 1895, Q. 11,447ff.

[98] *Ibid.*, Q. 11,438; *4 Hansard*, 73:640.

[99] *R. C. on Secondary Education*, 1895, I, 256ff.

[100] 62 & 63 Vict., c. 33; *4 Hansard*, 73:630.

[101] If the Government had proposed an outright transfer, there would probably have been even more insistent objections to vesting quasi-judicial functions in any administrative agency. On the other

However inconclusive the Act of 1899 may have seemed, at least it created within the field of education a single central authority, and this authority included in its province not only rate-provided institutions but those financed by charitable trusts. Any other solution would have been unthinkable, for by this time both types of school, especially at the elementary level, had become integral parts of the British educational structure. Here, in fact, was an instructive and prophetic example of the State's supplementing, guiding, and organizing the work of private philanthropists. It was a relatively small price to pay for unified supervision in the field of education that responsibility for charitable endowments would now be divided between two distinct agencies.

In the transfer of powers from the Charity Commission to the Board of Education the critical step was the Order in Council of 1901 which vested in the Board the scheme-making powers formerly exercised by the Commissioners. It was a relatively simple matter to transfer endowments which were purely educational in character, but a great many charities were "mixed" — that is, embodied both eleemosynary and educational elements. In some of these, the two were mingled so inextricably as to make any solution a purely arbitrary decision. Apprenticeship charities, for example, might contain educational provisions, while schools might sometimes be used for noneducational purposes, such as Sunday worship. The Charity Commissioners, whose duty it was to make the classification, wisely elected to begin with a tentative division of the income, leaving until later the more involved problem of the principal.[102] The whole transfer operation required seven or eight years and turned out to be a laborious assignment, since every endowment in the files of the Commission had to be examined. For most of these, of course, no more than a glance was necessary, but a large residue had to be scrutinized with some care. Some 9650 trusts were classified as wholly educational and nearly 2300 as partly so. Altogether about 12,000 charities were transferred from the Charity Commission to the Board of Education.[103]

Before the process had been completed, the situation was altered once more (and to a certain degree stabilized) by the Education Act of 1902, a notable landmark in the history not only of English education but of English philanthropy. In the years immediately preceding, matters had become even more complicated. For not only were county councils and county borough councils developing secondary schools under the Technical Instruction Act but local school boards were also establishing their own secondary classes under the authority of the Elementary Education Acts. The Cockerton judgment of 1899, upheld on appeal, went against the school boards, which were thus barred from the secondary field, and the way was opened for a comprehensive solution.[104] By the Act of 1902 the educational

---

hand, critics deplored the excessive caution with which the Government proceeded. (*4 Hansard,* 70:338; letter from Lord Cranborne, *The Times,* 28 July 1899.)

[102] *49th Ann. C. C. Rept.,* 1902, pp. 15–16; *51st Rept.,* 1903, pp. 15ff.

[103] *55th Ann. C. C. Rept.,* 1908, pp. 3–6.

[104] The judgment was given by T. B. Cockerton, auditor of the Local Government Board, in a test case brought against the London School Board. He held, in a word, that it was illegal for the Board to offer work above the elementary level.

process from kindergarten to university, much of which had been thought of as a quasi-charitable undertaking, was accepted as a public responsibility.[105] The Act substituted County Councils for school boards as local education authorities, and it associated the voluntary denominational schools with the state system — that is, they received a portion of the rates and submitted to a measure of control. This was an immense forward step and one whose significance was misjudged alike by its Tory-Churchman advocates and its Liberal-Nonconformist opponents.

For the Board of Education, especially for its legal staff, the Act of 1902 meant grave additional burdens. For one thing, voluntary schools were now eligible, on certain conditions, for aid from the rates, and they naturally made haste to qualify. If the Board had had to alter by formal scheme the trusts of all eleven thousand schools which applied during the first year, its machinery would have broken down completely.[106] What it did was to employ the simpler device of "final orders" to enable schools to qualify at once. There was also the annoying legal-technical problem having to do with the myriad of tiny elementary endowments, in number possibly fifteen thousand and with an income estimated at something like £300,000.[107] To make individual schemes for these infinitesimal trusts was out of the question. Yet they had been left without legal objects, and the consequence, as a Departmental Committee under the chairmanship of C. P. (later Sir Charles) Trevelyan concluded, "was a complete and universal failure of trusts such as . . . had never been experienced in the administration of charity law." [108] Though Trevelyan's Committee proposed in 1911 to delegate to the local education authorities the responsibility for dealing with such trusts, this required the sanction of Parliament, for which in 1914 the Board was still waiting.

From the point of view of this chapter, however, the principal point of interest in the Act of 1902 lies in the new recognition that it gave to secondary education. In the past, public agencies had been called upon to regulate schools established by private philanthropy, but the public purse had contributed only incidentally to their maintenance and expansion. The Endowed Schools Acts had assumed that endowments, combined with pupils' fees, would supply a sufficient basis for a civilized secondary school system. This had proved illusory, and the Act of 1902 fell back on a principle similar to that which the Act of 1870 had applied to elementary education. Henceforth secondary training was to be a public responsibility, as the elementary had been for more than thirty years, and it was now the

---

[105] "For the first time, the bill definitely includes as a public function education as education—not primary education only, or technical education only, but anything and everything that is education from the kindergarten to the university." (Sidney Webb, quoted by Elie Halévy, *History of the English People, 1895–1905* [London, 1929], p. 203.)

[106] Ministry of Education, *Education, 1900–1950* (Cmd. 8244), 1950, p. 14.

[107] *Departmental Committee on Endowments* (Cd. 5747), 1911, II, 219. This is an extrapolation based on the 1081 endowments in Cornwall, Gloucestershire, Durham, Kent, Northamptonshire, Staffordshire, and Wiltshire, which yielded a total of nearly £23,000 income.

[108] *Departmental Committee on Endowments* (Cd. 5662), 1911, I, 8. Trevelyan was a grandson of Sir Charles Edward Trevelyan, who figured in the previous chapter, and a son of the historian Sir George Otto Trevelyan.

duty of local authorities to take any measures necessary to assure adequate facilities.

This injunction was carried out by the combination of public and private effort that most foreigners have found so curious and confusing in the world of British education. Although endowed schools persisted in ample numbers, they became increasingly dependent on grants from the public funds and increasingly subject to state supervision. At the same time there was a spectacular growth in "provided" secondary schools — in American terms, public high schools. By the dawn of the new century education at all levels had lost most of its former character as a charitable activity and had taken on that of a public commitment. Sometime before 1914, in fact, the historian of philanthropy realizes that he has been carried outside his proper sphere and has become, by imperceptible degrees, the chronicler of a public service.

CHAPTER X

REMODELING ANCIENT TRUSTS: THE CITY OF LONDON CHARITIES

OR THE connoisseur of obsolete charities the mid-Victorian City of London offered an incomparable museum and for the charity reformer an irresistible challenge. Within the square mile of the ancient City lay the heaviest concentration of charitable endowments in the Kingdom. Their incomes had risen as their legal objects diminished or vanished altogether until the disparity became so marked that trustees found themselves suffering, in a literal sense, from an embarrassment of riches. Though they might resent and resist the drastic treatment that was ultimately applied, even City vestries did not deny the need for a degree of reform. It was, perhaps, the patent absurdity of the situation that made possible a statesmanlike solution, the amalgamation of most of these endowments into a single metropolitan trust, the City Parochial Foundation. Oddly enough, Britain's first general foundation was not the handiwork of an individual philanthropist but resulted from the consolidation of these obsolete, obsolescent, and underemployed City charities.

The City endowments to be considered are chiefly the parochial charities, that is, trusts administered by the City parishes. These parochial endowments by no means exhausted the charity resources of the City, for the Livery Companies also held massive funds in trust for charitable purposes. Not only that, but as will appear presently, their vast corporate wealth made them fair game for social and educational reformers, who looked forward to tapping this reservoir of idle endowments for their own causes. In the main, they were able to resist the pressure of the reformers — or more accurately, undertook a measure of self-reform as the price of immunity from public regulation.

The parochial charities were in a much weaker position, and they strikingly documented the *Times*'s definition of charity as "an institution which labours under a perpetual tendency to fall out of repair."[1] The maladjustments in the world of City endowments were the consequence of two centuries of social change which had proceeded at a constantly accelerating rate. Not only the charity arrangements but the whole parochial structure seemed sadly dated. The seven

[1] *The Times,* 3 Sept. 1880.

hundred acres of the City comprehended more than a hundred parishes.[2] These varied in size from St. John the Evangelist, which measured only four-fifths of an acre, to St. Botolph, Bishopsgate, with forty acres. Twenty-three of the parishes were under two acres in area and seven over twenty.[3]

The aggregate of charitable funds in the hands of the City parishes was not inconsiderable. The great bulk of the more than thirteen hundred trusts antedated 1700, the largest single group having been founded in the seventeenth century.[4] Even at best many of these would have been anachronisms — the funds for sermons celebrating the defeat of the Armada and the failure of the Gunpowder Plot, for the tolling of the bell of St. Sepulchre's before executions at Newgate, for the ransoming of Christian captives from the Turks or the Barbary pirates, for killing ladybirds on Cornhill, for an oil lamp at the corner of Billingsgate "for ever."[5] But the normal aging process of charitable endowments had been immensely hastened by a demographic revolution in the City. Throughout the mid-century, with the large-scale demolition of working-class quarters that accompanied "improvements" and with the conversion of whole parishes to public purposes, it was becoming increasingly clear that the City had no future as a place of residence. The Cannon Street Station accounted for the major part of All Hallows the Great, and the General Post Office for three-quarters of St. Anne and St. Agnes, while the Bank of England wiped out St. Christopher-le-Stock.[6] The effect on the resident population was almost catastrophic. In 1851 the census-taker counted 131,000 inhabitants, but his successor in 1881 reported only 52,000. However much City patriots might protest against the "midnight census" and urge that the *real* population was vastly greater than the *sleeping* population,[7] it was obvious that the City was well on the way to becoming little more than a gigantic countinghouse-cum-warehouse.

As the population of the City shrank, the income from its charitable endowments swelled. Between 1865 and 1876, a decade in which numbers of leases were apparently falling in and being renegotiated at substantially higher figures, the gross receipts of City charities rose by nearly fifty per cent to just under £100,000.[8] In wealth, as in population, there were enormous variations among parishes. By

---

[2] As usually given, the number varies from 107 to 112, the precise figure depending, apparently, on how combined parishes are counted. Although originally the parish had been both an ecclesiastical and governmental unit, the lines had become badly blurred. After the Great Fire there had been no attempt to rebuild all of the churches destroyed, with the result that only about sixty ecclesiastical parishes had been reconstituted.

[3] R. C. on the London Parochial Charities (C. 2522), 1880, I, 21–25.

[4] For figures on Tudor-Stuart charities in London, see W. K. Jordan, The Charities of London, 1480–1660 (London, 1960), p. 423.

[5] 3 Hansard, 261:1295; S. C. on the Endowed Schools Acts, 1886, Q. 640; R. C. on the Parochial Charities, 1880, Q. 2285, 7574.

[6] Ibid., Q. 1406, 267, 6176.

[7] Benjamin Scott, A Statistical Vindication of the City of London (London, 1867). The City, in fact, authorized a series of day censuses which were intended to dispose of "the assumption that it has lost some of its former standing and importance." (Report on the City Day-Census, 1881, p. 89.)

[8] In 1865 the total was £66,550; in 1870, £83,570; and in 1876, £99,575. (R. C. on the Parochial Charities, 1880, I, 20.)

1876, St. Botolph Aldgate and St. Giles Cripplegate each had a charity income of just under £10,000, the last's having more than doubled since 1865. The income of St. Martin, Ironmonger Lane, had also more than doubled — but from £2 to £4 10s. annually.[9]

The population upheaval, combined with the staggering increase in their resources, created a trying situation for City parishes. Churchwardens, vestry clerks, trustees, and other parochial administrators had the greatest difficulty in finding a use for their funds without committing a breach of trust, and indeed failure of objects was widespread among City charities. The bulk of these endowments had been left for the benefit of the poor of the parish — gifts of clothing, coal, or bread, apprenticeship fees, marriage portions, and the like — and they therefore assumed a poor population of some dimensions. But parish after parish appeared before the Royal Commission in 1878–79 to concede the virtual absence of eligible poor in the parish. There were, to be sure, stock figures like the old woman who was pleased to speak of herself as "the poor of St. Margaret, Lothbury," but some doubt existed as to whether she was a genuine resident.[10] Such a fund as Barber's Charity, for the marriage of "poor maids and widows in St. Botolph, Billingsgate," had been simply allowed to accumulate, since neither poor maid nor widow had presented herself for some twenty years.[11]

Parochial endowments fell into two broad categories, the ecclesiastical and the general. The former were intended for the upkeep of the church fabric, for the clergy and other functionaries, and for expenses connected with the services. These endowments may have represented something like two-fifths of the total, though in some reforming quarters there was a suspicion that, after the Great Fire, which destroyed so many documents, not a few endowments originally intended for charity turned up in the ecclesiastical pigeonhole.

Churches were no more able to spend their income usefully than were the civil parishes, for the City was heavily over-churched. It was easy enough to show that, on the whole, attendance at services was lamentably thin, in some churches averaging no more than ten. In these, the reformers charged, "on Sunday a solemn farce is performed, with . . . paid officials, and when there are any, almsmen, almswomen, and charity children" forming what a later generation would have called a captive congregation.[12] To dispose of their incomes, the better endowed parishes had to resort to curious expedients, supporting extensive cadres of functionaries — vestry clerks, organists, organ-tuners, pew-openers, bell-ringers, and the rest — as

[9] *Ibid.*, I, 18–20.
[10] *S. C. on the Parochial Charities Bill*, 1882, Q. 1185.
[11] *R. C. on the Parochial Charities*, 1880, Q. 4359.
[12] Sir Charles Trevelyan, "The City Parochial Endowments," *Social Science*, 1870–71, p. 438. In early May 1880 Sir Henry Peek, who was something of a reformer and who was animated by the Victorian's almost pathological respect for *facts*, took a survey of the attendance at City churches, exclusive of St. Paul's, the Temple, and the five largest parishes. The remaining fifty-five churches had congregations totaling 4837, but of these only 2784 could be called genuinely voluntary attendants. These churches had sittings for 27,500. (*Return of Objections to the Central Scheme* [*Parl. Pap.*, 1890], p. 23.)

well as maintaining and clothing choristers in overgenerous fashion, and sometimes embarking on unnecessary restorations of the church fabric. Where, as in the case of St. Michael's, Cornhill, it was a Wren building, the renovation was not only a frivolous waste of money but approached an esthetic disaster. Another Wren period church was saved from extensive restoration only by the spirited action of a parishioner.[13] All in all, no rational persons could doubt that the City of London had more than its share of ecclesiastical rotten boroughs.

On the civil side, charitable endowments comprised two main categories, those given for education and the much greater total for eleemosynary purposes, of which doles (outright gifts in money or kind) represented the largest element. This classification omits some of the more bizarre endowments, of which the fund to buy faggots for burning heretics may, perhaps, stand as the ultimate example.[14] Reformers felt not unkindly toward the £18,500 spent on education, chiefly on the charity schools which had been established in an earlier age, though they had little doubt that the money could be managed more productively. Of the miscellaneous charity income it is unnecessary to speak at length. The annual distribution in doles of upwards of £10,000 was generally regarded as pernicious, and especially so in parishes which no longer had a resident poor population.[15] In the latter situation one of two solutions would be adopted: either the income was bestowed on whoever applied, whether legally eligible or not, or it was simply diverted to other purposes. At dole time candidates used to flock to certain parishes "precisely as they now go hop-picking into Kent in the autumn, and when they got all the doles they could they went away, and we saw no more of them till the doles came round again." [16] Although by the 1870's some of the worst scandals had been checked, to reasonable observers City doles remained one of the least defensible forms of philanthropy.

Clearly it was impossible for City charity administrators to manage their endowments in strict conformity with founders' intentions. Some parishes, to be sure, had applied to the Charity Commission for a revision of their unworkable trusts, but more had simply developed their own rough and ready version of cy-près. Most of these, to say the least, would not have stood up in a court of law. With a good many dole charities, eligibility was interpreted so loosely that applicants had only to show some vague past connection with the parish to qualify for its bounty.[17] A not uncommon tactic was to make a contribution to

---

[13] 3 Hansard, 261:1295; 160:910–11; The Times, 1 Sept. 1883.

[14] This trust probably ought not to be taken too seriously, though it proved a serviceable weapon in the arsenal of reformers. Apparently the trust in question was Werk's Charity, an endowment of 6s. 8d. established in the parish of St. Anne and St. Agnes in the fifteenth century. It is not clear that the income was ever used for the object specified. (R. C. on the Parochial Charities, 1880, Q. 262.)

[15] Estimates of the amount distributed in doles vary widely, running from £10,000 to as high as the £31,000 cited by the London School Board when it was casting covetous eyes at the City endowments. (London School Board Minutes, 23 July 1879; 3 Hansard, 261:1293.)

[16] R. C. on the Parochial Charities, 1880, Q. 7566.

[17] Ibid., Q. 4805, 5064, 6388–92, 7401.

the poor rate from the charity income of the parish, so substantial in one or two instances as entirely to relieve the ratepayers of their legal responsibilities.

In the course of each year City parishes drew liberally on their charity funds to provide food and drink for the rector, the vestry, and sometimes the parishioners. The dinner or love feast at Greenwich or Richmond, justified as a means of improving relations within the parish, was a familiar function. St. Clement, Eastcheap, had an ancient endowment of 5s. for a love feast on Maundy Thursday to bring together parishioners who had fallen out; it also had £1 6s. 8d. "for some godly, virtuous, and well-disposed scholar" of Oxford or Cambridge. By the 1870's the five-shilling love feast had burgeoned into a handsome dinner at Richmond for the dignitaries of the parish and invited guests, while the "godly, virtuous, and well-disposed scholar" was still drawing his £1 6s. 8d.[18] The united parishes of St. Vedast, Foster Lane, and St. Michael-le-Querne reached what may have been the extreme in diverting charity funds when they used their income to pay the costs of legal proceedings against the rector, who had disagreed with the vestry and churchwardens about their handling of the trusts. Perhaps, James Bryce drily remarked in the House, they regarded this as a "*cy-près* application of the funds bequeathed for the combustion of heretics."[19]

2

The untidy clutter of City endowments stood high on the docket of charity reformers. In the course of the 1850's and '60's the most original and thoughtful of the Charity Commission's inspectors, Thomas Hare, turned in a set of reports covering the City parishes. To his 1860 report he attached a trenchant essay urging a fresh approach to the mélange of City charities. To attempt to keep these within the old parochial limits, he insisted, would be "an idle and a pernicious exercise of ingenuity."[20] Plainly what was needed was a reconsideration of the needs of the entire body of metropolitan poor. The outcome of such a re-examination, he hinted, might be a consolidated, or partly consolidated, administration of the City charities, without regard to parochial lines, to the boundaries of the City itself, or to conditions laid down by an Elizabethan or Stuart founder. The Charity Commissioners added their official, if rather cautious, support.[21] Although, as they noted, the disproportion between incomes and objects demanded a thorough recasting of City trusts, such a wholesale revision could not be managed through the ordinary scheme-making procedures of Charity Commission or courts. This was a condition which required the intervention of Parliament.

Merely calling a noisome situation to the attention of Parliament, as the Commissioners had done, was unlikely to lead to action. But other and less restrained voices were presently raised. The most vigorous critic was Sir Charles Trevelyan,

---

[18] *Ibid.*, Q. 540, 549–60.
[19] *Ibid.*, Q. 1303, 1978ff; *3 Hansard*, 261:1295.
[20] *R. C. on the Parochial Charities*, 1880, III, 2.
[21] *11th Ann. C. C. Rept.*, 1863, p. 5; *13th Rept.*, 1865, p. 3.

whose interest in charity reform had been stimulated by his activity in the Charity Organisation Society. Like other inquirers, he had been astonished to discover how many charitable trusts were so restricted as to be of little use in relieving social distress. The City endowments, it seemed to him, ought not to be monopolized by depopulated parishes but should benefit the poor of all metropolitan London. His two letters to *The Times,* later amplified in a paper before the London branch of the Social Science Association and published as a pamphlet, were typical of the assault of charity reformers.[22] Trevelyan's case was essentially correct and undeniably persuasive, though laced with a fair number of misstatements. For the twentieth-century reader, however, the effect is marred by his curious insistence that all charity real estate in the City ought to be sold and the proceeds invested in the public funds. No doubt, as administrators of such property, churchwardens and trustees left much to be desired, but it should have been impossible to miss the connection between the extraordinary affluence of City charities and the rise in value of urban land.

The agitation churned up by Trevelyan brought no immediate results. But throughout the 1870's the movement to reorganize City charities remained a live question, associated as it was with the broader issue of municipal reform in London. In their indictment of the City as the fortress of ancient and selfish privilege, municipal reformers did not omit its charitable trusts.[23] Successive returns of the income of City and Westminster endowments were called for and presented to Parliament, and the Charity Commissioners renewed more pointedly their demand for comprehensive action by the Legislature.[24] Throughout 1877 and 1878 Liberal members were prodding R. A. Cross, Disraeli's Home Secretary, who finally replied with a Royal Commission.[25]

This was not one of the century's more distinguished inquiries. Under the chairmanship of the aged Duke of Northumberland,[26] the Commission examined representatives from the hundred-plus City parishes, reviewing their charities one by one, with Thomas Hare's reports serving as a manual. Then it moved on to a succession of general and expert witnesses, of whom by all odds the most interesting was Sir Arthur Hobhouse, former Endowed Schools and Charity Commissioner. Hobhouse, to repeat, was considered an extreme representative of the school of thought advocating an extensive revision of old trusts, with current social needs rather than founders' wishes as the decisive criteria. On the essential issue facing the Commission he had no doubts. The principle of parochial ad-

[22] *The Times,* 17 June 1869, 26 June 1870; "The City Parochial Endowments," *Social Science,* 1870–71, pp. 437–51.

[23] A case in point is the two volumes by William Gilbert, *Contrasts* (London, 1873) and *The City* (London, 1877).

[24] No. 164 (1871) and No. 24 (1877); *24th Ann. C. C. Rept.,* 1876, pp. 5–6.

[25] *3 Hansard,* 233:665–66; 234:858; 235:594–95; 239:1694–1704; 241:327, 1244, 1852.

[26] Other members were Canon Rogers, a liberal clergyman, who had gained something of a reputation as an educational and parochial reformer at St. Botolph's Bishopsgate; Albert Pell, whose reforming interests expressed a strong self-help social philosophy; and Farrer Herschell, a future Lord Chancellor. See R. H. Hadden, comp., *Reminiscences of William Rogers,* 2d ed. (London, 1888), and Albert Pell, *The Reminiscences of Albert Pell* (London, 1908).

ministration should be abandoned forthwith and City charities combined into a single trust, whose benefits would be shared throughout the metropolitan area. The plan sketched by Hobhouse, in fact, was a reasonably accurate forecast of what finally emerged as the City Parochial Foundation.[27]

The proposals which the Commissioners submitted were less than revolutionary, and they were not received with unqualified enthusiasm in the City or outside.[28] Their plan for dealing with non-ecclesiastical endowments was an uninspired compromise between the claims of individual parishes and the patent impossibility of spending the City's charity income within the City, between a measure of deference to founders' wishes and admission that these could not be consistently followed. The essence of the scheme was, in a word, that only *surplus* parochial funds, as determined by a temporary commission, should go into a common pool.[29] If, in the Commission's plan, parochial interests fared better than they had expected, reformers were less happy. It was now James Bryce who took over the leadership of the reform cause, and in 1881 and 1882 he introduced bills which, drafted with the assistance of Hobhouse, went well beyond the wary proposals of the Commission. Although he would have left a few of the larger parishes in possession of their endowments, temporary commissioners should have wide discretionary powers with regard to the application of other funds. Bryce's bills, in short, were designed to free the great bulk of City trusts from both parochial control and founders' restrictions.[30]

City parishes at once mobilized against the threatened sacrilege. However freely they might admit the need for change, in the view of churchwardens and vestry clerks, this was not reform but revolution. They had previously urged that any alteration in the management of the charities "should emanate from the authorities of the City parishes themselves," [31] but only now appeared with a counter-proposal, and with a fund of £2000 for promoting it. Had the Charity Commissioners not objected emphatically, they might even have financed the fight out of charity income, as some parishes were inclined to do.[32] The obvious aim of the churchwardens' bill was to assure City interests of a preferred position. The bulk of charity property would have continued in the hands of existing bodies of trustees (as the Royal Commission had proposed), with only the "surplus" income being transferred to a central body — and even on this board the City would have a preponderance of members. Implicit in the City scheme, Bryce charged, was the notion that trustees enjoyed a vested right of sorts in the property they managed.[33] Throughout the controversy, moreover, the churchwardens and their allies talked as though the City parishes were living com-

---

[27] *R. C. on the Parochial Charities*, 1880, Q. 7751ff.
[28] *The Times*, 23 March 1880; R. H. Hadden, "The City Parochial Charities," *Nineteenth Century*, 9:324–37 (February 1881).
[29] *R. C. on the Parochial Charities*, 1880, I, 10–11.
[30] *3 Hansard*, 261:1296–97.
[31] *The Times*, 5 May 1881.
[32] *S. C. on the Parochial Charities Bill*, 1882, App. 1–4; 1883, App.
[33] *3 Hansard*, 261:1297.

munities, and they argued for the perpetuation of what was, in effect, an imaginary world. Unlike the parochial spokesmen, the reformers assumed that pious founders had intended to benefit the poor of London, and that they would have wished their benefactions to follow the movement of population — in other words, that they would have preferred to help the poor of Marylebone and Southwark rather than to maintain the vested interests of the City.

In the session of 1882 both bills passed the second reading. A Select Committee, presided over by Shaw-Lefevre and well seeded with municipal reformers, favored the more radical proposal, notwithstanding arguments from the churchwardens that their bill, rather than Bryce's was the legitimate heir of the Royal Commission. The claim was fair enough, but the Committee suspected it to be a stratagem to maintain an outdated regime, especially when the more active of the City clergy unhesitatingly aligned themselves against the churchwardens' bill.[34] Yet an accommodation between the two sides, the reformers realized, was obviously desirable. An out-and-out fight with the City interests would be both unedifying and time-consuming — and debating time was in short supply in the Parliaments of the 1880's. For the brilliant sabotage tactics of the Parnellites served to delay most of the debates on Bryce's bill until after midnight and some until three or four in the morning. Moreover, there was a growing suspicion in certain Liberal quarters that the assault on the parochial charities might further alienate the City from the Liberal Party.[35] When the two groups finally compounded their differences in the summer of 1883, Bryce had conceded nothing vital, though he agreed to certain face-saving clauses.[36] At 4:15 on the morning of July 31, 1883, the bill passed an exhausted House without a division and shortly after was accepted, substantially intact, by the Lords.[37]

The principle of the Parochial Charities Act was simple enough, though some of its ramifications could be infinitely complicated. Its essential purpose was to broaden the "beneficial area" of City endowments beyond the old London within the Walls to the new Metropolis and to adapt them to modern requirements. To this end, the Charity Commission, to be reinforced by additional Commissioners, would first review the entire mass of City charities, classifying each as "ecclesiastical" or "general."[38] The Act distinguished between what were tacitly regarded as live and dead City parishes and prescribed differential treatment for the two categories. The first schedule included five large parishes on the circumference,[39] with a combined population of over 31,000 and a total charity income of nearly £30,000, while in the second schedule were listed over a hundred phantom

[34] S. C. on the Parochial Charities Bill, 1882, Q. 2928ff; Charity Record, 29 June 1882.

[35] Ibid., 4 Aug. 1882.

[36] Bryce to Freshfield (solicitor to the churchwardens), 19 July 1883, in the office of the City Parochial Foundation.

[37] 3 Hansard, 282:1095–1104.

[38] In the case of mixed charities (which combined ecclesiastical and nonecclesiastical elements) the Commissioners were to assign each of the two funds its proper share.

[39] St. Andrew, Holborn; St. Botolph, Aldgate; St. Botolph, Bishopsgate; St. Bride, Fleet Street; St. Giles, Cripplegate.

parishes, whose endowments were sometimes heavy but whose population was exceedingly light. The five large parishes would continue to handle their own charities, though in conformity with new schemes to be framed by the Charity Commissioners. But the hundred-odd moribund parishes were to be relieved of their responsibilities, and their incomes applied throughout metropolitan London to such admirable causes as education, libraries and museums, open spaces, provident institutions, convalescent hospitals, and, in general, for the improvement of "the physical, social, and moral condition of the poorer inhabitants of the metropolis." [40] The preliminary work, largely of a legal character, fell on the Commissioners. Permanent management, however, would rest in the hands of a board of twenty-one members, the Trustees of the London Parochial Charities, on which both Crown and City Corporation would be well represented. Although the Bryce Act did little more than remove the legal obstacles to a solution, it accomplished that much admirably. It was now the responsibility of the Charity Commissioners to build a structure according to the general specifications of 46 & 47 Victoria.

3

Meanwhile, other City institutions were drawing even heavier fire from municipal reformers. For it was generally recognized that, if the City Corporation and its liberties were the major obstacles to a unified government for London, the resistance of the Corporation drew much of its strength from the wealthy and powerful Livery Companies, especially the Twelve Great Companies. With some exceptions, these had long since lost any connection with their original functions, but their immense endowments and their dominating position in the City assured them of an enormous residue of power. Their anomalous situation — great wealth and great public influence balanced by no public responsibility — made it inevitable that they should attract the critical attention of the reform party. For further annoyance, there were always the luxurious City dinners, of which green turtle soup was the classic symbol and which inspired such colorful attacks as *The Curse of Turtledom*.[41] The assault on the City Companies paralleled that on the parochial charities and reflected similar motives. In the 1870's a few voices were being raised in criticism, and in 1873, Gladstone himself spoke of the possibility of appropriating for more useful purposes the funds of the Companies, a threat probably not unconnected with the loosening of the City's old Liberal ties.[42] One of the first acts of the new Liberal Government in 1880 was to create a Royal Commission, on which, perhaps as a reassuring gesture, appeared the impeccable names of the Earl of Derby (chairman) and the Duke of Bedford.

The position of the Companies, legal and otherwise, was not as indefensible as the more eager reformers made it out to be. Their revenues, aggregating £750,000

[40] 46 & 47 Vict., c. 36, cl. 14.
[41] J. E. Woolacott, *The Curse of Turtledom* (London, 1894).
[42] J. F. B. Firth, *Reform of London Government and of City Guilds* (London, 1888), p. 90.

to £800,000, were of two kinds: first, the income from some eleven hundred trusts, which could be applied only in accordance with the will or deed of the founder (or as altered by a competent public authority), and secondly, the corporate income, which was the absolute property of the Company. The proportions between the two varied enormously from Company to Company, as is indicated by the revenues (shown in the table) reported to the Royal Commission by the Twelve Great.[43] The sixty-two Minor Companies accounted for something like £40,000 in trust and over £115,000 in corporate income.[44]

	CORPORATE	TRUST
Mercers	£47,341	£35,417
Grocers	37,736	500
Drapers	50,141	28,513
Fishmongers	46,913	3,800
Goldsmiths	43,505	10,792
Skinners	18,977	9,950
Merchant Taylors	31,243	12,068
Haberdashers	9,032	20,000
Salters	18,892	2,148
Ironmongers	9,625	12,822
Vintners	9,365	1,522
Clothworkers	40,458	10,000

Questions could be raised about the trust income of the Companies, but broadly speaking, their charities were better administered than most, with fairly scrupulous regard for the letter of the trust. In most instances management costs were paid out of corporate income rather than out of trust revenues.[45] Of the £200,000 charitable income, about three-eighths (£75,000) went for almshouses and pensions to poor members, since all of the Twelve and several of the Minor Companies had their own institutions. Another three-eighths of the Companies' charity income supported educational activities — in the neighborhood of a hundred scholarships and exhibitions at the old universities and a group of schools in and about London which prepared for the universities, together with a larger number described as "middle-class." In the former category one need only mention the Merchant Taylors' School; St. Paul's, confided by Dean Colet to the Mercers; Tonbridge in charge of the Skinners; and Oundle, of the Grocers. In administering their educational responsibilities the Companies had supplemented income from specific endowments with substantial appropriations from their corporate income.[46] Where the charitable trusts of the Companies seemed most out of tune with the times was in the £50,000 spent on miscellaneous objects, some

[43] R. C. on the Livery Companies (C. 4073), 1884, I, 26.
[44] Ibid., pp. 27–28.
[45] Ibid., p. 36.
[46] Ibid., pp. 33–34.

of which were thoroughly obsolete. Like other ancient charities, in and out of London, quantities of these trusts stood in grave need of revision. Still, in a limited sense the City Companies were more efficient charity administrators than were the bulk of trustees throughout the Kingdom, and had been so recognized by generations of benefactors who had left trusts to their management.

The corporate revenues of the Companies, three times as large as their trust income, raised issues of a different order. It was the belief of many, not only ardent reformers, that the public was morally entitled to a slice of these receipts, and they could cite the opinions of eminent jurists in support of the public's stake. Nor were they satisfied by the considerable sums which the Companies voluntarily donated to charities, their own and others, from their corporate income.[47] They believed not without reason, that corporate funds had grown more rapidly than trusts because certain increments that might justly have been claimed by the trusts found their way into the corporate coffer. A seventeenth-century benefactor, for example, might have left to charity £20 a year, assuming this to be the normal yield of a piece of property which, three hundred years later, might be producing several thousand pounds. In such a case the Companies would customarily pay only the specified sum, garnering the increase for their corporate funds. During the early century the courts tended to admit their right to such profits, though later decisions found more merit in the claims of the charities.[48] Here the issue was by no means clear-cut, and in facing their critics the Companies were in a strong legal, if not moral, position.

The argument really turned on the ambiguous status of the Companies. Were they simply private organizations, like Pall Mall clubs, as a Tory Solicitor-General had once implied, or were they quasi-public institutions?[49] There were items on corporate balance sheets that would have excited the virtuous avarice of any municipal reformer. Some of the expenditures of the Companies were to their opponents simply irresponsible extravagance, but none so appalling as the estimated £100,000 spent on "wasteful, and, it must be owned, for the most part, dull dinners, in hot close halls."[50] Nor were they appeased by the Companies' plea that many of these functions were means of extending to honored guests the semi-official hospitality of the City. In the eyes of the opposition, the Companies were simply practitioners of Thackeray's "monstrous belly-worship."

Critics were less prepared to complain about the £150,000 of corporate income

---

[47] *Ibid.*, pp. 36, 72–73. For a summary of Company giving see P. H. Ditchfield, *The City Companies of London and Their Good Works* (London, 1904), pp. 11–13.

[48] In Thomas Hare's reports on the eleven hundred trusts administered by the Companies he discusses the virtues and shortcomings of their trusteeship. His analyses drew enthusiastic comments from *The Times* (2 Feb. 1885). For relevant legal decisions, see Hare's evidence, *R. C. on the Livery Companies*, 1884, Q. 69–70; *Attorney-General v. Skinners*, 2 Russ. 438; *Attorney-General v. Grocers*, 6 Beav. 526; *Attorney-General v. Mayor of Bristol*, 2 Jac. and W. 294. On the other side, see *Attorney-General v. Wax Chandlers*, 6 Eng. and N., Ap. 1 (Kendall's Charity); *Attorney-General v. Merchant Taylors*, 11 Eq. 35 and 6 Ch. Ap. 512 (Donkin's Charity).

[49] *The Times*, 12 April 1877.

[50] *Ibid.*, 28 June 1884.

given to charity, though they were entitled to point out that some of this was the fruit of an eleventh-hour repentance. By the time of the Royal Commission's inquiry, the Companies were spending approximately £50,000 from their corporate income for educational purposes. In addition to supporting schools of their own and university exhibitions, the Companies were displaying a constructive interest in technical education.[51] In several West Riding cities the Clothworkers had identified themselves with the founding of institutions for training in the techniques of woolen manufacture. More important, shortly before the Royal Commission began sitting, some of the more enlightened Company members, led by Sir Sydney Waterlow and Lord Selborne, launched plans for the "City and Guilds of London Institute for the Advancement of Technical Education," an association to promote technical training. Over £100,000 was contributed to a building fund for the erection of Finsbury Technical College and the Central Institution in South Kensington, ultimately to become the Engineering Section of the Imperial College of Science and Technology. Not only that, but a group of Companies pledged annual gifts amounting to £25,000 a year.[52] These were projects eminently suited to the traditions and professed interests of the Companies.

Nor were their benefactions trifling in the vague area of miscellaneous charity. The Commission estimated these at about £90,000 annually, probably between £70,000 and £80,000 for benevolent and public purposes in the London area. The London Hospital in the East End, for example, received from the Grocers alone some £26,500 over a ten-year period, and other medical charities benefited handsomely.[53]

By the 1870's the Companies were beginning to admit some degree of public responsibility. If one accepted their claim that their corporate estates were private property pure and simple, then their benefactions were uncommonly generous. As a group (though with considerable differences among them) the Companies were not uncharitable, but they insisted on exercising benevolence in their own way and on objects selected by themselves. They were immensely resistant toward any threat to extend state power in their direction. In the 1830's some of them had flatly refused to supply information to the Municipal Commissioners, and their cooperation with the Royal Commission in the 1880's was less than cordial. There was some doubt, in fact, whether they would fill in the questionnaires sent by the Commission, and in the end their returns, insofar as these related to corporate funds, were submitted under protest.[54] Such matters were held to be nobody's business but their own. Yet as a whole the Companies, however reluctantly, provided the information required.

[51] Perhaps in response to appeals to reassert their connection with trade which they had once represented. See Hare's evidence, *R. C. on the Livery Companies,* 1884, Q. 87–89; memorandum by Hare, *ibid.,* pp. 105–106; *The Times,* 14 Sept. 1880.
[52] *R. C. on the Livery Companies,* 1884, pp. 38–39, 68–69.
[53] *Ibid.,* p. 39.
[54] *Ibid.,* p. 42.

For the Royal Commission the problem was not only the practical one of formulating a policy but also of justifying it legally and historically. Was the State entitled to intervene with respect to the corporate funds of the Companies? A majority of the Commission, disagreeing with the Lord Chancellor (who also happened to be a member of the Mercers' Company), answered in the affirmative on the general ground that these were at least semipublic institutions, as well as for a number of more specific reasons.[55] Three members rejected the reasoning of the majority — Sir Richard Cross, Sir Nathaniel de Rothschild, and Alderman Cotton, a former Lord Mayor and an unreconstructed City man, who added his own outraged protest to the more temperate dissenting report.

It followed that the Commission would recommend some kind of public control over the corporate funds of the Companies, though probably without yielding to the extreme reformers, who were urging virtual confiscation. The London School Board, searching as always for idle endowments which could be drafted into the service of education, had issued its reports on the Livery Companies, charging the misapplication of funds and citing examples of useless and mischievous charities which, the Board contended, should be appropriated to education under Section 30 of the Endowed Schools Act.[56] A prominent member of the Commission was J. F. B. Firth, most active of municipal reformers and often regarded as father of the London County Council. Between Firth and Alderman Cotton there was no possibility of agreement.

The majority report predictably took a middle path, one which *The Times* regarded as moderate and wise.[57] The Livery Companies should be conceived as analogous to Oxford and Cambridge, institutions which had already been brought under the scrutiny of the State and should be dealt with in similar fashion. The State, in short, should take the Companies in hand, but only for specific purposes — such as to prevent the alienation of their property,[58] to assure permanently the application of their corporate income to useful purposes, to revise trusts where desirable.

The Times might hold the majority report to be a well-considered solution of the dilemma posed by the Livery Companies, but its endorsement evoked no chorus of approval in the Company Halls. Though the moderates realized that the Companies had come out of it all with less damage than might have been expected, Liverymen of more traditional views could condemn the report as "unblushing spoliation . . . as naked as Adam and Eve in Paradise"[59] or, more elegantly, as "the demure rapacity of modern democracy."[60] A Company pamphleteer sadly reflected that "St. Martin of Tours gave half his cloak to the poor

[55] *Ibid.*, pp. 42–43. Lord Selborne was the Lord Chancellor.
[56] Benjamin Lucraft, *ibid.*, Q. 2161ff; London School Board Minutes, 17 Feb. 1881.
[57] *The Times*, 26 June 1884.
[58] That is, Companies should be forbidden to sell their property and divide the proceeds among the individual members.
[59] George H. Blakesley, *The London Companies Commission* (London, 1885), p. 43.
[60] Quoted in *The Times*, 2 Feb. 1885.

and needy, and was canonized for it; the City Guilds have done the same, and they are threatened with martyrdom." [61] Still, to reasonable men it must have seemed fantastic to denounce as revolutionary a document signed by Lord Derby, the Duke of Bedford, Lord Sherbrooke (Robert Lowe), and Lord Coleridge (Lord Chief Justice), to say nothing of Sir Sydney Waterlow, himself a former Lord Mayor and member of two Livery Companies.[62]

In the long run, the Royal Commission inquiry turned out to be cautionary and educative in its effects rather than punitive. As far as specific legislative restraints were concerned, its recommendations produced astonishing little result. For one thing, the fall of the Liberal Government in 1885 ushered in two decades of almost uninterrupted Tory hegemony, and there was little inclination among Conservatives to press the campaign against the Companies. By the time the Liberals returned to power, London had achieved its unified government and the London County Council was functioning. This served to divert into other channels some of the torrent that had been threatening to engulf the Companies. Occasionally there were isolated moves, within and outside Parliament, toward applying restraints. In 1885 Charles Dilke introduced a mild bill, and four years later, for the Corporate Property Committee of the new L.C.C., Lord (Sir Arthur) Hobhouse issued a report which aroused the City of London Guilds Defense Association, but only briefly.[63]

It would, no doubt, have seemed incredible to the reformers of the 1880's that the formal status of the City Companies in the Welfare State of the 1960's should be precisely the same as under Victorian high capitalism. Yet in their curious way they have continued to flourish, with some fourteen thousand Liverymen on their rolls and long waiting lists.[64] They are no more subject to state control than before the Royal Commission, nor have there been raids by public authorities on their corporate resources, the magnitude of which is as well concealed as ever. Although they regularly report to the Charity Commission and the Ministry of Education their charitable and educational trusts, no figures on corporate incomes have been published since those of the Royal Commission, and to this day the information forms from *Whitaker's Almanac* are returned blank.[65] A rough calculation, assuming that the trust and corporate branches remained in about the ratio of the mid-'80's (an excessively cautious assumption), would put the corporate income of the Twelve Great Companies at something over £1 million, probably substantially over.

Although they emerged relatively unscathed, the inquiry did serve to remind the Companies of their vulnerability and therefore of their public responsibilities. It is impossible to guess what proportion of their corporate income now goes for charitable or public objects, but the figure is obviously far from trivial. Aside

[61] L. B. S., *The City Livery Companies and Their Corporate Property* (London, 1885), pp. 57–58.
[62] George W. Smalley, *The Life of Sir Sydney Waterlow, Bart.* (London, 1909), p. 164.
[63] *3 Hansard*, 298:1791–93; L. C. C. Minutes, 7 May 1889; *The Times*, 22 May 1889.
[64] *Ibid.*, 8 March 1962.
[65] Evidence of the Clothworkers' Company before the Nathan Committee, 1951 (unpubl.), Q. 5184.

from their grants to schools, the Twelve annually contribute (from trust and corporate income) a sum estimated in excess of £500,000 to a wide assortment of charities.[66] Corporate funds are often used to supplement inadequate trusts and to provide for charitable enterprises requiring capital outlay.[67] The Cloth-workers, for example, have twice rebuilt two sets of their almshouses in Islington out of corporate funds.[68] Up to 1921 the Companies contributed over £1 million to the City and Guilds of London Institute, four of them accounting for nearly £600,000.[69] Individual Companies have established exhibitions, scholarships, and even chairs at the universities.[70] Some of their annual gifts from corporate funds are of such long standing and so traditional as to have become recognized commitments. Although as a group the Senior Companies have never developed long-range programs comparable to those of some of the larger foundations, many of their decisions about contributing to national objects are taken collectively — sometimes by setting up a single target for the Twelve and then, as the clerk of the Clothworkers put it, saying to themselves, " 'Now this is what we want to subscribe and how can we best do it?' "[71]

Aside from contributions by the Companies from their corporate funds, their charitable trusts remain one of the country's major resources for philanthropic purposes. To the Nathan Committee the Twelve reported an income, exclusive of school endowments, of about £320,000.[72] For administering this mass of good works, the Companies generally eschew the 5 per cent to which they might be entitled, thus contributing the equivalent of an additional £15,000 from their corporate funds.[73] The latter-day administration of their charities is considered vigorous and intelligent. It is typical, perhaps, that mid-century Britain, even Socialist Britain, should have shown little disposition to renew the attack on the Companies, though there are occasional complaints about their financial reticence. Apart from the element of pageantry and ceremonial that they add, they are recognized as institutions of genuine public value, monuments to the British talent for preserving anachronisms and putting them to work. Even Company dinners today excite less indignation than envy.

4

For their task of reorganizing the parochial charities of the City, the Bryce Act had equipped the Charity Commissioners with powers much greater than those under which they ordinarily acted.[74] In framing schemes for the more than

---

[66] *The Times,* 8 March 1962.

[67] The Clothworkers before the Nathan Committee, 1951, Q. 5049, 5057–58, 5184.

[68] *Ibid.,* Q. 5129.

[69] C. T. Millis, *Technical Education: Its Development and Aims* (London, 1925), p. 164.

[70] As have the Goldsmiths, whose more recent benefactions to education will be noted in Chapter XXI.

[71] Nathan Committee, 1951, Q. 5189.

[72] *Ibid.,* Q. 5016.

[73] *Ibid.,* Q. 5059–60.

[74] Two additional Commissioners were appointed to handle the work, Sir Francis Sandon, who had been Permanent Secretary of the Education Office, and James Anstie, Q.C., a Nonconformist barrister of some distinction, who proved to be the active member of the team.

thirteen hundred trusts, they were permitted to ignore founders' wishes and the canons of *cy-près* and to proceed on a utilitarian basis. But however attractive the authority, the assignment was exceedingly complex. To complete the task took nearly a decade and required two extensions of Bryce's Act beyond its original four-year term. Essential documents had been lost or had perished in that "convenient catastrophe, the Great Fire." Even when in existence and legible, they could be extraordinarily imprecise, as in the case of sums left "for the benefit of the parish." Vestry clerks were not lacking to argue that such benefactions were free of any trust and could be applied against the poor rates or for any other purpose that seemed good to the parish. At every stage there were parochial officials trying, not unnaturally, to salvage what they could for their own parishes.

A case in point is St. Sepulchre, Holborn, which carried on one of the more skillful and persevering actions. This parish, with some show of reason, felt aggrieved at having been omitted from the large parishes in the first schedule, for its charity income was greater than that of St. Andrew, Holborn, or St. Bride, Fleet Street. Outraged at the prospect of seeing its charities pass into a parochial pool, St. Sepulchre appointed a special committee, which proceeded to draw up schemes for reforming individual trusts, with the obvious aim of keeping them in the control of the parish. The list of parish functionaries who, the committee urged, had claims for continued emolument suggests that the attacks of reformers had not been overdrawn. These included a surveyor, sexton and assistant sexton, organ-blower, beadle, pew-openers, steeple-keeper, and gardener. Only gradually was St. Sepulchre convinced that Bryce's Act meant precisely what it said, and the special committee brought to acknowledge that its thirty-four meetings had been wholly unfruitful.[75]

By the autumn of 1887 the Commissioners had completed their initial task of classifying parochial endowments. In the 107 parishes of the second schedule they reported an income for ecclesiastical purposes of £35,459 and for general purposes of £56,567, while the five large parishes of the first schedule had incomes of £2,601 and £24,015. In all, then, the general charity funds yielded an annual revenue of about £80,000 and the ecclesiastical about £38,000.[76]

The other part of the task, that of deciding how the income was to be spent, brought its special embarrassments. From all directions worthy causes converged on the Commissioners with helpful proposals. In the late '70's the London School Board, combing the metropolitan area for resources that might be applied to education, presumably to the benefit of the school rate, admitted to designs on the parochial trusts, as well as on the Livery Companies. Its Educational Endowments Committee, for some time under the chairmanship of Helen Taylor, John Stuart Mill's stepdaughter, attempted, in fact, to stake out a claim to about £50,000, roughly half of the charitable income of the City parishes.[77] The cham-

---

[75] Minute Book of the St. Sepulchre Special Committee, 20 July 1886, 7 May 1888, Guildhall Library MS 7230.

[76] "Objections of the Open Space Societies," *Return of Certain Objections* (*Parl. Pap.*, 1890), p. 32.

[77] London School Board Minutes, 23 July, 6 Aug., 22 Oct., 19 Nov. 1879.

pions of open spaces — the Commons Preservation Society, the Metropolitan Public
Gardens Association, and the Kyrle Society[78] — made a persuasive case for a
large slice. Indeed, while the Commissioners were still putting their schemes in
order, the capital of the consolidated fund was tapped for the purchase of several
open spaces, the most notable being the 260 acres of Parliament Hill, adjoining
Hampstead Heath, which was in imminent danger of being sold for building lots.
By putting up £50,000 with the approval of Parliament, they were able to inspire
public authorities and private donors to contribute the additional £250,000 required.[79] Before the new Parochial Foundation was established, the Commissioners had bestowed, at the direction of Parliament, some £135,000 on open
spaces, a sum that primed the pump for a flow of over £425,000 from other
sources, public and private.[80]

The Commissioners were not hostile to providing open spaces for the congested
Metropolis, but they responded with greater enthusiasm to other projects. Above
all it was the opportunity to make a significant contribution to British technical
education (in American terms, trade schools) that kindled their imagination.
To many Englishmen, alarmed over foreign trade competition, technical training
could no longer be dismissed as expedient only for Continentals who had no
talent for British rule-of-thumb methods but had become a simple necessity.[81]
Uneasiness about Britain's industrial future was paralleled by a new concern
for working-class welfare. This interest, also, was embodied in the proposals of
the Commissioners, for, as will appear presently, the polytechnics they were
contemplating were to be not merely trade schools but working-class social centers
as well.

All this was true enough. Yet what explained, as much as anything, the Commissioners' espousal of the polytechnic movement was the profound impression
made on an Assistant Commissioner by one of the more appealing late Victorian
social-educational experiments. Henry H. Cunynghame, labeled by his biogra-
phers "The Unconventional Civil Servant" and certainly a man not bound by
traditional orthodoxies, had been charged with surveying the needs of the London
poor.[82] An incognito visit to the Regent Street Polytechnic, where Quintin Hogg,
a warm-hearted Etonian who had prospered as a sugar merchant in the City, was
supplying recreational facilities and technical instruction for numbers of lower-
middle- and lower-class boys, made him an enthusiastic advocate of Hogg's ideas.
The project had started as a Ragged School in the slums near Charing Cross and
had outgrown a succession of premises, finally arriving at the old Polytechnic
building on Regent Street, which had formerly been used for popular science

[78] Some account of these organizations will be given in Chapter XVIII.
[79] *Charity Record*, 17 Nov. 1887; George Shaw-Lefevre (Lord Eversley), *English Commons and Forests* (London, 1894), pp. 55–57. The Commissioners also contributed heavily toward the purchase of Clissold Park (Stoke Newington) and of the Lawn, Henry Fawcett's residence in Lambeth.
[80] "Objections of the Open Space Societies," *Return of Certain Objections* (Parl. Pap., 1890), p. 30.
[81] As evidenced by the *R. C. on Technical Instruction* (C. 3171, C. 3981), 1882–84.
[82] C. H. D. Ward and C. B. Spencer, *The Unconventional Civil Servant, Sir Henry H. Cunynghame* (London, 1948).

lectures and exhibitions. Over the years Hogg, it is said, spent on the work something like £100,000 of his own funds.[83] For Cunynghame, once he had inspected the Regent Street Polytechnic, the problem of what to do with the City parochial funds had been solved, and he succeeded in persuading the Commissioners, who in any case were pre-disposed to favor technical education.[84]

Meanwhile, their interest in offering social and educational advantages to the working classes was further stimulated by an unlikely influence, Sir Walter Besant's fantasy, *All Sorts and Conditions of Men*. This volume, appropriately subtitled "An Impossible Story," grew out of the author's tramps through the East End in 1880–81, in the course of which he became convinced of the need for an intellectual and social center in the London east of Aldgate Pump.[85] His utopian story pictured such a "Palace of Delight." In a social atmosphere that encouraged a sympathetic, and even sentimental, view of the slum-dweller, Besant's book struck fire and became, as he recalled, something of a beacon for the movement that founded the People's Palace in Mile End Road. Although the finances of the People's Palace were as chaotic as those of the Regent Street Polytechnic were well ordered, the Commissioners agreed to add it as a "kindred institution" to their circle of polytechnics.[86]

Not only was technical education, in the view of the Commissioners, an admirable cause in itself, but they suspected that it might attract the support of other donors, hopefully the City Companies. The self-reform of these bodies was already in progress, and some of them were giving considerable sums to educational purposes. In soliciting contributions from the Companies, Cunynghame appealed equally to self-interest and public spirit. To the Haberdashers he intimated that, "If you would take up this form of charity, it would, having received Governmental approval, be impregnable of attack." The Drapers, approached in somewhat the same fashion, committed themselves to £40,000, presently increased to £70,000, as endowment, in addition to the loan of £20,000, for building a technical school in connection with the Palace. Unhappily the troubles of the Drapers were just beginning. The People's Palace, for which they accepted special responsibility, proved insatiable in swallowing the Company's funds. In the years 1884–1917 the Drapers gave from their corporate funds nearly £960,000 to educational and other charities, a substantial fraction of which was accounted for by the East End institution.[87]

Although the central, consolidated scheme was the most original phase of City charity reform, the Commissioners dealt with the five large parishes in similar

[83] See Ethel M. Hogg, *Quintin Hogg*, 2d ed. (London, 1904), p. 215.
[84] Ward and Spencer, *Sir Henry H. Cunynghame*, pp. 180–81.
[85] Sir Walter Besant, *Autobiography* (London, 1902), p. 244.
[86] In the early 1930's the original People's Palace was destroyed by fire. It was rebuilt and since 1954 has formed a part of Queen Mary College of London University.
[87] The continuing interest of the Company in Queen Mary College is an outgrowth of this earlier connection with the People's Palace. (Ward and Spencer, *Sir Henry H. Cunynghame*, p. 185; *Reports to the Charity Commissioners* [County of London], VII, 452ff [*Parl. Pap.*, 1904]. A. H. Johnson, *The History of the Worshipful Company of the Drapers of London*, 5 vols. [Oxford, 1914–22, IV, 407] records the grants made annually to charity by the Company during the years 1884–1917.)

fashion. In each case, small trusts were amalgamated under schemes which put old funds to modern uses. Their plans for Bishopsgate and Cripplegate included libraries (one of these the now well-known Bishopsgate Institute which houses the Howell Collection of materials on Victorian labor history), and these were also promised subventions from the general fund. But even in some of the parishes that received specially favored treatment, the course of reform failed to run smoothly. Aldgate, perhaps the richest parish in London, with a charity income in the neighborhood of £10,000 a year, had fallen into the hands of a small ring, which managed the affairs of the parish to suit itself.[88] As the Commissioners prepared their scheme, the insiders attempted to forestall them by leasing three of the most valuable parish sites (presumably to themselves or their friends) at well below their value. At this point R. H. Hadden, the new vicar of St. Botolph's, reported the stratagem to the Commissioners, who, in turn, cited it to the Attorney-General.

With a parish as maladministered as this, the Commissioners did not hesitate to demolish the old order entirely, and from some three dozen trusts they created the Aldgate Freedom Foundation. For doles they substituted pensions; they provided generously for medical relief; and they assigned some £150 a year for the maintenance as an open space of the Tower Garden which adjoins the parish, with £50 for the churchyard. The approximately £8,000 of educational income went to re-establish the eighteenth-century educational charity of Sir John Cass as a technical institute. The school had been a cozy enterprise managed by a group of self-elected trustees who used every device to limit the enrollment in the school and preserve their own lush patronage. The Cass Foundation was hopelessly out of step with the times, and the Commissioners were on good ground when they argued that its usefulness had been unnecessarily restricted. Against the bitterest of opposition they went ahead with the reorganization until the parish not only became reconciled to the new departure but began to take pride in the reborn institution.

During 1889 the Commissioners unveiled their central scheme, which consolidated trusts with an aggregate income for nonecclesiastical purposes of about £50,000. At the outset they reduced the annual yield by making some grants out of capital, notably more than £160,000 to a series of polytechnics and kindred institutions. In addition, they directed that the new City Parochial Foundation shoud pay *in perpetuity* to the polytechnics about £22,500 a year — this in addition to £5,000 to be paid annually to a group of technical institutions still to be named. The future governing body of the Foundation, it appeared, might find its operations fairly well circumscribed.

The Charity Commissioners had labored long and earnestly, and in many respects their schemes showed sound judgment. But if they imagined these to be so obviously reasonable as to command immediate acceptance, disillusionment

[88] A. G. B. Atkinson, *St. Botolph Aldgate: The Story of a City Parish* (London, 1898), pp. 211–12 (chap. by R. H. Hadden).

followed promptly. Their decisions on the ecclesiastical fund aroused little complaint. On the whole, they had followed the recommendations of the diocesan
authorities and had allocated about half the total income in perpetuity to maintaining the fabric and services of fifty-five churches.[89] The general (or nonecclesiastical) fund was another matter. No doubt the Commissioners anticipated the
wail that went up from certain City parishes. Most of them held meetings to
protest against the withdrawal of Charity funds from City control, and vestry
clerks prepared to resist collectively threatened cuts in salary. The special committee of St. Sepulchre, Holborn, went into action again, requested the parish
solicitor to draw up a case, and finally attempted to bring the issue to the floor
of the House. The Bishop of London, far from encouraging the demonstration,
threw cold water on it by reminding the committee that the Commissioners had
followed his suggestions precisely and adding that, in the view of Fulham Palace,
some of the recent expenditures of the parish had seemed "hardly defensible." [90]

Such opposition the Charity Commissioners could take in their stride. What
was more alarming was the dissatisfaction among those who were highly sympathetic toward Bryce's Act and who might have been expected to give enthusiastic
support to the Commissioners' schemes. One might put down to self-interest the
protests from City parishes and Corporation, but the objections of Lord (Sir
Arthur) Hobhouse on behalf of the London County Council, from the associated
open space societies (signed by Shaw-Lefevre and Cardinal Manning among
others), and from the Charity Organisation Society could not be so easily dismissed. Still less easily could one shrug off the doubts of James Bryce himself,
who, as soon as he received the draft scheme, returned a temperate but critical
comment.[91]

Among the dissidents there was essential agreement about what was wrong
with the Commissioners' plans. The least crucial weakness, because the most
readily remediable, was the meager representation on the new governing body
given to the London County Council. Goaded by Hobhouse, who reflected all of
the reformer's buoyant confidence in municipal democracy as a solvent for
municipal ills, the Commissioners increased the Council's representation at the
expense of London University, which had been given overgenerous treatment.
Much more serious was the sweeping commitment to the polytechnics. These
represented an educational experiment, admittedly promising, but still an experiment. Only three of them were in actual operation; in addition, there was a
temperance music hall, the future "Old Vic," with which was connected Morley

[89] In addition, some £60,000 or £70,000 was taken from capital for repairing and restoring over
half of the City churches, an outlay for which the fund would be reimbursed in ten annual installments. Altogether it was a fair inference that in the immediate future no great increments would find
their way to the Ecclesiastical Commissioners.

[90] Minute Book of the St. Sepulchre Special Committee, 2 Feb. 1891, Guildhall Library MS 7230.

[91] All of these documents appear in the *Return of Certain Objections* (*Parl. Pap.*, 1890) except the
Charity Organisation Society's *The City Parochial Scheme* (London, 1889). Octavia Hill, in a letter to
the *Standard* (2 Oct. 1889), urged that more of the income ought to go to "charity," presumably
C.O.S.-approved.

College, an adult education venture. But, beyond these, the Commissioners also proposed permanent endowments for three polytechnics which were only projected. In short, there was a strong, and not unjustified feeling, that they had overdone their support of these institutions and that, in their implied bargains with City Companies and other donors, they had not only committed too large a share of their own funds but had also tied the hands of the future trustees.[92]

This suggests the third and most damaging question posed by the critics of the Commissioners. The new schemes specified in detail the uses to which the great bulk of charity property was to be applied, so much so that, according to Bryce's estimate, the new governing body would have only about £4,000 of free income to spend annually. One wonders that the Charity Commissioners, of all bodies, after their perennial complaints about the rigidity of testators' arrangements and their demand for more flexible machinery for revising trusts, should have assured annual grants to the polytechnics in perpetuity. Presumably they were convinced that in the polytechnics they had discovered an educational and cultural panacea, and they regarded a permanent commitment as necessary to gain the cooperation of Livery Companies and other donors. For the sake of their plan they did not hesitate to pledge virtually all of their income and, it seemed probable, to leave their future trustees with little more than routine duties.

Protests against such a long-term commitment were without effect. On the strength of the Commissioners' promises money-raising campaigns had already been launched for institutions to be established in Chelsea, Clerkenwell, Shoreditch, South London, and elsewhere, and these had received support from City Companies and others. As it turned out, the cost of this imposing ring of polytechnics far exceeded the Commissioners' generous provision for them, and those which had not been taken over by a City Company had to be rescued by the public authorities.[93] But this was in the future. On the immediate issue, Parliament was left with no practical alternative but to approve (as was done early in 1891) the Commissioners' schemes.[94] Yet in retrospect it is hard to disagree with the charges of their critics. Given the pledges made by the Commissioners, it seemed doubtful whether the Foundation would be left with a free income large enough to contribute anything of consequence to the improvement of the Metropolis or to enlist the efforts of able trustees. What disproved this gloomy and, at the time

[92] Another consideration was that, by the Technical Instruction Act of 1889, such enterprises as the polytechnics had been accepted as a proper charge on local rates — though London had shown little inclination to draw on the rates for this purpose.

[93] The benefaction from Parliament came in the form of "whisky money," explained in the previous chapter, through which the London County Council became the richer by £117,000. A good deal of this went to the polytechnics, whose prospects thus took a turn for the better, especially after the London Technical Education Committee, led by Sidney Webb, embarked on its work. An interesting sidelight on the results of the Government's unpremeditated aid to technical education is cast by the former farm laborer Joseph Ashby (M. K. Ashby, *Joseph Ashby of Tysoe, 1859–1919* [Cambridge, 1961], p. 227), who speaks of "the evening 'whisky money' classes in technical subjects" as exceedingly valuable to those who had left school. "Only keen pupils," he adds, "attended the evening classes and the special local committee could be asked to provide teaching in any 'technical' subject."

[94] *3 Hansard*, 349:1111–27.

reasonable, prediction was, of course, the enormous rise in the value of London property, so that the income of the City Parochial Foundation trebled between 1891 and 1950.[95] In the long run, therefore, the earlier decisions of the Commissioners did not fatally restrict the work of the trustees.

5

The Foundation took temporary quarters "until mid-summer next" at 3 Temple Gardens (its offices for the past seventy years!) and prepared to face the realities of its financial situation. In view of the earlier generosity of the Commissioners, it was out of the question that the Central Governing Body should consider new applications for grants. Yet the resources of the Foundation began to grow at once. By 1895 the gross income of the central (nonecclesiastical) Fund was nearly half again as large as four years before. As leases fell in during the 1890's, the trustees took the opportunity, wherever possible, to buy or get by exchange property adjoining their own and thus to improve the value of their holdings. By the early 1900's the capital of the Foundation had risen to roughly £4½ million, of which about £3 million, as might be expected, was solidly invested in City freeholds.[96]

In the early years the trustees were relatively undisturbed by their heavy commitment to the polytechnics. In addition to the compulsory payments, they regularly appropriated large sums out of their surplus income and continued to do so even after the County Council, as the education authority, had drawn the polytechnics into the state system. It was not until the 1920's that the Foundation became uneasy about its role as benefactor of rate-supported institutions (even though contributions had been chiefly for social and recreational facilities) especially when these were absorbing something like two-thirds of its income. The trustees were especially uneasy as they noted the changing character of the polytechnic clientele. There were some doubts whether the polytechnics were, in fact, patronized primarily by "the poorer classes of the Metropolis," though obviously, as long as some of the poor *did* attend, the Foundation could not be released from its statutory obligations. It could, however, reduce and finally withdraw its discretionary contributions. In the 1930's, therefore, the trustees took this step, canceling some £23,000 a year. Altogether in the sixty years 1891–1951 the polytechnics received roughly £2½ million from the City parochial endowments.[97]

The trustees have sometimes viewed their obligation to the polytechnics as a rather indefensible burden, but they have supported certain of the "kindred institutions" with marked generosity. To the noneducational activities of the People's Palace they contributed nearly £250,000. In the case of Victoria Hall and Morley College the Foundation was obligated by scheme to the amount of £1,000 a year. But as the Old Vic shed its trappings of a temperance music hall and made for

[95] Evidence of Donald (now Sir Donald) Allen before the Nathan Committee, 1951, Q. 5994–95; Donald Allen, "Charity," *London School of Economics Magazine,* July 1953, p. 10.

[96] *Nathan Report,* 1952, Par. 555.

[97] Donald Allen, Nathan Committee, 1951, Q. 5986.

itself a unique place in London's cultural life, the Foundation supported it with a total over the years of £133,000. The Whitechapel Art Gallery and the District Nursing Association were also well treated, and the old Chelsea Physic Garden, founded by Hans Sloane in the early eighteenth century and managed until the 1890's by the Apothecaries' Society, was saved from extinction when the Foundation took over the trust and supplied funds for carrying on the historic enterprise. The Physic Garden has served a dual purpose — educational, as a source of botanical specimens for schools and colleges, and social, as an open space for the residents of Chelsea. To salvage such a tract was especially appealing to the trustees, who have appropriated altogether about £500,000 for open spaces, recreation grounds, and playing fields in the metropolitan area.

Modern London, one must conclude, has done well from the old City endowments. Their capital has been astutely managed and the income applied to constructive ends. Almost from the beginning the Foundation employed the principle of the decreasing grant, and applications have been generally scrutinized with a highly critical eye.[98] It has been operated with an administrative superstructure that is modest almost to excess, and its record, in fact, suggests that Parkinson's Law may be less than universally applicable, since in seventy years the small staff has been augmented by only one member.[99] In recent years, like other major British trusts, the City Parochial Foundation has functioned, with no apparent loss of effectiveness, within the framework of the Welfare State. It now has specific hope of getting rid of its obligation to the polytechnics, which are adequately provided for by statutory agencies, and it is pursuing an interesting five-year program (1961–65) stressing work for the handicapped, preventive and educational action for the younger generation, and encouragement to investigations into "inadequacy," into the problem of coordination of official and voluntary action, and into the training of social workers. Measured by the Rockefeller or Nuffield yardstick, this is not a giant among philanthropies, nor does it aspire to rival them. Yet the City Parochial Foundation, though some of its policies have occasionally been criticized as lacking in novelty and daring, remains, perhaps, the most distinctively British of all the country's trusts. Its roots run deep into the Island's past, and it stands as a typical expression of the Englishman's instinct for meeting the challenge of the new by adapting the old.

[98] Minutes of the Central Governing Body, 14 Dec. 1896, Guildhall Library MS 8966.
[99] Donald Allen, Nathan Committee, 1951, Q. 6036.

CHAPTER XI

LAW AND ADMINISTRATION:
THE CHARITY COMMISSION

THE HISTORY of the Charity Commission is a record of frustration and disappointment balanced by a good deal of solid achievement. It was never armed with the kind of authority that would have enabled it to carry out a general rationalization of charitable endowments, nor would public opinion have tolerated such bureaucratic omnipotence. There was always bitter resistance to extending the powers of the Commissioners. Some of this emanated from the wealthier and more influential charities, the Royal Hospitals for example, who stubbornly fought any attempt to subject them to the kind of supervision that, they conceded, the small village charity required.[1] Some of it reflected the Englishman's traditional and instinctive suspicion of centralized direction and some of it his prejudice against interfering with a testator's "right" to leave his money as he wished. The pious founder may have been a semihumorous figure, but to limit his freedom would have bordered on sacrilege.

During the 1870's and early '80's the Commissioners looked forward with some confidence to an increase of authority. Encouraged by the powers granted under the Endowed Schools and the City Parochial Charities Acts, they ventured to hope that they might receive similar powers for dealing with other types of charity. They were encouraged by the talk of charity reform in the air, by the activities of the Charity Organisation Society, and by the demands, enunciated before the Social Science Association and in the books of Arthur Hobhouse and Courtney Kenny, for a liberalization of charity laws. At least one decision suggested that the courts might be moving toward a less restricted interpretation of the *cy-près* doctrine.[2] But these hopes proved illusory. Nothing of any consequence was done to broaden or increase the powers of the Commissioners. As a result, they themselves seemed to lose some of the vigor and initiative of their earlier years and to reconcile themselves to their limited authority. They became increasingly content to operate as a government office dealing with routine matters in a routine fashion. Still, the achievements of the Commissioners were considerable, and

---

[1] *S. C. on the Charitable Trusts Acts*, 1884, Q. 3668ff. (Christ's Hospital) and Q. 4176ff. (the Bridewell).

[2] The Campden Charities case, discussed later in this chapter.

during their first three or four decades they showed a good deal of vigor and imagination.

The Act of 1860 had established the Commissioners as a scheme-making authority and had armed them with powers equal to those of a "Judge of the Court of Chancery sitting at Chambers." But they could intervene, on their own initiative, to reorganize only those charities with an annual income of £50 or less, and in revising trusts they had, of course, to act in conformity with the canons of *cy-près*. In the case of the larger charities they could move only by invitation of a majority of the trustees. Although charities were supposed to submit accounts to the Commissioners, they never acquired the power of compulsory audit that the Select Committee of 1835 had recommended. Yet the Act of 1860 accomplished what was perhaps its cardinal purpose. It took the bulk of the small charity work, practically all that was of a noncontentious sort, away from the equity and county courts, and lodged it with the Charity Commission. The years after 1860 show a sharp falling-off in the charity business of the law courts. In the years 1861–67, the courts received only 78 applications for schemes (as against 1279 in the previous seven years), while 2070 were made to the Charity Commission.[3]

One of the more serviceable branches of the Commission's office and one which expanded steadily was the work of the Official Trustees. Here was an admirable solution of the problem of managing charity funds, at least those of the smaller charities. As their original fears were allayed, these increasingly discovered the advantages of placing their funds in the custody of the Trustees. For this was only a "bare trusteeship" — that is, the function of the Official Trustees was only to see that charity monies were properly invested and to pay the proceeds over to the local trustees. So useful was the device that a provision for transferring charity stock to the Official Trustees was almost invariably included in schemes made both by the Commissioners and the courts.[4] During the first quarter century of the Commission the funds in their hands reached nearly £8 million.[5] This was one activity of the Charity Commission about which little difference of opinion arose, save perhaps among treasurers of some of the larger charities who were alarmed lest their own financial independence be compromised.

From the beginning the Commissioners were troubled by the uncertain scope, as well as by the magnitude, of their supervisory duties. What was the actual number of charitable trusts for which they were responsible? Not only had the hand of British charity been active in the years since the Brougham survey, but the Report itself, it will be recalled, had omitted a good many trusts. Some of these had been specifically exempted from scrutiny; more had merely escaped the

---

[3] *25th Ann. C. C. Rept.,* 1877, p. 6.

[4] *S. C. on the Charitable Trusts Acts,* 1884, Q. 142, 1427, 4053–54.

[5] *25th Ann. C. C. Rept.,* 1877, p. 3. In their investment policies, the Official Trustees followed the practice of Chancery. By far the greater part of their resources were in the Funds. When the Court permitted itself greater latitude, the Commissioners also began to sanction such investments as railway debentures and India bonds, as well as municipal securities.

attention of the investigators. When the Commissioners began their work they had hopefully assumed that the annual accounts which endowed charities were now required by law to submit would provide them with a working inventory of trusts. But compliance was fitful and imperfect, so much so that in the mid-'70's they were receiving accounts from only a little over half the charities of which they had official knowledge.[6] If, in short, a usable roster of charities was essential, the Commissioners would have to supply it themselves. They therefore set about compiling a new analytical digest of English charities, expanding and supplementing the Digest of 1840. One of their perennial problems, incidentally, was that of keeping up to date their register of charities. Their only means of learning of new trusts, aside from scanning the columns of *The Times,* was by informal agreement with the Rolls Office for news of deeds creating charitable settlements and Somerset House for wills containing charitable bequests.[7]

The Commissioners did their work on the new Digest conscientiously, supplementing their regular sources of information by what they describe as "voluminous correspondence."[8] Their compilation, issued between 1868 and 1875, showed an impressive increase in the country's charitable resources, as the accompanying table shows.

CAPITAL

	Real property (in acres)	Stock	Mortgages and other personalty
Brougham Report	442,915	£ 5,656,746	£1,011,782
General Digest	524,311	17,418,250	2,197,478
Increase	81,396	11,761,504	1,185,696

INCOME

	Rent	Rent charges and fixed annual payments	Personality
Brougham Report	£ 874,313	£ 79,930	£255,151
General Digest	1,443,177	115,073	640,213
Increase	568,864	35,143	385,062

The total charity income of England and Wales, insofar as this lay within the jurisdiction of the Commission, thus amounted to about £2,200,000 and the

[6] *Ibid.* See the extracts on this and related subjects from the Annual Reports of the Commissioners, S. C. on the Charity Commission, 1894, App. No. 6. Figures compiled by the Commissioners necessarily understate the total of charitable trusts in the country, since numbers of them, including some of the larger — Oxford, Cambridge, their colleges, and some of the older public schools, for example — were exempt from their jurisdiction.

[7] S. C. on the Charity Commission, 1894, Q. 1866–69.

[8] *Explanatory Memorandum and Tabular Summaries of the General Digest,* 1877 (*Parl. Pap.*), p. 9.

increase to nearly a million sterling (£989,069). Of this, roughly half was attrib-
utable to an increase in income of foundations reported on by the Brougham
Commissioners and half to those not included. Of this latter category nearly half
(£226,000 out of £475,000) represented the income of charities founded since
the Brougham survey. During this period, 1338 trusts, yielding £110,000 had been
founded by deed, and 3467 (£116,000) by will.[9] Later in the century new endowments were being established at the rate of about five hundred a year.[10] Predictably enough, the industrial and urban areas showed by far the heaviest gains. The
income of West Riding charities had risen from £46,000 to £88,000, and Warwickshire (exclusive of Coventry) from £31,000 to £63,000, while that of Middlesex had virtually doubled.[11]

Compiling the Digest proved something of a strain on the office of the Commissioners, for under the terms of the early Acts they were entitled to only a
modest establishment. Successive Acts, which imposed additional responsibilities
on them, brought no comparable increase in staff. Whatever success they attained,
the Commissioners complained to Gladstone in April 1869, was only "at the cost
of severe and unremitting labour to ourselves and our principal subordinates.
We have no counsel to search out the Law . . . no solicitors (generally speaking)
to investigate the facts and put them into shape . . . Our only pleadings are frequently ill-written letters and memorials proceeding from ill-educated persons
destitute of any advice or assistance not supplied them by ourselves. Yet we have
to ascertain our facts accurately, to apply them to a difficult branch of Law, to
check the regularity of the procedure in all its stages, to construct our orders,
which frequently involve complicated schemes, to frame our judgments so as to
satisfy parties that their cases have been properly weighed, and to inform Courts
of Appeal on what grounds our decisions rest. In short, there is no legal work,
which any judge of any Civil Court has to do and which we have not to do;
while there is much other work done for other judges, which we have to do for
ourselves." [12]

As early as the mid-1860's the office was falling behind in its work so gravely
that the Commissioners, with only partial success, sought authority to increase
their establishment. In the years 1869–84 the work of the Commission increased
by more than 50 per cent and the staff by less than 20 per cent, and in 1894 the
Commissioners could testify that over the previous nineteen years official correspondence had grown by 70 per cent, the number of orders issued by about 50
per cent, and the financial work (Official Trustees) by more than 100 per cent,
while only 23 per cent more staff had been added.[13] The Charity Commission, in
fact, appears to have represented in an extreme form the understaffing thought

[9] *Ibid.*, p. 22.
[10] *S. C. on the Charity Commission*, 1894, Q. 239.
[11] *Explanatory Memorandum*, 1877, pp. 16–19.
[12] B. M. Add. Mss. 44,420, f. 90.
[13] *S. C. on the Charitable Trusts Acts*, 1884, Q. 936; *S. C. on the Charity Commission*, 1894, Q.
193.

by civil servants to be chronic in government offices.[14] No doubt this condition had something to do with the persistent complaint of delay in answering letters or performing routine services, a complaint that has been a constant in Charity Commission history. A correspondent writing to *The Times* in 1896 reported that the Commissioners had taken an average of two months in which to answer each of three letters, and another recalled that the execution of a simple deed, for which he had paid the stated fee, required nine months and fourteen days.[15] It must have been adding insult to injury when in 1887 W. H. Smith, as First Lord of the Treasury, charged that the Commission was top-heavy, with its six or seven full Commissioners. He appears to have overlooked the fact that the two Endowed Schools Commissioners and the two Commissioners for the City Parochial Charities held special and temporary appointments.[16]

The Commissioners, as a group, seem to have been capable, and, in some cases distinguished, equity lawyers. Advancement normally followed a *cursum honorem* within the office itself, a new appointee beginning as Third Commissioner and moving up to the post of Chief. It was thought mildly scandalous when Disraeli, instead of promoting from within the Commission, appointed as Chief Commissioner, Sir Seymour Fitzgerald, "one of Lord Beaconsfield's bad jobs," the *Pall Mall Gazette* put it.[17] During Fitzgerald's tenure the main responsibility was borne by Henry (later Sir Henry) Longley, the Second Commissioner, whose administrative abilities were beyond question. Longley, a son of the Archbishop of Canterbury and grandson of Sir Henry Parnell (Lord Congleton), served as Charity Commissioner for a quarter century, from 1874 to 1899, and as Chief for the last fifteen years of his tenure. Before entering the Commission, he had been one of the Poor Law Inspectors, to quote the Webbs, the most active and influential of the corps.[18] His 1874 *Report on Outdoor Relief in the Metropolis* was an able document, though resting on assumptions unappealing to twentieth-century readers. Reverting in effect to Chadwick's philosophy of the 1830's, Longley called for the practical abolition of outdoor relief and praised the workhouse test for its deterrent effect.[19] As Chief Commissioner, Longley showed a solid grasp of the work of the office. Occasionally a marked bureaucratic streak would come to the surface and his firmness could turn into something dangerously close to rigidity. Yet in the large his conception of the Commission's function (leaving aside his social philosophy) was sound enough, and in his appearance before Select Committees and Commissions he usually gave an excellent account of himself.

Though never achieving the freedom of action they sought, the Commissioners

---

[14] For a detailed picture of the office establishment and its operation, see *ibid.*, Q. 1769ff.

[15] 6 and 8 Jan.

[16] *S. C. on the Charity Commission*, 1894, App. No. 17.

[17] Quoted in the *Charity Record*, 16 July 1885, p. 233. In *The Times* (10 Dec. 1875), C. S. Roundell recalled that in the past a Government could award the Clerkship of the Pells "to the used-up Ancient of the Ministry of the Day," but deplored Disraeli's putting the Chief Commissionership into the same category as a sinecure clerkship.

[18] The Webbs, *English Poor Law History: The Last Hundred Years*, p. 374.

[19] Local Govt. Board, *3d Ann. Rept.*, 1874, App. No. 14.

were still able to reconstruct a considerable number of foundations. During the 1870's, for example, they were issuing about four hundred orders a year for the appointment of trustees or the establishment of schemes.[20] By the early '80's some four thousand schemes had been framed, the great bulk of these for charities with incomes under £50 and most of them with the consent of the trustees.[21] Some were simple enough, but scheme-making could be extraordinarily complex, even in the case of small charities. Where the foundation was ancient and wealthy the task could be staggering. Even though the Commissioners were not entitled to take the initiative in reorganizing such old and affluent endowments, they found many bodies of trustees who welcomed their assistance. As a result, they managed to reconstruct a number of the country's most notorious charity anachronisms.

Of such were the famous Tancred Charities, dating from the mid-eighteenth century and almost the classic example of the benefaction conceived in malice. The founder was Christopher Tancred, a Yorkshire squire, who was without sons and who thought his five sisters inappropriate legatees. Determined to perpetuate the name of Tancred, he established two charities. By one of these he created four studentships each in Divinity, Physic, and Law — at Christ's College, Caius, and Lincoln's Inn respectively, and he provided that in the halls of the three institutions public orations were to be delivered on the anniversary of his death "in perpetual remembrance of the said charity." This benefaction of Tancred's was estimable enough and no more consciously intended than many others to assure the earthly immortality of its founder.

The other branch of the foundation was a disaster. Tancred left his mansion-house and park at Whixley as a residence for twelve decayed gentlemen, clergymen, or commissioned officers, natives of Great Britain and members of the Church of England. The disinherited sisters naturally raised questions, and in the end it required an Act of Parliament to launch Tancred's Hospital.[22] A well-endowed almshouse for decayed gentlemen would inevitably be a hazardous undertaking, and almost from the beginning this one was chaos. Tancred's pensioners, mindful of their gentility and unreconciled to their decay, were a soured and truculent lot. According to the Charity Commissioners, the minutes and governors' books revealed "a state of quarrel, heart-burning, and misbehavior among the inmates, which appeared to have had little intermission, and which must have made the place wretched to its inmates, and highly unedifying to the neighborhood."[23] The autumn of 1865 saw something in the nature of a pitched battle among the idle and disgruntled pensioners. The proper course, the Commissioners were persuaded, was to liquidate the Hospital itself and use the income for pensions. Their first two schemes failed to gain Parliamentary approval (necessary because the Hospital was operating under a private Act). But the situation

---

[20] *25th Ann. C. C. Rept.,* 1877, p. 2.
[21] *S. C. on the Charitable Trusts Acts,* 1884, p. vi.
[22] *13th Ann. C. C. Rept.,* 1865, p. 7; 2 Geo. III, c. 15.
[23] *14th Ann. C. C. Rept.,* 1866, p. 24.

continued to deteriorate until trustees and pensioners, with one vociferous exception, were happy enough to see the Hospital demobilized.[24]

The Commissioners were also able to resolve some of the difficulties of Sir John Port's foundation in Derbyshire, which after three centuries seemed an almost ideal field for their activities. Unlike Tancred's bequest, there was nothing malicious about Sir John's charity. It was, however, a capital example of the ravages of time. Like Tancred's, the endowment had been intended to finance an almshouse and an educational benefaction. Sir John provided that six of the poorest of the village of Etwall should have 1s. 8d. a week, together with lodging in an almshouse, and that his trustees should establish a grammar school in Etwall or in Repton, four miles distant. Over the years, as the income increased (by the mid-1860's to about £3000 a year), the number of almsmen was raised to sixteen and their stipends increased. The fantastic feature of the Port charity was the composition of the board of management, which included the three oldest inmates of the Hospital, who, be it recalled, were selected from the "poor, needy, and impotent" of Etwall. Although the three no longer attended regular board meetings, they were annually transported to Repton, where they solemnly made their marks at the end of the school's accounts. At one time, the almsmen made up half the board, and one of them was custodian of the key to the muniment chest. This seemed an intolerable scheme of government for a school that was moving toward public school status.[25]

In spite of this incubus, Repton School was flourishing. But the ratepayers of Etwall and Repton demanded that the school, which enrolled about two hundred boys, be restricted to those from the two villages. They also demanded an increase in the number of almsmen, though there were only fifty-eight laborers in the entire parish. It seemed to have become a standard procedure that all old men of the parish died in Sir John Port's almshouse. When the Commissioners proposed not only to reorganize the governing body but also to extend the area from which residents could be drawn, the village was outraged, for in the local view, "the intention of the Founder" had been "to benefit in this respect the parish of Etwall alone." In the end the Commissioners were able to get their bill through Parliament, but only after making some damaging concessions to the opposition whipped up in the village.[26]

2

Although the Commissioners managed to accomplish a good deal, they felt keenly the limitations on their powers. In their annual reports they often alluded, sometimes tentatively but occasionally with emphasis, to the handicaps under which they labored. They were in no position to demand an extension of their powers, but they could remind the Government, as they frequently did, that

[24] *18th Ann. C. C. Rept.*, 1870, pp. 8–9.
[25] *14th Ann. C. C. Rept.*, 1867, pp. 8–9.
[26] Hobhouse, *The Dead Hand*, pp. 63–65.

without greater authority they could not get at some of the more objectionable anachronisms among endowments, notably the larger dole charities, those for poor relations, apprenticeships, and the like. Specifically the Commissioners were restive over three restrictions: first and most important, the fact that they were barred from dealing on their own initiative with charities whose annual income exceeded £50; secondly, their inability to compel an audit of charity accounts, a limitation which prevented their enforcing economical and efficient administration of charity funds; finally — and in a somewhat different category — their lack of authority to go beyond *cy-près* in revising trusts.

Of these clearly the most exasperating was the £50 ceiling. This provision not only barred the Commissioners from reforming certain individual charities which were capital candidates for their attention but it also formed a grave obstacle to projects for consolidating local charities. In more than one instance such plans were ruined by the reluctance of the larger charities to cooperate. Although the argument for amalgamation was not, perhaps, always as overwhelming as the Commissioners assumed, it was irrefutable when applied to dole charities managed by separate bodies of trustees. A case in point was Tewksbury, whose charities the Commissioners investigated at the invitation of the Board of Guardians. Here, out of a total charity income of £1300, some £700 was distributed in money, blankets, coal, and food by over thirty different agencies, apparently quite independently of one another. Indigents with initiative could readily obtain aid from several of the charities. To the Commissioners a consolidated foundation seemed the obvious prescription, and they succeeded in amalgamating thirty-one of the funds under a single body of trustees. But two of the larger, whose incomes amounted to about £600 a year, insisted on maintaining their freedom of action and continued, in the words of the Select Committee of 1884, "to dispense their funds in an objectionable manner." [27]

Walthamstow presented a similar situation. Of the £1166 charity income, £600 was marked for the poor in doles and widows' pensions and £193 for inmates of the almshouses.[28] Only about half of the thirty-odd charities would allow themselves to be included in the Commissioners' scheme providing for amalgamation under a single governing body. The others, which accounted for about three-quarters of the income, firmly declined to cooperate. Against such endowments the Commissioners were powerless, save, of course, where conditions were so bad as to justify legal proceedings. Their only chance was to inspire an application from a majority of the trustees — which they were sometimes able to arrange by committing themselves in advance to a scheme acceptable to the governing body.[29]

It is curious that the Charity Commission had so little success in lifting the £50 ceiling. Although the great London charities were bitterly hostile toward

[27] *S. C. on the Charitable Trusts Acts,* 1884, p. x; also Q. 368–85, 1920ff.
[28] *Ibid.,* Q. 2345.
[29] *Ibid.,* Q. 1810.

any proposal which might bring them more directly under the control of the Commissioners, they imputed no particular virtue to £50 as the critical figure, and they would probably not have opposed a considerably higher ceiling.[30] Yet the Commissioners could never raise the £50 limit. The fact is that there was little demand for and influential opposition to granting broader powers to the Charity Commissioners. Unhappily they had failed to commend their work either to charity trustees or to public opinion generally, and many were inclined to hail the defeat of any proposal on behalf of the Commissioners as a victory for the English way of life. While they looked hungrily at the powers they enjoyed under the Endowed Schools and the City Parochial Charities Acts and contrasted these with their meager authority under the Charitable Trusts Acts, others saw the question in different terms. As much as anything, it was the unpopularity achieved by the Endowed Schools Commissioners that hardened the resistance against bestowing greater authority on the Charity Commission.

Three times between 1881 and 1890 Charitable Trusts bills, with clauses providing for broader powers, reached the floor of the House of Commons.[31] When it was all over, the ceiling remained precisely where it had been, at £50. Each bill produced the usual indignation meetings of charity officials, petitions to the House, and deputations to Ministers. On the 1881 bill, Lord Shaftesbury, the very apotheosis of the Victorian charity worker, announced that he would not have given his labor, as he had done so devotedly, "if he had thought the money subscribed would be placed in the hands of the Charity Commissioners"[32]—an odd inference from a clause intended to facilitate the transfer of funds to the Official Trustees. In 1884 Shaw-Lefevre's Select Committee proposed not only to abolish the £50 limit but also to give the Commissioners certain powers exercised by the High Court of Justice.[33] These would have allowed the Commission to deal directly with mischievous or maladministered charities, rather than merely certifying them to the Attorney-General.

The absurdity of the Commissioners' situation was underscored by their impotence when facing such abuses as those which appeared in the management of Brown's Hospital at Stamford, a charity with £1200 annual income. For twelve almsmen the Hospital maintained a warden at £375 and a confrater at £200. With the onset of agricultural depression, the trustees were unable to support the twelve almsmen, but, perhaps in deliberate defiance of the Commissioners, proceeded to appoint a new confrater at the customary stipend.[34] Even such malodorous situations did not persuade the House, and the recommendations of the Select Committee remained in the realm of pious hope. In 1890 and 1891 bills sponsored

[30] Ibid., Q. 3684.
[31] These in addition to the bill brought forward by the Lord Chancellor in the Lords in 1878. (3 Hansard, 241:1427–28.)
[32] Charity Record, 19 May 1881.
[33] It was this Select Committee on the Charitable Trusts Acts that gave Sir Henry Longley what the chairman later described as probably the longest cross-examination to which a public officer had ever been subjected.
[34] 3 Hansard, 344:371; S. C. on the Charitable Trusts Acts, 1884, Q. 363–64.

by the public-spirited William Rathbone perished before the committee stage.[35]
The Charity Commission, it seemed likely, would have to be reconciled to a dual
existence, accepting as a fact of life the disparity between the limited powers
enjoyed by the Commissioners appointed under the Charitable Trusts Acts and
those of their colleagues who were working under the Endowed Schools or City
Parochial Charities Acts.

A second and less important extension of power for which the Charity Commissioners contended, especially in their evidence before the Select Committee of 1884,
was that of compulsory audit. There was no thought, of course, of subjecting the
whole mass of charity accounts to such scrutiny. Yet, as matters stood, the Commissioners could not intervene to check extravagant expenditures unless the
maladministration were extreme enough to certify to the Attorney-General. What
they sought was authority comparable to that of a Poor Law auditor, with power
to examine the accounts of a charity and to disallow objectionable items. Knowledge that their books might be inspected by the Commissioners would perhaps
serve to make trustees more circumspect in their expenditures, and might discourage such junkets as that of the eight trustees who spent £36 10s. on a trip from
London to Hastings to hold a manorial court for a manor whose annual produce
amounted to £41.[36] Yet, like the raising of the £50 ceiling, the power of compulsory audit remained in the realm of hope perennially deferred.

A third source of dissatisfaction on the part of the Commissioners had to do
with their lack of freedom in revising even those trusts where they had authority
to act. This was not so much a complaint against the Charitable Trusts Acts as
against the rules applied by Chancery. In revising trusts whose objects had failed,
the Commissioners were bound by the *cy-près* doctrine, since they were, for the
purpose, the *alter ego* of Chancery. No doubt there was historical justification for
adhering as faithfully as possible to the testator's wishes, but the Commissioners
chafed under the restriction. It seemed illogical to them that, when acting under
the Endowed Schools or City Parochial Charities Acts, they were entitled to
disregard *cy-près,* while under the Charitable Trusts Acts, they must observe it.
They could convert mischievous endowments, under certain conditions, to educational purposes but could not otherwise revise them.

If they wished to move against indiscriminate doles, which they held to be
iniquitous and injurious, they must remain within the ambit of *cy-près.* To
reconstruct the Jarvis charity, which, throughout the nineteenth century, had been
an engine of demoralization, would have been a blessing to English society. Outraged at his daughter's marriage, it will be recalled, George Jarvis had disinherited
his descendants and left £100,000 to the poor of three Hereford parishes. The
prospect of the income in doles attracted the poor and needy and greedy until,
according to Thomas Hare, the three villages deteriorated into something like
rural slums.[37] In one of their reports, the Commissioners cited, as evidence in their

[35] *3 Hansard,* 344:355–410; 350:808.
[36] *S. C. on the Charitable Trusts Acts,* 1884, Q. 524.
[37] Quoted in Hobhouse, *The Dead Hand,* pp. 209–10.

case against doles, the record of three Midland parishes. Out of a total population of 6345, nearly 50 per cent in the course of the year 1891 received between 7¼d. and 2s. 6d. in doles.[38] Even within the limits of *cy-près,* the Commissioners accomplished something in converting indiscriminate doles to more constructive uses, especially into pensions for the aged. Still they felt badly hamstrung by the obligation to apply the doctrine in its rigorous Eldonian form. From their point of view, among the more desirable provisions of the bills which failed to pass in the 1880's were those looking toward the conversion of doles.[39] By way of postscript, however, one may note the appeal which doles continued to make to philanthropists. In the early '80's, in apparent defiance of the Commissioners' advice, the novelist Charles Reade insisted on founding what the Chief Commissioner described as "a pure and simple dole charity."[40]

An equally disreputable, though less universal, form of benevolence, in the Commissioners' view, was the trust for the benefit of poor relations of the founder.[41] No doubt in some instances the poor-kin charity financed the education of deserving young men,[42] but it also led to such fantastic situations as that created in Norwich by the descendants of Alderman Norman. This charity, established in 1720, prescribed in a good deal of detail how the endowment was to be administered, but by the late nineteenth century these specifications had little relation to the actual management of the trust. When the Commissioners (under the Endowed Schools Acts) proposed to convert the charity into school exhibitions, protests resounded from the founder's kin. It then appeared that there were a thousand families on the rolls claiming Norman blood, and that they had organized themselves into a committee, with chairman and secretary — a formidable and determined pressure group of Normans.[43]

The seventeenth-century charity of Alderman Henry Smith, a London salter, supplies an almost perfect example of the kind of foundation that the fingers of the Commissioners itched to recast. One of the most thoughtful and statesmanlike (on Professor Jordan's authority) of Tudor-Stuart philanthropists, Smith created by deed and bequest a complicated series of trusts. Both in amount and in the judgment of the founder, by far the most important of these were for "the relief

[38] *40th Ann. C. C. Rept.,* 1892, p. 24. Longley reported to the Aberdare Commission in 1895 (*R. C. on the Aged Poor,* Q. 7596) that the parishes in question were three in Northamptonshire. See also Hobhouse, *The Dead Hand,* pp. 195–215.

[39] *40th Ann. C. C. Rept.,* 1892, p. 21.

[40] *S. C. on the Charitable Trusts Acts,* 1884, Q. 321.

[41] Lord Beveridge (*Voluntary Action*[London, 1948], p. 202) went to Oxford on a founder's kin scholarship.

[42] Because of their restriction to members of a particular family, founder's kin charities raised difficult legal questions. For their part the Commissioners regarded such trusts as "at variance with the general rules of law relative to settlements of property in this country . . . a kind of entail on a particular family." (*16th Ann. C. C. Rept.,* 1868, p. 5.) The courts, however, have usually sanctioned them as charities for a particular class of poor. (*Tudor on Charities,* 1906 ed., pp. 47–48.) In a decision in 1945 the Master of the Rolls made an interesting distinction between trusts for education (considered family trusts and not valid charities) and those for the relief of poverty (legal). The question is discussed by Beveridge, *Voluntary Action,* pp. 373–74.

[43] *S. C. on the Endowed Schools Acts,* 1886, Q. 1645, 2133ff.

and maintenance of poor towns" — a grand design of assisting the poor on a national scale — and some 219 communities profited from the London merchant's beneficence. There were smaller bequests, as well, including £1000 for the ransoming of captives of the Turks, and, what is directly relevant here, £1000 for "the poorest of his kindred." This was a magnificent contribution to Stuart social economy, but by the mid-nineteenth century it had fallen on evil days. The Smith charity had got itself divided into seventeen separate trusts with an income of nearly £16,000, about £13,000 of which belonged to the large general trust.[44]

Had Alderman Smith returned to earth in early Victorian times he would have discovered "the poorest of his kindred" to be faring handsomely. Not only was the capital sum of the trust invested in Kensington and Chelsea real estate that was rapidly rising in value, but in 1772 Parliament authorized the trustees to add the fund for Turkish captives to that for poor relations, so that in the 1860's the gross return was about £6800. The Smiths seem not to have been as fecund a race as the Normans, but by 1868 there were 412 claimants, including 104 whose relation to the founder might be expressed as great[10]-nieces or -nephews and 160 great[9]-nieces or -nephews. Obviously the trustees had an unhappy time in deciding among the masses of importunate Smiths, who to qualify for benefits were not above using "solicitation, importunity, testimonials, certificates, and all the apparatus of begging" and, for that matter, intimidation.[45] Certainly Alderman Smith's benevolent intention of leaving £60 a year to his genuinely needy kinfolk had borne curious and unintended fruit.

The main branch of the Smith charity had long since ceased to serve a useful purpose. By the 1860's some 209 places were sharing an income of over £8200, and in Surrey, Smith's native county, every parish was entitled to a share, the great bulk going for doles in money or in kind. In 1866, to take a typical year, the charity distributed £5580 to over 23,000 persons, at an average rate of 4s. 10d. a head. Probably the Charity Commissioners, like their contemporaries, were too ready to attribute pauperism to the pampering effect of indiscriminate charity, but it was difficult to see such doles as other than mischievous, at the least a waste of charitable resources and at worst a source of demoralization. It is little wonder that the Commissioners, facing the prospect of persuading 209 bodies of trustees to apply for schemes (and knowing that some of the wealthier funds would refuse), of framing 209 different schemes, and of carrying these through the various steps, decided to appeal for an Act of Parliament. The Legislature did not respond, and in the late 1880's a scheme established by the Commissioners served to make the administration of the charity more orderly and to curb some of its worst excesses. But poor kindred are still receiving relief from the office in Great Russell

[44] For an account of the origins of the Smith trusts, see Jordan, *The Charities of London, 1480–1660*, pp. 117–22. In the 1860's the endowment was the object of an investigation by the Charity Commissioners, and the results, which have to do both with the history and the current status of the foundation, are published in Part III of the Appendix (pp. 33–42) of their *16th Ann. Rept.*, 1868.
[45] *Ibid.*, p. 37.

Street, as are the poor of more than two hundred parishes. Meanwhile, the gross income of the Smith trust has risen to well over £200,000.[46]

3

The doctrine of *cy-près*, noticed briefly in an earlier chapter, raises a large and highly technical issue. Regularly denounced by the Commissioners in their earlier decades and a perennial object of attack by charity law reformers, it was regarded as one of the chief devices by which the Dead Hand retained its grip. Yet one may doubt whether, even if *cy-près* had been relaxed, the Commissioners would have undertaken any wholesale revision of trusts, certainly not of those outside the category of doles, poor relations, and the like. Invariably, when reformers put forward the thesis that ancient foundations must be made to serve the living rather than the dead, conservative opinion would rise to defend the sanctity of "founder's wishes."

The familiar statement of the *cy-près* doctrine is that of Lord Halsbury: "Where a clear charitable intention is expressed, it will not be permitted to fail because the mode, if specified, cannot be executed, but the law will substitute another mode *cy-près* that is, as near as possible to the mode specified by the donor. But there can be no question of the application *cy-près* until it is clearly established that the mode specified by the donor cannot be carried into effect and that the donor had a general charitable intention." [47] The doctrine has been in fact applied not only where the *mode* specified by the donor cannot be carried out but also where the specified charitable *purpose* fails. A more satisfactory statement might be that the disposition will not fail if the presumption is that the testator would have preferred that it not fail.[48] The points to be observed, in any case, are twofold: first, that the law will not intervene unless or until the trust becomes unworkable; and secondly, that in revising it, the wishes of the testator and not modern requirements must be decisive. These must be respected even though it is patent to all that the fund could be put to better use. The *cy-près* doctrine, in short, is a means of ensuring the perpetuity of a gift to charity even though the particular object should fail or the mode specified become impracticable or impossible.[49]

The doctrine of *cy-près* as it reached the mid-nineteenth century was a remarkably imprecise concept. As with other parts of charity law, the doctrine bore the strong imprint of Lord Eldon, and his influence was thrown on the side of strict construction. He would tolerate few liberties with the wishes of the testator. When a question was raised about applying the bulk of the notorious Jarvis bequest to direct gifts to the poor, Eldon stated flatly: "I have nothing to do with arguments of policy. If the Legislature thinks proper to give the power

---

[46] Jordan, *Charities of London*, p. 344.
[47] Halsbury's *Laws of England*, 2d ed., IV, Par. 323.
[48] As put by Professor Austin W. Scott in a MS Memorandum on Obsolescence, pp. 29, 45.
[49] Cf. the *Nathan Report*, chap. II.

of leaving property to charitable purposes, recognized by law as such, however prejudicial, the Court must administer it." [50]

Whatever the merit of Eldon's legal reasoning, some of his successors regarded the doctrine as absurd and ambiguous. During the latter half of the century, a number of the most distinguished equity judges attacked *cy-près* as indefensibly vague. Before the Taunton Commission Sir Page Wood (Lord Hatherley) urged that *cy-près* be thrown out the window, and Roundell Palmer (Lord Selborne) denounced it as an arbitrary concept, as what an American lawyer had termed "the imaginative department of the law of trusts." [51] Lord Westbury and Lord Romilly, Master of the Rolls, proved more cautious, though the latter thought the doctrine needlessly restrictive.[52] None could think of it as other than an extraordinarily loose concept, in that so much was left to the discretion of the court. Who could with assurance establish a *cy-près* application of Betton's or Henry Smith's or Lady Mico's charity for Christian captives? And where it had proved impossible to carry out some but not all the provisions of a charitable bequest, how was the court to decide which conditions should be fulfilled? The *cy-près* doctrine may have been one of "the ascertained principles of the law," but, as Lord Justice Davey remarked, it was evidently one "with a very ragged edge." [53]

In their work of revising trusts the Charity Commissioners were in a particularly vulnerable position. Since their orders were subject to appeal, they could not afford to be even as venturesome in interpreting *cy-près* as Chancery judges might on occasion turn out to be, though in uncontested cases they tended to stretch the doctrine farther than where opposition was likely.[54] The parliamentary scheme, which had been designed as their resource in cases not readily amenable to *cy-près* treatment, had proved of so little use that it had almost become a dead letter. In short, for the great bulk of their schemes the Commissioners were obliged to keep within the limits established by *cy-près* and to make the best of the situation.

During the 1870's they took some comfort from the opinion of Lord Westbury in *Clephane* v. *the Lord Provost of Edinburgh* (1869). Here the Court, distinguishing sharply between "the charity which is intended to be created and the means directed for its accomplishment," [55] declined to require the rebuilding of an almshouse to replace one which was demolished when the North British Railway was run through. The £10,000 compensation, the Court concluded, could be more usefully spent on pensions and other forms of outdoor relief. Westbury's flexible interpretation of the elusive doctrine gave to the Commissioners a sense of moderate security.

[50] 7 Vesey Jun. 324.
[51] *Schools Inquiry Commission,* 1867–68, Q. 12,857, 14,172; John D. Washburn, quoted in C. A. Chase, *Some Great Charitable Trusts of England* (Worcester, Mass., 1887), p. 48.
[52] *Schools Inquiry Commission,* 1867–68, Q. 16,666, 13,433.
[53] *S. C. on the Charity Commission,* 1894, Q. 4009.
[54] *S. C. on the Charitable Trusts Acts,* 1884, Q. 312.
[55] ⸱ L.R., S.C. App. 417.

This was confirmed and strengthened by Sir George Jessel's judgment in the Campden Charities case (1881), though only after they had been grievously alarmed by the decision of the Chancery Division in the first instance. The case had to do with the seventeenth-century charity of Lady Campden. Following instructions in her will, trustees had laid out in land a sum sufficient to yield £10 a year, half for the poor and needy and half for apprenticeship fees for Kensington boys. Since this was Kensington property, by the latter nineteenth century the charity found itself with an annual income that had grown to £2200, and the trustees applied to the Charity Commissioners for a scheme. The new plan not only made provision for relief of the needy, contributions to hospitals and dispensaries, and apprenticeship fees, but also included sums for educational purposes, as a *cy-près* application of some of the apprenticeship income. Residents of Kensington objected to admitting education to the charity, and Vice-Chancellor Hall agreed with them. To the Commissioners this judgment seemed to blight the hope that, through the decisions of Westbury and others, the *cy-près* doctrine was acquiring an acceptable degree of elasticity.[56] Unless it were reversed on appeal, they would be forced to proceed more cautiously than at any time since the Act of 1860.

They were not kept long on the anxious seat. Sir George Jessel, Master of the Rolls, not only reversed Hall's judgment but also laid down some principles, immensely satisfactory to the Commissioners, with regard to judicial supervision of their work. Far from criticizing the provision for scholarships and exhibitions, he found the Commissioners' scheme unobjectionable and consistent "with what is now the modern practice as to settling schemes." He went on to suggest that only in exceptional instances ought judges to revise schemes framed by the Charity Commissioners, "persons not only of great but of special experience in these matters." To justify interference, a judge "must be satisfied that the Charity Commissioners have gone wrong either by disobeying those rules of law which govern them, as well as they govern courts of justice, or else that there has been some slip or gross miscarriage which calls for the intervention of the court to set it aside and remodel the scheme." [57]

This judgment seemed to give the Commissioners as free a hand as they were entitled to expect and to provide them with some security against undue interference by the courts. Its tone was clearly such as to discourage appeals against them. The Master of the Rolls, in fact, had stretched the *cy-près* doctrine almost to the breaking point and certainly farther than any other judge had ventured to do. In insisting that *cy-près* properly had to do with "the principal object which the testatrix had in view" rather than "the means by which she wished that object carried out," he was sanctioning a rather wide discretion in the revision of trusts. The Commissioners, reasonably enough, could interpret Jessel's opinion as authorizing a review of a trust whenever the means, "by reason of changes which

[56] *28th Ann. C. C. Rept.*, 1880, p. 9.
[57] L.R., Ch. Div. 310.

may take place, either in the value of the endowment, in the circumstances of the locality, or the population for the benefit of which, the Charity is administered, — in the time, — in the habits of society, — in the ideas or practices of men, — have become unfitted to secure the end which the founder had in view." [58]

For three decades the Commissioners acted on the liberal interpretation implied by the Campden Charities decision without a serious check from the courts. In 1910, however, the decision of another Master of the Rolls threw them back on their heels. The Weir Hospital case had to do with a bequest for a dispensary cottage or convalescent home which the trustees, with the approval of the Commissioners, had converted into a home for nurses in connection with another hospital. The opinion of Cozens-Hardy, M.R., which invalidated the scheme, carried certain Eldonian overtones:

> The first duty of the Court is to construe the will, and to give effect to the charitable directions of the founder . . . The Court does not consider whether those directions are wise or whether a more generally beneficial application of a testator's property might not be found. There are many charitable purposes which, according to modern views, are productive of more harm than good — for example, doles in money or kind . . . Wherever the *cy-près* doctrine has to be applied it is competent to the Court to consider the comparative advantages of various charitable objects and to adopt by the scheme the one which seems most beneficial. But there can be no question of *cy-près* until it is clearly established that the directions of the testator cannot be carried into effect.[59]

The Commissioners interpreted this decision as a cautionary word addressed to themselves. Even though the courts again withdrew to the position outlined in the Campden Charities decision and limited their intervention to instances where the Commissioners had acted *ultra vires* or where their schemes contained something wrong in principle or in law, the Weir Hospital case had its effect.[60] Henceforth the Commissioners would hesitate before taking liberties with *cy-près*.[61] During the past half century, in fact, they have been so little inclined to take the initiative in reconstructing trusts that the fear of a charity dictatorship which they aroused in their earlier days seems fantastic.

The one significant increase in the powers of the Commissioners came almost fortuitously in 1914 in a bill introduced into the Lords by Lord Parmoor. It was directed to the dilemma created for city charities by the movement of population from the center to the outlying districts and the resulting difficulty of applying their income legally. Parmoor's bill, in a word, proposed to extend the beneficial area for such charities, and authorized the Commissioners to follow the principle

[58] *29th Ann. C. C. Rept.*, 1881, p. 9. Before the Select Committee of 1894 Sir Henry Longley appeared (Q. 345) to be moderately well reconciled to *cy-près* as interpreted by Jessel.
[59] 2 Ch. 124, 131, 132.
[60] *Nathan Report*, Par. 344.
[61] When giving evidence before the Nathan Committee, the Chief Commissioner had little criticism of the doctrine as it stood and seemed less interested (Q. 424ff) than was the Committee in its possible relaxation.

of geographical extension in framing their schemes. Not only that, but they were allowed somewhat more leeway in converting dole charities to more constructive purposes — roughly, to anything that relieved distress or sickness or improved the physical, social, or moral condition of the poor in the particular areas.[62] It was perhaps as well that the bill reached the Commons during the second week of August 1914, when it passed with virtually no debate.[63] To the Commissioners this increase in their powers was something of an unexpected windfall, but at least it enabled them to deal with some of the more pressing problems of unemployed charity income and useless doles in urban centers.

4

A major weakness in the position of the Commission was its anomalous constitutional status. It functioned under no responsible Minister, and its liaison with Parliament was always feeble. During most of its career the Commission could not count on being well defended in the House nor on having its decisions adequately interpreted. In its constitutional status, as well as in the hostility that its decisions aroused, the Charity Commission had a good deal in common with the Poor Law Commission in the days before it was placed under a Minister. For its link with the Legislature the Commission was dependent on the (unpaid) Fourth Commissioner, a member of the House of Commons, who would presumably prove an effective representative.

The theory was not beyond criticism and in practice the arrangement proved even more faulty. Ordinarily the Government designated one of its members as Fourth Commissioner, an absurd addition to the duties of a busy official. Up to 1874, in fact, Fourth Commissioners attended only nine meetings of the Board, and several failed to appear at all. Not until 1887 was a more rational plan introduced. Henceforth the Fourth Commissioner would be a Member of the House holding no other office under the Crown. He would thus be free enough to attend meetings, to visit the office, and otherwise to familiarize himself with the work of the Commissioners. With this reform, relations with Parliament became somewhat easier, for the new Fourth Commissioners could speak with greater knowledge and authority.[64] There was still, however, a difference of opinion as to whether the Commission ought not to be placed directly under a Minister, and in 1894 a Select Committee considered the question in some detail. The issue, however, remained unresolved until 1960, when, as will appear later, the Home Secretary added the Charity Commission to his far-flung and miscellaneous empire.

Their indifferent liaison with Parliament was one, but only one, explanation of the lack of public enthusiasm that the activities of the Charity Commissioners evoked. Certainly a good deal of unpopularity would have been the lot of any

[62] 5 *Hansard* (Lords), 15:422ff.
[63] 5 *Hansard* (Commons), 65:2294–95; 4 & 5 Geo. V, c. 56.
[64] *35th Ann. C. C. Rept.*, 1887, pp. 9–10; *S. C. on the Charity Commission*, 1894, Q. 133, 158ff.

administrative body whose duty it was to interfere with hallowed abuses and to disturb ancient habits. Yet it is also true that the Commissioners showed a certain ineptitude, to put it in the modern vernacular, in their public relations. They seem never to have regarded it as part of their responsibility to educate the public. Thinking of themselves chiefly as lawyers, they were little inclined to interpret their work to ordinary people in nontechnical terms, so that even among intelligent individuals who should have known better there flourished the most fantastic misconceptions of their powers. Robert Leader of Sheffield, giving evidence before the Select Committee of 1884, was made to look exceedingly silly when he announced that "these Charity Commissioners could come upon us of their own sweet will" and "we should be like children in the care of a very benevolent nurse, but a nurse not always fully informed." [65] Sometimes they seem to have given the impression of engineering a crusade against charity trustees, whom they tended to regard as their natural enemies, a contumacious lot who were stubbornly resisting the light. It was all more than a little reminiscent of the complicated antipathies between the Poor Law Commissioners and local bodies in the 1830's and '40's.

At the end of the century the movement for democratizing English local government altered the relations between the Commission and individual charities. Even before the Acts of 1888 and 1894 marked the triumph of the campaign, there were occasional demands for a more democratic control of charitable endowments, especially from places where vigorous and progressive municipal governments had been established. It was not, however, merely the pressure of municipal reformers that led to the growing democratization of boards of trustees. From the beginning it was an axiom of the Commissioners that adequate publicity was among the more powerful guarantees of honest, responsible charity administration. Anything that would broaden the base of a local charity and make it less of a hole-in-corner activity was obviously to be encouraged.[66]

During the 1880's, therefore, the Commissioners gradually introduced into their schemes provision for a representative element on boards of trustees. Although Britain still lacked local agencies wholly suitable for the purpose, the Commissioners conferred on various representative bodies — vestries, town councils, boards of guardians, and others — the power of appointing trustees. In the decade 1884–93, for example, in six sample counties, 176 new schemes provided for 549 co-optative, 352 *ex officio,* and 443 representative trustees.[67] The Commissioners, however, resisted the kind of rapid devolution urged by the more eager local democratic leaders. Not only did they consider co-optation a sound principle which ought to be preserved, but, until the Act of 1888 established the County Councils and that of 1894 the Parish Councils, they lacked appropriate appointive bodies, since they correctly regarded a public meeting as a less than ideal mecha-

[65] *S. C. on the Charitable Trusts Acts,* 1884, Q. 3953–54.
[66] *40th Ann. C. C. Rept.,* 1892, pp. 26–28.
[67] *S. C. on the Charity Commission,* 1894, App. No. 10, p. 362; Q. 3897ff.

nism for the purpose. Nor did they scruple to resist, with all possible firmness, what they suspected to be empire-building proclivities on the part of local corporations, town councils, and similar bodies.[68]

The reconstruction of local government effected by the Acts of 1888 and 1894 altered the Commissioners' position. Here at last were established the kind of local authorities whose absence had often been deplored both by them and by Committees of Parliament. At the least, the new bodies would meet the need for an intermediate authority standing between the Commissioners and the trustees of individual charities, and their existence might in the long run lead to a large-scale devolution of control in charitable trust administration. In the beginning the creation of the County Councils meant a substantial increase in business for the Commission. The new Councils were naturally interested in obtaining a reasonably accurate picture of the charity resources of the County, and the deluge of requests placed a heavy burden on the Commission's statistical and research facilities.[69] Not only were there appeals for information on specific endowments and for complete lists of local charities, with their financial accounts, but from some quarters at least there were suggestions that the Commissioners undertake a new survey on the scale of the Brougham inquiry, or perhaps reissue the Brougham Reports with supplementary material covering the last half century.

This latter project, the Commissioners agreed, was eminently worthwhile but out of the question without a heavy increase in staff and budget. Yet obviously there was useful work to be done here. Even since the publication of the Digest in the 1860's and '70's there had been a marked advance in charity income. Surveying nineteen counties in their 1891 Report, the Commissioners could point to an average increase in number of charities of about 30 per cent and in income of 27.16 per cent.[70] The question of expense was solved in part by the Charity Inquiries (Expenses) Act of 1892, which empowered local authorities to contribute toward the cost of inquiries conducted by the Charity Commissioners. When, therefore, a county had resolved on such a survey, it applied to the Treasury for a temporary increase in the staff of the Commission. Since expenses were to be shared between county (or other local authority) and central government, local authorities had to await their turn. Nevertheless, starting with Denbighshire, the Commissioners completed eight Welsh counties before 1900. The English counties

[68] A case in point was their action with regard to Lench's Trust in Birmingham, a Tudor foundation, whose income had now reached nearly £3500. The Commissioners used a minor crisis in the affairs of the charity to suggest that the time had come for a regulative scheme. The Birmingham Corporation, though it had been given opportunity to lodge its objections, was outraged when the scheme finally appeared. What gave the most offense was the provision for only four representative trustees (appointed by the Corporation) as against thirteen co-opted. The Commissioners were able to withstand this attack by citing the practice of Chancery and the fact that the Municipal Corporations Act of 1882 carried no implication of enlarged authority for corporations over charitable trusts within their jurisdiction. (S. C. on the Charitable Trusts Acts, 1884, Q. 1808ff; 45 & 46 Vict., c. 50, s. 133.) On the other hand, local oligarchies sometimes resisted the proposal of the Commissioners to introduce representative trustees. For an instance of this see Ashby, Joseph Ashby of Tysoe, p. 132.

[69] 38th Ann. C. C. Rept., 1890, pp. 12–13.

[70] 39th Ann. C. C. Rept., 1891, p. 21.

went more slowly, but by 1914 eight had been covered, wholly or in part, including London, Lancashire, and the West Riding. At this point the work was interrupted by the War and never resumed.

Incomplete as was the new "Brougham inquiry," it accomplished useful results. In the West Riding, an investigator reported, charities not previously known were brought to light in nearly two out of three parishes studied, some of them of considerable value. The inquiry also recovered many lapsed charities and rescued others in imminent danger of being lost. In this respect, charities whose endowment consisted of a rent charge on land, an exceedingly common device for small charities, were peculiarly vulnerable. These were easily lost sight of when property was sold, or they might be simply ignored (deliberately or inadvertently) by owners. In one Yorkshire parish four such charges were re-established after a lapse of more than sixty years.

The Commissioners also exposed a fair number of abuses, trivial or serious, in the handling of charity funds. They discovered sums remaining uninvested, invested in the name of a single trustee, or invested in unauthorized securities. They were also instrumental in recovering important legal documents relating to charities, sometimes retrieving them from private hands and sometimes tracing them after being lost or mislaid. On more than one occasion investigators appeared barely in time to save valuable documents from destruction, as in the parish where they arrived just as the vicar's daughter was about to destroy as useless lumber a box containing old deeds relating to local charities. Sometimes, unfortunately, the representatives of the Commission reached the scene of destruction too late.[71] But perhaps as important as these specific benefits was the opportunity that the inquiry provided for educating local charity administrators, especially members of the new Parish and Urban District Councils, and for bringing them into touch with the Commission. During the 1890's, in short, one of the genuine services of the Charity Commissioners was the guidance which they gave to the movement for democratizing local charity administration.

5

Although during the 1880's and '90's the Charity Commissioners failed to get rid of the restrictions that most annoyed them, Parliament moved to correct one of the more patent incongruities in charity law. Two Acts (1888 and 1891) disposed of some, though by no means all, of the mortmain incubus, which, since Sir Joseph Jekyll's Act of 1736,[72] had limited the benevolence of testators. The origins of this curious legislation have already been noted. What should be emphasized here is not merely the provisions of the Act itself but the extraordinarily tight construction placed upon it by the courts. It was restrictive enough when applied to gifts of land and buildings but when interpreted so as to bar securities in any way related to land — even those which in any common-sense

[71] *44th Ann. C. C. Rept.,* 1896, App. B.
[72] The Mortmain Act, 9 Geo. II, c. 36.

view would clearly be personalty — judicial logic seemed to have been pushed to a preposterous point. Lord Eldon, for example, decided that a mortgage of turn-pike tolls was no valid bequest on the curious ground that its consequence would be to "open a much larger field for charitable donations." [73] Even railway and canal shares fell under the ban, unless the Act establishing the company happened to have specified that these were to be considered personalty.[74] Likewise, bequests were invalid which directed that money be laid out in lands or from which such an intention might conceivably be inferred.[75] If a philanthropist who wished to found, say, a convalescent hospital were to miscalculate his life expectancy and to die before the site was actually bought, his charitable purpose might never be realized. This was precisely what happened to the Victorian philanthropist George Moore, whose £15,000 left for such an institution could not be used because land had not been acquired. It was equally illegal for a testator to leave land, even with instructions that it be sold. This could hardly be defended in rational terms if, as was often urged, the object of the statute was to prevent land from becoming inalienable.

Among the restrictions imposed by the courts' interpretation of mortmain, one of the more excessive, in the eyes of its critics, was the rule against the "marshal-ling of assets" in favor of charities. That is, where an estate is insufficient to meet a testator's legacies, the law normally throws on the real estate debts and other charges that would ordinarily be borne by the personalty, thus relieving the latter for the benefit of the legatees. Where a charity was involved, however, the court would permit no such indulgence.[76] Certainly in applying the Mortmain Act the courts could not be accused of undue favoritism toward philanthropy.

There had been no lack of protests, official and unofficial, against the Act. A Select Committee in 1844, presided over by Lord John Manners, failed to discover any conspicuous virtue in it and concluded that the statute had produced little but uncertainty, expense, and the frustration of those charitable impulses which society should seek to encourage.[77] Yet during the early 1850's the trend seemed, if anything, to be toward tightening rather than relaxing the law.[78] Here the controlling factor, to repeat, was the pathological fear of popery, always latent in Britain, which passed into a violent phase during the "papal aggression" scare. The doubtful legality of Catholic charities (since many were for "super-stitious uses") had made it necessary to exempt them from the jurisdiction of the Commissioners.[79] Although the law of mortmain had already been relaxed in favor of Queen Anne's Bounty and the Ecclesiastical Commission, as well as Oxford and Cambridge Universities, to liberalize it further would, in the view

[73] *Knapp* v. *Williams*, 4 Vesey Jun. 430, quoted in Kenny, *The True Principles of Legislation with regard to . . . Charitable . . . Uses*, p. 70.
[74] *S. C. on Mortmain*, 1844, Q. 49, 227.
[75] Cf. Kenny, *The True Principles of Legislation . . .* , p. 72.
[76] *S. C. on Mortmain*, 1844, Q. 230; *Report*, p. iv; *Kenny*, pp. 73–74.
[77] *S. C. on Mortmain*, 1844, p. viii.
[78] *S. C. . . . to Consider Extending the Law of Mortmain*, 1851–52.
[79] As has already been noted (Chapter VII).

of many, not only benefit the Roman Catholics in general but give official approval to charitable bequests for such superstitious uses as masses for the dead. Actually such dispositions, though illegal, had been extremely common. It was easy enough to leave property to an individual priest, who, though nothing may have been put on paper, would have no doubt of the donor's intentions. Most Roman Catholic charities, it was testified before the Nathan Committee, had been held on trusts orally declared.[80]

The problem of regulating Catholic charities was a more involved issue than can be profitably explored here. Among the complicating factors was the feud between the hierarchy and some of the old Catholic families, who showed themselves extremely suspicious of the influence thought to be exerted by priests over individual testators. Several of the Catholic witnesses before the Select Committee of 1851, in fact, urged a tightening of the mortmain law as a means of keeping the hierarchy under control.[81] A series of bills, some opposed and others favored by the Catholic community, were brought forward in Parliament, but all were stopped short of the statute book.[82] It was, at least in part, the difficulty over Catholic charities that postponed action on the mortmain laws until near the end of the century. What magnitude of loss the delay may have imposed on British charities it is impossible to guess. The record of Queen Anne's Bounty, which from 1803 was exempt from the restriction, suggests that the figure may have been of some consequence. This charity continued to profit from gifts and bequests of real property, its benefactions in land and houses (to take the years 1841–43 as a sample) amounting to more than half of those in money.[83]

During the latter part of the century it would have been hard to find defenders, lawyers or laymen, of the mortmain laws and the myriad absurdities of interpretation that had grown up around them. No one could possibly justify the reasoning which differentiated the bonds of the Corporations of Dewsbury and Wakefield, which might be given to a charity, from those of Oldham and Salford, which might not, or the even subtler distinction between the bonds of the Leicester Corporation (legal) and its 3½ per cent Redeemable Stock (illegal). Nor had any apparent logic governed the choice of charities to be exempted, by private Act, from the mortmain provisions. Gifts of land to some London hospitals had become legal, while such benefactions to other hospitals remained invalid.[84]

The first breach in the wall was made in 1888 by an Act which permitted assurances of land for charitable purposes by *deed*.[85] The donor still had to execute the deed before two witnesses at least twelve months before his death. Furthermore, the gift would take effect at once and must be made irrevocably and

---

[80] *S. C. (Lords) on the Charitable Uses Bill*, 1857 (2d Sess.), Q. 100; Nathan Committee (unpubl.) evidence, Q. 4181.
[81] *S. C. on the Law of Mortmain*, 1851, especially the evidence of Bray, Wale, Riddell, and Skirrow.
[82] Summarized in the *Dublin Review*, 34:428ff (June 1853).
[83] *S. C. on Mortmain*, 1844, Q. 1479.
[84] *3 Hansard*, 354:714–15.
[85] 51 & 52 Vict., c. 42.

with no reservation to the donor. The new enactment did not, however, deal with the more difficult matter of *bequests* of land. Here the problem, in the minds of some, was to find a formula which would allow a testator to leave his real property to a charity but which would not lead to larger accumulations of property in the hands of charitable corporations. It was apparently two physicians, Sir John Simon and Ernest Hart, who applied the necessary pressure. In October 1890 Hart, editor of the *British Medical Journal,* laid before the Parliamentary Bills Committee of the British Medical Association a memorandum setting forth the unhappy state of the law, and in the following month Simon published in the *Journal,* a paper entitled "Charitable Bequests Forbidden by Law." [86] The solution embodied in the bill prepared on behalf of the Hospitals Association and introduced into the Lords by Lord Herschell was, in all conscience, cautious enough. This was to permit bequests of land to charitable uses but to require (save where it was to be used for actual occupation, as, for example, land for a school building) that it be sold within a limited period. The Act of 1891[87] imposed on the Charity Commissioners the responsibility for seeing that these provisions were carried out — a task that forced them not only to deal with some fairly intricate legal questions but also occasionally to placate indignant trustees who could not understand why their land had to be sold regardless of market conditions and sometimes to the obvious disadvantage of the charity.[88] On balance, there was little reason to regard the Acts of 1888 and 1891 as a final settlement of the issues.

Opposition to the mortmain laws was only one phase, and a minor phase, of the broader movement for the reform of charity law. It is perhaps a little excessive to dignify the sporadic complaints of individuals and groups as a "movement," but throughout a good deal of the century there was dissatisfaction, latent or articulate, over the state of the law. Before the Mortmain Committee of 1844, for example, a legal witness could characterize as very injurious "the system at present allowed to all devisors of perpetuating their own personal whims and fancies." [89] Although something had been accomplished when the Charity Commission was established, its powers were not sufficient to give hope to those who looked for a sweeping modernization of trusts, still less to those who favored a curb on the rights of the testator. But from the 1860's through the '80's a succession of voices, some of them moderately influential, were raised to demand a fundamental revision in the law itself.

The sources of the movement were various. From its foundation in 1857 the Social Science Association supplied something of a focal point. The most effective of its sections, that on jurisprudence and amendment of the law, offered a forum for discussions on charity law, with barristers of experience and distinction leading the attack. Thomas Hare appeared frequently, Sir Arthur Hobhouse first pre-

[86] *British Medical Journal,* 1 Nov. 1890, pp. 1027–30; *Philanthropist,* December 1891, pp. 179–80.
[87] 54 & 55 Vict., c. 73.
[88] Memorandum to the Nathan Committee by the Charity Commission.
[89] *S. C. on Mortmain,* 1844, Q. 453.

sented several of the papers later published in *The Dead Hand,* and such distinguished lights of the equity bench and bar as Sir Page Wood (Lord Hatherley)
occasionally took part. At the 1859 meeting, Wood, who was then Vice-Chancellor, ridiculed the legal doctrine that guaranteed perpetuity to preposterous
bequests. Posthumous charity, he pointed out, was too often only another name
for vanity, sometimes carried to fantastic lengths, as with the testator who
directed "£300 a year to be paid out of my estate, to be applied for ever to the
payment of a man who has been unsuccessful in literature in the diffusion of my
opinions in my published works." [90] Later in the same congress he returned to
the charge, stressing the curious way in which the law permitted the imagination
of donors to run riot. In one parish, he recalled, a fund was left to trustees, half
to be distributed among fifteen maidens of the parish who should be the prettiest
and most regular in attendance at church, the other half among fifteen spinsters
over fifty with "like qualifications." This bequest was sanctioned as a valid charity
save for the qualification of "prettiest." [91] Even aside from such absurd night-
mares, there was, he argued, a strong case for restricting bequests in perpetuity
and subjecting them to periodic review.

Clearly, also, the movement for charity law reform owed something to public
concern for education, as in the days of the Brougham inquiry. The Royal Commissions which looked into elementary and secondary education in the 1860's
were no friends to the doctrine of perpetuity in charitable bequests, and two of
them came out flatly in favor of more systematic revision. The Newcastle Commission thought that the prescription of a founder ought to "be limited to the
period over which human foresight may be expected to extend. Without such a
limitation, foundations would be open to the condemnation passed upon them
by Turgot and other economists as creations of a vanity which imagines that it
can foresee the requirements of all future ages, and a credulity which supposes
that strangers, administering a founder's charity in distant times, will carry out
his favorite system with a zeal equal to his own." [92] The Taunton Commission
stressed the same themes, and the Endowed Schools Act of 1869, by its provisions
for converting certain types of obsolete trusts to educational purposes, further
drew attention to the need and possibility of reform.

Though even its author could not have taken its more extreme claims seriously,
Robert Lowe's perversely brilliant pamphlet *Middle Class Education: Endowment
or Free Trade* must have challenged intelligent readers.[93] Addressing himself to
the recommendations of the Taunton Commission (before which he had testified
in a similar vein), he professed surprise at the Commissioners' assumption "that
ordinary principles of political economy are inapplicable to the education of the
middle classes." Schooling, like trade, could properly be left to the operation of
economic law; bounties on education had become as archaic as bounties on foreign

[90] *Trans. Social Science Assn.,* 1859, p. 69.
[91] *Ibid.,* p. 188.
[92] *R. C. on Popular Education,* 1861, *Report,* p. 476.
[93] London, 1868.

trade. Teachers required the goad of active and ceaseless competition to be efficient — the prospect of a regular salary would sap their vitality. Even the public schools owed less to their endowments than to their system of private instruction based on pupils' fees. Presumably this reassertion of the verities of Turgot and Adam Smith by one of their more illustrious mid-Victorian disciples raised questions about the place of endowments in English society and their legal basis.

Other currents fed the stream of speculation and criticism. *The Times* attributed some of the interest to the furor aroused by Gladstone's proposal to remove the income tax exemption from charitable foundations.[94] The Charity Organisation Society, also, made its influence felt. Although legal reform was hardly a principal emphasis of the Society, no group committed to the promotion of "efficiency" in charitable relief could miss the spectacularly chaotic law which governed charitable endowments. Especially in their agitation against doles were the leaders of the C.O.S. brought up against the question of bequests in perpetuity, periodic scrutiny and revision of trusts, and a greater degree of state supervision. Sir Arthur Hobhouse, most outspoken of the law reformers, and Sir Charles Trevelyan, who set off the movement for reforming the City of London parochial endowments, were both members of the C.O.S. Council. Beyond such special influences on these, the campaigns carried on by the Society served to bring to public notice a variety of problems connected with philanthropy, including that of its legal basis.

The attack of the reformers centered largely on two related points. These had to do, first, with the extraordinary concessions made to donors and testators in their right to prescribe the conditions of the trusts in perpetuity, and, secondly, with the elaborate safeguards set up by the law for assuring the continued control of the testator and preventing a revision of the trust even when, on any reasonable basis, it was clearly needed. The reformers were protesting, in varying degrees, against the rule of the Dead Hand and attempting to break, or at least to relax, its grip.

At the outset there was the basic issue of whether, in its desire to encourage bequests to charity, the State had not conceded far too much. Few lawyers would argue anything inherent in the "right" of a testator to dictate in perpetuity the use to be made of his estate, and many were willing to consider limiting the privilege to a period of years, after which the trust might be reviewed and revised. It was disturbing enough that a testator might leave his property for a charity that, even with the most laudable intentions on his part, might become relatively valueless or obsolete in a few years. It was even more to be deplored, in the view of reformers, that the original bequest might be made for a purpose that, on any reasonable judgment, was socially useless or even harmful — but still in perpetuity. For a "charitable use" or "charitable intention" has no necessary connection with benevolence or with what is socially beneficial. To the lawyer, "charity" is a technical term and one that, on the periphery of its application, has always lacked

[94] *The Times*, 13 Oct. 1880.

precision. The interpretation of what constitutes a valid charity will, in some degree, vary from decade to decade and from court to court.

Nowhere is there an authoritative definition of the term. As we have seen, the preamble to the basic Elizabethan Statute of Charitable Uses lists a large number of such uses, a table "of charities so varied and comprehensive that it became the practice of the Court [of Chancery] to refer to it as a sort of index or chart." [95] In the early 1890's Lord Macnaghten, in what became the most influential formulation, attempted to restate the preamble of 43 Elizabeth in modern terms.[96] Of his four categories of charitable use, three would arouse little disagreement — the relief of poverty, the advancement of education, and the advancement of religion (though some questions might be raised about the definition of "religion"). The effect of precision in the three categories, however, was rather ruined by the vague, though necessary, fourth class: "trusts for other purposes beneficial to the community, not falling under any one of the preceding heads." This is about where the question remains today — if one adds the further proviso that all charitable bequests must benefit the community or a substantial fraction of it. To anticipate, the Charitable Trusts Act of 1960 leaves 43 Elizabeth still standing as the undoubted fountainhead of charity law.

From the reformers' point of view, numbers of trusts should never have been admitted as valid charities. They were fond of pointing to certain well-known endowments that owed their existence to no benevolence on the part of a pious founder but rather, as with the Tancred and Jarvis trusts, to sheer malice, a gesture of spite against his family. There were also charities created to gratify the whim, sometimes fairly bizarre in modern eyes, of the founder. Such, perhaps, was the gift to the vicar and churchwardens of St. Ives for the purchase of Bibles. They were to be distributed to the boys and girls on Whit Tuesday by a curious process of selection. After evening prayer, a table was moved in front of the altar and a half dozen boys and girls cast dice, those rolling the highest numbers winning the Bibles.[97] In the early 1880's one Cornelius Christmas died at the age of eighty-six, leaving the income from £16,000 to be distributed in bread, coals, and money "to the poor of Great Yarmouth, in the week before Christmas day, every year hereafter and at no other time, for ever." To the bequest he attached an anathema against the public authorities if they should "change or interfere with my gift I may make to the poor, then I do request my trustees *immediately* to *convert* all into cash, and distribute *without delay* all the same to the poor of this my native town — but not to give more than £20 to any one family; I trust and hope that they will never be driven to any such extremity." [98] Presumably Cornelius Christmas thought it a fitting memorial to himself that the distribution should take place during the week before December 25th.

[95] Lord Macnaghten, quoted in the *Nathan Report*, Par. 121.
[96] *The Commissioners of Income Tax* v. *Pemsel*, A. C. 521.
[97] H. L. Wayland, "The Dead Hand," *Journal of Social Science*, 26:84 (February 1890); *24th [Brougham] Rept.*, 1831, p. 37.
[98] *Charity Record*, 5 Oct. 1882.

The annals of philanthropy are not lacking in other self-advertising founders — indeed, a significant, and probably pardonable, element of vanity is present in a large share of charitable bequests. There was Greene, who perpetuated his memory by supplying old women with *green* waistcoats trimmed with *green* galloon lace, and Gray, who provided for garbing the poor in *gray*.[99] Someone has remarked on the mania of a certain type of donor for dictating the dress of the poor. A list of charitable bequests which from the beginning were harmful or useless or silly (and valid) could be extended indefinitely. Like others of his conceits, W. S. Gilbert's endowed corps of professional bridesmaids in *Ruddigore* seems only a little more preposterous than certain charities that were enjoying a full legal existence. These maidens, it will be recalled, found themselves so gravely underemployed that "the pious charity by which we exist is practically wasted," and disendowment, they feared, might be imminent. To dwell on the aberrations of the benevolent impulse, however, would distort the picture. Although, in the view of reformers, many charities from the day of their foundation conferred no apparent benefit on society, there was an argument against interfering with them immediately. What was objected to was the right enjoyed by the testator of imposing his crotchets or prejudices upon succeeding generations in perpetuity. The more extreme reforming spirits would have endorsed the dictum of Thomas Jefferson, "That our creator made the earth for the use of the living, and not of the dead; that those who exist not can have no use nor rights in it, no authority or power over it." [100]

In the hands of men like Hobhouse, Hare, and Lord Hatherley the case of the reformers did not lack for vigorous statement. In essence they demanded not only that the original purpose of a charitable bequest be scrutinized more critically but that its duration be limited to a specific period, perhaps fifty or sixty years, or, as Hatherley suggested, life in being plus twenty-one years. They regarded as the height of absurdity the principle under which a seventeenth-century testator felt entitled to threaten his trustees with eternal punishment if any fraction of his £100 bequest were "ever employed or made any other use of whatsoever so long as the world endureth." [101] To Hobhouse, whose ideas were admittedly more extreme than most of the others', two changes were fundamental. First, the public must no longer be compelled to take whatever a donor happened to offer, but should "as in other countries, have the right of considering whether that particular use which the Founder has fancied shall take effect, or whether the property shall be turned to some other public use, or given back to private uses." Some deference, he conceded, should be paid to the testator's wishes, but not to the point of interfering with the public welfare. Secondly, there must always be a responsible agency to manage charity property "according to the wants of mankind," presumably a public tribunal empowered to adjust "to new

[99] Chase, *Some Great Trusts of England*, p. 10; *17th [Brougham] Rept.*, 1826–27, pp. 296–97.

[100] Quoted by Wayland, "The Dead Hand," p. 88.

[101] L. R. Phelps, "The Use and Abuse of Endowed Charities," *Economic Review*, 2:88–89 (January 1892).

objects all Foundations which have become pernicious or useless." [102] These two principles he repeatedly emphasized and elaborated, most trenchantly in the three lectures delivered in 1868–69 during his tenure as Charity Commissioner. [103]

These lectures were to serve, in part, as a reply to John Stuart Mill's article in the *Fortnightly Review*. [104] What had set Mill off was Joshua Fitch's suggestion, growing out of his disillusioning experience as Assistant Commissioner for the Schools Inquiry Commission, that the right of charitable bequest had been allowed to run riot and perhaps was due to be curbed. Education and poor relief, he implied, ought to be administered according to a national policy to which private donors should be made to conform. This kind of talk, of course, stung Mill in his most sensitive spot. It seemed to run counter to all of his convictions about variety and experiment as the key to human progress. His was not the bigoted resistance that the reformers often encountered. On the contrary (and optimistically), Mill considered the right of the State to interfere with endowments as a matter that had been settled once and for all. In fact, he conceded so much that it is difficult to see why he should have become the whipping-boy of the reformers, when he might, not unjustifiably, have thought of his own views on charitable trusts as moderately radical. It would be quite sufficient, he agreed, to allow freedom to a testator to experiment for the length of time "which individual foresight can reasonably be supposed to cover," perhaps fifty to a hundred years, after which the endowment "should come under the control of the state, to be modified, or entirely changed, at its discretion." [105]

Mill's essay was a characteristically "yes-but-on-the-other-hand" formulation. His uneasiness about the social waste involved in unwise bequests and the manifest absurdity of deferring for all time to the wishes of a foolish testator was balanced by his fear of reducing human personality to a dull uniformity. Society, he continually insists, must leave an adequate field for imaginative experiment, even for enterprises which common opinion dismisses as preposterous. Actually Mill's views were not so different, save in emphasis, from those of such a zealous charity reformer as Thomas Hare. [106] Some of the passages from Hare's address before the Social Science Congress of 1869 might well have come from the utilitarian philosopher himself — or almost, indeed, from the head of a twentieth-century foundation: "I regard endowments as an important element in the experimental branches of political and social science. No doubt the nation at large may take on itself the cost of such tentative efforts, but this involves taxation; and the assent of the majority to increased taxes could not be justly demanded by philanthropist or projectors, and certainly would not be obtained until their speculations had taken such a hold upon the public mind as no longer to require an exceptional

---

[102] Hobhouse, *The Dead Hand*, pp. 120–21.

[103] *Ibid.*, chaps. I–III.

[104] "Endowments," *Fortnightly Review*, n.s., 11:377–90 (April 1869).

[105] *Ibid.*, p. 380.

[106] They had already developed something of a friendship as the result of Mill's espousal of Hare's plan of proportional representation.

support or propagation. The most important steps in human progress may be opposed to the prejudices, not only of the multitude, but even of the learned and leaders of thought in a particular epoch." [107]

This speech of Hare's stands as an impressive and prophetic statement of the role of charitable trusts in social advance. There was, he agreed with Mill, a strong argument for giving even a fatuous scheme a period of trial, for "an endowment is a standing protest on behalf of weakness against the negligence, indifference, or ignorance of power." [108] If they were to venture more courageously into fields where social pioneering was needed — for example, in cooperative labor organization, in cooperative agriculture, and in certain aspects of "industrial life that become daily of more interest and importance" — charitable endowments offered machinery for carrying on "experiments in sociology that may prove invaluable." To fulfill such a destiny, however, foundations must be guided by public officials (evidently a Charity Commission armed with greater powers) who would be "ministers not of the letter that killeth, but of the spirit that giveth life." Assured of reasonable freedom, they could give a lead by surveying social needs and experimenting with new techniques of organization. It would have taken a flight of fancy to accept Hare's vision of future Charity Commissions as such nonbureaucratic paragons of resourcefulness and tact. Yet in his imaginative outlook and his understanding of the worth of private philanthropy in an increasingly complex and democratic society, Hare was an exceedingly persuasive advocate of a more flexible charity policy.

In 1880 appeared two books which at once reflected and stimulated the growth of interest in charity law reform. Courtney Kenny of Downing College, Cambridge, and future Downing Professor, published his Yorke Prize essay, *The True Principles of Legislation with Regard to Charitable or Other Public Uses,* while Sir Arthur Hobhouse collected into a volume, *The Dead Hand,* seven addresses delivered during the years 1868–79. The speeches in book form proved an immensely effective piece of pamphleteering, though very likely Hobhouse's penchant for stating his views in extremely uncompromising terms gave alarm in quarters that might otherwise have been less hostile. The central theme was the text from which he had consistently preached, "that there is no inherent right belonging to those who have played their part in this world, to dictate in what manner their former worldly goods shall be used, so there is no wisdom in allowing them to do so except to a very moderate extent." In the sections devoted to replying to Mill, Hobhouse was inclined to exaggerate the differences between the two. He was entirely correct, of course, in denying Mill's too easy assumption that the more baneful manifestations of the Dead Hand had already been wiped out or could be easily obliterated. In practical measures, however, they were not so far apart; it was largely a difference in emphasis and philosophy. One of the more telling features of the Hobhouse volume was his collection of fantastic and

[107] *Trans. Social Science Assn.,* 1869, p. 135.
[108] *Ibid.*

devastatingly obsolete endowments which he used for illustrative purposes and which have found a place in the arsenal of every subsequent writer on charity reform.[109] More than any other Victorian, Hobhouse made himself the advocate of a drastic recasting of charity law, one which would reduce the rights of the testator nearly to the vanishing point.

A more judicious and balanced statement was that of Courtney Kenny, though he too would have applied to charity law the firm hand of the reformer. His is probably the most generally satisfactory book yet written on endowed charities in England from the point of view of legal arrangements and their reform. Rejecting such hostile analyses as those of Turgot and Robert Lowe, for whom the evil in charitable endowments outweighed the good, Kenny still discovers in trusts for charitable purposes peculiarities which demand special action by the State. In the first place, the Legislature must impose *restrictions* on certain categories of charity — foundations for doles, marriage portions, apprenticeship fees, or gratuitous schools, and must otherwise specify the terms on which charitable bequests can be made. In short, Kenny would disqualify as valid charities a number of types that had been of great importance historically. Secondly, the State must continue to exercise *supervision,* more closely than in the past, over endowments, since "foundations in themselves are usually good, but when left to themselves they usually become bad." [110] His praise of the Charity Commission — no other permanent commission had "ever proved so completely successful" [111] — approached the fulsome, and must have seemed excessive even to many who endorsed his conclusion that the powers of the Commissioners ought to be extended.

Finally, to counteract the tendency of charitable trusts to obsolescence, Kenny would have the State go about the business of *revision* in a more summary and determined fashion. It was nonsense, he asserted, to regard this as a violation of the inherent rights of property. If bequests were guaranteed a period of inviolability, the prospect of moderate revision in the future, far from discouraging intelligent donors, ought to reassure them that their bequests would be productively used. If it were understood, further, that, although the details of a founder's plan were considered alterable, the endowment would be retained in the particular province of philanthropy for which it had been intended, this would give donors an additional sense of security.

Where should this revising authority be lodged? Certainly neither in Parliament nor in the courts. Other things aside, the habit of mind of the equity judge disqualified him from carrying out this kind of revision, where moral and social considerations were heavily involved, along with the narrowly legal. Plainly this was a task for neither legislature nor an ordinary judicial tribunal, but for a body of experts, a special administrative department, presumably working under a responsible Minister. It is not clear whether Kenny's primary revising body would

[109] As in Lord Beveridge's "Charities' Chamber of Horrors," *Voluntary Action,* pp. 356ff.
[110] Kenny, *The True Principles of Legislation* . . . , p. 269.
[111] *Ibid.,* pp. 152–53.

be a reorganized and strengthened Charity Commission. But he has no doubt of the desperate need for a tribunal of revision "which, whilst allowing every wise Founder an adequate Term of inviolability for the undisturbed trial of the experiment he has planned, shall have power to save his gift from being wasted, and to correct his errors, as soon as the results of the trial demonstrate that his experiment has failed." [112]

The appeals of Hobhouse, Kenny, Hare, and other law reformers yielded no significant result. Indeed, after the mid-'80's, the issue seems to have faded out, and less was said about it than in the two preceding decades. It was partly, perhaps, the fact that the City Parochial Charities Act liquidated the most spectacular cluster of obsolete charities in the Kingdom and one to which a reformer could always point as a horrible example. The Campden Charities case seemed to point to a more flexible interpretation of *cy-près,* and the relaxation of mortmain restrictions in 1888–91 drew some of the sting from another perennial grievance. And the growing tendency of the State to take over responsibilities formerly left to private charity served, perhaps, to reduce the latter in importance and to make an effective policy of regulation seem less vital.

In addition to these factors, there was a noticeable change in the *esprit* of the Charity Commission itself. In the course of the 1890's one can sense a decline in the vigor and initiative of that body. The tone of the Commission's annual reports is a measure of the difference in temper. These became mostly formal in character, routine chronicles of the year's work, with particulars of major charitable bequests (an exceedingly useful feature, of course) and other statistical material. The sanguine and aggressive zeal with which earlier Commissioners had entered upon their work was conspicuously lacking, and their late-century successors seemed inclined to accept their situation uncomplainingly. Having been disappointed so frequently, they ceased even to ask for additional powers. Certainly Thomas Hare and Courtney Kenny would have failed to discover in the twentieth-century performance of the Commission an approach to the kind of active and imaginative charity administration that they had hopefully advocated.

[112] *Ibid.,* p. 274.

CHAPTER XII

LAW AND ADMINISTRATION:
FISCAL OBLIGATIONS

N EXT TO the right of perpetuity, the most important legal concessions enjoyed by British charities have had to do with their fiscal
liabilities. Although they have enjoyed less extensive immunities than
their American counterparts, these were still substantial, and during Victorian
times they were only occasionally challenged. After all, it was easy enough to
defend tax concessions on the utilitarian ground of public benefit, for private
charity was performing essential services in British society, some of which would
otherwise have fallen upon the State.

In three respects fiscal policy was of direct concern to nineteenth-century philanthropy. First and most significant, charity revenues were exempt from income tax.
Secondly, charity bequests received no such favorable treatment; on these Inland
Revenue collected legacy duty at the maximum rate. Finally, charity property —
the question never received a categorical answer — might or might not be liable
to local rates. Related to these was a fourth issue which emerged only in the
early 1920's. This had to do with income tax relief for donors to charity. The
outcome was the complicated device of the seven-year covenant, under which
taxpayers, by meeting certain conditions, receive what amounts to income tax
exemption on their charitable contributions.[1]

The exemption of British charities from the income tax dated from its inception. We can only guess as to the motives that inspired Pitt to include in his
Income Tax Act of 1799 a clause exempting charitable organizations, but it was
a natural enough decision.[2] To take a single example, grammar schools and free
schools were carrying the entire burden of popular education and thus performed
a public function of incontestable value. It would have been preposterous to tax
the income of such quasi-public agencies. When, after its lapse between 1816 and
1842, Sir Robert Peel reintroduced the income tax, he followed the precedent
established by Pitt.[3] Only rarely in the nineteenth century did the privilege come

[1] These categories ignore certain minor matters, such as liability for the stamp tax on various documents. See *Tudor on Charities* (1906 ed.), chap. XIII.
[2] 39 Geo. III, c. 13, s. 5. Specifically, the Act exempted the income of any "Corporation, Fraternity,
or Society of persons established for charitable purposes only."
[3] And continued by Addington in his Act of 1803 (43 Geo. III, c. 122, s. 68).

under fire, and, though viewed with little enthusiasm by such charity reformers
as Hare and Hobhouse, there was never serious danger that it might be withdrawn. Whatever the merits of the case, the philanthropic interests of the Kingdom, most conspicuously the great London charities, were not negligible politically
and, when necessary, could apply pressure. Ordinarily, therefore, it was taken
for granted that rents, dividends, and interest received by legitimate charities and
applied to charitable purposes should be free of tax.

The privileged status of charity income was not the subject of official attack
until Gladstone, as Chancellor of the Exchequer, threw out a challenge in his
Financial Statement of 1863.[4] This was apparently in the nature of a trial balloon,
for he offered no specific proposals. Rather he was content to argue in essence
that exempting charity income was inequitable in principle and so complex as to
be impracticable. When, a fortnight later, he brought forward his Customs and
Inland Revenue bill, it withdrew from endowed charities their exemption save
for the buildings occupied by hospitals, colleges, and almshouses.[5] Activities supported by voluntary contributions (rather than endowments) remained unaffected.

Gladstone's "deadly encounter with the so-called charities" (as he put it in his
diary) was introduced by a long and memorable speech. "Spoke from 5.10 to
8.20, with all my might, such as it was."[6] For some of his hearers the issue must
have been sharpened when he pictured the tax exemption as a subsidy of uncertain proportions granted by the State to institutions of questionable value. If a
fresh start were to be taken, he asserted, it was inconceivable that Parliament
would vote a subvention of the magnitude of £216,000 (his estimate of the value
of the tax relief) for enterprises, an astounding proportion of which were useless
or mischievous.[7] The policy was especially deplorable because the subsidy was
concealed and indiscriminate, a blind contribution, for the State applied few of the
checks and none of the scrutiny normally given to expenditures. There was
obvious substance in Gladstone's contention that "if we have the right to give
public money, we have no right to give it in the dark. We are bound to give it
with discrimination; bound to give it with supervision; bound as a constitutional
Parliament, if the Hospitals are to receive a grant, to bring them within some
degree of controul."[8]

One of the Chancellor's arguments, probably more persuasive in his time than
in ours, had to do with the different treatment given to endowed and voluntary
charities. On the whole, the latter, he held, were much the more admirable, for
they represented a measure of sacrifice by living men, while charitable trusts
were created predominantly by bequest, by "pious founders" seeking to immortal-

[4] 3 Hansard, 170:200ff; W. E. Gladstone, The Financial Statements of 1853, 1860–63 (London,
1863), pp. 330–408. The relevant material appears on pp. 365–71.
[5] S. 3. The speech was made on 4 May 1863. An excellent summary is given by Courtney Kenny,
The True Principles of Legislation . . . , pp. 251–53.
[6] John Morley, The Life of William Ewart Gladstone, 3 vols. (London, 1903), II, 65.
[7] Gladstone, Financial Statements, p. 435.
[8] Ibid., p. 458.

ize themselves. In his view, there was a grave anomaly in the fact that voluntary charities in effect were taxed (since taxes had been paid on the incomes of their contributors) while charities set up by the will of a dead person enjoyed their income tax-free. It was characteristic of the 1860's that no one suggested avoiding the anomaly by extending comparable advantages to those who supported non-endowed charities. Still, Gladstone scored a legitimate point when he complained that St. Bartholomew's, St. Thomas's, and Guy's were receiving more indulgent treatment than Charing Cross, University College, and King's College Hospitals.

Although his admiration for endowed charities was less than tepid, Gladstone freely admitted degrees of obliquity among them. Certainly much enlightened opinion would have approved his condemnation of small charities, whose income was distributed in minute amounts, chiefly as doles. These, he estimated, received a virtual subsidy of about £125,000 a year, whereas mere toleration was the most they ought to expect.[9] At the other extreme were a number of fantastically rich institutions, whose case for exemption was laughable — as well as a number of others, notably the great endowed hospitals, with less shaky claims. Few in the former category were more vulnerable than Christ's Hospital, an institution whose total income was now approaching £70,000 a year and which, though originally intended for the poorest of the poor, was drawing boys from higher social strata. Its system of donation governors allowed the donor of £500 to present a specified number of boys for education at the expense of the foundation, sometimes a convenient way of taking care of needy relatives. In Gladstone's view, the public purse was here being taxed to the amount of some £6000 to make possible the education of children not necessarily drawn from the ranks of the very poor.

Gladstone's plan elicited remarkably little support either within or outside the House. In the interval between his Financial Statement and his more detailed argument, charity interests had taken alarm and had mobilized to resist the threat. Even the Chancellor of the Exchequer, as he wryly noted, was struck "by the skilful manner in which the charitable army, so to call it, has been marshalled."[10] From the opposite side of the House his proposal was condemned as unsound in principle and inexpedient in practice. Disraeli drew applause when he proclaimed the curious doctrine that exemption "is not a privilege — it is a right."[11] No independent Member aligned himself with Gladstone, who prudently withdrew his measure with the debate still in progress. It was plain, as Palmerston observed, that outside the House local opinion had been aroused and organized, and within, Gladstone's eloquence had accomplished little beyond relieving his own conscience.

[9] *Ibid.*, p. 443.
[10] *Ibid.*, p. 438; *3 Hansard*, 170:1082.
[11] *Ibid.*, 1128.

2

No subsequent Government came as close to making the taxation of charities a part of its program, though occasionally Gladstonian private Members raised questions.[12] None of these attacks altered the fiscal position of charitable trusts, but they tended, at least in some circles, to increase the skepticism with which foundations were regarded. Among Gladstone's followers especially, there was a suspicion that certain major charities might be doing little to justify their privileges and that less tender treatment might stimulate them to more efficient performance. Some of these doubts were reflected in a memorandum from the Treasury to the Home Office a few weeks after Gladstone's speech in the House.[13] The Charity Commissioners, it was suggested, might usefully undertake a thorough inquiry into some of the large tax-exempt foundations of the Metropolis. In part this was what it appeared to be — a straightforward attempt to get more accurate information about the great London charities — but it was also inspired by doubt as to whether these institutions were really as their spokesmen in the House had pictured them.

The Commissioners required little prodding. They promptly set about investigating seven foundations, all but one in the London area.[14] Such institutions as Christ's Hospital, Bethlem, St. Thomas's, and the London Hospital were scrutinized with the kind of thoroughness characteristic of the Commission, and the reports, though perhaps less obviously critical than Gladstone expected, raised some searching questions. For example, Thomas Hare, after analyzing Christ's Hospital in an impeccably objective fashion, concluded by querying whether the Hospital estates ought to be "administered for the benefit of a small number of favoured persons [boys presented by the governors] or for the poorest classes and the common weal."[15] The significance of the Commissioners' investigation lay less in the domain of fiscal policy than in that of the broader relations between the State and the endowed charities. Their reports served to tear the veil from the operations of some of the greater metropolitan charities, to expose them to the critical gaze of whoever wished to see, and thus to invite the attacks of reformers. This was, in fact, a kind of reconnaissance for the battle between the Endowed Schools Commissioners and Christ's Hospital, probably the most complicated and stubborn case with which they had to deal.

Another consequence of Gladstone's gesture was to direct attention to the administrative side of income tax exemption. If nothing could be done about

[12] *Ibid.*, 205:1505ff; 245:1187ff. More often than not, the issue had to do with the expenses of the Charity Commission, whose establishment, it was widely held, ought to be financed by the charities themselves rather than by the Treasury.

[13] B.M. Add. MSS. 44,752, ff. 313–16 (25 July 1863).

[14] *Corr. between the Treasury, the Home Office, and the Charity Commissioners* (*Parl. Pap.*), 1865.

[15] *Ibid.*, p. 59.

the privilege in principle, perhaps it could be modified in practice. What, for example, was the legal status of trust funds whose income was to be applied in aid of poor rates and other regular parochial burdens? Could these be considered charities within the meaning of the law and thus entitled to exemption? Legal opinion on the point was conflicting and the Commissioners of Inland Revenue were gravely perplexed.[16] The Treasury for its part would have been happy to define more stringently the limits of exemption, but hesitated to alter long-standing practices by mere administrative regulations. In any case, Inland Revenue determined henceforth to examine more carefully applications from charities for refunds.[17]

Although this policy produced some feuding between Inland Revenue and foundations which thought themselves unfairly treated, it was not until the late 1880's that charities attempted resistance through the courts. At the time the Commissioners were showing a marked inclination to reduce the area of exemption, especially with respect to certain religious and educational trusts. Since the only legal classification of charities was nearly three centuries old and provided no readily applicable formula, they were moving toward establishing their own criteria at the cost, *The Times* protested, of usurping a function of Parliament.[18] Their position was made explicit in 1886 when they threw out the claim, previously admitted, of a Moravian trust. Two years later, a Scottish decision in the case of the Baird Trust appeared to support the position taken by Inland Revenue.[19] Meanwhile, the Moravian (Pemsel) case pursued its way through the courts with what Tudor describes as "a considerable diversity of judicial opinion." [20] In the end, the Law Lords held, four to two, that such trusts were legal charities and were entitled to income tax refunds.[21] Whatever the legal merits of the Pemsel decision, it not only overruled the Scottish court in the Baird Trust case but forced the Board of Inland Revenue to return to its earlier and more liberal policy.

The charities attempted to fight back on the political as well as the judicial front. While the Pemsel case was moving deliberately through the courts, Lord Addington spoke out on behalf of the Church Building Society, whose application had been refused, and demanded from Inland Revenue a statement showing the amounts on which income tax had been refunded to charities in 1886–87 and the claims rejected.[22] The protest was of little consequence in itself, since the courts were presently to settle the issue, but the figures submitted by the Board of Inland Revenue were exceedingly interesting. They indicated that refunds had been made

---

[16] Commrs. of Inland Rev. to the Treasury, 22 Aug. 1863, *ibid.*, pp. 1–5.

[17] The normal procedure was for the charities to apply for refunds after the tax had been paid.

[18] *The Times*, 4 Sept. 1888. For the types of application rejected, see *3 Hansard*, 334:1546–51.

[19] *Baird's Trustees* v. *Lord Advocate* (1888), 15 Sess. Cas. (Ser. 4) 688; see also *Tudor on Charities* (1906 ed.), p. 418.

[20] *Ibid.*, p. 419.

[21] It was in this decision that Lord Macnaghten developed his classic four categories of charitable use, as noted in the previous chapter.

[22] *3 Hansard*, 329:1384–86.

on something over £2 million of charity income. Also, the Board's return, as shown in the table, tells a good deal about the relative importance of the various categories of charity in the late century.[23]

Educational trusts	£ 778,528
Religious trusts	102,232
Hospitals	534,701
Pension funds	236,523
Almshouses	157,101
Doles	193,834
Miscellaneous	48,043
	£2,050,962

Following the Lords' decision in the Pemsel case, it was no longer expedient to discriminate for fiscal purposes among trusts that were charitable in law, to tax some categories and exempt others. Inland Revenue was obliged to grant exemption to any enterprise that was charitable within the technical meaning of the term. As a result, there have been not infrequent signs of uneasiness in official quarters both over the immunities enjoyed by activities unquestionably charitable in character and over the range of undertakings which must be considered legally "charitable." In 1920 the Colwyn Commission on the Income Tax showed concern over the privileges held by organizations which in the ordinary sense of the word were not charitable at all.[24] The paradox, the Commissioners thought, required that Parliament step in and establish *for income tax purposes* a special definition of "charitable use," without, however, attempting to alter the broader legal concept.

Thirty-five years after the Colwyn Report (to bring the story to the present), another Royal Commission reviewed the situation and found it highly unsatisfactory.[25] The Royal Commission on the Taxation of Profits and Income admitted to some sympathy with Gladstone's complaint that exemption in effect constituted a grant of public money for causes and activities over which Parliament exercised little authority. "There is," the Commission observed, "no public control of a charity from the point of view either of importance or of utility . . . Yet so long as the charitable purpose persists and is observed, the State automatically

[23] *Return on Income Tax Refund to Charities* . . . , *House of Lords Papers,* 1888, No. 289. The total on which refunds were paid, it will be noticed, was somewhat less than the approximately £2,200,000 shown as charity income in the Digest published by the Commissioners in the years 1868–75.

[24] *R. C. on the Income Tax* (Cmd. 615), 1920, Part III, sec. XIV. Appearing before the Nathan Committee in 1951, representatives of the Law Society showed some concern (Q. 5408ff) over the slightly different criteria employed by the Charity Commissioners and Inland Revenue in deciding whether to regard a trust as charitable.

[25] *R. C. on the Taxation of Profits and Income* (Cmd. 9474), 1955, Part I, chap. 7.

returns to the charity the tax on all its income — a concession which amounts at present rates to a virtually doubling of that income." [26]

What the Commission objected to was less the notion of income tax relief for genuine charities than the hit-or-miss way in which it operated. Because of the lack of a workable definition of charity, an astonishing range of activities had become eligible for exemption, many of which had no connection with charity as ordinarily understood. The Report reverted to the recommendation of the Colwyn Commission, proposing in somewhat more specific terms the framing of a statutory definition for tax purposes. Stated as a principle, the suggestion had obvious merit, but the procedure suggested was, to say the least, highly arguable. For if the Commission had its way, exemption would be restricted to the first three of Macnaghten's categories, somewhat enlarged, "the relief of poverty, the prevention or relief of distress, the advancement of education, learning, and research, the advancement of religion." But the miscellaneous and vague fourth class, "trusts for other purposes beneficial to the community" would be omitted, to the injury, the Commission admitted, of "a number of praiseworthy activities."

This was the view of the majority. Two members, Professor J. R. Hicks and Mr. Sylvester Gates, not only favored less indulgent treatment for charities but suggested new theoretical criteria for dealing with them.[27] Total exemption, in their opinion, could be justified only for charities performing functions which were recognized as a responsibility of the State. With the steady expansion of the public social services, the role of charity tended to shift from "that of the indispensable to that of the highly desirable." Yet, however defensible in theory, it would be clearly impossible administratively to separate foundations which were indispensable from those which were merely worthy. On the other hand, to go the whole way with Gladstone and sweep away all exemptions would not only handicap some useful enterprises but would invite increased pressure for public grants on behalf of agencies on which the Government had learned to depend. The conclusions of Messrs. Hicks and Gates were less revolutionary than their premises. What they proposed, in a word, was to give all charities some but not total exemption, a conclusion that was endorsed by three other members of the Commission in their long dissenting memorandum.[28]

3

The Royal Commission also scrutinized another category of income tax relief. This had to do with the special treatment given since the early 1920's to *donors*

---

[26] *Ibid.*, p. 56.

[27] "Reservation to Chapter 7," *ibid.*, pp. 352–53. The dissenters were Drummond Professor of Political Economy at Oxford and the Deputy Chairman of the Westminster Bank.

[28] Messrs. G. Woodcock, H. L. Bullock, and N. Kaldor, p. 417. The Hicks-Gates proposal was to tie the degree of exemption to the standard income tax rate. Specifically, all charities might be exempt up to 5s. in the £, after which they might pay at a rate equal to half the amount by which the standard rate exceeded 5s. With a rate, say, of 9s. in the £, charities would be liable for a tax of 2s.

to charity. The comparative advantage of the endowed over the voluntary charity, which Gladstone had deplored in the 1860's, had been wiped out, though certainly not in the fashion he had urged. Instead of imposing an income tax on charitable trusts, the State — quite inadvertently, to be sure — had made it possible for individual contributors to avoid paying a tax on the portion of their income given to charity. It was no part of the Government's intention to grant such a favor to donors. On the contrary, the concession was the wholly unforeseen result of a provision in the Revenue Act of 1922 designed to plug certain leaks in the flow of tax money. These had to do with the use of deeds of covenant, promises to pay for a specified term of years a sum of money out of an individual's income. It was an established principle that for tax purposes such sums could be deducted from the covenantor's income and added to that of the covenantee. The tax, in other words, would be paid by the recipient rather than by the giver. By the early '20's there was some concern lest this device develop into a mechanism for tax evasion, and into the Finance Act of 1922 was written a provision denying recognition to any covenant of less than six years.[29] Presumably this meant that one for more than six years was valid.

Like other productive ideas in the realm of charity, the original source of the seven-year covenant was Liverpool, and the earliest donor to make use of it was apparently one of the Rathbones, a family distinguished in the annals of local and national philanthropy.[30] That the 1922 Act could be made to serve the interests of charity was first sensed by Sir Godfrey Warr, son-in-law and solicitor to Hugh Rathbone, who pointed out the possibility to his father-in-law.[31] The critical point was that, although in the case of a covenant between two individuals, one of them was obliged to pay the tax, where the recipient was a charity no tax would be collected, since charity income was nontaxable. Transferring tax liability to a tax-exempt charity would, in effect, eliminate taxability altogether. Thus a donor who covenanted with a charitable organization to pay a given sum annually would deduct the standard income tax, certifying that he had done so. The charity would then be entitled to apply to Inland Revenue for a payment equivalent to that deducted by the donor and hence sufficient to bring the sum received up to the gross amount covenanted.

British charities saw their opportunity and exploited it, with the result that the seven-year covenant has become an important cog in the machinery of philanthropy. As the Royal Commission on Taxation noted, charitable enterprises had taken up the plan with enthusiasm; they encouraged donors to execute seven-year covenants; they explained the procedure and provided copies of the proper forms. In spite of the fact that a seven-year commitment is required, a measure of flexibility remains. Although a contributor must decide in advance what *sum* he

---

[29] 12 & 13 Geo. V, c. 17, s. 20.

[30] Some account of William Rathbone will be given in the pages on Liverpool philanthropy in Chapter XVI.

[31] H. R. Poole, *The Liverpool Council of Social Service, 1909–1959* (Liverpool, 1960), p. 46.

wishes to give to charity, he need not specify what individual *agencies* he proposes to benefit. He can make his covenant in favor of such an organization as the National Council of Social Service, which has established a special fund for the purpose, or one of the local councils and vary the objects of his philanthropy from year to year. Donors have made increasing use of these facilities. In 1953, to take a year at random, the Benevolent Fund of the National Council received approximately £250,000 in contributions under covenant, together with about £200,000 income tax on these contributions. A little over £450,000 was thus available for distribution to charities.[32]

The total amounts involved in seven-year covenants are impressive, even though since 1946 they have not served to reduce a subscriber's income for surtax purposes. In 1927 Inland Revenue paid out about £100,000 on account of seven-year covenants. By 1953–54 the figure approached £4 million and was made up of nearly 600,000 separate claims.[33] There has been some disposition to regard the seven-year covenant as hardly more than legalized tax evasion, and there have been doubts as to whether it is, in fact, a firm contract and whether trustees could take legal action against a defaulter. Such skepticism seems unjustified. Something like 90 per cent of the covenants appear to have been completed as scheduled, and included in the remaining tenth are a large number of cases where payment ceased because of the death of the covenantor. In spite of a certain dislike of the seven-year covenant in principle, the Royal Commission on Taxation thought it little abused in practice.[34]

4

If British charities had little cause to complain of their treatment under the income tax law, they enjoyed no such consideration with regard to legacies. At no time, from the first tentative introduction of a legacy duty in the early 1780's to the present, has the Government shown any disposition to distinguish between charitable and ordinary bequests. During the nineteenth century, in fact, charitable bequests were treated with exceptional severity and were liable to the maximum rate of duty — that is, the rate paid on bequests to those having no blood relationship to the testator. A legacy to a second cousin, for example, carried a lighter burden than one to Guy's Hospital.

Against the legacy duty the protests of charity interests were so feeble and sporadic as to have been almost negligible. In 1812 a motion to exempt charitable legacies was opposed by the Chancellor of the Exchequer on the ground that to give such encouragement to death bed bequests to charity might do injury to

---

[32] Natl. Council of Social Service, *Ann. Rept.,* 1953–54, p. 65.

[33] *R. C. on the Taxation of Profits and Income,* 1955, Par. 179. For three years ending September 1954, the annual amounts were £3,466,050, £3,812,628, and £3,749,620. Claims for repayment had grown from £294,306 in 1945–46 to £575,254 in 1953–54.

[34] *Ibid.,* Par. 182–84. The Commissioners were inclined to regard as preferable the American and Canadian procedure of giving the taxpayer an allowance for his charitable contributions, but they hesitated to recommend so drastic an alteration in the British system.

close relatives.[35] It was not until 1848 that the charities rallied for another attempt. The result was a petition from something over two hundred individuals and institutions in the metropolitan area. The petitioners found British policy less enlightened than those of the United States and Continental countries, where, they asserted, charitable legacies were allowed to pass untaxed. Nor did they hesitate to remind Parliament that philanthropic agencies relieved the State of responsibilities which must otherwise have fallen on the public purse.[36] This mid-century protest produced nothing beyond a brief and desultory debate in the Commons. The Chancellor of the Exchequer as guardian of the revenue and Sir Robert Peel as protector of the interests of testators' families declined to entertain any notion of reducing the duty.[37] The debate served only to make clear the fact that no one had even a vague notion of the revenue yielded by duties on charitable legacies, still less of the total amount that was passed on to charities by bequest.[38]

After this minor skirmish, there was little action. Harcourt's "death duties" Budget of 1894 produced some complaints and some tendency to ascribe an apparent falling-off in charitable bequests to the mounting imposts of the State.[39] The People's Budget of 1909 drew from the British Hospitals Association an appeal for exemption, which was given short shrift by the Chancellor of the Exchequer. It was inconceivable, Lloyd George replied crisply, that hospitals or any other single group of charities should be granted such a concession, however hard pressed they might be. In any case, they would suffer less than they imagined, he urged correctly enough, for charitable bequests were so generally made "free of duty" that it was the residuary legatee rather than the philanthropy that carried the burden.[40] But whatever the merits of the argument and counterargument, the truth is that British charities were never within striking distance of exemption from the legacy duty.

In 1949 the Labour Government simplified the death duty system. The result was a single inheritance tax, a graduated "estate duty" rising from one to eighty per cent and imposed on the principal value of all real or personal property which "passes" on death. No deduction is allowed for charitable bequests, though charitable gifts made one year or more before death are exempt — a provision which has been known to give charity officials a succession of anxious months. On occasion, the issue can be of material importance to the Government as well as to charity, as in the case of Calouste Gulbenkian. In the last year of his life the

[35] 1 Hansard, 21:319–20.

[36] This petition (dating from the spring of 1848) is in the London School of Economics Library.

[37] 3 Hansard, 100:1222–25.

[38] One by-product of the discussion was a statistical return from Inland Revenue giving the amounts of legacy duty paid at the various rates. Unfortunately the Board was unable to comply with the order of the Lords for the amount of legacy duty levied on bequests to charity. It was evidently impossible to separate charitable bequests from other bequests on which 10 per cent legacy duty had been collected. (Return to the House of Lords, 20 April 1848.)

[39] As in a letter from "Solicitor," in the Daily Telegraph, quoted in the Charity Record, 10 Sept. 1897.

[40] Ibid., 20 July 1912.

Armenian-born oil king founded the St. Sarkis Charitable and Religious Trust with shares valued at something over £300,000. Before the Trust had been established for a year, Gulbenkian died, and his gift thus became liable to estate duty.[41]

5

If the position of British philanthropies was reasonably clear with regard to income tax and legacy duty, their liability for local rates was another matter. This was an aspect of their fiscal obligations which never received statutory definition. The Elizabethan Poor Law, under which the poor rate was first imposed, offered no special guidance, though it was widely assumed that hospitals and other charitable institutions were exempt. The Act had merely authorized the Overseers of the Poor to raise a fund for the poor "by Taxation of every Inhabitant, Parson, Vicar and other, of every occupier of Lands, Houses, Tithes impropriate, Propriations of Tithes, Coal-Mines, or Saleable Underwoods." [42] Since charitable property had plainly not figured in the calculations of those who drafted the Act, only the courts could say whether or not it was legally rateable.

Judicial decisions, reinforced by custom in many parts of the country, inclined toward exemption of charity property, though even here there were counter-tendencies.[43] The principle most often invoked was that of "beneficial occupation": in order to be rateable, property must be "beneficially occupied" — that is, the occupier must derive pecuniary profit or personal advantage from his tenancy. It followed that property used purely for charitable purposes would be non-rateable, since there was no beneficial occupier — though school property seems not to have been so favored.[44] In establishing the principle of beneficial occupation, one of the more influential decisions was that of Lord Mansfield in the case of St. Bartholomew's the Less (1769). The local parish authorities attempted to impose on the St. Bartholomew Corporation £63 13s. in rates for new buildings which had been erected and for the hospital area created by pulling down a clump of old houses and shops. Lord Mansfield decided for the Hospital. The poor, he held, were the occupiers, and the poor were not rateable. "The general Rule of Law must be followed. That Rule is 'That you must *find an Occupier* to be rated.' The poor People (who are occupiers) *can not* be rated at all. The *Servants* can not be rated as *Occupiers:* Nor can the *Corporation* be charged, as Occupiers." [45]

Notwithstanding Mansfield's uncompromising decision, the rateability of charity property remained vague and uncertain. Local Improvement Acts sometimes included an exemption clause for charitable endowments, and in the mid-1840's

[41] *The Times,* 30 July 1955.
[42] 43 Eliz., c. 2, s. 1.
[43] *Tudor on Charities* (1906 ed.), p. 421.
[44] *S. C. on Public Establishments* (*Exemption from Rates*), 1857–58, Q. 962ff, 989ff. For American readers it should perhaps be recalled that in Britain local rates are normally paid by the occupier rather than the owner.
[45] *R.* v. *Inhabitants of St. Bartholomew's the Less,* 4 Burr 2435.

Parliament passed an Act specifically exempting property occupied by scientific and literary societies.[46] But parish authorities, especially in districts where hospitals, almshouses, churches, and other charitable institutions had proliferated, resented the notion that such establishments were entitled to immunity. In 1830 one of the City members introduced a bill designed to protect Bethlem and other Royal Hospitals from the exactions of parish officials.[47] Among opponents of the proposal there was a suspicion, not wholly baseless, that the resources of the Royal Hospitals were ample enough to cover ordinary parish rates. Why, it was asked, should Bethlem object, when Guy's had regularly met its obligation? Obviously such parishes as St. George's, Southwark, had a fiscal problem, especially when parish authorities were hesitant about challenging such prominent and affluent establishments as Bethlem. In the mid-century, in fact, twenty acres in St. George's were wholly exempt from rates, and the Overseers were much disturbed over the £6000 to £8000 assumed to have been lost annually by these immunities.[48]

During the first two-thirds of the century little was done to clarify the status of charity property, though some of the courts, notably Queen's Bench under Lord Campbell, tended to take a sterner view of exemptions. Yet legal decisions remained conflicting, and what happened in a particular situation depended, as much as anything, on local custom and the condition of the parish poor fund. Unfortunately for the charities, the question of their rateability got tangled in the courts with that of public establishments — dockyards and the like — and their special position received little attention. In 1857–58 a Select Committee of the House under the chairmanship of Sir George Cornewall Lewis, inquiring into the exemption of public establishments, reported in favor of a stiff policy for hitherto privileged institutions, public and charitable alike. The Committee would have abolished all exemptions, save for religious buildings, burial grounds, bridges, and a few other specified exceptions.[49]

The critical decision in altering the legal status of charity property, however, was that of the House of Lords in a case (or rather two cases) involving the Mersey docks, which, on the face of it, seemed to have no bearing on the rateability of hospitals and almshouses. The Liverpool Town Council was not unnaturally agitated by the exemption enjoyed by the docks which were operated under the Mersey Dock and Harbour Board and which accounted, it was estimated, for over £200,000 of rateable property.[50] There was little logic in the situation, for the Birkenhead docks across the river, managed by the same body, were unquestionably rateable.[51] When the local authorities proposed to rate the Liverpool

[46] 6 & 7 Vict., c. 36.
[47] No. 25 of 1830.
[48] 3 Hansard, 1:809–10; S. C. on Public Establishments, 1857–58, Q. 802ff, 989ff. The L.C.C. Survey of London, St. George's Fields, XXV (by Ida Darlington) documents the extraordinary concentration of charitable institutions in the area.
[49] S. C. on Public Establishments, 1857–58, p. ix.
[50] Ibid., Q. 764.
[51] Ibid., Q. 802.

docks, the Board resisted and managed to hold its position until the case reached the House of Lords on appeal.[52] Counsel for the Board argued that no beneficial occupation existed in the case of the docks, and, implying a similarity between the activities of the Board and those of a charitable institution, cited Lord Mansfield's opinions in the St. Bartholomew's and St. Luke's cases.[53] Where, he suggested, benefit was not confined to a particular locality or to a small, defined body of persons — that is, where the property was really public — it was not rateable.

Lord Westbury would have no commerce with such reasoning. Clearly his concern was to overrule the mass of previous decisions, including Mansfield's, which he considered ill-founded, conflicting, and impracticable. To Westbury no occupier was exempt save the Sovereign and the direct and immediate servants of the Crown. Such strict construction of 43 Elizabeth, c. 1, would obviously remove the exemption from the generality of property held for public purposes and from property held in trust for charitable purposes, "such as hospitals, or lunatic asylums, [which] are, in principle, rateable, notwithstanding that the buildings are actually occupied by paupers who are sick or insane." What emerged from the case was a drastic extension of the principle of "beneficial occupation." To be rateable, property need not be, in fact, beneficially occupied; it must be merely "capable of beneficial occupation" and, if let to a tenant, "capable of producing rent." In short, any property of commercial value was liable to rating, even though it might be used "under Acts of Parliament for the maintenance of works declared to be beneficial to the public."

It was bad luck for charities that they had been brought into the Mersey docks case at all. Obviously they had little in common with such an agency as the Mersey Dock and Harbour Board, but, given Westbury's interpretation of 43 Elizabeth, c. 1, there was little ground for excepting them. The significance of the decision was not lost on charity trustees, who at once took steps to protect their interests. At a public meeting, with Lord Shaftesbury in the chair, Archbishop Manning denounced the decision as contrary to the spirit of 43 Elizabeth.[54] Among attempts made in Parliament to mitigate the effect of the Westbury decision the most successful was an Act, passed over the opposition of Goschen, Gladstone's Chancellor of the Exchequer, exempting Ragged Schools and Sunday Schools.[55] But a bill, also introduced in 1869, to exempt hospitals had to be dropped, and the Government went so far as to threaten the abolition of all exemptions, save for churches and chapels.[56]

---

[52] (1866) 11 H.L.C. 443. There was some reason to think that the Act which created the Board had by implication exempted the trust from paying rates. In 1827 Lord Tenterden (following Lord Kenyon's decision in the Salters Lode Sluice case) held that, since Parliament had specified how any surplus of income over expense was to be disposed of and since poor rates were not explicitly mentioned, no part of the Board's monies should be so applied. This had the effect of exempting the docks from rates. (*S. C. on Public Establishments,* 1857–58, Q. 781–82, 799–801.)

[53] St. Luke's case (1760), 2 Burr 1053.

[54] *The Times,* 20 March 1867.

[55] 32 & 33 Vict., c. 40; *3 Hansard,* 196:1959ff.

[56] *Ibid.,* 195:1814–18.

Local authorities had no reason to hesitate further. Charitable institutions were now liable, and town officials, especially in the South, moved to gather the harvest. In Birmingham, for example, when charity trustees refused to pay a sum aggregating about £3000, distress warrants were issued and then a writ of *mandamus*.[57] It is impossible to make even an intelligent guess as to how generally charities were being rated in the 1870's and '80's. No doubt local officials were increasingly disposed to rate charity property, and their hands were strengthened by fresh court decisions.[58] Still, customary procedures which had been followed for a century or more did not give way readily, and in many places the exemption of charities continued to be taken for granted, or, if they were rated, it was only on a nominal valuation.

In fact, pressure from the Local Government Board was needed to bring some local authorities into line. A case in point was that of Liverpool, where the Town Council, though it had challenged the exemption of the Mersey Dock and Harbour Board, showed little interest in proceeding against bona fide charities. Liverpool opinion, official as well as public, was not eager to upset existing arrangements. And when in 1884 the Local Government Board auditor directed the Liverpool authorities to require payment of rates on charitable property, the Council clearly had little relish for the assignment. The charities were, of course, indignant, and their appeals against the assessments were treated with notable consideration by the local magistrates.[59] In London the managers of the large charities could summon only a moderate degree of sympathy for their Merseyside colleagues, since in the Metropolis they had been rated for a good many years, often heavily. Still, the Liverpool imbroglio seemed to open the way for concerted action against the state of affairs created by the Mersey Dock and Harbour decision. The impulse toward cooperation on the part of the Londoners was palpably strengthened by the Metropolitan Valuation Act, which closed another escape hatch. Overseers of the Poor, it appeared, had no authority to grant exemptions nor to list charitable property at a nominal value; they must deal with philanthropic institutions as with any other property.[60]

Late in 1885 some of the larger London hospitals took the lead in forming a Charities Rating Exemption Society, whose purpose was to regain the exemption from rates "which they enjoyed prior to the year 1866."[61] To achieve genuinely united action, however, seemed impossible. Institutions, among them one or two of the larger metropolitan hospitals, which felt themselves leniently treated by

---

[57] *The Times*, 5 Aug. 1870; *3 Hansard*, 206:593. It was this Birmingham crisis that lay behind the bill brought forward by Philip Muntz in May 1871. His proposal, in essence, was to leave the decision to the individual parish — that is, with the consent of the vestry, to exempt voluntary charities, together with hospitals and similar institutions — but the bill failed to survive a second reading. (*Ibid.*, 207:344–47)

[58] Notably a case involving St. Thomas's Hospital. (*Governors* v. *Stratton* [1875], 7 H.L.C. 477.)

[59] *S. C. on Hospitals (Exemption from Rates)*, 1900, Q. 729–36; *Charity Record*, 4 June and 17 September 1885; *Philanthropist*, October 1885, pp. 149–50.

[60] *Ibid.*, January 1886, pp. 5–6.

[61] *Charity Record*, 7 Jan. 1886.

local rating authorities, were not eager to call attention to their situation. A sharp difference of opinion thus emerged between those who could see no solution short of a definitive Act of Parliament and those who held to a more local and pragmatic approach.[62] The Liverpool charities had just demonstrated how effective the latter tactic could be, if aided by sympathetic officials. When the charity trustees protested against their assessments, the Liverpool magistrates responded by setting the valuation of their property at nil and thus maintaining their practical exemption.[63] Liverpool charities thus had good reason to doubt the wisdom of putting all their eggs in the basket of statutory exemption. They preferred to depend on the continued moderation of local authorities, applying such pressure as they could on behalf of individual charities in individual parishes. In the Metropolis, on the other hand, most of the institutions, having had less agreeable relations with rating authorities, could see no solution apart from an Act of Parliament. Of realizing this hope there was never a serious possibility. In 1886 and again in 1889, bills were introduced but failed to get beyond the earliest stages.[64]

The status of charity property, in short, remained about as it had been left by the Mersey Dock decision. In 1900 a Select Committee recommended exemption of hospitals, but the Royal Commission on Local Taxation promptly disagreed.[65] Even the Liverpool charities found their privileges crumbling when two out-townships were joined to the city and a uniform rating policy was introduced. This was not accomplished without a good deal of unpleasantness, protests to the magistrates, and seizure of property on the premises of at least one institution.[66] Yet even though attempts to alter the law had been spectacularly unsuccessful and though such islands of immunity as Liverpool gradually faded from view, English charities were still receiving special consideration at the hands of the rating authorities. In law, charity might be obligated to bear its share of the burden, but in practice it rarely felt the full weight of local taxation. In 1927, for example, charity properties were being rated well under their true values, generally at between 25 and 75 per cent.[67] Such valuations were far less favorable than the old-fashioned exemption or a merely nominal valuation, but they remained distinctly helpful.

Hit-or-miss procedures of this kind, however, became impossible after the Local Government Act of 1948 withdrew valuation powers from local authorities and vested them in the Board of Inland Revenue. Henceforth a uniform policy was to be applied to all property, charitable and otherwise, and many voluntary organizations faced the prospect of higher rates. Following the intercession of the

---

[62] Note, for example, the conflicting views of the *Philanthropist*, March 1886, and the *Charity Record*, 4 Feb. 1886.

[63] *S. C. on Hospitals*, 1900, Q. 730.

[64] *3 Hansard*, 305:701; 334:181.

[65] *S. C. on Hospitals*, 1900, p. iv; *R. C. on Local Taxation, Final Report* (Cd. 638), 1901, p. 50.

[66] *S. C. on Hospitals*, 1900, Q. 730; *The Times*, 11 July 1900, 22 Feb. 1902; *Charity Record*, 30 Oct. 1902.

[67] *Report of the Committee on the Rating of Charities and Kindred Bodies* (Cmnd. 831), 1959, Par. 21. This document (by the Pritchard Committee) gives an excellent summary of the entire problem. G. W. Keeton, *Modern Law of Charities*, chap. XVI, also analyzes the questions involved.

National Council of Social Service, the Government acted to offer some relief to apprehensive charities. Although, like most rating legislation, the Act of 1955 [68] was exceedingly complicated, the intentions of Section 8 with regard to charitable property are clear enough. The purpose was to maintain the existing level for charities during a period after the new valuation and to protect them against a sudden or excessive increase. This did well enough as a holding operation, but, the Pritchard Committee concluded four years later, as a permanent solution it was out of the question. What was called for, in the view of the Committee, was a uniform mandatory relief, and it recommended that, for the bulk of charities, this be set at 50 per cent.[69]

These categories — income tax, legacy duty, and local rates — cover most of the fiscal issues which have affected English charities. Measured by transatlantic notions, the British State has not been lavishly generous to charities. Only with regard to their incomes do British charitable organizations receive as favorable treatment as their American analogues, and even this did not go unchallenged. It was an article of faith on the part of the Victorians to question special privilege, even though privilege may sometimes have worked to the benefit of society. Charitable resources, it was argued, must therefore carry their proportionate share of the public load. Under British income tax law, charitable organizations themselves have managed well enough, but only for the past four decades and then only through the seven-year covenant have donors received concessions. Legacies, on the other hand, have been rigorously, almost punitively dealt with, while in the field of local taxation the traditional privileges of charities have been gradually eroded, though not entirely demolished.

Historically, as has been emphasized throughout this study, the well-being of British society has owed much to the benevolence of individuals. In spite of the many silly endowments which it fathered, philanthropy managed, through hospitals, almshouses, and schools, to meet a range of social needs now accepted as public responsibilities. In carrying out these quasi-public functions, British charities received a measure of encouragement from the State, but a measure which, for different reasons, neither critics nor friends thought wholly equitable. To anticipate a later chapter, during the past twenty years the dramatic expansion of the statutory services has altered the situation of charity and has, in some degree, weakened its traditional case for fiscal concessions. If, with the shift of the major responsibility for welfare from private to public agencies, the efforts of voluntary organizations have in fact become "highly desirable" rather than "indispensable," it would be quixotic to expect any substantial relaxation of the demands of the State. The premise is perhaps arguable — some voluntary activities remain nearly as essential, if not absolutely indispensable, as ever — but the conclusion can probably stand.

[68] Rating and Valuation (Miscellaneous Provisions) Acts, 4 & 5 Eliz. II, c. 9.
[69] *Pritchard Report*, Par. 84, 125. The Committee also recommended that the statutory exemption enjoyed by science societies (on the basis of the 1843 Act), voluntary schools (1944), and Sunday and Ragged Schools (1869) should be repealed.

CHAPTER XIII

PHILANTHROPY IN ACADEME

I N T H E hierarchy of eighteenth- and nineteenth-century philanthropic giving, higher education held a curious and uncertain position. Englishmen revealed no passion comparable to that of their transatlantic cousins for planting colleges and universities up and down the land. Nor for that matter did they approach the achievement of their own Tudor-Stuart ancestors, whose charity "literally founded a system of secular education in England . . . more competent and comprehensive than the nation was to possess again until deep in the nineteenth century."[1] Despite their ringing anthems in praise of education, the Victorians and their immediate predecessors had no such disinterested and sacrificial belief in its value. The charity school movement of the eighteenth century and the school societies of the nineteenth, as we have seen, enlisted widespread support, but during most of the period comprehended by this study, institutions of higher learning did not figure heavily in the calculations of philanthropic Britain.

Exceptions will come to mind at once. In the eighteenth-century Oxford acquired another college, Worcester, and Cambridge, Downing. In the nineteenth, Hertford was rehabilitated, and two new men's colleges took their places at Oxford and Cambridge respectively — these in addition to the six women's colleges founded at the ancient universities before 1900.[2] Earlier in the century the institutions that were to form the nucleus of London University made some appeal to the benevolent, and after 1850 the foundation of a half-dozen provincial colleges were laid, monuments to civic pride and middle-class dissatisfaction with the old universities, as well as a response to the growing demand of British industrialism for technical training. In these newer institutions certain philanthropic capitalists invested heavily, directly or posthumously. The names of John Owens and Sir Joseph Whitworth of Manchester come to mind at once, along with those of Sir Josiah Mason of Birmingham and Mark Firth of Sheffield, and, although he was

---

[1] Jordan, *Philanthropy in England,* p. 279. In the years 1480–1660, Englishmen devoted nearly 27 per cent of their benefactions to educational purposes — with Elizabethan donors the figure went to nearly a third — far more than was given for religious objects or social rehabilitation during the period. The newly established grammar schools accounted for about 14½ per cent (in Lancashire about 32 per cent), and the universities received nearly 7½ per cent. (*Ibid.,* pp. 282–83, 289, 295.)

[2] Two at Cambridge and four at Oxford.

not, like the others, a municipal philanthropist, Thomas Holloway and his college for young women. But most of this activity developed in the late century after the new urban centers had gained a certain maturity and cultural self-consciousness and industrialists had attained a breadth of vision which allowed them to look beyond ledgers and machines.

What seems indisputable is that, if there was a stream of academic philanthropy, relatively little of it flowed into the Isis or the Cam. With the exception of a few large gifts and bequests, such as Dr. Radcliffe's to Oxford in the early eighteenth century and Lord Fitzwilliam's to Cambridge a century later, neither university nor its colleges profited heavily from benefactions, nor, save when it was necessary to deal with some urgent crisis, did they solicit such aid. A celibate Fellow might leave a few hundred pounds (or even his entire estate) to his college, or Fellows' widows might remember the foundation, but it would have seemed absurd to an early Victorian that 1s. 6d. out of each £1 contributed to charity in Tudor-Stuart times should have gone to the universities. For almost half of the period that concerns us, the ancient universities, "for the most part sunk in a learned torpor,"[3] were cozy communities of clerical Fellows, who, it was taken for granted, could get along well enough on the yield from their estates, save, perhaps, when new buildings were required. Given the accepted notion of universities, their functions and responsibilities, this was not an unreasonable assumption.

The suspicion that, until well toward the end of the nineteenth century, the flow of benevolence to the older universities was not much more than a trickle is confirmed by scrutiny of the endowments of individual colleges. A review of the benefactions received by a sample group of Cambridge colleges[4] — three of the wealthier (King's, St. John's, and Trinity) and two of the less affluent (St. Catharine's and Magdalene) — failed to modify the picture in any essential particular, and it is doubtful whether a larger sample, which would have included some of the "middling" foundations, would have changed it. One finds isolated gifts and bequests — £20,000 to Peterhouse in 1817, from which Gisborne Court was built, and £25,000 to Clare in 1867, which financed two fellowships and five scholarships[5] — but such gifts were exceptional. Christ's College could report no considerable benefaction from the mid-eighteenth to the mid-twentieth century.[6] The author of the earlier philanthropy was Christopher Tancred, the Yorkshire squire already mentioned, whose almshouse for twelve decayed gentlemen, endowed with half of his estate, became one of the scandals of the charity world. Perhaps the twelve studentships to which he assigned the balance of his property — four in Divinity at Christ's, four in Physic at Caius, and

---

[3] V. H. H. Green, *Oxford Common Room* (London, 1957), p. 11.

[4] My choice of Cambridge rather than Oxford was partly accidental and partly the result of a somewhat greater familiarity with the former. It is also true that, as far as I am aware, J. W. Clark's helpful *Endowments of the University of Cambridge* (Cambridge, 1904), has no Oxford analogue.

[5] *Victoria County History, Cambridge*, III, J. P. C. Roach, ed. (London, 1959), 338, 342.

[6] *Ibid.*, p. 430.

four in Law at Lincoln's Inn — were sufficiently meritorious to take the curse off the other bequest.[7]

For King's, St. John's, and Trinity the theme showed only minor variations. The bulk of the King's College estates had been acquired in the mid-fifteenth century, and, although extended by gifts and bequests, there were few major changes, and virtually none between 1750 and 1914.[8] Most of the additions to the King's endowment were bequests from Fellows of the College, largely for specific purposes, such as a building fund (the debt on the Gibbs Building was not entirely wiped out until 1768, thirty-five years after occupancy had begun),[9] prizes, or upkeep of the Chapel, one of the perennial anxieties of the King's Fellows. A former Fellow, the Reverend Joseph Davidson, gave some £11,000 in all, by far the largest benefaction received by the College in the period studied. Part of this gift forms the basis of the maintenance fund for the Chapel.[10] Another former Fellow left (1866) £200, which is used for a brass standard for lights in the Chapel; a former Vice-Provost bequeathed £168 for choristers; and Dr. Thackeray, the powerful and determinedly conservative Provost of the first half of the nineteenth century, left £2000 to the Chapel for repairs and embellishment. He also, incidentally, left £300 to purchase plate for the Provost's Lodge, with the injunction that "my arms (in conjunction with those of the said College) be engraved on every piece of plate to be purchased as aforesaid." [11]

The records of St. John's benefactions are unusually complete and accessible, and they supply a reasonably solid basis for generalization.[12] Although in the eighteenth century the College appears to have been more fortunate than some other foundations, its benefactions conformed to the familiar pattern. They came largely from Masters and Fellows, and none was of startling dimensions — a number of advowsons, books for the library, endowment for exhibitions or studentships, or a fund for the upkeep of buildings. The nineteenth century repeats the story in essentials, though with some interesting variants. In 1817 the Regius Professor of Physic and Senior Fellow left £200 a year, urging that his money be used by the College to "execute with greater efficiency the visitatorial powers it then possessed over the schools of Sedbergh, Pocklington, and Rivington." Inasmuch as Pocklington was singled out by the Brougham Commissioners for distinctly unfavorable notice, Sir Isaac Pennington's concern seems not misplaced. Sometimes wealthy Fellows dealt with the College less than generously. In the late 1840's, for example, £5000 was received from an estate of £140,000 and only £1000 from one approaching £250,000, which was left by a Justice

---

[7] Some account of the Tancred charity has been given in Chapter XI above.

[8] *VCH, Cambridge*, III, 379–80.

[9] *Ibid.*, p. 392.

[10] King's College, *Trust Funds* (1875).

[11] *Ibid.*

[12] A. F. Torry, *Founders and Benefactors of St. John's College* (Cambridge, 1888) and the supplementary list kept in the bursary give all the essential information. I should like to acknowledge the helpfulness of the Master and the bursary in making the data available to me.

of King's Bench. On one occasion the College profited handsomely from the fact that a John's man served as executor for a philanthropic testator who had merely stipulated that his £27,000 estate was to be used for scholarships and studentships.

The benefactions which accomplished most for St. John's in the Victorian Age were gifts and legacies aggregating nearly £65,000 from James Wood, thirty-first Master of the College (1815–39) and Dean of Ely. Wood himself came of humble Lancashire origins and entered as a sizar. But his talents were considerable, and he achieved the double distinction of becoming Senior Wrangler and Smith's Prizeman.[13] He was the largest contributor to the Fourth Court of the College, reputedly giving £15,000, and he endowed exhibitions to the amount of £9000. As residuary legatee of Wood's estate, the College received about £40,000. Wood's benefactions not only comprise a significant chapter in Victorian academic philanthropy but also offer a suggestive commentary on the prizes to be gained from a successful conquest of preferments in the clerical-university world of Georgian times.

The Trinity situation has been succinctly described by the former Senior Bursar in terms which, one suspects, would be broadly applicable to the generality of Oxford and Cambridge colleges. Although gifts for special purposes were not unknown and were being received in increasing amounts during the nineteenth century, these had little to do with the day-to-day support of the College. Until the end of the century, says Mr. Nicholas, "so far as corporate revenue was concerned . . . the College continued to depend almost wholly upon the income produced by its ancient possessions, four-fifths of which was derived from agricultural land, either as farm rents or tithe rent-charge." [14] As long as land values were rising, agriculture was prosperous, and education proceeded largely in the simple, well-worn mathematical and classical channels, the College did not only well but handsomely. Like other foundations at both universities, the Trinity Fellows (though suffering less than King's or St. John's) learned a hard but salutary lesson in the agricultural depression of the 1880's.[15] To put such heavy reliance on the prosperity of a single industry was inviting disaster, and they moved gradually to diversify the investments of the College.

Henry VIII's Foundation did conspicuously well at the hands of its friends. Like those of the other Houses, Trinity benefactors were generally Masters or Fellows, and they gave or bequeathed, with some notable exceptions, relatively small sums for particular purposes — buildings, scholarships, or prizes. Two nineteenth-century Masters, Christopher Wordsworth and William Whewell, followed the example of their great predecessor Thomas Nevile (1593–1615) by

[13] D. A. Winstanley, *Early Victorian Cambridge* (Cambridge, 1955), p. 25.

[14] Tressilian C. Nicholas, "The Endowments of Trinity College, 1546–1914," *Trinity Review*, Michaelmas, 1959, p. 14.

[15] As, for example, did St. John's, *VCH, Cambridge*, III, 446; Queens', *ibid.*, p. 411; Christ's, *ibid.*, p. 435. Colleges with London property, such as Emmanuel (p. 479) seem to have been under less pressure.

making possible respectively the construction of King's Court and Whewell's Court.[16] In the latter half of the century one Vice-Master left two estates, the income to be used for lectures in English literature, and another bequeathed about £7000 for research in the natural sciences.[17] Of all the pre-1914 benefactions for special purposes, the most imposing was upwards of £50,000 from A. W. G. Allen. The fund was designated as endowment for additional fellowships to be called Ely Fellowships in memory of Allen's grandfather, who had been Lord Bishop of Ely and a Fellow of the College.

These increments were dwarfed by a windfall which in 1909 landed in the lap of the College. Not only was the bequest from Sir William Pearce, Bart., a Glasgow shipbuilder who had been at Trinity in the early '80's, enormous and unexpected, but it was also unrestricted as to purpose. There were complications, however. Although the bequest had been valued at better than £200,000, income was almost lacking, for the bulk of the estate consisted of common stock in two large armament and shipbuilding firms, which at the time were passing dividends in wholesale fashion. Rather than selling the shares for immediate income, the Fellows had the good judgment to hold on until the war enabled them to dispose of their holdings at fancy prices and to lay out the proceeds in less speculative stock. Actually the Pearce bequest had something of a revolutionary effect on Trinity finance. Here for the first time the College had in its own control a substantial block of negotiable securities, and had thus taken a long step away from the reliance on agriculture which had caused so much grief in the '90's.[18]

Since 1914 Trinity's benefactions, both to the Foundation itself and for special purposes, have mounted. One Fellow leaves £10,000, another £25,000, and a Vice-Master (D. A. Winstanley) the whole of his £45,000 estate. Among benefactions for special purposes one is notable not only for its size but also the aims of its donor. The philanthropist was W. W. Rouse Ball, a Fellow of the College, who not only established professorships in mathematics and English law, but who bequeathed (1927) to Trinity a total of over £100,000 chiefly for the promotion of research among members of the College under thirty. The Rouse Ball bequest has been used principally to finance the Junior Research Fellowships, which have added to Trinity's already great distinction as a center of research, especially in mathematics and the natural sciences.

St. Catharine's and Magdalene duplicate, in outline, the pattern traced by the more opulent colleges, though on a much smaller scale. Between 1700 and 1914 St. Catharine's received only a single benefaction of consequence. This came in the mid-eighteenth century at a time when the prestige of the College was slipping away, and, indeed, it is more than likely that Mrs. Mary Ramsden's legacy of her Yorkshire estates of nearly seventeen hundred acres prevented the dissolution

---

[16] Save where otherwise indicated, the information on Trinity is drawn from the *Commemoration of Benefactors*.

[17] W. G. Clark and Coutts Trotter.

[18] Nicholas, "The Endowments of Trinity College, 1914–1959," *Trinity Review*, Lent, 1960, p. 23.

of the College.[19] The property, which in the 1770's was bringing an income of £800 to £1000, was to provide six fellowships, ten scholarships, and twelve new sets of chambers. Yet, like other well-intentioned benefactors before and since, Mrs. Ramsden, obviously a strong-minded lady, almost nullified her charity by an absurdly detailed and restrictive set of "Rules and Orders," [20] which, by prescribing minutely for her new foundation, virtually created within the College a separate and self-contained body of Fellows. The Skerne Fellows, as the beneficiaries of her legacies were termed, received fixed stipends prescribed by the foundress, and much of the time these were below the income of the Foundation Fellows. As a result, if Mrs. Ramsden's benefaction rescued St. Catharine's from threatened destruction, it also equipped the College for a half century of unstable and quarrelsome existence.[21]

Magdalene's *Commemoration of Benefactors* reveals a larger number of gifts and bequests, but only one or two catch the eye by reason of size or novelty. With the exception of the Pepys Library, bequeathed in 1703, most of the benefactions were the conventional tributes from Master, President, or Fellows for augmenting fellowships, establishing prizes, or founding scholarships. A late eighteenth-century Master, however, Peter Peckard, who was also Dean of Peterborough, introduced one interesting variant. In addition to leaving property for founding scholarships and augmenting Master's and Fellows' dividends, he bequeathed £400 to accumulate for 112 years. It is agreeable to record that in 1923 the College established the Peckard Fellowship from the century-old bequest.[22]

Between the World Wars, Magdalene fortunes took something of a turn for the better. There was a contribution of £11,500 toward the Lutyens Building and £13,800 from the widow of Rudyard Kipling, who had been an Honorary Fellow.[23] But the most splendid series of Magdalene benefactions, as with other colleges, was identified with the name of a Master, in this instance A. C. Benson. As Vice-Master he had been busy with projects for improving the College architecturally and academically, and when in 1915 he was elected to the Mastership, Magdalene resources were augmented in a curious fashion. A wealthy American woman living in Switzerland, whom Benson had never met but who had found comfort in his books and in the letters with which he answered hers, offered to assist in his schemes for the College. Presently she turned over some £45,000 in cash and securities, and, in the words of Benson's brother, "his magnificent vicarious gifts to Magdalene began." [24] The anonymous benefactress later added

---

[19] St. Catharine's *Commemoration of Benefactors*; W. H. S. Jones, *History of St. Catharine's College* (Cambridge, 1936), pp. 267, 387, 390. In the autumn of 1920, the College sold about 850 acres for approximately £45,000. (*Ibid.*, p. 403).

[20] Reprinted *ibid.*, pp. 114ff.

[21] *VCH, Cambridge*, III, 417.

[22] *Ibid.*, p. 451.

[23] Magdalene College *Commemoration of Benefactors*.

[24] E. F. Benson, *Final Edition* (New York, 1940), p. 133.

£20,000, and the Master saw within his reach the wherewithal for virtually re-
founding the College.

With the unseen Lady Bountiful so committed to his plans, it is impossible to
separate Benson's own philanthropies from those in which he was merely acting
as her deputy. In any case the results for Magdalene were salutary. He founded
exhibitions, he planned Mallory Court on the farther side of Magdalene Street,
and he established a lectureship and a series of bye-fellowships. At his death in
1925, the College inherited more than £38,000, together with the copyright of his
published works.[25] There is little to indicate whether the legacy represented only
Benson's personal fortune or whether it may have included a residue of the lady's
two benefactions. If the former, the Master had himself been responsible for en-
riching the College by more than £100,000, and if the latter, by presumably no
less than £75,000. Whichever is the case, Benson is entitled to recognition as
primary agent in the rehabilitation of Magdalene — and the anonymous woman
philanthropist as his indispensable ally.

2

If Oxford and Cambridge colleges, by and large, could manage well enough on
their earlier endowments, the universities themselves were in a wholly different
situation. This is not the place to recall the attack of Victorian reformers on
education at the old universities and on their merits and shortcomings as centers
of learning. The controversy raised issues of collegiate strength and university
weakness, of teaching and research, and of the tutorial and professorial functions.
From the mid-nineteenth century on, with the encouragement of two Royal
Commissions in the 1850's and another in the '70's, a clear trend set in toward
strengthening the universities and requiring the colleges to provide more adequate
support for the undernourished central body.

This movement, however, was paralleled by no startling outpouring of fresh
wealth for professorships, research, or university buildings. Again, to look somewhat more closely at Cambridge,[26] in the course of the eighteenth century three
or four professorships had been established from property left to the University for
the purpose.[27] The early nineteenth century revealed no quickening pace. Not
until after mid-century (omitting the Downing Professorships of Law and Medicine which were established by a collegiate rather than a university benefaction)
was a new professorship founded at Cambridge. Then in the late '60's, the
Reverend Joseph Bosworth, Rawlinson Professor of Anglo-Saxon at Oxford (but
a Trinity man), provided £10,000 for a similar chair at Cambridge, and Felix
Slade bequeathed £45,000 for his famous Professorships of Fine Art at Oxford,
Cambridge, and London. After the turn of the century a new element is injected

[25] *Commemoration of Benefactors.*
[26] For which, to repeat, J. W. Clark's *Endowments* provides a guide.
[27] The Woodwardian Professorship in Geology, the Lowndean in Astronomy and Geometry, and
the Jacksonian in Natural Philosophy.

into Cambridge philanthropy when a business firm, the banking house of J. Henry Schröder & Company, endowed (1909) a chair of German, and in the following year Harold Harmsworth (Lord Rothermere) founded the King Edward VII Professorship of English Literature. From the will of John Lucas Walker (1887) the University received £10,000 for a studentship in pathology, Frank McClean endowed three Isaac Newton studentships with £12,000, and A. W. G. Allen (who also bestowed about £50,000 on Trinity College) left £10,000 for a University scholarship.[28]

Donors also established a number of University prizes, sometimes, one gathers, for the rewarding of disinterested scholarship and sometimes to encourage the propagation of views congenial to the benefactor. In the latter category there comes to mind the offer in 1845 of £500 by a servant of the East India Company for the best "Refutation of Hinduism, and Statement of the Evidences of Christianity in a Form suited to the Hindus." In the mid-'70's the will of a former Fellow of St. Catharine's left nearly £4000 for two half-yearly prizes for essays "upon the consistency or inconsistency of the law of primogeniture with the dictates of nature as well as with the spirit and precepts of the Christian religion: regard being had [as to] how far such law in its practical operation is in conformity with the reciprocal obligations so beautifully taught by our blessed Lord and Saviour in his answer to the question of the Lawyer as recorded in St. Matthew's Gospel 22nd chapter 30th verse." [29] The Masters of Trinity and Magdalene, who had been designated as trustees, backed off from the testator's conditions, and the University accepted the Yorke Prize only after Chancery had framed a scheme providing an award for an essay relating to the principles and history of the law of property. But for the historian of charities the Yorke Prize stands as a capital example of how even the eccentric, hobby-riding bequest can sometimes yield serviceable results. One of the first essays to win the award was Courtney Kenny's brilliant study of charity law and its needed reform.[30]

New university buildings might reflect either the bounty of individual benefactors or the collective effort of a subscription list. At Oxford the executors of the fabulously successful court physician Dr. Radcliffe, who died in 1714 and whose will included a series of handsome benefactions for his own college (University), supplied the University itself with the Radcliffe Library, Infirmary, and Observatory.[31] At Cambridge the building of the Senate House (1719–34) was financed by a subscription list headed by George I (£2000) and George II (£3000) and

[28] It is impossible not to notice the high proportion of University benefactors from Trinity College. The Royal Foundation was, of course, by far the largest of the colleges, but it is also possible that Trinity graduates were either more affluent or more university-minded than the generality of Cambridge men.

[29] Clark, *Endowments*, pp. 410ff.

[30] *True Principles of Legislation* . . . , of which some account has been given in Chapter XI.

[31] C. E. Mallet, *A History of the University of Oxford*, 3 vols. (London, 1924–27), III, 141–42. For the will and history of the Radcliffe foundations, see J. B. Nias, *Dr. John Radcliffe* (Oxford, 1918), pp. 101–38; and, more briefly, Campbell R. Hone, *The Life of Dr. John Radcliffe, 1652–1714* (London, 1950), chap. VII.

totaling £10,860.[32] For extensive additions to the University Library made in the mid-eighteenth century Cambridge depended on a group of something over fifty subscribers. George II (£3000) and the Duke of Newcastle (£1000) were the leading names on a list composed of dignitaries in Church and State who, with two small additional legacies, provided about £10,250.[33] Subscribers raised about £23,500 for Cockerell's Building (1837–40), and an unrestricted bequest of over £10,000 financed the Hancock Building. The Divinity School was the gift of William Selwyn, Lady Margaret Professor of Divinity, from whom £10,500 was received for the purpose. In the domain of the physical sciences, Richard Sheepshanks and his sister contributed £12,000 for improving the Observatory and promoting the study of astronomy, and the Duke of Devonshire, Chancellor of the University for thirty years (1861–91), built the Cavendish Laboratory, which was opened in 1874, at a cost of £6300. It would only be stating a commonplace to add that rarely has an academic investment returned more princely dividends.

What was called at the turn of the twentieth century the greatest single benefaction in either university "since Colleges ceased to be established by pious founders" came to Cambridge in 1816 by the will of Lord Fitzwilliam.[34] In addition to his pictures, engravings, and books, he left to the University the sum of £100,000 in South Sea annuities, with instructions that the proceeds be used for a building to house his collection. Owing to complications about the site, as well, perhaps, as a desire to allow dividends to accumulate for a time, construction was not actually begun until 1837 when some £40,000 in interest had been added. The new building, of which George Basevi was the architect, proceeded slowly, and not until 1848 was it sufficiently near completion to allow the collection to be installed.[35] The early history of the Fitzwilliam was not altogether placid, but no one would doubt that the noble benefactor had practiced far-seeing and productive philanthropy.[36]

Although during the late century the two universities developed a more genuine institutional existence and began to redress the balance between the One and the Many, they were still inadequately financed. After the Royal Commissions of the 1850's the colleges contributed, some of them substantially, to the university, and from '70's on, they were required to pay into a Common University Fund a fixed percentage of their income.[37] This was not sufficient, especially with the development of lecturing as a university, rather than a college, function, but until the turn of the century no serious consideration had been given at either Oxford or Cambridge to the possibility of an endowment fund for general university purposes. Cambridge was first in the field with its Cambridge University Association,

[32] Clark, *Endowments,* pp. 465ff.
[33] The list is printed *ibid.,* pp. 455–56.
[34] H. E. Malden, *Trinity Hall* (London, 1902), p. 201. The benefactor was the seventh Viscount Fitzwilliam of Meryon (1745–1816), a Trinity Hall graduate, and not one of the Earls Fitzwilliam.
[35] Winstanley, *Early Victorian Cambridge,* p. 140. On Basevi's death in 1845, Charles Robert Cockerell took over the architect's duties.
[36] See *ibid.,* chap. IX.
[37] Winstanley, *Later Victorian Cambridge* (Cambridge, 1947), pp. 318ff.

whose object was "to procure the better endowment of the University as a place of education, religion, learning, and research."[38] The appeal of the Association met with a degree of success. By 1903–1904 about £72,000 had been raised, of which £53,000 was unrestricted. The list was headed by the Chancellor (the Duke of Devonshire), W. W. Astor, and the House of Rothschild — each contributing £10,000 — and contained about three hundred names, most of whom had close connection with the University.[39]

The Oxford re-endowment drive owed a good deal to Lord Curzon, who as Chancellor declined to regard his office as merely honorific. His predecessor Goschen, characteristically enough, had interested himself in matters of University finance and of College-University relations, and T. A. Brassey, who had led a movement to add to the Balliol endowment, had already made some progress toward an endowment fund for the University.[40] At this point, in the spring of 1907, Curzon's election to the Chancellorship, with all of his restless energy and organizing gifts, assured the launching of a re-endowment appeal. Yet the new venture by no means revolutionized Oxford finance. Curzon's biographer is only stating the simple fact when he calls the campaign "rather a modest than a brilliant success."[41] Few large sums came in, and few large individual benefactors emerged. Although at the outset the drive seemed to be moving splendidly toward its target of £250,000, in the end less than £150,000 was raised, and of this some £33,000 was contributed by two of the City Companies, the Drapers and the Goldsmiths.[42] On the whole, the historian must write off the Oxford, like the Cambridge, endowment appeal as a helpful but not profoundly significant innovation.

Both universities emerged from the first World War in a precarious financial position and without the resources needed to meet the greater and more varied demands of the post-war world. College authorities and others became persuaded that a public grant offered the only way out, and, although few welcomed the prospect of accepting government money, they inclined to the view of the Master of Trinity who held "that the only alternative was to lose the efficiency of the University, and much as he disliked the receipt of money from the Government he disliked still more the idea of an inefficient University."[43] Emergency grants took care of the crisis temporarily, but a Royal Commission (1919–22) recommended annual grants of £100,000 (together with certain supplementary payments) to each of the ancient universities. The Commission was not entirely happy about its own proposal, and there was some expectation — or wishful thinking — that public grants would not be permanently needed. The views of

[38] Clark, *Endowments*, p. 597.

[39] *Ibid.*, pp. 598–608.

[40] Mallet, *History of Oxford*, III, 477; Earl of Ronaldshay, *The Life of Lord Curzon*, 3 vols. (London, 1928), III, 91–92; *The Times*, 2 May 1907; *Bodleian Quarterly Record*, II (January 1920), 296–97.

[41] Ronaldshay, *Lord Curzon*, III, 94.

[42] Mallet, *Oxford*, III, 477, n. 2.

[43] Quoted in *VCH, Cambridge*, III, 290.

Asquith Commission on the universities, in fact, had something in common with those of the Cave Committee of 1921, which attempted to prop up the tottering structure of voluntary hospitals. Although the Hospitals Committee was obliged to recommend assistance from the public funds, "any proposals for continuous rate or State aid should be rejected," while the Universities Commission, if less committed to the voluntary principle, still held "the real hope of future prosperity and development for the Universities" to lie in private benefactions.[44] Neither group proved to have the gift of prophecy. As it turned out, the Cave Committee marked a stage on the road that led ultimately to the National Health Service, while the Asquith Commission prepared the way for the University Grants Committee.

3

In the founding of new institutions the most significant steps (save in women's education) were being taken not at the ancient universities but in the Metropolis and the industrial cities of the provinces. Even so, during the two centuries Oxford acquired three new men's colleges and Cambridge two. At Oxford, Worcester College came into being through £10,000 left in 1701 by William Cookes, a Worcestershire baronet.[45] Hertford College had expired at the turn of the nineteenth century, and not until 1874 was Magdalen Hall, which in a curious fashion had succeeded it, transmuted by an Act of Parliament into a new Hertford College. Here the crucial benefactor was Thomas Baring, whose gift of an endowment for seventeen fellowships and thirty scholarships of £100 a year really effected the revival of the College. He had made his offer originally to Brasenose, but with such ecclesiastical strings attached that the Fellows felt obliged to decline it. The sponsors of Hertford were hardly in a position to be so scrupulous, and they accepted the Baring money on a semi-compromise basis.[46]

Two of the new Victorian foundations, Keble at Oxford and Selwyn at Cambridge, fall into a special category. Both were Church-oriented and were designed as institutions in which young men "now debarred from University Education" might be "trained in simple and religious habits." [47] Neither was the handiwork of an individual founder. The Keble promoters were able to raise £50,000 with relative ease, and the foundation stone was laid in 1868. Three years later the disconcerting Butterfield Gothic building was ready to receive students. Selwyn College, modeled on Keble and founded to commemorate the

[44] *Voluntary Hospitals Committee* (Cmd. 1335), 1921, p. 8; *R. C. on Oxford and Cambridge Universities* (Cmd. 1588), 1922, p. 54.

[45] Mallet, *Oxford*, III, 95–102.

[46] *Ibid.*, 423–26; Hastings Rashdall, "Hertford College," in Andrew Clark, *The Colleges of Oxford* (London, 1891), p. 459. Baring also imposed restrictions other than ecclesiastical, in favor of the county of Middlesex, Harrow School, founder's kin, and the sons of past Fellows of Hertford and B.N.C. — precisely the kind of thing, as Mallet observes, that the University Commission was doing its best to eradicate.

[47] Resolution of the Lambeth Palace meeting which launched the scheme for Keble Collegem quoted in Mallet, *Oxford*, III, 427.

pioneer Bishop of New Zealand, had harder sledding at the outset, but by 1881 about £30,000 was in hand.[48] The bulk of it came in small contributions — £3000 was by far the largest benefaction — and obviously from a Church constituency. With the laying of the cornerstone in June 1881 the new college was launched, not without arousing, as had Keble, some suspicion and hostility in the University. For it took courage, not to say temerity, only six years after the abolition of religious tests (for fellowships and professorships) to establish a college open only to conforming members of the Church of England.

Of all the new foundations during the period of this study, Downing College, Cambridge, has special claims on the historian of philanthropy. Not only does it offer the most characteristic example of the work of an individual founder, but, had circumstances been different, conceivably the Downing experiment might have pointed the way to reform throughout the University. About the Downing statutes there was much that was modern, tolerant, and liberal, but during its early decades, through no fault of its own, the College was little better than moribund and in no condition to exert any reforming influence. Thus, Winstanley remarks, "What was intended to be an encouragement of reform became a warning against it."[49]

The bequest that created Downing College was that of Sir George Downing (1684–1749), third baronet, but the estates were chiefly those accumulated by his grandfather, the first baronet. The elder Sir George, nephew of Governor John Winthrop of Massachusetts Bay and the second graduate of Harvard College, had an active and immensely lucrative career under both Cromwell and Charles II. The will of his grandson, made in 1717, left all of his considerable estates in Cambridgeshire, Bedfordshire, and Suffolk to a succession of cousins. In event of a failure of issue, the property was to be used to establish a college in Cambridge to be called Downing's College. We cannot trace the melancholy proceedings that followed the death in 1764 of the last eligible cousin. It is enough to say that, although judgment was rendered in favor of the College in 1769, the case was not finally settled for another thirty-one years, owing to resistance from other relatives. Delay followed delay, and frustration succeeded frustration, until it all seemed like a parody of an action in Chancery. By the time (1800) the Lord Chancellor finally pronounced in favor of the University, the costs of litigation and neglect of the estates had made heavy inroads on the College income. In 1802 the property was yielding about £6000 a year in rents.[50]

One would expect the Downing charter and statutes to mark a sharp break with the ancient formulas which governed the life of older Cambridge communities. After all, this was the first new college to be established since the foundation of Sidney Sussex at the end of the sixteenth century. But some of the Downing innovations, as well as the secular tone pervading the statutes, are striking in their

[48] A. L. Brown, *Selwyn College, Cambridge* (London, 1906), pp. 32–37.
[49] Winstanley, *Early Victorian Cambridge*, p. 7.
[50] *VCH, Cambridge*, III, 487–88.

modernity. The tradition, stated as fact by the Downing historian, is that "the general outline of the foundation is due to the younger Pitt," though there is no positive evidence to support this congenial belief.[51]

Whatever its source, the statutes diagnosed soundly enough some of the shortcomings of eighteenth-century Cambridge and made provision for avoiding them in the new foundation. In addition to the Master and Fellows, there was to be a professor of medicine and a professor of the laws of England, two branches of study which at the time were in less than flourishing condition. The majority of the fellowships, open only to laymen, were tenable for only twelve years, in the course of which both legal and medical Fellows must qualify professionally.[52] Lay fellowships, in a word, were designed as temporary assistance to younger men actively engaged in professional preparation, and were not intended as permanent refuges nor as a pleasurable interval between the taking of the degree and translation to a college living. Finally, both fellowships and scholarships were freed from some of the traditional restrictions. Any Oxford or Cambridge graduate, regardless of "place of birth or education," was eligible for a lay fellowship.[53] The Downing constitution not only provided for the award of fellowships and scholarships upon examination, but, in an attempt to break the monopoly of mathematics at Cambridge, permitted candidates to offer the classics and other subjects.

Unhappily the Downing plan, rational and promising as it was, never received a fair test. Throughout the century the College was desperately poor, the result in part of inept management by Chancery, which, unaffected by the shrinkage of the Downing estate during the years of litigation, approved building plans costing about £100,000, and directed that £3000 a year be set aside as a building fund.[54] This was a disastrous requirement, for it condemned the College to a hand-to-mouth existence, without usable endowment, scholarships, or exhibitions, and at times almost without undergraduates. In the latter part of the century, income sank to an extremely low level and the enrollment of undergraduates almost to the vanishing point. Not until after the first World War did the financial prospects of Downing take a recognizable turn for the better. The crucial benefaction, which finally reached the College in the 1940's, was an estate of some £125,000 from the will of S. W. Graystone. In an odd way, this was the return of bread cast upon the academic waters — for Graystone as an undergraduate had been sent down by Clare but had been admitted to Downing!

In retrospect, Sir George Downing's philanthropy appears to be one which, had the complications of its birth been less protracted, might have had an almost revolu-

[51] H. W. Pettit Stevens, *Downing College* (London, 1899), p. 65; *VCH, Cambridge*, III, 488.
[52] *Downing College Charter* (1837 reprint). Fellowships would be vacated "by those who are in the law line by their not being called to the bar within eight years after their elections, and by those who are in the medical line, by their not taking the degree of doctor of physic within two years after they are of sufficient standing."
[53] Winstanley, *Early Victorian Cambridge*, p. 4.
[54] Stevens, *Downing College*, p. 71.

tionary influence on the University. During much of its life the College has had
a certain appeal to more mature, serious undergraduates because of its liberal
scheme of organization, and names of great distinction, F. W. Maitland and
Courtney Kenny for example, have appeared among the Downing Professors.
Yet, owing to a series of misfortunes, until fairly recently Downing has been at
best a worthy poor relation of better endowed colleges and at worst, in conservative Cambridge opinion, a horrible example of what revised college statutes
might lead to.

4

If early nineteenth-century Oxford and Cambridge had been pretty well isolated
from the currents of change sweeping over British society, late Victorian times
found the two ancient universities rejoining, or at least approaching, the main
stream. It was partly pressure from reformers within the academic community
and partly the work of government commissions, but, in a broader sense, both of
these were agents of the Victorian belief in the necessity of progress. One straw
in the wind, though it must have seemed trivial at the time, was the emergence
in the 1870's of projects for the higher education of women. By the end of the
decade, in fact, Cambridge and Oxford each had two collegiate institutions for
women tenuously connected with the University. It will be sufficient, perhaps,
to take a single case and to recall the circumstances of the founding of Girton
College, the original institution of the group.

As with most projects of the kind, the active influence was a single dedicated
individual — in this instance, Emily Davies, who carried on her crusade as a
branch of the broader women's movement. Like her friend Elizabeth Garrett,
whose determination to be a physician was not unrelated to a desire to pioneer on
behalf of her sex, Emily Davies' agitation was meant to open up larger opportunities, intellectual and professional, for women and thus contribute to their
"emancipation." [55] She had been responsible for persuading the Taunton Commissioners to extend their investigation to girls' schools, and in 1866 she published
a book, something of a manifesto, on *The Higher Education of Women*. It was
in the autumn of 1866 that she formulated a "programme" calling for a college
for young women and at once began to investigate ways and means.

Girton College had no pious foundress (in a financial sense) but was built on
subscription-list philanthropy. In spite of the impressive committee assembled by
Miss Davies, benefactors failed to rally to the cause of women's education. By
mid-1868, after several months of activity, only £2000 of the £30,000 sought was
in sight, and half of this was the sum promised by Madame Bodichon (Barbara
Leigh Smith). By mid-1870 the situation was so little improved that the committee

---

[55] It was Emily Davies who had first proposed the study of medicine to Elizabeth Garrett, for she
"felt that her friend's health and strength would make her an admirable pioneer." (Barbara Stephen,
Emily Davies and Girton College [London, 1927], p. 55.) The following account of the founding of
Girton is drawn chiefly from the Stephen biography.

decided to go ahead as soon as £7000 was in hand. In point of fact, the College was opened at Hitchin before anything like that figure had been reached, and when in 1871 the move to Girton was in prospect it appeared that shortage of funds might be an insuperable obstacle. The committee appealed for £10,000, recalling wryly that the already handsomely endowed Harrow School had been showered with £78,000 during the past half century, and managed to raise £3000 in the course of the year. Meanwhile, the new building at Girton was to cost £7800, with the site still unpaid for. Here Sir Francis Goldsmid, philanthropist and first Jewish barrister, whose wife was an active promoter of the College, daringly advised borrowing on the security of a group of friends.[56] A guarantee fund was arranged, £5000 borrowed, and the move to Girton carried out.

Women's education, to repeat, made no irresistible appeal to British philanthropists, and the early years of Girton are recalled as "a monotonous story of subscription lists, loans, and mortgages."[57] To Newnham, which was also being launched in the early '70's, money appears to have come somewhat more readily. This may have had something to do with the fact that it was located in Cambridge itself, and the community seems to have accepted a degree of responsibility for the new venture. The sponsorship of Henry Sidgwick, distinguished philosopher and his wife, sister of A. J. Balfour, was also a powerful factor. When, after twice moving from rented premises, Newnham decided on a building of its own, the promoters formed a company and quickly disposed of £2800 in shares. With some additional receipts from subscriptions and donations, the prospect seemed sufficiently assured to justify leasing land and putting up a building. By mid-1876, about £10,000 had been raised, enough to finance the building itself, to furnish it, and to lay out a two-acre garden.[58]

As for Girton, it was not until the mid-'80's that the College turned the corner. What made the difference was the residuary estate of a surprise benefactor, Miss Jane Catherine Gamble. The bequest came to about £19,000 and allowed the College to buy seventeen additional acres of land (part of which was turned into a miniature park) and to provide rooms for twenty-seven more students.[59] Within a few years, the picture was further brightened by legacies of £10,000 from Madame Bodichon and £5000 from Madame Emily Pfeiffer, a minor Victorian poetess and widow of a wealthy German merchant.[60] In the late '90's Girton inaugurated a rather adventurous building program, estimated to cost £50,000. With only £8000 in subscriptions and another £8000 saved out of income by what must have been grinding economy, the decision was to go ahead. Predictably the

[56] *Ibid.*, pp. 257, 262–63.

[57] *Ibid.*, p. 314.

[58] Blanche A. Clough, *Memoir of Anne Jemima Clough* (New York, 1897), chap. VI.

[59] Stephen, *Emily Davies*, p. 315.

[60] Née Emily Jane Davis. Her benefaction was used entirely for scholarships and studentships. Almost from the beginning Girton had had a number of scholarships, for which she was indebted to private individuals, to the Gilchrist Educational Fund, and to several of the City Companies. (*VCH, Cambridge*, III, 492.)

buildings cost more than planned, and, although some £45,000 was paid over, the College was obliged to saddle itself with interest charges of about £1500.

For over a decade the debt was a burdensome millstone around the Girtonian neck, and to liquidate it required the cooperation of a variety of hands. As early as 1904, Rosalind, the dynamic and difficult Countess of Carlisle,[61] put up £2000, and a few years later former students of the College organized a campaign among their own group. The debt came down gradually — to £29,000 and in 1913 to £24,000. At that point Sir Alfred Yarrow, shipbuilder and marine engineer, offered to provide £12,000 if the College should raise the balance before 1 January 1914. This spurred the committee of former students to new efforts, and the City Companies, some of whom had previously shown their interest, again responded. In early January 1914 the mortgage was paid off, with a surplus of £1600, and the College relieved of punitive interest payments. Given the succession of crises that make up much of Girton's early history, it is not surprising that the women's colleges look with envy on the heavy endowments and well-to-do graduate constituencies of the men's foundations. To say the least, Princess Ida was not the favorite child of late Victorian philanthropy.

5

The century's most impressive investment in higher education, however, took place in the fast-growing urban centers, metropolitan and provincial, rather than in the historic university towns. Here some of the freshly acquired industrial and commercial fortunes could be tapped for the benefit of local projects. A variety of motives figured in the plans. There was, of course, a heavy component of civic pride, a conviction that civic dignity required a university college for its fulfillment, and some of the new rich, unimpressed by more disinterested educational arguments, could be appealed to in such terms. For them the role of civic benefactor was a congenial one.

Moreover, the provincial business classes tended to think of the older universities as not for them and to dismiss the classical-mathematical training as irrelevant to their special needs. They felt themselves excluded, spiritually or in fact, by their social background, their industrial orientation, and their Nonconformist religion. What was wanted, perhaps, was a group of local institutions tailored to local needs. Presumably these would offer a broader curriculum, with less stress on the old classical disciplines and with more room for the scientific and technical subjects thought to bear on industrial progress. The atmosphere of the new civic colleges would thus be freer, both socially and intellectually, and more secular than that in which the ancient universities had traditionally carried on.

Rather than Oxford and Cambridge, it was the pioneer college of London University that offered the most serviceable model. University College had been

[61] In addition to her lifetime services to the College, she bequeathed (1921) £20,000 for scholarships. (*VCH, Cambridge,* III, 492, n. 16.) For an intimate view of the Countess, see her daughter's biographical volume (Dorothy Henley, *Rosalind Howard, Countess of Carlisle* [London, 1959]).

established in the 1820's in protest against the social and religious exclusiveness of the older universities.[62] Its educational philosophy and practice derived from Edinburgh, supplemented by German and American influences, rather than from to call University College a philanthropic effort is justified only with qualifications. To raise the £150,000 that their venture was thought to demand, the promoters sold £100 shares. On paper the plan moved along handsomely, and during the summer of 1825 some fifteen hundred shares were subscribed. Henry Brougham, one of the chief projectors, himself sold two hunderd, writing "150 long letters" to friends and acquaintances and holding out, at least to some, the prospect of a six per cent return, "for we only call for sixty-six pounds, and pay four per cent. on a nominal hundred." [63] Although the collapse of 1825–26 proved a severe setback — the holders of some three hundred shares defaulted when the first installment of £25 was called for — by early 1827 all 1500 shares were in the hands of persons who apparently intended to fulfill their obligations, and nearly £34,000 cash was in hand. At this point the committee purchased land and began building operations.

Both University College and its Anglican analogue, King's College, had checkered financial histories. The former got off to a shaky start because of its heavy dependence on the fees of students, who appeared in far smaller numbers than had been forecast. A number of benefactions eased the pressure, and for two or three decades crises were avoided. But at the end of the century the College was some £30,000 in debt to its bankers. What saved the situation and enabled University College to enter on a period of development and expansion was a series of large benefactions in the decade 1902–12 amounting to nearly £420,000. These included £100,000 from Sir Donald Currie (Union-Castle Line) for quarters for the School of Advanced Medical Studies and a Nurses' Home.

For much of the century the financial record of King's College paralleled that of the Bloomsbury institution. As with University College, the initial capital was to be raised by subscriptions to shares and donations. The original appeal went swimmingly. The Anglican faithful in London and the provinces responded so generously that about a month after the inaugural meeting in the summer of 1828, £102,000 had been either paid or promised. What shattered the auspicious harmony of the effort was the surrender of Wellington and Peel on Catholic Emancipation and the refusal of the ultra-Protestants, notably Lord Winchelsea, to have further commerce with an institution of which the Duke of Wellington was a patron. When £25 a share was called in, King's (for different reasons) had as much trouble collecting from Church of England men as University had had with Dissenters and secularists.

Life was precarious for the College in the Strand. Deficits were regular, endowment was lacking, and few benefactors appeared to ease the situation. During

[62] This brief account of University College is based largely on H. H. Bellot, *University College, London, 1826–1926* (London, 1929).

[63] Quoted *ibid.*, p. 32; New, *Lord Brougham*, p. 364.

a crisis in the '70's, so desperate that the secretary had been authorized to sell the College silverware, the council managed, in the course of a half-dozen years, to raise £11,000 (out of a hoped-for £30,000).[64] Two of the City Companies, the Clothworkers and the Drapers, who, alarmed over the attacks of municipal reformers, were beginning "to buy less turtle, and to endow schools, colleges, chairs, and charities," [65] now helped the College to weather the storm. But in the '80's and '90's the deficit went from bad to worse, until the finance committee reported that "the borrowing powers of the council are exhausted." [66] This occurred after the council had appealed for an endowment fund of £50,000 — and had got £526 5s. from two City Companies!

In the end there was no way out for the determinedly Church of England institution but to abolish religious tests in order to qualify for grants from the pubilc authorities. Behind this decision lay a record of successive appeals for funds that had turned out to be embarrassing fiascos, like that of 1902, which produced £30,000 out of the £500,000 sought.[67] Here, as in other sectors of the philanthropic world, private benevolence proved unequal to the task. Once the decision against religious tests had been taken, Treasury grants, supplemented by others from the London County Council, "converted the college from a condition of resigned adversity to progressive prosperity." [68]

No single formula will cover the origin of English provincial universities. In some instances (Manchester and Birmingham, for example) a single philanthropist supplied the principal impetus; in others (Liverpool) it was a group of promoters with their subscription list, sometimes assisted by a grant from municipal authorities; and in still others (Nottingham and Sheffield) the founding of a college was connected with the university extension movement. Certain provincial institutions (Leeds and Newcastle) were conceived at the outset as auxiliaries of the regional economy and were supported by industrialists on that basis, while others were regarded chiefly as additions to the cultural resources of the city. What was common to the entire group was their local constituency, local both in support and clientele. Unlike wealthy merchants of the Tudor-Stuart era, who after accumulating a fortune in London might endow a grammar school in their native town in Somerset or Cheshire, the Victorian philanthropists — a Josiah Mason in Birmingham or a Joseph Whitworth in Manchester — were investing in indigenous educational ventures riches acquired in local business enterprises. These institutions were, in short, expressions of Victorian provincial culture and were promoted and supported as such.[69]

[64] F. J. C. Hearnshaw, *The Centenary History of King's College, London, 1828–1928* (London, 1929), pp. 283–84.

[65] *Ibid.*, p. 285.

[66] *Ibid.*, p. 355.

[67] *Ibid.*, pp. 409–10.

[68] *Ibid.*, p. 413.

[69] For an account of the provincial universities as a group, see W. H. G. Armytage, *Civic Universities* (London, 1955).

The rise of Redbrick forms a complex and varied story. Here it must suffice merely to note some of the different manifestations of the Victorian philanthropic impulse as reflected in the financing of provincial universities. As the first of the new institutions,[70] and one with as distinguished a record as any, Manchester will perhaps offer an instructive sample. Unlike Josiah Mason, whose benefactions of over £200,000 to Birmingham were described at the time as "without parallel in the annals of modern education," [71] John Owens, the merchant whose bequest laid the foundation for Manchester, remains a shadowy figure. Why this moody and antisocial bachelor should have left about half of his estate, over £96,000, for nonsectarian higher education is by no means clear today.[72] Although the Manchester community had displayed enthusiasm when Owens College first opened its doors in 1851, until more than halfway through the '60's Cottonocracy made no move to supplement the Owens bequest.[73] It is curious that in its intellectually most vigorous and commercially most prosperous days (save for the Cotton Famine in the early '60's), Manchester took so little interest in an institution which some observers even thought to be on the verge of collapse.

The second founder of Owens College was Thomas Ashton, one of the distinguished cotton dynasty of Hyde and a leading citizen of Manchester. It was he, more than anyone else, who was responsible for making the College a public cause — and ultimately getting subscriptions for more than £200,000. Once the College was accepted as a valuable civic institution, support was forthcoming in amounts which make King's College and even University College, London, seem like moderately poor relations. Between 1850 and 1914 Manchester received nearly £700,000 in benefactions of £10,000 or more.[74] Some were of imposing proportions — £100,000 from Charles Frederick Beyer (1877) for professorships in science; gifts totaling about £150,000 from the residuary legatees of Sir Joseph Whitworth, engineer and munitions manufacturer, whose firm later merged with Armstrong to form Armstrong, Whitworth & Co., Ltd.;[75] £75,000 from Mrs. E. A. Rylands, founder of the John Rylands Library; and £33,000 from Professor R. C. Christie, one of Whitworth's legatees, who gave and endowed the Christie Library from his own resources. Since universities are notoriously insatiable, Owens College (which in 1900 became part of the federal Victoria University and

[70] With the exception of Durham, an institution thoroughly untypical in its origins. Here the pious founder was the cathedral chapter, which, in its alarm over the prospect of church reform and possible confiscation of ecclesiastical revenues, hastened to invest some of its accumulated surplus in a college.
[71] H. F. W. Burstall and C. G. Burton, *Foundation and Development of the . . . University of Birmingham, 1880–1930* (Birmingham, 1930), p. 11. Mason's philanthropies are described in a separate essay in Chapter XV.
[72] Edward Fiddes, *Chapters in the History of Owens College* (Manchester, 1937), pp. 6–7. Apparently his friend, George Faulkner, a Conservative Anglican, had something to do with suggesting a nondenominational university as a suitable use for Owens's fortune.
[73] Except to raise £10,000 for a chemistry laboratory.
[74] Exclusive of grants-in-aid from public authorities. (H. B. Charlton, *Portrait of a University* [Manchester, 1951], App. III.)
[75] Whitworth left his residuary estate to his widow and two friends with the understanding that the bulk of it would be applied to public purposes. (Fiddes, *Owens College*, pp. 125–26.)

in 1904 acquired independent university status) may have been supported less lavishly than it deserved. But at least, by contemporary standards, the Manchester community did exceptionally well by the College and enabled it to climb to a distinguished, and at some periods perhaps a pre-eminent, position among English academic institutions.

The record of other provincial foundations diverges to a greater or less degree from the Manchester experience, but in virtually all of them fortunes made in local industry were heavily involved. At Sheffield the decisive influence was a sizable contribution from Mark Firth, a leading figure in the manufacturing community, who had been Master Cutler for three successive terms and was Mayor of the city at the time when concern about the town's educational facilities was growing. His family had already built Ranmoor College, at the cost of £5000, as a training school for Methodist ministers, and Firth himself had contributed about £30,000 for building and endowing thirty-six almshouses.[76] What aroused his interest in the founding of a college in Sheffield was a series of university extension lectures given by a group of Cambridge dons in the years 1875–77. When it appeared that these had been thought of as laying the ground for a permanent local institution, Firth accepted the challenge. He bought land and put up a building at the cost of about £20,000, and contributed a further £5000 for the endowment of Firth College, which was later merged in the University College of Sheffield (and in 1905 in the University of Sheffield). His death in 1880 at the age of 61 was apparently something of a blow to the College, whose officers had looked forward to further expressions of his benevolence.[77]

Even allowing for its shorter history, Sheffield received less bountiful support than Manchester. From the founding of Firth College in 1879 to 1918, large gifts and bequests to capital (£10,000 or more) totaled nearly £262,000.[78] Of this figure by far the largest increment came from Sheffield business leaders or their firms, the exceptions being £14,000 from the Duke of Norfolk (the principal ground landlord of the city), £27,000 from the Sheffield Trustees, £16,000 from the Drapers' Company, and about £15,550 from Dr. Hunter, son of the historian of Hallamshire. In the 1930's and '40's the University had some success in enlisting the direct support of industry, with £50,000 from the Staveley Coal & Iron Company, Ltd., for chemical research laboratories; £30,400 from the United Steel Companies, Ltd.; and £24,900 from the English Steel Corporation, Ltd. A fund of £40,000 contributed by the glass industry provided new quarters for the Department of Glass Technology, a cooperative venture of the University and the industry. During the early 1950's some ninety firms were subscribing about £20,000 annually for the work of the department.[79]

To comment on other provincial universities as objects of civic philanthropy

---

[76] Alfred Gatty, *Sheffield: Past and Present* (Sheffield, 1873), pp. 330–31.

[77] Arthur W. Chapman, *The Story of a Modern University* (Oxford, 1955), chap. I.

[78] *Ibid.*, pp. 518–20. Where the benefactions of an individual or a firm over a period of years added up to £10,000, I have considered the total as a single gift.

[79] *Ibid.*, p. 273.

might prove more repetitious than illuminating. Yet one ought perhaps to recall some of the circumstances of origin and growth which make each a special case. Liverpool, for example, was launched on a spontaneous wave of civic interest. In 1879 a town meeting persuaded the Corporation to supply a site, £50,000 was raised by subscription, and for its building the College acquired an abandoned lunatic asylum in a slum district. At Nottingham the civic authorities proved extraordinarily cooperative. Here it was a university extension course held in the rebuilt Mechanics Institute that set things in motion. An anonymous donor agreed to give £10,000 on condition that the Nottingham Corporation would erect a suitable building. The authorities not only spent £100,000 on a building, but they levied a 3½d. rate for maintenance.[80]

Bristol's beginning was unique in that two Oxford colleges were involved. Canon Percival of Bristol had been urging Oxford colleges to convert some of their fellowships into professorships in provincial colleges still to be founded. Both Balliol and New College offered their cooperation and contributed financially. Yet local people, notably the Fry family (chocolate), were the most active of the founders and the principal early benefactors. More recently the Wills family (Imperial Tobacco) has taken over as the University's most munificent friend, and its members have presented a series of handsome buildings and made other impressive gifts. On Founders' Day each year the list of benefactors whose names are recalled contains six Willses, two Frys, and only three not obviously related to either of these clans.[81]

Among provincial institutions Leeds has had better than average success in drawing the business community to its support.[82] Formed initially from rather curious ingredients — an older medical school and the Yorkshire College of Science — it has achieved the kind of distinction in technological subjects, as well as in pure science, that would serve to enlist the patronage of industry. Between the two World Wars, especially, the resources of the University, in buildings and endowments, grew markedly. Like the Willses in Bristol, certain Leeds families, such as the Tetleys (Joshua Tetley & Son, Ltd.), contributed generously and frequently, to the amount of about £160,000. Some of the wealthier and more enlightened business leaders in the West Riding also came to regard contributions to the University's teaching and research as a productive investment. Lord Brotherton of Wakefield, a major figure in the British chemical industry, was the source of £220,000, his firm of another £39,000, and his brother of £65,000 more. In the mid-'30's Frank Parkinson, head of a large electrical engineering firm and former Baines Scholar of the University, gave £250,000 — £50,000 for scholarships and £200,000 for the central block (Parkinson Building) of the new plant. Among great business enterprises with no special West Riding connections, Im-

---

[80] Armytage, *Civic Universities,* pp. 225–26.

[81] Basil Cottle and J. W. Sherborne, *The Life of a University* (Bristol 1951), p. 116.

[82] A. N. Shimmin, *The University of Leeds* (Cambridge, 1954), chap. VI, the financial data in which is drawn from E. J. Brown, *The Private Donor in the History of University of Leeds* (Leeds, 1953).

perial Chemicals provided (1948–53) nearly £80,000 for research fellowships, in addition to considerable sums for laboratory equipment, and Courtaulds, Ltd. were the donors of £60,000 for a building devoted to rayon technology.[83]

Altogether, in the course of its history (to 1953), Leeds received something over £2 million in donations and legacies of £10,000 and upwards.[84] Paradoxically enough, the most munificent benefactor was no modern limited liability company or captain of industry but the Worshipful Company of Clothworkers, founded in 1528. The interest of the Company in matters of higher education in Leeds was aroused early, and the response was generous — £130,000 for capital development and £420,000 in annual grants. Lest such figures, however, create a distorted notion of the relative weight pulled by private philanthropy in university education, it is well to recall the specific figures. In 1952–53, 71 per cent of the Leeds income came from Treasury grants, another 5 per cent from grants from local authorities, 13 per cent from fees, and only 11 per cent from "other sources." [85] Here, as elsewhere in what was once the domain of the private philanthropist and the self-maintaining individual, the statutory sector has expanded strikingly as the voluntary has shrunk.

6

One of the services most commonly identified with modern foundations is that of financing research, especially in the natural and social sciences. This is not, of course, a traditional object of charitable endowments but one that has emerged only in more recent decades as the dimensions of knowledge have been enlarged and research has become a systematic and organized pursuit. Certainly no marked demand that research be recognized as an essential intellectual concern and receive suitable support antedated the latter nineteenth century. No doubt its appearance was in some degree connected with the controversy in the ancient universities over the relative emphases to be placed on teaching and research, on the proper balance between the tutorial and professorial functions. An interesting contribution to the debate was a volume by a group of Oxford dons, *Essays on the Endowment of Research,* published in 1876, with an introduction by Mark Pattison. They argued, in essence, that Oxford had been delinquent in adding to human knowledge, especially in the physical sciences, and they urged that college endowments ought to advance learning and not merely provide tutors for undergraduates — nor, for that matter, simply to equip old tutors with new professorial titles.[86]

It would be out of the question to follow the rise of scientific research as an accepted object of philanthropy. Although only in the past seventy-five years or so has it bulked significantly, many earlier gifts aided the cause directly or in-

[83] Shimmin, *University of Leeds,* p. 109.
[84] *Ibid.,* pp. 215–16. Unlike the figures quoted for other universities, not all of this amount consisted of gifts to capital.
[85] *Ibid.,* p. 214.
[86] Mark Pattison, "Review of the Situation," pp. 24–25.

directly. Subscriptions to teaching hospitals promoted discoveries in medical science, and equipping universities with laboratories provided scientists with necessary facilities for their work. The record of the Royal Society sheds light of a sort on the chronology of the trend. During the first half of the nineteenth century the Society received some gifts from Fellows, but these did not much exceed £10,000 in all. Only after the mid-century, when, in the words of its historian, "the Society was being rapidly converted into a scientific institution," did support flow in more freely, the bulk of it from scientists who were Fellows.[87] The first large gift (£15,000) reached Burlington House in 1871, and for the half century 1851–1900 the total topped £50,000.[88] Yet the really massive increments did not arrive until the inter-war period. In 1912 the income from the Society's research funds was about £2400. By 1939 it had risen to about £20,000, exclusive of Parliamentary grants, and the list of benefactions contains items of £127,000, £57,000, and £67,000.[89] During this period gifts to the Royal Society were paralleled by those to universities — from private individuals, industry, and foundations. Since 1945, as in the United States, subventions to science from such sources have become inconsiderable beside the streams flowing from the public treasury.

The more traditional channel by which philanthropy has served research has been through the provision of books. Here, naturally enough, the record of the philanthropist has been long and creditable, longer than can be here recalled. In a funeral sermon in 1629, Robert Willan saw in books "the rivers of Paradise watering the earth; the deaw of Hermon making the vallies fertile," and appealed to the powerful and opulent of London to establish a library comparable to those of Athens and Alexandria.[90] If the charitable of the age failed to respond as spaciously as he had urged, at least libraries were founded and augmented, both within and independently of institutions of formal learning.[91]

For our period three or four examples, taken mostly from the Victorian Age, must be sufficient. Throughout the century Oxford and Cambridge colleges received additions to their libraries of greater or less consequence. In the early 1860's William Grylls bequeathed some ten thousand volumes, including a complete set of Shakespeare folios, to the library of Trinity College, Cambridge, only a few years after the widow of Archdeacon Julius Hare had given about half as many volumes, largely theological.[92] Probably the most impressive of all modern benefactions to Oxford-Cambridge libraries was Dr. Robert Mason's bequest to the Queen's College, Oxford, of £30,000 for the purchase of books, with the provision that the entire sum was to be expended within a decade.[93] This was a

[87] Sir Henry Lyons, *The Royal Society, 1660–1940* (Cambridge, 1944), p. 281.
[88] *Ibid.*, p. 297; *Record of the Royal Society*, 4th ed. (London, 1940), chap. IV.
[89] *Ibid.*, p. 119.
[90] Jordan, *Charities of London*, p. 398, n. 175.
[91] I am not here concerned with reading libraries for the general public, only with collections which can claim the status of research institutions.
[92] *VCH, Cambridge*, III, 465.
[93] J. R. Magrath, *The Queen's College*, 2 vols. (Oxford, 1921), II, 172.

librarian's dream come true, and the College, spending the legacy with intelligence, accumulated one of the distinguished libraries of Oxford.

Among the more outstanding private collections of the century was that belonging to Dr. Martin Routh, the almost indestructible President of Magdalen. Throughout his long life — he died at the age of ninety-nine, having held the Presidency for sixty-three years — Routh had been a book collector, and his shelves held over sixteen thousand volumes, among which, he liked to point out, were two hundred which the Bodleian lacked. The library, rich in patristic material and English history, was said to have cost him £8000.[94] In the early 1840's he had been prepared to sell his printed volumes to the Queen's College for £10,000, but negotiations broke down over Routh's insistence that the library remain with him for the balance of his days. In the end it was the newly founded Durham University that won out, to the regret of the Oxford community. As a loyal Churchman, Routh had taken an active interest in the launching of a new college in the County Palatine, and by deed of gift discovered in his papers after his death, he left the collection to Durham, "for the purpose of promoting the Glory of God through the advancement of good learning." [95]

Of the country's two leading research collections, the British Museum and the Bodleian, little need be said. For the Museum the early Victorian Age was made memorable by the bequest in 1847 of the Grenville library of over twenty thousand volumes. During most of his life Thomas Grenville was an avid and knowledgeable bibliophile, and the collection that he willed to the Museum, said by him to have cost £50,000, was almost certainly worth more. As Panizzi, the able and inexhaustibly vigorous Principal Librarian, told the Trustees, the Grenville library, with its wealth of incunabula and Italian and Spanish literature, "placed it [the Museum] in some classes at the head of all libraries, and in others second only to the Royal Library at Paris." [96] Panizzi had reason to point with pride, for in a large measure it was Grenville's admiration for the Italian refugee that persuaded him to leave his treasures to the Museum. Also, apparently, he felt an obligation, certainly a Victorian rather than an eighteenth-century impulse, to return to the nation some of the riches that a well-paid government sinecure had allowed him to acquire. In the course of the next century, similar motives — a twinge of social conscience or awareness of a debt of sorts owed to society — would turn rich men on both sides of the Atlantic to large-scale philanthropy.

Such advances as the Bodleian made in Victorian times owed little to the intervention of benefactors. The only notable addition of the kind was £40,000

[94] R. D. Middleton, *Dr. Routh* (London, 1938), p. 250; A. E. Boyle, "Martin Joseph Routh and His Books," *Durham University Journal,* June, 1956, p. 106; A. N. L. Munby, *The Formation of the Phillips Library from 1841 to 1872* (Cambridge, 1956), pp. 77–78.

[95] Middleton, *Dr. Routh,* p. 255. Not only did the heirs decline to challenge the bequest (which was legally vulnerable), but they even permitted Durham to keep volumes acquired by Routh during the two years and a half between the date of the deed and his death. (Boyle, "Routh and His Books," p. 106.)

[96] Arundell Esdaile, *The British Museum Library* (London, 1946), p. 196.

from the same Dr. Robert Mason who had done so handsomely by his own College, the Queen's.[97] In the course of the century the Library's income grew, mainly through increased contributions from some of the colleges, but its funds, especially those for book purchases, were gravely inadequate. T. A. Brassey, who had proposed and indeed launched the project of an endowment fund for the University shortly before Curzon became Chancellor, had thought of the Bodleian as a first charge on such a fund. He himself had contributed £10,000. From the endowment appeal, however, Bodley's foundation profited only to the extent of £24,000, and the Hebdomadal Council of the University determined to try for £50,000 additional endowment. The decision could not have been more unfortunately timed, for two months later war broke out, and only £1400 of the hoped-for £50,000 was realized.[98]

What a general appeal could not accomplish was managed by a single benefactor. The third in the line of Bodleian benefactors, the first two being Sir Thomas himself and Robert Mason, was Walter Morrison, a bachelor of enormous and far-flung business interests, who had already given away large sums — for example, an annual gift of £10,000 to King Edward's Hospital Fund, £10,000 to the University of Leeds, and £15,000 to finance the British Museum's Hittite excavations. In the latter part of the century Morrison's philanthropies tended to center on Oxford, and he gave to the University, first, £30,000 for a readership in Egyptology and other purposes, and then, in 1920, his crowning benefaction, £50,000 for the Bodleian.[99] Owing to Morrison's benefaction and a series of smaller bequests, the income of the Library from investments trebled between 1912 and 1923.[100] In the 1930's the crisis in storage space that had been looming for years could no longer be held off. For the building of an extension the Rockefeller Foundation offered to provide three-fifths of the cost, on condition that the University would find the balance, about £340,000. Instead of attempting a general appeal the authorities chose to rely on college contributions (£65,000) and other expedients. The trustees of the old Curzon Endowment Fund assigned their entire balance, £48,000, and within a year nearly £250,000 had been given or pledged — and the balance guaranteed by the University Chest. A joint effort of ancient and modern philanthropy thus assured the Bodleian of its new facilities.[101]

At the end of the century research in the humanities was brilliantly reinforced in an unexpected quarter and by rather unlikely hands. Few Englishmen would have looked to Manchester as a natural site for a great collection of priceless rarities — sixty-two genuine Caxtons, for example, thirty-six of them perfect — that give special distinction to the John Rylands Library. The Library stands as a memorial to the builder of one of the city's fabulously successful business firms.

[97] Sir Herbert Edmund Craster, *History of the Bodleian Library, 1845–1945* (Oxford, 1952), p. 35.
[98] *Ibid.*, pp. 164, 260.
[99] *DNB*, XXIV (1912–21), 388–89.
[100] Craster, *The Bodleian Library*, p. 260. Among the donors of the period was Kenneth Grahame, who left to the Bodleian his residuary estate, together with the copyright to his works and royalties.
[101] *Ibid.*, p. 327.

John Rylands' own literary interests, like those of most of his hardworking contemporaries, were limited and were, in part, an outgrowth of his own Dissenting piety. He spent considerable sums in having prepared and distributed on the Continent and in Britain special editions of the Bible and other religious works, and when his widow first began to plan for the Library it was to have, in a broad sense, a religious and theological tone.[102]

What enlarged her conception was the opportunity to purchase from Earl Spencer the incomparable "Althorp Library" of about forty thousand volumes. This collection, described by a French bibliographer as "the most beautiful and richest private library in Europe," cost Mrs. Rylands about £250,000. A few years later, for nearly as great a price, she was able to add the six thousand illuminated and other manuscripts of the Earl of Crawford. How many hundreds of thousands Mrs. Rylands lavished on the Library is difficult to estimate. In addition to the cost of erecting and equipping the neo-Gothic building in Deansgate, she spent nearly £500,000 on the Althorp and Crawford collections alone, to say nothing of the thousands of other volumes bought before the opening of the Library in 1899. Between that date and her death in 1908, she added something like £200,000 to her original gift, and in her will she left Rylands Ltd. debentures worth more than their nominal values of £200,000.[103] Mrs. Rylands' benefactions made possible the establishment in the North of England of an institution with resources comparable, for some types of scholarly investigation, to those of the British Museum and the Bodleian and in a measure vindicated the claims of Cottonopolis to cultural eminence. In the twilight of the reign, they contributed a brilliant epilogue to the less than dazzling record of Victorian philanthropy as an agency for "the advancement of good learning."

[102] Henry Guppy, *The John Rylands Library* (Manchester, 1935), pp. 8–9.
[103] *Ibid.*, p. 88; *The Times*, 15 Feb. and 27 March 1908. Even with all of her benefactions, Mrs. Rylands left net personalty of about £3½ million, on which death duties amounted to £650,000.

CHAPTER XIV

"PHILANTHROPY
AND FIVE PER CENT":
HOUSING EXPERIMENTS

O F A L L the branches of Victorian philanthropic activity, none, says Sir John Simon in his classic *English Sanitary Institutions,* was more productive than the efforts to improve working-class housing.[1] The most distinctive achievement of these philanthropists and quasi-philanthropists, he indicates correctly enough, was not the dwellings for which they were directly responsible. Their lasting contribution was a matter of education rather than material construction, for they had something to do with persuading not only other private builders but the State itself that urban working-class housing could not be left entirely to the mercies of the market. More recent students have discovered less to exult over. Elizabeth Macadam could find "no subject on which philanthropy has so signally failed either to do the job itself or to stimulate the State to do it adequately." Not only that, but housing ventures, all of them on a relatively small scale, "tended to obscure the magnitude of the real problem by a false sense of achievement."[2]

The judgment is severe but not without substance. The issue has to do chiefly with the success of the housing societies in enlisting other forces, since their own improved dwellings never accommodated any considerable number of working-class families. For years it was their comfortable illusion that commercial builders would follow the example set by the model dwellings projects — "we must remember how influences radiate from every centre"[3] — and a large-scale improvement in urban housing would follow gradually. Clearly, as in so many other areas, the private philanthropist underestimated the dimensions of the evil. Yet, when all criticisms have been leveled, it was he who first resolved to do something about the appalling state of working-class dwellings and who cast about for ways and means. Ultimately it became evident that the task far exceeded the power of private agencies — individual philanthropists, housing trusts, and the half-philanthropic, half-commercial companies (the "philanthropy and 5 per cent" under-

[1] London, 1890, pp. 443–44.
[2] Elizabeth Macadam, *The New Philanthropy* (London, 1934), p. 138–39.
[3] Bernard Bosanquet, *Essays and Addresses* (London, 1889), p. 44.

takings) — even with the negative cooperation of the State, and from the latter years of the nineteenth century the burden came to rest increasingly on public authorities. In the end both the accomplishments of private agencies and their patent inability to do more than nibble at the edges of a gigantic problem were not without effect in inducing the State to move in. Whether private philanthropy hastened or delayed this decision is, after all, a matter of opinion.

As it unfolded, the housing problem was discouragingly complex, but it was the product of factors, which, reduced to their lowest terms, were apparent to all. The nineteenth-century slum, with its crowding, disease, squalor, and filth, was one of the more pernicious consequences of the growth of population and, more particularly, of urban population. In the course of the four decades 1841–81, numbers of cities — London, Bradford, Leicester, and Sheffield, for example — doubled in population, and by the end of Victoria's reign three-quarters of the English people were residents of urban areas.[4] But it was not a simple matter of disparity between city population and total available dwellings, of the failure of housing to keep abreast of population growth. Hardly less crucial was the fact that the older sections of Victorian cities were the scenes of almost continuous revolution. Clearly the semimedieval character of business districts and streets was incompatible with the bustling expansion of nineteenth-century commercial life. The larger cities, especially during the latter half of the century, were in a perpetual ferment of "improvements," both those inspired by public authorities and those carried out by private interests. In either case, the poor residents were probable sufferers. As old cottages and small houses made way for business blocks, masses of tenants were inevitably displaced to increase the congestion of neighboring areas. A railway or railway station might cause the demolition of hundreds of cottages and reduce thousands of persons at least temporarily to homelessness.[5]

The activities of public authorities were no less catastrophic as agents of change. They accomplished much toward making Victorian cities more presentable and habitable, but sometimes at the expense of a multitude of slum dwellers. As a mid-century student of working-class life noted, "Public improvements which *should* ameliorate the condition of the poor, are often one of their greatest afflictions."[6] London, as we implied in connection with the parochial charities of the City, was the scene of a series of large-scale upheavals. During the first half of the century such improvements as the new London Bridge and its approaches displaced numbers of poor residents. New Oxford Street was cut through a squalid slum area, Victoria Street was laid down, and Trafalgar Square redesigned and extended, while, to the east, Cannon Street was rebuilt and Liverpool Street felt the firm hand of the improver.[7] After the Metropolis Management Act of 1855 had created the Metropolitan Board of Works, a new wave of improvement was

---

[4] G. R. Porter, rev. by F. W. Hirst, *Progress of the Nation* (London, 1912), p. 17.

[5] See R. C. on the Housing of the Working Classes (C. 4402), 1884–85, pp. 714–16, for figures on railway bills and the destruction of laborers' dwellings.

[6] James Hole, *The Homes of the Working Classes* (London, 1866), p. 5.

[7] R. H. Mottram, "Town Life and London," in Young, ed., *Early Victorian England*, I, 177.

launched. Such thoroughfares, as Queen Victoria Street, Shaftesbury Avenue, Charing Cross Road, Northumberland Avenue, and Clerkenwell Road were driven through, again uprooting thousands of inhabitants.[8] When one tries to follow these unfortunates to their new habitation, the distance ordinarily is short. Since most of them must live close to their work and could pay only a minimal rent, they were likely to take refuge in a nearby rookery, adding further to its indescribable filth and hopeless congestion. In a greater or less degree the larger provincial cities followed a similar course. Urban improvements, in the long run a benefit to the poor as to other citizens, often spelled personal disaster for the residents of the improved area, and at the outset they aggravated rather than eased the problems of working-class housing.

In its origins the movement to improve the condition of working-class dwellings was one of the more beneficent by-products of the New Poor Law, more specifically an outgrowth of the investigation undertaken by the Poor Law Commissioners into the sanitary condition of the laboring population. The project owed more to motives of economy, by no means shortsighted economy, than to humanitarianism as such. The Commissioners had reached the unassailable conclusion that epidemics and disease were a major factor in keeping the poor rate at what was regarded as an excessive level. It was inevitable that the three investigators — Drs. Neil Arnott, J. P. Kay (Kay-Shuttleworth) and Southwood Smith — in their survey of the "physical causes of fever" should raise questions about overcrowding, drainage, and the like. Southwood Smith's "Account of a Personal Inspection" of Bethnal Green and Whitechapel was eloquent in its documentary simplicity, and his conclusion irrefutable. Plainly, such matters as sewerage, the arrangement of streets, and the proper planning and construction of houses merited "the serious consideration of those who labour for the improvement of the physical conditions of the poor."[9] Other and more elaborate studies followed on the heels of this relatively modest inquiry. During the early 1840's, in short, public health was in the news, and the revelations of the Blue Books smote certain not insensitive upper- and middle-class consciences.

The two pioneering efforts among Victorian housing organizations dated from the early 1840's, and both derived, in a large measure, from these distressing but productive investigations. The first to enter the field was the Metropolitan Association for Improving the Dwellings of the Industrious Classes, which was formed in 1841, with Charles Gatliff as the moving spirit. He took office as secretary and for more than forty years his name was almost synonymous with the Association. The new society had as its aim that of "providing the labouring man with an increase of the comforts and conveniences of life, with full compensation to the capitalist."[10] Specifically the Association proposed to build blocks of flats for multi-family occupancy (for one of the graver evils of slum

---

[8] William A. Robson, *The Government and Misgovernment of London* (London, 1939), pp. 62–63.
[9] Poor Law Commission, *4th Ann. Rept.*, 1838, p. 94. Smith's reports appear as App. A., No. 1, Suppl. 2 and 3.
[10] Charles Gatliff, "On Improved Dwellings," *Journal of the Statistical Society*, 38:33 (March 1875).

living, as the various inquiries had shown, was the tenement house, the converted one-family dwelling), dormitories for nightly lodgers, and separate dwellings for families.

From the beginning, Gatliff's organization was cast in the mold that became typical of the semiphilanthropic, semi-investment housing societies, and, indeed, it had a good deal to do with setting the pattern. Its promoters held that the Association must be self-supporting, and they made no attempt to begin construction until capital was in sight. Their early years, therefore, were given over to publicizing the principle of their society and selling shares. By 1845 subscriptions had reached £20,000, and the Association received a royal charter. The distinctive provision of this document was a clause limiting the dividend rate to 5 per cent and stipulating that any surplus profits were to go toward expanding the operations of the Association.[11] By the end of the decade, three buildings, two in Spitalfields and one in St. Pancras, had been put up at a cost of more than £47,500 These housed 216 families comprising nearly 1200 individuals and yielded over £3300 annually in rents.[12] In 1849 *The Times* could hail the annual meeting of the Association as an exception to the misgiving with which the public has learned to approach "a meeting of shareholders and a meeting for charitable purposes." [13] As a venture which combined "profit with benevolence," the Metropolitan Association merited enthusiastic support.

Three years after the launching of the Metropolitan Association, the Society for Improving the Condition of the Labouring Classes began to interest itself in working-class housing. The Society was an outgrowth of an earlier body, the Labourer's Friend Society, founded in the early 1830's by the Bishop of Bath and Wells to provide allotments for rural laborers. In 1844 new life was breathed into the moribund organization by a group of men hitherto unconnected with it. Obviously the public health inquiries had impressed them deeply. At the organization meeting in May 1844, references to the *Sanitary Report* of 1842 cropped up often, and there were audible suspicions that, unless charity softened the acerbities of the New Poor Law, the tensions in English society might become insupportable.[14]

The new group, led by Lord Ashley and including Leonard Horner, Monckton Milnes, Sidney Godolphin Osborne, the Dorsetshire parson and champion of the rural laborer, and others, set for itself aims different from those of the Metropolitan Association. Its leaders were not sanguine about creating an organization which would house large numbers of the poor in its own buildings. What they proposed rather was a series of pilot schemes, model dwellings for various categories of tenant. They hoped, by experiments on a relatively small scale, to work out types of accommodation suitable for different classes of occupant, and also to demonstrate that dwellings to house working-class families in reasonable

[11] *Ibid.*, p. 34.
[12] *Ibid.*, pp. 50–51.
[13] 13 Dec. 1849.
[14] For example, from Monckton Milnes, *Labourer's Friend*, June 1844, p. 23.

comfort and decency could be built and operated at rentals within the range of these families.[15] Here, in short, was a body of philanthropists consciously assuming a tutorial responsibility in their society, seeking to lay out for less venturesome souls the lines on which the problem of housing the working classes could be attacked most effectively.

Specifically the Society was to provide three forms of assistance to the poor. There was, in the first place, no thought of abandoning the stress on allotments. Consistent with the Society's view of its own function, a series of demonstration allotments would be established near the Metropolis, where they could be exhibited to the numbers of landed proprietors who habitually spent part of the year in London. There was also the proposal to found a loan fund for the poor, perhaps a model benefit society. More important for the present purpose was the decision to build for working-class tenants a series of buildings or cottages combining comfort with economy and, their sponsors hopefully predicted, offering better accommodations for two or three shillings a week than those for which working-class families normally paid four to six shillings. The Society for Improving the Condition of the Labouring Classes (or The Labourer's Friend Society, as it continued to be called) was thus duly launched, with Lord Ashley as chairman of the committee and with the normal complement of Lords Temporal and Spiritual as vice-presidents. A few months later the Prince Consort himself accepted the presidency.[16]

In its activities the Society was less committed to strict "business principles" than was the Metropolitan Association. Instead of selling shares, the committee received contributions, which during the first year amounted to more than £4500.[17] The initial venture was to be a series of dwellings at Bagnigge Wells, near Gray's Inn Road, to accommodate twenty families and thirty single residents and to cost £6200. The committee, with an optimism that turned out to have been excessive, estimated on the basis of a yearly rental of £400 an annual return of 5½ or 6 per cent.[18] As is a constant with such enterprises, unexpected expenses took their toll, and after the first year, the committee concluded that 5 per cent would be doing well enough.

As president, the Prince Consort was no *roi fainéant,* content to exhibit a merely formal interest. As was his wont, he took his obligation seriously and contributed a good deal of time and energy. In the spring of 1848, it occurred to Ashley and his colleagues that presenting the Prince at a public meeting might be a publicity coup for working-class housing. There had been indubitable progress, but it had been less spectacular than the leaders had hoped for.[19] The Prince, Ashley suggested, might first visit some dwellings of the poor and then preside

[15] Lord Shaftesbury, "The Mischief of State Aid," *Nineteenth Century,* 4:934 (December 1883).
[16] *Labourer's Friend,* June 1844, pp. 1–3; Hodder, *Shaftesbury,* II, 155.
[17] *Labourer's Friend,* July 1845, p. 243.
[18] *Ibid.,* June 1846, pp. 85ff.
[19] The Society had now spent £13,000 to £14,000 and in 1847–48 had collected about £850 in subscriptions and gifts.

at Exeter Hall at the fourth annual meeting of the Society. Overruling the protests of Lord John Russell, who, in view of the agitated temper of the working
classes, regarded the spring of 1848 as an unhealthy season for aristocracy and
royalty, the Prince visited St. Giles and spoke at Exeter Hall. "Ay, truly," exulted
Ashley, "this is the way to stifle Chartism."[20] For Albert the inspection tour
marked the beginning of a new and more practical stage in his interest in working-class housing, and he presently set about embodying his ideas in a small block
of model dwellings. The result was the rather forbidding structure that was
erected not far from the Crystal Palace as a part of the Great Exhibition and now
stands in Kennington Park.[21]

The most elaborate of the early projects of the Society was the large building in
Streatham Street, Bloomsbury, which required an investment of nearly £8000.
Today, as one detours a block or so from the normal route from New Oxford
Street to the British Museum, his curiosity is aroused by the gloomy, prison-like
structure, and, viewing it through his twentieth-century spectacles, he may think
it incredible that such an edifice should have been regarded as a model anything.
Yet in its time the Streatham Building was exceedingly advanced — five stories
of fireproof construction and with external galleries for additional fire protection.[22]
The basement was equipped with workshops, wash-house, and bath. Whatever
defects may be discovered a century later, those for whom the flats were intended
found little fault. Long before the building was ready, 140 applications had been
received for forty-seven dwellings, designed to rent at between 4s. and 6s. 6d. a
week.[23] To Ashley and his enthusiastic committee, the opening of the Streatham
Building marked a substantial step toward the Society's goal of "Improving the
Condition of the Poor."

The earliest undertakings of the Society were intended to furnish a pattern of
housing for families and single women, but Ashley was also deeply concerned
about the plight of the male lodger. It was in part his experience with the Society
that lay behind the bill which he introduced in 1851 for the licensing and inspection of all common lodging houses.[24] The Society's direct contribution to the
problem was a model lodging house in the ghastly St. Giles district, which was
built at a cost of £5000 to accommodate 104 men and opened in the summer of
1847.[25] It also renovated three tumble-down houses in the notorious Drury Lane
area for by-the-night lodgings for the lowest class of transient laborers.[26]

[20] Hodder, *Shaftesbury*, II, 249.
[21] C. R. Fay, *Palace of Industry — 1851* (Cambridge, 1951), pp. 144–47.
[22] Society of Arts, *Report on the Statistics of Dwellings Improvement* (London, 1864), p. 17. This
interesting document gives (pp. 37–43) in tabular form statistical information on most of the working-
class housing projects in the Metropolis.
[23] *Labourer's Friend*, May 1850, pp. 83–85.
[24] 14 & 15 Vict., c. 28. He was largely responsible also for an Act (14 & 15 Vict., c. 34) designed
to encourage local authorities to build houses by empowering them to raise a rate for the purpose.
The Act, which was merely permissive, accomplished little, for only one municipality (Huddersfield)
made any move to take advantage of it.
[25] *Labourer's Friend*, July 1847, p. 106.
[26] *Ibid.*, p. 107.

In the course of its first decade, the Society for Improving the Condition of the Labouring Classes had not succeeded in revolutionizing working-class housing, but it could take a limited satisfaction in what had been accomplished. In 1851 Ashley could announce to the House of Commons that in seven years the Society had spent £20,750 on new buildings and £2250 in renovating older dwellings and could claim a net return of 5½ per cent on the former and 6 per cent on the entire investment.[27] He could legitimately hold, moreover, that some of the hopeful experiments being carried on elsewhere had profited from the Society's pilot schemes.[28]

2

The 1850's and early '60's saw a modest upsurge of interest in housing questions, with three new metropolitan ventures reinforcing those of the '40's. Of these probably the least significant from the angle of wider influence was the work of that insatiable philanthropist Angela Burdett-Coutts, in this, as in other instances, apparently prompted by Charles Dickens.[29] Nova Scotia Gardens in Bethnal Green, anything but the garden spot that its name implied, was an irrefutable argument for slum clearance. It was here that Miss Burdett-Coutts and her architect H. A. Darbishire put up, at a cost of £43,000, four Gothic blocks of dwellings, complete with clock tower, for 183 families. This enterprise, different in spirit and practice from the run of housing associations, was philanthropy pure and simple, without the 5 per cent — for the buildings yielded only 2½ per cent. Nor was the beneficent owner much interested in such details. She did not hesitate to sacrifice rent-producing space to add to the comfort of her tenants.[30] One unique feature of these Columbia Square Buildings was the welcome given to costermongers, often regarded as one of the more raucous and less desirable classes of tenant. Not only were they not discriminated against at Columbia Square, but the buildings provided them with accommodations for their donkeys, always a critical issue in the housing of this colorful and boisterous guild. One of Miss Burdett-Coutts's treasured possessions was the silver donkey presented to her by the Costermongers' Club which she had founded.[31] The Bethnal Green project, in short, offers an admirable example of individual Victorian philanthropy in action, but critics were entitled to discount its long-run importance.[32] It depended too exclusively on the eagerness of a wealthy woman to give away large sums of money. Only if one assumed the existence of numbers of com-

[27] *3 Hansard*, 115:1268. There is reason to suspect that a more rigorous accounting system might have reduced this rate.

[28] Hodder, *Shaftesbury*, II, 225; *Labourer's Friend*, September 1847, pp. 168–69; March 1850, pp. 41–42; April 1850, p. 75.

[29] Clara B. Patterson, *Angela Burdett-Coutts and the Victorians* (London, 1953), p. 104. Baroness Burdett-Coutts is one of the "Gallery of Victorian Philanthropists," whose work is described in Chapter XV below.

[30] Society of Arts, *Report on the Statistics of Dwellings Improvement*, pp. 23, 41.

[31] *DNB*, XXIII (1901–1911), 263.

[32] Sir Sydney Waterlow, *R. C. on the Housing of the Working Classes*, 1884–85, Q. 11,953.

parably well-to-do and similarly motivated individuals could this be considered a productive experiment.

In a different category, though reflecting impulses no less philanthropic, were the plans of Alderman Sydney Waterlow, head of a large firm of printers and stationers and himself one of the more attractive figures in the world of Victorian philanthropy.[33] A City man, Waterlow was especially distressed at the uprooting of thousands of working-class residents by railway construction and street improvements. He was aware, of course, that the remedy lay beyond the resources of any single individual. At this stage he seemed to have suspected that experiments carried on by individuals and organizations would be important chiefly as examples to public authorities. Waterlow's pressure on the Common Council had something to do with the decision of the City government to enter the housing field on its own account.[34]

Before daring to approach his friends about contributing to a building society, he must satisfy himself that his ideas were practicable. Waterlow's earliest housing experiment, therefore, was carried out in 1862 on his own responsibility and at his own expense. Obtaining a site in Mark Street, Finsbury, he laid out £10,000 for four blocks of dwellings to accommodate eighty families. His collaborator was a master builder of working-class origins, Matthew Allen, with his own interesting notions about housing the poor. The two worked up their design by means of cardboard models, drawing for some of their ideas on the Prince Consort's building at the Great Exhibition. The new blocks embodied advanced ideas of construction, an external staircase, on which Waterlow was insistent (though an eminent architect objected because of the difficulty of getting "a coffin up and down the staircase")[35] and walls and floors of fire-resistant materials. These buildings, if possible, were to be less institutional than Angela Burdett-Coutts's severely whitewashed apartments at Columbia Square.

Waterlow's trial run was so encouraging that he proceeded to his larger plans. From fourteen friends he raised £25,000 as the initial capital for his Improved Industrial Dwellings Company. This figure was later increased to £50,000, then to £100,000, and finally to £500,000, as investors discovered the Company and became convinced of its soundness. At the outset, Waterlow told the Royal Commission on the Housing of the Working Classes (1884–85), his gravest difficulty had been that of capital. Although later money came more easily,[36] he was persuaded that the dimensions of the problem made it inevitable that sooner or later the State should intervene. And, as will appear presently, he took the initiative in persuading the Treasury to make available, through the Public Works Loan Commissioners, funds which eased, if they did not wholly meet, the capital requirements of the housing associations.

[33] An account of some of his philanthropic activities is given in Chapter XVIII.
[34] George Smalley, *The Life of Sir Sydney H. Waterlow, Bart.* (London, 1909), pp. 63–69.
[35] *Ibid.*, p. 63.
[36] Q. 11,908.

The philanthropy represented by the Burdett-Coutts blocks was little concerned with long-range effects; Sir Sydney Waterlow,[37] though his motives were as philanthropic as any, never doubted that unless his Improved Industrial Dwellings Company attained financial success it would have little permanent usefulness. Between the two stood the Peabody Donation, perhaps the most dramatic event in the history of Victorian housing. It originated in an act of individual philanthropy unparalleled in its time, and the donor attached almost no strings to his benefaction. The trustees, however, though they were not interested in a net return above 3 or 3½ per cent, managed the undertaking in such a way as regularly to produce a substantial surplus for further expansion.

The donor was, of course, George Peabody, the American merchant and philanthropist, who had been a resident of London since the late 1830's. His gift, originally £150,000 and increased by a series of additions to £500,000,[38] was conceived both as the repayment of a debt of gratitude to the city which had welcomed him a quarter of a century before and as the fulfillment of his own solemn resolution to share with his fellow men whatever fortune he might acquire. His purpose, as the letter to his trustees stated, was "to ameliorate the condition and augment the comforts of the poor" of London. Beyond that, the trustees enjoyed a wide discretion, save that there was to be no discrimination against claimants "on the grounds of religious belief or of political bias," nor, indeed, was there to be any flavor of sectarian religion or party politics. Though the trustees were aware of Peabody's views and he continued in close touch with them until his death, he made no positive requirement that they devote the gift to the housing of the poor. The donor was content simply "to throw out for your consideration . . . whether . . . to apply the fund, or a portion of it, in the construction of such improved dwellings for the poor." [39] Not only was the gift itself munificent, especially so since, as was noted with some surprise, this was a *gift* and not a *bequest,* but Peabody's liberal terms offered an agreement contrast to the restrictions with which donors often straitjacketed their trustees.

The London press was enthusiastic, though into the hymn of praise occasionally crept a note of regret that it had been left to an American to pioneer with such imaginative generosity. In a single act Peabody had insured better Anglo-American relations (greatly to be desired in 1862) and had compensated "for the foolish ravings of scores of American journalists who never set foot on English soil . . . How can England ever go to war with a nation whose leading man among us sympathises with and blesses the poor." [40] The Sovereign offered a baronetcy or the Grand Cross of the Bath, which Peabody gracefully declined, but Oxford awarded him a D.C.L., and the City of London an assortment of honors. There was no word of criticism when his statue was granted a place in Threadneedle

---

[37] He received a knighthood in 1867 and a baronetcy six years later.

[38] 1862, £150,000; 1866, £100,000; 1868, £100,000; 1873, £150,000 (by bequest).

[39] *The Times,* 26 March 1862.

[40] *Sun,* 27 March 1862, in a collection of leaders printed in a pamphlet, *The Peabody Donation* (London, 1862).

Street close by the Royal Exchange, so that an American philanthropist for nearly a century has been sitting "on the most costly chair in the British Empire." [41]

The trustees, five in number, included the American Minister (Charles Francis Adams), Lord Stanley, Sir James Tennent, and Junius S. Morgan, Peabody's business partner. But by far the most active of the group was Peabody's close friend, Curtis Lampson, under whose management the Peabody Trust became virtually a one-man corporation. A transplanted Vermonter, whose fur-trading interests had brought him to London originally, Lampson was known for his labors on behalf of the Atlantic cable, for which he received a baronetcy. The trustees got down to business promptly, working out their policies in consultation with Peabody himself, arranging for sites, and planning buildings. Within six years they had erected four groups of buildings to house a population of nearly two thousand individuals. [42] Thirty-five years later, with a capital outlay of over £1,250,000, the Trust was housing nearly twenty thousand persons in over fifty-one hundred separate dwellings. [43] Although, as will appear later in the chapter, Peabody policies did not escape criticism, this can still be regarded as one of the more original and productive philanthropies of a century that, with all of its humanitarian and charitable concern, was not conspicuously inventive in its giving.

3

Interest in housing was not a metropolitan monopoly. In the provinces, however, probably the most noteworthy undertakings were the work of enlightened employers facing the practical problem of accommodations for their working force. Earlier in the century Robert Owen had made a memorable attempt to plan a factory community at New Lanark, and throughout the century the more enlightened provincial employers (as well as the London owners of Prices' candle factory at Battersea) had shown concern with the dwellings of their work-people. Two of the better known, before the days of Port Sunlight and Bournville, were probably Titus Salt's factory community, Saltaire, three or four miles from Bradford, and Edward Akroyd's model village near Halifax.

Saltaire came about as the result of Salt's decision to move his large and thriving worsted factory from Bradford to a site on the River Aire not far from Shipley. On the left bank he erected a huge factory "in the Italian style," along with warehouses and weaving sheds, and on the opposite bank he laid out a residential community for his nearly four thousand operatives. The move to Saltaire took place in the early 1850's, and by the mid-'60's Salt had completed nearly six hundred dwellings at a cost of more that £100,000, exclusive of the land. [44] By the

[41] P. W. Wilson, George Peabody, Esq. (n.p., 1926), p. 58.
[42] Phebe A. Hanaford, The Life of George Peabody (Boston, 1870), p. 140.
[43] Peabody Trust, 33d Ann. Rept., 1897.
[44] Hole, Homes of the Working Classes, p. 67; Robert Balgarnie, Sir Titus Salt, Baronet (London, 1877), p. 136. For Hole and his work, see J. F. C. Harrison, Social Reform in Victorian Leeds: The Work of James Hole (Thoresby Society, Leeds, 1954)

early '80's the figure had risen to eight hundred.[45] In addition to cottages for the workmen, Saltaire had its full complement of public and "welfare" institutions — the Saltaire Club and Institute, with reading room, library, classrooms and recreation rooms; a park and playing fields; a series of schools — "handsome buildings," a visitor commented in the early '70's, looking "not unlike some Oriental temple, and you half expect to see a gorgeously appareled procession of dervishes or swarthy priestesses issue from the ornate portals" [46] — and forty-five almshouses for the aged and infirm. In mapping out his community, moreover, Salt showed an exceptional sense of scenic values, of vistas and squares, of the importance of well-arranged planting, and of the asset represented by the River Aire (whose course he changed so that the prospect from Saltaire would include graceful curves). Altogether this was a significant early achievement in town-planning and a noble expression of the philanthropic impulse — or of exceedingly enlightened self-interest. For at the rents he charged, Salt could not hope to receive more than 4 per cent on his investment.[47]

Edward Akroyd's project, though materially less impressive than Salt's, has some special points of interest. Although the original 112 houses that Akroyd built in connection with his Copley works were intended for his own work force, his next venture went beyond the familiar pattern. The Halifax employer seems to have had a taste for social experiment. He regularly attended the meetings of the Social Science Association and was the founder of the Yorkshire Penny Bank. Having launched his housing venture at Copley, Akroyd began to meditate on schemes which might have a broader application. He was skeptical alike of ordinary capitalist enterprise and of the benevolence of philanthropists as answers to the question of working-class housing. What he sought was a plan by which a relatively small sum of philanthropic capital could be made to accomplish results far out of proportion to its volume, so that, in his words, it might "materially assist in raising the general standard of working men's houses in any locality to an extent far beyond the original capital employed." [48]

The answer, Akroyd convinced himself, lay in helping the Halifax Union Building Society to increase its benefits. Specifically, if he were to buy the land, employ a competent architect to design blocks of dwellings, and persuade groups of working-class families to take the various units, then the Building Society might be expected to advance three-quarters of the capital required. In other words, this capitalist-philanthropist undertook to provide site and plans, to carry the overhead of contracts and supervision, and to assure purchasers that the contract would not exceed the estimate. Not only that, but where a buyer of good character could not find the necessary 25 per cent of the purchase money, payments would be spread over fifteen years, with Akroyd himself guaranteeing the first three years' installments and thus indemnifying the Society against loss.

---

[45] Anon., *Fortunes Made in Business*, 3 vols. (London, 1884), I, 318.
[46] George M. Towle, "Saltaire and Its Founder," *Harper's Magazine*, 44:834 (May 1872).
[47] Hole, *Homes*, p. 68.
[48] Quoted, *ibid.*, p. 72.

The fruit of Akroyd's idea was the model suburb of Akroydon. Although the community never quite justified its founder's rosy hopes, the plan had some influence on other undertakings. In Halifax itself, John Crossley, of the carpet-manufacturing firm which supplied the city with its other principal family of benefactors, started a similar scheme, West Hill Park. At Leeds, inspired by Akroyd's example, nine public-spirited citizens formed a "Society for the Erection of Improved Dwellings." Like the others, it cooperated closely with the local building society, but without such obvious philanthropic elements as were present in Akroydon.

4

By the mid-'60's a suspicion was growing among those interested in housing questions that philanthropy must discover more powerful allies. Urban improvements, especially in London, were proceeding apace, and the tempo of working-class evictions was accelerating. There was a limit, it appeared, to what could be accomplished by philanthropy, with or without the 5 per cent, unless the State were prepared to assist, and little hope could be placed in the activities of speculative builders. "Charity and speculation," the House of Commons was informed, "are but crutches at the best."[49] The Yorkshireman James Hole could conclude that philanthropy "may give the impulse but the work must be conducted by wise organisation and on ordinary commercial principles."[50] This, it seemed, was not easy to manage, and some of the semiphilanthropic ventures had failed to return dividends of even 4 per cent. Moreover, whatever may have been accomplished for the "solid artisan class," none of these efforts had reached down into the stratum of the very poor. The housing problems of these most necessitous city-dwellers remained substantially untouched, for even the modest rents imposed by, say, the Peabody Foundation, were well beyond their resources.

The most stubborn obstacles facing those concerned with housing were twofold. The operations of some of the organizations were cramped by their inability to obtain capital at low rates, while, with metropolitan real estate values skyrocketing, all were having trouble in acquiring suitable sites — at prices which would permit a rent level within the means of working-class tenants.[51] The suspicion, amounting to a conviction, was growing that such problems would continue insoluble as long as private agencies were left to fend for themselves, though how heavily the State ought to be involved remained for decades a matter of acute controversy.

The 1860's marked the initial stage in public intervention, when the Government was persuaded to take a modest step toward easing the capital shortage. When appealed to by Sydney Waterlow, the Treasury shied away from making loans to housing enterprises, save as these differentiated themselves sharply from

[49] By W. T. McCullagh Torrens (*3 Hansard,* 181:819).
[50] Hole, *Homes,* p. 91.
[51] Some revealing figures are given in *3 Hansard,* 218:1962. No one interested in housing could doubt that the critical obstacle was sites. See M. G. Mulhall, "The Housing of the London Poor," *Contemporary Review,* 45:231–37 (February 1884).

ordinary commercial ventures. This was no discouragement to Waterlow, who was entirely willing to fix his own dividends at a maximum of 5 per cent, a figure that was approved by the Treasury and written into the Labouring Classes Dwellings Act of 1866.[52] It was, in part, willingness to take advantage of this Act that accounted for the rapid expansion of Improved Industrial Dwellings as compared with the Peabody Trust. For whereas Peabody's expansion was financed entirely out of its own profits, Waterlow's method was to borrow from the Public Works Loan Commissioners on the security of his completed buildings.[53]

All this left the even graver problem of sites unsolved. There was good reason to doubt whether working-class dwellings could be built in central locations unless land were bought below its market value. Certain metropolitan landowners — Westminster, Northampton, and Portman — had leased land at low figures, but such indulgence on the part of noble landlords offered little permanent hope.[54] Apparently the essential condition of further progress in housing was the right of compulsory purchase by public authorities. This was the conclusion reached, somewhat reluctantly perhaps, by the Dwellings Committee of the Charity Organisation Society, which submitted its report in 1873. The Committee was suspicious of philanthropy as an approach to working-class housing, for "the free operations of capital would be embarrassed, and serious injury would be inflicted on the very classes for whom it is intended to provide." [55] Still, the housing societies could not go it alone, and the only agency which could aid them effectively was municipal government. In short, the ordinary incentives of the market place must continue to operate, but the way must be cleared for them by the State. What this meant was that a suitable authority must have powers of compulsory purchase in working-class districts, with, of course, full compensation to the owner.[56]

This principle was embodied in the bill which the Home Secretary, R. A. Cross, introduced in 1875, and the so-called Cross Acts (1875–79) empowered a local authority, where nothing short of razing and rebuilding a neighborhood would serve, to buy the property and arrange for a scheme of reconstruction. The high hopes aroused by this step proved largely illusory. During the first six years the Metropolitan Board of Works purchased, at a cost of over £1½ million,

[52] Relevant documents are printed in Hole, *Homes,* pp. 187–90 and summarized by Smalley, *Waterlow,* pp. 71ff. The Torrens Act of 1868, often regarded as something of a milestone in the history of working-class housing legislation, was of little significance for the housing societies. Although it increased the power of local authorities to hold owners of property to a decent standard, it applied only to individual dwellings.

[53] *The Times,* 26 March 1869.

[54] David P. Schloss, "Healthy Homes for the Working Classes," *Fortnightly Review,* n.s., 49:529 (April 1888).

[55] *Report of the C.O.S. Committee on the Dwellings of the People* (London, 1873).

[56] Since London still lacked a comprehensive municipal government, the City Corporation and the Metropolitan Board of Works would presumably serve as authorities for buying land. In 1867 a local Act had empowered Manchester authorities to close, without compensation to owners, dwellings unfit for human habitation. Until 1906, however, it was their custom to pay £15 for every such dwelling torn down. (William Ashworth, *The Genesis of Modern British Town Planning* [London, 1954], p. 105.)

fourteen areas totaling about forty-two acres and housing a population of over twenty thousand.[57] Six of these sites were sold to the Peabody Trust on terms which some of the other housing organizations regarded as scandalous. The Board of Works had allowed the Trust to buy land, by private agreement, at a price not only below the market value but even, it was suggested, well below what a quasi-philanthropic body would have paid.[58] This sacrifice, there was reason to believe, had been made for the benefit of tenants who would turn out to be much higher in the social scale than those whom Parliament had in mind.[59] Outside London, several municipalities, of which Birmingham is best known, hastened to take advantage of the new powers.

When the Select Committee of 1881–82 and the Royal Commission of 1884–85 reviewed the situation, they could find little cause for self-congratulation. In the Metropolis in the early '80's something over 50,000 individuals, to be sure, were living in "model" dwellings administered by a dozen different agencies. Of these the bulk were accommodated by the Peabody Trust (nearly 10,000), Sir Sydney Waterlow's Company (15,750), and the newer Artizans', Labourers', and General Dwellings Company which had been established under the Companies Acts (1855–62) and specialized in suburban cottage developments. The *Annual Chari ties Register and Digest* listed about thirty organizations interested in metropolitan housing. These included associations concerned with improving old buildings rather than building new, as well as a considerable number of units managed on Octavia Hill's system. Yet if there had been solid progress, there were also excellent grounds for skepticism, and little support for the buoyant confidence of a few years back that philanthropy plus 5 per cent would be enough to turn the trick. Octavia Hill recalled in 1875 that the total number housed during the previous three decades (26,000) was only a little more than the semiannual increase in the London population.[60] A new C.O.S. Committee on Dwellings, meeting in 1880–81, could find little reassurance, and a minority took an even gloomier view, tending to dismiss as hopeless the prospect of extensive housing developments in the central areas. Perhaps the proper procedure was to encourage the movement of the working population to the suburbs.[61]

The Royal Commission of 1884–85, under the chairmanship of Charles Dilke, carried on its work in a social atmosphere suffused with sympathy for the poor and with a certain sense of public guilt. *The Bitter Cry of Outcast London* had appeared only the year before, and the West End was evincing a new interest, compounded of pity and curiosity, in the condition of the East. Some of this concern resulted in nothing more constructive than to make slumming a fashionable diversion, but that was not the whole story. These were the years when the founding of Toynbee Hall and Oxford House witnessed to the hope that the chasm

[57] *S. C. on Artizans' and Labourers' Dwellings Improvement Acts*, 1882, p. v.
[58] Robert Vigers, *ibid.*, 1881, Q. 4449.
[59] G. W. Richardson, *ibid.*, Q. 5678.
[60] Cited in J. D. Chambers, *The Workshop of the World* (London, 1961), pp. 185–86.
[61] *Report of the C.O.S. Committee on Dwellings* (London, 1881), p. 141.

between rich and poor, educated and ignorant, could be narrowed by establishing groups of university men in slum districts. It was, in part at least, the furor aroused by *The Bitter Cry,* with the publicity given it by W. T. Stead in the *Pall Mall Gazette,* that led to the appointment of the Commission.[62]

Distinguished as was its membership, the Royal Commission set off no revolution in housing policy. There was some recognition that a parting of the ways had been reached and that private effort, even aided by the Cross Acts, was not doing the job. By this time the pattern was tragically familiar. Useful as the housing companies may have been in providing dwellings for numbers of artisans, they had completely failed to meet the needs of the poorer classes — costermongers, dockers, and casual labor of all sorts. And slum clearance projects, even when accompanied by a commitment to rehouse the poor, generally made their last state worse than their first. The evidence showed that in such cases the new dwellings, more often than not, were occupied by a higher class than those evicted, while the latter simply added to the housing miseries of neighboring districts.

Admittedly companies like Sir Sydney Waterlow's housed tenants above the lowest class, as they had been designed to do. But there was an evident suspicion of Peabody policies both on the part of other housing agencies, who regarded the competition of a subsidized undertaking as unfair unless it reached down to a stratum well below that of their own clientele, and on the part of "pure" philanthropists, who doubted that the Trust was fulfilling its founder's purpose.[63] Nettled by the criticism, the trustees included in their 1881 Report an earlier statement from Peabody himself approving their administration of the fund. No tenants earning more than 30s. a week, the management assured the Commission, were admitted to the buildings, though it was natural to select the most orderly and industrious of the applicants, who were always far in excess of the vacancies to be filled.[64] This assurance did not satisfy the critics (especially when the 30s. class was well above the lowest), and in the 1890's an outraged journalist could call attention to the net profit of nearly £725,000 in rent and interest harvested by the Trust on an original capital of £500,000.[65]

The Dilke Commission turned out to be something of a battleground for conflicting social philosophies. These ran all the way from the inexorably moralistic individualism of Octavia Hill to the Secretary of the London Trades Council, who most accurately sensed the direction in which the current must flow. "Private enterprise," he asserted, "aided by enlightened philanthropy, has done a great deal . . . Nevertheless, and without wishing to detract from these noble efforts, it is totally impossible that private enterprise, philanthropy, and charity can keep

[62] Helen M. Lynd, *England in the Eighteen-Eighties* (New York, 1945), p. 148.

[63] *R. C. on the Housing of the Working Classes,* 1884–85, e.g., Q. 5074, 11,912; *S. C. on Artizans' and Labourers' Dwellings Improvement Acts,* 1881, Q. 4072–74 (Gatliff); 1882, Q. 1192, 1278 (Canon Gilbert). See also the *Charity Record,* 20 Dec. 1883, p. 394, which reports an attack on Peabody policies by Lord Claud Hamilton at the Mansion House meeting on dwellings.

[64] *R. C. on the Housing of the Working Classes,* 1884–85, pp. 54–55.

[65] George Haw, *No Room to Live* (London, 1900), pp. 47–48.

pace with the present demands, and those involved in the rapid increase of population . . . But what the individual cannot do the State and municipality must
seek to accomplish." [66] He went on to assert that *permitting* public authorities to
act had produced only meager results. The next step must be to apply compulsion
to them.

The Commission's recommendations produced no sharp change in the direction
of housing policy. The Housing Act of 1890 served chiefly to consolidate what
had been spread on the statute books during the previous four decades. These
developments pass beyond the scope of this study, for increasingly housing became
the responsibility of public authorities. To this trend the creation of the London
County Council contributed markedly, for one of the obstacles to action by public
bodies in the Metropolis had been lack of a suitable authority.[67] Although private
philanthropists and quasi-philanthropists continued to interest themselves in working-class dwellings — in the years before 1914 there was a marked activity among
such undertakings — no one thought of these newer ventures, as some of the
Victorians had regarded their particular schemes, as the key to the problem.

4

One of the conclusions that emerged unmistakably from the inquiries, parliamentary and private, of the 1870's and '80's was the utter failure of housing
philanthropies and model-dwellings societies to reach the neediest and poorest
of the slum-dwellers. The only enterprises that deliberately sought a less respectable class were those identified with Octavia Hill,[68] a name of immense prestige
in the world of philanthropy. Of all the later Victorians few are more baffling
to a twentieth-century interpreter. Her achievements were formidable, and some
of them, notably her battle for open spaces and her pioneer efforts on behalf of
the National Trust, can be praised unreservedly. But of the work into which she
put her greatest energy and to which she devoted her undeniable gifts of organization, one must speak in more qualified terms. Though her contemporaries
regarded her as an oracle on working-class housing and her accomplishments in
the field were, in fact, staggering, they no longer command unquestioning admiration. If they were the achievements of a woman of impressive stature, they were
also expressions of a social outlook that today is almost incomprehensible and even
in the 1880's and '90's was being vigorously challenged. At the turn of the century
she could attack the London County Council for itself undertaking to put up
dwellings for the poor and thus discouraging private enterprise.[69] Her own work
placed Octavia Hill not in the vanguard of the main army but, one might almost
say, in charge of a diversionary operation.

The granddaughter of Dr. Southwood Smith, whose report on Bethnal Green

[66] *R. C. on the Housing of the Working Classes,* 1884–85, Q. 12,859.
[67] As Thomas Hare had emphasized in the early '60's. (*Usque ad Coelum: Thoughts on the Dwellings of the People* [London, 1862].)
[68] Save for the Burdett-Coutts buildings which accepted some types of tenant unwelcome elsewhere.
[69] *The Times,* 4 and 6 March 1901.

and Whitechapel had helped to set off the public health movement in the 1840's, she had some reason to know of the consequences of evil environment. But her first contact with the poor occurred when, as a mere girl of fourteen, she took charge of a group of Ragged School children who were engaged in toymaking as a cooperative venture under Christian Socialist auspices. The interest and sympathy that these children aroused in Octavia Hill was intensified in the late '50's, when she became secretary of classes for women in connection with F. D. Maurice's Working Men's College. She had visited the unspeakable homes of her toymakers, and she was not unfamiliar with the dwellings of some of her Working Women's College pupils. And when, after combing the parish of Marylebone, she was still unable to find tolerable accommodations for a poor family with young children, the issue of housing took on a burning urgency for her. While she was turning the question over in her mind, John Ruskin, whom she admired intensely and for whom she had done work in the days when she had looked toward a career in art, was also facing a dilemma. This was the agreeable problem of disposing of a substantial patrimony. Octavia's counsel pointed the way not only out of Ruskin's difficulty but her own. He would finance her housing experiment.[70]

This began in 1865 with three dilapidated houses in Paradise Place, Marylebone, followed a year later by an even more abandoned row in the same district, and at the end of 1866 by "the four very worst houses I have ever had to deal with." [71] A less resolute character would have been tempted to give up in advance. But during these early days, as she saw to the repairing of old houses and the reforming of drunken and shiftless tenants, she was working out the techniques that distinguished her plan from the ordinary model-dwellings society. Ordinarily she did not build new buildings but bought what were generally run-down, though not irreclaimable, dwellings, which she renovated by degrees. They were more manageable, she concluded, if relatively small, and her largest building in the mid-'80's contained only forty-nine tenements.[72] "If I build a large block of model buildings upon these sites I should have rather respectable, nice, working people coming to me . . . leaving the people [in] these courts which are difficult to deal with, and among whom my duty and that of my fellow-workers lies." [73] Since her tenants, as she put it, began "with as low a class as have a settled abode," [74] she held firmly to the principle that rebuilding ought to be neither too rapidly nor too elaborately carried out. In other words, improvement of the material environment must be accompanied by a parallel improvement in the tenants.

In the philosophy of Octavia Hill, better dwellings were an instrument for building character. When Sir Richard Cross, chairman of the Select Committee of 1881–82 queried, "I believe your particular plan of working has been the im-

---

[70] E. Moberly Bell, *Octavia Hill* (London, 1942), pp. 72–73.
[71] *Ibid.*, p. 77.
[72] *R. C. on the Housing of the Working Classes*, 1884–85, Q. 9062.
[73] *S. C. on the Dwellings of the Poor*, 1882, Q. 3361.
[74] *Ibid.*, Q. 3410, 3273.

provement of individual houses," she replied, "Yes, I think my particular plan has been that of improving tenants in old houses." Yet it was difficult to assign priority to either chicken or egg, for, "when both tenants and houses had improved, as far as I could carry them with the old buildings, I have had several houses rebuilt." [75] If she had been forced to commit herself, she would have held that "the aborigines of the East End" [76] lived in their unutterable squalor primarily because of their own moral weakness, and, without a moral reformation, no amount of superior housing would permanently better their lot. Octavia Hill never sentimentalized the poor, but neither did she shrink from raucous, destructive applicants when she came to select her tenants. She would never have endorsed the practice of the Peabody superintendent who told Beatrice Webb: "We had a rough lot to begin with; had to weed them of the old inhabitants; now only take men in regular employment." [77]

In the Hill system the chief agent in transmuting improvident savages into solid citizens was the corps of volunteer rent collectors. They were, in Octavia's view, the indispensable mechanism for dealing with the lowest class.[78] These ladies, as trained by Miss Hill, could be better described as social workers, who used their weekly call for the rent (regular weekly payments were an essential part of the plan) as a channel for establishing friendly relations with the tenants and discovering how they could best be helped to self-respect and independence. Once her enterprise was well launched, the limiting factor proved to be not capital, of which she always had an adequate supply, but these volunteer workers. As buildings were offered to her to manage (on a 5 per cent commission)[79] by individuals and in 1884 by the Ecclesiastical Commissioners, who gave into her charge large properties in Southwark and Deptford, the pressure for competent workers became heavy. For the duties of a volunteer rent collector, though they offered an outlet for young ladies who wished to be of use in an era when there was little that most of them could do, required qualities that not all possessed, however estimable their intentions. Among other things, it was no easy matter to strike a balance between the conformity to her system that Octavia, of course, required, and the degree of initiative which she also looked for.

Through her talent for leadership and her business ability, which commanded general confidence, Octavia Hill developed an admirable esprit de corps in her organization. Her *Letters to Her Fellow Workers,* as well as personal contact with her, inspired them with some of her own sense of mission. But this was a benevolent despotism, with no nonsense about committees or consensus. No one can miss the will to power, mingling with an unselfish dedication, which informed the work of this charming and determined little lady. With neither "fellow workers" nor tenants could there be any doubt about who was in charge.

[75] *Ibid.,* Q. 2980.
[76] The expression is Beatrice Webb's (*My Apprenticeship,* p. 265).
[77] *Ibid.,* p. 266.
[78] *R. C. on the Housing of the Working Classes,* 1884–85, Q. 8942–43.
[79] *Ibid.,* Q. 9013ff.

In her evidence before parliamentary inquiries her prejudice against committees emerged frequently.[80] The pronoun was invariably "I," never "we."

With the tenants the despotism was so transparent and the despot so convinced of her own wisdom as to be almost disarming. "I do not say I will not have drunkards. I have quantities of drunkards; but everything depends on whether I think the drunkard will be better for being sent away or not. It is a tremendous despotism, but it is exercised with a view of bringing out the powers of the people and treating them as responsible for themselves within certain limits." [81] She was devoting herself, as she believed, to training backward and delinquent individuals to stand on their own feet, and, committed as she was to the *mystique* of the Charity Organisation Society, she interpreted poverty and squalor largely in terms of personal failure. In her resolve to inculcate in her tenants the self-reliance and sobriety esteemed by the C.O.S., she would take any necessary measures to re-create them in the approved image. There was something infinitely school-mistressy about it all. If she "had been less of an individualist," Elizabeth Macadam remarks, "less of an intensive artist bent on her own particular performance and more of a prophet, she might have left behind her a really great scheme on big lines." [82] As it was, Octavia Hill was confident that she had the answers, and she must discipline her tenants until they too had learned them.

One of the appealing features of Octavia Hill's system was its efficiency. She watched details and gave close supervision to all of her extensive operations. Her apparent success and her confidence that she could continue indefinitely to earn at least 5 per cent persuaded owners of semiphilanthropic impulses to entrust their property to her management. By the early 1880's, seventeen years after she had taken over her first house, 378 families, numbering nearly two thousand individuals, were living in dwellings administered on the Octavia Hill system.[83]

Although she herself had little interest in collective housing ventures, at least as applied to the poorest classes, her success inspired one such effort. This was the East End Dwellings Company, formed in 1884 with a capital of £200,000 to provide dwellings for those too poor to qualify for the Peabody Trust or Improved Industrial Dwellings. The leading spirit in the new agency was the Reverend Samuel Barnett, the remarkable clergyman who was Vicar of St. Jude's and first Warden of Toynbee Hall, supported by several of Octavia Hill's former workers.[84] In the social atmosphere of the early and mid-'80's there was ample goodwill toward such ventures, and the fund of sympathy was augmented by such revelations as those of the Royal Commission on the Housing of the Working Classes and, on another level, by the shocking findings of the Sanitary Committee of the Jewish Board of Guardians. A direct outcome of this latter inquiry was

[80] *Ibid.,* Q. 8966.

[81] *Ibid.,* Q. 8967.

[82] *The New Philanthropy,* p. 140.

[83] *Report of the C.O.S. Committee on Dwellings,* 1881, pp. 70–75.

[84] Samuel Barnett, *R. C. on the Housing of the Working Classes,* 1884–85, Q. 8850; Henrietta Barnett, *Canon Barnett,* I, 134.

the Four Per Cent Industrial Dwellings Company, in which Lord Rothschild's was the guiding hand. The first of the six-story "Rothschild houses" was opened in 1886, and by the mid-'90's the "Four Per Cents" were sheltering nearly three thousand persons.[85]

The initial achievement of East End Dwellings was Katharine Buildings, close by St. Katharine's Docks, which were described by Beatrice Webb with a singular lack of enthusiasm. The structure had, in fact, only the merits of cheap rents and reasonably adequate sanitary arrangements. Beyond this it was almost numbing in its bleak sameness, a splendid example of what Charles Masterman called the "Later Desolate" style.[86] After serving for a period as volunteer rent collector, Beatrice concluded the buildings to be "an utter failure." Apparently potential tenants agreed, for as late as 1890 there were said to be a large number of vacant dwellings.[87] Beatrice Webb's view of the tenants was as little flattering as Octavia Hill's, but she did not share the older woman's confidence in the lady collectors, whose service she dismissed as "an altogether superficial thing. Undoubtedly their gentleness and kindness brings light into many homes: but what are they in the face of this collective brutality, heaped up together in infectious contact; adding to each other's dirt, physical and moral?"[88]

Whatever difficulties the Company experienced at the outset, it enjoyed a moderately prosperous and presumably a useful career. By 1900 it was claiming for its buildings a population of over 5600 and was paying dividends of 6 per cent on a profit of nearly £12,000.[89] Indeed, like most of the housing associations mentioned in this chapter, East End Dwellings still carries on.

With the exception of George Peabody's famous gift and, on a lesser scale, Angela Burdett-Coutts's Columbia Square buildings, great benefactions from individual philanthropists played only a negligible part in the model-dwellings movement. For several decades after the founding of the Peabody Trust no major endowments were established to finance housing. But the years around the turn of the century saw the launching of three such enterprises centered chiefly in the London area — the Guinness, the Lewis, and the Sutton Trusts — as well as a number in other parts of the Island, such as the Rowntree Village Trust's New Earswick outside York. The Guinness Trust, created in 1889 by Sir Edward Guinness, later Lord Iveagh, whose philanthropies in other fields were also memorable, comprised a fund of £200,000 for dwellings in London and another £50,000 for a similar purpose in Dublin.[90] The Lewis Trust developed out of the will of Samuel Lewis, chastely described by *The Times* as "money lender," and by

[85] Lloyd P. Gartner, *The Jewish Immigrant in England, 1870–1914* (London, 1960), pp. 155–56; V. D. Lipman, *A Century of Social Service* (London, 1959), p. 128.

[86] Quoted in Bruce, *The Coming of the Welfare State*, p. 119.

[87] Beatrice Webb, *My Apprenticeship*, p. 277; *The Times*, 5 Feb. 1890.

[88] Webb, *My Apprenticeship*, p. 277.

[89] *The Times*, 27 Jan. 1900.

[90] In addition, he gave £250,000 for destroying London slum property, £250,000 to the Lister Institute of Preventive Medicine, and Ken Wood House, together with part of the estate and the art collection.

the *Charity Record* as "well-known money lender," who in 1901 bequeathed to various charitable objects a sum which in the end amounted to about £1½ million.[91] The bulk of it was left with a reversion to his wife, who lived until 1906. The largest Lewis benefaction, £400,000, was to provide housing for the poor.[92] Obviously he had taken note of Sir Edward Guinness' arrangements, for the administration of his own bequest, he stipulated, was to follow that of the Guinness Trust, though it was not to be limited to the poor of London.

Like the Lewis, the Sutton Trust, the largest of the three, was intended to be all-English in its scope. Its source lay in the considerable fortune built up by William Sutton who organized a system of goods carriage on Victorian railways. Sutton & Co., Ltd., prospered mightily, and when Sutton died in 1900, he left the major part of his estate to finance low-rental dwellings for the poor of London and other "towns and prosperous places" in England. Owing to litigation over the will and entanglement in Chancery, it was not until 1927 that the Sutton Dwellings Trust went into full operation. Before that the Trustees had to proceed cautiously, obtaining the Court's permission for any step of consequence. Most of their pre-1914 building was in the London area, with blocks of dwellings in Bethnal Green, City Road, and Chelsea. In 1918 they opened a block at New-castle-upon-Tyne, and at the same time laid out their first cottage estate, in this case at Birmingham. At the outbreak of the second World War, the properties of the Trust numbered twenty-three, six of them in the metropolitan area, the others in large cities from Newcastle to Plymouth. At the end of its first half-century the Trust was housing nearly thirty thousand individuals in about eight thousand separate rentals, and was receiving a gross income from rents of nearly £250,000.[93]

In the fifty years since Sutton's legacy, the situation of charitable foundations for housing the poor (and others), as well as that of the building societies, has altered profoundly. Like education, though in a far less sweeping fashion, housing has been accepted as a public service, and the old semiphilanthropic agencies are no longer the advance guard that they once appeared to be. It is difficult to esti-mate their achievement fairly. Plainly their "model dwellings" had only a feeble impact on the housing problem itself. In London shortly after the turn of the century, their buildings in all were sheltering fewer than 150,000 persons,[94] and at no time did their programs keep pace with the increase in the metropolitan working population, to say nothing of reducing the original mass of congestion. Conceivably, also, their theory of working-class accommodations exerted a baneful influence, in that they put their stamp of approval on high-density housing as hygienic, comfortable, and economical, at a time when overcrowding may have

---

[91] *The Times*, 26 Jan. 1901; *Charity Record*, 18 Oct. 1906. In 1903 the estate was revalued at 2½ million, from which charity received about £1½ million. (*Ibid.*, 3 Sept. 1903.)

[92] The two other large benefactions in Lewis's will were £250,000 to the Prince of Wales Hospital Fund and £100,000 to the Jewish Board of Guardians.

[93] *Report of the Sutton Trust*, 1950, pp. 13, 21.

[94] Bruce, *Coming of the Welfare State*, p. 119.

been the gravest evil of urban life. To lodge as many individuals as possible within a given area at a tolerable level of sanitation became a conscious aim in drawing up plans.[95] This was natural enough — probably inevitable, given their economic assumptions — for even with buildings that took up every square inch of a site, so astronomical was the cost of land that the societies had to resort to every practicable economy to make their 5 per cent. There is, in fact, some suspicion that more sophisticated accounting methods might have shown them, at times, to have been less successful financially than they professed to be. After studying the statements of the two oldest building organizations in London, a competent student concluded that in the 1850's neither was doing as well as its annual reports proclaimed. The Metropolitan Association's return appeared to be 3⅛ per cent, while the Labourer's Friend was well below its alleged 4½.[96]

The most damaging criticisms, however, have to do not with the failure of philanthropists and five per cent societies themselves to cope effectively with the complicated issues of working-class housing. Rather, it is implied, by misjudging the proportions of the problem and by raising expectations that were quite impossible of fulfillment, private agencies were delaying rather than contributing to the ultimate solution. This line of argument puts the question in a false perspective. Conceivably the leaders of the model-dwellings movement might have spent their time and energy more productively in moving to arouse public sentiment in favor of a state housing policy. If private philanthropists had not attempted to check the further deterioration of London slums, it is at least hypothetically possible that the State might have been forced to intervene at an earlier stage.

Yet only with a flight of the imagination can one picture British Governments in the 1860's and '70's committing themselves to a comprehensive policy of working-class housing, especially without the object lesson supplied by the record of the building societies. As elsewhere in the world of philanthropy, one of the more significant functions of these voluntary organizations was education, both positive and negative. In this case, any decisive intervention by the State must rest on the presumption that working-class housing could not be handled by private enterprise, charitable or commercial, and this presumption gradually took on the certainty of conviction. Notwithstanding the most creditable of intentions and some considerable accomplishments, year by year the model-dwellings agencies were demonstrating that they were unequal to the task. It was charitable and public-spirited individuals who first exposed the hideous squalor of the slums and who founded organizations to improve the dwellings of the working classes. In the course of it, they accumulated a fund of experience on which statutory authorities have drawn, to the immense benefit of public housing projects. But it is also true that their relative impotence in the face of a complex and vast problem offered an irrefutable argument for responsible action by the State.

[95] William Ashworth, *The Genesis of Modern British Town Planning* (London, 1954), p. 85.
[96] Computation of Henry Roberts, *Trans. Natl. Social Science Assn.*, 1860, p. 771.

CHAPTER XV

A GALLERY OF
VICTORIAN PHILANTHROPISTS

O SELECT from the host of Victorian philanthropists a half-dozen (seven to be precise) for special mention calls for a measure of justification. Why this particular group of portraits rather than another? The prudent curator will begin with the admission that in a large degree his is an arbitrary collection and that another and equally representative gallery could be readily arranged. Joseph Rowntree, for example, would do as well as George Cadbury; William Rathbone of Liverpool might, perhaps, replace Passmore Edwards, and one of several Anglo-Jewish philanthropists might appear instead of F. D. Mocatta.[1] Numbers of Victorian businessmen made money and gave it away in much the same fashion as did Samuel Morley, though not many disposed of such large amounts.[2] Thomas Holloway and Angela Burdett-Coutts, one is tempted to urge, are unique and irreplaceable.

If there is much that is arbitrary and subjective about the selection of these portraits, there was also deliberate intent. I have purposely avoided some of the more obvious figures, the classic monuments of Victorian philanthropy, the Shaftesburys and Octavia Hills, who come to mind at once. Such men as George Cadbury, Samuel Morley, and Josiah Mason, though certainly well known, fall into a somewhat different category. For one thing, they meet the rather high pecuniary qualification established for inclusion. Philanthropist and humanitarian, as here conceived, are by no means synonymous (though the Victorians often used them interchangeably), and a life devoted to the service of society, such as that of Louisa Twining (workhouse reform and children's welfare) or Benjamin Waugh (N.S.P.C.C.), would not meet the conditions. The subjects of these portraits were all Victorians with ample fortunes, mostly of their own making, a large part of which they insisted on giving away. Their motives and the objects of their benevolence were as diversified as human need itself. A principal purpose, in fact,

---

[1] Rowntree and Rathbone will receive attention in Chapter XVI.

[2] An extreme example of "scatteration" philanthropy is George Moore, whose biography was written by Samuel Smiles (*George Moore*, 2d ed. [London, 1878]). In Bernard Bosanquet's words (*Essays and Addresses*, p. 8), Moore "had a sort of rage for collecting money for charitable and religious institutions; he collected for them just as he used to canvass customers for his firm." In this essay, entitled "Two Philanthropists," Bosanquet compared Moore with the Frenchman Leclaire, somewhat to the disadvantage of the former.

of this excursion into the byways of biography is to illustrate some of the varieties of the philanthropic impulse. For, within the group of seven, motives ranged from religious commitment through humanitarianism, social idealism, civic patriotism, and personal satisfaction to an undeniable, though not necessarily ignoble, desire for self-perpetuation. Like other worlds, it took all kinds to make that of philanthropy.

THOMAS HOLLOWAY
(1800–83)

The fortune accumulated by Thomas Holloway, the patent-medicine king, was a monument to unremitting effort and a talent for shrewd promotion. When he came to give it away, his approach had something in common with that of certain Elizabethan and Stuart *nouveaux riches* philanthropists and, indeed, of some latter-day American millionaires. For, unlike many of his well-to-do contemporaries, Holloway was little tempted to scatter his wealth semi-anonymously over the charity terrain. Instead, he elected to put the bulk of it into bricks and mortar (and endowment) for the two institutions that he founded. On one of these, Royal Holloway College, he lavished both his fortune and his personal energies over a period of years. He not only gave the closest kind of supervision to the building of the physical plant, but, with the aggressive assurance of some self-made men, he unhesitatingly laid down regulations—not all bad, by any means—on aspects of the institution's work of which he had little understanding. Although he would not necessarily reject advice when *he* had asked for it, his philanthropies were one-man affairs in which all the essential decisions were Holloway's own.[1]

Holloway's career was almost the apotheosis of the Victorian success saga, but one in which the theme was not production but publicity. For it was his talent for advertising, combining as it did a genuine, if mystifying, belief in the worth of his innocuous product with an acute sense of how best to appeal to his fellow countrymen, that spread the fame of Holloway's proprietary medicines from Cork to Singapore. When, at the age of twenty-eight, he left his native Cornwall in the time-honored fashion to seek his fortune in London, there was little about him to suggest a millionaire in the making. It was his association with an Italian vendor of pills and ointments that started Holloway on the road to affluence. On Albinolo's death, he began to manufacture the remedies on his own account and thus to build the fortune which grew steadily throughout the next half-century.

One might wish that such initiative and toil as Holloway and his wife expended on their vocation of selling patent medicines had been put to more productive purposes. But that would be to miss the heroic strain in this "epic of pills and ointment." At their home-factory-office just outside Temple Bar, the couple worked sixteen or eighteen hours a day, the long periods of indoor labor relieved

[1] Save where otherwise noted, material on Holloway is taken from the privately printed semi-centennial volume, *The Royal Holloway College, 1887–1937*, specifically from two chapters: "The Founder," by Hilda Johnstone (pp. 9–15), and "The Buildings," by C. W. Carey (pp. 16–20).

by daily visits to ships moored at nearby docks or longer expeditions into the country. As a salesman, one householder recalled, the impression that Holloway made was "not in the least that of the pushing canvasser, but of a quiet, kindly man convinced of the merits of the goods he recommended."[2]

The epic of Holloway's pills, however, was written not so much in his personal exertions in manufacturing and selling as in advertising copy brilliantly calculated to catch the attention of the middle- and working-class audience. All of the emotions exploited by twentieth-century Madison Avenue were adroitly played upon — fear, hope, vanity, keeping-up-with-the-parade, and the rest — and by a variety of devices the impression was conveyed that users of Holloway's pills belonged to the more enlightened section of the human race. In 1842 he was already spending £5000 on advertising; forty years later the total had risen to £45,000.[3] One pamphlet, whose cover carried Hygeia in flowing draperies standing on a step emblazoned "Holloway's Pills," contained helpful hints, some of which were hardly the sentiments to be identified with the future founder of a college. Holloway advised his customers, if they would keep their health, to "avoid heated assemblies" and to "read and study but little." The same pamphlet apprised shippers and merchants that the manufacturer would supply his remedies with directions for use in any of twenty languages, including, besides the ordinary European languages, such exotic tongues as Turkish, Armenian, Persian, Arabic, Hindustanee, Gozzerattee, Bengalee, Tamul [sic], Japanese, and Chinese.

One of the foundations of Holloway's astonishing success lay in the worldwide scope of his operations and in the skillful way his advertising emphasized the fact. It was almost as though Holloway's pills were paralleling — and even moving out ahead of — the expanding perspectives of the British people. On one advertising triptych of the early 1880's the center panel was composed of the young Britannia, who appeared to be a twin sister of the young Victoria, flanked by a bearded sailor and a guardsman each holding aloft a banner. Below them stood a Red Indian and a Zulu, in front of whom squatted a turbaned Oriental sandwiched between tablets proclaiming the virtues of "Pillules Holloway" and the "Onguent Holloway." The side panels illustrated Holloway's operations in the Near and Far East respectively, with veiled Muslim ladies on the one side and Chinese ladies on the other being supplied with the coveted remedies. This was the outside of the triptych; the inside struck a more personal note — and emphasizes the fact that Holloway did not shrink from publicizing his good works. For here was a portrait of the proprietor himself occupying the center panel and standing between panels descriptive respectively of the company's advertising policy and of the "Collège Holloway et Sanatorium Holloway."

Carried along by his untiring industry and artful publicity, Holloway's pills moved from strength to strength. On one occasion during the early days, his excessive commitments for newspaper advertising led to bankruptcy, but in the

[2] Johnstone, "The Founder," p. 10.
[3] *DNB*, IX, 1075.

end, all of his creditors (save the newspaper which had pushed him to the wall) were repaid, together with a ten per cent bonus. In 1867, to make way for the neo-Gothic Law Courts, the business moved from the Strand to an ornate five-story building in New Oxford Street. The proprietor and his wife had their living quarters on the top floor, and the firm's offices occupied the ground floor. In between were the manufacturing and packing departments, where, the *Pall Mall Gazette* reported,[4] a corps of young women could be seen filling boxes "from small hillocks of pills each containing a sufficient dose for a whole city." The profits from the business are said finally to have reached £50,000 a year. Holloway proved as shrewd in investing as in advertising, and the fortune, founded originally on his proprietary remedies, expanded rapidly through his financial operations. Holloway's Bank, concrete evidence of his talents as a financier, was a successful enterprise, even though it was liquidated after the death of its founder.

Meanwhile, a growing fortune brought its own problems. Without sons or daughters to inherit his wealth and with neither respect nor affection for his own brothers and sisters, Holloway canvassed various avenues by which his money could be turned to public benefit. Speculation on his precise motives would, no doubt, turn out to be of little profit. Beyond the negative factor of childlessness (the starting-point of a good many careers in philanthropy), we may assume that the Holloways shared with their fellow Victorians the belief that, though wealth represented a fair enough measure of industry and ability, it carried obligations as well. One of the heroes of the Victorian epic was the self-made man who used his substance, or a reasonable fraction of it, in improving the life of those about him. The efficiency of good works was an essential element in the Victorian ethos, and there is no reason to doubt that Holloway's acceptance of it was as genuine as his belief in his own success. He obviously enjoyed the twin satisfactions of contributing to social progress and wielding power, albeit in the interests of benevolence.

There was nothing impulsive about his choice of philanthropies. On the contrary, he studied the possibilities with exemplary deliberation, took counsel from a variety of advisers, and reached his decision only after years of reflection. Apparently he saw in the benefactions of George Peabody, the American, a challenge and even a rebuke to wealthy Englishmen. From the beginning he made it clear that he would concentrate on one or two important projects of national utility rather than scatter his resources on a variety of minor schemes. Once word of Holloway's intentions got around, through announcements in *The Builder* and at the Social Science Association, the old man's search was at an end. Some seven hundred communications, each with a solution to his difficulty, are said to have streamed in on him.[5]

Two schemes drew his attention. Some time before, in 1864, Lord Shaftesbury had aroused in Holloway an interest in the claims of sufferers from mental

[4] Quoted by Johnstone, "The Founder," p. 10.
[5] *Philanthropist,* December 1884, pp. 181–82.

disease.[6] What was most needed, he came to feel, was better provision for members of the middle and professional classes, whose conditions were not beyond cure. It was two decades before this idea was embodied in the Holloway Sanatorium at Virginia Water, with its twenty acres of ground and nearly five hundred rooms. Like Holloway's other decisions, this was based on study and reflection, with visits to institutions for the mentally ill on the Continent and in the United States. The new Sanatorium was not to be simply another insane asylum. It was to be a curative institution, chiefly for middle-class patients in the incipient stages, for professional or business people who might be saved from a complete collapse by timely treatment. The whole establishment, with its endowment, cost the donor approximately £350,000, and it marked a departure of some consequence in the care of mental patients.[7]

Another project captured Holloway's imagination more decisively and permanently. What turned his attention to the higher education of women and made him, in the Gilbertian phrase, "all wild to found an University for maidens" we cannot be certain. Very likely he drew some inspiration from Tennyson's Princess,[8] but a more immediate influence was his wife. She had shown interest in a women's college as a possible field for their joint philanthropy, and after her death Holloway naturally returned to the plan as the most appropriate of memorials to her. For counsel he turned to a group of eminent and able advisers which included such men as Kay-Shuttleworth and Henry Fawcett. With their encouragement he began to make plans for a women's college to be laid out on far more spacious lines than any then existing in the Kingdom. For, one must recall, Girton and Newnham were still in their infancy in the mid-'70's, while at Oxford, Somerville and Lady Margaret had not yet opened their doors.

In Holloway's somewhat grandiose thinking, his new institution would be more than an ordinary college. It would, he was confident, develop into a women's university, administering its own examinations and awarding its own degrees. The obvious arguments in favor of locating the new institution in one of the university centers made little appeal to the donor. Holloway's expansive energies would have felt stifled in the Oxford or Cambridge environment, and certainly the chateau that he was about to build would not have fitted easily into the pattern of Girton and Newnham — or, for that matter, of most other colleges. More than that, though naturally enough Holloway was relatively innocent of useful ideas on the higher education of women, by temperament he was something of an innovator. The new women's colleges at Oxford and Cambridge, *The Times* held, were simply creating men's colleges for women students — doubtless a salutary and indeed inevitable step.[9] But Holloway was looking toward a scheme of education, though with little precise notion of what he was about, that might not follow the masculine model so unquestioningly.

---

[6] Holloway called on him in the spring of 1864. (Hodder, *Shaftesbury*, III, 123.)
[7] *Charity Record,* 21 July and 6 Oct. 1881.
[8] R. C. K. Ensor, *England, 1870–1914* (Oxford, 1936), p. 150.
[9] *The Times,* 19 Dec. 1887.

Admittedly his own interests centered around the bricks-and-mortar rather than the intellectual aspect of his undertaking. Holloway's remark that he worked harder in spending his money than in making it was, of course, a picturesque exaggeration, but no one could take exception to the energy with which he threw himself into planning for the college. A relative was dispatched to the United States on reconnaissance, while Holloway himself went to the Continent. Whatever doubts may plague one who confronts Holloway's version of Chambord-in-Surrey, at least he did not succumb to the epidemic of Ruskin Gothic. Apparently it was Thomas Henry Wyatt, brother of Digby Wyatt and an architect himself, who encouraged the donor to consider French Renaissance. With Holloway it was love at first sight, and he and his brother-in-law[10] returned from a trip to the Continent more than half committed to French chateaux, a commitment that became final when an architect submitted illustrations of several. He would house his new college in a replica of Chambord, and he instructed the architect to measure the sixteenth-century building "from bottom to top." The order was carried out with relentless precision. Crossland, the architect, with an assistant, spent weeks at Chambord, submitting during the final two days to a checking-over by Holloway, who came to France to assure himself that no dimensions had been missed. Actually, the story goes, only a small and inaccessible dormer window on the east front was lacking in the architect's notebook, but he was required to remedy the omission at once.[11]

It would be redundant to comment on Holloway's judgment in building for his college a foot-by-foot duplicate of a French chateau, still less on his taste in imagining that the magnificent stone palace could be acceptably reproduced in brick. Admittedly there is a certain splendor about the *ersatz* chateau, especially when seen from a distance great enough to soften the incongruities and allow the observer to focus on outline and proportion. But whatever his esthetic shortcomings, the founder's determination was beyond criticism. Twelve years elapsed between the purchase of the estate at Egham and the opening of the College in 1886, three years after Holloway's death. The contract, let for £257,000, did not include land, auxiliary buildings, landscaping, and internal fittings, so that the cost of the whole establishment, exclusive of £200,000 for endowment, reached about £600,000.[12] The building was laid out on spacious lines, as spacious, necessarily, as Chambord itself, with external dimensions of 550 by 376 feet. Through the period of construction, Holloway required the architect to remain on the ground, and, though rarely coming closer than the nearby road, he himself received daily reports from the brother-in-law who was his deputy.

One bizarre feature of the building operation was the cash-and-carry basis on

---

[10] Although Holloway had little use for his own brothers and sisters, his wife's brothers became his principal assistants, and in his will he left the bulk of his estate, not already disposed of, to an unmarried sister of his wife. This amounted to more than £550,000. (*DNB*, IX, 1076.)

[11] Carey, "The Buildings," in *Royal Holloway College*, p. 16.

[12] These are the figures given by Carey. They differ in some respects from those in the *DNB*. What seems beyond question is that the undertaking cost Holloway between £700,000 and £800,000. The *Charity Record* (3 June 1886) gives the higher figure.

which the founder insisted. The patent medicine king could never forget his earlier experience with bankruptcy, and the notion of going into debt seemed to strike terror to his soul. In his business he had paid the employees daily, and in building the College (according to a story which, one concedes, is difficult to credit) he tried to employ the same principle. But "the contractor simply found himself unable to deliver the tale of bricks and the bill for them on one and the same day, and Holloway agreed that it would be sufficient if the account appeared on his breakfast-table next morning." [13]

The whole undertaking, *The Times* observed on the formal opening of the College, "had a wilful air about it from the beginning." [14] The building itself, magnificent or absurd, left much to be desired for utility. The semicircular rooms in the turrets of the chateau were awkward and impractical, and in some undergraduate suites the windows were well above the eye level of the occupants. Uninhibited by any understanding of academic procedures, Holloway provided only a single lecture hall, and no laboratories whatever.[15] The latter defect was remedied, by no means ideally, by equipping rooms in the basement and elsewhere for laboratory work. There might also have been questions about some of the nonutilitarian facilities of the College, notably the art gallery on which Holloway spent about £85,000 and which he stocked largely with the canvases of Victorian painters.[16] The examples of Landseer's and Millais' work evoked general admiration, but the irreverent found Long's "Babylonian Marriage Market" a curious subject for a community of young women pursuing the life of the intellect.

Obviously there were criticisms to be made of Holloway's one-man and, in a sense, irresponsible philanthropy. No doubt, to establish an institution on such a magnificent scale and with such a fanfare of publicity (it was formally opened in June 1886 by Queen Victoria herself) would give something of a fillip to the cause of women's education. But to locate it in such an academically isolated spot — more isolated, of course, then than now — seemed preposterous to some observers. There were those, moreover, who considered that the thousands lavished on bricklayers and masons could have been better spent in improving the instruction in existing institutions, and indeed that the whole plant had been built in too costly a fashion. "Luxuries which are not missed at Somerville and Girton," *The Times* asserted, "will not be enthusiastically prized at Holloway." [17]

Yet in some respects the founder's ignorance of academic matters was an asset to the young institution. *The Times* was less than fair in criticizing Holloway, "whose munificence is as innocently neutral as are said to be his own drugs," for the slowness of the College in determining its curriculum.[18] Actually, though he

---

[13] Johnstone, "The Founder," in *Royal Holloway College*, p. 10.

[14] *The Times*, 1 July 1886.

[15] Information from Professor Helen Cam, a graduate of Holloway; Carey, "The Buildings," pp. 18–19.

[16] *DNB*, IX, 1076.

[17] *The Times*, 16 July 1887.

[18] *Ibid.*

did not hesitate to lay down academic specifications, the Deed of Foundation (1883) showed a certain experimental attitude. Holloway may not have been clear as to what he wanted, but he was not to be hamstrung by tradition. He was prepared to believe that disciplines other than the classics and mathematics might have value, and he insisted on a curriculum that would not "discourage students who desire a liberal education apart from the Latin and Greek languages." Nor did he align himself with those who looked on the training of teachers as the primary aim of women's education. His College, he prescribed explicitly, was not to be regarded as "a mere training-college for teachers and governesses." [19] Not the least of the founder's legacies, it turned out, was the degree of freedom with which he endowed the College and which allowed it to develop in its own way. Holloway's ambitious dream, or fantasy, of a women's university remained unfulfilled; the currents of higher education were flowing in a contrary direction, toward less separation of the sexes. Yet as one of the member colleges of London University, Royal Holloway has been able both to maintain its distinctive character and to take its part in the affairs of a great University. With this outcome the founder himself could have found little fault.

It would be unrewarding to try to picture a "typical" Victorian philanthropist, but clearly, if a portrait could be drawn, it would bear little resemblance to Thomas Holloway. He seems, perhaps, to have less in common with his English contemporaries than with certain American multimillionaires, who during most of their careers were concerned only with business success and whose sense of social responsibility flowered late. For Holloway lacked the interest in a profusion of good works that marked the characteristically charitable Victorian, and religious motivation, if it existed at all, was not conspicuous in his activities. Yet measured by the total of his benefactions, which totaled well over a million pounds, the patent medicine magnate was certainly one of the two or three preeminent philanthropists of this time. The editor of the *Charity Record,* a knowledgeable enough observer, supported that judgment, asserting at the time a baronetcy was being talked of for Samuel Morley, that Holloway had done more than Morley and Sir Josiah Mason combined.[20] Such opinions are difficult to confirm. What is beyond doubt is that Holloway's decision to concentrate his gifts on a limited number of highly constructive objects makes him a memorable figure in the story of Victorian philanthropy.

SAMUEL MORLEY
(1809–86)

In his aims and methods Samuel Morley belongs well toward the opposite end of the philanthropic spectrum from that occupied by the pill-and-ointment chieftain. For him charity was no afterthought in the evening of a life given over, al-

[19] Johnstone, "The Founder," p. 14.
[20] *Charity Record,* 1 Sept. 1881. These two philanthropists are the subjects of the sketches that follow next in order.

most without letup, to building his fortune. As the heir to a well-established business, Morley was under no such pressure. But more than that, his outlook on philanthropy, as on other matters, reflected his devout Nonconformist faith, and his gifts tended to flow toward causes lying within the ambit of Dissenting piety. To Morley, with his convictions on Christian stewardship and his own simple, even austere, habits of life, charitable giving was a continuous obligation, not a single magnificent gesture. He was not the innovating philanthropist, but rather the well-to-do, benevolent individual who responded to the initiative of others. He was the resource which could be invoked when all others had failed.

With a single exception, Morley's charities hold no great interest for the student of philanthropy, restricted as they were to those causes, religious and reforming, so dear to the heart of Victorian Nonconformity. No doubt it would astonish the pious businessman to find himself remembered today as a kind of patron saint of the Old Vic, the single instance in which he deviated markedly from his established pattern of giving. After all, few, including Morley himself, could have seen in the "wholesome amusement" for the working classes which he helped to introduce in the disreputable old music hall a foretaste of the latter-day Old Vic.

For Samuel Morley the world of Victorian business was not quite the grim struggle that it had seemed to first-generation entrepreneurs. The firm of J. and R. Morley, hosiers, of Nottingham and London, had been flourishing for some decades before Samuel entered it. From shortly before the turn of the century, when his father established the London branch (leaving a brother in charge of manufacturing operations around Nottingham), prosperity had rained on J. & R. Morley in almost embarrassing abundance.[1] The fortunes of the firm were founded, of course, on the hand-operated stocking frame and the labor of hundreds of domestic framework knitters, for power machinery effected no sudden revolution in the hosiery trade. Even after it was clear that the future lay with the machine, the Morleys continued to maintain handicraftsmen who turned out work of conspicuously high quality. One of their silk knitters was said to have fashioned stockings for the Queen on her Coronation and, at the age of eighty-four, for her Golden Jubilee.[2]

The decision of the Morley brothers, John and Richard, to divide their forces meant that Samuel was to be born a Londoner rather than a Nottingham man. The youngest of six children, he spent his early years in Homerton, one of the northeast suburbs in which Nonconformists tended to cluster. At the age of sixteen, after periods at two boarding schools, he entered the Morley counting-house. Though he acquired the necessary grasp of the business as a whole, it presently appeared that Samuel's talents ran less to buying and selling than to finance. He took charge of the accounts, handled credit arrangements with the

[1] Edwin Hodder, *The Life of Samuel Morley*, 2d ed. (London, 1887), pp. 3–4.
[2] *Ibid.*, p. 7.

banks, and, modifying the ultra-cautious practices of his father, showed much skill in turning to the advantage of the firm changes in the money market.[3]

In the early '60's Samuel Morley became sole head of the business, the Nottingham as well as the London branch. It was under his hand that the firm made the transition to the factory system. At its greatest extent the house of Morley, the largest establishment of its kind in the Kingdom, had seven factories in the Midlands employing about three thousand hands. Partly as a philanthropy and partly because it continued to produce hand-wrought hose of high quality, the firm retained in its employ a number of old framework knitters. These had first claim on the remarkably advanced pension scheme established by Morley under which no less than £2000 was disbursed annually.[4] J. & R. Morley offers a capital example of the firm, astutely administered by successive directors, which rode the expanding waves of Victorian economy.

If hosiery supplied the materiel for Samuel Morley's philanthropy, it was Nonconformity that largely prescribed the conditions of its expenditure. The bulk of his benefactions went either directly to Dissenting organizations or to reform activities with which Nonconformist interests were closely identified. Only during his later years did Morley's philanthropic concerns transcend narrow sectarian limits. Throughout most of his life he was the patron of evangelism and chapel-building, the friend of a myriad of Congregational and nondenominational evangelical organizations. This was a rather tight Gospel-philanthropy, a reflection of his own uncomplicated religious faith, his contribution to the evangelical campaign against sin and ignorance. But Morley's social vision expanded along with that of his fellow Independents, some of whom during the 1870's were showing uneasiness about what an earlier generation had called the "condition of England question." Obviously the Two Nations had not been united, and there was some suspicion that Christians might have a heavier responsibility than they had hitherto admitted.

It is not a simple matter to deal in specific terms with Morley's aims and methods in philanthropy. Not a man of constructive imagination, he was, as the *Spectator* put it at the time of his death, "just an average English Dissenter of the strong type, with a great business faculty, much decision, a clear though narrow judgment, and a royal kind of capacity for giving." [5] Yet he was not one of those wealthy individuals who thought to discharge their obligations with "an easily drawn cheque." To Morley, however busy he may have been, philanthropy meant not only pecuniary assistance but personal service, a continuing commitment. He sometimes took office or labored actively behind the scenes in organizations to which he gave financial aid, and he was accustomed to follow up his gifts with personal inquiry, invariably in the case of the larger ones. On occasion he would employ the exemplary principle, favored by many present-day

[3] *Ibid.*, p. 34.
[4] Hodder tells the story of Morley's business career in chap. XII.
[5] *Spectator*, 59:1205–1206 (11 Sept. 1886).

philanthropists, of making his gifts on such terms as to attract contributions from others — or even making his own conditional on such support.

The character of Morley's giving precludes even a rough guess as to its total. There is no reason to dissent from the *Spectator's* suggestion that his philanthropies "would have made in the aggregate a great family fortune." [6] But the number of items making up the aggregate would have been enormous, for Morley's individual donation, on the average, was relatively small. There are gifts of £5000 or £6000, though these were few in number. Gifts in the £100 to £1000 bracket bulked large in his charitable expenditures, while his assistance to individuals might be given in almost any amount. Typically, though not invariably, he waited until appealed to by others before giving aid, and one looks in vain for interesting ideas from the philanthropist himself.

His official biographer, vaguely admitting this defect, finds justification in the pressure placed upon Morley by appeals from others. Letters "were perpetually pouring in, asking his aid on every conceivable subject. The result was, that his time was completely broken up in furthering the labours of others." [7] However little he may have taken the initiative himself, those who appealed to him had little cause to complain of casual or unsympathetic treatment. Morley carried over into his giving the same methodical habits that governed his business practice. Apparently he managed to read the hundreds of appeals which came annually to his desk, making the appropriate notation for his secretary on each. The various degrees of rejection might be designated by "litho" (lithographed form letter or refusal) — "No," "Impossible," "Unable" — while other marks indicated the amount to be given. [8] Naturally enough, Morley's reputation for generosity laid him open to wholesale persecution by organizations and individuals, deserving and otherwise. He could never escape from the flood of appeals, nor apparently did he wish to, and the black morocco bag from which he was never far separated always bulged with unanswered requests and other material demanding his attention.

For much of his life Morley's giving was heavily Nonconformist in flavor. He contributed handsomely to the building of chapels, especially in Wales, and assisted others to clear themselves of debt. In the years 1864–70 he put nearly £15,000 into chapel-building. Toward purchasing Exeter Hall for the Young Men's Christian Association he gave £5000, and £6000 for the Bicentenary Memorial Hall in Farringdon Street, which commemorated the Dissenting Ministers ejected from their pulpits in 1662. Not surprisingly the secular causes that attracted him were those that stood high in the Nonconformist-Liberal affections. A dedicated Gladstonian and for the last twenty years of his life a Liberal M.P. for Bristol, Morley was, of course, a free trader, an opponent of Church rates for Dissenters, an active champion of temperance, and a vigorous member of the

[6] *Ibid.*, p. 1205.
[7] Hodder, *Morley*, p. 144.
[8] *Ibid.*, p. 288.

Financial Reform Association. An alphabetical section from the list of the hundred religious and philanthropic organizations which sent deputations to his funeral will give the flavor of Morley's interests more adequately than any general description: "Earlswood Asylum, Early Closing Association, Evangelical Continental Society, Evangelistic Mission, English Congregational Union, Finsbury Radical Association, Gohehyb Memorial Chapel, Hackney College, Hackney Juvenile Mission, Homerton College, Hospital Saturday Fund, Howard Association, International Arbitration and Peace Association." [9]

Gifts to organizations and institutions by no means exhausted Morley's benevolence. Unlike some of his fellow philanthropists, he was ready with aid to worthy individuals — widows, orphans, and hard-pressed Nonconformist ministers. On one occasion, for example, he rescued a minister who, in his innocence, had requested plans for a new chapel from several architects and then found himself with a series of bills, each demanding 2½ per cent of the estimated cost. At another time he started a subscription list on behalf of George Cruikshank, the artist and caricaturist, himself contributing a goodly sum. [10]

To picture Morley, however, as simply the pious, evangelical businessman would do less than justice. In his later years particularly, without losing interest in the good works that had hitherto engaged him, he seemed disposed to move out in new directions. As some of his peppery personal qualities mellowed and some of his rigidities softened, his social outlook became less restricted. He often found himself well to the left of his fellow middle-class Liberals. He did not hesitate to preside at an Exeter Hall meeting where Joseph Arch was the speaker, and, during the agricultural lockout of 1874 in the Eastern Counties, he contributed £500 to the relief fund and joined with George Dixon of Birmingham in attempting to bring about a settlement. He championed the cause of franchise reform, and was, in fact, the chief financial support of the Reform League. [11] His apparent flirtation with political radicalism went far enough, one gathers, to arouse a mild uneasiness among some of his middle-class friends. [12]

Educational projects, realistic and visionary, also enlisted Morley's efforts. He gave handsomely to Congregational education, as well as to such secular institutions as the University College at Aberystwyth and the University College at Nottingham (£2000 each). What aroused more enthusiasm with him, however, was a characteristically Victorian scheme of providing sons of the middle classes with a taste of higher education and university life. Again, Morley was not the source of the idea, but he became one of its warmest and most munificent supporters. Cavendish College in Cambridge was set up as the capstone for a series of "county schools," privately supported institutions which would give to the sons of the middle classes some of the advantages that the public schools con-

[9] *Ibid.*, p. 500.
[10] *Ibid.*, pp. 316, 319.
[11] H. J. Hanham, *Elections and Party Management* (London, 1959), p. 333.
[12] W. H. G. Armytage, *A. J. Mundella* (London, 1951), p. 117.

ferred on their social superiors. Some of the top products of these schools, it was imagined, would profit from a year or two in Oxford or Cambridge.

Morley espoused the cause with the eager dedication that he brought to all of his philanthropies and took the lead in raising money for the new institution. The results were disappointing and, to him, mystifying — all of which, perhaps, underscores a certain lack of imaginative understanding in his make-up. Conceivably the same undefined pressures that caused Morley himself to send his sons to Trinity College, Cambridge, and later to set himself up as a country squire in Kent, accounted for the dramatic lack of interest displayed by his friends in higher education for the middle classes. Cavendish College turned out to be the sort of well-intentioned venture that was an anachronism even before it was solidly established.

A convincing symptom of Morley's more relaxed outlook was the enthusiastic support he gave to the Old Vic as a working-class recreation center. During the middle years of the century the old playhouse was anything but a reputable Temple of the Muses. Its specialties were the more lurid varieties of melodrama and ribald music-hall turns. Not only were the Vic's stage presentations of a singularly unsavory genre, but, as its historians suggest, we may reasonably "assume that it discharged its functions of bar and brothel with something like the maximum of grossness."[13] From this low estate it was rescued chiefly by Emma Cons, one of the more resolute and resourceful of Victorian social workers. A close friend and associate of Octavia Hill in her housing activities, Emma Cons had acquired an intimate and realistic view of the London poor. In fact, her attention was first directed to the question of nonalcoholic entertainment by the Monday morning harvest of black eyes which she encountered, the consequence of Saturday night in pub and music hall. To set up a counterattraction seemed an obvious prescription.

The Coffee Palace Association had already had some success in providing facilities for nonalcoholic refreshment. It was Emma Cons's plan to extend the same formula to entertainment and to establish a temperance music hall. The Vic, bankrupt and run-down, seemed an obvious site, and the Coffee Music-Halls Company (with Arthur Sullivan, Carl Rosa, and Julius Benedict, among others, on the council) raised the several thousand pounds required to put it into shape.[14] On Boxing Day, 1880, the old theater reopened, with fumigated variety as the main attraction and without liquor and ladies. The venture, though wholly on the side of the angels, lost £2800 in the first eight months.[15] It looked as though the poorer classes were determined to resist improvement. To many, respectable and disreputable alike, the notion of an antiseptic variety show seemed a contradiction in terms.

Although the Vic managed to hold on, catastrophe was never far distant. Dur-

[13] Cicely Hamilton and Lilian Baylis, *The Old Vic* (London, 1926), p. 169.
[14] *Ibid.*, p. 180.
[15] *Ibid.*, p. 183.

ing the early years, its program was a potpourri of variety shows, ballad concerts, temperance and educational (particularly technical and scientific) lectures. These latter aroused interest and led, first, to more systematic instruction at the Vic itself, and later to the founding of Morley College nearby. Again in 1884 crisis loomed, and here it was Samuel Morley who intervened so decisively that, in the judgment of its historians, to him "the Vic owes only less than it owes to its founder, Emma Cons." [16] With little of the frivolous in his own make-up, he had shared some of the familiar puritan prejudices against "worldly amusements," but with advancing years tolerance was coming more readily to him.

As long as the Vic specialized in music-hall performances, however decorous, Morley was little interested. But when concerts and lectures began to bulk larger, he convinced himself that this was an institution that, even in its lighter activities, merited support. In 1882 he began to contribute £500 a year, and two years later, when the Vic was facing collapse, he joined the executive committee in response to an appeal from Miss Cons. Though seventy-five years old at the time, he threw himself with his usual energy and perseverance into the business of establishing the Vic on a less precarious financial basis. He began by contributing £1000 toward buying up the remainder of the lease; he canvassed, made speeches, and reassured the workers that they were not to "worry about money" — and in the course of it all found himself enjoying some of the entertainments.[17]

Morley's "happy partnership," as he called it, with Emma Cons was cut short after two years by his death. It would be too much to say that his efforts relieved her of any occasion for worry, but certainly the Vic's prospects had become much less gloomy. Even after his death Morley's executors made a sizable gift toward buying the freehold property so that the Royal Victoria might become eligible for a grant from the new City Parochial Foundation. Presently the more specifically educational activities left the old building and acquired an autonomous status as Morley College. Morley's services were recalled in a tablet in the Vic, which proclaimed no more than the simple truth: "In memory of one who held his wealth in trust for the benefit of others."

There were few sour notes in the hymn of praise sung by editors and others to the philanthropy of Samuel Morley. All agreed that he was remarkably accessible to appeals for aid. Moreover, owing perhaps to "some inner nobleness or surpassing self-denial," he not only gave them a thoughtful and sympathetic hearing, but once he had decided that a cause was worthy, he adopted it as his own. All this was splendid. Yet at least one critic doubted whether, in the long run, Morley's tactics represented philanthropy at its most constructive. In an article entitled "Diffuse Benevolence," the *Spectator* deplored the failure of wealthy and charitable Victorians to "think of deliberately carrying out a definite and circumscribed plan of usefulness . . . A man of Mr. Morley's resources and largeness of liberality might, by a steady limitation of effort, do a really grand

[16] *Ibid.*, p. 187.
[17] Hodder, *Morley*, pp. 437–38.

bit of work in the world, might cover his county with free libraries, or give its whole population a chance of high education . . . He might, within certain towns, completely change the conditions of existence for poor children, or make life bearable for the aged poor, or relieve finally, and in all cases, some condition of physical suffering." [18] Practitioners of such catholic charity as Morley's might be more admirable and human individuals than those who, like Holloway, limited their operations. But the *Spectator* doubted whether in the long run their work was as constructive. Though it would be unduly cynical to suggest an inverse relation between the unselfishness of the donor and the ultimate utility of his philanthropy, a religious or moral compulsion to contribute, as far as possible, to every good cause could get in the way of more imaginative uses of the money. The *Spectator's* judgment was not without point: "We honour Mr. Morley for giving to all these things, but we should like some day to see a Mr. Morley concentrate his wealth and his powers on some immortal deed."

SIR JOSIAH MASON
(1 7 9 5 – 1 8 8 1)

Josiah Mason might or might not have met the ideal of a philanthropist who concentrated "his wealth and his powers on some immortal deed." Certainly there was nothing diffuse about the philanthropy of the Birmingham manufacturer. Not only do Mason's claims rest on two benefactions, a large orphanage and, more significantly, Mason College, the nucleus around which the University of Birmingham took shape, but during most of his life he was at pains to conceal such inclinations toward charitable giving as he may have had. More than that, he lived so simply and inconspicuously that, although there were vague rumors of riches, no one was prepared for the two large gifts amounting, between them, to nearly £500,000. Manifestly, in aim and method Mason's philanthropy had more in common with Holloway's than with Morley's.

Mason was as perfect an example of the self-made man as any of the giants of the eighteenth-century industrial revolution. The son of a Kidderminster weaver. as a boy and a young man he tried his hand at a bewildering succession of occupations. At the age of eight, he began peddling cakes and rolls, and then, with the aid of a donkey christened Admiral Rodney, he sold fruits and vegetables. Turning from distribution to production, he became successively a bootmaker, blacksmith, carpenter, and house-painter. Meanwhile, encouraged by attending Unitarian and Wesleyan Sunday Schools, he taught himself to write. About Mason's shifts from trade to trade there was little of the classic rolling-stone behavior. Rather these suggest the restless energy of the born entrepreneur. A turn at carpet-weaving, the staple industry of Kidderminster, convinced him that his

---

[18] *Spectator,* 59:1206 (11 Sept. 1886).

native city offered little prospect of fame or fortune, and he determined to seek a wider field.[1]

Success did not rush to meet Mason when he established himself in Birmingham. Shabbily treated by an uncle whose small workshop he managed, at the end of seven years he found himself not a rising young businessman but simply one of the unemployed. What set him on the road to riches was an almost fortuitous encounter with Harrison, a manufacturer of split (key) rings. At his suggestion, Mason moved in, took charge of the business, and at the end of a year when the older man retired, bought it for the nominal figure of £500. This was hardly more than a gift on the part of Harrison, who had quickly developed respect and affection for his younger partner. The split ring business proved moderately lucrative, and Mason, who combined a degree of mechanical ingenuity with business talent, improved the process and increased the profits. But the eye of the ambitious young entrepreneur was scanning the Birmingham horizon for greener pastures.

More by accident than design, he was drawn to a branch of manufacture whose expansion was being made inevitable by nineteenth-century social change. The spread of literacy and the growth of trade, with the large volume of business correspondence and the more elaborate accounting systems that it entailed, created a demand for improved writing materials. With the supply of quills already inadequate, the expanding economy depended increasingly on the production of cheap, efficient steel pens in quantity. Harrison, Mason's partner, had introduced him to the problem, having years before made some pens for his friend Dr. Joseph Priestley, who complained of the lack of satisfactory writing implements. During the 1820's, three or four manufacturers in London and Birmingham were experimenting with improved nibs. Mason happened to buy some made by James Perry of London. These he thought so poor that he hurried home to turn out an improved variety, which he sent at once to the manufacturer. Forty-eight hours later Perry appeared in Birmingham, prepared to thrust a contract at Mason. The upshot was an agreement which tied the two men in an exclusive relationship. For many years Mason manufactured only for Perry, and all of the pens sold by the latter came from Mason's works, though they continued to bear the stamp "Perry, Red Lion Square, London."

Even after the factory began to sell quantities abroad, these usually bore the stamp of the foreign wholesaler rather than of the manufacturer. As a result, the extent of Mason's operations was largely concealed from the trade itself, and even more from the pen-buying public. Yet his was the world's largest business of its kind. When he first began to manufacture for Perry in 1829, shipments were small, not more than twenty or thirty gross at a time. Forty-five years later, the

---

[1] John T. Bunce, *Josiah Mason* (Birmingham, 1882), chap. I. See also *Fortunes Made in Business* (London, 1884), I, 131–83. From internal evidence it is clear that the chapter on Mason was written by Bunce.

factory was producing thirty-two thousand gross a week, and employing about a thousand hands. Something like sixty tons of pens were constantly moving through the factory, and when one recalls that a ton of steel yielded about a million and a half pens, it is hard to conceive an army of consumers large enough to use such a quantity.[2]

If few realized that Mason was the dominant figure in pen manufacturing, even fewer connected him with one of Birmingham's more interesting industrial innovations, that of electroplating. The pioneers, of course, were the brothers Elkington and a group of associates. When George Elkington decided to go into manufacturing on his own account rather than grant licenses to others, his ally in the venture was Josiah Mason, who, Bunce remarks, played Boulton to Elkington's Watt. Mason had financed some of the earlier experiments, and now he took over much of the responsibility for planning and arranging the factory. His shrewd eye saw that "art products" and handsome showrooms were all very well, but for its main support the firm must depend on humbler creations — knives, forks, and other household wares. Once more Mason's business judgment had served him well. His partnership with the Elkingtons, which lasted from 1842 to 1857, proved immensely profitable. It would not have occurred to most of his Birmingham neighbors to associate the inconspicuous pen manufacturer with the Mason who seemed to be involved in the new electroplating establishment. Others, better informed, recognized his superlative business talent. On more than one occasion Herr Krupp offered him a partnership in the Essen plant, a temptation which, apparently, Mason found easy to resist.

As with successful entrepreneurs, Mason's money bred money. Though he had little of the plunger about him, he never held with half-measures. Once convinced that an undertaking promised well, he did not stint on his investment. From split rings he had moved on to become the world's largest producer of steel pens, a partner in a great electroplating establishment, and, with Elkington, the proprietor of copper-smelting works in South Wales. Here the owners had not only to erect a smelting plant, but, since the site had been little more than "a lonely and desolate rabbit warren," they had to build a community, with cottages and schools, in order to attract workpeople. In addition to the businesses in which he was actively involved, Mason invested in other ventures and in Birmingham real estate. He was, in fact, almost the archetype of the first-generation Victorian businessman, never flagging in his entrepreneurial energy, and with few interests beyond making money and (later) giving it away. This, he would have said, was enjoyment enough for anyone.

Unlike Samuel Morley, whose whole life was an exercise in philanthropy, Josiah Mason had passed the age of sixty-five before he took his first major step. What impelled him we cannot be sure. Obviously, as with Thomas Holloway, childlessness was a factor. He had had the usual unhappy experiences with

[2] Drawn largely from Bunce. See also Gill and Briggs, *History of Birmingham*, I, 300–302.

charity impostors and had discovered the evils of indiscriminate giving. But beyond all this — and possibly enhanced by his own childlessness — Mason's love of children was deep and genuine. As a young man, he had abandoned his street trade and taken up shoemaking in order to care for a crippled brother. It was not unnatural, therefore, that his first large benefaction should be an orphanage of imposing size.

As a late-blooming philanthropist, Mason had the advantage of never having acquired a special reputation for benevolence. His was not one of the names to which all charitable organizations addressed appeals as a matter of course. Not only that, but his unassuming ways and his modest scale of living served as something of a protective screen. When at the time the orphanage project was taking form in his mind, he sought the counsel of the rector of St. Martin's, the principal Birmingham parish, he was treated rather brusquely by the reverend doctor. One could not get very far, the rector cautioned him, with a donation of £20 or £50. It was the clergyman who was embarrassed when Mason replied casually that what was contemplated would be of the order of £100,000. The scheme, however, foundered on religious differences, and in the end he built his orphanage at Erdington without benefit of clerical advice.

This was a charitable establishment of some magnitude, with a building designed for three hundred children and costing £60,000. To this Mason added an endowment of approximately £200,000. The Erdington institution was the end product of a series of plans. Originally the donor had contemplated merely a small orphanage (which was actually built), but this donation served only to whet his appetite for philanthropy. He began to think of an institution first for a hundred, then for two hundred, and finally for three hundred children. The massive building, begun in 1865 with remarkably little fanfare, was completed four years later, a stately and indeed somewhat overpowering monument in Ruskin Gothic or "Lombardic," as a contemporary described it. About one matter Mason felt strongly. He had no objection to religious teaching of a nondogmatic sort, but there was to be no teaching of "catechisms, formularies, or articles of faith," nor any discrimination among applicants on the ground of religious persuasion — or for that matter, of class, condition, or locality. This was, in short, a well-endowed [3] institution administered, in accordance with the donor's instructions, on enlightened principles.

In founding an orphanage, Mason was following a well-established convention for one-man philanthropies. His other great benefaction, a scientific and liberal arts college, contributed to the revival of an old but relatively dormant tradition — for few foundations for higher education had been established by individual philanthropists in the eighteenth and early nineteenth centuries. His decision owed something to the awareness of a self-made man of the deficiencies

[3] The endowment, chiefly in land, was expected to yield an income of £10,000, and perhaps more, since a good deal of it was close to the expanding city. Unfortunately other portions were farming land, and during the agricultural depression of the late century the income of the orphanage suffered.

in his own education, but it also reflected the civic pride and industrial optimism of the Midland metropolis.

Birmingham was moderately well-equipped with institutions of other grades, notably the magnificent King Edward VI School and the Midland Institute, a successful venture in adult education, chiefly for artisans. But the civic leaders of Joseph Chamberlain's renovated city looked enviously at Manchester and Liverpool to the north, where colleges had been already founded. To a much greater degree than these, Birmingham's institution was the creation of a single benefactor. Twenty years after the cornerstone of Mason College had been laid, it was incorporated as a university college and a few years later received a royal charter as the University of Birmingham.[4] Meanwhile, the cause of higher education had been adopted by the community and had profited from the gifts of numbers of local manufacturers and businessmen. The original impulse, however, came from the self-educated pen magnate.

Mason's essential purpose was to meet the special educational needs of the Birmingham district, a problem that at the outset he saw in rather limited terms. He seems to have conceived of his new foundation largely as an institute of technology, a center of "practical scientific knowledge," which would benefit the industries of the Midlands and help England "maintain her position as the manufacturing center of the world."[5] His initial deed of foundation therefore provided only for instruction in science and in the English, German, and French languages. Fortunately he did not long insist upon such a restricted curriculum, but by later deeds gave the trustees all the latitude they could wish, with a single qualification. The reservation, as one might guess, derived from Mason's abhorrence of religious doctrine. There were to be "no lectures, or teaching, or examinations" on theology, and likewise none on issues which "for the time being shall be the subject of party political controversy," a condition which the "said Josiah Mason doth declare to be fundamental."[6] Save for this restriction the new foundation was scarcely touched by the Dead Hand.

Progress on the building was slow. Although Mason's ideas had been fairly well formed by 1868, it was not until four years later that sufficient land could be obtained in the Town Hall area, so complicated and confused were the legal rights. To work out satisfactory building plans also took time; one gathers that both the founder and his trustees found a good deal to query and alter in the architect's specifications. When it came to construction, the founder would have nothing to do with the contract system. Instead, the builder, who happened to be Mason's relative by marriage, handled the assignment under the day-to-day supervision of the architect and his staff. The foundation stone was laid in 1875, on the founder's eightieth birthday, and five years later the red brick Gothic pile (the style is described as thirteenth-century French) was opened with exercises

---

[4] Gill and Briggs, *Birmingham*, II, 110.
[5] Mason's remarks on laying the foundation stone. (Bunce, *Josiah Mason*, p. 212.)
[6] Quoted *ibid.*, pp. 219–20.

at which T. H. Huxley was the principal speaker. By a single stroke, costing him about £200,000 in building and endowment,[7] Mason assured Birmingham of an outstanding position among regional centers of higher learning.

Mason's approach to philanthropy raises no vastly perplexing questions. His giving was, in fact, an authentic expression of his character, and somewhat analogous to his behavior as a businessman. He had none of the religious devoutness that made such men as Samuel Morley susceptible to appeals to their Christian duty, and he was little tempted to dribble out his resources in small gifts. The substantial investment he thought as sound in philanthropy as in business. He gave to potential investments in charity much the same kind of hard-headed scrutiny that he applied to business openings — and on these his decisions were made with quick insight and assurance. Looking at his shrewd, determined face, with mouth and eyes that could be grim but could also relax in kindly humor, one has no difficulty in crediting his reputation as a formidable bargainer and a businessman of constructive gifts. These qualities he carried over into his philanthropy. For, if Samuel Morley was happiest when assisting organizations already carrying on, Josiah Mason wished himself to be a creative force.

BARONESS BURDETT-COUTTS
(1814–1906)

If one were to compile even a relatively short list of exceptional Victorians, Angela Burdett-Coutts would have an almost unimpeachable case for inclusion. Among her other claims to distinction, she may well have been, in aggregate contributions to charity, the premier Victorian philanthropist.[1] Certainly none of her philanthropic impulses were frustrated by lack of financial resources. Granddaughter of Thomas Coutts, founder of Coutts's Bank, she inherited, in a rather roundabout way, his vast fortune. At the age of eighty and only a few days after the death of his first wife, Grandfather Coutts had scandalized his three daughters by marrying Harriot Mellon, a thirty-eight-year-old actress to whom he had been devoted for some years. Harriot, who appears to have been clever, kindly, and unaffected, though without pedigree, was received by her new stepdaughters with resentment and hostility. Tom Coutts's will, leaving his entire fortune (he had already made some provision for his daughters) to the new wife added injury to insult. A few years later Harriot's marriage to the young Duke of St. Albans provided her with social position to match her enormous wealth.

In all of the Coutts connection it was only the young Angela who found her step-grandmamma agreeable company. A curious bond of sympathy developed between the rather unattractive girl and the plebeian old Duchess. For them the family feud did not exist, and they spent a good deal of time together, in driving

---

[7] The endowment was largely in local land, buildings, and ground rents. The College received part of the endowment as Mason's residuary legatee.

[1] The impression in the 1880's was that she might have given away £3 or £4 million. (Sarah Bolton, *Lives of Girls Who Became Famous* [New York, 1886], p. 320.)

tours around the country and country-house visits. Even so it came as a surprise
to everyone, including Angela, when, by a will signed only a fortnight before her
death in 1837, the Duchess left the whole of her fortune, including her large
interest in Coutts's Bank, to Angela.[2] In the view of the family, this was nearly
as great an indignity as the will of Tom Coutts himself, who had disinherited
his daughters in favor of the wife of his old age, and Angela's father, the
crotchety sometime radical Sir Francis Burdett, was so outraged at his wife's
being passed over that the young heiress had to take temporary refuge with a
former governess.[3]

At the age of twenty-three Angela thus found herself the possessor of enormous
wealth, with an income of the order of perhaps £80,000.[4] She promptly became a
public figure, the most coveted of marital prizes, at whose feet half of the country's eligible young men cast themselves with eager hope. They received little
encouragement. Angela was shrewd enough to realize the source of her appeal.
Though an intelligent, admirable young woman, she was rather too tall, with
an indifferent complexion and little of the charm that conventionally kindles
romance. As an heiress of more modest fortune, Angela would not have been
swamped by proposals of marriage. She was little tempted by any of them.
Among the friends of her early days of affluence, it was only the venerable Duke
of Wellington with whom she was on easy and affectionate terms and whom,
with more encouragement on his part, she might well have married.[5] Disparity in
age was not regarded in the Coutts connection as a serious obstacle to marriage,
and forty years later Angela herself was to add a slightly bizarre epilogue to
the tradition when at the age of sixty-seven she married the twenty-seven-year-old
William Ashmead Bartlett.

To administer such a fortune as Angela Burdett's (or Burdett-Coutts's, as she
had become by royal license) would have taxed the business ability and wisdom
of older heads. In general, though inclined to be a bit headstrong and proud,
she handled her affairs with method and judgment. Whether she had much influence on policy at the Bank is doubtful. She has been credited, however, with
seeing that the future lay with the joint-stock rather than the private bank and
with persuading Coutts & Company to reorganize. Her main concern was with
spending her income in a useful fashion, and here she showed herself generous
and sensitive to the misfortunes of others. In its leader on her death *The Times*
plainly exaggerated when it implied that "mainly to her example . . . the modern

[2] Harriot provided the Duke with a life annuity of £10,000 (with the reversion to Angela). Most
of the estate was left unconditionally, but, under pressure from Coutts partners, Harriot willed the
Bank stock to Angela with remainder to her elder sisters if she should die without issue. (*DNB,
1901–1911*, I, 259.) The Duchess had always made it clear that the bulk of the estate would return
to the family and had planned on making the son of Lady Bute (Angela's elder sister) her heir. But
when the young man married the daughter of Lucien Bonaparte, he was promptly disinherited. (Edgar
Johnson, *Letters from Charles Dickens to Angela Burdett-Coutts* [London, 1953], p. 13.)
[3] Clara Burdett Patterson, *Angela Burdett-Coutts and the Victorians* (London, 1953), p. 26.
[4] *Ibid.*, p. 25.
[5] *Ibid.*, pp. 77–78.

conception of judicious charity is due." [6] But at least she recognized the social responsibility of wealth and admitted an obligation to use her own for constructive purposes.

Angela's addiction to philanthropy is sometimes attributed to the influence of her father, the public-spirited but erratic radical politician, Sir Francis.[7] This is a credible inference. Obviously she thought of herself as heir to a family tradition that embodied not only the financial caution and canniness of Thomas Coutts but the passionate, if sometimes unpredictable, sympathy for the underdog of Sir Francis Burdett. It would have been impossible, of course, for a highly publicized heiress to avoid some involvement with London charity. She was the recipient of hundreds of appeals each month, legitimate and otherwise, from the begging letters of individuals to solicitations from well established institutions. What distinguished Angela Burdett-Coutts from monied young women of charitable inclinations was not only the volume of her benefactions but the fact that, to a considerable degree, she made philanthropy her profession.

In guiding her benevolence the influence of Charles Dickens was probably decisive. He was, his biographer concludes, "not only the creative imagination behind many of Miss Coutts's efforts, but their directing force and executive arm." [8] Two years before Angela's inheritance came to her, they had met at the home of a banker who was shortly to become a Coutts partner. The young woman with the means to aid her fellow humans and the resolution to do it discovered an adviser and ally in the twenty-three-year-old reporter with a burning hatred of social injustice. As their friendship grew, Dickens was able to broaden her charity horizons beyond the church work in which at the outset she was engrossed.[9] This she continued, of course, and her gifts to the Church of England, in its various branches, reached a formidable total. She founded and endowed the colonial bishoprics of Cape Town and Adelaide, and in the late 1850's the bishopric of British Columbia, the latter with gift of £50,000.[10] St. Stephen's Church, Westminster, with schools and vicarage, which was built in memory of her father in the constituency which he represented for thirty years, cost over £90,000. She furnished Bishop Blomfield with £15,000 for church-building in his London diocese, and at her own expense put up a church in a poor section of Carlisle. Almost certainly, as Howitt remarked, no other woman below the rank of Queen had done so much for the Church, and (to allow him his picturesque exaggeration) had she so served the Catholic Church, "she would undoubtedly be canonised St. Angela." [11]

No one could complain that, throughout her career as a whole, Miss Coutts's philanthropic interests were overspecialized. On the one hand, she was always

[6] *The Times*, 7 Jan. 1907.
[7] Johnson, *Letters from Charles Dickens*, p. 11; Patterson, *Angela Burdett-Coutts*, p. 26.
[8] Johnson, p. 18.
[9] Patterson, p. 151.
[10] *DNB, 1901–1911*, I, 261.
[11] *Northern Heights of London*, quoted in the *DNB, 1901–1911*, I, 261.

eager to relieve personal distress, and her private charity must have been enormous, though by no means indiscriminate. For some years Dickens served as her almoner, screening applications and separating the worthy from the undeserving. "Mr. Tolfrey," he advises her, "is *not* a fit subject for your generous aid," but "with a smaller sum, my dear Miss Coutts, I think I can do, on your behalf, an infinitely greater service" for a case where £30 "will be like Help from Heaven." [12] When Dickens' other responsibilities became too demanding, his successor (recommended by himself) was W. H. Wills, assistant editor of *Household Words,* who served as her secretary for twelve years until a hunting accident in 1868 forced his retirement. [13]

To recall Angela's public charities would be almost to box the compass of Victorian philanthropy. Her benevolence comprehended a myriad of causes, both palliative and genuinely productive. Her interests extended to education, fallen women, housing, emigration, child welfare, and what would now be termed urban improvement or redevelopment. About her philanthropy there was some of the omnivorousness characteristic of her fellow Victorian humanitarians; the difference lay in the magnitude of her resources. And although Dickens and his successors carried a good deal of the burden of suggesting and weighing opportunities, beyond any doubt the Baroness (for such she became in 1871) herself was the key figure in her philanthropic activities. Not only did she try to read every letter sent to her — sometimes to the number of three or four hundred a day [14] — but the ideas for the projects which she financed often originated with herself. And once having made a charitable investment, she worked indefatigably in supervising it.

Rather than attempt a catalogue of the multitudinous Burdett-Coutts benefactions, it will be enough to note a number of her chief areas of activity. This will mean passing over some of her better-known philanthropies, such as Urania Cottage, the home for fallen (and other unfortunate) women at Shepherd's Bush, for whose founding and administration Dickens was largely responsible. Although interesting enough as an illustration of Dickens' social conscience and of an enlightened attitude toward prostitutes, the experiment left the broader problem about where it had been. The complexities of managing Urania Cottage were so great as to seem out of proportion to its achievements, and the venture was abandoned after ten years or so. [15]

Among the objects of her benevolence none bulked larger in the eyes of this childless philanthropist than child welfare and education. As a result of Dickens' investigation of the Field Lane Ragged School, she had become a convinced and generous patron of the Ragged School Union. This led by natural stages to other types of work for neglected children. She pioneered in forming shoeblack brigades

---

[12] Johnson, *Letters from Charles Dickens,* pp. 71–72; see also Osborne, *Letters of Charles Dickens to the Baroness Burdett-Coutts,* pp. 127–28.

[13] Johnson, *Letters,* pp. 310–14; Patterson, *Angela Burdett-Coutts,* pp. 152–53.

[14] Osborne, *Letters,* p. 3.

[15] *Ibid.,* p. 175.

for boys salvaged by the Ragged Schools. Lord Ashley's project of training homeless boys for the life of a seaman appealed alike to her humanitarian and patriotic
sides, and she contributed £5000 to the *Goliath*, which, with the *Chichester* and
Arethusa, made up the little training fleet.[16] The Destitute Children's Dinner
Society, dating from 1864, was started as an auxiliary of a Westminster Ragged
School, and within a few months had established over fifty centers (some of them
short-lived) where penny dinners were served.[17] Notwithstanding the penny
charge, which in some districts it was impossible to collect, the work was never
self-supporting, and the cost was borne by Angela, for many years president of the
Society, and other sponsors.

The Baroness was heavily involved in the founding, in 1884, of the London
Society for the Prevention of Cruelty to Children, which was modeled on a similar
effort in Liverpool and, less directly, on two associations in the New World. Her
chief collaborator, Sarah Smith ("Hesba Stretton"), who was associated on the
Sunday Magazine with Benjamin Waugh, the dynamic force in the protect-the-
children movement, published a letter in *The Times* pointing to the need for
such a society. The consequence was a meeting, attended by Baroness Burdett-
Coutts and Lord Shaftesbury among others, from which emerged the London
S.P.C.C. For a decade she remained one of the most stalwart of the Society's
supporters. What led to her unhappy withdrawal in 1894 was, in general, her
reservations about converting the Society into a national organization but, more
specifically, her opposition to certain clauses in the royal charter for which the
Society was applying.[18]

For the Baroness education constituted a primary charge on the interest of
philanthropy. In Westminster, even before her new St. Stephen's Church had been
dedicated, she was already building schools to be run in connection with the
Church. A quarter century later (1876) she was able to expand those facilities
through a bequest which had been left to her discretion and through further gifts
of her own. In the 1890's she established the St. Stephen's Technical Institute,
which in 1901 she turned over to the London County Council as the Westminster
Technical Institute. Her educational benevolence extended to such diverse locales
as Carlisle, Ramsbury and Baydon (Wilts.), and Stepney, where she founded or
contributed heavily to school ventures.[19] Among the more interesting categories of philanthropy connected with the Burdett-Coutts name was a series of
projects, not all of them successful, of urban improvement. The Columbia Square
housing development was described in the previous chapter. Since, to repeat, the
buildings never came close to breaking even, nor would their donor have expected it, they had little value as a "pilot project." Columbia Square was also
the site of one of Angela's expensive errors, indeed, her only complete failure.

[16] *Ibid.*, p. 5.
[17] M. E. Bulkley, *Feeding of School Children*, pp. 3–4.
[18] Rosa Waugh, *The Life of Benjamin Waugh* (London, 1915), pp. 129, 179; Arthur Morton, *Early
Days* (London, 1954), pp. 27–28.
[19] Patterson, *Angela Burdett-Coutts*, pp. 206–7.

This was the consequence of her decision to build a fish and vegetable market free from the tolls collected at other London markets and thus to supply the poor of the district with cheaper food. Armed with a private Act of Parliament (1866), she began the construction of a huge neo-Gothic edifice, complete with decorated windows, majestic vaulting, and granite columns, which was to cost £200,000 — and to stand, in the end, as a moving example of the Victorian difficulty in adapting style to use. *The Times* was more than justified in its suspicion that this cathedral of plaice and cabbage would turn out to be far too exquisite for the ordinary wear-and-tear of a market.[20]

The main problems, however, had to do with the opposition of other markets. Although the Columbia Market must be put down as a mistake, at least it drew attention to the archaic privileges under which an additional tax was, in effect, imposed on Londoners' food. Angela's enterprise had a curious and checkered history, operating under a succession of managements, including that of the London Corporation (which, however, gave up after three years). The magnificent gift turned out to be an imposing white elephant, though conceivably, as the *DNB* insists, it may have pointed the way to more efficient and rational methods of food distribution.

The interest of the Baroness in Westminster, evidenced originally by her gift of St. Stephen's Church and again in her educational work, extended to other areas of community welfare. In connection with the Church and schools, she financed a variety of activities, some of them forecasting those of the late-century settlement house — clubs, friendly societies, and a soup kitchen which in the course of a few years served over 70,000 meals.[21] She contributed to the public library and the swimming bath in Great Smith Street. To improve the housing of the Westminster slum population was more of an assignment, but at least the Baroness could make a modest beginning. Dickens had called her attention to the abysmal conditions in certain neighborhoods, particularly to a block of 150 dwellings which lacked water and drainage and whose sanitary state was deplorable. An ingenious proposal was made to the eighteen owners: If they would proceed (on the basis of exceedingly low estimates) to install sanitary facilities, Miss Coutts would stand responsible for any excess.[22]

One ought, perhaps, to stress once more the range of her activities. For example, the middle-class residential community, Holly Village, which she established on her Holly Lodge estate at Highgate, gives her some standing as a pioneer of the garden suburb. Nor did her benevolence stop at the water's edge. Her robust belief in the overseas mission of Britain was tempered by none of the hesitancies of the Little Englander. To her friend Rajah Brooke of Sarawak she gave generous support, among other benefactions buying a gunboat for him and maintaining a model farm in his principality, and she aided the African explorations of Moffat,

[20] 29 April 1869.
[21] Johnson, *Letters from Charles Dickens*, p. 206n.
[22] *Ibid.*, p. 216.

Livingstone, and Stanley.[23] She supplied Abeoukuta (in Southern Nigeria) with cotton-gins and provided hospital equipment and nurses during the Zulu War of 1879. Altogether, the Victorian Empire could have had few more ardent and useful friends than the Baroness.

Some of her more inventive philanthropies were directed toward mitigating the distress and improving the economy of depressed areas in and out of England. When the Cobden-Chevalier Treaty of 1860 dealt a blow to the silk weavers of Spitalfields, her East End Weavers' Aid Association assisted some to find new employment at home and others to emigrate to Queensland and Nova Scotia. At the end of the decade she sent some twelve hundred Ayrshire weavers to Australia. Her most elaborate operations, however, took place in John Bull's Other Island. During the famine in 1880, especially calamitous in Galway and Mayo, her offer of £250,000 for seed potatoes had something to do with pushing the Government into action on its own account. But the fishing district of the southwest was her particular care. It was an appeal from a parish priest in the early '60's that opened this chapter in her history of good works. The Baroness responded with relief supplies and with assistance for those who wished to emigrate to Canada. More constructive were her efforts to revive the fishing industry by making advances for capital equipment. As a result of the modern fishing boats and gear that she supplied, within a few years the Baltimore fishing fleet came to represent an investment of some £50,000. It is reassuring to read that, under the supervising eye of Father Davis, the fishermen repaid much of the capital advanced by the Baroness. To continue the work she established at Baltimore a fishery training school for four hundred boys, which was opened in the summer of 1887 by the "Queen of Baltimore" herself.[24]

To large sections of the British public the name of Baroness Burdett-Coutts became almost synonymous with large-scale charity. Many must have regarded her as Madame Philanthropie herself. For this, no doubt, both the volume and variety of her benevolences were partly responsible. More than with most of her wealthy contemporaries, she considered the practice of philanthropy to be almost a professional commitment, and, no small element in a reputation, her career as a philanthropist covered nearly three quarters of a century. Inevitably contemporaries found her a fascinating figure, with the touch of eccentricity that adds color — the fabulously wealthy heiress, strong-minded and shrewd, devoting her resources to improving the life of her time. The peerage in her own right, the freedom of the City of London and four City Companies, and her singular marriage at the age of sixty-seven (complete with bridal veil and three little bridesmaids) added to the legend. There is no reason to doubt the story that, when she died in her ninety-second year, some thirty thousand Londoners filed past her coffin as it lay

---

[23] The relationship between the two is detailed in the letters edited by Owen Rutter, *Rajah Brooke and Baroness Burdett-Coutts* (London, 1935); see also Steven Runciman, *The White Rajahs* (Cambridge, 1960), p. 154.

[24] Patterson, *Angela Burdett-Coutts*, p. 210.

in state at One Stratton Street. Her span of life comprehended, with something to spare at both ends, not only the Victorian Age but the life of the Queen herself. And in the course of the century the Baroness, too, had become an institution.

FREDERIC DAVID MOCATTA
(1 8 2 8 – 1 9 0 5)

In the goodly company of Anglo-Jewish philanthropists the name of Frederic David Mocatta merits a special place. This is not so much because of the volume of his charities, though these were great, as because of a dedication to the cause of philanthropy so sweeping as to be almost unique. More than any other member of his community Mocatta was heavily involved in both Jewish and non-Jewish charities, and he saw the issues in less sectarian terms than did some of his fellow Jewish philanthropists. He was never president of the Jewish Board of Guardians — that office, more often than not, went to a member of the Cohen dynasty[1] — but for nearly two decades at the end of the century he served as a vice-president and was always one of the dominant voices in the policies of the Guardians. More than any other individual, Mocatta provided a liaison between Jewish and non-Jewish philanthropy, especially between the Board of Guardians and the Charity Organisation Society, in which he was also a leader.

The problems of Jewish charities differed in essential respects from those of Christian and secular organizations.[2] For one thing, it was out of the question that members of the community, with their special observances and dietary laws, should be allowed to fall back on the Poor Law workhouse, and they therefore, whatever the cost, must be taken care of by their co-religionists. Far more important was the factor of immigration. The essential source of Jewish poverty in London was the successive waves of needy immigrants from Eastern Europe coming to Britain to escape persecution or to better their situation. Often at the outset their lot was little improved, for, because of prejudice, their foreignness, and religious restrictions on their working schedules, they were barred from entering ordinary occupations. They must work perforce for Jewish employers or carry on independently with such skills as they may have brought or become street sellers or peddlers. By the mid-century the unhappy situation described by Patrick Colquhoun more than fifty years before had shown improvement.[3] Jews were no longer, as in his day, obliged to live by their wits or to enter a career of crime for lack of alternative occupations. For one Fagin there were thousands of self-respecting, industrious Jewish poor, whose neatness and sobriety, as compared with the shiftless misery of the non-Jewish destitute, drew favorable comment from more than one observer.

---

[1] Five of the seven presidents of the Board between 1859 and 1947 were descendants of Louis Cohen (1779–1882). None served for less than eight years.

[2] Readers of V. D. Lipman's admirable history of the Jewish Board of Guardians (*A Century of Social Service,* 1859–1959 [London, 1959]) will be aware of how heavily dependent on his work is the account that follows.

[3] *Police of the Metropolis,* 5th ed. (London, 1797), pp. 158–60.

Certainly the charitable institutions — schools, orphanages, apprenticeship charities, and numbers of relief agencies — created for Dutch, German, and Polish
immigrants had some connection with the change. In the course of the eighteenth
century the Sephardim had established for their relatively small body of poor
an almost excessive number of charities, so well supported as to raise some
suspicion of attracting further immigrants from the Continent,[4] but it was only
after the turn of the century that the newer arrivals received much assistance
from their fellow Jews. Originally, looking after the poor was a function of the
synagogue, with the "strange poor" (recent immigrants not attached to any
particular congregation) the responsibility of the three synagogues.[5]

What is relevant here, however, was the formation of voluntary organizations
to serve the German, Dutch, and Polish groups — most conspicuously the German — which were similar in scope and methods to the non-Jewish agencies
that were sprouting so luxuriantly. Several of these institutions had notable careers,
such as the Jews' Free Schools, opened in 1817, which by 1850 had over eleven
hundred children enrolled. A tabulation of Ashkenazi charities, which ministered
to the newer immigrants, shows more than twenty-five agencies, exclusive of
schools and friendly societies, in operation by the mid-century.[6] At this stage
organized Jewish charities may have been responsible for a total outlay of £30,000
a year.[7]

In their virtues and defects alike these agencies conformed fairly faithfully to
the nineteenth-century norm. They were mostly voting charities, in which an
annual subscription would give the philanthropist a vote in choosing beneficiaries,
and they showed the same tendencies as did non-Jewish agencies to proliferate in
an anarchical fashion. There was no little uneasiness in the Jewish community
over the chaotic charity regime, and the 1840's and '50's brought forth a number
of remedial suggestions. Among these the most trenchant was a series of articles
in the *Jewish Chronicle* urging a central committee — "we will call it for want
of a better name a Board of Guardians"[8] — representing the three synagogues
and the voluntary bodies. The decisive proposal, however, was that of Ephraim
Alex, generally honored as the founder of the Jewish Board of Guardians, who
favored broadening the activities of the Conjoint Board of the three City Synagogues, which, since the mid-1830's, had superintended the machinery set up to
deal with the "strange poor."

Although its beginnings were modest enough, the Board of Guardians marked

[4] Sir John Fielding, quoted by M. D. George, *London Life in the XVIIIth Century*, p. 128; Neville
Laski, *The Laws and Charities of the Spanish and Portuguese Jews Congregation of London* (London,
1952), chaps. IV–V; V. D. Lipman, *Social History of the Jews, 1850–1950* (London, 1954), pp.
52–53, gives a tabulation of both the Sephardic and Ashkenazic charities about 1850, with their dates
of foundation. Most of the former were established before 1780.
[5] The arrangements among the three synagogues (the Great, the Hambro', and the New) are
explained by Lipman, *Century of Social Service*, pp. 15–16.
[6] Lipman, *Social History*, pp. 52–53.
[7] The estimate of the editor of the *Jewish Chronicle*, cited by Lipman, *Century of Social Service*,
p. 20, n. 3.
[8] Quoted *ibid.*, p. 21.

an important development in charity practice. The philosophy of charity which
the Guardians consciously applied was familiar to mid-century philanthropists
but had not yet been embodied in an organization of such dimensions.[9] The
principles which informed their work — thorough investigation, detailed case
records, adequate relief, and home visiting — were later to be more aggressively
publicized by the Charity Organisation Society, but the Jewish Board antedated
the C.O.S. by ten years and the Liverpool Central Relief Society by four. The
Board was more strategically situated than was the C.O.S., and within its appointed sphere its obligations and powers alike were much greater. As the principal charitable and social agency of London Jewry, it must accept responsibility
for the entire body of Jewish poor, even for the "undeserving," who plainly could
not be left to the mercies of the secular Poor Law if that involved workhouse
residence. Unlike the C.O.S., however, the Guardians not merely aspired to a
coordinating role but were a great operating charity, the outstanding Jewish
welfare organization, which was directly concerned with administering relief
and with managing a variety of enterprises. They were thus in an excellent position to influence welfare policies throughout the metropolitan Jewish community.

Although its sphere as originally defined was highly limited, the leaders of the
new Board had no intention that it should remain so. Ephraim Alex as president
and Lionel Louis Cohen as secretary and future president[10] looked forward to taking over from individual synagogues the relief of their own poor and even to
entering such areas as medical care, training immigrants in useful trades, and possibly housing. Not only that, but they were resolved to seek financial support beyond the regular payments from the associated synagogues and to build up a
corps of individual subscribers and contributors. In this latter aspiration they were
wholly successful, and the fraction of the Board's revenue represented by synagogue
payments sharply declined.[11]

We cannot here follow the growth of the Board's services or detail the procedures followed. What is clear is that, as mid-Victorian charities went, the Jewish
Board of Guardians was managed with exceptional intelligence and efficiency.
Very likely Dr. Stallard's volume comparing Jewish and Christian poor relief to
the marked disadvantage of the latter was overenthusiastic,[12] but there could be
no doubt that the accomplishments of the Board, even at this early date, were
considerable. By the early 1870's the Board was relieving something like half of
the Jewish poor of the Metropolis and was experimenting with new services —
medical care, sanitary inspection of the homes of the poor, and loans instead of

---

[9] Although some features were characteristic of the M.V.R.A. and other visiting societies.

[10] Senior partner in Louis Cohen & Sons, foreign bankers and stockbrokers, who was first hon.
secretary (1859–69) and then president until his death in 1887. Cohen was the planning and
organizing genius of the Board for nearly three decades.

[11] Lipman, *Century of Social Service,* p. 39. As early as 1861, two years after the formation of the
Board, payments from the synagogues represented only one-seventh (£440 out of £2922) and by
1879 had fallen to less than a tenth (£1274 out of £15,128).

[12] J. H. Stallard, *London Pauperism amongst Jews and Christians* (London, 1867).

outright relief (for unlike the Poor Law authorities and some Christian agencies, the Board tended to think of the able-bodied applicant as a genuinely unemployed person who might be tided over by a small loan).[13]

The Guardians only partly realized their ambition to serve as the coordinating agency for Jewish charities. In the early '70's the Statistical Committee was complaining of the lack of communication among the more than thirty-five Jewish relief organizations.[14] But among Jewish, as well as non-Jewish, voluntary bodies, the resistance to outside control was stubborn, and the Board discovered that it must be prepared to make haste slowly. Over the years the Guardians have, in fact, absorbed a number of Jewish charities and have developed cooperative working agreements with others, so that today, perhaps more than ever, the agency holds a pre-eminent position in the Jewish charitable world.

Like other agencies, the Board was unhappy over its failure to draw support from a broader constituency. Yet, although its subscription list was relatively short, through the annual contributions of certain large donors and even more from special gifts — legacies, memorial offerings, and the like — the total resources of the Board grew impressively, partly the result of the prudent policy of funding all such receipts of more than £10. In 1889, obviously an exceptional year, out of a total revenue of nearly £33,000, the Board managed to invest £10,000.[15] But the flow of expendable income grew less strikingly, and in the years after 1890 the Board was in frequent, almost perpetual, financial difficulty, with activities expanding more rapidly than income.[16] A succession of heavy deficits left no apparent alternative but to dip into capital and suspend the traditional policy of funding legacies. The 1920's and '30's brought no improvement. Unhappily, as the Board often reflected, it had been unable to develop a broad base of support in the Jewish community; about half of the amount contributed annually came from forty individuals. For the Jewish Board of Guardians, as for numbers of other voluntary agencies, the Welfare State meant a measure of deliverance.

Among the leaders in the work of the Board none has a stronger claim on the student of charities than Frederic David Mocatta, "the *beau ideal* of the Anglo-Jewish philanthropist."[17] His interests were more comprehensive than those of most of his associates, and his appetite for philanthropic activity, Jewish and non-Jewish, was insatiable. As the writer of an obituary notice observed, he would race all over Greater London to attend dull committee meetings, and would willingly take on all sorts of equally dull duties.[18] It was philanthropy rather than "Jewish" philanthropy as such that engaged his efforts, and he was evidently a major

[13] For a brief account of the policies and procedures of the Guardians, perhaps a bit too favorable, see Young and Ashton, *British Social Work*, pp. 82–84.
[14] Table of Metropolitan Jewish Institutions (exclusive of educational) in the Mocatta Library, University College. Incomplete figures of income show an annual revenue of over £17,000 for the group.
[15] *Charity Record*, 20 Feb. 1890.
[16] Lipman, *Century of Social Service*, p. 107.
[17] *Ibid.*, p. 138.
[18] *Charity Organisation Review*, February 1905, p. 107.

channel by which the Board was kept in touch with developments in the theory
and practice of charity.

For the last thirty years of his life Mocatta was literally a full-time philanthropist, lavishing time, money, and energy on a multitude of institutions, organizations, and, when properly accredited, individuals. For nearly two decades (1861–
78) he served as chairman of the Board's Visiting Committee, which supervised
its casework service, and he acquired a far more realistic knowledge of East End
conditions than most well-to-do philanthropists. Every social worker in the area,
testified Rabbi Stern, became as a matter of course an almoner for Mocatta, and
on no occasion "during the 18 years of my ministry" did his generosity fail "in
response to any appeal I addressed to him." [19] Of all Mocatta's organizational
causes, the Charity Voting Reform Association, in which for years he was the
leading spirit, was perhaps the one that enjoyed his most uncompromising and
even militant support. When on his seventieth birthday he was presented with
an address signed by eight thousand persons representing some 250 organizations,
he was said to have remarked privately, "I should prefer if they would have
promised not to give any more to voting charities." [20]

The Mocattas were no recent immigrants to Britain. When the Jews were
driven from Spain, the family had divided, one branch settling in Venice and the
other in Holland. In the latter half of the seventeenth century the Dutch Mocattas
took up residence in London, where their fortunes prospered in a more than
satisfying fashion. Frederic David's grandfather founded the firm of Mocatta &
Goldsmid, bullion brokers to the Bank of England, which his son and grandson
entered as a matter of course.[21] The young man was educated privately and thoroughly. His father taught him Latin and Hebrew, while tutors added other
subjects. The result was a man of scholarly tastes and a patron of learning, widely
traveled and a genuine cosmopolitan. The author of two volumes on Jewish
history and affairs, he also collected a library of over five thousand titles, preeminently Hebraica, which now make up the Mocatta Library in University College, London.[22]

His interest in philanthropy was present almost from the beginning. Before he
had come of age he was heavily involved in Jewish charities, notably the Jews'
Infant School and the Jews' Free School. Conceivably his lack of family responsibilities created a void to be filled, and certainly it left him with more leisure for
public concerns than could be had by a man engaged in rearing a family of
children. Mocatta's wife, daughter of Frederick David Goldsmid and sister of
Sir Julian Goldsmid, was a semi-invalid, and they had no children. For him, in a
sense, his charitable interests took the place of a family, so much so that, at the

---

[19] *Jewish Chronicle,* 20 Jan. 1905.
[20] *Charity Organisation Review* (see n. 18 above).
[21] Most of the biographical details on Mocatta are taken from the "Memoir" by the Reverend
Isidore Harris in Ada Mocatta, ed., *F. D. Mocatta* (London, 1911).
[22] An account of the Library (which suffered heavily from enemy action in 1942) is contained in
Paul H. Emden, *Jews of Britain* (London, 1944), pp. 126–28.

age of forty-six, after over thirty years in Mocatta & Goldsmid, he retired to devote all of his time to philanthropy and scholarship. Henceforth charity was his occupation, not only in London but internationally. The precarious situation of the Jews in Eastern Europe was a source of perennial anxiety to him, and as vice-president of the Anglo-Jewish Association, founded in the 1870's to assist in protecting persecuted Jews, he took a leading part in formulating and carrying out plans for their relief.

By and large, Mocatta's ideas of charitable work were those that enjoyed the greatest vogue among progressive philanthropists in his middle years. He was, first of all, a convinced charity organizer, with a horror of overlapping and duplicating agencies. On more than one occasion he managed to unite Jewish organizations engaged in similar activities, as when the Jewish Workhouse joined with the Hand-in-Hand Asylum to form the Home for Aged Jews, perhaps the favorite charity of Mocatta, who became president of the united institution. He was an indefatigable champion of sound administrative practice in charitable enterprise, and in fact conceived of philanthropy as a complex practical science that demanded concentrated study of those who would understand its problems. As a result of this belief in rational organization, he did not hesitate to invest many man hours in "helping institutions over crises of stress and difficulty, bringing public bodies into form, creating order out of chaos, and retiring from view when the desired state . . . was brought about." [23]

Mocatta's hatred of voting charities derived both from his essential humanity and his contempt for messy, imprecise administrative procedure. It was, he held, the duty of charity managers to choose their beneficiaries on the basis of merit and need and not to allow subscribers to pervert the selection process into electioneering campaigns. In his will, which distributed about £35,000 among some seventy-five agencies, he pointed to some of the unregenerate bodies. He had originally intended to remember the Hospital for Incurables (Putney), the Asylum for Idiots (Earlswood), and other institutions, but, given their system of electing beneficiaries, he deemed it a "duty not to leave legacies to any institution which adopts this system." With the Jews' Hospital and the Orphan Asylum he was less uncompromising, and to them he held out the carrot of £1000 each if, within ten years of his death, they were to abolish the voting system. [24]

Although Mocatta in general shared the outlook of his C.O.S. associates, one can sense a slightly different texture in his social thinking. He lacked the hard, cocksure dogmatism of, say, a Helen Dendy Bosanquet, and he was less ready to find in moral weakness a satisfying explanation of social distress. This canon of C.O.S. orthodoxy was, in fact, hard to square with the experience of the Jewish Board of Guardians. The Jewish poor as a class were sober, frugal, and hardworking, and it would have been preposterous for the Board to accept poverty as *"prima facie* evidence of idleness or depravity." [25] Like the C.O.S., the Board

[23] Harris, "Memoir," in Ada Mocatta, ed., *F. D. Mocatta*, p. 16.
[24] *Jewish Chronicle*, 17 Feb. 1905.
[25] Lipman, *Century of Social Service*, p. 74.

worked on the premise that assistance in individual cases was the essential instrument of social improvement, but in Jewish circles there was a growing suspicion that the problem must be defined in other terms. Possibly without further mass immigration the prescription of individual relief might have sufficed for the Jewish community. What made it hopelessly inadequate were the successive waves of immigrants and the marginal and seasonal character of the only trades open to them. This condition, rather than the shiftlessness of individuals, created the gravest problems that confronted the Board of Guardians.

During the 1880's and '90's the Board's machinery and philosophy alike received a cruel testing. The reign of terror which swept through South Russia in the early '80's and the anti-Jewish laws that followed ushered in an era of persecution which continued, as a reality or a lowering threat, for the better part of three decades. Unfortunately the pressure of immigrants was heaviest at a time when the British labor market was in no condition to absorb numbers of new workers. Given a public temper not at its most hospitable toward immigration, Jewish leaders had to proceed cautiously lest the State intervene to impose a formal restriction. At the outset the business was not handled by the Board itself. This was perhaps just as well, for its procedures, one gathers, had failed to keep pace with the newer ideas of social casework. The agency primarily in charge of the refugees was a Conjoint Committee of representatives of a Mansion House fund and the Board, which during its first year (1882) handled cases involving about 2750 individuals. Though the United States or Canada was the goal of most of the immigrants, the number remaining in England reached a substantial total. An index of this inflow is the growth in the Jewish population of London, which trebled between 1880 and 1914, while applications to the Board for assistance rose from fewer than 2500 in 1880 to more than 5000 in 1894. Of these applicants only about 10 per cent were native-born.

The pressure of immigration raised agonizing questions for English Jews. Was it conceivable that they should raise barriers against their co-religionists fleeing to freedom? Yet this was a complex matter. Not only was there danger that immigration might be restricted by law, but by no means all of the immigrants were clearly fugitives from persecution. Some of the British leaders urged prudence and discrimination, but the warm-hearted Mocatta, whose knowledge of international Jewry was more extensive than that of his fellows, would have none of such caution. He had favored large-scale emigration from Russia and had himself offered to contribute £10,000 of the £1 million thought necessary, if the world-wide Jewish community would find the rest.[26] This sum was never realized, but Mocatta provided more than a comparable fraction of the £108,000 collected by the Mansion House Committee. Actually, though for him it was unthinkable that English Jews should do other than welcome and assist the Eastern European refugees, he would not himself have taken steps to encourage it, and he did not protest when the Board went to some lengths to warn prospective immigrants

[26] Harris, "Memoir," p. 19.

of the widespread unemployment in England. Perhaps the Guardians' fear of public opinion made them unduly stiff-necked in dealing with the new immigrants, and their policies earned for them respect rather than affection. There is reason to believe that their cable name " 'Rachmonem' — the compassionate" was regarded as a misnomer by numbers of necessitous immigrants.[27]

Mocatta's remedy for social distress in England, as for Russian pogroms, was large-scale emigration, a formula to which he clung with a kind of desperate hopefulness. Like other humane and thoughtful Englishmen, he was deeply troubled by the social restlessness of the 1880's, but unlike some of his C.O.S. friends, he was little inclined to make light of the *malaise*. His faith in the patient treatment of individual cases as a solution of the social problem was, in fact, badly shaken, and what saved him from flirting with collectivist remedies was chiefly his overdeveloped reverence for "economic law." He was aware how pitifully impotent were English charitable agencies to meet the needs even of the "deserving and helpable" cases, the unfortunates whose claims to consideration were indisputable. Beyond these lay the more basic question of poverty, which, he sadly concluded, was "far too large to grapple with." [28]

A series of letters from Mocatta to C. S. Loch in the 1880's and '90's written while on holiday in France reveals the bewilderment of one of the most unselfish and single minded of philanthropists as he reflected on the discontents of British society. At times he seems to go well beyond C.O.S. orthodoxy, only to draw back as he realizes the implications of his proposals. Contemplating the possibilities of a social revolution, he concludes that, in spite of the widespread prejudice against state interference, "the care of suffering should be incumbent on society as a whole, and not left to chance as it is now." Then he goes on to propose what amounts to a graduated income tax. "I am aware that such an idea will be called Communism, or Socialism, or that it may be considered as subverting every rule of political economy, but things must not be allowed to remain as they are." [29] Four years before he had reminded Loch how much had been done toward palliating poverty and how little toward eradicating it. What could be more absurd than to expect a man receiving 20*s*. a week for the support of his family to put anything by for the future! At the end of his long life Mocatta was demanding more aggressive action by the State in certain areas of public health, and he took an amused satisfaction in referring to his proposals as "socialistic." "My [C.O.S.] friends, with whom I usually act and agree, think me a little unsafe and crotchety on these points, but I believe we shall 'come to it,' and that it will be the right thing." [30]

Yet such notions were hardly more than passing deviations on the part of a humane individualist who thought "all labour laws, such as the eight hours movement . . . so many absurdities" and who was appalled that the London County

[27] Lloyd P. Gartner, *The Jewish Immigrant in England, 1870–1914* (London, 1960), p. 164.

[28] Mocatta to Loch, 1886, Ada Mocatta, *F. D. Mocatta*, p. 31.

[29] *Ibid.*, p. 33.

[30] *Charity Organisation Review*, February 1905, p. 106.

Council should consider undertaking working-class housing.[31] To Mocatta the
idea of state-aided pensions for the aged was "a damning heresy, which all
thoughtful people should be bound to oppose with all their might." [32] Given
Mocatta's recognition of widespread destitution and his rather naive faith in the
inflexibility of "economic law," it was natural that he should be drawn to emigration as the solution. "I know," he wrote in 1886, "the distress is chronic, is increasing, is terrible, and is destructive. . . . Nothing short of removing some hundreds
of thousands of people can make things better." [33] Repeatedly he points to the
surplus of labor in terms reminiscent of an early nineteenth-century Malthusian
and can find no way out other than the removal of vast numbers to the colonies.[34]

It would be an error to picture Mocatta's social views, in spite of an occasional
mild heresy, as markedly advanced. His ideas had been formed during the middle
quarters of the century, and they were thoroughly mid-Victorian in spirit. Yet to
stress the limitations of Mocatta's social thinking would be to miss his real distinction. No Victorian practitioner of philanthropy, not even Lord Shaftesbury, gave
more lavishly of his time and money, and none more effectively combined personal service and monetary benevolence with concentrated, almost excruciating,
effort to gain an understanding of the larger issues. It was well known in charity
circles that his generosity prompted him often to anticipate his income, and the
list of agencies in which he took an active part reads almost like a directory of
metropolitan charities. Mocatta stands, in short, as an exceptionally satisfying representative of mid-Victorian philanthropy, "the most eminent English Jew in
nobility of character," who, "far from mere giving . . . was almost restless in
doing good." [35]

J. PASSMORE EDWARDS
(1 8 2 3 - 1 9 1 1)

Among the late Victorian philanthropists, Passmore Edwards will survive
critical examination better than most. Not only were his motives above reproach,
as selfless as Samuel Morley's, but his benefactions expressed deeply held and
intelligent convictions about the conditions of progress in his society. It was not
enough that he should respond to the appeals of hard-pressed organizations. His
own philanthropies rested rather on a considered view of the needs of working-
class England, which brought him out at a point midway between the "Diffuse
Benevolence" (to recall the *Spectator's* epithet) of Morley and the highly concentrated giving of Holloway and Mason. The libraries, hospitals, and convalescent homes planted by Edwards in the London area, Cornwall, and elsewhere
suggest a notion of philanthropic strategy akin to that of Andrew Carnegie, with
whom he had collaborated — a brief and uneasy partnership — in a venture in

---

[31] Ada Mocatta, *F. D. Mocatta*, pp. 36, 45.
[32] *Ibid.*, p. 39.
[33] *Ibid.*, p. 35.
[34] See, for example, his "Poverty and Duty" and "Social Aches and Pains," *ibid.*, pp. 79–82 and 87.
[35] Claude Montefiore, quoted by Lipman, *Century of Social Service*, p. 139, n. 1.

popular journalism. It was probably not wholly fortuitous that the beginning of Edwards' career as a major philanthropist coincided with the appearance in the *North American Review* of Carnegie's famous article, which was presently reprinted in the *Pall Mall Gazette* as "The Gospel of Wealth." [1]

In one sense, however, Edwards' philanthropies were a natural outgrowth of his experience as journalist and publisher. He had always conceived of his publications as vehicles of mass education and liberal views, and his whole career was dedicated to the three causes of journalism, philanthropy, and reform, all of them, as he insisted late in life, parts of a broader purpose. Born in 1823 in Blackwater, Cornwall, the son of a carpenter and publican, Edwards began to write with the benefit of no formal education beyond that offered by the village school. His youthful devotion to the anti-Corn Law cause brought him his first opportunity in journalism as Manchester representative for the *Sentinel,* a new and ephemeral anti-Corn Law paper published in London.[2] The paper failed, and Edwards received £10 for his fifteen months in the service of the free-trade press.

This painful experience did not shake Edwards' faith in the cause of liberal reform. After all, he was young and sanguine and earnest, and the Victorian world offered rewards for such qualities. When in 1845 he went to London with only a few shillings in his pocket, he was taking the road to ultimate fortune, but it was a long and twisting path. He first supported himself by writing for the newspapers and lecturing on behalf of reform movements, such as the Peace Society and the Early Closing Association, which attracted his support, and in five years had managed to save enough to launch his first publication. *The Public Good,* a two-penny monthly, did well enough in circulation and esteem, but, as Edwards ruefully recalled, "The praise I received did not butter parsnips." [3] The young publisher was trying to operate on too slender a margin, and his attempt to shore up his enterprise by adding other publications — the *Biographical Magazine,* the *Peace Advocate,* and the *Poetic Magazine* — only postponed the inevitable disaster. In three years his health broke, and he was forced to go into bankruptcy, paying five shillings in the pound.

The story had a happy ending for Edwards and his creditors. He managed to recover his position enough to pick up for a nominal sum the *Building News,* which was losing money for Kelly of the *London Directory* but which Edwards turned into a profitable property. What the *Building News* did for construction workers the *Mechanics' Magazine,* also bought by Edwards in the '60's, did for artisans and amateur mechanics. Both turned out to be substantial money-makers, and he was able to settle his old debts in full. It was a pleasant and graceful gesture when his creditors, at a dinner in his honor, presented Edwards with a watch on which was inscribed their appreciation of his "integrity and honor."

Edwards was now out of the woods, but his real ascent to fortune began only

---

[1] Burton J. Hendrick, *The Life of Andrew Carnegie,* 2 vols. (New York, 1932), I, 340.

[2] E. Harcourt Burrage, *J. Passmore Edwards, Philanthropist* (London, 1902), pp. 14–16; *DNB, 1901–1911,* I, 613.

[3] Burrage, *J. Passmore Edwards,* p. 27.

after he had invaded the field of daily journalism. It was his achievement to pioneer successfully in supplying the working classes in London with a halfpenny daily. The *Echo,* which was started by Messrs. Cassell in 1868 and reached Edwards' hands seven years later, was an interesting attempt to meet the reading needs of the British workingman for whom popular education was opening a new world. The publisher's road was not easy, and his paper was not received with universal acclaim. Unattractively printed on colored paper, it was not, most respectable observers thought, an ornament to British journalism in either format or content. Newsdealers refused to stock the paper, and even the newsboys, apparently, did not bay *"E-cho"* with the gusto that they accorded to other journals.[4] Nor did Edwards hesitate to use his paper as a pulpit from which to preach his favorite causes — temperance, peace, education, and the rest. But the greatest test of the *Echo*'s hold on working-class affections came when, after some hesitation, he decided to exclude racing news and tips from its columns. Actually the decision seems to have produced nothing more serious than a wave of grumbling, though one may doubt whether it had a perceptible effect on working-class betting habits.

The year 1883–84 marked a curious interlude in the history of the *Echo,* during which Edwards became, somewhat unintentionally, an accomplice in Andrew Carnegie's project to bring republicanism to Britain. The "Star-Spangled Scotchman," enemy of hereditary privilege and champion of working-class democracy, had acquired a chain of popular newspapers, chiefly in the Northeast and Midlands, as vehicles for his reformist and republican propaganda. His active partner was Samuel Storey, a flamboyant radical, M.P. for Sunderland, and owner of two halfpenny papers, the Sunderland *Echo* and the Tyneside *Echo.* What was essential in the Carnegie-Storey plan was a suitable London medium, a need which Edwards' paper, the original *Echo,* seemed predestined to fill. In late 1882 the syndicate bought a two-thirds interest for $250,000.[5]

This was not a happy association, and, indeed, Carnegie presently discovered that Britain could not be led down the republican road by a band of pipers, however handsomely financed. Even before the syndicate had fallen apart, Edwards repented his bargain and proceeded to buy back his two-thirds interest for $500,000, double what he had received a few months before. What Carnegie made in buying and selling the London *Echo* must have done a good deal to compensate for losses the syndicate was suffering elsewhere.[6] As for Edwards, he had had an expensive and presumably instructive experience. But however uncomfortable he had found the company of Storey and Carnegie, his ideas on

---

[4] Hendrick, *Andrew Carnegie,* I, 261.

[5] The chronology here is not entirely clear. Edwards' own *A Few Footprints* (London, 1905) gives 1884 as the year in which Carnegie and Storey took over. A letter from Carnegie to Storey, however, d. 3 Jan. 1883 (Hendrick, *Andrew Carnegie,* I, 267), leaves no doubt that the two had already bought the *Echo,* presumably in late 1882.

[6] Hendrick, I, 270.

philanthropy seem to have been influenced by the latter's. Some of his activities as a donor suggest a smaller-scale Andrew Carnegie.

Despite his costly encounter with the American Scotsman, Edwards' fortunes were prospering during the 1880's, and by the end of the decade he was ready to dispose of some of his accumulation. Like Carnegie, he found unappealing the prospect of dying a rich man. The American multimillionaire, in fact, hailed the Londoner as a convert to his Gospel of Wealth and could congratulate himself that "Passmore Edwards of the *Echo,* formerly M.P., has recently begun to walk as a disciple." [7] Whatever the source of his ideas, during his latter years Edwards was almost the full-time philanthropist, and he went about his calling with a shrewd eye as well as a humane spirit.

Edwards was clear that the working classes, who had first claim on philanthropy, could be best helped by institutions to promote their physical welfare and their self-cultivation. In other words, his special concern would be hospitals, convalescent homes, and orphanages on the one hand, and public libraries on the other. Not only that, but he would try to see that these were located at points of maximum usefulness. For, unlike some of those who pointed to the aggregate of Britain's welfare institutions, Edwards was aware how unequally and sometimes erratically these were distributed. In short, he would consciously try to improve Britain's network of hospitals and libraries, planting his benefactions in needy communities.

It would be pointless to recall Edwards' individual gifts. Like many provincials who had made their fortunes in the Metropolis, his first thought was for his native district. What channeled his benevolence toward libraries in the first place was a series of bequests, inadequate in themselves, which had been left to a number of Cornish towns. To Edwards it seemed an obvious step to double these £2000 Ferris bequests in order to make possible the building of libraries. In all, Edwards provided his native Cornwall with twelve such institutions, in whole or in part, and stocked them with books — these in addition to a series of other community benefactions. The total, he recalled late in life, approximated £30,000.[8]

Altogether Edwards was responsible for well over twenty-five library buildings (and part of their contents) in the London area and Cornwall. He shared with some of his contemporaries a sense of guilt as he contemplated the squalor of the slums, and he had long held "that the East of London has stupendous and uncancelled claims on the wealthy and well-to-do people of the West End." [9] The spearhead of the movement for public libraries in the East End was Canon Barnett of Toynbee Hall, and he found in Passmore Edwards a loyal and generous ally. When Barnett appealed to him on behalf of the Whitechapel project, he offered to pay the whole cost of the new building, nearly £6500. The Whitechapel

[7] *Ibid.,* p. 345. Edwards sat for Salisbury as a Liberal during the years 1880–85.
[8] Burrage, *J. Passmore Edwards,* p. 37.
[9] Henrietta O. Barnett, *Canon Barnett,* II, 5.

institution turned out to be the pioneer undertaking in a sequence which established Passmore Edwards libraries in St. George's-in-the-East, Limehouse, Mile
End, Poplar, East Ham, Shoreditch, and other East London districts.

The Barnett-Edwards team scored again in the Whitechapel Art Gallery. The
Barnetts had been arranging showings of pictures for the benefit of their Whitechapel neighbors, but their hope of getting from the parish authorities more
permanent facilities proved to be illusory. In the end Barnett determined to strike
out for himself, and he appealed for £20,000 for an art gallery. It was Edwards'
initial gift of £5000 that launched the campaign on its successful course and,
indirectly, the Whitechapel Art Gallery on its brilliant career. Lord Rosebery's
remark at the opening of the Whitechapel Library stated only the plain fact:
"Wherever he [Passmore Edwards] goes, a suspicion of benevolence dogs his
steps." [10]

The same belief in technical education which led Edwards to contribute generously to a number of working-class institutions made him a substantial benefactor of one of the world's most distinguished centers of research and teaching
in the social sciences, the London School of Economics. It was apparently the
Technical Education Board of the London County Council, led by Sidney Webb,
that turned his attention to the lack of commercial education of the higher sort
in London. When in 1899–1900 London University was reorganized and the
School of Economics admitted as a constituent faculty, the old accommodations
in Adelphi Terrace became painfully inadequate. At this point Passmore Edwards
came forward with an offer of £10,000 (later raised to £11,000) for a building in
the neighborhood of the Strand, and vested it in three trustees, of whom one was
Sidney Webb. For the new building the London County Council provided the
site, some four thousand square feet in Clare Street, Clare Market, and the Technical Education Board agreed to an annual grant of £2500.[11] Passmore Edwards
Hall thus became the physical nucleus of a rapidly growing School of Economics
and Political Science.

Since working-class advance was impossible without a minimum of physical
well-being, hospitals and convalescent homes figured heavily in Edwards' philanthropic plans. He financed a chain of hospitals in Cornwall and Greater London,
together with convalescent homes for metropolitan hospitals and workingmen's
organization, including one for railwaymen and another for the printing trades.[12]
When, after three years, Charing Cross Hospital had made little progress in its
plan for a convalescent home, Edwards intervened with an offer of £5000 and an
undertaking to supply whatever else might be required.[13] *Punch* was wholly
justified in hymning his wide-ranging benevolence:

---

[10] Quoted by Burrage, p. 53.
[11] *Ibid.*, pp. 134–35; *Calendars of the London School of Economics.* The only other large donor
was Rothschild & Sons who gave £5000.
[12] Edwards, *A Few Footprints.*
[13] Burrage, *J. Passmore Edwards,* pp. 75–76.

"Oh, Passmore Edwards, you beyond contention
Are worthy of Punch's 'Honourable Mention' . . .
There's scarce a project schemed with kindly sense,
But profits by your large benevolence." [14]

It is unnecessary to recall in detail Edwards' miscellaneous benefactions — the drinking fountains, the more than eighty thousand volumes presented to libraries and reading rooms, the Passmore Edwards Scholarship at Oxford, or the Sailors' Palace on Commercial Road given to the British and Foreign Sailors Society. The gift to Mrs. Humphry Ward for her settlement house falls into a different category. Not only was this one of Edwards' larger benefactions — £14,000 altogether — but the institution that finally emerged became one of the best known monuments to the philanthropist himself. The forerunner of the Passmore Edwards Settlement was University Hall, opened in 1890 in Gordon Square by Mrs. Ward and a group of Unitarian leaders. The new institution, dedicated by the author of *Robert Elsmere* and her associates to reinterpreting Christianity to the masses, was too relentlessly intellectual to carry any broad appeal, and some of the younger residents, chafing under the heavy educational emphasis of the Hall, started a more typical social settlement in an old building east of Tavistock Square.

Mrs. Ward was faced with the problem of reattaching the flourishing Marchmont Hall to the faltering University Hall. Obviously an indispensable condition was better physical facilities. The first response to her appeal for a building fund of £5000 (an amazing underestimate) came in the form of a £4000 check from Passmore Edwards.[15] In the course of the next two years he raised his original offer from £4000 to £7000 and then to £10,000. Here he hesitated, disturbed by the apparent indifference of others who might have been expected to contribute. When, however, Mrs. Ward herself added £1000, Edwards donated a further £2000, capping his series of gifts with £2000 more on the night of the formal opening of the Passmore Edwards Settlement, as the new building was inevitably named.[16]

To hazard a total figure for Edwards' philanthropies would be little more than an exercise in guesswork. The aggregate might lie in the neighborhood of £200,000 to £250,000. When one recalls that he was involved in the founding of over eighty institutions, in few of which he had invested less than £2000 and in several as much as £10,000 to £15,000, the higher figure seems not unreasonable. Though he did not die poor in any absolute sense (his estate came to a little under £50,000), he shared the view popularized by Carnegie that it was "disgraceful to die a rich man." [17] His philanthropies were thus matters of personal decision and planning rather than of testamentary bequest, and these he conceived

---

[14] Quoted *ibid.*, p. 61.
[15] Janet P. Trevelyan, *The Life of Mrs. Humphry Ward* (London, 1923), p. 91.
[16] *Ibid.*, pp. 120–21.
[17] Hendrick, *Andrew Carnegie*, II, 331. Actually Carnegie's condemnation was less unqualified than the familiar tagline would suggest.

as part of a larger pattern of social betterment to which his own professional work as a publisher and the expanding state services also contributed. To Edwards the institutions and agencies that he was financing were "so many links in the chain of endeavour now being forged by individual, municipal, and Government activity to raise the social life and improve the industrial capacities of the nation . . . And so, in a way, I have realized a triple-tinted dream — first by possessing publications read by many; by threading such publications with an educating and elevating purpose, and by devoting industrial gains so obtained to building useful institutions."[18] It was fitting that two Sovereigns should offer him a knighthood, and it was characteristic that he should respectfully decline the honor.

GEORGE CADBURY
(1 8 3 9 – 1 9 2 2)

For many Englishmen and Americans the name of George Cadbury, and indeed of the Cadbury family, has been almost synonymous with early twentieth-century British philanthropy. With the Rowntrees and the Frys, their fellow Quakers and friendly competitors for the custom of British and foreign consumers of chocolate, the Cadburys wrote a new and exciting chapter in British giving. George Cadbury brought to the practice of philanthropy not only the self-sacrifice and self-denial which were common enough among those in whose religious philosophy charity held a central place but also a concern for ultimate consequences that was almost unique. In spite of his deep compassion, Cadbury was not much interested in relieving temporary distress, nor in applying what he thought of as palliatives. He could deplore the way in which philanthropists seemed satisfied to deal only with "superficial evils," and, as will appear presently, he formed the *Daily News* trust to assist "those who are seeking to remove their underlying causes."[1] Such expressions as "superficial evils" and "underlying causes" were commonplaces in the vocabulary of charity reformers, but to George Cadbury they conveyed something very different from what they meant to Charles Loch and the Charity Organisation Society.

It is impossible to estimate the sum of his benefactions. He was not one to parade his benevolence, save where the publicity might benefit the cause.[2] Moreover, his business and philanthropic careers were so closely intertwined as to make it difficult and unprofitable to classify some of his decisions. The magnificent schools, with which he equipped Bournville at a cost of some £30,000, were to him neither charity nor extravagance but simply a "rich man's view of economy." To an extent that his business contemporaries found more than a little mysterious, almost traitorous, Cadbury's whole career was, in the broad sense, a venture in philanthropy. He was contemptuous of the rich men who devoted the morning and noon of their lives to making money and the evening to giving it away, and

---

[18] *A Few Footprints*, p. 43.
[1] A. G. Gardiner, *Life of George Cadbury* (London, 1923), p. 235. As will be apparent, this essay is based largely on the Gardiner biography.
[2] *Ibid.*, pp. 139–40.

of those who kept their money-making and their benevolent activities in well-insulated compartments. Though he would have agreed with Carnegie that to die rich was a sin, his views on accumulating a fortune and, indeed, his whole scale of ethical-social values had little in common with those of the Scottish American. His conception of the factory and the factory community as a social laboratory recalls a much earlier philanthropist and humanitarian, Robert Owen and his New Lanark venture. Cadbury's substantial contributions to the anti-sweating and old age pension campaigns, among his other causes, marked him as something of an alien spirit among late Victorian philanthropists and proclaimed his sharp deviation from the main tradition of Victorian philanthropy.

Cadbury's uniqueness was a matter of aim as well as act. Among the benevolent rich men of his day he was not only the most creative and daring in his giving but also the most articulate. His notions of business achievement would never have been admitted to the orthodox Victorian canon. "Both in England and America too much is made of men who are successful in business. Success in business is not a test of fine character . . . It is not even a test of a man's diligence." [3] Almost alone among his fellow philanthropists Cadbury was concerned with the long-range implications of his gifts for society. He wished to further the social values in which he so firmly believed, and he had not deluded himself into believing that private charity was sufficient, even though he gave away virtually his entire income. Stiff death duties seemed to him the most obvious kind of device for returning to the nation what men had not given during their lifetime, and he enthusiastically supported the graduated income tax.[4]

As with many of his contemporaries, the dynamic of Cadbury's philanthropy was heavily religious. The notion of stewardship for God was to him a working principle, not merely a pious ideal. To accumulate vast wealth he regarded as a sin. The Quaker Discipline warned him not to "strive or covet to be rich in this world, in these changeable things that will pass away." [5] More than that and almost alone among the business leaders of his time, Cadbury made of his firm itself a quasi-philanthropy; he saw it as a pilot experiment in social welfare which, if successful, might provide a model for industry as a whole. And, like Robert Owen a century before, he demonstrated that such unconventional views were by no means incompatible with a wildly profitable business.

Although not the founders of the Cadbury firm, George and, to a less degree, his brother Richard were in fact its creators. Their father, John Cadbury who was something of a figure in Birmingham local government and reform causes, had branched out from a tea and coffee business to establish a small chocolate factory in Bridge Street. With the death of John's wife and his own failing health, the firm fell on evil days, and, as a young man, George Cadbury had to rehabilitate a shaky business before he could afford to interest himself in public questions. At the time George was twenty-two, the product of four generations of Quaker

---

[3] *Ibid.*, p. 116.
[4] Letter to the Reverend Charles Gore, 10 Nov. 1906, *ibid.*, p. 119.
[5] *The Book of Christian Discipline of the . . . Friends* (London, 1883), p. 125.

tradition and a devout, puritanical upbringing. The varieties of austerity practiced in such families, though numerous, were a bit unpredictable. George's father, though fond of music, gave up his flute in deference to his parents' wishes and until late in life would have no truck with pianos, though music boxes escaped the ban. Nor, until he had passed the age of seventy, would he permit an easy chair in the house. Yet, though to keep a carriage was an effete luxury, ponies were provided for the boys.[6] Such an environment would inevitably have its effect. The adult George Cadbury was not a man of broad cultivation; among his relatively restricted interests there was little place for the arts or letters. To be sure, his second marriage in 1888 to Elizabeth Taylor brought into his life an influence which, no less earnest in its Quakerism, had outgrown some of the ascetic rigors of the Quaker tradition — even to having dancing at her 1910 New Year's party.[7] Still it is true, as his biographer suggests, that the energies of George Cadbury's mind flowed in relatively few channels, but within these they ran deep and powerful.[8]

These energies he threw into the salvaging of the chocolate business. The brothers staked all of their combined capital of £10,000. If that were not enough, the business would have to go, for they had no intention of contracting obligations which they might be unable to repay. The combination of new capital and unremitting toil was effective, and in the fourth year (1864) they turned the corner. From that time on the story of the Cadbury firm was a chronicle of repeated triumphs. One of their early strokes was the decision to sell pure cocoa rather than the hair-raising mixture of cocoa, potato starch, sago, and treacle that was the standard commercial product. In this instance virtue and material success coincided, and before the end of the century Cadbury Brothers were processing about a third of the cocoa imported into the country.[9]

To George Cadbury this achievement as such seemed neither especially remarkable nor admirable. For him ability to make money, as we have seen, had little necessary connection with the more desirable qualities of mind and character. What made Cadbury an innovator was the way in which he turned a successful business into an instrument of social reform. It was impossible for one of his background to accept the notion of a "cash-nexus" as the vital link between employer and workpeople. In his view, the employer's responsibility was not discharged when he paid standard wages; he must also make some provision for light, ventilation, space, and decent living conditions outside the factory — for precisely the essentials that could not be assured in Birmingham, the growing, sprawling, congested Midland metropolis.

Through his interest in the adult school movement Cadbury had received something of an education in the seamier side of working-class living. As a teacher in

---

[6] Gardiner, pp. 13–14.

[7] Richenda Scott, *Elizabeth Cadbury, 1858–1951* (London, 1955), p. 120.

[8] Gardiner, p. 23.

[9] The growth of the business and the welfare activities associated with it are described by Iolo A. Williams, *The Firm of Cadbury, 1831–1931* (London, 1931).

the Severn Street School, he was able to get on an intimate footing not only with members of the "respectable artisan class" but also with others whose way of life was anything but respectable — vagrants, ex-convicts, and drunkards. His Class XIV, which he took over as a group of youngsters in 1863 and carried on for half a century, developed into what was virtually a welfare club of some three hundred members or even a home missionary society, and it fathered a number of branches in the city and the suburbs. But with the success of Class XIV came a sense of frustration, a familiar emotion among social workers whose efforts on behalf of individuals were doomed by the hard facts of environment. It is not enough, Cadbury often said, to talk to a man "about ideals. How can he cultivate ideals when his home is a slum and his only possible place of recreation is the public-house? . . . To win them to better ideals you must give them better conditions of life." [10]

The decision, taken in the late 1870's, to move the factory into the country, was not made solely in the interests of the workpeople's welfare, though that was a major factor. The truth was that the firm had so prospered (though still employing fewer than three hundred hands) as to put the issue of future expansion directly up to its owners. Should they seek more space in the heart of the city itself or should they transplant the whole establishment to the country — or the suburbs, as it turned out — where there was plenty of space, fresh air, and good water? There were disadvantages, of course, and these were not missed by critics of the Cadbury decision. Even with cheap railway tickets, getting to the factory was going to be a difficulty for the working force, for the plan of a residential community in connection with the plant must be for some time a future ideal rather than an immediate prospect. Even so, when in late October 1879 the move was made to the new site, about four miles from the center of the city, Cadbury workers found a cricket and football field for the men and a playground for the girls all ready for use.

It would be impossible — and relatively superfluous, since this is a familiar story — even to sketch the growth of the Bournville enterprise or to elaborate the philosophy of business and welfare that was embodied in it. To repeat, making money and giving it away formed for George Cadbury a single pattern, and making it could be as constructive socially as giving it away. No amount of philanthropic giving could take the curse off a fortune that had been accumulated carelessly or without regard for the welfare of the workpeople who had labored for it. The Cadbury Brothers factory was there not only to produce chocolate and a fortune for the Cadburys but also to serve as an industrial laboratory, an experiment in management and welfare. It was partly, in fact, the desire of the Cadburys for freedom in which to test their ideas without interference by shareholders that deterred them from incorporating as a public limited liability company. Such features as medical and dental care, a pension fund (to which the firm itself contributed heavily), handsome athletic facilities, and schemes for

[10] Gardiner, p. 48.

regularizing employment in a seasonal trade made Cadbury Brothers almost unique in the British industrial world. In 1899, on the death of Richard, the firm converted to a private limited company, with a board of directors, and responsibility passed in some degree from George to the younger generation of Cadburys. Very likely the tremendous growth of the business demanded of the new regime policies less personal, perhaps less paternalistic, than George Cadbury had followed, but he showed none of the proprietary attachment to his own methods that aging innovators often exhibit. Change and experiment were always welcomed by him, possibly, his biographer suspects, as a demonstration in the realm of the common life of the Quaker doctrine of continuous inspiration.[11]

Of all the enterprises connected with the name of George Cadbury, no doubt Bournville Village is the best known. Its influence on the whole garden city movement has been so often emphasized as to need no repetition here. We can only note in passing some of the circumstances of its origin and some of the principles by which it was administered. Like most of the good works of George Cadbury as industrialist, he would have denied to Bournville Village the character of a philanthropy. Actually it represented a fusion of philanthropy and higher self-interest, both of them highly beneficial to the workpeople. In a sense some such decision was thrust on Cadbury Brothers if they were not prepared to see the advantages of their move away from the city pretty will nullified. What had been the country in the late '70's was rapidly becoming a suburb as the city spread out in its compulsive, uncontrolled fashion, and Cadbury could see the specter, if not of slums as bad as those of Birmingham, of a speculative rise in land values and ultimately the covering of the whole area with the handiwork of the jerry-builder. The employees of the firm itself, now numbering nearly twenty-seven hundred,[12] alone made up a fair-sized town. A dual purpose, Gardiner points out, animated George Cadbury, in that "his abstract desire to give an object lesson in housing, therefore, was reinforced by an immediate need of saving the industrial experiment from disaster."[13]

In his plan of establishing a village community he could follow no existing model. Although Ebenezer Howard was beginning to preach the garden city ideal, this was still the vision of an enthusiast, and Cadbury was obliged to work out empirically the principles on which the community would operate. His initial step was to protect the future by buying 120 acres of land, to which he gradually added until in about ten years, the estate exceeded 500 acres. One difficulty for which he had not bargained emerged at once. He sold the first 143 houses at such a modest figure, in terms of the market, that some of the purchasers at once resold at a fancy profit — a blessing that Cadbury, a champion of heavy taxation of land values, had not intended to confer. A change in procedure was indicated if he did not wish to serve the interests of speculators.

[11] *Ibid.,* p. 115.
[12] Scott, *Elizabeth Cadbury,* p. 47n.
[13] Gardiner, p. 142.

Cadbury's solution was to convert the enterprise into a charitable trust. In late December 1900 he turned over to trustees property valued at about £175,000 and comprising about 500 acres and some 370 houses, of which 143 were owned by purchasers and the remainder let for a weekly rent. Two decades later, both the number of houses and the value of the trust property had approximately doubled, and Bournville, as the pioneer town-planning venture, had undertaken missionary work and had invested in both Letchworth and the Hampstead Garden Suburb.[14]

Although technically a charitable trust, this was not intended to be a "charity" in the ordinary use of the word. Nor was it primarily an expedient for solving the housing problem of Cadbury Brothers, though admittedly helpful in this connection. In the early years of the Trust only about 40 per cent of the residents were Cadbury employees, the bulk of the others working in Birmingham proper. George Cadbury saw Bournville as contributing rather to the larger problem of providing civilized housing for Englishmen, and as evidence that such housing could be made to yield a fair return on capital. He would not for a minute have claimed sole honors as prophet of town-planning. Yet Bournville exerted a perceptible influence on the garden city movement in England and abroad, and, less directly, on such large-scale public housing developments as the New Towns. One may share some of the present-day doubts about the garden city as the answer without belittling the importance of the Bournville experiment. Against the bleak background of Victorian industrial housing, living arrangements in the community seem incomparably gracious — the ample space for gardens and playgrounds, the healthful surroundings, the layout of the Village with its wide roads and shade trees and the calculated irregularity in the placing of houses, the excellent schools and other community facilities. The Village Trust, brought into existence through a large capital outlay of Cadbury's, offers a capital example of "seminal philanthropy." Here the Quaker manufacturer was consciously inaugurating an experiment which, he believed, might show numbers of Englishmen a way of escaping from the squalor of slum living.

One of George Cadbury's most conspicuous traits as a philanthropist was the breadth of his interests. Few good causes, political, social, or religious, appealed to him in vain, especially if they seemed to hold promise for the future. Not only was he a rich man, but he put practically his entire income beyond living expenses into good works. Unlike some of his contemporaries who, by their childlessness, had charitable wills virtually thrust upon them, Cadbury not only gave his money away as he made it but did so notwithstanding a large family. At the time he created the Bournville Trust, he pointed out that the gifts comprised the bulk of his property (other than the business) and went on to record his belief that "my children will be all the better for being deprived of this money. Great wealth is not to be desired, and in my experience of life it is more a curse than a blessing to the families of those who possess it. I have ten children. Six of them are at an

[14] *Ibid.*, pp. 145, 160.

age to understand how my actions affect them, and they all entirely approve." [15]

Most of Cadbury's smaller and miscellaneous philanthropies must remain unidentified. His benefactions abroad included such narrowly pious causes as the Reverend Hudson Taylor and his China Inland Mission, but, along with Sir William Lever, he also assisted the London Missionary Society with its Papuan Native Industries, Ltd., an agency formed to protect the natives of New Guinea from the cruder sort of commercial exploitation. He was acutely sensitive, also, to the needs of the Birmingham district itself. He provided £6500 for a site for the Birmingham Y.M.C.A., and along with his wife, who, as one who had been influenced by Christian Socialism, had something to do with guiding his social views, he put up in Bournville Village a rest home and Woodlands, a home for crippled children said to have cost £15,000. Although Cadbury disapproved of ordinary almsgiving, no doubt he relieved a good many individual cases of distress. To more constructive ends, he sometimes helped support those engaged in social experiments that he thought important or assisted needy Members of Parliament in the days before they received compensation from the State.

Some of George Cadbury's more costly and statesmanlike philanthropies, in fact, had a marked political tinge. He was a convinced Liberal, believing firmly in the obligation of men of goodwill and substance to encourage an enlightened public opinion and to guide the nation to upright, high-principled decisions. Such efforts he was always ready to finance. In 1891 he bought four weekly suburban papers in Birmingham to serve as media of education in civic affairs, and early in the Boer War he paid for printing and distributing nearly a million copies of a leaflet issued by the National Arbitration League. For Cadbury, indeed, the War marked almost the beginning of a new career. As with so many anti-imperialists, it seemed to challenge all his principles of international morality, to say nothing of his Quaker antipathy to war, and the hysterical behavior of his fellow countrymen called into question the Liberal confidence in rational progress through democratic processes. The War made something of a national figure out of the Birmingham manufacturer, who hitherto had been known chiefly to those who shared his special religious and social reform interests. But Cadbury's fortune now became an important asset for the "Pro-Boer" Liberals in their effort to stem the tide of Jingoism.

Their fight was gravely handicapped by lack of an adequate platform from which to state their case. The British press was overwhelmingly and shrilly for the War. In London the change of front of the *Daily Chronicle,* followed by the resignation of its editor, H. W. Massingham, left the Pro-Boers with only the *Morning Leader* among metropolitan dailies, and Lloyd George was casting around for means of acquiring the *Daily News.* Cadbury did not answer the appeal at once, deeply as he felt the Government's South African policies to be iniquitous. His Birmingham interests, business and philanthropic, were sufficient to engage all of his energies. He was in the course of launching Bournville Village

[15] *Ibid.,* p. 117.

as a trust, and the affairs of the firm had been complicated by the death of his brother Richard. Moreover, both George and Elizabeth Cadbury were much interested in encouraging the new current of the Social Gospel that was stirring the Quaker community, and they conceived the idea of an informal college for the study of Quaker social thought. The outcome was their decision to give for the purpose their house "Woodbrooke" (which became the first of the Selly Oak colleges), together with an endowed lectureship and a number of scholarships. But notwithstanding these other commitments, Cadbury could not allow the *Daily News* project to fail, and he supplied the necessary £20,000. When, at the close of the War, the paper found itself in serious trouble, he had to choose between permitting it to collapse and buying out another director, who, like himself, had put in £20,000. He decided to go ahead and thus assumed full responsibility for the Liberal daily.

Though newspaper ownership may well be regarded as a highly peripheral philanthropy, Cadbury undertook its duties in precisely the same spirit that informed his other charitable activities. His investment in journalism, he assured his sons, was money that "would otherwise have been given to charities. I had a profound conviction that money spent on charities was of infinitely less value than money spent in trying to arouse my fellow countrymen to the necessity for measures to ameliorate the condition of the poor, forsaken and downtrodden masses which can be done most effectively by a great newspaper." [16] In his own way Cadbury had arrived at certain convictions with regard to the limited utility of private charity, and the *Daily News* editorial policy did not trumpet the doctrines of classical Liberalism. Old age pensions, the expansion of small holdings, and an attack on sweated industries — these were the chief areas of social reform in which the paper was active.

It was Cadbury himself who financed the *Daily News* exhibition of sweated industries in Queen's Hall in May–June 1906, a brilliant stratagem for dramatizing the evil and arousing public feeling. A cause championed even more warmly was that of old age pensions, a need, which, he was convinced, could never be met even by such excellent private pension schemes as that of Cadbury Brothers. It was Cadbury who supplied half of the sinews of war for the National Old Age Pensions League and the campaign that led to the Old Age Pensions Act of 1908.

We need recall the uneasy career of the *Daily News* itself only to note that for Cadbury himself it was a costly philanthropy.[17] In spite of A. G. Gardiner's admirable editing, the paper seems to have lost between £20,000 and £30,000 a year — partly, perhaps, because of the quixotic policy of excluding racing news and liquor advertising. In 1910 he added the *Morning Leader* and the *Star,* which continued, somewhat to the distress of Cadbury's Quaker friends, to print racing news. Yet the *Star* had acquired a position both as an advocate of social reform and a purveyor of racing information, and, in Cadbury's view, "the *Star* with

[16] *Ibid.,* p. 236.
[17] *Ibid.,* pp. 220–21, 228.

betting news and pleading for social reform and for peace was far better than the *Star* with betting and opposing social reform . . . So with great reluctance, I consented to take some part in the purchase, but with the idea that in the course of year it might be possible to do without betting forecasts." [18]

The energies of George Cadbury, who had already exceeded the Biblical span of life, were severely taxed by the strain of these negotiations, and it seemed to him an appropriate time to convert his newspaper holdings into a trust. To the deed creating the trust he attached memoranda which comprised something of a social testament and revealed how closely, in the good works of this Quaker chocolate magnate, private philanthropist and radical social reformer collaborated. For both were offspring of a Christian faith in which religion was inseparably bound up with social morality. "I desire," he wrote, "in forming the *Daily News* Trust that it may be of service in bringing the ethical teaching of Jesus Christ to bear upon National Questions, and in promoting National Righteousness; for example, that Arbitration should take the place of War, and that the spirit of the Sermon on the Mount — especially of the Beatitudes — should take the place of Imperialism and of the military spirit . . . Much of current philanthropic effort is directed to remedying the more superficial evils. I earnestly desire that the *Daily News* Trust may be of service in assisting those who are seeking to remove their underlying causes."

He recognized that reforms which he considered especially vital — broadly speaking, those which tended to transfer wealth from the rich to the community — might not be so regarded by the trustees or might in years to come recede in importance. To Cadbury, the Christian Liberal, the Dead Hand of the reformer was no more tolerable than any other form of dictation by the past. It was only to be expected that he would authorize the trustees "to follow their own conscientious convictions [for] circumstances change, but the spirit of Christ's teachings is unchangeable." [19]

[18] *Ibid.*, p. 231.
[19] *Ibid.*, p. 235.

CHAPTER XVI

BENEVOLENCE BEYOND
THE METROPOLIS:
YORK AND LIVERPOOL

T HIS STUDY has necessarily had much to say about the charities of the Metropolis and about philanthropic movements centered there. Both in its income from endowed charities and in the number and revenue of its voluntary organizations London was unrivaled in the Kingdom. Yet such an emphasis may have been excessive and may perhaps have distorted the picture. The Metropolis, after all, had no monopoly. The provinces did not invariably take their cue from London but in some types of effort themselves gave the lead. One need only recall that the Sunday Hospital Fund came from Birmingham, that industrial and reformatory schools owed much to Mary Carpenter's work at Bristol, and that district nursing was a Liverpool idea. Obviously *caritas* is no respecter of places.

To do something toward restoring the balance, we shall attempt a survey of the charity structure, endowed and voluntary, of two major provincial communities. These carry different types of appeal but between them they serve to underscore, in a fashion none can miss, the debt owed by London to the provinces. York, with its ancient endowments and its modern philanthropies associated with the Rowntree family, is an obvious choice. Here is a community that, drawing on an ancient tradition of benevolence and guided by wise leadership, has emerged as something of a model for other cities. Liverpool has other points of interest. Not abundantly equipped with charitable foundations, Merseyside has been the source of influential ideas and techniques of action for voluntary bodies. From the mid-nineteenth century on, partly in consequence of her special situation as the nation's great port city, Liverpool developed schemes of cooperation and various procedures, which, if they did not solve the local problems, at least suggested points of attack for other cities.

These two communities do not, of course, exhaust the possibilities. Almost any of the larger provincial centers and some of the smaller would have their special attractions for the historian — Bedford, for example, with its great educational foundation; Coventry with its heavy income from charitable endowments; or Bristol with its variety of trusts, ancient and modern. One might move down to smaller towns and villages, most of which would exhibit, in a greater or less degree, elements both typical and individual. But at least to notice York and Liverpool should be enough, along with what has been already pointed out, to suggest that London both drew from and gave to the rest of the country.

YORK

The city of York has enjoyed a double or triple distinction as a center of philanthropy. During the last half-century the public-spirited benevolence of the Rowntree family, who with the Cadburys and the Frys make up the famous triad of Quaker chocolate manufacturers, has added new chapters to the history of philanthropy. But long before the city took to cocoa, pious donors had equipped it handsomely with charitable endowments. Although the endowed income was less per capita than that enjoyed by Norwich or Coventry, when voluntary charities were included, York was better provided for than either of the others.[1] Moreover, to look ahead to a third point of distinction, the consolidation of York charities which was finally managed in the mid-1950's offers something of a model scheme, reconciling, as it does, the advantages of combination with those of flexibility.

At the turn of the century York was a city of about 78,000. Industry had never invaded in force, and the character of the city as an ecclesiastical and residential center had been modified only to a degree by the intrusion of railway works and cocoa and confectionery factories. As with many ancient communities, to repeat, York could boast a large and variegated array of endowed charities (today something over 350 in number),[2] the oldest of which dated from medieval times. In 1907 investigators for the Poor Law Commission computed the endowed charity income of the city at nearly £9000[3] and the voluntary at nearly £13,000. Since they were concerned only with charities which affected the poor more or less directly, they took no account of purely medical and educational agencies. With these included, the charities of York, endowed and voluntary, could have been credited with an income of upwards of £30,000.[4]

The situation in York, in some respects, was reminiscent of that in the Metropolis. Three-quarters of the endowments were general — that is, applicable to the entire city — but above a quarter were limited to one or more of the nearly thirty parishes. Among these appeared the same disparities that prevailed in the City of London. At the turn of the century the wealthiest York parish enjoyed a charity income of £380 and the poorest received only 6s. 8d. Not only that, but as in

[1] A. C. Kay and H. V. Toynbee, "Report on Endowed and Voluntary Charities," *R. C. on the Poor Laws* (Cd. 4593), 1909, App. XV. Figures on which the calculation is based are taken from the 1901 Census.

[2] Manuscript copy of a report prepared by W. K. Sessions for the Nuffield Committee on the Problems of Ageing, and so on, p. 19.

[3] This figure should be greater by at least £1700, for the Yorkshire School for the Blind is counted as a voluntary charity in spite of a considerable endowment.

[4] The York County Hospital accounted for more than £6500, though this was not, strictly speaking, a city of York enterprise.

London the movement of population away from the center had left some parishes with a grave excess of charity income. In 1931 the inner parishes, with 18 per cent of the population, received 64 per cent of the yield of parochial endowments.[5] It was a condition similar to, though, of course, less extreme than, that which in London had made inevitable the City Parochial Foundation.

The pious founders of York reflected faithfully enough the charitable interests of the age in which they lived, and the endowments of the city included all of the major causes for which the benevolent were accustomed to give or leave their money. By far the largest category had to do with the care of the aged. York was famous for its almshouses. At the turn of the century these provided a refuge for about 145. With the almshouses, about twenty separate institutions, must be coupled the pension charities, in which the City abounded, with about 115 beneficiaries.[6] Sometimes these endowments formed a branch of an almshouse foundation, sometimes they were entirely distinct, and sometimes they were administered so as to benefit inmates of under-endowed almshouses. In fact York was, and still is, a kind of Mecca for the aged; no other English city has such adequate — and in some cases sumptuous — almshouse facilities.

Founded over six centuries, York almshouses presented a scene of enormous variety. The earliest, St. Thomas's and St. Catherine's, dated from the Middle Ages; the latest with which we are here concerned (though several handsome establishments have been built more recently) were founded in the 1890's.[7] Their income ran from a pitiful £16 a year (for four almspeople) to more than £325 with which the reasonably affluent Wandesford's Hospital provided for ten unmarried gentlewomen of the Church of England. Altogether York almshouses accounted for an annual income of £2550.

One of the perennial problems of trustees — that of maintaining inmates in almshouses that could offer nothing beyond shelter — was solved in part by York's pension charities, with an annual income of over £1150.[8] This income appears to have been managed, on the whole, systematically and responsibly. The roster of York charities also abounded in doles of the classic sort, to the amount of nearly £1800 a year.[9] These were largely parochial, and more than two-thirds of the income reached the poor in the form of direct money doles. There were, of course, the traditional Christmas doles, tickets for coal and bread, and a few funds for outfitting apprentices (though none for apprenticeship premiums, since these were not commonly paid in York) or providing clothes for the needy.[10]

---

[5] Sessions report (n. 2 above), p. 16.

[6] Kay and Toynbee, "Endowed and Voluntary Charities," p. 16.

[7] Nuffield Survey Committee, *Old People* (Oxford, 1947), App. 13.

[8] In some cases trusts left for almshouse purposes had been converted into pension charities. Agar's Charity (1735), for example, originally an almshouse, was revised in 1877 to provide pensions for six widows. Allen's Charity, intended for a hospital, was supplying pensions for thirteen.

[9] The discrepancy between this figure and the £3700 given by Kay and Toynbee (p. 15) is explained by their inclusion of voluntary charities for the poor, such as certain church collections.

[10] A novel element in the charity structure of York was a series of funds resulting from the strays or pasture lands held by the Corporation in trust for the freemen of the four wards. At the time

York's special distinction lay in its endowments. In its voluntary and mixed [11] charities the city strikes one as virtually a pocket edition of the metropolitan world, with agencies and organizations representing most of the causes to which generations of Victorians and pre-Victorians gave of their time and substance. Among the medical charities the oldest and most imposing was the York County Hospital (1740), one of the earliest of the great provincial institutions established during the eighteenth-century wave of hospital-building. By the turn of the century it was enjoying an average gross income of over £9000 (including legacies and special gifts) and a regular income of about £6550, voluntary contributions and endowment each yielding about £2500. The dispensary movement of the latter eighteenth century produced the York Dispensary (1788), which, a hundred years later, had an income, voluntary and invested, of over £1600.[12] As we have already seen,[13] in the treatment of insanity York played something of a pioneering role. On the eve of the twentieth century both the (Quaker) Retreat and the rehabilitated Bootham Park Asylum were substantial quasi-charities, the former with an income of over £23,000 and the latter with over £10,000. Although most of this revenue was realized from patients' fees, both were in part the products of an earlier philanthropy and both continued to receive poor patients.

York also offered assistance to other varieties of disability. The Yorkshire School for the Blind (not primarily a city of York charity), founded in 1833, had invested property of the order of £50,000 and income (counting about £1800 from the education authorities and £4250 from the sale of goods) of nearly £9000.[14] The York Emanuel, established in 1782, offered treatment for ministers and their families who were afflicted with blindness or "idiocy."

There would be little profit in enumerating the other institutions and organizations which made up the corpus of York charities. There were, of course, the old charity schools — the Blue Coat for boys and the Grey Coat for girls — with an endowed income of over £1800 and subscriptions and donations amounting to over £600. The York Benevolent Society, Wesleyan-managed, which dated from 1793, was a good example of an early visiting society, while the Discharged Prisoners' Aid Society disbursed the income of the old York Castle Prison charities as well as its own voluntary income. For the rest there were the standard charities — for wayward and friendless girls, for the sick and needy, and for semi-delinquents — agencies typical, in a greater or less degree, of the English county town at the turn of the century. But rather than such organizations, it was York's

of our survey, the strays, which returned an annual income of nearly £1700, were about to be put on a more regular basis. Freemen's rights to the most profitable of these lands, the Micklegate Strays, had just been extinguished by Act of Parliament (1907) in return for an annual payment of £1000 to be made by the York Corporation to a committee of Micklegate freemen, the income to be applied for the benefit of freemen and their families under a scheme of the Charity Commissioners.

[11] Meaning, of course, charities which depended in part on income from endowments and in part on subscriptions and donations.
[12] *Burdett's Hospitals,* 1906, p. 516.
[13] Chapter IV above.
[14] Kay and Toynbee, "Endowed and Voluntary Charities," pp. 127–28.

charitable endowments, especially those for the care of the aged, that gave the city its eminence as a center of philanthropy.[15]

2

No serious step toward modernizing and consolidating the management of these ancient foundations was taken until the first decade of the new century. What raised the issue was the study of the charities of a dozen communities carried out by two Assistant Charity Commissioners, Messrs. Kay and Toynbee, for the Poor Law Commission. In their report they noted similarities in the charity situation of York and Norwich and recommended a consolidated administration for the endowments of both cities. When, therefore, the Charity Commissioners put through an elaborate scheme for amalgamating Norwich charities, they took steps to test sentiment in York.[16] The result was a draft scheme covering about 250 separate trusts which, in preliminary form, they sent to the York City Council in July 1910. The scheme called for consolidating all but five of York's charities for the benefit of the poor and for administering their income in four branches covering almshouses, pensions, advancement (aid to deserving and necessitous children), and the poor.

If this was the kind of rational arrangement which in the abstract was unimpeachable, it was also one that would inevitably outrage a variety of local interests. Even such a manifestly sensible notion as that of combining parochial charities so that they could serve the poor of the entire city, a plan approved by the Archbishop, would be viewed with little enthusiasm by the more affluent parishes. If the Commissioners anticipated trouble, their premonitions were wholly justified, and they felt obliged to hold a public inquiry. A. C. Kay, who was placed in charge of the proceedings, held a hearing at York in May of 1911. His two days in the city must have been exceedingly uncomfortable, for it became abundantly clear that York trustees were bitterly opposed to giving over their endowments to a central body. They attacked along a half-dozen fronts — from "duty to uphold the wishes and directions of the pious founders" to claims that the proposed body of trustees would be too large for efficient work. Certainly among the more articulate of charity trustees there was strong resistance to the Commissioners' plan.

Very likely the Commissioners were overoptimistic about their prospects in York. Though they received some support from elements that might be described loosely as Liberal-Labour and Free Church, this was plainly a minority view. They had indulged in wishful thinking and had insisted on putting a favorable construction on what were in fact hostile votes by the City Council. In any case, their hopes of consolidation were conclusively dashed in the summer of 1912, when

[15] Cf. Nuffield Survey Committee, *Old People*, App. 2 ("Survey of Endowed Charities for Old People in York") and App. 13 (W. K. Sessions, "Report on the Almshouses of York").

[16] Information on the 1910–11 amalgamation scheme is taken from a manuscript account (in the offices of the Joseph Rowntree Memorial Trust) of an inquiry held at York in May 1911, by A. C. Kay, an Assistant Charity Commissioner.

the York Council rejected the scheme by a two-to-one vote, and for another four decades the York charities continued along their separate paths.

What revived interest in the possibility of effective cooperation was the epoch-making report on the care of the aged issued in 1947 by a committee of the Nuffield Foundation. This committee — the chairman was Seebohm Rowntree — singled out York, with its twenty groups of almshouses and its other endowed charities for the aged, for special treatment in appendices.[17] With such assets as these, it appeared, York might give the lead to other communities in working out more productive methods of caring for their aged citizens and conceivably in persuading individual charities to unite in a common attack on the problem. The drastic expansion in the welfare activities of the State, moreover, was altering the situation of voluntary agencies. Perhaps, the Lord Mayor suggested at a meeting in the spring of 1947, "by a partnership between voluntary and statutory organizations, a scheme of old people's welfare may be evolved which will serve as a pattern for the country as a whole." [18] And cooperation among endowments for the aged might point the way to more concerted action in other sectors of the charity front.

Within the complex of York philanthropies was a group of "municipal charities," formerly managed directly by the City Corporation, but since the reforms of the 1830's by a special body of trustees.[19] A study of the institutions under their own supervision persuaded these York Charity Trustees that a good deal of readjustment would be needed, readjustment which, they suspected, might be usefully extended beyond their particular bailiwick. What they proposed, in a word, was a consolidation of the York municipal charities, together with as many other endowments as wished to associate themselves with the new body. The Charity Commissioners at first shied away from the idea, apparently under the misapprehension that this was to be a compulsory amalgamation of the whole mass of York charities. They had had their fill of schemes which trenched upon vested local interests, and they viewed with little relish the prospect of protest meetings of trustees, parishioners, and clergy. Eventually, however, they discovered some merit in the modest proposals from York, and they agreed to draft a scheme for Parliamentary action — for obviously a change involving so many trusts which had not "failed" in a legal sense could be effected only through Parliament.

It was inevitable that proceedings should be held up during the inquiry of the Nathan Committee. Promoters of the York scheme — Messrs. L. E. Waddilove of the Rowntree Village Trust and W. K. Sessions — who testified before the Committee were reassured to sense support for precisely such flexible plans as theirs. As for the Charity Commissioners, the Nathan Report proved something of a tonic, and they pushed ahead with the scheme on the terms agreed upon. The

[17] *Old People*, Apps. 2 and 13, by W. K. Sessions, whose father, a City Councillor, had supported the consolidation scheme of the Charity Commissioners in 1911–12.

[18] Information in this section is drawn from manuscript materials supplied me by Mr. L. E. Waddilove.

[19] The municipal charities accounted for less than 10 per cent of the York endowed income.

outcome was a bill consolidating some forty-six charity funds. These comprised a substantial fraction of the city's charitable capital, though from it were missing some of the better-established almshouses, as well as the mass of small parochial charities. The sponsors of the scheme, strongly as they believed in better administration, had no desire to fit all York charities into a strait jacket. There were obvious virtues in consolidation, but there was also great value in the attention which an individual group of trustees could give to an individual charity. This was a permissive amalgamation, consciously designed to conserve such useful energies as this.

The York City Charities, as set up by the Act of 1956, accounted for an annual gross income of about £2800, leaving something over £4000 to be administered independently.[20] As in Norwich the income is spent for three broad categories of object corresponding more or less closely to the original purposes of the individual endowments — through the Advancement, the Poor's, and (by far the largest) the Almshouse and Pension Branches. As with all schemes of the Charity Commissioners since the 1880's, management is vested in a body of trustees divided between a representative and a co-optative element. The York plan, in fine, appears to have reconciled administrative cooperation in the area where it was most needed with the preservation of personal initiative where that was still flourishing.

3

To most people, mention of York philanthropy is less likely to recall its extensive charitable endowments than the benefactions and the humanitarian interests of the Rowntree family. This dynasty of chocolate manufacturers has proved worthy heirs of the Quaker tradition of well-doing, as embodied in the Gurneys, the Frys, the Hoares, and others of an earlier generation. Even to enumerate the projects for public betterment which enlisted the efforts of Seebohm Rowntree, the most distinguished social servant of the clan, would be out of the question. His survey of York working-class life in 1901 (*Poverty: A Study of Town Life*) and his complementary *English Life and Leisure* (1951) enclosed a half century of exertion for the English common life that is almost unique. Here we can only glance at one of the more interesting and permanent of the family philanthropies, the Rowntree Village Trust (now the Joseph Rowntree Memorial Trust) which financed an experiment in community-building similar, though with significant differences, to what was already on the way to realization at Bournville, Port Sunlight, and the garden cities.

The founder was Joseph Rowntree (1836–1925), under whose management the family business had made its greatest expansion.[21] Like others of his Society, "J.R." interpreted his growing prosperity as a trust vested in him by God.

---

[20] Manuscript report by W. K. Sessions for the Nuffield Committee, p. 9. These figures cover non-educational and nonmedical charities.

[21] A recent biography is Anne Vernon, *A Quaker Business Man: The Life of Joseph Rowntree, 1836–1925* (London, 1958).

Throughout his life Rowntree devoted much time to public interests, notably the control of the liquor trade, but as he approached seventy he resolved to make over the bulk of his fortune to causes that had been increasingly engaging his attention. All three of the trusts that he established at the time reflected, in some degree, Rowntree's uneasiness over the superficial and casual character of contemporary philanthropy, the facility, for example, with which money could be raised for famine sufferers in India as compared with the difficulty of financing research into the causes and prevention of famines. In agreeable contrast to the immemorial propensities of donors — and, indeed, against the counsel of his legal advisers, who wished to tie the trustees more rigidly — he granted his trustees a wide latitude. " 'New occasions teach new duties,' " he recalled. "I have given to the Trustees and Directors of these foundations very wide powers and very few directions of a mandatory nature as to their exercise." [22]

Two of the trusts were intended to make possible social investigations (such as Seebohm Rowntree's), to further the work of the Society of Friends, and to support certain social and political activities of a reforming sort. The third was of direct and material benefit to York itself. The Rowntree Village Trust was not, of course, a unique venture but was associated with the movement that developed around the turn of the century and that owed a good deal to Ebenezer Howard's propaganda for garden cities.[23] Before he had decided to establish the Trust, Joseph Rowntree had already bought an estate of about 150 acres three miles from York, and Seebohm had engaged the services of Raymond Unwin, one of the more original and influential of the town planners.[24] This earliest unit, designed by Unwin and his partner Barry Parker at a time when the land for Letchworth was just being purchased, was remarkably prophetic. In his first plan, the architect gave evidence of an exhilarating indifference to convention. He would have no commerce with a community divided by parallel roads, enclosing tightly packed blocks of houses — a chunk of the city translated to the country. He refused to sacrifice to roads valuable land that could be better used for open spaces and garden plots, and he distributed his houses so that living rooms would receive a decent supply of sunlight, without much concern as to whether or not they faced on a main street. The Rowntree community, in short, was an imaginative attempt on the part of donor and architect to break away from the familiar formulas of working-class housing and to provide accommodations combining economy with a reasonable degree not only of physical but of esthetic and social comfort as well.

This is not intended to be a history, nor even a thumbnail sketch, of the Rown-

[22] (L. E. Waddilove) *One Man's Vision* (London, 1954), pp. 1-4. This account of the Village Trust is drawn largely from Mr. Waddilove's volume.

[23] *To-morrow: A Peaceful Path to Real Reform,* published originally in 1898 and republished in 1902 as *Garden Cities of Tomorrow.*

[24] Cf. Lewis Mumford's tribute to Unwin (quoted by Waddilove, *One Man's Vision,* pp. 133-34) in which he credits the pioneer planner with demonstrating that even from an economic standpoint there is "Nothing Gained by Overcrowding."

tree Village Trust and its New Earswick community.[25] All that can be noted here is some of the more distinctive features of the Trust as a philanthropy. Although New Earswick owed something to the Cadbury's Bournville, the problems of the two were by no means identical. York was not Birmingham. Whereas housing developments near large cities had to compete only with wretched slum property and were thus able, without too much difficulty, to attract numbers of tenants, the situation of New Earswick was more complicated. York was not primarily an industrial city, and its housing as a whole was far from intolerable. As a result, though applications from potential tenants were never in short supply, the Trust made little progress with the lowest rental groups. With this qualification, the community — nearly six hundred houses in 1954, with twenty-six more under construction — has always represented a fairly adequate social cross section. The founder was not primarily interested in creating a housing facility for Rowntree employees, despite its proximity to the Works, and during the 1950's fewer than a third of the tenants belonged in this category.

Denying any intention of establishing a perpetual philanthropy, Rowntree hoped to demonstrate that housing for the lower-paid workers could be made to yield a minimum commercial return. This goal the Trust was never able to achieve completely, though it did not fall short by far. The total assets of the Trust, originally about £62,000, by 1953 exceeded £950,000, and the total expenditure made on land, houses, and necessary services had come to something like £450,-000. To trace the financial history of New Earswick would involve us in unnecessary detail. It must suffice merely to note some of the stages through which its policies have passed. The experiment, to repeat, was not to bear "the stamp of charity" but was to serve as a pilot demonstration for public authorities and private landlords. Before 1914 it seemed to be meeting these conditions admirably and, in accordance with the founder's intention, was financing the expansion of the community from income. But this early financial success was in part illusory. Only because repairs on new buildings were so relatively minor was it possible to carry out expansion on the basis of the extremely low rents that were charged. During the period between the two World Wars the situation changed, and rocketing building costs forced the trustees to finance new construction by borrowing, while collecting government subsidies under the various Housing Acts of the 1920's. Some 225 dwellings were put up on these terms as against only 34 financed wholly by the Trust. During these years, with the aid of the subsidy, the net return on capital rose substantially.

Since 1945 the position of the Village Trust, like that of many British philanthropies, has been markedly altered. The day had passed when experiments in working-class housing were needed to give a lead to the State. The State, in fact, had seized the initiative, and with local authorities undertaking housing projects

[25] Mr. Waddilove's volume gives the relevant facts including many technical details of plans, rentals, and costs, as well as information on the corporate life of the community. A brief account is given by Anne Vernon, *Quaker Business Man*, pp. 147ff.

on a large scale and offering dwellings within the reach of low-paid workers, the problem that had harried the Village Trust from the beginning now ceased to bother. The trustees could accept with a clear conscience a tenant population whose lowest economic stratum was somewhat above the minimum and could adjust their rentals accordingly. As a result, they found themselves with resources which they could apply to some of the broader social purposes contemplated by the founder.

All along, the Trust had been making such grants as it could for the benefit of the "wider community" — for social investigations, for gardens and open spaces in York, and for housing reform — and had been providing amenities of various sorts for New Earswick itself. The schools of the village, for example, were from the beginning of superior quality and were a justifiable source of pride.[26] Since the War the trustees have been involved in a variety of experimental ventures. Of such are their grants for research in the handling of the "problem family," a difficulty which such private undertakings as New Earswick might avoid but which public housing authorities must deal with. After a period of studying matters of rural health, the trustees acquired a mobile maternity and child welfare center which they turned over to the Health Authority and which has been serving some twenty villages in the area. The National Assistance Act of 1948, as well, perhaps, as Seebohm Rowntree's chairmanship of the Nuffield old age study, turned the attention of the trustees to the aged members of their own community. Their conclusion, reached in cooperation with the public authorities, tended to show that old people could be maintained in small local homes at reasonable cost, thus avoiding the evil of uprooting and transplanting them to larger city establishments.

Such accomplishments by no means exhaust the record of the Trust. Certainly both trustees and residents would discover something especially satisfying in the community life of the village, with its organs of self-government expanding their functions year by year. Rowntree's enterprise, never designed as a paternalistic charity, became even less so with the passage of time, and it has supplied an admirable example of a private philanthropy changing with the years and functioning effectively in an age of social concern and growing state responsibility. In the early days, in common with other housing philanthropies, a primary aim was to influence private landlords of the better sort — to provide evidence that a reasonable return on capital was not incompatible with superior housing — and to give encouragement to the garden city movement. Then the focus shifted to the public authorities, agencies responsible for building new working-class communities, and these the Trust was eager to serve.

Since the War, however, emphases have altered even more sharply. At the end

---

[26] Waddilove, p. 143. Although the Education Act of 1944 altered the terms of the problem, schooling at New Earswick (in 1952) was about 40 per cent more costly than in North Riding schools as a whole. The contribution of the trustees amounted to about half the sum contributed by the Local Education Authority, the additional outlay being used chiefly to make possible smaller classes.

of a half century of housing experiment, the Rowntree trustees found themselves with an income of about £100,000, more than half again their total original assets and far greater than the founder had contemplated. Meanwhile housing had been so widely taken up by public authorities and others that there seemed little excuse for reinvesting the resources of the Trust in new estates. The solution, registered in a Private Act of Parliament,[27] was to alter the terms of the trust to permit a greater range of social research and experiment. The Joseph Rowntree Memorial Trust (as the Village Trust has now become) has supported such diverse undertakings, its first (1960) Report reveals, as a survey of prenatal mortality, a five-year study of the impact of legislative controls on housing facilities in the United Kingdom, and an inquiry looking toward the establishment of Citizens' Advice Bureaux in Rhodesia — in addition, of course, to continuing the regular and experimental activities at New Earswick.[28] Among all of the assorted institutions and organizations that go to make up the British charitable world, none has shown a livelier awareness of "the new occasions" which "teach new duties,"[29] or a more imaginative understanding of the uses of private philanthropy in semicollectivist Britain.

LIVERPOOL

The claims laid upon the historian of philanthropy by the great port at the mouth of the Mersey are strikingly different from those of York. Liverpool is not a city of ancient foundations, and, as compared with older centers, there are relatively few endowments for almshouses, pensions and doles, or other classic charitable objects. Even the sixteenth-century grammar school, a monument to Tudor philanthropy, had been absorbed by the Blue Coat School, which was founded at the turn of the eighteenth century by a humane ship captain.[1] In spite of the exemplary public spirit of some of its leading families — the Rathbones, the Holts, and others — no single dynasty of philanthropists dominated the scene as did the Rowntrees in York. The Merseyside was, of course, the source of splendid gifts and bequests — the Tate Gallery and the David Lewis Trust,[2] for example — and critical citizens demanded of their wealthy compatriots a decent concern for local good works. When Sir William Brown (Brown, Shipley & Company) gave the Brown Library, a journalist could remind his readers that the prospect of a baronetcy rather than any native generosity had inspired the gift, and even then the donor "gave it under pressure, after much judicious handling, grudgingly — somewhat like the famous cow which first yielded milk, but afterwards kicked over the pail."[3] Sir Andrew Barclay Walker, the brewer and distiller,

[27] The Joseph Rowntree Memorial Trust Act, which received the Royal Assent on 29 July 1959.
[28] As noted in the *First Report* of the Trust, 1960.
[29] To recall the familiar words of James Russell Lowell with which Rowntree concluded his original charge to the trustees.
[1] George Chandler, *Liverpool* (London, 1957), p. 389.
[2] Asa Briggs, *Friends of the People* (London, 1956), p. 99.
[3] B. Guiness Orchard, *Liverpool's Legion of Honour* (Birkenhead, 1893), pp. 213–14.

who provided Liverpool with its art gallery, was regarded with no more enthusiasm by this abrasive commentator. Walker's philanthropies, he intimated, were planned as instruments for his own social and political advancement, first to a knighthood and then to a baronetcy.[4]

Liverpool's distinction in philanthropy, however, lies less in large foundations established by individual donors than in its organized voluntary effort. Local critics may have felt, correctly enough, that evils of Liverpool life were not being adequately grappled with, and Mrs. Simey can characterize Liverpool charitable activity as a story of alternate hope and frustration. But with all of the discouraging chapters in its record, Liverpool philanthropy has been the source of ideas, forms, and devices which have powerfully influenced charity practice in London and elsewhere. Though it would be too much to suggest that, in the realm of voluntary charity, "what Liverpool thinks today, the rest of the country will think tomorrow," some of the more significant principles and techniques of nineteenth- and twentieth-century philanthropic action did in fact originate at the mouth of the Mersey.

The emergence of the port of Liverpool was an eighteenth-century phenomenon, beginning with the construction of the first wet dock in 1709 and proceeding so rapidly that by the end of the century a city of seventy-five thousand was handling nearly five thousand ships a year.[5] This was, in short, a commercial, not an industrial, society. The leading men of the city were merchants rather than manufacturers, and their political and social outlook, broadly speaking, was that of the eighteenth-century mercantile aristocracy. Nor was Liverpool's working class typically South Lancashire. There were no large masses of semipermanently located factory hands; the great merchant princes presided over relatively small labor forces made up chiefly of casual workers with whom the employer had little need to work out a stable relationship. In 1885–86, for example, nearly 21 per cent of the applicants for relief were dockers and 13 per cent porters.[6] The city's laboring population was made up, in a large measure, of floaters — masses of Irish driven out by distress or attracted by hope of bettering their lot, and migrants from Wales or the country districts of the Midlands and the North. Add to such casuals the numbers of seamen held in port by unfavorable winds or off-seasons and the stream of emigrants which flowed into Liverpool en route to the New World and one can readily appreciate why, even among early Victorian cities, Liverpool should have been thought of as especially abandoned in its congestion, filth, and disease.

More even than in the industrial centers, social contact between the classes was minimal. Liverpool employers were not obliged by the circumstances of their business to accept the kind of responsibility for their workers that even the less

---

[4] *Ibid.*, p. 689.

[5] Margaret Simey, *Charitable Effort in Liverpool*, p. 7; J. A. Picton, *Memorials of Liverpool* (London, 1873), I, 252.

[6] Central Relief Society, *Ann. Rept.*, 1885–86, p. 6.

humane factory-owner was often forced to assume. Their attitude toward the classes below them could be described, in the words of a Liverpool historian, as "indifference slightly tempered by philanthropy." [7] Yet if relative isolation bred indifference in the upper classes of Liverpool, it did not encourage the hostility toward their inferiors characteristic of some of the new industrial centers. The merchant aristocracy sensed no challenge to its own position, and its members might therefore take the lead in reform or humanitarian undertakings. Some of the great merchant families, mostly "Renshaw Street Unitarians," developed a strong and enviable tradition of civic leadership.

To chronicle the methods by which Liverpool humanitarians sought to assist the poor and sick of their city would be merely to summarize Mrs. Simey's volume.[8] Although its social structure and economic orientation imparted something of a distinctive character, in the large the stream of Liverpool philanthropy paralleled the currents flowing in the Metropolis and elsewhere. During the early century there was the same zeal for district visiting and the same fecundity of voluntary societies, together with extraordinarily devoted individual effort. A remarkable young Unitarian clergyman, the Reverend John Hamilton Thom, who came to the Renshaw Street Chapel in 1831, persuaded his well-to-do flock to establish a Domestic Mission and to appoint a Minister to the Poor. The committee was guided providentially to the Reverend John Johns, a Devonshire man and no less exceptional a person than Thom, who served as Missioner until his death in 1848 from cholera contracted in the course of his duties. It was Johns's achievement to reveal to his sponsors, in the eloquent, sensitive prose of his annual reports and in his personal appeals, the conditions of life of the Other Nation and to implant in them his own conviction that the dismal state of Liverpool slum-dwellers was due less to their own moral defects than to the failure of society to provide a physical minimum for civilized living. However minor may have been the specific results of Johns's ministry, at least he left to his Renshaw Street constituents the "legacy of uneasy mind and troubled conscience." [9]

Even in the early century Liverpool could claim priority in some types of organized effort. The Liverpool Night Asylum (1830) was a pioneer charity of its kind, and Kitty Wilkinson, an alumna of the Greg apprentice house and wife of a porter in Rathbone's warehouse, took the initial step in the movement for wash-houses and public baths. During the epidemic of 1833 she collaborated with Mrs. William Rathbone in setting up facilities in her cellar for washing the clothing and linen of cholera victims.[10] There were, as elsewhere, fitful attempts to

---

[7] Brian D. White, *A History of the Corporation of Liverpool, 1835–1914* (Liverpool, 1951), p. 4.
[8] Above, n. 5. A list of about 125 Liverpool agencies, together with financial particulars about each (for the year 1905) appears in the *R. C. on the Poor Law* (Cd. 4835), 1909. App. IV, 543–49.
[9] Simey, *Charitable Effort*, p. 44. For Thom and the Domestic Mission, see Anne Holt, *A Ministry to the Poor* (Liverpool, 1936), chap. III.
[10] Simey, pp. 26–27; Chandler, *Liverpool*, p. 409.

introduce some degree of order into the anarchy of Liverpool almsgiving, and there was distress over the narrow social base of charity financing.[11] There were the familiar waves of sentimental philanthropy which periodically engulfed the upper middle classes of the city, as elsewhere in the Victorian world. But as for Liverpool's distinctive contributions to philanthropy, the bulk of these took place during the latter half of the century.

2

Liverpool was notable in the world of mid-Victorian philanthropy for its pioneering efforts in charity cooperation, in which it anticipated by several years the London Charity Organisation Society. The city was also the source of one of the more constructive mechanisms fashioned by the Victorian Age for the medical care of the poor. In both of these developments — charity cooperation and district nursing — the driving force was William Rathbone VI, paragon of Liverpool merchant-philanthropists, in whom a sensitive social conscience and the compulsions of Christian obligation were in some degree frustrated by the class assumptions of his age. More reflective and articulate than most of his fellows, Rathbone's ascendancy among the civic-minded of his city was unchallengeable. And his labors in philanthropy, together with his philosophy of social reform, offer what is perhaps the most useful introduction to the attempts of Liverpool to deal with its social *malaise*.

Rathbone's outlook owed a good deal to his family background. During the eighteenth century the family had risen to prominence and wealth as a merchant house, and his father, William Rathbone V (1787–1868), had himself been something of a pillar of Liverpool charity. The marriage of William V to Elizabeth Greg of the distinguished cotton dynasty not only reinforced some of the admirable qualities of the Rathbone stock and added new ones but also had something to do with the final shift in the family religious allegiance from Quakerism to Unitarianism. Elizabeth and her eldest son, much alike, shared an overflowing vitality and a gift for instinctive good judgment, a practical cast of mind, William's daughter recalls, "amounting almost to the genius of common sense." [12]

His eminently practical talents and his driving energy predestined William VI for the family business, and he set a steady course, interrupted only by a year of study at the University of Heidelberg. During the early days of their partnership in the firm, William and his brother Samuel devoted themselves largely to rebuilding the business. For, although Rathbone Brothers & Company was in no critical situation, it had failed to keep up with the procession in Liverpool. The two young men were aware that, without a prosperous and respected business behind them, their voice would carry little weight on public issues. Although William tended, both from personal taste and a sense of duty, toward the frugal,

---

[11] William Grisewood, *The Collection of Subscriptions to Charitable Institutions* (Liverpool, 1906), p. 3.

[12] Eleanor F. Rathbone, *William Rathbone: A Memoir* (London, 1905), p. 40.

his realistic eye could not miss the fact that, among middle-class Englishmen, the influence carried by a man's words depended in a large measure on his success in managing his own affairs and that, at least with businessmen, this was equated with their wealth.[13]

From the beginning Rathbone had strong views on the making and spending of money. He thought it essential for the young man to form habits of saving and giving — not merely to do good to others but to improve his own character. To postpone developing these habits until wealth had been acquired would be fatal and would produce a "pecuniary paralysis." It was his formula, followed by himself and prescribed for others, to give "for the sake of practice" even while one's resources were scanty. Then when greater wealth came, it would be natural and relatively painless to increase not only the amount but the proportion of one's income used for social betterment. In fact, the really conscientious and public-spirited man, as his wealth increased, not only would give a progressively larger proportion to charity but might reasonably establish a ceiling for his private expenditures, devoting the surplus to public causes.

Even during his early years as a partner in the business, William Rathbone practiced his own precepts by giving generously. Not only that, but also, to his considerable profit, he served an apprenticeship of sorts as a social worker, an experience which brought him into more or less systematic contact with the poor and modified some of his preconceptions about them. The District Provident Society, which Rathbone served as a voluntary worker, stands as a typical enough specimen of the early nineteenth-century visiting charity, one of the favorite recipes of the age for the growing isolation of classes in urban society, where "on both sides, the connecting links of love and interest, the sympathy, are wanting."[14] The purpose of those who in 1829 organized the Society was to re-establish some of the bonds between rich and poor, in a sense to provide a mechanism by which the well-to-do could inculcate in the poor the habits which might enable them to attain self-respect and independence.

In its operations the Society managed to combine elements of a working-class savings bank, a house-to-house Bible mission, and social casework. Some two hundred voluntary visitors called regularly in the quarters assigned to them, collecting savings (the Society offered sixpence premium for every ten shillings saved), and issuing Bibles. Rathbone's beat was some of the more unsavory courts in the Lime Street area, where he collected pennies and sixpences and offered such counsel as he was able. The Society's visitors often encountered resentment and suspicion, and some of them emerged from the experience confirmed in their notion that the poor were irreclaimably shiftless and were living the kind of lives they deserved. As a result, Mrs. Simey suggests, the District Provident tended to become a society "for the suppression of vice rather than the

[13] *Ibid.*, p. 113.
[14] James Shaw, *An Account of the Liverpool District Provident Society* (Liverpool, 1834), quoted in Simey, *Charitable Effort*, p. 30.

promotion of virtue," and, in spite of its claim to be "a field where rich and poor may meet together," increasingly stressed its thrift and anti-mendicity activities.[15]

William Rathbone's most memorable legacy to the well-being of Liverpool's poorer citizens lay in the domain not of friendly visiting but of medical care. More than anyone else, he was the founder and promoter of the district nursing movement, which Charles Booth considered the most "directly successful" of all the forms of charity.[16] Rathbone's experiment grew directly out of the death in 1859 of his first wife and his desire to establish a suitable memorial for her. Employing as his agent the skilled nurse who had taken care of his wife, he arranged for her to visit the sick poor in their homes for a period of three months. The trial, in Rathbone's judgment, was so undeniably successful that he determined to expand the service.

The most distressing obstacle faced by the founder was not financial stringency — he himself was going to finance the undertaking, at least in its infancy — but the total lack of trained personnel. One need only recall the dismal state of the nursing profession, just beginning at the end of the '50's to show the results of Florence Nightingale's labors, to realize how unlikely it was that Rathbone should find recruits among the handful of adequately trained nurses. In the end he had to appeal to Miss Nightingale herself, who came up with the common-sense solution of starting a training school in Liverpool, presumably in connection with the Royal Infirmary.[17] Four years after Rathbone had sent Nurse Robinson on her novel mission, the Liverpool Training School, built at his expense, was preparing nurses for the new service, as well as for the Infirmary and private patients. In each of the eighteen Liverpool districts the nurse was supervised and assisted by a lady superintendent, usually with a committee of ladies, who agreed to arrange for her lodging and to enlist public support. Although it was the responsibility of each locality to finance its own nursing service, in point of fact nearly half of the districts were wholly maintained by lady superintendents and their immediate families.[18]

His growing interest in medical care for the poor led Rathbone to persuade the Liverpool authorities to introduce trained nursing into the parish infirmary on Brownlow Hill. To finance the venture in its experimental stages he put down £1200 for twelve Nightingale nurses and a matron.[19] The latter was Agnes Jones, Florence Nightingale's "best and dearest pupil," who, in the three years between assuming her new post and her premature death from typhus in 1868, wrote one

[15] Simey, pp. 30–32.
[16] Quoted in Rathbone. *William Rathbone,* p. 155. The most recent account of the movement is Mary Stocks. *A Hundred Years of District Nursing* (London, 1960). There is also William Rathbone's own *Sketch of the History and Progress of District Nursing* (London, 1890), and a good brief account (chap. V) in Eleanor Rathbone's memoir of her father.
[17] Cecil Woodham-Smith, *Florence Nightingale, 1802–1910* (London, 1950), p. 460.
[18] Simey, *Charitable Effort,* p. 73.
[19] Woodham-Smith, p. 463.

of the epics of Victorian nursing. Her achievement with the fourteen hundred pauper patients in the Liverpool Infirmary immensely strengthened the hands of those who were contending for more adequate care of Britain's workhouse population.

Meanwhile, the Liverpool District Nursing Society flourished exceedingly and provided something of a model for other communities. Manchester, Leicester, and Birmingham followed within a few years, and two societies were formed in the Metropolis. Here plainly was a form of philanthropic effort which not only met a genuine need but which was realistically conceived and managed. Yet even Rathbone, with all his faith in the movement, could hardly have foreseen that, seventy-five years after his first tentative experiment, over a thousand district nursing associations, employing nearly seventy-three hundred nurses, would cover 95 per cent of the population of England and Wales.[20]

The original impulse toward a national association for district nursing came not from Rathbone himself but from the English branch of the Order of St. John of Jerusalem, which was especially concerned with establishing a visiting nursing service in the Metropolis. But when called into consultation, he at once assumed a position of leadership in the discussions from which in June 1874 emerged the National Association for Providing Trained Nurses for the Sick Poor (later the Metropolitan and National Association). It was Rathbone also who served as chairman of the Association's subcommittee to survey the need for and the current state of district nursing. In its report the subcommittee took its stand on the principle of a thoroughly trained staff of visiting nurses, working under the supervision of more highly qualified nurses and in close touch with medical men. These views were essentially those of Florence Nightingale, who, Rathbone admitted, "in any matter of nursing is my Pope and I believe in her infallibility." Miss Nightingale had no doubt that the visiting nurse must be "a sanitary missionary, not an almsgiver" and that those who became "merely clothes-givers, soup-givers, beef-givers" had missed the road.[21] Rathbone's thorough, well-considered report was, perhaps, the major influence in determining that district nursing in much of the country "should run in a broad, well-defined professional channel, instead of meandering through the countless runnels of parochial and sectarian philanthropy."[22]

William Rathbone's services to the nursing profession were not yet completed. When in 1887 the Queen decided to devote the bulk of the "Women's Jubilee Gift," amounting to some £70,000, to the cause of district nursing, he joined the three trustees to work out preliminary plans. Clearly Rathbone had a good deal to do with establishing the policies and making the practical arrangements for the new Queen Victoria's Jubilee Institute for Nurses (later the Queen's Institute

---

[20] Constance Braithwaite, *The Voluntary Citizen* (London, 1938), p. 201.

[21] Woodham-Smith, pp. 567–68. Miss Nightingale's views are summarized in an interesting letter to *The Times*, 14 April 1876, having to do specifically with the provision of homes for nurses.

[22] E. F. Rathbone, *William Rathbone*, p. 175.

of District Nursing), of which he remained vice-president until his death in 1902. A decade later the resources of the Institute had increased by £132,000 — £48,000 from the Queen and £84,000 from other donors.[23] By standardizing the training of district nurses and by providing a center for the movement, the Institute effectively turned "a scattered service into a national system."[24] Within fifteen years of its foundation, district associations were employing about 1240 Queen's Nurses at an annual cost of about £115,000.[25]

Though plainly the work of many hands, English district nursing was in a special sense the creation of the Liverpool philanthropist, and it is a memorial that became him well. In its structure and policies the district nursing system almost perfectly expressed Rathbone's own combination of qualities — his driving energy and daring, controlled by an intuitive feeling for the practical, a social idealism balanced by a both-feet-on-the-ground understanding of human realities. All of these contributed to the movement which remains one of the more solid philanthropic achievements of the Victorian Age.

3

The primacy of Liverpool in district nursing is indisputable; its claim to priority in the charity organization movement, though defensible enough, is perhaps less conclusive. The Liverpool Central Relief Society, formed in 1863, did in fact antedate the London Charity Organisation Society by several years, but something of the kind was in the air during the 1860's in most large cities. Not only that, but the merger which created the Central Relief Society owed a good deal to the special situation of Merseyside charities. As a port city, Liverpool's problem with casual and semicasual labor was particularly acute. Employment was subject to the wildest of fluctuations, and Liverpool businessmen are said often to have been faced by queues of beggars (and presumably unemployed workers) outside their office doors demanding their shillings and half-crowns.[26] Much duplication and overlapping was present in the work of the three existing relief agencies — the District Provident Society, the Strangers' Friend Society, and the Charity Society — all of which permitted their subscribers to recommend needy persons to the organization. Inevitably some of their more enterprising clients discovered that relief could be obtained safely enough from all three.

The spring of 1855, when a long-continued east wind kept incoming ships in port and a severe frost stopped work in the outdoor trades, dramatized the unsatisfactory relief arrangements. Crowds of unemployed gathered around the Exchange, the hearts of the benevolent were touched, and a fund of about £5000 was raised. Unfortunately to distribute relief through employers was no guarantee against duplication, since dockers and porters ordinarily worked for several em-

---

[23] Arthur Shadwell, *The Times*, 27 Sept. 1926, whose articles appearing 27–29 Sept. provide a good brief summary of the movement.
[24] *Ibid.*, 28 Sept. 1926.
[25] E. F. Rathbone, *William Rathbone*, p. 182.
[26] Central Relief Society, *Ann. Rept.*, 1902–1903, p. 5.

ployers.[27] The experience with the 1855 relief fund led to a more critical examination of the methods of the three societies and launched a movement for consolidating their work, a trend that was further strengthened by the cooperative
effort required to raise and distribute the huge Cotton Famine relief fund.[28] By
January 1863 the committees of the older societies were convinced that amalgamation offered the only reasonable solution, and the Central Relief Society came into
being. Unlike the London C.O.S., the Liverpool Society conceived of itself as a
relief agency, not merely as a charity holding company or clearing house. To raise
and disburse funds for the relief of the "distressed and deserving poor," with
thorough investigation and appropriate action in all cases, and to repress mendicity
and expose imposture, these were the aims of the new Society — a nice balance of
the benevolent and the punitive.

Three years after its founding William Rathbone supplied what could be interpreted as a rationale for the Relief Society in his *Social Duties* — or, as his own
preference would have been, "Method versus Muddle and Waste in Charitable
Work." He was disturbed, as were other thoughtful observers by the disruptive
influence of large-scale industry on the social fabric and the impersonal character
of urban life, and he was interested in exploring new ways of re-establishing relations between classes. No doubt special responsibility lay with the rich, and he
appealed to his well-to-do contemporaries in the name of both self-interest and
moral obligation. But through what channels could they best express their social
concern? Obviously random almsgiving was no answer; philanthropy was not
a field in which donors "have a right to indulge their caprice."[29] Nor was the
world of voluntary charity, taken as a whole, such as to encourage the intelligent
philanthropist. Whether on balance charity did more good than harm, no one
could ever describe it as a system, for regularity and rational planning were
precisely what was lacking.

Rathbone outlined a scheme for introducing order into the anarchy of mid-
Victorian giving. His proposal, in essence, called for the marshaling of voluntary
effort along the lines later followed by Charity Organisation Societies — central
committee, district committees, and the rest — with the object of systematically
covering the needy poor, while preserving the values, the humanity and kindli-
ness, of personal charity. Rathbone was confident that this organization would
create a framework within which the benevolent individual could more readily
"come into contact with his suffering brother," and he would have resented that
notion that his plan might lead to an overemphasis on machinery. Yet, though
he did not himself lack in human warmth and he passionately believed in the
efficacy of ungrudging sacrificial service to the poor, his own approach to charity,
both as practiced by himself and as reflected in *Social Duties*, was notably un-

---

[27] William Grisewood, *The Liverpool Central Relief and Charity Organisation Society* (Liverpool, 1899), pp. 28–29.
[28] Liverpool raised more than £100,000 (E. F. Rathbone, *William Rathbone*, p. 188).
[29] *Social Duties* (London, 1867), p. 37.

emotional.[30] However much Rathbone and the other prophets of charity organizations may have done to improve procedures for dealing with the poor, they were also a bit prone, as critics charged, to confuse the husk with the kernel and, at least in appearance, to lay greater store by the mechanics of charity than by its substance.

It would not do to pass a sweeping judgment on the work of the Central Relief Society. From a reading of the annual reports one gets the impression of a body somewhat less complacently doctrinaire than the London C.O.S., perhaps because, as the only general relief agency in Liverpool, it was closer to the poor themselves. During bad times, when mass unemployment swept the city, the Society was in no position to stand on the niceties of C.O.S. procedure (though in 1874 it had become the Liverpool Central Relief and Charity Organisation Society) but must move with promptness and decision. Late-century proposals of old age pensions to be financed by contributions from worker, employer, and State did not make C.R.S. leaders turn livid.[31] Yet C.R.S. philosophy represented no very serious dilution of the C.O.S. gospel. In 1897, for example, the Society carried out through its visitors an inquiry into the condition of the Liverpool poor. "As might have been anticipated," the Annual Report concluded, "drink, improvidence, and neglect of family obligations, were amongst the chief causes," though, it was conceded, "testimony was not wanting to the fact of poverty and suffering overtaking many through irregularity of employment, sickness and other causes, for which they could not be held to blame." [32] The remedial measures proposed were less than revolutionary — more friendly visiting, provident dispensaries, encouragement to saving, and personal reformation were the ingredients in the familiar prescription. One might readily infer that if the poor would not drink so much, would use the savings banks, and would wash more frequently, social distress would at least be markedly alleviated.

From the beginning the C.R.S. carried out relief operations on an impressive scale. During the bad year 1866–67 the soup kitchens which had been placed at the disposal of the Society were exceedingly busy, and nearly twenty-seven thousand cases were relieved (at a cost of £4025 out of about thirty-four thousand visited — all this from a total income of about £6750.[33] No one could charge the Society with administering its relief with overlavish hands. For William Rathbone the new organization held great promise, but he disapproved of certain features, especially the paid agents on whom the C.R.S. relied chiefly for investigating and distributing relief. His own plan, sketched in *Social Duties,* assigned a primary position to the voluntary worker, with the central agency responsible for raising money and organizing the corps of volunteers. An earlier visit to Elberfeld confirmed him in his conviction of the importance of the unpaid worker, and in 1888 he arranged for a delegation (composed of a Local Government Board In-

---

[30] Simey, *Charitable Effort,* pp. 90–92.
[31] William Grisewood, *Friendly Visiting and Charity Organisation* (Liverpool, n.d.), p. 3.
[32] *Ann. Rept.,* 1896–97, pp. 16–17.
[33] *Ann. Rept.,* 1866–67, p. 7.

spector, the chief agent of the C.R.S., and Charles Loch) to make an on-the-spot survey.[34] This, if ever, was a propitious time for a change, for the severe unemployment of 1887 had brought about a near-collapse in the existing relief mechanism.

The result of it all was the decision to apply the Elberfeld system throughout the city. It was a heroic, almost quixotic, scheme of recruiting an army of "friendly visitors" and assigning to each of these responsibility for a segment of "the poor." At one time as many as three hundred visitors were enlisted, working under twenty-three district committees — a far cry from the twenty-five hundred Rathbone had pictured. The initial response, indeed, was not overwhelming, and disenchantment followed.[35] To say the least, the attempt to transplant the Elberfeld system to Merseyside turned out badly. Perhaps, as Miss Rathbone suggests, the basic differences between the two communities had something to do with it, but, in retrospect, what seems remarkable was not the Liverpool collapse but the Elberfeld success.[36] No one who has been responsible for assembling and directing large numbers of volunteers will find anything particularly mysterious in the failure of the Elberfeld plan to take hold in Liverpool.

The motives that originally created the C.R.S. were, in a large degree, prudential. As a weapon against the indiscriminate charity, which, in the mid-Victorian view, lay at the root of much social maladjustment, the Society made a solid record, and it annually distributed temporary relief to several thousands of "deserving" cases. But the premise on which the C.R.S. was built turned out to be less impeccable than it had seemed, and uncomfortable suspicions began to intrude. To continue providing emergency relief for the masses of men periodically employed in Liverpool, it was suspected, might be simply pouring money down the proverbial rat-hole; to turn them over to the Poor Law authorities as congenital paupers would be even more absurd. Perhaps the C.R.S. ought to experiment with more constructive remedies.

The Society's projects on behalf of the unemployed, neither of which proved a resounding success, were familiar enough mid-Victorian prescriptions. The firelighter factory — "each winter bringing with it the same tale of unmitigated, if not increased distress among the working classes" — never became self-supporting, and in the end was used chiefly as a labor test to separate the deserving from the "mendicant." [37] The Society also attempted to relieve the local labor market by shipping destitute families to manufacturing districts. At the turn of the century the secretary of the C.R.S. could profess pride in the 2050 persons who (in twenty-eight years) had been transplanted "from poverty and hardship in Liverpool to independence and comfort elsewhere." Very likely, as he maintained, their re-

[34] E. F. Rathbone, *William Rathbone*, p. 372.

[35] Simey, *Charitable Effort*, p. 111. Notwithstanding the sanguine report given to the Royal Commission on the Poor Laws by the secretary of the C.R.S., who spoke hopefully of expanding the corps of visitors from 250 to 500 (William Grisewood, *R. C. on the Poor Laws*, 1909, IV, Q. 37,145).

[36] It is also true that in Elberfeld the plan operated under semipublic auspices, with public funds to be drawn upon.

[37] *Ann. Repts.*, 1868–69, p. 9, and 1873–74, p. 8.

moval benefited themselves, but that, "by lessening the competition for work here," it improved employment conditions in Liverpool is more than questionable.[38]

For the present study one of the more significant activities of the Central Relief Society had to do with its efforts toward greater financial cooperation among charities. The decision to establish a central office for receiving subscriptions was, in part, the result of uneasiness about the relatively small body of subscribers from which Liverpool philanthropies drew their support and, in part, of a desire to make collection as painless and economical an operation as possible. The somewhat narrow financial base on which the charities of the city rested was often cited as a remediable weakness in the structure of good works. In the early 1850's, the Reverend A. Hume's study of twenty major charities had shown them to be maintained by 1810 subscribers, half of whom subscribed to only a single charity. Fifty per cent of the total subscribed was contributed by 689 persons.[39] Two decades later a study of another thirty-eight agencies yielded similar results. Of the 6668 subscribers, 52 per cent gave to a single charity, while half of the £28,000 received in subscriptions by the charities came from fewer than seven hundred individuals.[40] Conceivably a single collection agency might handle the business more efficiently and at the same time give better publicity to the cause of Liverpool charities as a whole.

Some of the charities balked at the notion of turning over their collections. Most of them employed collectors, professional or part-time, who were rewarded with a percentage of their take. A number of agencies, however, agreed to go ahead on a tentative basis, permitting the C.R.S. office to receive subscriptions but reserving to themselves the right to collect the unpaid balance. For five years (1877–81) the plan operated in this fashion, and by the latter year over two-fifths of their subscription revenue reached sixty-six charities via the C.R.S. office.[41] In 1882, at the request of a number of charities, the Society agreed to handle the whole of their collections. For subscribers it was a distinct advantage to make only a single payment, while the charities profited from the fact that the C.R.S. commission — usually 4 per cent on the full list — was below that demanded by regular collectors. In the course of three decades (1877–1906) Liverpool charitable agencies received more than half of their subscription income (£668,000 out of £1,250,000) through the Society's office, together with about £95,500 in donations.[42]

---

[38] Grisewood, *The Liverpool Central Relief and Charity Organisation Society*, pp. 31–32. An idyllic picture of the situation of the emigrants is given by a C.R.S. official who visited the factory communities in the summer of 1907. (*R. C. on the Poor Laws*, 1909, App. IV, 563–64.)

[39] Rev. A. Hume, "Analysis of the Subscribers to the Various Liverpool Charities," *Trans. Lancashire and Cheshire Historical Society*, VII (1854–55), 25.

[40] Grisewood, *The Collection of Subscriptions to Charitable Institutions*, p. 4; reprinted by the *R. C. on the Poor Laws*, 1909, App. IV, 557–60.

[41] *Ibid.; Ann. Rept.*, 1885–86, p. 42. In that year about £15,000 of of about £35,000 was paid through the C.R.S.

[42] At the outset only twenty-nine agencies were involved in the total collection plan. By 1906 the number had risen to about fifty.

One would not deny the constructive purposes that inspired the formation of the Central Relief Society or disparage the heroic labors of its leaders and some of their followers. Yet during the later years it is impossible to miss, amid the self-congratulation and official optimism of the annual reports, a note of disappointment that the C.R.S.–C.O.S. formula had not effected a more revolutionary improvement in the life of the poor. The Society's efforts had not demonstrably succeeded in reducing the volume of poverty and suffering nor in setting the marginal poor as a class on the path to sturdy independence.[43] By the early 1920's the Society had plainly lost its momentum. National social policy had moved well beyond the line at which the army of charity organization had entrenched itself, while on the local scene a new and broadly based body was increasingly taking over the more creative functions of the C.R.S.

4

The Liverpool Council of Voluntary Aid (or the Council of Social Service as it became in 1933) was a by-product of the Royal Commission on the Poor Laws, whose Majority Report had proposed the founding of such local bodies. Hampstead with its Council of Social Welfare was first in the field, but Liverpool, following a year later, provided a model that was widely adopted in the United Kingdom and elsewhere in the English-speaking world.[44] The Council of Voluntary Aid took form in 1909, financed at the outset by the families whose names more often than not figured heavily on Liverpool subscription lists — Rathbone, Holt, Bibby, Lever, and the rest.[45] A hundred charitable agencies were represented on the Council, with fifty additional seats held largely by public officials and co-opted members. Its purpose was, of course, to further the interests of Liverpool charities and to promote cooperation among them. In the latter connection a central register of cases was set up which in the course of a few years grew to almost staggering proportions. By the mid-'30's the files contained records of about 170,000 cases.[46] For the first few years the Council was closely affiliated with the C.R.S., whose support had been tactfully enlisted. By 1913, however, the new organization was sufficiently well established to strike out on its own, and the balance of influence gradually shifted to the Council until in 1932, after a Scriptural life of three score years and ten, the Central Relief Society allowed itself to be absorbed.

What is perhaps most impressive in the record of the Liverpool Council is its

[43] In 1896 the secretary could maintain, legitimately enough, that the Society had given great assistance to individuals, but he was forced to concede that "the problem of removing poverty and suffering remains as great as ever." (Quoted by Simey, *Charitable Effort*, pp. 137–38.)

[44] L.C.S.S., *Ann. Rept.,* 1947, p. 3. This section was in draft before the publication of the semicentennial history of the Council by its present secretary, Mr. H. R. Poole (*The Liverpool Council of Social Service, 1909–1959* [Liverpool 1960]). I have made a few changes of detail, but in the large I have allowed my account to stand as written.

[45] L.C.V.A., *Ann. Rept.,* 1913, p. 19.

[46] L.C.S.S., *Ann. Rept.,* 1934, p. 27. The growth can be indicated as follows: 1911, 24,600 cases; 1926, 88,600; 1931, 105,000; and 1934, 169,200.

financial services to local charities. The fact that it was the custodian of substantial funds for selective distribution to other agencies enabled it to exert an influence beyond what would have been otherwise possible. Not only that, but would-be donors could find in the Council a judicious and discreet almoner. Most of the business of the C.R.S. as charity middleman now passed into the Council's hands, and in the early '30's about £75,000 a year was being paid through its office at a cost of collection and distribution of about 1½ per cent.[47]

A turning-point in its fortunes came in 1918 when an anonymous donor (finally identified in 1955 as John Rankin) presented the Council with £50,000 for Liverpool charities. Others added to the fund until by the mid-'30's it had reached the figure of about £150,000, from which some £5000 was distributed annually to constituent agencies. It was the Council's policy, while allocating a fraction of the income to charities in proportion to their subscription list, to reserve more than half for special grants to agencies planning capital expenditures or starting new activities. In the words of the present secretary of the Council, the Charities Fund "as a primer of the pump has been a major factor in the endless succession of new schemes, ideas and services which have originated in Liverpool during the last forty years." [48]

The Council also proved itself vigilant and resourceful in promoting the fiscal interests of local agencies. Liverpool, as we have seen,[49] was the source of the seven-year covenant, and it was the Council which first worked out a mechanism to assure the philanthropist a reasonable flexibility within the framework of the covenant. A covenant made with the Council itself would allow the donor to instruct the office annually as to the specific charities that he wished to benefit, and these might vary from year to year. During the first dozen years of the arrangement over £450,000 reached charitable objects through the Council of Social Service, and in 1946, for example, nearly £100,000 was distributed from 762 tax-free covenants.[50]

The Council's statistical work was so thoroughly carried out that from the year of its foundation one has fuller information about the character and magnitude of philanthropy in Liverpool than in any other provincial city. Here the special genius was the statesmanlike Frederic D'Aeth, who not only was the principal hand in founding the Council but who served the cause of social welfare throughout the country with memorable distinction. In the early years as director of reports and for two decades as secretary of the Council, he issued a stream of special reports, as well as the regular *Quarterly Papers,* which were full of information, statistical and otherwise, on philanthropic activities. In fact, an important preliminary step to the founding of the Council was D'Aeth's exhaustive survey of Liverpool charities, and his results proved a convincing argument for better coordination

[47] *Ibid.,* p. 17.
[48] Poole, *Liverpool Council,* p. 44.
[49] As described in Chapter XII above.
[50] *Ann. Repts.,* 1934, p. 18, and 1946, pp. 12–13.

among the 241 agencies which annually raised more that £175,000 in subscriptions and donations and whose annual income exceeded £450,000.[51]

The Council's conscientious adherence to the basic premise of its foundation — that its office was to be "a repository of accurate information about voluntary effort in Liverpool" [52] — has made available a body of data which illuminates some of the trends in charity-financing.[53] During the inter-war period the money income of Liverpool charities reached impressive totals (though, of course, changes in the price level made the real increase much less significant). Between 1905 and the late '20's receipts more than trebled, until in some years they approached the £1 million figure.[54] But as often with such gross figures, these tend to conceal rather than clarify the complexities of the situation. For one thing, annual subscriptions increased only slightly; in 1929, to take a typical year, they represented only between 6 and 7 per cent of the total revenue. Not only that, but for some types of agency, notably hospitals, receipts from subscriptions actually declined during the inter-war years. It is Miss Braithwaite's conclusion that annual subscriptions and donations, taken together, fell short of offsetting the increase in prices. Legacies held up more satisfactorily, and some agencies became heavily dependent on their continuance. In its twenty-five year report, the Council points out that the general average of legacies for the decade 1924–33 was nearly double that of subscriptions — about £120,000 to £62,000.[55] This was, however, a precarious resource, especially when most organizations were forced to treat legacies as income. Their distribution among agencies was extremely uneven, and there was enormous fluctuation from year to year. Looking back over the quarter century, the Council also discovered evidence of a shift in the order of preference of private donors. What was most striking, apparently, was the emergence of new voluntary services — institutions and organizations for the promotion of social welfare — which now competed with hospitals for the charity pound. Although medical charities still held first place, their lead was plainly being reduced.[56]

The most significant new factor on the income side of the ledger was not, strictly speaking, charitable at all. This covered payments made for and by inmates of hospitals and other institutions, together with industrial receipts. In 1929 this figure ran to about £425,000, a sum which included nearly £115,000 from public authorities.[57] The dependence of certain types of voluntary agency on the statutory authorities was to increase until, after the drastic expansion of the state social

---

[51] F. G. D'Aeth, Report . . . on the Charitable Effort in Liverpool (Liverpool, 1910), p. 19.

[52] Poole, Liverpool Council, p. 8.

[53] Braithwaite, Voluntary Citizen, chap. VIII, analyzes the Liverpool figures in some detail.

[54] I have used the figures for 1905 given by the R. C. on the Poor Laws, 1909, App. IV, 543–49, rather than D'Aeth's more comprehensive statistics for 1908. His survey covered a larger number of agencies than did the later Annual Reports of the L.C.S.S., and to use them would distort the comparison. (The Poor Law figures, incidentally, are for 1905 and not 1907, as Miss Braithwaite states.)

[55] L.C.S.S., Ann. Rept., 1934, p. 17.

[56] Chiefly with respect to subscriptions. Of subscriptions made to standard Liverpool charities, the share of the medical group declined from about 53 per cent in 1924 to about 43 per cent in 1932.

[57] Braithwaite, Voluntary Citizen, p. 121.

services in the late '40's, they could survive only through substantial support from public sources.

It would not do to picture the Liverpool Council of Social Service as primarily a statistical office. Its range of activity has been wide, and it has not only served as a coordinating agency but has often taken the initiative in inaugurating new services — for example, the Liverpool Boys Association, the West Lancashire Association for Mental Health, and its own Personal Service Committee, which developed into the Personal Service Society and formed an important forerunner of the Citizens' Advice Bureaux.[58] It has, moreover, labored with energy and judgment for social reform through state action as well as through voluntary effort. By common consent, the Council deserves a good deal of the credit for the continued pre-eminence of Liverpool's voluntary services.

[58] On the Personal Service Society see Dorothy C. Keeling, *The Crowded Stairs* (London, 1961).

CHAPTER XVII

THE RANGE AND RESOURCES
OF PHILANTHROPY

HERE IS reason to think," exulted the Charity Commissioners in 1895, "that the latter half of the 19th century will stand second in respect of the greatness and variety of the Charities created within its duration, to no other half-century since the Reformation."[1] In the light of Professor Jordan's evidence it may be doubted whether the late Victorians were investing in charity as large a proportion of the national income as did their Tudor-Stuart ancestors, but in absolute terms the Commissioners were only stating a simple fact. Going back over their records for the two previous decades, they could list thirteen new trusts of over £100,000 each and could report an average of five hundred new endowments a year.

Such benefactions, of course, accounted for only a small fraction of what the British public, by gift or bequest, was pouring into the philanthropic hopper. The Commissioners' sample list took account only of *new* foundations, whereas some of the larger bequests, such as the £118,000 left to a group of charities by an Islington auctioneer,[2] went to existing institutions, with or without trust provisions. Not only were endowments multiplying, but the annual income of voluntary charities was growing and new societies were being formed with the reckless abandon characteristic of the Victorian Englishman bent on good works. In the mid-1880's, in one of its half-jubilant, half-rueful leading articles on the charitable activities of Englishmen, *The Times* could note that the income of London charities was greater than that of several independent governments, exceeding the revenues of Sweden, Denmark, and Portugal, and double that of the Swiss Confederation.[3]

Philanthropy apparently was reaping, or at least sharing in, the harvest of Victorian prosperity. Successful businessmen as a class were under less unrelenting pressure than in the early days of industrialism, when the twin demands of

---

[1] *42d Ann. C. C. Rept.*, 1895, p. 17.

[2] R. A. Newbon (*Charity Record*, 31 Dec. 1891; *Daily Telegraph*, 26 Dec. 1891). Actually, according to the Nathan Committee (*Report*, Par. 44), the number of charitable trusts founded since the Brougham Commission and known to the Charity Commissioners increased from 9154 in 1880 to 22,607 in 1900.

[3] 9 Jan. 1885; *Burdett's Hospitals and Charities*, 1912, p. 76, made a similar claim, adding Bulgaria, Greece, and Norway to the list of states with budgets substantially below British charity receipts.

founding a business and a family left little surplus for large-scale philanthropy. But the second and third-generation industrialist (who may well have withdrawn from active connection with the family business) tended to view his position in society and his responsibilities rather differently from his grandfather. There is good reason to believe that industrial wealth was developing a quasi-aristocratic sense of obligation, that the plutocracy was doing its best to attain the status of aristocracy. Indeed, all the pressures of the English social structure, as well as the Victorian ethos, worked toward this end, for munificence not only earned the gratitude of society but, more concretely, assisted in the ascent of the social ladder. Possibly, in the growing social discontent of the late century, some of the more perceptive among the rich could foresee a day when wealth itself would be on the defensive and could subscribe to Chauncey Depew's rationale of philanthropy as "an insurance policy of wealth [which] promotes social order and good feeling."[4] This would be to attribute to British philanthropists a self-protective motive that hardly existed, certainly not consciously. Still, there was a pervasive suspicion that the voluntary contribution of money and effort for the public good was one of the glories of British civilization and one of the forces that made for social stability.

To reach a satisfying quantitative measurement of philanthropic giving in the Victorian Age is clearly out of the question. Not until well toward the end of the century are even moderately informed guesses available. The figures of the Charity Commissioners, to repeat, offer little help. Their jurisdiction extended only to charitable endowments (not to charities maintained by subscriptions and contributions) and even here some important areas, such as the old universities and their colleges, two ancient public schools, and Church endowments, lay outside their province. With regard to legacies to charity, sample groups of wills can provide a basis for reasonable inference, but what is more difficult than estimating bequests and large gifts to capital — and, indeed, quite impossible — is arriving at a convincing total of voluntary, year-by-year giving to charitable causes. It is an obvious approach, therefore, to begin with bequests, where the ground, though slippery enough, is a little firmer than with annual subscriptions and casual donations.

For the bulk of their capital resources, as well as for part of their current income, British good works relied heavily on legacies. Most large wills included some bequests to charity, though the behavior of testators varied so sharply as to make averages relatively meaningless. Out of an estate of over £300,000, one niggardly philanthropist could find only £900 to divide among five hospitals, while J. T. Morton, oil exporter and manufacturer of preserved foods, left his entire residual estate of about £575,000 to a group of charities, religious and otherwise.[5] Some of the well-to-do, taking the advice of the Quaker Joseph Pease, who urged "everyone to be his own executor in all charitable gifts," had deliberately made their principal benefactions while living.[6] For that reason the wills of certain

[4] *Charity Record*, 1 Sept. 1898.
[5] *Ibid.*, 18 Nov. 1897, 17 Sept. 1903; *47th Ann. C. C. Rept.*, 1900, p. 18.
[6] *Charity Record*, 15 April 1886.

wealthy and indubitably philanthropic individuals, like Miss Ryland, whose benefactions to Birmingham were said to have approached £180,000, contained only
minor bequests to charity.[7] Clearly the provisions of wills, useful as they are,
offer no infallible yardstick for measuring the dimensions of late Victorian philanthropy.

The most revealing sample of late-century wills is perhaps the fifty or sixty listed
annually during the 1890's by the *Daily Telegraph,* 466 in all.[8] These disposed of
nearly £76 million in personalty, of which £10,200,000 or over 13 per cent was
left to charitable uses. In commenting on the *Telegraph's* figures, *The Times*
pointed out that the record of the 150 women was distinctly higher than that of
the 316 men, presumably because of the large number of spinsters and widows
without family obligations.[9] Whatever the explanation, the ladies bequeathed, on
the average, a little over 25 per cent of their estates to charity, while the men left
only 11 per cent. Two years before the *Telegraph* published its figures, another
newspaper had approached the question from a different direction. Taking all of
the wills reported in the newspapers in 1889, the *Standard* discovered that about
one in seven contained charitable bequests. Out of an aggregate personalty of
£58,760,000 charity received £1,080,000 or about 1.84 per cent. The *Standard*
conjectured that unreported wills might account for between £400,000 and £500,-
000 and that the total left annually to charity might thus be in the neighborhood
of £1½ million.[10]

This is probably an underestimate, certainly so for the 1890's. The *Daily
Telegraph* figures for the years 1891-98 give an annual average of better than
£1¼ million. No doubt these larger bequests comprised the bulk of personalty
left to charity — in 1891, for example, 40 wills out of the 120 listed accounted for
nearly 92 per cent of the total [11] — but there were, of course, numbers of smaller
bequests unreported in the press. What allowance ought to be made for these is
pure guesswork. If the £800,000 suggested by *The Times* as a reasonable figure is
accepted, the annual total of charitable bequests would amount to about 1½ per
cent of the aggregate personalty bequeathed, and for the years covered by the
Telegraph data, the amount might average about £2 million annually, or, more
specifically, would vary from about £1,760,000 (1894-95) to £2,420,000 (1891-
92).[12]

After the turn of the century the harvest gathered from wills rose strikingly.
The Times estimated that the four years 1906-1909 brought in a total of £18½
million, or an annual average of more than £4½ million.[13] A relatively small
number of estates accounted for the bulk of the increment. The years 1906 and
1907 saw some exceptionally large charitable bequests, such as £1,800,000 from

[7] *Ibid.,* 7 Feb. 1889.
[8] These figures appeared during the last week of December each year from 1891 to 1898.
[9] 25 Sept. 1899.
[10] Quoted in *The Philanthropist,* July 1890, p. 108.
[11] *Daily Telegraph,* 26 Dec. 1891.
[12] 25 Sept. 1899.
[13] 4 Feb. 1910.

Alfred Beit (in addition to the £1,200,000 which was to comprise the capital of the Beit Trust for Rhodesia, and handsome gifts made during his lifetime, including the Beit Professorship at Oxford) and £1 million from the draper William Whiteley for homes for the aged. But the objects of most of this benevolence, noted the *Charity Organisation Review,* were fairly standard, save for the anti-vivisection movement, which was enjoying a grotesque but unmistakable prosperity.[14] Hospitals and church societies continued to attract a steady flow of funds, while orphanages and children's charities held their own. Altogether, with some exceptions, this was not a period of marked inventiveness in the world of private philanthropy. Millionaires continued to subsidize the "deserving poor" and to support "our cadging hospital system." Only occasionally did they seem inclined to follow Shaw's ironic counsel never "to give the people anything they want; give them something they ought to want and don't." [15]

2

Late-century British philanthropists turn out to be remarkably resistant to generalization. In background and aim they cover a broad spectrum. One might, for example, juxtapose the names of W. P. Hartley and George Herring. Hartley, a devout Primitive Methodist, had built up the well-known preserve business, with factories at Aintree and London employing over three thousand workers, for whom he had established a profit-sharing scheme. Obviously Hartley thought of his wealth in the Biblical context of stewardship, and his benefactions included a range of Primitive Methodist and other religious enterprises, as well as a large group of Lancashire hospitals.[16] George Herring's habitat, another world from that of the Primitive Methodist chapel, was the track, where, in the words of the *DNB,* he waxed prosperous as "a turf commission agent and owner of race-horses." Thence he moved into the City and added to his already considerable fortune, finally becoming chairman of the City of London Electric Lighting Company. But in Herring's later years his consuming interest was London hospitals, especially the Great Northern Hospital, which he served as treasurer, and the Hospital Sunday Fund, in which for years he was the leading spirit. In addition to large contributions to the Fund during his lifetime, Herring's charitable bequests exceeded £900,000, mostly to medical charities.[17]

London charities, in fact, did rather well from the track. During the 1890's, Baron Hirsch, the Jewish financier and member of the Marlborough House set, was giving all of his turf winnings to charity — his gross receipts, one should note. On the advice of George Herring, he channeled most of these sums to the London hospitals, which thus found themselves receiving handsome windfalls, as

[14] March 1920, pp. 113–14.
[15] G. B. Shaw, "Socialism for Millionaires," *Contemporary Review,* 69:217 (February 1896).
[16] *Charity Record,* 4 July 1908.
[17] *DNB; Charity Record,* 15 Nov. 1906.

much as £30,000 in 1892, the *Charity Record* reported.[18] There was rubbing of hands in hospital offices when the Hirsch colors appeared to be having a good year, and gloom when his horses were running badly, though at such times he might supplement his winnings so that the charities would not lose too heavily. Hirsch, indeed, has been credited with total benefactions in the neighborhood of £20 millions.[19] One of the more engaging philanthropic by-products of the turf was the row of almshouses at Welbeck built for widows on the estate by the sixth Duke of Portland to commemorate the victories of "his racehorses Ayrshire (Two Thousand Guineas and Derby), Donovan (Derby and St. Leger), Memoir (Oaks and St. Leger) Semolina, and others." [20]

If charity profited from the turf, the professions also contributed. The rise of new professions and the increasing importance of the old was obviously a cardinal development in the Victorian social pattern, and this was reflected in a number of sizable gifts and bequests to charity. The benefactions of professional men were, of course, far outstripped by fortunes made in industry and trade, and, indeed, some of the larger donations and legacies, such as those of Fellows of colleges and certain clergymen, had no apparent connection with the professional labors of the donor. Still, in going down the list of late-century benefactors, one discovers physicians, lawyers, university dons, and an occasional engineer, architect, or artist. Among the major legacies of the period were three from clergymen and one from the wife of a bishop, herself, however, a banker's daughter.[21] Sir Erasmus Wilson, dermatologist, surgeon, and author of a history of the Middlesex Hospital, who defrayed the cost of bringing Cleopatra's Needle to London, founded a chair and museum of dermatology in the College of Surgeons, as well as a chair of pathology at Aberdeen, added a chapel and wing at the Margate Sea Bathing Infirmary, and left (1884) about £200,000, with the College of Surgeons as the chief beneficiary. Another benefactor from the professions was David Edward Hughes, electrical engineer and inventor, whose will established the Hughes Hospital Fund with a capital of over £300,000.[22]

Among the testamentary philanthropists of the period there was the usual complement of eccentric and malicious types. In some instances charity profited from family feuds, as with the Kensington woman who left her estate of more than £50,000 to Protestant charities because of her repugnance for the doctrines of the

---

[18] 19 Jan. 1893. This banner year was chiefly owing to the performance of the Hirsch filly la Flèche, which won the Oaks, the St. Leger, the One Thousand Guineas, and the Cambridgeshire. (*The Times,* 30 Dec. 1899.)

[19] Paul H. Emden, *Money Powers of Europe* (London, 1938), p. 322. Hirsch's will is not included in the lists published by the *Daily Telegraph* presumably because both his fortune and his benefactions were so heavily international in character. For example, the Jewish Colonization Association, with a capital of £2 million, was founded by him, as well as the Baron de Hirsch Fund for the relief of Jewish immigrants in the United States and a Galician foundation.

[20] *Charity Record,* 15 Nov. 1906.

[21] The Reverend James Spurrell (1892) left more than £500,000, the Reverend Francis Jacox (1897) about £85,000, the Reverend Edward Pochin (1898) about £80,000, and Mrs. James Fraser, daughter of John Shute Duncan, who had promoted the savings bank at Bath, some £150,000.

[22] *Charity Record,* 21 Aug. 1884, 22 March 1900.

Roman Church "in which to her great grief her grandsons were being brought up." [23] Occasionally a testator might use his estate as a gesture of defiance of the Government and man-made law, as did Cornelius Harley Christmas of Great Yarmouth, who, it will be recalled,[24] instructed his executors, should the authorities move to interfere with the bequest, to convert the entire £61,000 into cash and distribute the proceeds to the poor of the town. At least one philanthropist ventured to challenge not the Government but death itself, and lost. Henry Dodd, a wealthy and eccentric dust contractor, remembered in his will a group of charities, including £5000 to the Fishmongers Company to provide silver and gold cups for barge races on the Thames. To his doctor Dodd offered £2000 on condition that he keep him alive for two years and, should he manage that, £3000 for three. Unfortunately both Dodd and the doctor lost out, for the former died in less than a month and the latter received nothing.[25]

Yet the chief impression left by late-century bequests is not that of eccentricity but of conventionality. Few wills contained anything particularly venturesome or imaginative. Money went, on the whole, to maintain established institutions or to create new ones of the same sort. Hospitals, orphanages, almshouses, church organizations, such eminently respectable national charities as the R.S.P.C.A., and the Royal National Life-boat Institution — these were the philanthropies that commonly figured in wills, together with an occasional public park, gift to a library or art gallery, or scholarship or university chair. More than anything else, it was medical charities that dominated the scene. The insatiable demands of the voluntary hospitals, especially the London hospitals, may in fact have been partly responsible for guiding philanthropy into such familiar channels. Even after receiving their lion's share of public support, these were in a precarious state in the 1880's and early '90's. To be the responsible financial officer of a large London hospital in these years called for steady nerves and inexhaustible persistence.

Still, one does not look for imaginative philanthropies in the will of the average testator, Victorian or otherwise.[26] The well-established, well-advertised charities had a clear advantage, and most people with money to leave preferred to divide their benefactions among a number, sometimes an absurd number, of such institutions. An agency like the Royal National Life-boat Institution, to take one instance, did handsomely from legacies. Its activities, as we have seen, made a powerful appeal to a maritime nation, it filled an undeniable national need, and its publicity was astutely handled. For the comparatively modest sum of £1000 the Institution would supply a memorial in the form of a lifeboat. One clerical testator left £3000 for three lifeboats, *all* to be named for himself, while a Yorkshire cloth manufacturer left £5000 for a small fleet of five, to be named for

[23] *Ibid.*, 20 June 1907.
[24] *Ibid.*, 5 Oct. 1882. Described in Chapter XI.
[25] *Ibid.*, 16 June 1881.
[26] Thus the will of a Proper Bostonian might include the Boston Symphony Orchestra, the Boston Public Library, the Museum of Fine Arts, Harvard College, the Athenaeum, and one or more hospitals. An analogous list could be offered for many American cities.

a sister, three brothers, and himself.[27] The National Society for the Prevention of Cruelty to Children, whose founding in the mid-'80's has already been noted, also developed into a conspicuous favorite of those making wills and indeed into a major national charity. In 1959–60 the Society was spending over a half million pounds and receiving over £200,000 in legacies.[28] No doubt many charitable bequests represented the judgment of family solicitors, not a notably daring race, rather than that of testators themselves. The importance of the solicitor, in fact, was so generally recognized that his good offices were not infrequently invoked by this or that worthy organization when it came to advising will-making clients.

There was dissatisfaction in some quarters over the behavior of British philanthropists. A critic might complain of the "great lack of originality on the part of rich men in the disposition of their wealth," and another, on the distaff side, might discover a similar failing in the case of rich women. *The Times* was inclined to credit American testators with greater liberality and more interesting ideas than their British counterparts. The bulk of British bequests, the editor insisted, came from childless persons, with no family responsibilities, and went for pretty conventional objects.[29]

This was not wholly fair. Most American novelties in philanthropy came from a few men of enormous wealth; the mass of American bequests to charity were no more original than were the British. And British wealth from the South African diamond deposits was presently to create in the Rhodes Trust one of the more imaginative philanthropies of modern times, while two fortunes made in Canada were to be of critical importance in putting on its feet King Edward's Hospital Fund, which from 1897 on provided indispensable financial support for the London hospitals.[30] As for the complaint of *The Times* that large landowners rarely left substantial sums to charity, this should have been no occasion for surprise during the late-century agricultural depression, at any rate. In a list of about a hundred names of those who between 1881 and 1914 bequeathed at least £100,000 to charitable objects, there are only two whose interests appear to have lain chiefly in the land.[31] The others are about what one would expect — bankers and City men, brewers and wine merchants, manufacturers of various sorts, two architects, a solicitor or two, two doctors, two clergymen, and at least five retailers (David Lewis, William Whiteley, William Debenham, Frederick Gorringe, and Blundell Maple). Altogether this segment of the philanthropic public was a fairly mixed lot, composed predominantly of members of the commercial, industrial, and financial communities. But there was no striking difference between the objects

[27] *Charity Record,* 6 Aug. 1891, 2 Oct. 1890.
[28] *Ann. Rept.,* 1959–60, p. 15.
[29] 25 Sept. 1899.
[30] Frank D. Long, *King Edward's Hospital Fund, 1897–1942* (London, 1942), pp. 24–25. Lord Strathcona and Lord Mount Stephen together contributed £400,000 to the "Coronation Gift" of 1902. The latter's legacy to the fund amounted to £815,000 and his gifts to £500,000.
[31] The Earl of Moray and Lady Forester. The list was compiled from reports of bequests published in the *Charity Record.*

of benevolence favored by the wealthier donors and those which attracted the less affluent. A few brilliantly novel departures emerge — for example, the National Trust (1894–95)[32] — and certain other benefactions, already noted, broke through the conventional ring of hospitals, orphanages, almshouses, and church enterprises. Yet these were exceptions to the formulae that commonly guided the actions of the benevolent in late Victorian times.[33]

3

If estimates of legacies and large gifts to capital fail to command great confidence, those purporting to measure run-of-the-mill subscriptions and contributions are even less credible. Moreover, because of differences in methods of compiling figures and in the numbers and types of agencies covered, it is impossible to compare one set of estimates with another. The first serious attempt at a comprehensive view of the income and expenditure of British charities came at the end of the Victorian Age, when the editor of *Burdett's Hospitals and Charities* collected figures covering the finances of 1867 charities for the year 1896, including some in Scotland and Ireland. A decade later such tables became an annual feature of the publication. By 1910 some 2126 agencies were being polled, and the income, which in 1896 had totaled a little over £8 million, had now risen to nearly £13 million.[34]

Another source for statistics on Edwardian giving is the Royal Commission on the Poor Laws. The Commission collected figures for 1907, admittedly incomplete, and published them in an appendix to the Report.[35] This information, covering twenty-six categories of charity in thirty-one cities plus an unspecified number of towns, shows a total income of over £10 million and offers an illuminating panorama of the philanthropic enterprises of middle- and upper-class Edwardian England, almost a relief map of charitable giving. At about the same time the Charity Organisation Society began to include in its *Annual Charities Register* tables of data on provincial, in addition to metropolitan, charities. But even a casual comparison of the three sets of statistics suggests that such compilations cannot be regarded as more than the roughest of approximations.

More satisfactory than national estimates are figures relating only to the charities of the Metropolis. This in spite of the fact that such statistics are distorted by contributions reaching London from all over the Kingdom for the support of good works which belonged to London only administratively. Still, the London figures cover a longer period and include a larger proportion of charitable agencies than do the various national estimates. From mid-century on there were frequent

[32] A brief account of the National Trust is given later in this chapter.
[33] On the whole, though certainly not universally, living donors were more likely to be the source of interesting philanthropies than were those who established theirs by bequests. The former frequently showed more careful thought on the part of the donor, as well as, in some instances, a degree of sacrifice.
[34] *Burdett's Hospitals and Charities*, 1912, pp. 82–83.
[35] *R. C. on the Poor Laws, 1905–1909*, Cd. 5078, 1910, App. XXVI, pp. 75–76.

attempts to draw a statistical picture of the charities of the Metropolis. Since most of these were the work of editors of one or another of the various charity directories, who sometimes followed fairly captious and arbitrary methods and, in any case, were limited by untrustworthy data supplied by charitable agencies, the aggregates will not bear close scrutiny. Yet these lists do give an intimation of the range and volume of British benevolence, and they tell us something of the financial side of the jungle of duplicating, conflicting, proliferating charitable agencies in London, over a thousand of which were being listed in directories in the 1880's and over seventeen hundred in the 1905 edition of the C.O.S. *Annual Charities Register*.[36] It was all very well to point to London as a modern Philanthropolis, but critics could reasonably urge that this was a singularly chaotic and anarchical realm.[37]

For the late-century decades the least unsatisfactory London figures are probably those published by William F. Howe in his *Classified Directory*. Yet these were not only incomplete — Howe was able to get returns from only about 75 per cent of the agencies — but they also fail to distinguish between voluntary income and that from investments and property. The totals, therefore, are less significant as absolute amounts than as indicating the rate of growth in charity income. The accompanying table gives the total receipts in round numbers (in £000) for five sample years from the mid-1870's to the mid-'90's.[38]

YEAR	INCLUDING MISSIONARY, BIBLE, AND TRACT SOCIETIES	EXCLUSIVE OF THESE AGENCIES
1874–75	£3940	£2250
1879–80	4200	2525
1884–85	4450	2560
1888–89	5060	2930
1893–94	5290	3150

The first reasonably reliable view of London charity finance, unhappily for the present purpose, is Edwardian rather than Victorian. It is that offered by the *Annual Charities Register* of the C.O.S., which in 1905 began to publish tables of estimated income and expenditure of metropolitan agencies. Not only was the coverage more extensive (though not, of course, complete) than in previous

[36] Exclusive of the 117 "spiritual institutions."

[37] *The Times*, 14 April 1884.

[38] The statistics are based on between seven and eight hundred of the approximately one thousand organizations of whose existence Howe was aware. Gifts to such agencies, "public charities," do not, of course, tell the whole story of British philanthropic giving. There was still an enormous volume of personal almsgiving, and considerable sums were raised and distributed by parish churches and Nonconformist chapels. The total volume of giving through religious agencies was, of course, tremendous. William Howe, who deplored "telescopic charity," was distressed by the fact that during the 1880's the income of twenty-three missionary societies was running well ahead, by a quarter of a million in 1882–83, of the receipts of ninety hospitals (*Classified Directory*, 1884, p. xxi). And according to figures cited by Kitson Clark (*The Making of Victorian England*, Cambridge, Mass., 1962, p. 170), in the period 1860–85 voluntary contributions for various Church of England purposes amounted to £80½ million.

directories and the editorial work more scrupulously done, but income was analyzed according to source. The table below shows (in £000), for a sequence of four years before 1914, the sources from which charitable income was derived.[39]

YEAR	CONTRIBUTIONS	INTEREST	LEGACIES	OTHER	TOTAL
1908	3825 (45.1)[a]	1034 (12.2)	1181 (14.0)	2438 (28.7)	8479
1909	3823 (45.1)	1063 (12.6)	1034 (12.2)	2549 (30.1)	8469
1910	3719 (44.1)	1095 (13.0)	990 (11.7)	2626 (31.2)	8430
1911	3817 (44.6)	1122 (13.1)	949 (11.1)	2677 (31.2)	8565

[a] Figures in parentheses indicate percentage of total.

Something less than half the total receipts of metropolitan charities came from year-by-year contributions (subscriptions and donations). The balance was made up by interest and legacies, amounting to roughly 25 per cent, and "other sources," a category comprising two chief elements — payments by and for beneficiaries (26 per cent in 1911) and receipts from industrial work (4.8 per cent). Such gross percentages, of course, tend to conceal the tremendous variations from one type of charity to another and from one institution to another. State-aided reformatories and asylums might draw 80 per cent of their revenue from payments for inmates. Homes for the aged could count on interest from investments to carry about a third of their costs, while with day nurseries this source accounted for only about 2.6 per cent and with penitentiaries (refuges for girls and women) only 6.3 per cent.[40] Since agencies located in or officially based on London received a preponderant share of the country's benevolence, something over 60 per cent, presumably these proportions do not gravely misrepresent the situation of the voluntary charities throughout England and Wales.[41]

Business firms as firms do not appear to have contributed heavily to philanthropic undertakings. One finds business houses often listed among the contributors to emergency and special funds, and sometimes as donors to provincial universities, but regular corporation giving was little known in Britain (save in the case of such ancient and inactive corporate bodies as the City Companies);[42] this in spite of the fact that the legal basis for such giving is found chiefly in an English case, one which, incidentally, had nothing to do with ordinary philanthropy. Agreeing that to contribute to charity as such was not permissible for a business corporation, Lord Justice Bowen then proceeded to leave the door wide

---

[39] *Annual Charities Register and Digest,* 1906, 1913.

[40] See the table for 1911, *ibid.,* 1913, p. ccclviii.

[41] *R. C. on the Poor Laws,* 1905–1909, Cd. 5078, 1910, App. XXVI, pp. 75–76. Behind London in contributions in 1907 came Liverpool (£152,000), Manchester £(129,000), Birmingham (£78,000), and Bristol (£71,000). The London percentages are substantiated in the large by the figures in *Burdett's Hospitals and Charities,* 1908, pp. 82–83, and the figures collected by the Poor Law Commission and the Charity Organisation Society for 1907 and 1911 respectively indicate about the same dependence on contributions—45 per cent in 1907 and 43.8 per cent in 1911—as obtained in the Metropolis.

[42] Further reference will be made to this question in Chapter XX.

open: "It is not charity sitting at the board of directors, because as it seems to me charity has no business to sit at boards of directors *qua* charity. There is, however, a kind of charitable dealing which is for the interest of those who practice it, and to that extent and in that garb (I admit not a very philanthropic garb) charity may sit at the board, but for no other purpose."[43] Nothing suggests that British business hastened to enter the door. Plainly there was more of such giving than can be readily identified, but for specific evidence one can only cite a return to the House of Commons in 1909. These figures indicated that British railway companies, during the previous year, had given some £17,500 to the charities of the United Kingdom, including over £7500 to hospitals, £1150 to church funds, and £1100 to schools and technical institutes.[44]

An important question has to do with the relative shares of the charity pound received by the different branches of philanthropy. Here, although the figures may vary with the year and the source consulted, the main purport of the evidence, to repeat, is clear — that medical agencies were more generously supported by the British public than any other secular charities. On the basis of the statistics for 1907 and 1911 cited above, it appears that medical charities (excluding homes for incurables, the blind, cripples, and so on) were receiving something over eight shillings of every pound contributed and over eleven shillings of every pound bequeathed.[45] Next, but well behind in receipts, with less than 13 per cent of the total, come homes for the young, followed by miscellaneous relief agencies. Perhaps because these were mostly endowed institutions, homes for the aged were well toward the bottom with respect to voluntary contributions. As a footnote to philanthropy's benefactions to organizations and institutions, one ought to recall also the imposing sums collected to meet disasters and public emergencies. Of these the fund of £135,000 raised in 1879–80 for Irish famine sufferers by the Duchess of Marlborough's committee can stand as a fair enough example.[46]

4

The generality of contributors to late Victorian charity must remain an anonymous mass, for there is little evidence as to their identity, their numbers, and their motives. Apparently they represented a fairly small fraction of the community, even of its moderately prosperous segment. This at least is the conclusion emerging from the only study made of the question during the period. In the mid-1880's a member of the Manchester Statistical Society discovered that out

[43] *Hutton v. West Cork Railway Company*, 23 L.R., Ch. Div., 1883, p. 654, quoted in F. E. Andrews, *Corporation Giving* (New York, 1952), pp. 229–30.

[44] *Return of . . . Amounts Contributed by Railway Companies* (d. 19 Aug. 1909), *Parl. Pap.,* 1909.

[45] These figures, it should be noted, do not include endowed charities, save in cases where income from endowments is administered by a voluntary organization. No account is taken, for example, of legacies left to endowed schools. Both the Poor Law Commission and the C.O.S. figures have to do chiefly with charities for the benefit of the poor.

[46] Norman D. Palmer, *The Irish Land League Crisis* (New Haven, 1940), p. 89.

of about 10,500 subscribers, nearly 8200 (78 per cent) subscribed to only one charity, 1065 to two, and only 420 (4 per cent) to more than five.[47] These conclusions were even more discouraging than those reached thirty years before in Liverpool by the Reverend A. Hume.[48] The plea for broader support of local charities, with which both investigators concluded their reports, pointed to an inference which it would have occurred to neither to draw. Conceivably, as applied to some of the more essential social services, such reliance on voluntary charity tended to turn "into an individual virtue what ought to be regarded as a public duty," [49] and thus enabled numbers of well-endowed citizens to avoid their share of the burden.

Keeping English charities supplied with funds was no minor undertaking. There were the annual appeals, the bazaars, and the familiar charity dinners, where, as earlier in the century, astute managers noted the correlation between quality (and quantity) of food and wine and volume of response. Fortunate the organizer who could stock his head table with well-known peers or, still better, could adorn it with a member of the Royal Family. Snob appeal, after all, was one of the more efficient handmaidens of good works. The costly duplication and institutional rivalry of the charities themselves were reflected in their money-raising practices. Collectors, paid and voluntary, were crossing and recrossing each other's trails throughout the Metropolis, frequently calling on the same individuals on behalf of identical varieties of charitable endeavor. After the mid-1890's they could follow a printed directory of known charity subscribers. No doubt there had been plenty of informal lists to guide charity secretaries, but this volume, *The Charitable Ten Thousand,* was a grand index of potential contributors, almost a philanthropic "sucker-list," fitted with blank interleaves for additional names.[50] Evidently this publication was a composite of all the subscription lists on which the editor could lay his hand. The gloomy meditations of a *Times* leader writer fifteen years before were prophetic enough: "When a name has once been printed on a subscription list, its owner becomes a marked man. He has joined, by his own act, the unhappy class to which an appeal can be made with some chance that it will be met. From that day forward his persecution will never cease." [51]

The employment of professional or semiprofessional collectors was common enough, though not universal. For their efforts these laborers in the charity vineyard received something like 5 or 7½ per cent of their harvest, and even hospital secretaries often got a generous commission on the money they raised. On one

[47] Fred Scott, "The Need for Better Organization of Benevolent Effort in Manchester and Salford," *Trans. Manchester Statistical Society,* 1884–85, pp. 127–80. Scott's study, of course, took into account only annual subscribers and did not consider casual contributors.

[48] *Trans. Hist. Soc. of Lancs. and Cheshire,* 7:22–26 (1854–55).

[49] *Saturday Review,* 101:745 (18 June 1906).

[50] Publ. by H. Grant, London, 1896.

[51] *The Times,* 1 July 1880.

occasion the unexpected success of a collector involved the charity in an embarrassing lawsuit. A canvasser for the Royal National Hospital for Consumption at
Ventnor, working on a 7½ per cent commission, aroused the interest of one
donor to such an extent that the latter left the Hospital some £70,000 in his will.
The collector demanded his 7½ per cent or other suitable compensation. This the
Hospital refused on the ground that the arrangement applied only to subscriptions
and donations, an argument that was accepted by the court. The collector's claim
of upwards of £5000 may have been preposterous, but the charity itself appeared
in a fairly unattractive light, if, as seems to have been admitted, the bequest came
as a result of its canvasser's representations.[52]

One of the traditional financial resources of some, especially the older, institutions was the privilege which could be held out to subscribers of selecting the
beneficiaries of the charity. By the late century the voting charity had become, in
the view of its critics, a complete anachronism and was, beyond question, one
of the more vulnerable features of Victorian charity practice. With such charities
a panel of eligible candidates was generally drawn up by a committee and then
voted on by the whole body of subscribers, each casting votes proportional to the
amount of his subscription. This, Florence Nightingale remarked to Sir Sydney
Waterlow, was "the best method for electing the least eligible."[53]

The system had other defects. The labor of canvassing subscribers for votes,
ending year after year in failure and frustration, was an absurd expenditure of
energy and money for both candidates and sponsors. Sir Charles Trevelyan reported that at the November 1868 election, there had been 307 candidates for the
Royal Hospital for Incurables, many of whom had been up ten to sixteen times
and only about twenty of whom could be chosen.[54] In February 1882, 383 candidates competed for fifteen pensions offered by the United Kingdom Beneficent
Association.[55] At one charity election, with 235 candidates standing for ten places,
all but twenty-three had been up more than once; indeed, seventy-seven had stood
more than ten times.[56]

As objectionable as the campaigning were the elections themselves, held usually
at the London Tavern in Bishopsgate or the Cannon Street Hotel. The atmosphere of these proceedings recalled the Stock Exchange or a race meeting. One
hears that the walls of the London Tavern were placarded with the names of

[52] H. N. Hardy, S. C. (*Lords*) *on Metropolitan Hospitals,* 1890, Q. 1094; *The Philanthropist,* June
1885, pp. 84–85.
[53] Smalley, *Sir Sydney Waterlow,* p. 133. Even such a high-minded person as John Stuart Mill,
however, did not hesitate to make use of the voting charity. See the account of Mill's, Mazzini's, and
Jane Welsh Carlyle's attempt to get a female orphan into the Orphan Asylum in Francis E. Mineka,
ed., *The Earlier Letters of John Stuart Mill,* 2 vols. (Toronto, 1963), II, 548, 569–70, 603.
[54] Sir Charles Trevelyan, "Charity Electioneering," *Macmillan's* 29:171–76 (December 1873).
[55] *Charity Record,* 16 Feb. 1882.
[56] Henry Carr, "The Selection of Beneficiaries to Charitable Institutions," a paper read before the
London Social Science Association, 1 Dec. 1873 and reprinted in *Papers Relating to the Election of
Beneficiaries* (Charity Voting Reform Association, 1874).

candidates, sponsors offering to exchange two "Idiots" for a "Governess" or three "Governesses" for one "Female Orphan."[57] At least one lawsuit resulted from the failure of a trader to deliver the votes he had agreed to exchange.[58] About it all there was a certain excitement and an appeal to the sporting instincts of the sponsors. To pick a winner, to bring one's candidate through at the head of the poll was akin, in a morbid fashion, to any triumph on the track, the playing field, or the stock market. Admittedly there were degrees of culpability in the practices of various agencies. Some described cases; some advised voters on the most deserving; some frowned on canvassing, while others encouraged it and held a public polling day when some of the most brazen trading of votes occurred.

The organized protest against the iniquities of the voting charity was set off by a subscriber to the Royal Hospital for Incurables at Putney, an institution in which the system was deeply entrenched. He formed a committee of his fellow subscribers, who discovered what they identified as widespread dissatisfaction among the supporters of the Hospital. Meanwhile the paladin of integrity in charity practice, Sir Charles Trevelyan, entered the lists, and in early December 1872 published in *The Times* a short letter on "Charity Electioneering," later expanded into a magazine article, in which he attacked the enemy in his usual vigorous, even headlong, fashion.[59] But the managers of the voting charities showed no inclination to set forth on the path of reform, for, after all, the acquiring of votes was one of the chief inducements traditionally held out to potential subscribers. The consequence of their intransigence was the founding of the Charity Voting Reform Association, with the backing of the Charity Organisation Society and with two of its leaders, Sir Charles Trevelyan and F. D. Mocatta, as the moving spirits.[60]

This was a campaign conducted with a good deal of moderation and under auspices of unimpeachable respectability. In 1878, for example, the president was the Duke of Northumberland, and in the bevy of vice-presidents appeared the names of Salisbury, Shaftesbury, Derby, Brassey, Russell Gurney, Louisa Twining, Sir Sydney Waterlow, and four bishops.[61] At the outset the Association took no absolutist position; its leaders would have been satisfied by a removal of the abuses with which the voting charity had become encrusted — such things as trafficking in votes, canvassing, and public polling. Gradually the more objectionable practices were modified, and finally the voting procedure itself was abolished, save in a handful of agencies. How much credit for the disappearance of the voting charity should go to the Association is uncertain, for clearly, as with most successful reform movements, it served as the channel through which the "spirit of the age" was brought to bear. At least in its unreconstructed form the voting

[57] "Proceedings of the C.O.S. Council on Voting Charities," *ibid.*, p. 29.
[58] *Bolton* v. *Maddox, The Times*, 5 Nov. 1873, cited *ibid.*, p. 66.
[59] *The Times*, 3 Dec. 1872; *Macmillan's*, December 1873, pp. 171–76.
[60] Mocatta's interest has already been noticed in Chapter XV.
[61] *Charity Electioneering*, 1878, publ. by the Association.

charity was an anachronism, utterly incompatible with the newer conceptions of the voluntary organization and its responsibilities.

5

In the world of medical charities both old and new institutions made heavy demands. The latter half of the century, in fact, spawned hospitals in a lavish fashion. Of the approximately 550 general and special hospitals in the provinces (exclusive of those for infectious diseases) listed in *Burdett's Hospitals and Charities* for 1906, more than four hundred were founded after 1850. In the Metropolis, although virtually all of the great general hospitals date from an earlier period, an extraordinary number of new special hospitals appeared in central London and a variety of institutions in the suburbs. Not only had the period seen the creation of new institutions but there was widespread renovation and extension of older plants.

Yet however imposing the British hospital system may have been, there was much about it, especially in the Metropolis, to disturb a philanthropist who liked his charitable activities conducted with a decent degree of efficiency and solvency. In neither respect were British hospitals, voluntary or endowed, beyond criticism. As the medical committee of the C.O.S. never tired of stressing, there was a lamentable lack of uniformity and coordination in the policies and practices of the institutions that made up the metropolitan medical complex. For example, the relation between the general hospital, with its special departments, and the special hospitals had never been defined. The latter had been burgeoning throughout the country, often in response to no genuine need and distributed on no optimum basis. Founding a hospital could be as individualistic an operation as starting any other charity, and some of the newer ones were viewed with a skeptical eye by certain observers, among them general practitioners.[62] In any case, whether useful or superfluous, they siphoned support from essential and better-managed institutions.

What sharpened the issue, of course, was the perennial financial difficulties in which hospitals as a whole, especially the large general hospitals, found themselves. One might ordinarily have tolerated rivalries, incompatible policies, grave differences in administrative efficiency, and accounting systems which made it virtually impossible to compare one institution with another. When, however, hospitals had got themselves into such a financial pickle that they could not admit patients to fill their beds — Guy's had a hundred out of six hundred beds vacant in 1890[63] — this called for investigation. Before the mid-'80's at least two of the great endowed hospitals, St. Thomas's and Guy's, had fallen back on the expedient of allotting blocks of beds to paying patients, a shocking departure to those who

---

[62] See, for example, the evidence of H. N. Hardy, *S. C. (Lords) on Metropolitan Hospitals*, 1890, Q. 1092.
[63] E. H. Lushington, *ibid.*, 1890–91, Q. 9812.

thought of the old endowments as the patrimony of the poor.[64] *The Times* considered the position of the hospitals so precarious as to bring them close to one of two unthinkable alternatives, collapse or state intervention.[65]

From its original attack on abuses in out-patient departments, the energetic medical committee of the C.O.S., as we have seen, had been led on to look critically at the larger world of metropolitan hospitals. Surely there were adequate facilities to take care of the sick poor of London (a questionable inference, since the ratio of beds to population in 1893 was 1.91 per thousand as against 3.85 in Berlin),[66] given the Poor Law infirmaries and the hospitals themselves. Yet something must be wrong if, on the average, nearly 17 per cent of the 5272 beds (1887) in the general hospitals were unoccupied, owing chiefly to the financial stringency of the institution.[67] What was needed, in the Society's view, was not so much new resources as better management of the existing plant, endowment, and staff. If these assumptions were correct, here was an incomparable field for charity organization.

The Lords' Select Committee on Metropolitan Hospitals (1890–92), appointed largely under C.O.S. inspiration,[68] effected no significant change in procedures, but at least it assembled a mass of interesting information on the financial condition of London hospitals. The bulk of them, save where rescued temporarily by legacies, were showing heavy annual deficits. Earlier in the 1880's one hears of St. George's, Westminster, King's College, and University College Hospitals being obliged to sell securities to remain above water, the last named, indeed, was said to have unloaded £17,000 worth in the years 1880–83.[69] Of the endowed hospitals Guy's was in the most desperate plight, a victim, in part, of mismanagement, and in part, of the agricultural depression. For the bulk of Guy's endowment was in farming land in Hereford, Lincoln, and Essex, about 28,000 acres, on which the gross income dropped from about £50,000 to about £26,000.[70] St. Thomas's fared better owing to its holdings of London property, but to fill all of the Hospital's 569 beds, the Steward testified, would require an additional £6000 to £7000 of income.[71] St. Bartholomew's, under the astute financial management of Sir Sydney Waterlow, had less to worry about. Its income of £70,500 was drawn largely from London real estate, together with about 13,000 acres in Essex, Kent, and Hampshire.[72] The voluntary or mixed (part voluntary and part endowed) institutions

[64] *Charity Record,* 20 Jan. 1881; *The Philanthropist,* August 1884, pp. 121–22.

[65] *The Times,* 20 Dec. 1886.

[66] Sir Henry Burdett, quoted by B. Kirkman Gray and B. L. Hutchins, *Philanthropy and the State, or Social Politics* (London, 1908), p. 230. The London ratio was, of course, more favorable than that of the country at large.

[67] C. S. Loch, "Medical Relief in London," *Murray's Magazine,* 7:448 (April 1890).

[68] As indicated in Chapter VIII.

[69] *Charity Record,* 2 March 1882; *Fry's Royal Guide,* 1883–84, p. xix.

[70] E. H. Lushington, *S. C. (Lords) on Metropolitan Hospitals,* 1890–91, Q. 9805, 9808, 9809.

[71] Robert Brass and F. Walker, *ibid.,* Q. 10,884, 10,983.

[72] Sir Sydney Waterlow, *ibid.,* 1890, Q. 2586.

showed similar degrees of solvency or the reverse. The fact was that the large London hospitals were leading a precarious, hand-to-mouth existence.

In the face of such unremitting pressure, they could afford to ignore no possible source of revenue. To be sure, they did not rise to George Newnes's offer to distribute £10,000 among them if the average circulation of *Tit-Bits* should reach half a million! But his circulation-building stratagem gained the enthusiastic support of *The Philanthropist,* which pointed out that ten thousand nurses, each persuading eight friends to subscribe could easily provide the additional eighty thousand copies needed.[73] During the 1890's Baron Hirsch's turf winnings helped out, but since, on the advice of George Herring, he generally recognized only fifteen to twenty institutions, each distribution left behind it a wake of bitterness on the part of those which had been passed over.[74] Yet, however ruinous their situation, London hospitals were little inclined to engage in cooperative fund-raising. Until the end of the century the only significant venture in common financing was that connected with the Hospital Sunday and Saturday Funds. For some decades the annual allotment from the Sunday Fund was an increment on which hospital managers came to depend and which enabled a number of them to keep their institutions in running order.

It is hardly worth while to try to single out the originator of the Fund. The honor has been claimed for two Birmingham men, and Birmingham was, in fact, first in the field with a church collection for its hospitals in 1859.[75] No doubt, such offerings were not unknown in pre-Victorian Britain. From 1784 on, to cite an instance, the Aberdeen Infirmary benefited from such a collection taken on the first Sunday of the year.[76] In establishing Sunday Funds a number of cities — among them Sheffield, Nottingham, Carlisle, Manchester, Newcastle-on-Tyne, and Liverpool — anticipated the Metropolis.[77] In London the moving spirit was un-questionably Sir Sydney Waterlow, who from the inception of the Fund handled the touchy problem of distributing the money collected among the eligible insti-tutions.[78] The idea was, of course, simplicity itself. On a specified day each June let a collection for the benefit of hospitals and dispensaries be taken in every place of worship and the proceeds divided according to their "needs and merits."

The Fund got off to a flying start in 1873 when nearly £28,000 was collected from 1072 congregations. A quarter of a century later about £39,000 was being drawn from 1834 congregations, together with £14,000 in legacies and special gifts.[79] One can doubt whether the increase achieved in the 1880's and '90's was

[73] *The Philanthropist,* October 1889, pp. 147–48.

[74] *Charity Record,* 9 March 1893.

[75] Rev. J. C. Miller (1814–80), later Canon of Rochester, and Thomas Wright (1809–84), surgeon.

[76] *Charity Record,* 6 Jan. 1881.

[77] *Burdett's Hospitals and Charities,* 1906, pp. 124–25.

[78] Smalley, *Sir Sydney Waterlow,* chap. XIII.

[79] These figures represent the annual average for the five years 1898–1902, taken from *Burdett's Hospitals,* 1906, p. 119. The average in the legacy and special gift category was much reduced by the launching of the Prince of Wales Fund in 1897–98.

commensurate with the additional effort invested in the campaign. But in the decade before 1914 the fortunes of the Fund took a turn for the better. What accounted, as much as anything, for the large totals was a marked rise in special gifts and legacies, notably the annual gifts of George Herring. During the years 1899–1901 he annually put £10,000 into the Fund, without, however, inciting the regular Sunday donors to significantly greater openhandedness. Then he shrewdly decided to use his gift as bait, agreeing to give five shillings for every pound collected on Hospital Sunday. It was this device, according to Burdett, which was responsible for extracting from the congregations nearly 40 per cent more than they had been contributing.[80]

The work of the Fund was marked by occasional differences of opinion. The *Charity Record,* which, of course, existed on advertising from individual agencies and served as something of a press agent for them — at least those of which the editor approved — deplored all "centralizing" tendencies.[81] In some quarters there was a suspicion that a certain type of contributor tended to discharge his obligation to all medical charities through a small gift to the Fund. Still, even apart from its financial assistance, the Fund exercised a salutary influence, especially on marginal institutions. To qualify for a grant each hospital had to submit its accounts in a form prescribed by the Fund. In the office of the Fund these were analyzed, and compared with the costs of other hospitals. The applications of some were rejected entirely; others were required to appear and defend their claims. In a sense, this was a kind of unofficial grants committee which made its aid conditional on meeting certain minimum standards. As Sir Sydney Waterlow put it, "holding the power of the purse in the name of the public, we have an influence over them [hospitals] which it would be difficult to exercise in any other way."[82]

The London Sunday Fund dwarfed those of the provincial cities, even though a few of these had a higher per capita record. With the Saturday Fund, designed to tap the working-class population, other centers, especially industrial centers, made a better showing. In most of the larger cities the Saturday Funds took their rise in the 1870's, obviously inspired by the Sunday Funds. The professed aim of their sponsors was to give the working classes an opportunity to contribute to the hospitals from which they received so much benefit.[83] But collections, taken in factories and other places of employment or amusement, never reached the volume that the more optimistic supporters of the Fund had predicted. In London in 1890 some £20,500 was contributed in 4300 establishments; ten years later the

[80] *Burdett's Hospitals,* 1906, p. 121.
[81] *Charity Record,* 7 July 1887.
[82] S. C. (Lords) *on Metropolitan Hospitals,* 1890, Q. 2766.
[83] R. B. C. Acland, *ibid.,* 1890–91, Q. 22, 841. The Saturday Fund was in itself an admission that the working classes were not, in general, attending church and were therefore inaccessible to the Sunday Fund appeal. The impression was apparently justified, as K. S. Inglis has demonstrated on the basis of the Census of 1851 ("Patterns of Worship in 1851," *J. Ecclesiastical History,* 11:74:86 [April, 1960]). See, also, his book, *Churches and the Working Classes in Victorian England* (London, 1963), Introduction.

Fund had grown to only about £23,000.[84] This was creditable enough, for the Saturday Fund had none of the special gifts and legacies that supplemented the Sunday collections. But obviously the key to hospital solvency did not lie in such expedients as these.

They did not, in fact, succeed in getting London hospitals out of the red. In 1895 the deficits of 122 institutions totaled between £70,000 and £102,500 (depending on the basis of computation).[85] In some quarters there was genuine apprehension lest financial stringency open the way to subventions from public funds and a weakening of the voluntary principle. Such a fear seemed not altogether baseless when the editor of the *Daily Chronicle* could query whether the care of the sick and disabled ought not to be assumed by the community rather than being left to the sporadic mercies of private zeal.[86] What brought a measure of stability to the hospitals was the extraordinary outpouring of philanthropy evoked by the Queen's Diamond Jubilee Year. Among its more significant results was a project for putting hospital charity on a more regular foundation than the *ad hoc* operation of the Sunday and Saturday Funds permitted.

The Prince of Wales, whose responsibility it was to decide among the various proposals for a national memorial, had an authentic and long-standing interest in hospitals. Here an important influence was H. C. (later Sir Henry) Burdett, the editor of *Hospital* and *Burdett's Hospitals and Charities*, who two years before had presciently issued a volume on the welfare activities of Edward and Alexandra under the alliterative title, *Prince, Princess, and People*.[87] Burdett's project of a permanent fund for the London hospitals differed sharply from the annual Sunday collections. From the beginning its sponsors thought in long-range terms. Not only did they hope to make available something approaching £150,000 a year but they also proposed to accumulate a permanent endowment. This, in short, was to be a kind of central hospital foundation, whose directors would not be content merely to dole out money to worthy establishments but would intervene in hospital affairs in a positive fashion.

Its identification with Jubilee Year helped to produce for the Prince of Wales's (after 1902, King Edward's) Hospital Fund an initial year's income of over £200,000.[88] The Prince's accession to the throne was celebrated by gifts totaling over £425,000 toward endowment, £86,100 in ordinary income, and a special coronation offering of more than £600,000. What the King's Fund had that the Sunday Fund lacked was the ability to attract larger sums, either as legacies or gifts.[89] In 1901 Samuel Lewis bequeathed £250,000, together with a share in his residuary estate (a legacy which in the end yielded over £525,000), and three

---

[84] *Ibid.*, Q. 22,806; *Burdett's Hospitals*, 1906, p. 74.

[85] Loch, "The Prince of Wales Hospital Fund," *Macmillan's*, 75:401 (April 1897).

[86] Quoted in the *Charity Record*, 5 Jan. 1890.

[87] London, 1889. For the circumstances of the founding of the Prince of Wales Fund, see Frank D. Long, *King Edward's Hospital Fund*, chap. I.

[88] *Burdett's Hospitals*, 1906, p. 74.

[89] For some of the larger benefactions see Long, *King Edward's Hospital Fund*, p. 25.

years later the Canadian railway magnate Lord Mount Stephen donated £200,000, having, with his associate Lord Strathcona, already given £400,000. The latter's gifts amounted to £500,000, and his legacy to £815,000.[90] The Fund, in fact, did everything possible to apprise testators of its existence. A recent chairman of the management committee admits to having written "twenty of my personal friends [solicitors] once and saying 'when asked by your clients what charities they should put in their wills, do please remember King Edward's Hospital Fund.' "[91] Presently donors became aware of the Fund and discovered in it a highly satisfactory method of contributing to medical charities; some, indeed, thought it an effective technique for improving hospital efficiency. From Andrew Carnegie came £100,000 to be used as seemed best but "the more strenuously for reform the better."[92] At the end of its first fifteen years the Fund had distributed about £1,635,000, and had accumulated investments of about £1,700,000, so that in most years after 1905 interest on capital exceeded donations and subscriptions.[93]

Enthusiasm for the new idea was by no means unanimous. Managers of individual hospitals showed alarm lest the Fund should divert subscriptions from their own institutions. This, as it turned out, was an accurate premonition, at least in the case of certain corporate subscribers. From 1907 some of the City Companies ceased contributing to individual hospitals and instead made substantial gifts to the King's Fund, a course that was followed by the City Parochial Foundation as well.[94] There were also those who feared that the Sunday Fund would be gravely injured by the new agency. This may perhaps have been the case, but it is at least arguable that the growing popularity of the out-of-town week-end and shrinking church attendance had as much to do with the decline in the Sunday Fund as did competition from the King's Fund.[95] For the two, in a considerable degree, engaged in different tasks. The one was reasonably effective in luring the small, semicasual offering, while the other stalked bigger game. Whatever the early objections to the Fund, defenders of the voluntary hospital system had good reason to be grateful to it. One could make a persuasive case to show that for a period of years only the Fund stood between the London hospitals and a financial collapse that would have brought the State in to salvage and control them.

Lord Beveridge characterized the King's Fund as a "new model" charity — that is, one of those which allowed a good deal of discretion to the trustees. At an early stage the Council and its committees resolved that the Fund should be employed as a constructive instrument for improving hospital methods, and they did not hesitate to lay down the law in unambiguous fashion. Within a few years, by

[90] *Ibid.,* pp. 24–25; *Burdett's Hospitals,* 1905, p. 83.
[91] Sir Ernest Pooley before the Nathan Committee (unpubl.), Q. 2319.
[92] *Charity Record,* 7 Feb. 1905.
[93] *Burdett's Hospitals,* 1913, p. 87.
[94] Sir Ernest Pooley before the Nathan Committee (unpubl.), Q. 2323, 2324.
[95] Sunday collections dropped from nearly £50,000 in 1905 to about £36,000 in 1912. The total income of the Sunday Fund reached its peak (£78,000) in 1907 (*Burdett's Hospitals,* 1913, p. 139).

enabling hospitals to reopen closed wards, they had added 450 beds to London's facilities for the sick, and they had persuaded their beneficiaries to adopt a uniform accounting system.[96] To qualify for grants a hospital was expected to maintain a high standard of performance. Officials of the Fund took pains to acquire a first-hand knowledge of the strong and weak points of each institution, and they moved in to curb the expansionist ambitions of some hospital boards when these were tempted to make "ill-considered expenditures on bricks and mortar." [97] Altogether the King's Fund supplied the London voluntary hospitals with a desperately needed lifeline.

It was comforting to conclude with Burdett that the financial soundness of the voluntary system had now been assured that it would maintain itself in spite of the socialism in the air.[98] Yet only a decade after the Fund had been launched, the *Saturday Review* pondered the dilemma of the voluntary hospital and decided that the time had come for state aid. "Individual effort and benevolence may be extolled, but . . . what is the natural work of the community cannot be left to the uncertain and sporadic goodwill of individuals. The lunatic hospitals and the poor-law hospitals are not supported by charitable contributions; and it is only a confusion of ideas that the general hospitals are supposed to be on a different footing." Other advantages aside, to call in the State would be to distribute the burden more fairly and would "mean that the people who are able to contribute and who ought to contribute but do not, would as citizens have to contribute." [99] This analysis, heretical enough in 1906, was to appeal to an increasing number of Englishmen as no more than simple common sense.

6

When the Prince of Wales issued his original appeal for the Fund, he stressed not only its humanitarian side but also the role of hospitals in advancing medical science. In pointing to the importance of medical research he was noting a cause that hitherto had made little specific appeal to British philanthropists but one which would increasingly engage their attention.[100] Not until the 1890's were there significant indications of a rising interest in expanding medical knowledge as such, especially in improving the methods of treating such afflictions as tuberculosis and cancer. Endowing medical research as such was a novel conception; the Rockefeller Institute, a conspicuous milestone, dates only from the turn of the century.

At about the same time, though on an infinitely smaller scale than that of their

[96] *Ibid.*, 1905, p. 83; *The Times*, 3 Feb. 1947.
[97] *Burdett's Hospitals*, 1910, p. 88.
[98] *Ibid.*, p. 84.
[99] *Saturday Review*, 101:745 (18 June 1906).
[100] They had given help to medical education in the form of endowed professorships, and presumably they believed that some of their gifts to hospitals, particularly to the newer special hospitals for the treatment of such diseases as tuberculosis, would help in the progress of medical science. But clearly the dominant motive in most of the philanthropic giving in the medical field was directly humanitarian rather than scientific.

gifts to hospitals, British philanthropists began to direct their benefactions toward research. In 1892 Richard Berridge left more than £150,000 to medical charities, including £20,000 for a British Institute of Preventive Medicine (with £20,000 more if the public were to provide £40,000 for site and buildings), and £10,000 for a chair in pathology at University College, London.[101] Six years later Lord Iveagh (Edward Guinness) offered £250,000 to the Jenner Institute of Preventive Medicine for research at an advanced level in bacteriology or other areas of biology.[102] In Liverpool, Thomas Sutton Tommis, who had already built a chemistry laboratory for University College, gave £10,000 for systematic research into the origin and cure of cancer, and in London, Mrs. Lloyd (the Kensington lady who had been outraged over the rearing of her grandsons in the Catholic faith) bequeathed a like amount for the cause.[103]

A rather appealing example of the new philanthropic interest is that offered by E. G. Bawden, a retired stockbroker of Clapton, who explained his situation as follows: "I am 76 years old . . . and I am without family ties. Therefore I felt that, as I should like to do something good with my money, it was time that I should take steps in that direction."[104] With the counsel of Edgar Speyer, the banker-philanthropist, he set up the Bawden Trust of £100,000, more than half of which was to be devoted to medical causes, part to hospitals and part to research. It was Bawden's conviction that humankind was on the verge of great discoveries in the treatment of certain diseases, and he was determined to aid in the quest. *The Times,* in applauding his generosity, pointed to other needs in the same area, such as research scholarships in London hospitals. In 1909 the appeal was answered by Otto Beit with £215,000 for thirty research fellowships at London University as a memorial to his brother Alfred.[105] As compared with the tremendous flow of gifts to hospitals, the funds for research were only a drop, but they were a drop that would start, if not the deluge, at least a goodly stream.

One quasi-medical problem to which private philanthropy made a signal contribution was that of provision for the blind. Organized work for this handicapped group, as we have seen, took its rise in the late eighteenth century and expanded, like other British humanitarian efforts, broadly but erratically. By the mid-1870's Howe's *Classified Directory* could list about twenty-five London agencies for the blind with an annual income of about £45,000. A number of developments, one of which, the Gardner Trust, has special relevance to the theme of this study, marked the latter half of the century.[106] There was, first of all, conspicuous progress in the education of the blind. Less and less were they to be dealt with as helpless objects of pity but as potentially useful and responsible members of the

---

[101] *Charity Record,* 20 Oct. 1892.

[102] *Ibid.,* 29 Dec. 1898.

[103] *Ibid.,* 5 Feb. 1903, 20 June 1907.

[104] *Daily Chronicle,* quoted *ibid.,* 7 Sept. 1905.

[105] *Ibid.,* 6 Jan. 1910.

[106] For an account of the progress in the treatment of the blind during this period, see Madeline Rooff, *Voluntary Societies and Social Progress* (London, 1957), chap. XV.

community. For sons of the upper classes there was Worcester College for the Blind, a public school founded in 1866 to offer a classical education and prepare for the universities and the professions.[107] The moving force behind the Royal Normal College and Academy of Music, opened at Norwood in 1871, was Dr. Thomas Rhodes Armitage, son of a Leeds ironmaster, who had to abandon his medical practice because of failing eyesight and who became one of the more imaginative and indefatigable champions of the blind. The new institution embodied some of his educational theories, especially his notion that music was a pursuit for which the blind were peculiarly suited.[108] Into the school Armitage is said to have poured some £40,000 of his own, and he had the satisfaction of seeing it develop into one of the more constructive and successful ventures of its kind.[109]

By all odds the most memorable benefaction for the blind was the Gardner Trust of £300,000, established by the will of Henry Gardner of London, himself blind in his last years. The bequest marked something of a departure in such philanthropies, since his concern was with the problems of the blind, especially with their education and training, not with an individual institution or particular locality, and within the broad terms of the Trust the trustees enjoyed a good deal of discretion. A legacy of such dimensions put the situation of the blind into a rather difficult focus. As one of their advocates remarked, it lifted them from obscurity and transformed them into interesting persons.[110]

The provisions of the will were so general that they seemed to invite suggestions as to the use of the money, and there was no lack of proposals. A close relative of Gardner's urged the founding of a "Gardner Institute for the Blind." C. S. Loch, on the other hand, to whom the trustees appealed, opposed the idea of a new institution and concluded that the situation called rather (in consonance with C.O.S. philosophy) for an agency which would take as its major task that of adjusting the inequalities, supplementing the resources, and coordinating the efforts of other charities.[111] In 1882, three years after Gardner's death, the Trust began its operations, applying its income at the outset largely to musical instruction, education (including grants for printing books for the blind), and pensions.[112] Sponsoring the magazine *The Blind,* assisting in local activities of various

[107] In the course of its first three decades the school sent to the universities nearly fifty boys, many of whom graduated with honors and several with first class honors.

[108] Through the British and Foreign Blind Association (later the National Institute for the Blind), of which he was the principal founder, Armitage had been largely responsible for the adoption of Braille and Moon type throughout the Kingdom.

[109] *Fry's Royal Guide,* 1884–85, pp. 16–17. For a brief sketch of Armitage and his work, see Beveridge, *Voluntary Action,* pp. 173–74.

[110] S. S. Forster, *The "Gardner" Bequest* (London, 1880), p. 1.

[111] C. S. Loch to the Gardner Trustees, 29 Jan. 1880, in a volume of documents on the Gardner Trust in the library of the Family Welfare Association.

[112] In 1894 the trustees obtained from the Charity Commissioners an order still further liberalizing the scheme under which the Trust was administered, so that a third of the income would be available for whatever purpose seemed most promising. (H. J. Wilson, *R. C. on the Blind* [C. 5781–II], 1889, Q. 4417; H. J. Wilson, ed., *Information with Regard to Institutions for the Blind in England and Wales,* 2d ed. [London, 1896].)

sorts, encouraging better understanding among voluntary organizations and between these and the statutory authorities — for it was inevitable that before many
years the State would have to assume primary responsibility — in these and other
ways the Trust marked itself as a creative force in late century philanthropy.[113]

7

The movement for preserving from enclosure the commons, especially those
on the edge of urban centers, and for maintaining open spaces in crowded cities,
looked to the future even more than to the immediate present. Earlier in the
century there had been a volume of protest against the wholesale enclosure of
commons, and occasionally one finds pressure for preserving them as recreation
areas for town dwellers. But it required a threat to the commons in the neighborhood of London to bring about an organized resistance. When a Select Committee
in 1865 rejected their case for enclosure (based largely on the ancient Statute of
Merton), landlords moved to take matters into their own hands.[114] In Berkham-
sted, Plumstead, Tooting, and parts of Epping Forest enclosures were actually
carried out, though later reversed by legal action. With the price of urban and
suburban building land climbing sharply, the threat to the commons became so
general as to make almost inevitable some defensive action on behalf of the public.

This took the form of the Commons Preservation Society organized in the
autumn of 1865, with such leaders as John Stuart Mill, Charles and T. Fowell
Buxton, Thomas Hughes, and with Shaw-Lefevre (Lord Eversley) as chairman.
The initial suggestion for organized opposition had come from P. H. Lawrence,
a solicitor and resident of Wimbledon, who had been active in resisting the sale
of Putney Common and who, along with Shaw-Lefevre, had drafted the report
of the Select Committee. For the first three years Lawrence served as honorary
solicitor to the Society. When he accepted a government post, his successor was
Robert (later Sir Robert) Hunter, who became perhaps the most commanding
figure in the whole commons preservation movement. The original leaders were
reinforced in the course of time by such public-spirited citizens as Sir Charles
Dilke, Octavia Hill, James Bryce, Lord Thring, and others.

In most instances householders adjoining the commons themselves raised funds
and organized committees to fight the enclosure. Sometimes wealthy individuals
who possessed rights in a particular common led the fight on behalf of the whole
body of freeholders, as did Gurney Hoare in the case of Hampstead Heath, Sir
Julian Goldsmid for Plumstead Common, and Sir Henry Peek for Wimbledon.
But strategy and direction remained largely in the hands of the solicitor to the
Society, who planned the legal campaign with marked astuteness. Lawrence arranged that the cases should be brought up in the most favorable order, the strongest ones first, and he showed excellent judgment in employing counsel, Sir Roun-

---

[113] For the beginnings of a public policy, see Rooff, *Voluntary Societies and Social Policy,* pp. 196ff.
[114] *S. C. on the Public Use of Commons,* 1865. A good deal of the following section is based on
George Shaw-Lefevre (Lord Eversley), *English Commons and Forests* (London, 1894).

dell Palmer, later (as Lord Selborne) Lord Chancellor, handling most of the earlier cases. Not only that but the successive solicitors managed to have several of the cases heard by notably enlightened judges, such as Lord Romilly and Sir George Jessel. It was a skillful war that the Society waged, and, with two or three exceptions, it was uniformly successful.

It was also a costly war, and the Society was fortunate in having a membership roll of greater than average wealth. Among those subscribing £100 in 1867 were Thomas Baring, Thomas Brassey, Angela Burdett-Coutts, Charles Buxton, Frederic Goldsmid, Samuel Morley, H. W. (Sir Henry) Peek, and Lawrence himself.[115] In the lengthiest piece of litigation, that with regard to Epping Forest, the Society managed to enlist the support of the London Corporation, which provided altogether about £240,000, of which about £33,000 went for legal and parliamentary expenses.[116]

The problem was not merely one of financing litigation. Even though the Commons Preservation Society might reject the view that the rights over the commons of a lord of the manor had to be purchased, in some instances large sums were necessary to buy land held in fee and thus to enhance the utility of the common. An instructive case is that of Hampstead Heath and Parliament Hill, which brought together in an unusual fashion the Society, private donors, the City Parochial Foundation, and several public bodies.[117] Action became necessary when, apparently in a deliberate attempt to precipitate the issue, the lord of the manor began to build a number of houses on the Heath, planting them on the most conspicuous sites. Even before this gesture, the Metropolitan Board of Works had taken alarm, and had explored the possibility of buying the lord's rights. But the price asked was £400,000 (£1600 an acre for about 250 acres), a figure that was clearly out of the question. Sir Thomas Wilson, the lord of the manor, would have to be checked in the courts if the Heath were not to become another real estate development. The Commons Preservation Society took the lead in encouraging the commoners to resist, in organizing a local committee, and in persuading Gurney Hoare, as representative of the commoners, to ask for an injunction restraining the lord of the manor.

For reasons that need not be detailed here, the Hampstead Heath case did not run its full legal course. In 1868, however, Sir Thomas Wilson died, and his successor proved to be a more accommodating character. It appeared that he might be willing to dispose of his lord's rights at a reasonable figure. The final price paid by the Metropolitan Board of Works was £45,000 a little over a tenth of what Sir Thomas had asked. About this transaction the Society had mingled feelings. Obviously it was a bargain if one were to accept (as the Society had never done) the lord's contention as to his rights. The Hampstead common saved

---

[115] In a volume of pamphlets and letters on the Commons Preservation Society in the London County Council Library.

[116] Shaw-Lefevre, *English Commons and Forests*, p. 158; Minutes of the Common Council, 4 Feb. 1886.

[117] Shaw-Lefevre, chap. IV, gives a detailed account.

for the public by this purchase was not the whole magnificent tract now known as Hampstead Heath. To repeat, it comprised a bit less than 250 acres, and these were broken at some points by the intrusion of private property. Without the two adjoining tracts of Parliament Hill and Ken Wood, the estate of Lord Mansfield, the Heath would lose much of its spacious beauty. There was in addition a smaller plot of some sixty acres owned by Sir Spencer Wilson, the lord of the manor, and already on its way to being cut up for building lots, a destiny evidently intended also for Ken Wood by Lord Mansfield's heir. In this situation, of course, legal action could accomplish nothing. To save the Heath in its larger form would mean raising a sizable fund and buying the adjoining estates.

A paper presented by Octavia Hill in early 1884 at a meeting at Grosvenor House supplied the necessary impulse and led to the formation of a committee to make arrangements for the purchase of the property.[118] Something under three hundred acres was involved. The committee, of which the Duke of Westminster served as president and Shaw-Lefevre as chairman of the executive committee, had undertaken no easy commission. In addition to carrying on delicate negotiations with the owners, there was the problem of enlisting the support of various public and semipublic bodies. For plainly the larger fraction of the £300,000 required would have to come — and indeed should come — from public sources. Eventually, in spite of the standoffish attitude of the Board of Works, a schedule of contributions was worked out, under which the Board agreed to provide half of the total, and Hampstead and St. Pancras, the two parishes most directly interested, £50,000. Of the remaining £100,000, Parliament ordered £50,000 to be taken from the funds that were about to form the capital of the City Parochial Foundation — somewhat to the annoyance of the City Corporation, which took exception to the method rather than to the object.[119]

These official and semiofficial contributions left slightly more than £50,000 to be raised by public subscription. It was no handicap to have the Duke of Westminster, a peer whose interest in good causes had already been demonstrated, so actively concerned, and other members of the nobility followed his lead — the Duke of Bedford with £3000, Lord Portman and his daughter with £1000 each. Baring Brothers, Lady Angela Burdett-Coutts, and W. H. Smith each assisted with £1000, and within a few weeks the larger share of the required amount had been pledged. During the following year (1888) Octavia Hill, a host in herself, and the other leaders succeeded in finding the balance in smaller contributions.[120] The whole campaign had taken five years, from the forming of the committee to the final signing of the contracts in March of 1889. This extension of Hampstead Heath was accomplished by the joint action of public and private agencies, though we must note that public participation was enlisted, and virtually forced, by individ-

---

[118] E. Moberly Bell, *Octavia Hill*, p. 223. In this account, however, raising the money is made to appear an individual achievement of Octavia Hill, an interpretation which would be hard to sustain.
[119] Minutes of the Common Council, 16 Dec. 1886.
[120] *Charity Record*, 17 Nov. 1887; Bell, *Octavia Hill*, pp. 224–25.

uals who organized for the purpose. Of the necessary funds, two-thirds came from public sources, while the remaining third was provided by private philanthropists, living or dead, intentionally or unwittingly. Presumably most of those whose ancient benefactions to City parishes made up half of the private increment would have been astonished at the use now being made of their gifts. Yet the Dead Hand, one must conclude, has rarely been brought to life with results more beneficial to an urban population.[121]

The publicity received by the Commons Preservation Society and the success of its court actions convinced social reformers that something might be done in related areas. Here one can point to the experience of Octavia Hill, who did not join the Society for more than a decade after its founding. What brought her into the movement was the failure of her attempt to save Swiss Cottage Fields (now Fitzjohn's Avenue) from the hand of the builder.[122] The episode raised larger questions in her mind, specifically that of open spaces in cities, and, since most of the donors to her save-Swiss-Cottage-Fields fund elected to leave their contributions in the hands of the committee, she found herself equipped with a war chest. The critical need, in her view, was for small open spaces in congested districts, "open air sitting rooms for the poor," where they might escape from their crowded rooms and narrow, squalid courts. She was appalled that the London School Board closed its fifty-seven playgrounds on Saturdays and in the evening, and she respectfully suggested that owners of private squares might open them at certain times.[123] Her most immediate point of attack, however, was the church yards, to the distress of those who regarded burial ground as hallowed. Why should such open spaces not be employed to make more tolerable the lot of the living?

Octavia Hill carried on her crusade with the almost pathological energy for which she was becoming known. She assaulted public authorities and private bodies with appeals that they cooperate by acquiring new open spaces or by making available those that existed. As a champion of open spaces, she is a much more sympathetic figure than as the last-ditch opponent of old age pensions; here she ceased to be the doctrinaire individualist and became the advocate of planning and public action. Some central body, she finally concluded, must decide on the location of open spaces, for, if initiative were left to individual residents, the wealthier districts would inevitably do better than the needier, as was in fact

[121] Although most of the earlier operations of the Society had to do with commons not far from London, before many years the leaders realized that the danger was not confined to the metropolitan area. The Society found itself involved in cases in Hampshire, Dorset, and the West (Malvern Chase and the Forest of Dean). Not only that, but largely through the influence of Henry Fawcett the Society developed an interest in rural commons throughout the country. (Leslie Stephen, *Life of Henry Fawcett*, 5th ed. [London, 1885], pp. 327–34; Shaw-Lefevre, *English Commons and Forests*, pp. 286–87.)

[122] When it looked as though she might manage to raise the ten thousand guineas required to buy the land, the contractor repudiated the agreement and the Fields were lost. (Bell, *Octavia Hill*, pp. 143–46.)

[123] Octavia Hill, *Our Common Land* (London, 1877), pp. 130ff, 137ff.

already the case. In the western semicircle of the Metropolis, comprising the area four miles to the west of Charing Cross, there was one acre of open space for 682 residents, while in the eastern it was one for 7481.[124]

These were the figures for 1888. A decade later the situation had improved perceptibly. Through the action of local bodies, the London County Council, the City Parochial Foundation, the open-space societies, and a number of private donors, the common estate of Londoners had been notably increased. Sir Sydney Waterlow gave Lauderdale House, Highgate, together with twenty-nine acres; G. T. (Sir George) Livesey gave Telegraph Hill in the Peckham-Hatcham suburban area; and twenty-eight acres adjoining Epping Forest came from Edward North Buxton, himself active in the Commons Preservation Society.[125] The acreage included in the parks and open spaces contributed throughout the Kingdom by Victorian philanthropists would, it is clear, reach an imposing total.

Of the organized groups active in the cause probably the most noteworthy, next to the Commons Preservation Society, was the Kyrle Society, of which Octavia Hill's sister Miranda was the principal architect. The Society (which narrowly escaped being christened "The Society for the Diffusion of Beauty")[126] was named for Pope's Man of Ross, who had brought beauty to his own city. To introduce beauty into the lives and dwellings of the London poor was the aim set for the Society, an object which in retrospect seems to carry more than a whiff of Ruskinian sentimentality. To crass modern eyes some of the Society's projects appear almost whimsically romantic, such as that of decorating walls through the city with elevating sentiments — Octavia proposed Kingsley's words "Do noble deeds" for a wall near Waterloo Station.[127] Yet it would be hard to take exception to the labors of the committee on open spaces. Where necessary to save a desirable lot, the Society might raise a fund for its purchase, and before turning it over to a vestry or other local body, would see to putting the property in shape, with suitable planting and benches. Altogether, when credit is assigned for acquiring open spaces, especially the smaller spaces, for Londoners, the Kyrle Society will be entitled to more than an insignificant fraction.

8

By the late 1890's the battle for the small open space in congested urban districts had been pretty well won, but there was still much to be done on other fronts. Especially, as Octavia Hill urged in an article outlining a future program for the movement,[128] was it vital to hold for the public some of the lovelier and more historic spots throughout the Island. The National Trust, for which the article was in part a bit of publicity, was an outgrowth of the save-the-commons move-

---

[124] Octavia Hill, "The Open Spaces of the Future," *Nineteenth Century*, 46:27–28 (July 1899).

[125] *Ibid.*, p. 26.

[126] Bell, *Octavia Hill*, p. 151. For an account of the founding of the Kyrle Society, see C. E. Maurice, ed., *Life of Octavia Hill as Told in Her Letters* (London, 1913), pp. 316–17.

[127] Bell, *Octavia Hill*, p. 152.

[128] Hill, "The Open Spaces of the Future," *Nineteenth Century*, 46:27–32 (July 1899).

ment and indeed a device for remedying one of its weaknesses. Since none of the societies had corporate status, none could acquire land and pass it on to future generations. What was needed was a responsible body, nation-wide in its operations, in whose custody ancient buildings or picturesque tracts could be safely placed. The solution was provided by three individuals: Sir Robert Hunter, master strategist of the Commons Preservation Society; Octavia Hill, who incidentally contributed the word "Trust"; and Canon Rawnsley, Vicar of Wray in Westmorland, who had labored vigorously to protect his own Lake District from devastation. At a meeting at Grosvenor House in the summer of 1894, the outlines of a scheme were agreed upon, and by January 1895 the Trust was officially in business.

Like other philanthropic bodies, the Trust found it simpler to raise money for specific causes than for the general purposes of the organization. Although a decade after its founding subscriptions to the general fund had reached only about £400 a year, the Trust was the owner of twenty-four properties totaling nearly 1700 acres, including 108 acres on Derwentwater, for which £7000 had been collected, and 750 acres of Gowbarton Fell overlooking Ullswater.[129] By the eve of the first World War its estate amounted to about 6000 acres in sixty different pieces of property, and total receipts to something like £45,000.[130]

The Trust sought always to operate in a flexible fashion, using whatever means seemed most appropriate for a particular end. Its leaders explored the possibility of persuading private individuals or firms to take over ancient buildings, as with the Prudential Insurance Company and Staple Inn; they appealed to Parliament for legislation to facilitate the preservation of places of historical and natural interest; and they did not hesitate to work cooperatively with public bodies, as when, to save Geffrye's Almshouses in Shoreditch, they extracted £16,000 from the London County Council and £3000 from the Shoreditch authorities, raising the remaining £5000 themselves.[131] One of the more fruitful strategies was that of encouraging county and local societies with similar aims, and the new lease on life taken by numbers of these bodies owed something to the lead given by the central organization.

No doubt, as was freely conceded, the spectacular success of the Trust was possible only because it gave a corporate, concrete form to ideas that were already in the air. Until the first World War the normal pattern was for the Trust, through gift or purchase, to take over full ownership of a piece of property. This procedure continued, of course, but by the 1930's it had become increasingly difficult to raise large sums of money through special appeals. On the other hand, owners of historic and picturesque (and income-producing) property, however sympathetic, could not afford simply to turn it over to the Trust. An experimental covenant, made during the war years with Sir Thomas Dyke Acland, proprietor

[129] *Ann. Rept.*, 1905–1906; James Lees-Milne, ed., *The National Trust* (London, 1945), p. 123.
[130] *Ann. Rept.*, 1913–14.
[131] *Ann. Rept.*, 1908–1909, pp. 12–13.

of over seven thousand acres near Exmoor, suggested the possibility that, through an agreement with the owner, the Trust might in some instances attain its ends at much less expense than through outright purchase.[132] That is, an owner, while retaining proprietorship of his land, might give or sell to the Trust the right to control building on or development of the land in question. This plan, tried out in 1934 in the Buttermere Valley, was later widely extended, until by the mid-'40's about 40,000 of the Trust's 110,000 acres were held under protective covenants.[133]

During the past two decades the National Trust has become a major British philanthropy, and a large, diversified business. In 1937 an Act of Parliament supplied the necessary powers for preserving country houses and parks. What this meant, among other things, was that the Trust was obliged to enter the field of estate management on a more extensive basis, for with houses often came lands from which income had to be drawn. There were tenants to be managed, agriculture and stock-raising to be supervised, and old buildings to be renovated. Currently the work of the Trust has to do more with administering its extensive properties than with acquiring new ones or "preserving" natural beauties in the traditional sense. In fact, the cost of maintaining property obtained at no expense makes it necessary to pick and choose carefully among the various pieces offered. Obviously, save where the property itself is income-producing, no gift can be accepted unless accompanied by a fund for maintenance. This hard reality has, of course, stood between the Trust and many desirable acquisitions, and it has frustrated would-be donors, philanthropists by force of grim circumstances, who, unable themselves to carry on, had hoped to see their estate in the custody of a public-spirited trustee.

No doubt the Trust has made its mistakes and no doubt it is still, and will continue to be, beset by staggering difficulties — troubles with nature, with the public, and, not least, with official bodies. Yet Britons and visitors from abroad alike have reason to bless the agency that, in a period of catastrophic social change, has been able to maintain so much of historic and natural England without making it, in the words of G. M. Young, into a series of "potted landscapes," and without "Putting England under a Glass Case." [134]

The character of late-century philanthropy suggests a focus that was shifting, perceptibly even if not drastically. In a large degree the benevolence of the early century reflected simple humanitarian concern with human misery and misfortune, an impulse to ameliorate the lot of its victims and to set individuals on

---

[132] *Ann. Rept.,* 1916–17, pp. 5–6. The agreement with Sir Thomas Dyke Acland took the form of a five-hundred-year lease, under which he and his successors retained the rent, profits, and the ordinary rights of an owner but lost power to develop the land for building purposes or otherwise to change it radically.

[133] Lees-Milne, *National Trust,* pp. 123–24.

[134] Quoted *ibid.,* p. 9. The societies mentioned above by no means include all of the organized effort to preserve the countryside and the nation's ancient monuments. For others see (Leslie) Patrick Abercrombie, *The Preservation of Rural England* (London, 1926), and Richardson Evans, *An Account of the Scapa Society* (National Society for Checking the Abuses of Public Advertising), London, 1926.

the road to self-sufficiency. With this was sometimes mingled a measure of anxiety to check destitution and suffering in the lower classes before it reached the stage of widespread desperation. During the latter years the emphasis tended to shift toward prevention, conservation, and rehabilitation. The pre-eminence of medical charities in the hierarchy of philanthropic interests and the emergence of medical research, the founding of university colleges and colleges for women, the enhanced appeal of housing projects, the City Parochial Foundation, the save-the-commons movement and the National Trust — all of these mark a change in orientation. Some involved a greater degree of government participation, active or passive, than would have been thought appropriate fifty years earlier. The save-the-commons movement, for example, forms an instructive case not only of a philanthropy conceived in more comprehensive terms than would have attracted the charitable giver of the early century, but also of constructive cooperation, financial and otherwise, between private philanthropists and public authorities. This latter trend, only fitfully apparent at the time, was to gather strength as the years passed until the initiative shifted decisively to the public side. To a philanthropist of the 1850's the social and welfare activities of the British State in the 1950's would have been inconceivable. Private philanthropy continued to function to good effect, but the basic social tasks were increasingly turned over to the State. Even here, however, the stamp of voluntary effort was unmistakable. Public policy often followed along lines previously laid down by voluntary organizations, and public agencies often depended on them to carry it out.

CHAPTER XVIII

APPROACH TO
STATE PARTNERSHIP

THE MID-VICTORIANS, we have observed, tended to find in individual shortcomings the source of many of their social problems. If their diagnosis was adequate, there could be little complaint about their remedy. Surely, in their view, what could fairly be called *legitimate* distress did not exceed the resources of private charity! In the Metropolis, hundreds of agencies, endowed and voluntary, stood ready to respond to the deserving appeal. The income of the nation's almshouse and pension charities, about £550,000 in 1877, and the £364,000 for "the general use of the poor" would be sufficient, it seemed obvious, for such old-age pensions as were genuinely required, if this considerable sum could be systematically applied to that end.[1] And in special crises the pockets of the charitable would be opened promptly to relieve suffering.

Few intelligent mid-Victorians would have doubted that the essential instruments for dealing with their social problem were the spread of public enlightenment and such further assistance, in the way of penalties and rewards, as might encourage the working classes in their advance toward responsibility and self-respect. In this pattern private charity held a vital place, and it was assumed to be a permanent and even indispensable element in the system. For one thing, whereas state aid was inevitably limited, standardized, and mechanically administered, the charity of individuals could be as discretionary as one wished. But more important, Professor Burn suggests, was the value of charity as discipline for the donor himself. In making a choice among possible objects of his benevolence — indeed, in having to decide whether to contribute at all — the individual was receiving the kind of moral training that he would never get merely by paying his poor rates.[2] Only after a long and furious battle would the Victorian agree to relinquish any substantial fraction of that freedom of choice which figured so heavily in the social thinking of his age.

The function of the State, then, was strictly circumscribed. It would act, through

---

[1] Sir Henry Longley, R. C. (*Aberdare*) *on the Aged Poor* (C. 7684), 1895, Q. 7553.

[2] In *The Age of Equipoise,* chap. II, "Getting and Spending," Professor W. L. Burn has an illuminating discussion of some of the issues of wealth and poverty, state aid and private charity, free competition and philanthropic benevolence in mid-Victorian times. Unforunately I was not able to examine the volume until this study was already in proof.

the Poor Law administration, only to succor the most desperate cases. The main responsibility lay in the private sector — with individuals who would exert themselves to better their own situation and with groups of philanthropists who would assist them. It was not until the 1880's and '90's brought a change in the social temper that this mid-Victorian prescription was seriously queried. But even before the basic questions were raised, some slight measures of cooperation between statutory authorities and voluntary agencies had already developed. As in other areas, practice moved ahead of theory. The most conspicuous example, elementary education, is a familiar story — and something of a special case because of the denominational factor — that needs no retelling here. It is enough to recall that from 1833, when the two great Societies first received grants from the public funds, the stake of the State in education increased, slowly but perceptibly. School inspectors, grants for building schoolhouses, teacher-training and capitation grants all marked a growing public involvement. Whatever the inadequacies of these arrangements, they plainly foreshadowed the kind of public-private enterprise that English education has remained.

Some of the earlier forms of joint effort were by-products of the police function of the State, as, for example, the government grants to societies for aiding discharged prisoners.[3] A more instructive case, noticed in a previous chapter,[4] is that of schools for the care and rehabilitation of juvenile offenders. The pioneer agency was, of course, the Philanthropic Society, a purely voluntary body, whose sphere of activity, however, inevitably brought it into close contact with the Home Office. In the mid-1840's Sir James Graham proposed that the Philanthropic Society and the Refuge of the Destitute, both of which were receiving boys who had been pardoned under the Parkhurst Act, join in establishing a central reformatory school to be financed and supervised by the Government.[5] Since this would have cost the Society much of its freedom of action, the Philanthropic declined the offer and a few years later made the move to Redhill.

The institutions for juvenile delinquents operating in the 1840's and '50's all represented the voluntary principle, and yet in a sense they formed an auxiliary, if not an integral part, of the penal system of the nation. The partnership, it will be recalled, was made explicit by the Youthful Offenders Act of 1854,[6] which, while leaving the schools under independent management, extended to them the financial assistance of the State and brought them under its supervision. Industrial schools, originally intended as asylums for vagrant children where they could be trained in habits of industry, were taken under the wing of the State in a similar fashion.[7] On paper these decisions created an unlikely system, but one which, in practice, turned out to have substantial merits. Even though a good deal of their

[3] Rev. G. P. Merrick, *Report to H. M. Commissioners on Discharged Prisoners' Aid Societies* (C. 8299), 1897.
[4] In Chapter IV.
[5] *Report of the H. O. Committee on Reformatory and Industrial Schools* (C. 8204), 1896, II, 176.
[6] 17 & 18 Vict., c. 86.
[7] 20 & 21 Vict., c. 48.

financial support presently came from public sources, the schools retained much of their character as independent philanthropic agencies. The public was thus able to profit from the activity of such dedicated and adventurous pioneers as Mary Carpenter and Matthew Davenport Hill, while contributing to the partnership the funds necessary to make their work more widely effective.

Such developments as these were clearly exceptional. In the same category belong the tentative approaches to public medical care made by certain of the Poor Law authorities. If its police responsibilities led the State into cooperation with private philanthropists in maintaining reformatory and industrial schools, its concern with matters of public health opened the way for timid experimentation with public hospitals. To replace the old workhouse sick wards, Poor Law authorities in a number of large towns had built infirmaries, and others, challenged by recurrent cholera epidemics, had established special hospitals for fever patients, thus relieving the voluntary hospitals. Meanwhile Disraeli's Public Health Act of 1875, consolidating and extending previous legislation, vested substantial powers in the new local sanitary authorities, including that of providing hospitals out of the rates.

Such steps implied no conscious decision on the part of the State to develop a welfare policy or to share the burden with voluntary bodies. Neither public authorities nor philanthropists were disposed to demand a closer union of forces, save in special areas. They agreed, on the whole, that the proper concerns of the State lay within the ambit of "politics" and that matters of social betterment were best left to voluntary effort. But during the last quarter of the century signs of uneasiness multiplied, and there were nagging suspicions that private philanthropy might prove unequal to the task. Perhaps, if the real sources of distress were embedded in the structure of society, alleviation ought not to be left to groups of charitable individuals.

Some might reasonably doubt, for example, whether personal savings, even if supplemented by assistance from relatives, offered a realistic solution to the problems of old age. A few skeptics might wonder whether the voluntary hospitals, so much admired by chroniclers of philanthropic achievement, were in fact capable of carrying out their colossal assignment. And such years as 1886, when trade union unemployment exceeded 10 per cent and when 22.2 per cent of the Boilermakers and Iron Shipbuilders drew out-of-work pay,[8] inevitably produced a reaction against the comfortable doctrine that nothing much could be done about such things anyway. Mass unemployment could hardly be attributed to personal inadequacy, nor could workers, especially marginal workers, be reasonably expected to save for such a succession of rainy days as the bad years of the '80's turned out to be. Indiscriminate emergency relief, as the C.O.S. correctly urged and as the Mansion House Fund unhappily and prodigally was to demonstrate,

---

[8] Clapham, *Economic History of Modern Britain*, II, 453; Helen M. Lynd, *England in the Eighteen-Eighties*, p. 55.

supplied no answer; but the methods of the Society, with their stress on meticulous individual investigation, were as little adapted to handling vast numbers of unemployed. Here, apparently, was a form of social distress which the 1880's and '90's were beginning to view in a different way.

It is unnecessary to recapitulate the evidences of a changing social outlook. One must, of course, speak of "indications" and "symptoms" rather than of a decisive revolution in social philosophy. The balance did not shift abruptly or conclusively, nor was there sudden and general acceptance of the notion of state responsibility for welfare. Yet the sky was full of portents, many of them as yet barely visible. One might, for one thing, point to the increasing initiative taken by local authorities, encouraged by Disraeli's legislation of the mid-'70's, in undertaking projects of municipal improvement; of these Chamberlain's achievements in Birmingham, though perhaps the most dramatic, were not unique. At Westminster the decade was notable for a series of royal commissions on social and economic issues. Not since the 1830's and '40's had the Government embarked on so many systematic inquiries into the life of its citizens. And in the realm of ideas and their application to the problems of the common life, more audacious questions were being asked both at the universities and in the discussions of a variety of groups, informal and organized. Of these the Fabian Society can stand as repre sentative, though it by no means monopolized the field.

A more direct influence in turning public opinion toward a positive social policy was the growing accumulation of data on the conditions of life of the lower classes. By 1900 the upper ranks — at least those with eyes to see — could command far more accurate knowledge, personal and statistical, of their social inferiors than was possible a quarter of a century before. Some of this new understanding was unsystematic and individual: the experiences reported by residents of the settlement houses, which took their rise in the 1880's, the sympathetic interest aroused by the Dock Strike of 1889, and even the practice of "slumming," a fashionable diversion of the period — all these contributed in obscure ways to the changing attitude. The lower classes, in short, became an object of intense and often sentimental (if somewhat unpredictable) concern, and the East End a bit less *terra incognita* to the West. Of this sympathetic curiosity a magazine published in the mid-'80's can stand as a sufficiently expressive symbol. It was called *Eastward Ho!* and was founded to interpret the two Londons to each other.

Among the more effective instruments for shocking the well-to-do and reminding them of their responsibilities was a penny pamphlet by an East End Congregational minister. *The Bitter Cry of Outcast London* by the Reverend Andrew Mearns, a fairly sensational document, owed some of its influence to the publicity received in the *Pall Mall Gazette*. The newspaper had recently come under the editorship of W. T. Stead, one of the great figures among popular, reforming journalists. He later pointed to the pamphlet, as publicized by the *Pall Mall,* as a major factor in the appointment of the Royal Commission on the Housing of the Working Classes (1884–85) "from which modern social legislation may almost be said to date." [9]

2

It was inevitable that more intimate knowledge should produce dissatisfaction with the self-help-cum-private-charity formula. In Whitechapel, as we have seen, Samuel and Henrietta Barnett were discovering the inadequacy of private philanthropy and were becoming aware, in Beatrice Webb's words, of "a deeper and more continuous evil than unrestricted and unregulated charity, namely unrestricted and unregulated capitalism and landlordism." [10] As Warden of Toynbee Hall, Barnett invested time and energy in advocating a series of welfare measures, most conspicuously pensions for the aged—his "practical socialism"—to be financed and administered by the State. This same uneasiness, the growing suspicion of private philanthropy as a preventive of destitution, aroused in Charles Booth the thoroughly Victorian determination to get at the facts. For amid all the clashing counsels it was apparent to any detached observer that the statistical basis necessary for sound conclusions was utterly lacking. The well-disposed citizen had no basis for judging, say, between the sensational claims of *The Bitter Cry of Outcast London* and the vigorous rebuttal of the champions of self-help. From Booth's dissatisfaction emerged the most elaborate inquiry into British urban society yet undertaken and a magnificent addition to the social data of the late century. [11] To many, the seventeen volumes of *Life and Labour* seemed to demonstrate the failure of private charity in some areas of social well-being and the necessity for a less hesitant public policy.

Beatrice Webb, one of the more perceptive of Booth's assistants and his cousin by marriage, pictures him as "perhaps the most perfect embodiment of . . . the Victorian time-spirit—the union of faith in the scientific method with the transference of the emotion of self-sacrificing service from God to man." [12] Certainly Booth, a product of the distinguished Unitarian shipowning and manufacturing community in Liverpool, entered upon his grand inquiry (which incidentally he financed out of his own pocket) resolved to carry through a rigorously objective investigation. Later generations have developed more sophisticated techniques of inquiry and analysis; no investigator has undertaken his work in a more genuinely scientific spirit. And his conclusions, stated cautiously and unemotionally, carried conviction where more fervid claims would have aroused skepticism. Even to those who had little conception of the scope or methods of the inquiry, the terrifying figure of "thirty per cent" of Londoners living below the bare subsistence level seemed a shocking revelation—especially when it was presently confirmed

---

[9] Whyte, *W. T. Stead*, I, 105.
[10] B. Webb, *My Apprenticeship*, p. 207.
[11] For the immediate circumstances out of which the Booth inquiry grew, see T. S. and M. B. Simey, *Charles Booth, Social Scientist* (London, 1960), pp. 68–70.
[12] Webb, *My Apprenticeship*, p. 221.

by studies of other cities, among them Seebohm Rowntree's epoch-making survey of York.[13] On Booth's evidence, in short, about a million inhabitants of the Metropolis were dependent on a family income of 20s. a week or less.[14] In the face of such a statistic as this, however much it might be questioned and qualified, the burden of proof would henceforth lie with those who continued to find in private philanthropy a satisfying solution to the social problem.

Indeed, the most distinguished convert of the Booth survey was none other than the chief investigator himself. For his study transformed the Conservative individualist into a collectivist of sorts, who would remove from the struggle of competitive society the "very poor class," in London amounting to three hundred thousand, and would make them into virtual wards of the State. Was it not reasonable, he queried, "for the State to nurse the helpless and incompetent as we in our own families nurse the old, the young, and the sick, and provide for those who are not competent to provide for themselves?"[15] And he defended the proposal on the curious ground that, if this small and weak element were placed under the tutelage of the State, it would be possible to avoid "socialistic interference in the lives of all the rest."[16] This, in a word, was to be a homeopathic preventive of socialism and as such was a sound enough Tory prescription. But few Conservatives of the time would have contemplated social homeopathy on the scale recommended by Booth.

Plainly Booth's proposals went far beyond what the 1890's regarded as practical politics. Of more immediate inportance was his conviction, confirmed by the mounting evidence of his survey, that poverty was "essentially a trouble of old age" (though of course many were poor before they were old) and that the State must care for the aged on terms more generous than those laid down by the Poor Law.[17] Here, in fact, was the first major field of social welfare, save education, where numbers of Englishmen discovered that private charity was not enough and found themselves moving hesitantly toward a more positive public policy. The old age pension, in the Simeys' words, became "the symbol of the most urgent moral dilemma of the Victorian era; namely, the reconciliation of collective action designed to remedy social abuses, and promote the well-being of the individual, with the maintenance and encouragement of personal responsibility and initiative."[18]

From the late 1870's, Canon W. L. Blackley, probably entitled to be considered the father of the movement, had been preaching the gospel of old age pensions

---

[13] *Poverty, a Study of Town Life* (York, 1902). Booth's "thirty per cent" comprised "the poor," whose weekly wages varied from 18s. to 21s., and the "very poor," whose earnings fell below even that minimum.

[14] Webb, *My Apprenticeship*, p. 248.

[15] Quoted *ibid.*, p. 254.

[16] Quoted *ibid.*, and Simey, *Charles Booth*, p. 109.

[17] Booth, *Pauperism, a Picture; and the Endowment of Old Age, an Argument* (London, 1892), p. 148.

[18] *Charles Booth*, p. 5.

with incredible perseverance and an engaging Irish humor.[19] In the mid-80's his efforts, together with those of the National Providence League, brought about the appointment of a Select Committee — before which representatives of the large Friendly Societies registered their violent opposition to any universal, compulsory scheme. Although by the early '90's there were other proposals in the field, Booth's had certain special virtues. For one thing, it was extraordinarily simple, since it involved no complicated contributory features. What Booth was urging, in a word, was universal, state-provided pensions of 5s. a week beginning at the age of sixty-five, payments which, being universal, would carry none of the stigma of poor relief. The sum of £17 million, his estimate of initial cost, which admittedly would mount as the number of old persons in the population increased, he conceded to be "a terribly large" sum, though partly offset by something like a third of the £8½ million being spent on poor relief.[20] Yet was there any other answer? His investigations in the East End had persuaded him that neither abolishing outdoor relief nor more generous charity provision by the benevolent would meet the need.

Among the half-dozen plans, Booth's represented the maximum of state participation. Others managed to fill in the spectrum from the purely voluntary to the wholly public in financing. Politically the most prominent was the scheme associated with the name of Joseph Chamberlain, who in 1891, in the course of a spring by-election, made an eloquent appeal for the aged. The Unionist leader had not missed the significance of the Bismarckian social program, and almost from the beginning he had been convinced that British parties — Liberal or Conservative — must turn a more sympathetic ear to working-class demands. During the summer and autumn of 1891, with an unofficial committee of members of both Houses, he drafted a plan which, shorn of detail, was calculated to encourage voluntary provision for old age by granting state aid to those who through saving had taken steps to provide for themselves.[21] For the first time a political figure of national stature had ventured to take up the cause of the aged and to offer them something more than exhortations to frugality.

The agitation worked up enough steam to justify the appointment of a Royal Commission. This body, which sat through 1893 and 1894 under the chairmanship of Lord Aberdare, included among its members the customary variety in points

[19] Canon Blackley had first come out with a plan in an article, "National Insurance: A Cheap, Practical, and Popular Means of Abolishing Poor Rates," in *Nineteenth Century*, 4:834–57 (November 1878). An extract is given by Michael Goodwin, *Nineteenth Century Opinion* (London, 1951), pp. 76–78. Shortly after Blackley's article appeared, R. B. Hookham issued a pamphlet, *Outlines of a Scheme for Dealing with Pauperism* (London, 1879). This dealt largely with agricultural laborers, who, the writer argued, could not possibly provide for old age. He urged a universal plan of state pensions. On the movement for old age pensions see Williams, *The State and the Standard of Living*, chap. II, and for the early stages see Ronald V. Sires, "The Beginnings of British Legislation for Old-Age Pensions," *J. Econ. Hist.*, 14:228–53 (1954).

[20] Booth, *Pauperism . . . and . . . Old Age*, pp. 200, 205. Booth first unveiled his plan before the Royal Statistical Society in November 1891. The paper, "Enumeration and Classification of Paupers, and State Pensions for the Aged," appeared in the *Royal Statistical Society*, 54:600-43 (1891).

[21] J. L. Garvin, *The Life of Joseph Chamberlain* (London, 1932–34), II, 508–14.

of view. Booth and Chamberlain represented the interventionists, while C. S. Loch stoutly defended the traditional Victorian verities, and Henry Broadhurst and Joseph Arch spoke for the working classes. Although no decision of consequence emerged from its deliberations, the Report of the Aberdare Commission remains an important document for the student of philanthropy. Here for almost the first time in the century the two philosophies of welfare (if one can use the term) confronted each other on an approximately equal basis. Should the country continue to rely on the tried methods of the Poor Law supplemented by private benevolence or, by introducing what Loch rather ungenerously called "outdoor relief in a new guise," go down the road toward mass dependence and wholesale pauperization?[22] Or to put the issue in language acceptable to the other side, why should not Englishmen rid themselves of the old inhibiting dogmas and look realistically at the problem of the aged poor?

A question which naturally engaged the attention of the Commission had to do with the degree of assistance to be expected from endowed and voluntary charities. In the mid-'90's, according to the estimate of Sir Henry Longley, Chief Charity Commissioner, almshouses and pension trusts might account for a total income of about £660,000.[23] But these endowments were unevenly distributed, so that the aged poor of one city might receive fairly handsome, if not luxurious, treatment, while in another place little would be done for them. Not only that, but charities for the aged often carried fancy trust restrictions, religious and otherwise, like the Bristol almshouse "for five old bachelors and five old maidens 'who are not inclined to Roman Catholicism.'"[24] As always, the Charity Commissioners looked wistfully at the mass of dole charities, something like £400,000 annually for the "general uses of the poor," much of it applied in ways thought to be futile, if not actively pernicious. Were they by some miracle to be given a free hand, Longley conceded, they might liquidate two-thirds of these trusts, but this, he was aware, was sheer fantasy.[25] It required, in short, a sanguine nature to see in the nation's almshouse and pension charities—unevenly distributed, as they were, and infinitely varied in their legal and administrative arrangements — a promising basis for a welfare policy for the aged. Merely to compare the cities of Norwich and Coventry, both exceedingly well endowed, is to underline the difficulties. The former, with some £10,000 a year for almspeople, was almost lacking in pension funds, while Coventry, with about £9500 for pensioners and only about £1000 for almspeople, represented the opposite condition.[26]

Throughout the course of the Aberdare Commission, Loch and the tradition-

[22] Barnett, *Canon Barnett*, II, 267.

[23] Sir Henry Longley, *R. C. on the Aged Poor*, 1895, Q. 7559.

[24] Mary Clifford, *ibid.*, Q. 6418.

[25] *Ibid.*, Q. 7553, 7557, 7662.

[26] The figures were, for Norwich, about £10,000 for almspeople, £480 for pensioners, and £5500 for doles, and for Coventry about £9500 for pensioners, £1000 for almspeople, and £2600 for doles. These statistics were compiled for the Royal Commission on the Poor Laws, 1905–1909, and appear in App. XV of the *Report*, pp. 9, 20.

alists sought to show that a more rigorous Poor Law administration, together with pensions provided from endowments and donations, would do all that was necessary. Something was made of the three East End Unions (Stepney, Whitechapel, and St. George's-in-the-East) which had drastically reduced outdoor relief, while the slack was taken up by charitable organizations. To the progressives this was a dubious advance. When the clerk of the Whitechapel Guardians boasted that cutting down on outdoor relief had stimulated private charity, they declined to hail it as an occasion for rejoicing.[27] And Canon Blackley, whose plan was to be launched with a fund supplied jointly by the State and private charity, rejected Loch's suggestion that the latter might provide the entire amount. Not merely was this impracticable but, in his view, it was inequitable to exempt from their obligations "the vast number who never give a farthing."[28] Yet to point to the unfairness of saddling the charitable with a burden that belonged properly to the whole body of rate-payers was to attack a theorem taken as axiomatic by British philanthropic leaders from Thomas Chalmers to Charles Loch. That the giving and accepting of charity (under proper conditions) should be considered an ennobling transaction while state aid was inevitably pauperizing stands in retrospect as one of the more curious articles of Victorian belief.

A number of witnesses, of whom Octavia Hill was the best known, held high the banner of individualism. To Booth, indeed, one of the more painful features of the inquiry was the way in which it appeared to align him against his friends Loch and Octavia Hill. It is difficult to see how their friendship could have survived Miss Hill's appearance before the Commission (though his wife assures us that it remained unaffected),[29] for she was at her most offensively doctrinaire, bristling with moral superiority and censoriousness, more than ever the self-appointed school mistress of the lower classes. She and her C.O.S. associates alone held the key to the problems of the poor, young and old, and she could dismiss Booth's plan as "the most gigantic scheme of inadequate relief ever devised by a human being."[30] During her appearance before the Commission Octavia Hill showed little of the persuasive enthusiasm and charm that she unquestionably possessed, and if one's judgment were to be based solely on this evidence, her immense prestige in matters concerning the poor would be quite inexplicable.

If the official school of charity *expertise* would have no commerce with Booth's plan, at least qualified praise came from unexpected quarters. Alfred Marshall thought it immensely preferable to things as they were. Unfortunately, as he saw it, no mechanism had been provided for liquidating the scheme as poverty itself disappeared, an objection that would have occurred only to the most buoyant of social optimists. To Marshall, with his sturdy Victorian faith in human improvement, poverty was "a mere passing evil in the progress of man upwards." In

---

[27] William Vallance, *R. C. on the Aged Poor,* 1895, Q. 2538.
[28] Canon W. L. Blackley, *ibid.,* Q. 12,945, 12,947.
[29] Mary Booth, *Charles Booth: A Memoir* (London, 1918), p. 149.
[30] Q. 10,466.

other respects, however, the great economist's grasp of social reality was solid enough, as when he reminded the Commission that "while the problem of 1834 was pauperism, the problem of 1893 is the problem of poverty . . . extreme poverty ought to be regarded, not indeed as a crime, but as a thing so detrimental to the State that it should not be endured." [31] These were dangerous sentiments, even though Marshall conceded them to be only a counsel of future perfection.

To give even a skeletal account of the movement for state pensions would be irrelevant to the present purpose. Our concern is with the retreat of private philanthropy from certain areas, with the increasingly apparent inadequacies of private charity as a corrective for the more deep-seated ills of industrial and urban society, rather than with the development of a public welfare policy. It is enough to recall that, though the Aberdare Commission produced few specific results, it was not without influence. In writing the report the individualist majority was under heavy pressure, and five members, led by Chamberlain and Booth, presented a strong minority report. Henry Broadhurst, for his part, added a special report (written by Sidney Webb) calling for noncontributory pensions. From this time on, it became a practical possibility that the State might move with greater decision into a field that had hitherto belonged exclusively to self-help, private philanthropy, and the Poor Law.

Two other official bodies — a Departmental Committee under the chairmanship of Lord Rothschild (1896) and Henry Chaplin's Select Committee (1899) — worked over the familiar ground once more.[32] Neither marked a decisive step forward, though the Chaplin Committee did propose a scheme of pensions for the "deserving poor" to be administered by the local Poor Law authorities. But at least the lightning appeared to be coming closer, close enough to alarm the Charity Organisation Society. Partly to counter Charles Booth's National Committee on Old Age Pensions, the C.O.S., as we noticed earlier,[33] formed its own Committee on [against] Old Age Pensions. Against the sinister proposal the Society invoked the authority of Dr. Chalmers himself: "A systematic provision for old age in any land is tantamount to a systematic hostility against its virtues, both of prudence and of natural piety." [34] What was called for was not state pensions, with the inducement to mass pauperism that they held out, but careful individual treatment — meaning, of course, application of C.O.S. methods.

The Liberal sweep in the General Election of 1906 brought the likelihood of favorable action measurably closer, and in the course of the next year it became evident that resistance in the House had greatly diminished. No one would suggest that the Liberal Government's measure, the far from revolutionary Act of

[31] Q. 10,356, 10,358.
[32] *Report of the Committee on Old Age Pensions* (C. 8911), 1898; *S. C. on the Aged Deserving Poor*, 1899. For the Chaplin Committee the historian Lecky offered as a draft report a document that would have brought a blush to the cheek of the Herbert Spencer of *Man versus the State*. It was rejected by the unanimous vote of the rest of the Committee.
[33] In Chapter VIII.
[34] N. Masterman, ed., *Chalmers on Charity*, p. 83.

1908, solved the problems of superannuation, but at least it established the principle of noncontributory assistance apart from relief through the Poor Law mechanism. On the one hand, of course, the new departure owed something to the tradition established by generations of charitable individuals, the founders of almshouses and pension funds; and another philanthropist, Charles Booth, was an active force in the campaign that led to the Act. But it also stood as an admission that old age, as a problem in the modern world, lay beyond the reach of private endowments and formed, in a sense, a legitimate charge on society itself. Even if the income of almshouse and pension charities reached a total of £1 million, this looked fairly insignificant against the £10 million plus estimated as the initial cost of the system proposed in 1899 by the Chaplin Committee.[35] Here plainly was a task of social engineering which required the larger capital and the more comprehensive machinery of the State itself, though even so the new structure would build on the foundation laid by private philanthropists and would draw freely on their goodwill and experience.

3

If voluntary philanthropy could offer no comprehensive protection against the hazards of old age, its shortcomings were even more apparent with respect to unemployment. Impotent old age, after all, was a far more familiar and definable problem than was inability of large numbers of men to find regular places in the complex world of modern industry. To the Victorians, to be out of work either implied spinelessness or incompetence on the part of the individual, or it marked him as the victim of abnormally depressed conditions of trade. They were painfully familiar with the mass unemployment that came with "bad times," but they thought of it as exceptional and fortuitous. In such emergencies the obvious step was to provide outdoor relief more generously or, if the situation became critical, to take more drastic measures, presumably raising a special relief fund. Of the irregularity of employment and the chronic underemployment, which by some heretics was held to be "the characteristic disease" of modern capitalism, the Victorians had little understanding. And insofar as they recognized the existence of unemployment, they viewed it fatalistically, as simple a part of the nature of things.[36]

It is generally assumed to have been the bad years of the 1880's and '90's that forced unemployment upon the late Victorian consciousness. Perhaps more significant than the numbers actually out of work was the growing acceptance of the notion that unemployment on such a scale was an unhealthy condition and that it merited study and investigation.[37] True, the public authorities had always acknowledged a form of obligation toward those who were unable to earn a

---

[35] Sir Arnold Wilson and G. S. Mackay, *Old Age Pensions* (Oxford, 1941), p. 36. The estimate is based on the 1901 Census.

[36] Webb, *English Poor Law History: The Last Hundred Years,* pp. 631ff.

[37] Lynd, *England in the Eighteen-Eighties,* p. 56.

living, but claims to assistance from the rates derived not from the fact of unemployment but of destitution. To the Poor Law, the jobless were simply able-
bodied paupers and were entitled to relief on the same terms as any other member
of that class. During the latter half of the century these terms varied enormously
from decade to decade and place to place. Few generalizations can be offered,
save that little distinction was made (except perhaps in time of extraordinary
distress) between the genuine out-of-work and the able-bodied pauper.[38]

It was the bad years of the mid-'80's that started the British State hesitantly and
almost involuntarily along the road that would lead to a new and comprehensive
policy. Joseph Chamberlain, the first British statesman to think of unemployment
as a special problem, was the active agent. As President of the Local Government
Board, Chamberlain found shocking the plight of large numbers of ordinarily
industrious workmen who, though out of work and in desperate straits, had not
applied for parish assistance. In his famous circular of 1886 he distinguished
sharply between the classes of the needy — on the one hand, the vagrants and
perennial paupers who might properly be left to the mercies of the Poor Law and,
on the other, the legitimately unemployed, who "chose to make great personal
sacrifices rather than incur the stigma of pauperism." [39] What the circular did, in
a word, was to authorize local authorities to provide work for the unemployed outside of and apart from what was offered under the Poor Law. Unfortunately
Chamberlain remained in the Government only three months, and he had no
opportunity to develop the policy that he had announced. The consequence was
that, although works for the unemployed became a familiar feature of the
municipal landscape, such experiments added little to the theory or practice of
unemployment relief.[40] Yet whatever their shortcomings, at least they helped to
encourage the belief that the unemployed were wholly different from paupers and
that the former must be dealt with in such a way as to prevent their turning into
the latter.

Though its intentions were unexceptionable, in the nature of the case private
philanthropy could make relatively little contribution to a realistic handling of unemployment. Indeed, as soon as the terms of the problem were more accurately
defined, it was seen to lie well beyond the scope of voluntary agencies. Possibly the
biggest single contribution of philanthropists was that made by such investigators
as Booth and Rowntree, whose wealth of fresh data added what was almost a new
dimension to discussions of the evil. Apart from such studies, philanthropic effort
was brought to bear on the problem through three principal channels: in the
special relief funds that were enthusiastically raised in seasons of exceptional
distress; in the founding, under private charitable auspices, of a few labor colonies,
none of which promised much as an answer to the larger question; and in the

[38] Sir William Beveridge, *Unemployment* (London, 1930 ed.), pp. 150–54, gives an account of the
various forms of relief.
[39] Webb, *English Poor Law History*, pp. 645–47.
[40] See Beveridge, *Unemployment*, p. 155, for a description of these activities, and Williams, *The
State and the Standard of Living*, pp. 190–93.

activities of the Charity Organization Society and those who shared its views. Although the Society did useful work with unemployed individuals and families, C.O.S. leaders tended, as we have seen, to minimize the distress and to urge that the thriftless and idle among the unemployed be handled through the Poor Law machinery in a thoroughly deterrent fashion. The steady and respectable, meanwhile, would rely on voluntary charity without recourse to public relief works or public funds.[41]

The most characteristic instrument of private philanthropy for the relief of the unemployed was, of course, the special funds raised at times of unusual distress. The latter half of the century was marked by a succession of such efforts, the two best known, perhaps, being the relief funds collected during the Lancashire cotton famine and the Mansion House Fund of the mid-'80's. The cotton fund is not entirely typical, for the crisis was thought of as a national disaster rather than as unemployment resulting from the normal vicissitudes of trade or even from "bad years." Still, private charity bore the main burden. The Poor Law system broke down completely, and, although the Government empowered local authorities to borrow from the Public Works Loan Commissioners for constructing public works, there was little support for a more extensive plan of national assistance.[42]

To the challenge of the emergency Lancashire responded magnificently. The most impressive achievement was the series of funds totaling over £1,275,000 (of which over £1 million was collected in Britain) which became the chief resource for alleviating the disaster. To set up, under emergency conditions, a reasonably efficient system for disbursing a fund of such proportions was a staggering assignment; merely to see that relief reached the genuine victims of the national calamity and not habitual paupers or impostors taxed the discretion of the administrators. Yet on the whole both central and local committees seem to have done their work soundly, though hardly meriting the accolade of the chief engineer of the Local Government Board, who praised the "admirable and perfect system of relief administered so liberally yet so wisely." [43]

This was only one — and one of the better managed — of the funds raised to prevent the starvation of workmen during periods of sharp unemployment. Throughout much of the century, indeed, Victorian England relied on such emergency collections to offset the consequences of unemployment. It was almost routine in the larger industrial cities, the Royal Commission on the Poor Laws was told, "to ask the Mayor to open a Fund whenever there was an outcry as to unemployment. He issued an appeal in the Press or by letter, the response to which in the form of donations was of course very uncertain, varying with his personal popularity, as well as with the general opinion of the wealthier classes

---

[41] *37th Ann. Rept.*, 1904–1905.
[42] W. O. Henderson, *The Lancashire Cotton Famine, 1861–1865* (Manchester, 1934), p. 68. This paragraph is based largely on Henderson's chap. IV.
[43] Quoted *ibid.*, p. 92.

as to the existence of exceptional distress."[44] The same technique was followed in the case of severe winters or other natural disasters. London saw a succession of "Mansion House Funds," and during the depressed years of the '80's most of the larger centers broke into a rash of emergency collections. The three metropolitan funds, collected between 1860 and 1886 and totaling about £135,000, all went for direct temporary relief, with little attempt to distinguish the bona fide unemployed from the chronic loafers.[45]

The most notable, or notorious, of these funds was the nearly £80,000 raised to meet the crisis of 1885–86. At the outset the committee established an admirably cautious set of rules for relief, with ample checks against abuse by chronic mendicants and other impostors. But unhappily one member on his own responsibility issued thousands of handbills announcing the fund. As always with such misleading publicity, committees were swamped by applications, some of which had nothing to do with unemployment — appeals for the Thimble League Society, the Universal Beneficent Society, and the diffusion of vegetarianism.[46] The proclaimed purpose of the fund, "for the temporary assistance of the unemployed poor" turned out to be a phrase of incredible elasticity. Among the members of the central committee there were few illusions about the achievement, even though, in fact, their administration marked something of an improvement over previous operations of the kind.[47] The final report deplored such funds, save in the gravest of emergencies, and held that chronic or semichronic distress was the responsibility of the Poor Law machinery. Despite the fact that it did rescue a good many worthy and desperate cases, few would have chosen to repeat the 1885–86 Mansion House Fund experience. Its principal lessons for the future, the C.O.S. committee was entitled to urge, were of a cautionary sort.

Subsequent Mansion House ventures took a drastically different direction. The first of these, carried on in 1892–93, was of narrow scope and was designed to deal with a small and reasonably identifiable group, the labor surplus of dockland. With a fund raised by the Lord Mayor, a committee (composed of trade unionists, C.O.S. representatives, and others) established a temporary work project on forty acres of waste land near the Abbey Mills pumping station. A probationary period at Abbey Mills would presumably fit the individual for a new occupation at home or abroad. Whatever its modest successes, the project is of no more than limited interest. Only about 225 men were actually employed, of whom about a hundred were permanently established, with or without the assistance of the committee.[48] The final Mansion House Fund, the £4000 raised in 1903–1904, even more ob-

[44] Jackson and Pringle, "Report on the Effects of Employment . . . Given to the Unemployed," R. C. on the Poor Laws (Cd. 4795), 1909, App. XIX, quoted in Webb, English Poor Law History, p. 640.
[45] Report of the C.O.S. Committee on the Relief of Exceptional Distress, 1886.
[46] Report of the Mansion House Relief Fund, 1886, p. 18.
[47] Beveridge, Unemployment, p. 158.
[48] Board of Trade, Report on the Agencies and Methods for Dealing with the Unemployed (C. 7182), 1893, pp. 238–61.

viously forms a chapter in the history of labor colony experiments rather than of special relief collections and as such can be reserved until some of the earlier projects have been noticed.

To most intelligent Englishmen in the 1890's the idea of a labor colony for the unemployed was identified with the social program of the Salvation Army.[49] In the perspective of the 1960's the violent emotions aroused by General William Booth's schemes seem exaggerated, to say the least. Yet his *Darkest England,* aided by publicity from W. T. Stead and others, had a sensational sale and aroused enormous interest. To one group his farm, city, and overseas colonies seemed promising; to the other, pernicious and delusive. Clearly the plan justified neither extravagant enthusiasm nor alarm, and the furor would have been inexplicable save in the hypersensitive social atmosphere of the time. A few months after the appearance of *Darkest England* nearly £130,000 had poured in to finance the plan. It was a development that scandalized those who, like T. H. Huxley, regarded the project itself as "mere autocratic Socialism, masked by its theological exterior" and the leaders of the C.O.S. who saw in it everything they considered most iniquitous among social remedies.[50] Booth lost no time in getting his scheme under way. In the year 1892 nearly eleven thousand persons registered in the Army's London labour exchanges. Of these, 6650 were provided with work, mostly of a temporary sort. Of more general interest was the farm colony established in 1891 at Hadleigh, Essex, on an estate of over fifteen hundred acres. During the first two years about a thousand colonists passed through the farm, the majority remaining something under a year.[51]

Such farm colonies turned out to have an importance not contemplated by their projectors, for they formed one of the avenues by which the State, indirectly and hesitantly, moved toward an unemployment policy. The Mansion House Fund raised in 1903–1904 had been intended by its sponsors — the Bishop of Stepney, Canon Barnett, and others — to finance the families of men who elected to work on a farm colony. It was a short-lived experiment, lasting only three or four months. The main result, Beveridge suggests, was to reveal the immensity of the problem — and, one may add, to underline the growing suspicion that the solution lay beyond the powers of private agencies, however earnest.[52] But the Government showed no great eagerness to take over. The first expedient, Walter Long's Unemployment Fund scheme of 1904–1905, virtually vested responsibility for the metropolitan unemployed in committees drawn from borough councils, Poor Law Guardians, and social workers, whose activities were to be supported

---

[49] By 1893 the Labour Homes of the Church Army, first established in 1889, numbered sixteen. They assisted several hundred individuals but added nothing to an understanding of the disease or its treatment. (*Ibid.,* pp. 173–78).

[50] Huxley, *Social Diseases and Worse Remedies* (London, 1891), p. 7; see also Loch, Bosanquet, and Dwyer, *Criticisms on "General" Booth's Social Scheme.*

[51] Board of Trade, *Report on . . . the Unemployed,* 1893, pp. 167–72.

[52] *Unemployment,* p. 160.

largely by voluntary contributions. Most of the thirty-five hundred men recommended by the committees for relief were employed on the grounds of London parks or other public projects or they were rusticated to one of the farm colonies. At this stage even the Government viewed farm colonies with sufficient hope to authorize an investigation by Rider Haggard of those run by the Salvation Army in North America and at Hadleigh.[53]

Among the farm communities for the unemployed one of the more interesting was the colony at Hollesley, the gift of the American philanthropist and soap manufacturer Joseph Fels, who had already befriended the Barnetts at Toynbee Hall. Along with numbers of his contemporaries who were shocked as they came to appreciate the realities of urban working-class life, Fels found a possible solution in restoring city dwellers to an agrarian way of life, a kind of hopeful, even desperate dream, Halévy implies, of recapturing the imagined stability of Merrie England.[54] He had already bought a hundred acres at Laindon, which he leased to the Poplar Board of Guardians for three years at a rent of one peppercorn. And when the London Unemployed Fund was created, he offered to lend, rent-free for three years, an estate of some thirteen-hundred acres at Hollesley Bay, Suffolk, for which he proposed to pay more than £30,000.[55] Fels's offer was readily accepted by the Fund, and the experiment was quietly launched.

Thus far the Government had hardly done more than dip a tentative toe in the pool of unemployment. The next step, though it amounted to little more than making official Long's Unemployment Fund plan of 1904-1905 and extending it throughout the country, in fact meant a heavier involvement for the State. What the Unemployed Workmen Act of 1905 did, in a word, was to require the establishment in every municipal borough and urban district of fifty thousand inhabitants of a Distress Committee similar to those already functioning in the Metropolis. In their financial arrangements, as in their membership, they represented an odd amalgam of public and private effort. Some expenses could be defrayed from the rates, but for providing work, committees at the outset could rely only on voluntary contributions.

Only in a limited sense does the Unemployed Workmen Act fall within the scope of this survey. In his classic study, *Unemployment,* Beveridge explains its rationale and weighs its record.[56] The Act, he observes, suffered from its own timidity, attempting little that was new. On the administrative side, it represented an unstable partnership of Poor Law Guardians, municipal authorities, and voluntary agencies, and the philosophy of relief on which it operated was, to put it bluntly, the same old thing — municipal relief works, a bit of deterrence drawn from Poor Law practice, and an attempt to guide the flow of charity more produc-

[53] H. Rider Haggard, *Report on the Salvation Army Colonies* (Cd. 2562), 1905.
[54] *A History of the English People, 1895-1905* (London, 1926), p. 368.
[55] Mary Fels, *The Life of Joseph Fels* (New York, 1940), pp. 60-63.
[56] Pages 162ff.

tively. The notion that a semipublic system of this kind should have relied for its support on the donations of the benevolent seems fantastic, and, in fact, this inconsistency presently disappeared.

Queen Alexandra's appeal in November 1905 brought contributions of over £150,000, of which £125,000 went to the various Distress Committees. This was a splendid display of national concern, but no one believed that it could be repeated annually. In the following year Parliament stepped in with an Exchequer grant of £200,000, which was renewed in 1907 and 1908. In the course of these years, therefore, the financial basis of the scheme was radically altered. Philanthropy withdrew as the State moved in, and the plan became, to all intents and purposes, a publicly financed affair. As for the Hollesley Bay Colony, this also became a public institution when the Fund purchased it from Fels.[57] Indeed, as it worked out in practice, the Unemployed Workmen Act came to look less and less like a joint attack by statutory authorities and voluntary agencies and increasingly took on the aspect of an effort, halting and confused, on the part of the State to grapple with the problem of joblessness.

In the late century, as we have seen, one of the more persuasive voices influencing public attitudes on social policy was that of the Charity Organisation Society. In its implacable hostility to measures which appeared to shift responsibility from the individual to the community, it spoke for a recognizable, though steadily diminishing, body of opinion. Since the C.O.S. position on unemployment has already been sketched,[58] it is necessary only to recall some of the main emphases. Given its basic outlook, the Society could hardly regard unemployment as a critical issue, and, insofar as the problem was admitted, there must be a sharp distinction between "ordinary" unemployment and "exceptional distress." With the former the C.O.S. had no concern, for it was an article of faith that, in the large, there was sufficient work for everyone. If a man found himself unemployed in normal times, it would strengthen his moral fiber to hunt for another job. To the Society it was comforting to believe that "only by his thrift can he meet the irregularities of trade and the regular periods of winter slackness." [59]

What was regarded as "exceptional distress" naturally required different treatment, but even here, however widespread the trouble, relief should be administered with discrimination and understanding of the individual case. The main tenor of C.O.S. thinking about unemployment, to repeat, was to minimize it or ascribe it to factors other than economic. "Almost all of these men and women are weak," Loch told the Mansion House Committee. "If anybody could care for them two years, with a definite object all the time, something might be done for them. You [would then] know what is wrong with them . . . the circumstances of their character and weakness." [60] Before the Royal Commission on Labour in 1893, he suggested that the volume of unemployment had been exaggerated and

[57] Fels, *Joseph Fels*, p. 63.
[58] In Chapter VIII.
[59] *19th Ann. Rept.*, 1887, p. 33.
[60] 8 June 1885. Manuscript notes in the library of the Family Welfare Association.

that greater foresight would have enabled many applicants for relief to weather the storm on their own savings.[61] The difficulty, insisted the C.O.S. committee of 1904, "is only partly industrial and economic. In great part it is a problem of social competence and moral responsibility." [62]

4

The Majority Report of the Royal Commission on the Poor Laws (1905–1909) marked a kind of Indian summer in the prestige of the Charity Organisation Society. Although its traditionally ruthless individualism appeared in a somewhat modified form, one can fairly regard the Report as an exposition of C.O.S. views —perhaps more accurately as a fusion of the Society's ideas with those of the Poor Law officials and administrators on the Commission. The relevance of the inquiry to the theme of this study is, of course, only peripheral. But both Majority and Minority paid some attention, a good deal in the case of the former, to the place to be assigned to charity in the welfare structure for which each was drafting blueprints. The Majority Report, apparently at the instance of Loch, included a long section on "Charities and the Relief of Distress," and the Commission went to some effort to obtain statistical material on the resources of British charities, endowed and voluntary. Two of the Commission's investigators, after studying sixteen communities, returned with anything but a reassuring picture of the achievements of private philanthropies for the poor.[63] Yet the income of these was still formidable and, if efficiently managed, could be of immense benefit to the British community. But what place were such charities to occupy vis-à-vis the various statutory authorities? On this point Majority and Minority found themselves in sharp disagreement.

It has never been entirely clear why an expiring Tory Government chose to initiate a large-scale inquiry into the Poor Law and related issues. Apparently the decisive pressure came from a new and vigorous head of the Poor Law Division, who hoped that a Commission might rationalize the administrative framework and might recommend a return to the solid "Principles of 1834" — that is, re-establish deterrent tests as a condition of relief. Gerald Balfour, President of the Local Government Board, was also thought to favor an inquiry, recognizing as a philosopher "the public advantage of a precise discrimination between opposing principles." [64] He could hardly have imagined how sharply opposed they would turn out to be.

The Commission, whose chairman was Lord George Hamilton, included a half-dozen C.O.S. members, among them Loch, Octavia Hill, and Mrs. Bernard Bosanquet; nine Poor Law administrators, assorted clergymen, and academic

[61] R. C. on Labour (C. 7063–1), 1893–94, Q. 5809.

[62] The Relief of Distress due to Want of Employment, 1904, pp. 48–49.

[63] Kay & Toynbee, "Report on . . . Endowed and Voluntary Charities," R. C. on the Poor Laws (Cd. 4593), 1909, App. XV.

[64] B. Webb, Our Partnership (London, 1948), p. 317; A. M. McBriar, Fabian Socialism and English Politics, 1884–1914 (Cambridge, 1963), p. 263.

men; and three representatives of the labor and socialist movements — George Lansbury, Francis Chandler, and Beatrice Webb, the most purposeful and resourceful of the group, working as always in the closest harmony with the Other One. Through the confused and often frustrating activities of the four years, the partnership operated with telling effect, with Sidney as a relatively silent partner. Though the Minority Report was a joint production, it was actually penned by him.[65]

The quarrel between the signers of the two Reports lay less in the realm of immediate measures than of ultimate objectives. No doubt the tactics of Mrs. Webb, whom the Commission must have found to be a fairly indigestible morsel, made the differences seem even more irreconcilable than they were. Throughout it all the clash of principles was hardly less important than the conflict of personalities. The C.O.S., notes one critic, could be infuriatingly smug, lacking in imagination and humility, while Beatrice Webb, the only member who knew precisely where she wished to go, felt superior to her colleagues and behaved with that "higher kind of unscrupulousness which belong to nearly every effective, driving personality," alternately wheedling and browbeating, making of herself, as she conceded, "something of a handful." [66] When she concluded that the Majority would not accept her views and determined to write her own Report, she gave little further time to the Commission itself. Conceivably, though lacking the architectural coherence of Mrs. Webb's plan, the Majority Report offered a program better adapted to the immediate situation. The failure of the two sides to reach any mutual understanding, Miss Cormack argues, destroyed the possibility of building a comprehensive, reasonably well-articulated system of social services.[67]

This is probably to take too sanguine a view of the rather eclectic proposals of the Majority. Beatrice Webb's essay sketched, more or less consciously, a welfare policy for a Fabian state, while the Majority, a rather variegated group, offered a series of expedients thought to be practicable. Still, the surprising thing was the relatively large measure of agreement on immediate reforms, especially structural reforms. Under pressure of the facts unearthed by the Commission's investigators, the C.O.S. representatives moved a long way. By the time the Report was written, they had lost any hankering for a return to the "Principles of 1834," and instead recommended a substantial extension of the social services, under or outside of the Poor Law, for the sick, the aged, children, unemployed, and mental defectives.[68] The Majority Report, in fact, went farther than Beatrice Webb expected or wished, and she found its initial favorable reception, as against that of her own, astonishing and more than a little unnerving.

Yet there was, as she insists, a fairly sharp difference between the philosophies

[65] Margaret Cole, *Beatrice Webb* (New York, 1946), p. 109.
[66] Una Cormack, *The Welfare State: The Royal Commission on the Poor Laws and the Welfare State Our Partnership*, p. 358.
[67] Cormack, *The Welfare State*, pp. 21, 32–33.
[68] For a summary of the points of agreement, see Webb, *Poor Law History*, pp. 528ff.

of welfare that informed the two reports. She invokes the authority of one of the opposition, Professor Bosanquet, who, agreeing that "the antagonism cannot be put too strongly," saw as the basis of the Majority Report the familiar C.O.S. premise of personal inadequacy as the cause of destitution. The necessitous (the term preferred by the Majority), thus seen as a distinctive social category, required treatment different from that offered to people who were "maintaining themselves in the normal course of life." [69] It may perhaps have been this assumption that led the Majority, while scrapping the old form of Poor Law, to retain the principle of a general relief authority (with local public assistance committees) rather than introducing the specialized agencies dealing with, say, medical care, old age, or education as favored by the Minority.

Though the Majority proposal was not without merit — certain categories of personal and family problems, it is now accepted, can be most effectively handled by an undifferentiated agency[70] — to Mrs. Webb it simply meant perpetuating the old evils behind a new façade. Her formula called for the more vigorous development of the "Framework of Prevention" that had been built up since 1834 — the public health services, municipal hospitals, medical care of children in elementary schools, and the rest. The growth of such activities had led to confusion and large scale overlapping between the newer bodies and the old Poor Law authorities. Nothing would serve, the Minority Report argued, but to break up the Poor Law altogether and assign its former duties to education committees, health committees, and pension committees under the County Councils, and to create for the jobless a national unemployment authority. The burden of Beatrice Webb's hostility to the Majority Report was her conviction that "only by redistribution of the services can you obtain curative and restorative treatment." [71]

For her the take-off point was "an attack on" or "a consideration of" not pauperism — that was only a symptom — but destitution. The underlying principle of the Minority Report, though not specifically mentioned, was clearly the ideal of a national minimum. To Mrs. Webb the essential issue had to do not so much with rehabilitating a pauper class as with assuring adequate treatment for "every case in which, from whatever cause, any person fell below the prescribed National Minimum of Civilised Life." [72] This notion of a national minimum meant, of course, that the Minority would assign to voluntary effort a radically different place from that marked off by the Majority. It was only in some of their subsequent writings, however, that the Webbs developed their ideas on the point.[73]

In the Poor Law Report, the plan offered by the Majority was more explicit and elaborate. Its thesis, in essentials, was what the Webbs have called the "parallel bars" theory. According to this formula, as embodied in the Poor Law Minute of 1869 and accepted by the C.O.S. as a basic policy, the Poor Law and private

[69] *Sociological Review*, II, no. 2 (April 1909), quoted *ibid.*, p. 545.
[70] Cormack, *The Welfare State*, pp. 23–24.
[71] *Our Partnership*, p. 426.
[72] The Webbs, *English Poor Law History*, pp. 545–46.
[73] See especially *The Prevention of Destitution* (London, 1911), chap. VIII.

charitable agencies had their distinctive spheres, and each would labor in its own bailiwick without encroaching on the other's. Yet by the time of the Commission's inquiry there was good reason to doubt whether the "parallel bars" theory had proved an adequate formula. Not only had the distinction between "deserving" and "undeserving" turned out to be far less obvious than had been assumed, but private charity had proved unable to care even for those who were admittedly "deserving."

The solution of the Majority, however, was a new and more elaborate version of the "parallel bars" arrangement. Some of the old distinction should be retained between the "more deserving" (to be relieved by voluntary agencies) and the "less deserving" (to be handled by the Poor Law authority). Fundamental to this procedure was the principle that the lot of the latter class would be "in some way less agreeable" [74] than the former. To this end the plan called for two coordinate authorities within each public assistance area:[75] on the one hand, a public assistance committee, a statutory body financed by public funds, and, on the other, a voluntary aid committee, composed of charity trustees, clergymen, social workers, and others. Behind it all lay a genuine belief that, in the large, charity could act more constructively than could the State — partly because the State was thought of largely in terms of Poor Law agencies.

In some quarters this recommendation of the Majority was hailed as a new triumph of the voluntary principle in social welfare and as a fruitful fusion of private and public effort. Others could attack it as an attempt to smuggle in by the back door the old deterrent doctrine of "less eligibility" and as a piece of empire-building on the part of the C.O.S. To create a series of voluntary aid committees precisely coordinate with the public assistance committees was to institutionalize the "parallel bars" theory in a way that would have astonished Goschen himself. Not only that, but the Majority foresaw the time when voluntary aid committees might screen "the great majority of cases before they reached Public Assistance." [76] In a word, these charitable agencies not only were to be made responsible for dealing with large categories of the "necessitous poor" but would determine through what channels the individual could be most appropriately relieved.

To the "parallel bars" theory the Webbs opposed their own notion of the "extension ladder." This they implied rather than developed in the Minority Report but expounded at some length two years later in the *Prevention of Destitution*. In the Report itself, it was alleged, they had left little scope for volunteers. This criticism they sharply rejected. As the Dean of Norwich (Beatrice's only convert on the Commission) put the point, "What we want is the volunteer as *aiding and supplementing* the Public authority; never as a substitute or alterna-

---

[74] *R. C. on the Poor Laws* (Cd. 4499), 1909, p. 425.

[75] Their initial coverage was to be the old Poor Law Union, but at some future date they would be made to coincide as nearly as possible with regular Rural or Urban Districts. (*Ibid.*, p. 606.)

[76] *Ibid.*, p. 624.

tive . . . We of the Minority strongly object to any *charity standing between* an applicant and the Public Authority, and depriving him of his *right* to public aid." [77] The Minority, too, held to the principle of close cooperation between voluntary and statutory bodies, but not of the kind which would involve separating the poor into two classes, one to be handled exclusively by a public agency and the other by a private. Rather there would be a systematic partnership between voluntary and statutory effort, each in its special sphere.

The Webbs' "extension ladder" formula suggests the nature of these spheres. To maintain and improve the national minimum was, of course, the responsibility of the public authorities; voluntary organizations would carry on in the area above this basic level. Public agencies, in the nature of things, must concern themselves with the normal and regular, rather than the exceptional, and rigid procedures and bureaucratic routines are for them a condition of existence. Against all this, voluntary bodies formed a countervailing force. The Webbs's case was essentially a preview of that now made for voluntary effort (to be examined in the following chapter) as an indispensable element in the complex of Welfare State services. What they demanded was that the "extension ladder" be "placed firmly on the foundation of an enforced minimum standard of life." That being settled, voluntary agencies would carry "onward the work of the Public Authorities to far finer shades of physical, moral, and spiritual perfection." [78] To lay the foundation was the duty of the community, but it remained for philanthropic individuals and groups to build a fitting superstructure. Plainly the Heavenly City of Beatrice Webb was vastly different from the Beulah Land of the Charity Organisation Society. Still, whatever one's views of the relative merits of the two Reports, none can deny to Mrs. Webb an extraordinarily prophetic vision. In not a few respects, the Minority draft turned out to be a prospectus for the mid-twentieth century Welfare State.

[77] *The Sphere of Voluntary Agencies under the Minority Report,* p. 19, issued by the National Committee to Promote the Break-Up of the Poor Law, the propagandist body organized by the Webbs to push their Minority Report. The Reverend Henry Russell Wakefield, Dean of Norwich and future Bishop of Birmingham, was one of the four signers of the Report. The others were the Labour men, George Lansbury and Francis Chandler, who could hardly be considered converts.
[78] *The Prevention of Destitution,* p: 252.

PART FOUR

THE "NEW PHILANTHROPY"
AND THE WELFARE STATE
1914–1960

"Anticipate charity by preventing poverty . . .
This is the highest step and summit of charity's golden
ladder."

—Maimonides

"While a society is alive and growing it will not make
rigid choices between state action and voluntary action,
but both alike will expand as the common expression
of its vitality."

— *Nathan Report*

T O T R Y to establish the historical origins of the Welfare State would be a relatively unrewarding pursuit. It is one of those inquiries whose outcome would be determined largely by the assumptions and criteria of the seeker. Plainly some of the essential foundations of the welfare structure had been laid well before the Beveridge Report provided comprehensive blueprints and before Messrs. Attlee, Bevan & Company became its principal builders. The campaign for old age pensions in the 1890's and the social legislation of 1905–1911 proclaimed unambiguously that a new era was at hand.[1] By the 1920's and '30's the more perceptive philanthropists and social workers not only recognized that their own position was changing but suspected that, as the trend to state action accelerated, it might even be revolutionized. When the focus shifted from "the Poor" and what could be done to relieve their distress to poverty and what could be done to abolish it, then it became inevitable that the State should intervene more decisively and that the scope of private charity should be correspondingly altered.

The new departures created problems of adjustment, not immediately or universally recognized, for voluntary agencies. A network of statutory services was being fashioned which would make necessary a fresh definition of the role of the voluntary organization. In ante-bellum Britain, as we have noted repeatedly, welfare arrangements depended chiefly on the voluntary effort of individuals and groups, self-supporting and self-governing, which carried on their work with little interference from or contact with the public authorities. But in the inter-war world of expanding services it appeared at once that neither public nor private agencies were sufficient unto themselves. Of necessity they drew closer together, and the weight of responsibility gradually passed from the voluntary agencies to the statutory services.

Admittedly this was a rather uneasy, ill-defined partnership. Some leaders in the world of philanthropy were determined to defend the voluntary principle to the last ditch. Others, less immured in their Victorian preconceptions, could view developments more objectively. The new association was first described in detail in 1934 by Elizabeth Macadam, a distinguished social worker and teacher of social workers, in her volume *The New Philanthropy*,[2] a thoughtful and influential analysis of the growing interdependence of statutory and voluntary services. To

[1] See Maurice Bruce, *The Coming of the Welfare State* (London, 1961), chap. V.
[2] London, 1934.

those whose experience had been restricted to one corner or another of the realm of social welfare, her systematic account of voluntary-statutory relations came as something of a revelation. Not only that but she insisted that "this unique partnership which I have called the new philanthropy"[3] had come to stay, and she appealed to voluntary agencies to cooperate to better effect with the public services.

Miss Macadam accepted as inevitable and desirable the further expansion of the State's role, but she could hardly have foreseen the sweeping changes that came in the wake of the Second War. The new legislation, which in the large followed the proposals of the Beveridge Report and was animated by the hopes that it had aroused, assured to each citizen a minimum of well-being in income maintenance and employment, in health and education, and in old age — to mention only the most obvious areas in which the Welfare State functions. Not only did the State emerge as the predominant partner, but for a time there was grave doubt as to what might be left for its older but now junior associate. Yet as the situation became more stable, the voluntary agencies found themselves as heavily occupied as ever, in some cases carrying on much as before, in others closely meshed with the statutory services, and in still others moving into new and unfamiliar areas. It was not parliamentary rhetoric but considered policy when Lord Pakenham, for the Labour Government, assigned to voluntary organizations "a part . . . as essential in the future as they have played in the past."[4]

Whatever its special impact on different branches of philanthropy, the Welfare State is obviously the cardinal fact in the world of mid-century charities. In one way or another it conditions the work of all and poses questions of philosophy and procedure for which no conclusive answer has yet emerged. The outlines of the new situation and some of the issues are sketched in the chapters that follow. It is enough here to emphasize that charities, large and small, have had to redefine their objectives and reconsider their programs. Even the great general trusts—the Nuffield Foundation is perhaps the most familiar example — have been guided, in some degree, in their planning by the needs of the statutory services. Admittedly their contribution has been of considerable magnitude; they have carried on systematic studies of problems of the common life, have engaged in pilot experiments, and have supplemented the statutory arrangements at particular points.

In another area the adjustments taking place throughout the world of philanthropy created a favorable occasion for re-examining the legal provisions governing charitable trusts. The outcome was the exhaustive inquiry undertaken by the Nathan Committee in 1950-52 and the Charities Act of 1960, the first comprehensive statute on the subject for a century and, in Professor Keeton's words, "possibly the most important enactment upon the law of charities" since 1601.[5] Altogether the postwar years have proved hardly less revolutionary in the voluntary than in the public sector of social welfare.

[3] Page 287.
[4] 5 *Parl. Deb.* (Lords), 163:120.
[5] *The Modern Law of Charities*, p. v.

CHAPTER XIX

JUNIOR PARTNER
IN THE WELFARE FIRM

D URING the decade after Versailles British philanthropies shared in the adversity experienced by British economy. Not only did hard times and high taxes affect charitable giving, but wartime drives, which had been dazzlingly successful, seemed to have drained off some of the support that would normally go to voluntary organizations. At the same time the charities themselves were crippled by rising prices and heavier operating costs. Comprehensive statistics on charity receipts are, of course, lacking, and one must rely on local figures which cannot themselves be considered as more than approximations. Those for London are more nearly adequate than for other British cities (save possibly Liverpool), and they have the further advantage of covering many agencies which are, in fact, national in their scope.[1] These suggest that in the early '20's the real income of London charities fell to a point well below the prewar level, and only after 1923 did it revive. Roughly speaking, by the mid-'20's metropolitan charities had about recovered their prewar financial position.[2]

More significant perhaps were the shifting proportions among the components of charity income. Charitable contributions — donations and subscriptions — tended to lag behind the increase in costs. Legacies, too, formed a smaller proportion of the total receipts than before the war, though they held up fairly well. What took up the slack was the rise in payments made by or for beneficiaries, from individuals, insurance funds, or public authorities. From about £1.75 million in 1908 this increment grew to an annual average (1922-27) of more than £4 million, comprising over 28 per cent of the total revenue of London charities.[3] By 1934, it has been estimated, something like 37 per cent of the total income of

---

[1] The total charity receipts of the Metropolis, stated in index numbers (1908 = 100) rose from 102 in 1912 to an average of 172.43 in the years 1922–27, an increase of nearly 70 per cent. But if allowance is made for the rise in prices the gain will seem much less impressive. These calculations are Miss Braithwaite's (*The Voluntary Citizen*, chap. VII). Her figures are drawn from the C.O.S. *Annual Charities Register and Digest*.

[2] Admittedly the margin of error in estimating the "real income" of charities is great. Such devices as a "cost-of-living" index number can have only a limited and uneven application to a mass of organizations whose expenditures exhibit such bewildering variety.

[3] As compared with 21 per cent at the earlier date. The gain is even more spectacular if 1904 is taken as the base point. Then, as Miss Rooff notes (*Voluntary Societies and Social Policy*, p. 259), the rise would be from 12 to 28 per cent.

English charities was being received as payment for services.[4] Here, clearly, was a small-scale preview of the statutory-voluntary relationship that has figured so heavily in the postwar Welfare State, with voluntary agencies assisted on a vast scale by grants from public authorities.

Throughout the inter-war period there was more than a little uneasiness about the failure of ordinary income to keep pace with rising costs. Many voluntary agencies were forced to rely in a greater measure on exceptional sources of revenue — special appeals, large individual gifts, and legacies (treated as current income) — rather than on annual subscriptions and donations.[5] The secretaries of some charities, foreseeing an inevitable drying-up of the larger reservoirs of benevolence, called (as their predecessors had been doing for at least half a century!) for broadening the base of support. They complained that too large a proportion of the charitable resources of the country were being squandered in the appeals of a myriad of "collecting" charities, often irresponsible, fly-by-night organizations, and there were demands for public machinery to screen and regulate these agencies.[6] A Home Office Committee, however, declined to recommend any comprehensive plan of supervision.[7]

The most critical postwar issue was that posed by the financial plight of the voluntary hospitals. During the First War these had been under the severest kind of pressure, and at its close they lacked the funds even to maintain their buildings and equipment, to say nothing of financing urgently needed improvements. In the London area the hospitals were facing a combined deficit of well over £350,000.[8] The situation was grave enough to call for the appointment of a special Committee on the Voluntary Hospitals, the Cave Committee, whose report pictured the whole structure as threatened with imminent collapse. Unswervingly dedicated to the voluntary principle, the Committee vigorously dismissed any thought of regular state assistance: "If the voluntary system is worth saving [and of this the Committee had no shred of doubt], any proposals for continuous rate or State aid should be rejected."[9] What would do the trick, the Committee held, was such temporary assistance from public funds as would restore the hospitals to their 1914 position. After that, presumably, they could carry on as before.

The Cave Committee recommended £1 million, but the Government would provide only £500,000 in an Exchequer grant, piously exhorting the hospitals to develop "fresh and permanent sources of revenue."[10] In retrospect it is tempting

---

[4] Braithwaite, *The Voluntary Citizen*, p. 171.

[5] For the experience, not atypical, of one major charity, the Jewish Board of Guardians, see V. D. Lipman, *A Century of Social Service*, pp. 155–56.

[6] L. G. Brock, "A Censorship of Charities," *Fortnightly Review*, 120:113ff (July 1923); A. Carr-Saunders and D. Caradog Jones, *A Survey of the Social Structure of England and Wales* (London, 1927), p. 177.

[7] *H. O. Committee on the Supervision of Charities* (Cmd. 2823), 1927.

[8] *Voluntary Hospitals (Cave) Committee* (Cmd. 1335), 1921, p. 5.

[9] *Ibid.*, p. 8.

[10] *Voluntary Hospitals Commission: Terms of Appointment* (Cmd. 1402), 1921.

to conclude that Committee and Government were mistranslating the handwriting on the wall. There were signs that the voluntary hospitals were not merely victims of a passing emergency, and both governmental agencies and the hospitals themselves might well have taken a harder, more objective look at these. Would voluntary support, in an age of increasing taxes and inflationary prices, expand sufficiently to pay for a medical service that was constantly becoming more costly?[11] This seemed unlikely, especially when measured against the estimate of the Voluntary Hospitals Commission (whose duty it was to distribute the Exchequer grant) that at least ten thousand more hospital beds would be needed if medical care were to be at all adequate. To make up ground lost during the previous decade, the Commission concluded in 1925, the State would have to provide more substantial assistance than had been seriously contemplated.[12]

Yet the issue was hardly as clear at the time as it seems in hindsight. No general conclusion about the financial position of British hospitals is worth much. These, after all, were individual institutions, and they revealed every degree of solvency and penury. Some could manage current expenses satisfactorily enough but were unable to provide for desperately needed capital expenditure. Not only that but the inter-war period showed a good deal of variation from year to year. Though in the early '30's deficits were conspicuous, the year 1934 showed an aggregate surplus, owing chiefly to the spread of contributory schemes, the increase in the number of pay beds, and payments from local authorities.[13] Indeed, champions of voluntarism could take comfort from some of the developments of the '30's. Altogether the picture presented by the hospital world between the Wars was a spotted one, but it contained new and disturbing elements that were largely ignored by those who sang hosannas to the voluntary principle.

During the 1930's, in fact, the State moved gropingly toward a more affirmative policy. Here the decisive change came about through the Local Government Act of 1929, which by implication imposed upon local authorities some responsibility for meeting the hospital needs of their districts, either by public institutions or by arrangements with voluntary hospitals.[14] Although their response was various, the net result was a rapid expansion of the public sector, so that a decade later fewer than a third of the hospital beds in England were under voluntary management.[15] In the late '30's the condition of the hospitals became increasingly precarious. Among other things, they had been caught in one of those periods of revolutionary change in medical science, and this one, in Professor Titmuss' words, "represented to most of the voluntary hospitals in Britain a sentence of death."[16] The outbreak of war found the voluntary hospitals on the verge of bankruptcy, and it was apparent to all but the most hardened voluntarists that

[11] Harry Eckstein, *The English Health Service* (Cambridge, Mass., 1958), p. 73.
[12] Quoted by John Trevelyan, *Voluntary Service and the State* (London, 1952), p. 23.
[13] P.E.P., *Report on the British Social Services* (1937), p. 232.
[14] Sir Arthur S. McNalty, *The Reform of the Public Health Services* (London, 1943), pp. 41–42.
[15] R. M. Titmuss, *Problems of Social Policy* (London, 1950), p. 66.
[16] R. M. Titmuss, *Essays on the Welfare State* (London, 1958), p. 153.

private philanthropy would never restore them to solvency. In the face of sharply mounting pressure, gifts from private sources remained roughly constant, accounting for only about a third of the income of London hospitals. It is enough to underline Professor Eckstein's conclusion that "the voluntary hospitals were kept alive, toward the end of their existence, only by extensive government payments."[17]

The hospitals, perhaps, offered the most striking example of a voluntary service already somewhat dependent upon public support and inevitably to become more so. But the trend was present, to a greater or less degree and with uneven incidence, throughout the world of voluntary effort. In 1929, to cite two instances, Liverpool charities were receiving 13 per cent of their income from public sources as payment for services, and in 1938 public money was providing 17 per cent of Manchester's charitable receipts.[18] There was, however, little uniformity about it all. Public authority grants to the Mental After-Care Association could rise from an annual average of £607 in 1920–24 to nearly £17,000 in 1935–39, while London County Council grants to charities for the blind dropped from about £112,000 in 1934–35 to about £33,000 in the following year — the explanation being the Council's decision to operate on its own account most of the necessary services for the blind.[19]

Yet there was an obvious drawing closer, financially and otherwise, of statutory and voluntary. A case in point is the National Council of Social Service, formed in 1919 not only to encourage and coordinate voluntary social work but also to cooperate with government departments and local authorities. In this project there was explicit recognition of the fact that voluntary and statutory agencies were concerned with similar problems and that a working understanding, if not a formal partnership, was essential. This is not the place to trace the growth and expanding services of the Council. Its pre-war development can be measured by recalling that its expenditure increased more than tenfold (from £3323 to £37,210) in the period from 1926 to 1936–37.[20] Although the sharp rise in income was only in part the result of grants from public authorities for particular purposes, these were coming in increasing volume. In welfare work for the unemployed, for example, Government and Council worked out a fruitful collaboration. An experimental grant of £20,000 made in 1933 enabled the Council to expand its clubs for the unemployed, so that about four hundred of these, with perhaps 250,000 members, came into being in the course of the next two years.[21] In 1936–37 the Ministry of Labour granted over £100,000 and the Commissioner for Special

---

[17] *English Health Service*, p. 72. On the eve of the War, about 50 per cent of the income of London hospitals (including 8 per cent from the public authorities) was received in payment for services rendered.

[18] Constance Braithwaite, "Statistics of Finance," in H. A. Mess. *Voluntary Social Services since 1918* (London, 1948), pp. 200–1.

[19] Rooff, *Voluntary Societies and Social Policy*, pp. 166, 212.

[20] John Morgan, "The National Council," in H. A. Mess, *Voluntary Social Services*, p. 81.

[21] H. A. Mess, "Social Service with the Unemployed," *ibid.*, p. 42.

Areas over £200,000 to the Council for work among the unemployed.[22] Altogether, during the 1930's the Council must have received from government sources not less than £1 million.

It is hardly possible to formulate useful generalizations about philanthropic giving on the eve of the War. In such a decade to look for a significant rise would be absurd. One gets the impression of a group of voluntary services that, as a whole, were not able to do much more than hold their own, and of a volume of giving that was rising, if at all, far less than they required.[23] On the other hand, there is no evidence of an absolute shrinkage. Neither increase in taxation nor the extensive social services provided by the State seem as yet to have had a disastrous effect on individual contributions. What is true is that these were now serving a somewhat different purpose and were increasingly a means of subsidizing a service rather than of carrying it in full.[24] It was a reasonable prediction, moreover, that the welfare activities of the State would continue to advance, though probably at a fairly deliberate pace. Such calculations were radically altered by the War, which broadened the social vision of Englishmen and revived their sense of community in the face of common danger. Without this new impulse, Britain could hardly have created "a nation-wide scheme of mutual assistance and care" out of a miscellany of uncoordinated social services.[25]

2

The postwar Welfare State was brought into existence by a series of enactments intended to establish a social minimum below which no member of the community would be allowed to fall. To attribute these exclusively to the new Labour Government would do less than justice. Some of the schemes had been forecast by National Government commissions and committees. Those having to do with freedom from want were sketched in Beveridge's brilliantly persuasive *Report on Social Insurance and Allied Services,* the report of a committee appointed by a Labour Minister in the National Government. In outlining his proposals, Beveridge explicitly denied that these were enough. When freedom from want had been assured, "Disease, Ignorance, Squalor, and Idleness" would remain to be dealt with. Indeed, he premised his scheme of social insurance on an adequate plan of children's allowances, on comprehensive health and rehabilitation services, and on machinery for maintaining employment.[26] The Report thus offered, directly or by implication, something of a preview of the services that make up the Welfare State.

For our purpose the critical decisions were those embodied in the National Health Service Act (1946), setting up a comprehensive plan of medical care; the

---

[22] Either under its own auspices or to be distributed to organizations carrying on similar activities.
[23] Save for certain large foundations, whose record will be reviewed in the following chapter.
[24] Braithwaite, "Statistics of Finance," in Mess, *Voluntary Social Services,* pp. 202–3.
[25] M. P. Hall, *The Social Services of Modern England,* 4th ed. (London, 1959), p. 6.
[26] *Social Insurance and Allied Services,* pp. 153ff.

Children Act (1948), providing for a service for children without normal home life and thus supplementing the Family Allowances Act (1946); and the National Assistance Act (1948), designed to fill such gaps as were left by the National Insurance Act (1946) and incidentally wiping out the last vestiges of the Poor Law. What was being laid down here was a second line of defense against want, one that would assist those not qualified for insurance benefits — the aged, the long-term unemployed, and the variously handicapped.[27] One ought also, perhaps, to take note of the Education Act of 1944, which, in a sense, opened educational opportunity at all levels and which, by radically extending public responsibility, forced certain educational philanthropies to take stock of their position and to redefine their functions.

Although for some decades the statutory services had been encroaching on areas traditionally assigned to voluntary effort, this postwar legislation was conceived on such a vastly broader scale as to involve what was, in effect, a new principle. Henceforth the sick poor (along with the rest of the British population) would receive medical care as their right and would not be dependent on the voluntary hospital and its free clinic; the aged, though they might still, possibly, find shelter in a privately endowed almshouse, would draw pensions under the National Insurance scheme or receive payments under the National Assistance Act; and British families with more than one child would be subsidized by weekly payments under the Family Allowance Act. All this meant that Englishmen could now look to the State for a basic social minimum, and it aroused uneasy suspicions that in at least some sectors private philanthropy might be on the way to redundancy. For American readers the point can be sharpened by recalling the "Hundred Neediest Cases" for whom each Christmas the *New York Times* requests contributions. In December 1952 the list was reprinted in London by *The Times,* with the comment that in England only ten of the hundred would have required private charity. The others would have claimed assistance as their right.[28]

The impact of the broadened statutory services on voluntary agencies was naturally erratic. Those whose sphere of action was untouched by the new legislation might continue almost as though nothing had happened. Cases in point were the well-financed R.S.P.C.A. and the Royal National Life-boat Institution, a service that *a priori* would seem an obvious public responsibility. The National Trust, too, carries on its admirable work without direct aid from public funds. At the opposite pole certain other charities were left with no function whatever. Of these the classic example was that of agencies founded originally to provide surgical appliances — crutches, braces, trusses — for poor patients, equipment now supplied by the National Health Service. Between the two extremes lay the vast mass of British charities contemplating an uncertain future. Some would be obliged to curtail their services; others, surprisingly enough, would find greater

---

[27] Hall, *Social Services,* p. 50.
[28] Daisy L. Hobman, *The Welfare State* (London, 1953), p. 105.

opportunities than before; but most of them would face problems of readjustment of greater or less gravity.

On the one hand, voluntary agencies were entitled to feel uneasy about their financial prospects. Was it reasonable that donors, already harried by staggering taxes, should continue to support voluntary effort? This would be asking them to make a double contribution, since, through their taxes, they were already carrying what they might consider their share of the load. Would the Welfare State, in short, drain the pools which historically had watered British philanthropy? Even more immediate was the matter of working relationships between voluntary agencies and the enormously expanded statutory services. The Government had proclaimed its adherence to the principle of partnership, and some of the specific enactments, notably the Children Act (1948), had accepted it.[29] But its terms, which would vary from area to area and from year to year, were still to be worked out.

On the roles which private philanthropy can appropriately play in a social service state there is substantial agreement. These have been enumerated time and again by social workers, thoughtful civil servants, and scholars, as well as by the Nathan Committee, with remarkable consensus.[30] None doubts that the old doctrine of the mutual exclusiveness of voluntary and statutory services, the "parallel bars" formula, has long since been (to recall Disraeli's repudiation of agricultural protection) "not only dead but damned." Even the "extension ladder" image fails to suggest what has been taking place. The fact is that over large sectors of the welfare front the purely voluntary agency has disappeared and the assault on disease, distress, and ignorance has become a combined operation in which in many instances statutory and voluntary forces are closely integrated. Although voluntary bodies have been converted from principals into auxiliaries — Miss Hall thinks it possible "that, except on a very limited scale in pioneer or very controversial work, the days of the strictly voluntary organization . . . are at an end" [31] — no knowledgeable observer would undervalue their services. This is a genuine partnership in which neither the statutory nor the voluntary component could be readily dispensed with. The Nathan Committee put the point with sound emphasis: "So far from voluntary action being dried up by the extension of the social services greater and greater demands are being made on it. We believe, indeed, that the democratic state, as we know it, could hardly function effectively . . . without such channels for, and demands upon, voluntary service." [32]

[29] Samuel Mencher, "Voluntary and Statutory Welfare Services," unpubl. diss., New York School of Social Work, p. 165.

[30] For example, Hall, *Social Services*, pp. 343ff; Rooff, *Voluntary Societies*, pp. 276ff; Braithwaite, *Voluntary Citizen*, pp. 68ff; Eyre Carter, "The Partnership between the Statutory and Voluntary Social Services in Postwar Britain," *Social Service Review*, 23:158–75 (June 1949); S. K. Ruck, "The Place of Charity in the Welfare State" (unpubl.), Nathan Committee; also, S. K. Ruck, *J. Royal Society of Arts*, 12 June 1953, pp. 523–24; *Nathan Report*, Par. 55.

[31] Hall, *Social Services*, p. 357.

[32] Paragraph 63.

Among the contributions to be made by nonstatutory agencies none can be more significant than those growing out of their freedom to experiment, to carry on pioneer activities which, for one reason or another, a government department is unable to undertake. This is not, of course, an entirely new role for them. The annals of charity are full of examples of services started on a small scale by private effort, which, sometimes by their success and sometimes by their palpable inadequacy, pointed the way to state action on a comprehensive scale. To quote the Nathan Committee again, "historically, state action is voluntary action crystallized and made universal."[33] In the nature of the case, statutory agencies must hesitate to spend public money on uncertain (or heavily controversial) ventures, and, broadly speaking, they have shown greater initiative in adapting schemes pioneered by voluntary agencies than in creating wholly new services.[34]

Plainly the opportunity, indeed the obligation, to experiment remains with voluntary bodies. Here it is perhaps the larger foundations, sometimes through their own operations and sometimes through grants to other bodies, which have most deliberately gone about the business of accumulating a fund of experience to be offered to the statutory authorities as a contribution to social policy.[35] It would be manifestly unfair to picture the state services as slaves of bureaucratic routine, for whom the voluntary organizations are constantly opening new vistas.[36] Yet nonstatutory agencies, both the well established and the as yet unproved, are carrying on interesting and productive experiments of a kind in which statutory bodies could hardly engage. What limits them is less a lack of opportunity than a financial stringency which not only prevents their entering upon new projects but sometimes even imposes a curtailment of their regular services.[37]

Voluntary effort also meets a major need in supplementing, quantitatively and qualitatively, the regular statutory system.[38] Voluntary organizations may find themselves administering schemes too amorphous and ill-defined to fit neatly into the public welfare framework or certain services which by statute must be handled by nonofficial bodies (mobile meals and clubs for the aged are cases in point). They may contribute funds and workers to round out the statutory arrangements, filling gaps or reaching into corners unoccupied by the statutory services. Where flexibility is a special requirement the contribution of voluntary agencies can be of critical importance. State services must, in general, follow established routines; their rules of procedure cannot take into account the emergencies that crop up nor cover the infinite variations in the human plight. Designed to handle the "average" case, they lack discretionary power to deal

[33] Paragraph 39.
[34] Hall, *Social Services*, p. 353.
[35] As will be described in the following chapter.
[36] See T. H. Marshall, "Voluntary Action," *Political Quarterly*, 20:34 (January–March 1949).
[37] Rooff, *Voluntary Societies and Social Policy*, p. 275.
[38] In these paragraphs on the contribution of the voluntary services I have drawn heavily on Eyre Carter's article (n. 30), Samuel Mencher's unpublished thesis (n. 29), and his Loch Memorial Lecture of 1954, *The Relationship of Voluntary and Statutory Agencies in the Welfare Services*.

with the atypical. For the latter — those which fit into no specific category or for whom an application of the rules would constitute a grave hardship — voluntary bodies, with their "right to be inconsistent," [39] have proved an indispensable adjunct to the statutory services.

For an illustration we may turn to the Family Service Units, whose special province is hard-core problem families. These families, highly resistant to re-habilitation, lie beyond the reach of the regular agencies, their difficulties too complex and interrelated to fall within the scope of any one body. The Units grew out of the wartime experience of pacifists in Liverpool, who, wishing to serve the community in some fashion, worked among bombed-out families who were considered unbilletable by the authorities. As constituted in 1961, F.S.U. comprised some thirteen local units, with seventy full-time trained social workers making over forty thousand visits a year to problem families. Among these pri-marily local agencies there are substantial differences from city to city. Some are wholly financed by statutory bodies; others rely chiefly on voluntary support. Virtually all of F.S.U.'s problem families are referred by other workers, perhaps most commonly by statutory agencies. There is, in fact, good reason to believe that such families, whose conditions of life are well below the minimum standard accepted as tolerable by the community, require the kind of attention that only a voluntary body can give.[40]

A social domain remote from that of the problem family offers another example of philanthropy's supplementing statutory arrangements, in this instance the state scholarship system. One of the ancient Livery Companies, no longer needing its scholarship funds for their former objects, has discovered new and original educational uses for the income. Since the 1880's, when the Goldsmiths amalga-mated a mass of their eleemosynary endowments into a consolidated fund, they have allocated considerable sums to university scholarships and exhibitions. The Company is justly proud of its roll of exhibitioners, on which appears the name, fittingly enough, of Christopher Pascoe Hill, the new Chief Charity Commissioner. In addition to their scholarship grants, the Goldsmiths showed concern with other educational causes. They endowed readerships (now professorships) at Oxford and Cambridge, made grants to various institutions at the old universities and London, and purchased for the University of London Professor Foxwell's famous collection on economic and social history known since as the Goldsmiths' Library — all this in addition to more than £400,000 subscribed by the Company to the City & Guilds of London Institute.

The Education Act of 1944, by vastly augmenting the provision of state scholar-ships, altered the nature of the problem. The Goldsmiths could therefore dis-continue their university exhibitions and apply their resources to other purposes, among which the financing of study in overseas institutions took a primary place.

---

[39] *Report of the Working Party on Social Workers (Younghusband Report)*, (H.M.S.O., 1959), par. 1038.

[40] F.S.U. Catechism (mimeographed) and interview with Mr. David Jones, the Director.

One of their more inventive programs has had to do with vacation travel grants for London University students. These grew out of a suspicion that some promising undergraduates, shuttling back and forth between home and lecture hall, were getting from their university experience little more than "book-learning" in the narrowest sense. It was the hope of the Goldsmiths' Committee that such grants might serve to introduce these earnest students to unfamiliar places and people and lift their horizons beyond the daily bus trip and the library. No doubt this use of their endowments would have surprised pious founders who had left bequests for the "poor of the Company," but they could not complain that their charities had been made obsolete or redundant by the expansion of statutory services.[41]

Again, the function of explaining and interpreting to the ordinary citizen the complicated mechanism of the state services is one that has fallen naturally to voluntary effort. Here the chief agencies are the Citizens' Advice Bureaux, which have become invaluable as guides for the helpless individual through the confusing thicket of, say, social insurance procedures or housing regulations. Not only that, they are constantly called upon for counsel on personal and family difficulties not directly connected with the social services. They stand as a kind of wise and experienced uncle, who may or may not provide the solution at once but who will at least canvass the problem with understanding and sympathy.

Like other agencies which have proved of permanent value, the Bureaux were created originally to meet an emergency situation, in this case the social dislocation expected to follow the declaration of war in September 1939. Two decades later some 430 were in operation, with a total staff of more than two thousand volunteer workers.[42] The National Council of Social Service supplies advice and assistance, but the stress throughout is on local initiative. Most of the Bureaux received grants, small or substantial, from local authorities, but government policy on aid to the Council for central services has been an up-and-down affair. On balance there appear to be compelling reasons, some of them inherent in the nature of their work, why the Bureaux should remain a voluntary service. Their essential function, the N.C.S.S. points out, is that of communication — "explaining to authorities the needs of the citizen, to the citizen the intention of the authorities."[43] Such mediation would be out of the question for other than a nonofficial body.

Finally, voluntary bodies can perform an inestimable service in stimulating, restraining, and criticizing the proceedings of statutory authorities. In the words of the Nathan Committee: "They are able to stand aside from and criticize state action, or inaction, in the interests of the inarticulate man-in-the-street."[44] Their

---

[41] *The Worshipful Company of Goldsmiths* (London, 1958), pp. 18–19; interview with Mr. Walter Prideaux, Clerk of the Company. Other Companies, such as the Drapers, also launched overseas scholarship programs. (Hugh Dalton, *Memoirs, 1945–60: High Tide and After* [London, 1962], p. 442.)

[42] Hall, *Social Services*, p. 146.

[43] N.C.S.S., *Ann. Rept.*, 1958–59, p. 25.

[44] Paragraph 55.

intervention, the Committee goes on to note, can take the form of assisting individuals (as through the Citizens' Advice Bureaux) in their dealings with officialdom or of attacking broader issues. They can also continue, as their predecessors have done for decades, to gather data on particular evils or social needs, and then to set in motion the familiar machinery of democratic agitation and pressure until the evils are corrected or the needs met. No doubt it is in the nature of even benevolent bureaucracies to become over self-assured, to behave as if they had all the answers. Their performance will be the better for an occasional bit of prodding or curbing, and voluntary bodies, with their understanding of the problems that engage the statutory authorities, are appropriate agents.

The pattern of prospective voluntary-statutory relationships was traced in broad outline by Herbert Morrison when, in the late '40's, he addressed the London Council of Social Service: "There are," he said, "certain services which, because they are or should be universal, are the special responsibility of the statutory authorities. At the other extreme are what might be called the 'unique' activities of associations and concerns. They represent the pioneers who point the way and the critics who keep us up to the mark. In between are a great variety of other services where statutory and voluntary effort can co-operate effectively." [45] Nothing occurred in the following decade to invalidate Morrison's analysis.

3

The picture sketched in the preceding paragraphs would be generally accepted as a summary of the uses, actual and potential, of voluntary bodies. The statutory services, however comprehensive, were not intended to establish a state monopoly of welfare, and even such zealous champions of state action as Herbert Morrison were committed to preserving voluntary effort as "fundamental to the health of a democratic society . . . These people who care about causes; the adherents, the supporters, the belongers; the Chairmen, the Treasurers, Secretaries, Committee Members; they have a special significance in our society." Nobody, in short, wished to cripple the voluntary agencies, but for many of them the future seemed to hold more problems than promise. With some the critical issues had to do with finding their place in a society that itself was providing for basic needs, but with numbers of others the question was the simple one of survival — that is, whether the community would continue to give financial support to voluntary organizations.

Admittedly the situation remains cloudy and complex. Data are meager and less than satisfying. Although few voluntary organizations have, in fact, been obliged to shut down, many have encountered heavy weather. As Sir John Wolfenden told the National Council of Social Service Annual Meeting in 1956, "With a few exceptions, they carry on under conditions which are crippling to good work. Every year their costs increase, largely for reasons outside their control. Each year they must increase their income considerably merely to maintain the

---

[45] Quoted by Eyre Carter (n. 30), p. 175.

work of the previous year, and many of them cannot do this . . . The community must recognise that the voluntary movement as a whole needs far greater support if the quality of social life is to be maintained." [46] Yet there are solid reasons for doubting whether this greater support is likely to be forthcoming, certainly not from the classes which have traditionally financed British charities.

Evidence on postwar charitable giving is fragmentary and often contradictory. For example, the Royal National Life-boat Institution recorded a rising income through most of the 1950's, apparently documenting the theory that, to the mass of givers, the most appealing causes in order of preference were sailors, animals, and children. [47] But it is impossible to miss the heavy dependence on legacies, which, unless they carry trust provisions, are treated as income. In 1958 subscriptions and donations amounted to about £375,000, and legacies (474 in number) exceeded £550,000. In the following year, surplus turned to deficit owing to the fact that legacies fell below £400,000. [48] The experience of the N.S.P.C.C. has been similar. In 1958–60 legacies reached a new high, but regular subscriptions made up an almost negligible proportion of the £500,000 received by the central office and its branches. [49]

With a single exception there have been no studies of postwar giving which contribute significantly to more general conclusions. The exception is a comparative analysis of the income for the years 1938 and 1951 of the receipts of between 250 and 300 Manchester-Salford voluntary organizations, an attempt to measure both quantitative and qualitative changes in philanthropic practice. [50] The figures (admittedly a simple comparison in terms of £'s is misleading) show an increase of nearly 5 per cent in charity income over the thirteen years, but this was more than accounted for by larger grants from public authorities. If only subscriptions, donations, and legacies are considered, the two years are almost identical — £418,000 and £419,000 respectively — and these made up 40 per cent and 38 per cent of the total. A drastic shrinkage in subscriptions of the traditional sort was offset by a substantial increase in legacies and donations. What is clear, on balance, is that Manchester and Salford charities were kept afloat not by any expansion in individual giving — this did not begin to offset the rise in costs — but by grants from statutory bodies.

Within the charity world, too, there was some redistribution of income, resulting primarily from the altered status of the hospitals. In 1938 these received 78 per cent of the subscriptions, 45 per cent of the donations, and 83 per cent of the legacies. By 1951 subscriptions had shrunk to 22 per cent and donations to 19 per cent, but legacies to hospitals still amounted to 70 per cent of the bequests to Manchester-Salford charities. [51] This continued appeal of the hospitals, three years

---

[46] 25 Sept. 1956.
[47] Beveridge, *Voluntary Action*, p. 302.
[48] R.N.L.I., *Ann. Rept.*, 1958, 1959.
[49] The Society received only £9146 in covenanted subscriptions (*Ann. Rept.*, 1959–60, p. 10).
[50] Irene Green and G. W. Murphy, "Income of Voluntary Social Services in Manchester and Salford," *Social Welfare*, 9:78ff (1954).
[51] And reached a total half again as great as in 1938.

after their "take-over" by the State, is less mystifying than at first appears. Some of the benefactions were gifts deliberately made to a special service or activity of the hospital. Others, presumably, resulted from wills that were never changed or reflected habits of giving carried over from the day when hospitals depended on the support of private donors.

Few charity officials will doubt that the pool from which the voluntary services have drawn their sustenance — the upper and upper-middle-class subscription list — is drying up. Legacies still come in, but these too are likely to dwindle as the years pass. In some charity circles there has been a burgeoning hope, not as yet fully justified, that the way out might be to democratize philanthropy, as the Hospital Saturday Fund attempted. Obviously the redistribution of income in the British community has altered the conditions of charity finance. Perhaps the sound policy would be to exploit the new situation and rely on support from a multitude of small donors rather than on the conventional subscription list.

Within limits the expectation is not unreasonable. The "new rich," it has been established, will respond to appeals for certain types of cause, especially if these are astutely organized and well publicized. The N.S.P.C.C. has always put a good deal of store by house-to-house collections, flower days, and the like. Heart and cancer funds have effectively tapped working-class pay envelopes, and the National Spastics Society, which also takes the man-in-the-street as its constituency, has given £100,000 to Guy's for cancer research and hopes to have raised £2 million in the course of the next few years. World Refugee Year, for which the working classes felt a special responsibility, also turned out to be a huge success. Of the £35 million plus raised in ninety-seven countries, Britain contributed over £9 million, more than four times the original target figure.[52]

Emergency appeals produce a generous response, sometimes embarrassingly large. The Lord Mayor's National Flood Fund for the relief of those who suffered in the Lynmouth disaster of 1952 and that for the victims of the Gillingham bus disaster in 1951 yielded sums considerably greater than the need.[53] Yet to persuade the small, casual donor to contribute his shilling to a cause that appeals to his imagination — saving children from cruelty, discovering a cure for cancer, or relieving the sufferers from fire or flood — is very different from gaining his support for the ordinary workaday agency, especially when it is providing services which, he holds, are now the responsibility of the State.[54] From the record thus far there is little to suggest that this can be readily accomplished, though in some cities schemes for regular weekly contributions of working people to local charities have shown promise.

Another source of hope for hard-pressed philanthropies has been a growing inclination of industry and commerce to help out. The point was raised a few years ago by the chairman of the Provincial Insurance Company in a letter to

[52] *Manchester Guardian Weekly*, 20 July 1961.

[53] Interview with officers of the N.C.S.S., 30 Aug. 1960.

[54] See the Mass Observation report on current attitudes toward charity in Lord Beveridge and A. F. Wells, *The Evidence for Voluntary Action* (London, 1949), pp. 55ff.

The Times.[55] It would be too much to describe the response, at least the visible response, from business houses as warm and enthusiastic. There were complaints that British tax laws were less favorable than those in the United States, where corporate giving was said to be common, and that anyway more than half of the profits of most companies went into taxes from which the social services were financed.[56] The flurry of correspondence continued for a month. If he could not boast of specific results, its instigator could at least assert that "discussion has already started round many board room tables." [57]

More revealing were the results of a survey carried out in 1957 by the Economist Intelligence Unit on behalf of Arthur Guinness, Son & Company.[58] The question put to more than nine hundred firms was this: "Are industrial and commercial bodies in this country taking the place of the private philanthropist, as is happening — or so it is often claimed — in the United States?" What emerged from the 380 questionnaires that were returned was a widespread belief that industry ought to "do something" but a good deal of confusion about standards and policies. Some firms made their decisions on a purely *ad hoc* basis, as appeals were received, often yielding to those that could apply the heaviest pressure. Few professed a consistent policy, though some set aside a fixed sum annually. Only a quarter of those who described their methods made donations by seven-year covenant, which would, of course, have meant substantial savings. Among the tangled motives that seem to have inspired contributions, the aim of indirectly benefiting the industry, the company, and its employees stood out — even though expenditures designed to benefit the staff directly were excluded. The number practicing "pure" philanthropy on a significant scale was relatively small; one firm, with unconscious humor, included in its donations account a section headed "disinterested Philanthropy." [59] There was some suspicion, the study concluded, on the part of businesses "that they might have been giving less than they should," and an eagerness to discover a "yardstick" which would assist them in measuring their obligations.

Corporate giving in Britain is still in its infancy. How far it can be expected to develop is an open question. In some knowledgeable quarters hopes are high. The National Council of Social Service, for example, has been splendidly supported by business firms, with about £50,000 in 1957–58 and again in 1958–59.[60] Some of the larger donations in 1957–58 bear the names of Unilever (£3693), Courtaulds (£2156), Imperial Chemicals (£2000), Imperial Tobacco (£1879). Yet one may doubt whether other charities would fare proportionately as well.

[55] F. C. Scott, 3 Oct. 1955.

[56] 4, 5 and 15 October.

[57] 28 October.

[58] *Business and the Community,* prepared for Arthur Guinness, Son & Company, by the Economist Intelligence Unit, 1957.

[59] *Ibid.,* p. 13.

[60] *N.C.S.S. Subscription Lists.* The totals, £51,160 in 1958–59 and £53,377 in 1959–60, comprise gifts from trusts and organizations as well as from business houses, but the bulk came from the latter.

Not only is the Council in a special position as a central body representing the corpus of British voluntary effort, but it profited from the vigorous leadership of Sir John Wolfenden as chairman, who had a good deal to do with enlisting the efforts of certain industrial leaders. Subscription lists of other bodies, of course, include the names of business houses. That of the Jewish Board of Guardians, for example, contains a number, but without exception their contributions are relatively trivial. Causes with a special public or national interest sometimes have appealed to good effect for business contributions. Some provincial universities, we have seen, received substantial support for special projects. The Historic Churches Preservation Trust, the *Times* correspondence brought out, had drawn about half of its large gifts from companies.[61] Altogether, the world of business has been explored only superficially by philanthropic enterprise, and until this is done more thoroughly it would be imprudent to look to the market place for salvation.

4

Thus far neither the shillings of the workingman nor the guineas from British business have markedly relieved the pressure on philanthropic agencies.[62] Of infinitely greater consequence has been the emergence of the State itself as a major philanthropist and benefactor of the voluntary services. It is impossible to get an accurate notion of the dependence of voluntary agencies on statutory financing, for this varies enormously from service to service. Some important bodies receive no government money and pride themselves on remaining purely voluntary undertakings. Others draw their chief support from public funds — from the Home Office, the Ministry of Health, or a local authority — and approximate the position of an agency under contract to the Government. Sometimes in this welfare partnership, it is the voluntary agency which serves as the managing partner in immediate charge of the work, while the statutory partner supplies the bulk of the working capital and gives general oversight. Services for children, the aged, and the handicapped are, of course, heavily subsidized. In 1959 the Jewish Board of Guardians drew from statutory sources about £90,000 of the £143,000 required by its Welfare Departments, and the National Council of Social Service received about a third (£49,000) of its total income in government grants.[63]

To regard these involved arrangements as a novel form of outdoor relief for voluntary organizations, a means of rescuing them from threatened collapse, would misrepresent the situation. This has been a mutually advantageous partnership. The existence of the voluntary services, with their financial resources and their staffs of workers, professional and voluntary, saved the State money and reduced the administrative complications inherent in setting up a statutory system. Clearly the experience, equipment, and financial support of private philanthropy

---

[61] Letter from Ivor Bulmer-Thomas, *The Times,* 19 Oct. 1955.

[62] This statement refers to direct contributions by business firms, not to grants from foundations, which, of course, were the product of business activity.

[63] Jewish Board of Guardians, *Ann. Rept.,* 1959, p. 45; N.C.S.S., *Ann. Rept.,* 1959–60, p. 41.

were distinct assets in the building of the new Welfare State. Conversely, cooperation with the public authorities relieved some voluntary bodies of the necessity of
penny-pinching and enabled them to improve their services and facilities — indeed,
in certain areas this was a requirement in order to qualify for grants. Unquestionably they have profited, through technical counsel as well as financial aid,
from their association with a national service.

Since the terms of the partnership are so various, we can expect little uniformity
in the methods by which it is financed. Grant-aid may come from the Central
Government or from local authorities; it may comprise lump sums for experimental ventures or capital construction, or may consist of per capita payments
for the care of children or aged persons; it may defray a large or small fraction
of the total cost of the service.[64] Broadly speaking, Central Government and local
authorities have different ends in view in their subsidies. Grants from the Home
Office or the Ministry of Health may be designed to lay the foundation for a new
service, meet a special need, or deal with a temporary situation. As a general thing,
they allow greater discretion to voluntary agencies than do those from local
authorities. Since the latter are ordinarily made to finance services which otherwise
the authority itself would have to furnish, voluntary organizations are expected
to stick fairly close to the prescribed paths.

Voluntary bodies appear to regard as reasonably satisfactory, and some as almost
ideal, the structure of statutory-voluntary cooperation that has been built up since
1945. A senior official of the Jewish Board of Guardians, comparing the plight of
his agency in the 1930's, when it was staggering under a tragic burden of unemployed and refugees, with its condition in the 1950's, remarked, "For me this is a
dream come true." [65] Subsidies flowing from statutory sources to voluntary bodies
have already had an undeniable influence on the latter. Some have expanded
notably under the stimulus of statutory grants; some have altered the scope of
their work in order to qualify for subsidies; some have simply carried on, and
very likely improved, their regular services. But on other agencies, it would be
idle to deny, grant-aid has had a stultifying effect, though conceivably some of
these had long since lost their momentum. There are instances where subsidies
have been so large that voluntary sponsors have lost interest in the undertaking.
No doubt the Government acts wisely — voluntary societies generally agree — in
requiring the voluntary agency itself to make more than a token contribution to
the cost of service. Not only does the fact of a financial stake give to sponsors and
workers a larger sense of responsibility but it also seems to entitle the officers of
the charity to greater voice in determining its policies. They are less likely to
become (or to feel that they are becoming) simple agents for carrying out plans
developed in statutory offices.

[64] This paragraph and those immediately following owe a good deal to Dr. Mencher's 1954 Loch
Memorial Lecture, *The Relationship of Voluntary and Statutory Agencies*.
[65] Mr. Mark Fineman, Assistant Secretary, in personal conversation.

One of the issues still unresolved has to do with the degree of overlapping and duplication to be tolerated in the welfare structure. No one has yet established an acceptable line dividing the statutory from the voluntary spheres. At best it is a borderland whose area and location will be perpetually changing.[66] Some overlapping is not by definition undesirable. The Nathan Committee deliberately rejected the notion of sharp separation of the two domains and declined to recommend the transfer of private charitable resources to state agencies.[67] Yet, though cooperation is admirable and coexistence unobjectionable, there is obviously a point at which the duplication of voluntary and statutory effort becomes highly uneconomic. One wonders how much longer the public will continue to give to voluntary organizations which are appealing for support precisely as they did before the growth of the statutory services. Dr. Barnardo's Homes, perhaps the most sensational charity success story of the Victorian Age, have persisted in their traditional money-raising policies and (at least in the early 1950's) were preferring to draw the vast bulk of their support from voluntary benefactors — more than 90 per cent, exclusive of legacies, in 1949 — rather than from statutory sources.[68] This disclosure gave the Nathan Committee some uneasiness, especially when it appeared that the Homes were not much concerned about adequate statutory assistance, "because our job is caring for children and not arguing finance with local authorities." [69]

There are, and will continue to be, masses of unresolved questions growing out of the voluntary-statutory partnership. It would be a mistake to discover the promise of long-term stability in the existing balance. Ministers have pointed to voluntary agencies as indispensable parts of the welfare mechanism, and grant-aid has flowed to them. But there is little evidence of long-range thinking in Whitehall or in local government circles about the future place of voluntary effort in the total welfare scheme and, indeed, little attempt to define, from the statutory point of view, the function of a voluntary body.[70] All this makes it more essential than ever for alert and vigorous voluntary groups to be continually reassessing their own function. British society will change, and new social needs will emerge; the weight of welfare responsibility will probably shift even more heavily to the statutory side. Voluntary bodies must therefore be always ready to adapt their activities to fresh circumstances. They will not even shrink from the possibility that further growth of the statutory agencies may make some of their own work redundant and that they had best move on to new problems.

[66] As Sir Hubert Llewellyn Smith observed in his 1937 Sidney Ball Lecture, *The Borderland between Public and Voluntary Action in the Social Services.*

[67] S. K. Ruck, a member of the Committee, in *J. Royal Society of Arts*, 12 June 1953, p. 523.

[68] Donations and collections, £650,000; legacies, £500,000; statutory subsidies, £55,000.

[69] Q. 6850.

[70] Mencher, *Relationship of Voluntary and Statutory Agencies*, p. 17. One aspect of the problem, that of "Social Workers in the Local Authority Health and Welfare Services," has been thoroughly canvassed in a report (1959) previously cited, by a Ministry of Health Working Party under the chairmanship of Miss Eileen Younghusband.

5

To bring into sharper focus the outlines of voluntary-statutory relations we may take for illustrative purposes two of the main areas covered by the great welfare Acts — the national hospital service and arrangements for the care of the aged. In their different ways both mechanisms remain heavily dependent on voluntary effort.

In persuading the voluntary hospitals to coordinate their operations, the Second World War accomplished what exhortations and warnings from a variety of sources had failed to do. Plainly British hospitals, whether voluntary or public, had to be treated as a common resource of the nation, and in the end the demands of war "produced ideas as relevant to the needs of peace as of war." [71] It was taken for granted that the country could not return to the chaotic individualism of the prewar hospital service. At the end of the War when government subsidies were withdrawn and the hospitals were faced with fantastically mounting costs of medical care, there could be little doubt that the era of voluntarism had come to an end.[72]

Under the National Health Service Act the vast majority of the nation's hospitals, some 1143 voluntary and 1545 municipal, were transferred to the Ministry of Health.[73] The administrative structure set up for them was, however, a curious but thoroughly workable combination of statutory and voluntary elements. Although title and ultimate control would now lie with the Government, there was no intention of creating a full-dress official bureaucracy for the hospital service. Administrative responsibility would be vested not in civil servants but in voluntary committees, their duties and status defined by the Act itself. This has been hailed as "the first example in this country of a public service which is financed almost entirely by public funds being operated by a government department and voluntary service in partnership" — with, one may add, the responsibility for the annual expenditure of over £300 million.[74]

With the exception of the teaching institutions, for which the Act makes special provision, the hospital service is administered through fourteen regional groupings, each under the direction of a regional board. At the next lower level are the hospital management committees, who may be responsible for a single major hospital or a group of smaller ones. All of these committees and board members, some seven thousand of them as early as 1949,[75] serve voluntarily and without remuneration. Curiously enough, this administrative structure, which at first glance suggests excessive decentralization, involves a good deal of central control.

---

[71] Titmuss, *Problems of Social Policy*, p. 504.

[72] *Ibid.*, pp. 456–57; *Essays on the Welfare State*, pp. 152–53.

[73] The only institutions exempted were hospitals operated for profit (nursing homes) and those "disclaimed" by the Ministry, chiefly denominational hospitals, neither category accounting for more than a trivial fraction of the whole.

[74] Trevelyan, *Voluntary Service and the State*, p. 33; Hall, *Social Services*, p. 79.

[75] P.E.P., *Planning*, XVI, No. 303 (1949), p. 96.

The writ of the Minister, PEP points out, runs through the hospital service more effectively than through nationalized industry. One explanation lies in the fact that board and committee members are not elected but appointed by the higher authority. The Minister himself appoints regional boards, which in turn appoint managing committees. Even though, as must inevitably be the case, active administration remains largely in the hands of salaried officials, hospital boards and committees offer a striking example of voluntary-statutory partnership. What remains to be seen is whether the supply of able and qualified members will hold out, especially for assignments that require more than attendance at occasional committee meetings.[76]

When the voluntary hospitals were transferred to the State, with them went the bulk of their endowments, the charitable trusts which witnessed to two centuries of concern for the sick and helpless. A claim to retain control of funds given originally for their benefit was disallowed save in the case of the thirty-six teaching hospitals, which were to continue as semiautonomous units within the national system. They were to be administered by boards of governors independent of regional committees and responsible only to the Minister, and their endowments remained with the governors for "purposes relating to hospital services or research." As a result, some of the better endowed teaching hospitals suddenly attained a state of almost embarrassing affluence. With ordinary running expenses now borne by the State, endowment income was released for financing research, improving facilities, or providing amenities for patients and staff.[77] Yet, in a day of sharply rising costs and especially of rising costs of medical research, one ought not to stress the point unduly.

Even the nonteaching hospitals were not entirely shorn of their free funds, specifically trusts whose objects were partly for hospital and partly for non-hospital purposes. Of such were the so-called "Samaritan Funds" for assisting convalescent patients after leaving the hospital. More often than not, these funds have remained in the hands of hospital management committees. Then, too, the National Health Service Act specifically permitted hospitals to accept donations and legacies. This was enough to inspire some institutions to undertake money-raising activities of their own, until a cease-and-desist order from the Ministry put a stop to official solicitation. Yet "free money" from gifts and bequests, in the spending of which hospital committees enjoy a wide latitude, is of undoubted utility. It may finance special "amenities" — tea and buns for out-patients, a television set for the nurses' home, or a billiard table — and may help to preserve, even within a standardized system, a measure of individuality.

To imply that voluntary service disappeared with the setting up of the National Health Service would do violence to the facts. Both the need and the impulse of Britons to help have continued, if not unabated, at least on a substantial scale. The St. John Ambulance Brigade, for example, carries on much as ever, though

[76] Acton Society Trust Report, *Hospitals and the State,* quoted by Hall, *Social Services,* p. 79.
[77] Trevelyan, *Voluntary Service and the State,* p. 112.

now grant-aided by local authorities. Its total strength — men, women, boys, and girls — exceeds a hundred thousand. More remarkable, perhaps, has been the formation of organized groups to aid particular hospitals by financial contributions and personal service. The 450 local Leagues of Hospital Friends have assisted not only by supplying extras of a material sort but also by creating a reservoir of persons who are not complete strangers to hospital administration.[78]

Of all the larger medical charities, King Edward's Fund perhaps offers the most illuminating example of adjustment to a situation radically different from that which originally called it into existence. In a sense the coming of N.H.S. converted the Fund from a successful but rather humdrum money-raising and money-distributing organization (though astutely using its financial power to improve hospital efficiency) into a mechanism for financing pioneer projects and meeting new needs. The special charitable interest of the Royal Family, the Fund was so well supported that during its first sixty years (1897–1957) hospitals received a total of £17¼ million, of which over £15 million took the form of grants to London institutions.[79] To the Fund the passing of the National Health Service Act came as both a shock and a relief. What had been held to be its chief function was swept away, but its income was now available for other purposes. On the appointed day the Fund could point to capital resources of over £6 million (by 1959 this had risen to £9½ million), while having been freed of most of its regular commitments.[80]

A brief period of uncertainty was followed by realization that the opportunities for the Fund had, in fact, expanded. "Released from financial responsibility for maintenance," the 1948 Report concluded, "it has gained freedom to initiate and develop activities which, not being part of the National Health Service, will yet increase the efficacy of the Hospitals' provision for the sick."[81] In short, save for minor grants to "disclaimed" hospitals in the London area, the Fund would withdraw from what for a half century had been its chief activity and would devote its income to undertakings which could not be carried on by the statutory authorities, such enterprises as staff colleges for hospital administrators, ward sisters, and matrons. There are still grants to hospitals, but for special purposes not included in the official program — experimental equipment for wards; a house at the Royal National Orthopaedic Hospital, where mothers of patients can spend a few days; recreation halls for patients and staff. The Fund's conscious policy is to use its grants to call attention to "this or that need which seems to be escaping its due measure of support from public monies."[82]

The Fund is much more eager to find constructive uses for its income than to add to its capital, but this too is taking place. The subscription list, which was never very large since the Fund avoided entering into direct competition with the

[78] National League of Hospital Friends, *Ann. Rept.*, 1957.
[79] King Edward's Fund, *Ann. Rept.*, 1959, p. 8.
[80] *Ibid.*, 1950, p. 6, and 1959, p. 8.
[81] In its new program the Fund quite deliberately took as its model the Rockefeller Foundation.
[82] *Ibid.*, 1959, p. 6.

hospitals themselves, has shrunk materially. Business houses which formerly subscribed to the Fund rather than to individual hospitals have naturally withdrawn
their contributions. Legacies, however, have continued to come in — £80,000 in
1950, £52,500 in 1955, £225,000 in 1958 (an exceptional year, of course), and
£31,000 in 1959.[83] Such additions to capital have helped to swell the annual income
to about £450,000. No doubt the Fund will be less popular as an object of charitable
bequests in the future than it has been in the past. Some of those recently received
came presumably from pre-N.H.S. wills; yet even with its present resources King
Edward's Fund has marked out for itself a creative role in the statutory-voluntary
hospital partnership.

On balance, the transfer to the State of the voluntary hospitals has not excluded
private philanthropy from the field of medical care, though inevitably its content
and emphasis have shifted. Voluntary service endures, a King's Fund Report
suggests, "not for sentimental reasons but . . . because it is needed and will continue to be needed." [84] Very likely Mr. John Trevelyan's claim can be admitted
when he attributes "the humanity and vitality of the hospital service to-day . . . to
the decision of Parliament . . . to make full use of voluntary effort." [85] Since
1945 the personal contribution of philanthropy has necessarily outweighed the
pecuniary. Although nonstatutory money still serves a variety of useful purposes,
it is no longer the bread and butter of the hospital service. With the hospitals,
traditionally the most voracious of the country's secular charities, no longer claiming the lion's share of British benevolence, some of these funds have been released
for other causes. Philanthropists especially concerned with medical care are no
longer obliged to see their gifts swallowed up in the running expenses of hard-
pressed hospitals, but are free to support more interesting ventures in research,
training, or administrative experiment.

6

Far less orderly than statutory-voluntary cooperation in the hospital service are
the relationships involved in the care of the aged. On the statutory side, primary
responsibility lies with scores of local authorities, while at the center ultimate
control is vested in no single government office. On the voluntary side, an analogous situation has prevailed. Unlike child care, which is dominated by a few
powerful national organizations, agencies having to do with the welfare of the
aged, many of them local and relatively weak, exhibit a bewildering multiplicity
and diversity.[86] The National Assistance Act (1948) assumed a joint voluntary-
statutory effort. In the course of the debate on the Bill, Aneurin Bevan alluded to
the Government's intention "to make full use of voluntary organizations," [87] and
he accepted certain amendments safeguarding the voluntary position. This accom-

[83] *Ann. Repts., passim.*
[84] *Ibid.,* 1951, p. 6.
[85] *Voluntary Service and the State,* p. 122.
[86] Mencher, "Voluntary and Statutory Welfare Services," p. 189.
[87] 5 *Hansard,* 450:2136.

modating attitude was not entirely disinterested. Obviously the facilities and resources of voluntary bodies would be an important asset to the nation-wide scheme
of welfare. Not only were local authorities empowered to provide "residential
accommodation" for the aged and infirm through voluntary agencies, "which
they may either subsidize or employ as their agent on agreed terms," but they
were urged to do so and to work out plans collaboratively.[88]

The National Assistance Act coincided with a fresh appreciation of the problem
of the aged. Growing awareness of changes in the age structure of the population,
together with wartime disclosures of the conditions under which numbers of the
elderly were forced to live, underlined the need for a coherent and comprehensive
social policy. Once again in this branch of social welfare, one traditionally holding
special appeal for the pious and philanthropic, some of the most fruitful pioneering
was being done by voluntary organizations. The National Old People's Welfare
Committee, founded in 1940–41 by the National Council of Social Service, with
Eleanor Rathbone as its first chairman, held a general commission "to study
the needs of old people and to encourage and promote measures for their well
being." [89] It was one of the wartime achievements of the Committee to obtain
from the Assistance Board a supplementary allowance for old people in voluntary
homes and thus to enable pensioners to contribute toward their own maintenance.
This arrangement brought about a remarkable expansion in the number of small
voluntary homes and, in fact, set the pattern for later statutory-voluntary relations.[90]

Probably the most decisive nonofficial influence, however, was that of the Survey
Committee of the Nuffield Foundation, which in the autumn of 1946 submitted
its report on "the problems of ageing and the care of old people." [91] The membership of the Committee — the chairman, it will be recalled, was Seebohm Rowntree
— commanded confidence, and the report *Old People* turned out to be a model of
its kind, thorough, balanced, and concise. From the point of view of this study,
the most striking feature of the report was its assumption that providing for the
aged called for the combined efforts of statutory and nonstatutory agencies. The
Committee went to great pains to get a reasonably occurate inventory of the
country's charitable activities, endowed and voluntary, for the aged. Basing its
estimate on some 3300 questionnaires, which covered about 86 per cent of charities
for the aged, the Committee put their total income at not less than £5 million.[92]
These included nearly 1500 residence charities with accommodations for over
26,000 and over 1800 pension charities with more than 75,000 beneficiaries.[93] But

[88] Ministry of Health Circular 87/46, quoted in National Old People's Welfare Committee, *Age Is Opportunity* (London, 1961), p. 62.
[89] *Ibid.*, pp. 13–14. An account of its first decade is given by Dorothy Ramsey, "The National Old People's Welfare Committee," *Social Service*, 25: pp. 26–28 (1949).
[90] By June 1949 there were nearly 650 voluntary homes for the aged, most of them antedating 1948 (Mencher, "Voluntary and Statutory Welfare Services," pp. 178–79).
[91] Nuffield Survey Committee, *Old People* (London, 1947).
[92] The Committee sent out over forty-eight hundred questionnaires but for one reason or another was obliged to exclude more than fifteen hundred from the final calculation.
[93] *Old People*, pp. 26–27 and App. 1. These were not all separate endowments (in fact, some of

like earlier investigators and critics, the Rowntree Committee was disturbed by the chaos it discovered in the world of endowed charity, the lack of reliable information, especially about parochial charities, and the undiscriminating, slipshod fashion in which income was often distributed.

On the whole, the public assistance institutions, which cared for more than two-thirds of the ninety thousand aged citizens receiving residential care, failed to measure up to the smaller, more informal voluntary homes. They were typically large, impersonal institutions housed in monumental but bleak Victorian structures and administered by rigid regulations. Such accommodations, to say the least, were not sought after, while the demand for places in voluntary homes far outran the supply. Some twenty-six religious bodies, of which the Little Sisters of the Poor, the Sisters of Nazareth, and the Salvation Army were by far the most considerable, housed over 6200 in 98 homes, while 120 secular societies, accommodated about 2750.[94] This was a creditable enough showing, but well short of the demand. Nor was it reasonable to suppose that voluntary bodies could expand their facilities on a scale commensurate with the need. Yet the Committee had no doubt that the small home, voluntary or statutory, was far preferable to the larger institution.

The most direct outcome of the Rowntree inquiry was the formation of the National Corporation for the Care of Old People, financed by the Nuffield Foundation and secondarily by the Lord Mayor's Air Raid Distress Fund, which had come out of the war with a substantial balance. As we have seen, the National Assistance Act imposed on local authorities the duty of providing for the aged and empowered them to arrange with voluntary agencies for accommodations. The Corporation proposed to assist voluntary bodies, by grants-in-aid, help in planning, and pilot schemes, in carrying out their side of the partnership. There was no intention of relieving statutory authorities of their responsibilities under the Act — indeed, they were obliged to pay for the maintenance of individual residents at an agreed rate. This was relatively simple. What produced greater complications was the business of extracting from local authorities capital grants for the improvement of facilities. At the same time, voluntary agencies faced increasing difficulties in raising money independently, having "always to overcome the argument put forward by their subscribers that this is a statutory service which is paid for by rates and taxes and that individuals cannot be expected, nor indeed, can they afford, to contribute twice to the same object."[95] To meet the problem of capital cost of new homes or equipment, during its first two years the Corporation allocated nearly £340,000 to voluntary bodies.[96]

The Corporation has successfully resisted the temptation to use its resources to

them, such as certain religious homes, were not endowed at all). The same endowment, as was frequently the case with almshouse charities, might provide for both accommodations and pensions.

[94] *Ibid.*, pp. 67–68.

[95] *2d Ann. Rept.*, 1949, pp. 3–4.

[96] The funds of the Corporation were augmented by £170,000 from the £1 million gift to the people of Great Britain from the people of South Africa, an increment that was to be used for special projects.

support voluntary organizations on a semipermanent basis. As a result, its record reveals frequent and calculated changes of policy. At the end of five years marked by heavy grants-in-aid for the construction or renovation of homes for the able-bodied and by interest in homes for the infirm, rest homes, and nonresidential clubs, the Corporation was ready to move on to new fields.[97] Henceforth a chief point of emphasis was to be on plans for maintaining the aged in their own homes, pilot schemes which might later form the basis for a more general policy.[98] During its fifteen years the Corporation has admirably exemplified its own philosophy of the pioneering agency in social welfare, indefatigably searching for new and promising approaches or for difficulties which an organization with its wealth and prestige might help to resolve.

Few would have questioned the desirability of maintaining the aged in their own homes as long as practicable, and old people as a class were known to be almost unanimous in their reluctance to be moved.[99] Clearly this was an area where voluntary effort was conspicuously appropriate. The National Assistance Act (s. 31) had recognized this, and had virtually reserved certain domiciliary services to voluntary agencies. The Act empowered local authorities to contribute to the funds of voluntary organizations providing recreation or meals for old people but did not authorize them to establish such services on their own account. If in furnishing homes for the aged, voluntary bodies (even though receiving per capita maintenance payments from local authorities) were contributing to a statutory service, with such activities as "meals-on-wheels," [100] the pattern was reversed. Here statutory authorities were financing what was essentially a voluntary service.

Curiously enough, the Welfare State in general and the National Assistance Act in particular have given a new lease on life to the most traditional of institutions for the care of the aged, the almshouse. Among these foundations are numbered some of the architectural treasures of the Island — Christ's Hospital at Abingdon or the Almshouses at Chipping Camden — monuments to the piety and humanity of earlier generations. Yet it is a mistake to think of the almshouse merely as a vehicle for the charity of remote ages. Actually the latter half of the nineteenth century was one of the more productive periods in the founding of almshouses, and even the years since the Second World War have seen the establishment of a number of handsome modern units. At the close of the War the Rowntree Committee discovered almshouses to be sheltering more old people than the entire body of communal homes, religious and secular.[101]

---

[97] *5th Ann. Rept.*, 1952, p. 4.

[98] *6th Ann. Rept.*, 1953, pp. 7–8.

[99] The Corporation, though favoring home maintenance, was not convinced that this would necessarily be less expensive than providing for them in an old persons' home. Obviously the relative costs would depend on the kind of domiciliary service thought suitable. See B. E. Shenfield, *Social Policies for Old Age* (London, 1957), pp. 169–71, and Hall, *Social Services*, p. 287.

[100] A mobile service providing meals for the aged in their own homes or other places of residence.

[101] About 12,000 to 10,000. The National Association of Almshouses estimated (*An Account of Almshouses*, p. 7) the almshouse population at upwards of 35,000. This figure was, however, a

Although almshouses were carrying a large share of the load, in many instances they were doing it badly, usually through no fault of their own. Numbers of them, always small and underendowed, had decayed until they were plainly unfit for human habitation. Others, once adequately financed, now found themselves caught in the squeeze of rising costs, shrinking income, and higher standards of housing. There was also the complaint, not entirely unjustified, that almshouse endowments had been raided for the benefit of education.[102] At all events, scores of almshouses, some of architectural distinction, had reached a sad state of deterioration and lacked the funds necessary to keep the buildings in a decent state of repair, to say nothing of introducing such elementary improvements as running water and indoor sanitation. In its early years the National Corporation for the Care of Old People had considered financing a program of almshouse modernization but concluded that even the necessary minimum outlay would be so staggering as to preclude other projects.[103]

For almshouse trustees the National Assistance Act both created an opportunity and precipitated a crisis. On the one hand, almshouses now became potential auxiliary agents of the State in carrying out its welfare policies. Not only that, but payment by the National Assistance Board of supplementary allowances to old people in need relieved some of the pressure on almshouse income. In many institutions it was possible to reduce pensions to the residents and to accumulate a modest surplus for repairs and renovation.[104] On the other hand, the Act empowered local authorities to require a standard of comfort and sanitation which, unfortunately, many institutions could not meet without extensive improvements.

With the future thus uncertain, representatives of metropolitan almshouses came together to form a London Association of Almshouses, which in 1951 was expanded into a National Association. Aided by a grant from the National Corporation and with energetic leadership and a council in which architectural and social interests are nicely balanced, the Association has proved to be an astute and resourceful general staff for the almshouse interest. It acts as an intermediary between individual institutions and government offices; it supplies advice, architectural and financial, to trustees faced with problems of renovation; and it has successfully appealed to private donors, among them the Commonwealth Foundation, the Dulverton Trust, and the Joseph Rowntree Memorial Trust, which has

---

conjectural one based on the 500 houses, with their 8000 residents, known to the Association. For American readers it may be useful to distinguish between the almshouse and the ordinary communal old people's home. The almshouse is ordinarily a self-contained apartment, which offers to its occupants an opportunity to live an independent life. Board is not provided, and residents are neither expected nor required to practise community living, though some almshouses are equipped with a chapel and reading and recreation rooms.

[102] Peter Winckworth for the London Association of Almshouses, Nathan Committee, Q. 4059ff; *An Account of Almshouses*, p. 5. It is true that, when the Endowed Schools Commissioners in the 1870's undertook to split an almshouse-cum-school trust, they were rarely charged with undue partiality toward the eleemosynary side.

[103] *2d Ann. Rept.*, 1949, p. 8.

[104] Nathan Committee, Q. 4006–4008.

characterized the work of the Association as "beyond praise." [105] In the rehabilitation of the almshouse, ancient charity, modern voluntary effort, and statutory stewardship have joined hands in fruitful partnership. Hiram's Hospital has become, to a degree, an instrument of the Welfare State.

In perspective, there can be no question of the value of the contribution made by voluntary organizations to the care of the aged. During the past fifteen years they have proved an almost indispensable supplement to statutory arrangements. But it is also impossible to miss the growth and qualitative improvement in the statutory services, and impossible, also, to avoid the suspicion that the public sector is due to expand and the voluntary to contract, at least in a relative sense. On the statutory side, the bulk of the responsibility rests with the local authorities rather than with Whitehall, and on the voluntary, the characterisic organization is also local — a home, society, or committee. The pattern is variegated but, broadly speaking, homes for the aged are heavily dependent on local statutory financing. As long as there is a shortage of accommodations, this support will continue, but homes administered by local authorities themselves have increased in a spectacular fashion. As early as 1954 only about 11 per cent of the total number of aged cared for by local authorities were in voluntary homes.[106]

Conceivably voluntary effort may find its distinctive field in providing a wide range of domiciliary services rather than offering an alternative system of residential care. Here local Old People's Welfare Committees — nearly thirteen hundred in England and Wales[107] — and other groups have carried a heavy burden with considerable success. Often a local authority pays the bills while a voluntary organization carries on the service through its unpaid personnel. Admittedly the mobilization of voluntary workers on such a scale has been impressive.[108] Yet it would be too much to imply that in old age welfare the voluntary-statutory partnership is one between equals. Financial power, prestige, and public acceptance have given the statutory partner the dominant position and brought about the growing dependence of voluntary bodies.[109] More than in certain other parts of the welfare world, the great mass of voluntary organizations serving the aged must conform to statutory policy — so much so that they can be regarded as "voluntary" only in a qualified sense.

To venture predictions about "the future of British philanthropy" would be tempting but foolhardy. Welfare legislation has by no means created a static situation in British society. Further change and constant adjustment are inevitable, and these will continue to affect the giving of money and personal service to meet both older and newly discovered needs. Presumably the status and role

---

[105] *1st Ann. Rept.*, 1960, p. 31.

[106] Mencher, *"Voluntary and Statutory Welfare Services,"* p. 201.

[107] *Younghusband Report*, 1959, Par. 250.

[108] Mrs. Shenfield (*Social Policies for Old Age*, p. 177) discovers "the most heartening feature" in the recent record of voluntary organizations to be "the mobilization of so much practical voluntary help at local levels, even in the smallest community."

[109] Mencher, "Voluntary and Statutory Welfare Services," p. 282.

of voluntary agencies will vary a good deal, as at present, from area to area. Where the State has entered in force, voluntary organizations may well find their position reduced to that of rather minor and dependent auxiliaries. At the least their activities will necessarily be carried on within the framework of the statutory services, and essential policies will be established by the public authorities. Not only that, but there is reason to believe that local authorities will continue, perhaps at an accelerated rate, to take over established services formerly left to voluntary hands.[110] Yet however much the traditional channels of philanthropy may be altered — and narrowed — they are not likely to run dry.

At a guess, one may suspect that future voluntary effort will be especially productive at two widely separated points, almost at opposite ends of the philanthropy spectrum. On the one hand, personal service, given informally or through a voluntary organization or under statutory auspices,[111] will persist and perhaps expand. Plainly the growth of the public welfare system has not only left ample room for voluntary helpfulness, organized as well as individual, but in some respects it has even broadened the opportunities for men to serve their fellows. At the opposite pole are the large general foundations, whose value to the Welfare State is beyond question. Unlike smaller voluntary bodies, such trusts have not only the resources but also the prestige needed to interest ministries, government agencies, and voluntary organizations in their experimental projects. As will appear in the following chapter, not only are the older foundations collaborating with statutory bodies to good effect but their number is still being augmented. At least one major trust[112] has been established on the basis of a fortune accumulated in large part since the War. A kind of volunteer intelligence service, these larger philanthropies form an almost indispensable auxiliary of the official welfare army.

[110] *Younghusband Report,* Par. 1037–38.

[111] *Ibid.,* Par. 1034, which speaks of "the ferment of experiment in the use of voluntary workers in health and welfare departments." For a statistical view, by regions, of the use of voluntary organizations by local authorities, see Table 56 (p. 365).

[112] The Isaac Wolfson Foundation.

CHAPTER XX

AUXILIARIES OF
THE WELFARE STATE:
SOME TWENTIETH-CENTURY
FOUNDATIONS[1]

T HE LARGE charitable trust whose commission allows it to range widely over the world of human affairs holds a special place in the history of philanthropy. And its utility, if anything, has been enhanced rather than diminished by the postwar expansion of the statutory services. Yet the general foundation was no indigenous development in British charity but was transatlantic in its origins and its most luxuriant flowering.

Trusts of substantial size, it is true, were established in Britain around the turn of the century — the Sutton and Rhodes Trusts, for example — but these were directed to special purposes. Nor does the first of the major general foundations, the City Parochial Foundation, stand as typical of the *genre*. For this trust was not the creation of a contemporary philanthropist but an amalgam of obsolete endowments, and its "beneficial area" was limited to metropolitan London. King George's Jubilee Trust, founded in the mid-1930's, came about through vast numbers of contributions rather than a single large benefaction. It was not until the second World War had run more than half its course that a home-grown philanthropist, Lord Nuffield, set up a large foundation with relative freedom in its choice of activities, and today, of those founded originally as general trusts, only the Nuffield and the Isaac Wolfson Foundations, along with the more specialized Wellcome Trust, rest on British-made fortunes.

In this branch of philanthropy it was the United States, where the new industrialism was piling up wealth for its most successful practitioners, that supplied the model. The establishment of Carnegie Corporation in 1911, with an original capital of $125 million, set a capstone on the series of more specialized foundations already created by the Scottish-American philanthropist. The same decade saw the emergence of The Rockefeller Foundation, which continued and branched out from the work carried on by the General Education Board, a Rockefeller trust set up in 1903. The Foundation itself was incorporated in 1913, after three years of what now seems like a preposterous controversy.[1]

---

[1] F. Emerson Andrews, *Philanthropic Foundations* (New York, 1956), p. 43. The application to

The growing penchant of certain American multimillionaires for giving away their money through a general foundation was responsible for the first two such trusts in Britain. Both were based on fortunes made in America, though the donors — both, incidentally, had Scottish antecedents — admitted to motives of filial piety in their philanthropies. In 1913 Andrew Carnegie set up the Carnegie United Kingdom Trust with $10 million in United States Steel Corporation bonds. This followed some years after the establishment of his Scottish Universities Trust in 1901, the Dunfermline Trust (for the benefit of his native town) in 1903, and the Carnegie Hero Fund. The Pilgrim Trust, founded by Edward S. Harkness[2] in 1930, had a curiously informal origin. As told to the Nathan Committee by Lord Macmillan, who with John Buchan and Sir James Irvine had been a guest at a small dinner given by Harkness at Claridge's, the first intimation came when "our host turned to us and said, 'Gentlemen, I am a hundred per cent. American, five generations in the States, but I have never forgotten the rock whence I was hewn. My people came from a little village in Dumfriesshire in Scotland and there are the graves of my ancestors. I have been blessed with this world's goods to a quite inordinate extent and have spent my life in philanthropy . . . Now my heart has turned to the country of my origin. I know you are passing through a period of great financial difficulty and you may lose some of the most valuable things in your country, your national heritage, just through want of a little timely help . . . Now will you gentlemen accept £2 million just to do with as you think right. You know the things that are needed. I do not.' That was the Trust." [3]

As financial operations these British trusts are relatively modest. Even the largest of them, the Nuffield Foundation with 1963 assets of over £36 million (market value), seems unimposing when measured against the roughly $3944 million of the Ford Foundation, the $632 million of The Rockefeller, and the $268 million of Carnegie Corporation.[4] The Nuffield Foundation's grants for 1954–55 came to less than 4 per cent of the Ford's nearly $50 million, about 11 per cent of The Rockefeller's $17 million, and 38 per cent of Carnegie Corporation's $5 million.[5] If the dimensions of British trusts seem rather small in comparison with their American opposite numbers, they are also dwarfed by government-supported trusts in Britain itself. In 1953 the British Council, for example, was receiving an annual income from public funds of over £3 million, and the Arts Council an annual Treasury grant of £785,000. This latter amount exceeded the annual outlay of the Nuffield Foundation, and the former equaled the total expenditures of the

---

Congress in 1910 for a charter produced "a storm of protest," and in the end the Foundation was incorporated under the laws of the State of New York.

[2] The father of E. S. Harkness had been a partner of Rockefeller in the Standard Oil Company.

[3] Nathan Committee, Q. 2180.

[4] Letter from F. Emerson Andrews, 31 Dec. 1963.

[5] The percentages were computed by Miss Evelyan Janover in my 1957–58 Harvard-Radcliffe seminar. At this stage, it should be pointed out, Ford policies were not fully developed, and the total of grants was relatively small. In 1963 these reached $171 million, with administrative costs accounting for another $8 million.

Foundation in the previous five years. In 1954–55, when the Foundation spent a record total of over £680,000 in grants, the State bestowed on colleges and universities about £28 million, with over a million more in research grants in the arts and sciences and nearly £2 million more to the Medical Research Council.[6]

Yet to be unduly impressed by such comparisons would be to miss the significance of foundations in the structure of British life. In Britain the cleavage between private philanthropy and state action is less marked than in the United States; in some of the areas which are normally of concern to foundations, British trusts carry a perceptibly smaller share of the load than do their transatlantic counterparts. Nor do Englishmen share American suspicions of government spending as a step to government control. The British Council, the Arts Council, and the University Grants Committee, quasi-official bodies, go their beneficent way with little opposition in principle. Some of their specific decisions may incur criticism, but it will be errors in judgment rather than sinister motives that are charged.

Relations between the larger foundations and the Government are, in fact, exceedingly close and are carried on in an atmosphere of mutual confidence. The concentration in London of government, finance, intellectual *expertise* (with the ancient universities not two hours distant), and the resources of philanthropy has made for a certain understanding, even coziness, in the handling of their common concerns. This was specifically contemplated in the plans of organization of some of the larger trusts. Though not required to follow official views on any question, the Managing Trustees of the Nuffield Foundation were "enjoined to consult the appropriate Ministries or departments of State in connection with any matters of major importance in which they may become interested,"[7] and a similar doctrine governs the trustees of the younger Isaac Wolfson Foundation.

One hears of Treasury officials dining at Nuffield Lodge and suggesting things which needed doing but which the Government could not or ought not to undertake. The foundation's program of rheumatism research, for example, was proposed by the Ministry of Health.[8] Conversely, in 1946 the offer of the Pilgrim Trust to contribute £50,000 to buy the Hirsch music library for the British Museum apparently inspired the Chancellor of the Exchequer to add £60,000.[9] Few rivalries or jealousies appear to have marred the cooperation between the public branches of the welfare forces and their private allies. In major campaigns, it is conceded, the main brunt must fall on the statutory armies, but these will rely, in some degree, on philanthropic foundations for their intelligence service, mobile units, and other auxiliary strength.

[6] Guy Keeling, *Trusts and Foundations* (Cambridge, 1953), pp. 5, 17; *Whitaker's Almanac*, 1955, p. 596.
[7] *Manchester Guardian*, 13 Feb. 1943.
[8] Interview with Mr. W. A. Sanderson, Assistant Director, June 1956; *Report on Grants, 1943–53* (Oxford, 1954), p. 37.
[9] Nathan Committee, Q. 2220.

2

Foundation executives think of their greatest single function as that of operating a "first-run experiment station." The larger trusts have, in fact, pioneered in countless projects, some of long-range significance. Most of them are interested only in the experimental stages of a program (and in spot grants for special purposes), and they reject applications that involve continuing grants. As a group, they are committed to a philosophy of risk-taking, and they like to think of the large foundation as the "venture capital" of society. The now classic remark on the subject was made to the Nathan Committee by the Secretary of the Carnegie United Kingdom Trust, "I think it is the business of trusts to live dangerously." [10]

For them the most welcome vindication of their policies comes when Government or voluntary bodies take over a scheme which the foundation has seen through the pilot stage. Sometimes, indeed, projects have been designed expressly as demonstration aids for public authorities. Thus, as its contribution to the problem of housing the aged poor, the City Parochial Foundation in 1948–49 built an experimental unit, Isleden House, at a cost of £275,000, incorporating in it every imaginable facility for the comfort and care of the elderly. Local authorities, it was realized, could not afford to model their undertakings on Isleden House. What was intended was to offer them an "ideal" unit, which would serve as a source of ideas for those who had to plan for the care of the aged. In 1953 the establishment was bought by the London Corporation.

The adoption by the Government of a successful foundation experiment has become a familiar enough phenomenon. A case in point is the experience of the Carnegie United Kingdom Trust, which, in cooperation with local authorities, established libraries up and down the Island. By 1935, however, the Trust had concluded that public agencies were sufficiently committed to doing what remained to be done and moved on to other interests. The Arts Council developed out of the Committee for the Encouragement of Music and Art (CEMA), which was founded by the Pilgrim Trust in 1939 and was later taken over by the Government. Again, shortly after the second World War the Nuffield Foundation financed a series of scholarships to make possible a period of training in England for Colonial Service officers of Colonial or Dominion origin. The hope of the Foundation that the Colonial Office would take over the scheme was realized when the Colonial Development and Welfare Act of 1948 included a provision for such scholarships.[11]

The same Foundation sponsored the visits of young British farmers to the United States, Canada, the Netherlands, and elsewhere to observe methods in branches of agriculture of special interest to them. Eventually what amounted to a post-graduate travel course in farming received the support of the National

[10] *Nathan Report*, Par. 59.
[11] *Report on Grants*, 1943–53, p. 169.

Farmers Union and the various regional associations. The Nuffield Provincial Hospitals Trust (which antedated the Foundation) made a valiant attempt to coordinate the hospital services on a regional basis and, positively or negatively, prepared the ground for a national system. Most far-reaching of all, perhaps, was the influence exerted by the Foundation, through the Rowntree report and the National Corporation for the Care of Old People, on public opinion and on the policies of statutory and voluntary bodies. As we have already seen, the Rowntree inquiry had something to do with thrusting the problem of old age into the forefront of postwar social issues.

Other services rendered by large foundations are, in a sense, functions of their independent status. In some instances they have served as intermediaries, almost as mediators, between the Government and interested groups. Some years ago farming circles were disposed to criticize the Agricultural Advisory Service of the Ministry of Agriculture. To test the validity of their complaints and to canvass possibilities of improvement an official of the Nuffield Foundation brought a team of experts to the United States to study the agricultural extension service and submitted to the Ministry a report of its findings.[12] In another domain, that of scientific research, it is of obvious value to have a "second opinion" on projects which may have been rejected by the official agency. Since the Medical Research Council enjoys a virtual monopoly of government funds for supporting medical research and its membership is roughly identical with that of the Clinical Research Council, nonacceptance by these two bodies amounts to a final veto. In such instances both government agencies and citizens who have reason to query their decisions can be well served by the disinterested opinion of a responsible foundation with resources of its own.

Not all of the larger trusts have been as consciously experimental as Nuffield. Some have preferred to assist established institutions by providing facilities which lie outside the scope (or immediate capabilities) of statutory support. Of such are the gifts by the Wolfson Foundation to universities and colleges for the endowment of chairs and for needed physical equipment, and those of the Pilgrim Trust for the preservation of ancient buildings and historical records. In terms of practical policies there is no necessary conflict between the "gap-filling" and "venture capital" principles, as long as filling the same gap does not become a perennial commitment. Many grants involve elements of both, and most foundations, in varying degrees, are interested alike in discovering new needs and in closing existing gaps in statutory or voluntary arrangements. The Pilgrim Trust may conceive of itself, properly enough, as a "salvage corps," but in fact some of its salvage operations have been highly original and imaginative and have led to action by other bodies.

Both approaches have their merits and dangers. On the one hand, determination to "live dangerously" can sometimes lead to the financing of marginal or overambitious projects. Money poured into "inter-disciplinary" attempts "to elu-

---

[12] Interview with W. A. Sanderson.

cidate some problems of contemporary importance" has not always been productive. Thus the *Ninth Report* of the Nuffield Foundation concedes that "most of [such] projects have had to be initiated by the Foundation itself, since it seems that people with different skills do not readily and spontaneously combine to seek solutions to current questions." [13] Such ventures may be prosecuted at the cost of allowing other enterprises of proved value to languish. Yet no one would deny that the measure of a foundation's achievement lies not only in its judgment in choosing among proposals presented to it but in searching out new and vital areas of usefulness.

On the other hand, gap-filling carries hazards of its own. It can easily deteriorate into a convention of supporting only established and safe projects — in short, of making grants which will become the means of lubricating "the gears of the status quo." [14] To assist in work of demonstrated value is an unobjectionable policy if pursued in moderation. The danger is that it may lead to "scatteration" philanthropy — spending too small amounts on too many agencies or individuals, deserving enough in themselves, as is said to have been done by the Pilgrim Trust in its early days,[15] and to renewing grants with such regularity that agencies and institutions come to regard the foundation almost as an annual subscriber. The larger British trusts, virtually without exception, have resisted these temptations. Their common practice, to repeat, is to review their policies every five years, and not infrequently drastic shifts are made for the ensuing period. Not only that, but many grants are, of course, made as lump sums for specific purposes — £250,000 for a residence hall for Commonwealth students at London University or £50,000 "to save Durham Castle from falling into the river." [16] As with American foundations, such benefactions are often conditional on the raising of a specified sum by the applicants themselves.

British foundations have not escaped the dilemmas of their kind. Yet on the whole the judgment must be that the nation receives good value for such concessions, legal and fiscal, as it extends to them. They appear to operate with a minimum of administrative superstructure; their overhead tends to be rather lower than that of the leading American foundations. In the mid-'50's Nuffield's was running about 7½ per cent and the Pilgrim's about 5 per cent as against 10 per cent for the Ford Foundation (without its improvident satellite, the Fund for the Republic), 7 per cent for Carnegie, and 13 per cent for Rockefeller.[17] British

[13] Page 64.

[14] Dwight Macdonald, *The Ford Foundation* (New York, 1956), p. 49.

[15] H. A. Mess, *The Voluntary Social Services*, pp. 181–82.

[16] The first by the Isaac Wolfson Foundation (*The Times*, 31 July 1958) and the second by the Pilgrim Trust (Nathan Committee, Q. 2185).

[17] Dwight Macdonald, *The Ford Foundation*, p. 72; Nuffield Foundation, *10th Rept.*, 1954–55, p. 108. Nathan Committee, Q. 2210. These percentages are based on the ratio of grants to administrative expenses. The calculation for the Ford Foundation takes no account of grants of $35 million to its three subsidiaries. Too much significance, however, ought not to be attached to these figures. Overhead costs will depend, in part, on the kind of work undertaken by the foundation, the size of grants which it awards, and a number of other variables.

foundation resources appear to have been skilfully handled, and they have increased satisfactorily, in some instances strikingly. In fact, the large trust is able to carry on its range of undertakings and to risk some of its income in unproductive experiments not only because its resources are great but because they grow. The Nathan Committee was impressed by the difference between small and large endowments in this respect. While the small charity rarely rose in value and often declined, the assets of the larger foundations had increased strikingly. In the sixty years from 1891 to 1951 the income of the City Parochial Foundation grew from £80,000 to £230,000. By mid-century the endowment of the Pilgrim Trust was half again as large as at its creation in 1931, and the Carnegie United Kingdom Trust doubled its capital in less than forty years.[18] In 1959 the Rowntree Village Trust, as we have seen, found itself with an income more than 50 per cent greater than its original assets, and so ample as to encourage the foundation to move into areas other than housing.[19]

All in all, British foundations, if not absolutely indispensable, have plainly made a place for themselves in the structure of the welfare society. The extension of state responsibility has not seriously impaired their social utility, and may even have enhanced it. Certainly they still enjoy the unique advantages summarized by Edwin Embree a decade ago in an article criticizing the policies of American foundations, and, in the large, they have shown themselves alive to the obligations implicit in their position. These agencies, he pointed out, "are unique in their opportunity to pioneer. They have free funds and freedom of operation. Not restricted to narrow purposes, their mobile resources can be used on any front for any cause that presents special need or special opportunity. They do not have to cater to a standardized constituency by doing the popularly accepted things . . . If their experiments do not come up to expectation, there is no social catastrophe. If they succeed, the work is taken up by the state or by general giving, leaving the foundation free to move on to pioneering in other fields."[20]

3

Although relatively few in number and, in comparison with their American counterparts, relatively weak in financial resources, British foundations manage to cover a good deal of territory. Partly intuitively and partly by informal arrangement, each occupies its own sector of specialization, so that there is little overlapping or duplication. Admittedly this can be overdone. There has been some uneasiness at Nuffield Lodge over the fact that the Foundation remains practically the only source of support for research in the social sciences. Here some competition might be salutary.[21] Yet on the whole the efforts of the various foundations

[18] *Nathan Report,* Par. 555; Nathan Committee, Q. 2723.

[19] The Trust had grown from total assets of about £62,150 in 1904 to an *income* of about £100,000 in 1959 (*1st Rept.,* 1960).

[20] Edwin R. Embree, "Timid Billions: Are the Foundations Doing Their Job?", *Harper's Magazine,* 198:29 (March 1949).

[21] As suggested by W. A. Sanderson.

mesh satisfactorily, aided by occasional conferences of the chief administrative officers, who sometimes consider borderline applications as a group.[22]

During the past decade the Carnegie United Kingdom Trust has concentrated on various branches of social welfare, while the Nuffield has promoted research in the social sciences and medicine, and has maintained special connections with the Commonwealth. Its subsidiary, the National Corporation for the Care of Old People, continues to support research into the problems of age, and King George V's Jubilee Trust specializes in work for youth. The Pilgrim Trust is heavily involved in preserving the national heritage, especially the architectural heritage, and the City Parochial Foundation with a variety of projects in the Metropolis. Of the most recently established trusts, the larger Isaac Wolfson grants have gone chiefly to colleges, universities, and research institutions, while the Gulbenkian, not technically a British foundation but one on which Britain has special claims, has taken the support of the arts as its particular province.

The Carnegie Trust was first in the field, an expression of its founder's desire to benefit his native country more broadly than was possible under his three previously established British trusts. This was, however, a Scottish charity, not an English, and it is not subject to the jurisdiction of English courts or of the Charity Commissioners.[23] In fact, some pressure was necessary to dissuade Carnegie from placing the administration of his new foundation in the hands of the trustees of his Dunfermline Trust, a purely local body which was hardly equipped to deal with the wider field now contemplated. The compromise saddled the United Kingdom Trust with a rather cumbersome administrative structure, thirty to forty trustees and an executive committee of sixteen.[24] To finance his British foundation, Carnegie made the novel proposal of withdrawing $10 million from the bonds belonging to Carnegie Corporation of New York, which he had founded two years before. On being reminded by Elihu Root that such a trust, once made, was irrevocable and that the bonds were in the legal custody of the Corporation's trustees, the undiscouraged philanthropist dug into his personal reserve for the necessary sum.[25]

The terms of the Trust were unobjectionably liberal: "The improvement of the well-being of the masses of the people of Great Britain and Ireland by such means as are embraced within the meaning of the word 'charitable' according to Scotch or English law and which the Trustees may from time to time select as best fitted from age to age for securing these purposes, remembering that new needs are constantly arising as the masses advance." In spite of their inclusive assignment, during the early years the trustees tended to follow the donor's special interests.[26] This meant, on the one hand, giving vigorous support to the library movement as a whole — financing a rural library service, municipal libraries, and certain special

[22] Nathan Committee, Q. 2718 (Carnegie U. K. Trust).
[23] Ibid., Q. 2565.
[24] Ibid., Q. 2571.
[25] B. J. Hendrick, Life of Carnegie, II, 351–52.
[26] A brief account of the Trust to the 1940's is given in Mess, Voluntary Social Services, chap. XI.

collections, and helping to improve the quality and professional status of librarian-
ship — and, on the other, encouraging a variety of musical interests. Here the
trustees did not share the founder's enthusiasm for church organs as a means of
fostering love of music, but they discovered other — and, as they thought, more
productive — ways of accomplishing the end in view. They subsidized the publication of contemporary and of Tudor music, and they arranged for the performance of good music, by professionals and amateurs, in rural districts. Up to the
end of 1949 the Trust had spent on its library interests about £1,640,000, or more
than two-fifths of its total grants of nearly £4 million, and it could take pride
with having created, in the words of King George V, "a National University
which all may attend and none need ever leave." [27]

The Trust has held consistently to the practice of framing its policies in five-year
blocks, and its special emphases show a good deal of change from period to
period. All in all, there were sound grounds for satisfaction in the Carnegie record
as one of constructive pioneering, for in instance after instance experiments of
the Trust influenced government policies. Libraries, of course, became public
undertakings; an investment of about £250,000 in the National Playing Fields
Association led to the Physical Training and Recreation Act of 1937; land settlement, in which the Trust was especially interested in the late '30's, passed over
to the Ministry of Agriculture; and the Ministry of Education took over the
scheme of providing village halls and rural community centers which the Trust
had originally financed.[28]

More recently the Trust has put a considerable fraction of its income of approximately £135,000 into projects connected, in a direct and practical sense, with
social welfare. It does not finance research in the social sciences as such. The
Carnegie Trust regards expert investigation as simply the first stage in a planned
sequence comprising inquiry, pilot experiment, and finally application of the
results on a larger scale by public authorities or other agencies. For example, the
Trust has collaborated with the National Council of Social Service in sponsoring
a study of the problems of social growth in new communities, the New Towns
as well as other types. With the completion of Dr. J. H. Nicholson's report, *New
Communities in Britain: Achievements and Policies* (1961), the second stage was
reached, and for the five years 1961–65 the Trust has allocated a substantial sum
to support pilot schemes, some of which, it is presumed, will turn out to be of
general relevance.[29] Looking back over nearly a half century of philanthropy, the
United Kingdom Trust can summarize its achievements in these terms: Of a
total disbursement (1916–60) of over £6 million, about 36 per cent went to educational services, chiefly libraries; 18 per cent to community services; 11 per cent

---

[27] *36th Rept.*, 1949, p. 14. This document contains an interesting summary of the library work of
the Trust.
[28] Nathan Committee, Q. 2633–38.
[29] *47th Rept.*, 1960, pp. 26–27.

to the arts, music, and drama; 11 per cent to physical and mental welfare; 8.3 per cent to youth services; and the balance in non-grant expenditures.[30]

The early emphases of the Pilgrim Trust, in order of chronology the next of Britain's general foundation,[31] were heavily conditioned by the situation in Britain at the time of its founding. If, as the trustees interpreted the wishes of the founder, their charge was "to come to the rescue of the things that mattered in our country," they could hardly ignore the distress of the unemployed thousands and especially the black distress that pervaded such areas as South Wales, Lancashire, and the Tyneside.[32] Here plainly was important work for a "salvage corps," and the trustees invested heavily in agencies working in depressed areas. They established holiday centers, craft industries, and clubs, and they paid the salaries of numbers of organizers and trained workers. In the course of it, they made grants to a large, perhaps an excessive, number of organizations. In 1936, for example, eighty-four agencies (including some federal bodies which would redistribute their grants) received about £66,000 out of a Trust income of roughly £125,000.[33]

The trustees, however, were not unmindful of the other side of their salvage operation, that of preserving the national heritage in architecture, historical records, and, in broad terms, the nation's memorabilia. For the first twenty years their grants break down as follows (in 000's):[34]

Preservation (buildings, records, countryside)	£ 779
Art and learning	408
Social welfare	660
	£1,847

Since the War the balance has shifted heavily toward "preservation" as the primary commitment of the Trust. In 1948, for example, grants (exceptionally small that year) in this category came to nearly £39,000 as against a total of less than £22,000 for the other two.[35] No visitor to English cathedrals or parish churches can be unaware of the achievement of the Trust. Between 1930 and 1949, over £112,000 was provided for the repair and preservation of nineteen cathedrals, and 159 parish churches were assisted with grants totaling £86,000.[36]

To illustrate Pilgrim policies, we may look at one of the early postwar years. In 1948 the trustees decided against grants-in-aid to parish churches, having become convinced by the deluge of applications that the situation lay beyond the means

[30] Ibid., App. XI.
[31] I am omitting the City Parochial Foundation since it has been covered in an earlier chapter.
[32] Nathan Committee, Q. 2185.
[33] Mess, Voluntary Social Services, p. 181.
[34] Memorandum by the Pilgrim Trust, Nathan Committee.
[35] 18th Rept., 1948, p. 2.
[36] Memorandum to the Nathan Committee.

of a private foundation. But if parish churches were deferred, three cathedrals were included, Chester and Bristol for help in schemes of restoration and York for reinstalling its ancient glass. Westminster School received a grant for work on its famous dormitory, and the Merchant Adventurers of York for restoring their buildings and preserving their records. Through a Pilgrim grant the National Trust was able to acquire Arlington Row at Bibury in the Cotswolds and the Guild Hall group at Lavenham, Suffolk. The trustees purchased two ancient documents — the earliest known minute book of the Order of the Garter, presented to the Knights, and the Sherborne Chartulary for the British Museum. The Linnean Society of London and the Society of Antiquaries in Scotland were assisted in special crises, and the new Severn Wildfowl Trust was started off with a grant toward its initial capital expenditure. In "art and learning" the Trust continued its sponsorship of *Recording Britain* and of Radzinowicz's *History of English Criminal Law*. Small grants in the social welfare category went to the Free Legal Advice Centres maintained in London by Cambridge House and the Mary Ward Settlement. These were intended as a kind of holding operation until the Legal Advice and Aid Bill (1948) should make unnecessary further private financing.[37]

The Trust's special interest in "preservation" does not naturally predispose it to a "pioneering" role. For obvious reasons Pilgrim grants less commonly lead to action by statutory authorities than do those from foundations whose concerns are more directly social and political, and fewer Pilgrim projects are taken over by the State. This was not the case in the 1930's, but as the sphere of welfare legislation broadened after the war, the trustees deliberately shifted their emphasis to "those things which cannot call for public money." Yet the value of the Pilgrim contribution is beyond question. A foundation which can act quickly and decisively enough to prevent the possible dispersal of Sir Isaac Newton's library performs a service as real as the body which carries on a pilot study of juvenile delinquency. As the chairman of the Trust tells the story:

I suddenly heard one day from Dr. Trevelyan of Trinity College [who] wrote me a letter and said 'Have you seen that Sir Isaac Newton's library has been discovered in the possession of some family in England who are going to sell it? It would be a disaster if Sir Isaac Newton's books were to leave the country and not to be preserved intact; won't you do something?' So simple and flexible is our administration that I was able to act at once . . . I said to my secretary . . . 'Go down and prevent them selling. We are in this.' We were able in a few days so to arrange matters that we bought Sir Isaac Newton's library for £5,000 containing among other things his own copy of the *Principia* with his own manuscript emendations in the margin, his own copy of the famous *Optics* — in short, all the books which represented his daily surroundings in his library . . . You can now see [them] in a bay of the Trinity College Library . . . It is a charming thing to have been able to do.[38]

[37] *18th Rept.,* 1948, *passim.*
[38] Lord Macmillan, Nathan Committee, Q. 2185.

The work of the Pilgrim Trust, in sum, admirably complements that of other foundations. Obviously the social economy of the Welfare State requires agencies which conserve as well as those which conceive their chief function to be pioneering.

In two respects King George's Jubilee Trust is atypical of the general foundation. On the one hand, its purpose is to promote the "welfare of the younger generation," and the terms of its trust deed limit its activities to this broad object. On the other, not only was the original capital supplied by numbers of contributors rather than a single philanthropist, but the Trust has continued to receive donations and subscriptions. King George's Trust has never hesitated to spend in excess of its funded income, although it has sought to maintain its capital fund at the original level. The Trust dates from 1935 when the Prince of Wales appealed for a national thank-offering in honor of King George's Silver Jubilee, the proceeds to be devoted to advancing the welfare of youth. The original appeal produced about £1 million, but increments continued to be received. In the decade 1939–49, for example, the Trust was enriched by about £67,000 in donations and subscriptions, £188,000 from legacies, and £59,000 from the sale of publications.[39] Able to look forward to additional support of a more or less regular sort, the Trust has boldly overspent its assured income during periods of special pressure. In each case the tactic succeeded, for a series of windfalls served to maintain the holdings of the Trust at a point somewhat above the £1 million norm.

Although King George's Trust works chiefly through grants to existing youth organizations, in a few instances it has initiated new ventures. King George's House in London, a hostel built at a cost of about £75,000 for boys between fourteen and eighteen, had about 180 residents in 1938. The Trust also took the lead in establishing a model youth center at Scunthorpe in Lincolnshire.[40] As a central headquarters for all of the forces engaged in work for youth, the Trust has sponsored a series of studies attempting to survey the field and define its problems.[41] But by far the lion's share of Trust expenditure has been in grants. with virtually no strings attached, to national youth agencies. Of the fifty-seven organizations and institutions receiving grants in the years 1935–49, eight beneficiaries account for over two-thirds of the total of nearly £700,000,[42] and two of these — the National Associations of Boys Clubs and of Girls Clubs — received over £260,000. All this suggests that the role of King George's Jubilee Trust is rather more passive than that of some of the other foundations. In general, it has chosen to support established organizations and does not hesitate to assist them on a semipermanent basis.

With the Wellcome Trust we reach a new category of foundation. Not only

[39] *5th Rept.*, 1949, p. 41.
[40] Constance Braithwaite in Mess, *Voluntary Social Services*, p. 185.
[41] *5th Rept.*, 1949, pp. 31–32.
[42] Excluding the £76,150 to the Youth Hostels Association for King George's House.

are its resources considerably greater than the endowments thus far considered but these are drawn entirely and directly from the profits of the large pharmaceutical house, Burroughs Wellcome & Company. In this the Trust resembles the Carlsberg Foundation (Carlsberg Breweries) in Denmark. The founder was Henry Solomon Wellcome, born in Wisconsin in 1853 and brought up in Garden City, Blue Earth County, Minnesota, who took up the serious study of pharmacy largely as a result of his contact with the May brothers of Rochester. Traveling abroad for McKesson & Robbins, he fell in with Burroughs, whom he had met before, and their interest in the British market inspired them in 1880 to form Burroughs Wellcome & Company. The partnership lasted for fifteen years when, after the death of Burroughs, Wellcome found himself the sole proprietor.

One of Wellcome's signal assets was his profound belief in the importance for the pharmaceutical enterprise of independent research. The series of institutes that he established — the Wellcome Physiological Research Laboratories (1894) and the Wellcome Chemical Research Laboratories (1896) — had no regular connection with the firm, nor did the later Wellcome Laboratories for Tropical Medicine, the Historical Medical Museum and Library, and the Museum of Medical Science. These were personal ventures of Wellcome, though some of them obviously contributed much to the business, and it therefore became necessary to clarify the relationship between the two. The solution was a company registered in 1924 under the somewhat misleading name of the Wellcome Foundation Limited with a theoretical capital of £1 million, all owned by Wellcome himself. This new arrangement included the parent firm, the whole body of subsidiaries and branches, and all of the laboratories, museums, and libraries that Wellcome had maintained. It is not surprising that the distinction between the Foundation and the Trust has been a difficult one for the uninitiated. As for Wellcome himself, he died in 1936 loaded with honors, a knight, an LL.D. (Edinburgh), and a Fellow of the Royal College of Surgeons and of the Royal Society.[43]

There is reason to believe that Wellcome expected that the trustees appointed in his will would administer both the business and the charitable projects that he had in view. Obviously this was out of the question, and the early years of the Trust were confused and troubled — by the problem of setting up machinery to handle the business, by estate duty complications, and by the destruction of the War. A curious difficulty was created by Wellcome's bequest of $400,000 for a memorial in Garden City, Minnesota, which would include a public library, an assembly hall, and a playground. But contrary to his expectation, Garden City had not grown appreciably but had remained a farming village of some two hundred inhabitants, in which the only substantial building was a consolidated school. The trustees were therefore obliged to have the trust modified so that the more useful features of the bequest, such as the assembly hall, could form a part of the school plant.

Their early problems were so involved that the trustees got into action slowly.

---

[43] Wellcome Trust, *1st Rept.*, 1937–56, pp. 9–17.

During the first twenty years of the Trust the grants totaled only £1,170,000, all but a little under £50,000 going to medical research. Although this is the primary purpose of the endowment, the trustees do not construe it in a limited fashion, but continue to invest considerable amounts in medical history, one of Wellcome's primary interests. More recently the Trust has been gathering momentum, with over £1 million in grants in 1956–58 and about £1,200,000 in 1958–60.[44] The bulk of these, again, went for medical research broadly construed. The Trust has financed special projects, given individual grants, established research chairs, and built buildings. Their policy, the trustees point out, is "one of opportunism"[45] — that is, of searching for gaps in existing research facilities and for needs being unmet by other agencies.

Two other trusts, both the creation of the mid-'50's, qualify for inclusion in a list of general foundations. The first of these, the Calouste Gulbenkian, is something of a special case. Established under the will of an Armenian-born, naturalized British subject who spent most of his later years in Lisbon, the Foundation is technically Portuguese and its main offices are in Lisbon. But Britain and the Commonwealth are specified among the areas of special interest,[46] and a London branch is vested with initial responsibility for Commonwealth grants. The resources of the Foundation are less determinable than those of most trusts, for the main source of revenue (originally put at over £5 million a year) consists of a 5 per cent share in the output of the Iraq Petroleum Company. At the outset the trustees recognized a certain precariousness in their financial position — their income was, in fact, reduced in 1956–57 by the cutting of the pipelines in Syria — and they determined to set aside and fund "a substantial part" of their annual receipts.[47]

The terms of the Gulbenkian trust are sufficiently broad to comprehend almost any legal charitable purpose — learning, the arts, science, welfare. But in its grants to Britain and the Commonwealth the Foundation leans heavily toward learning and the arts, especially the latter. One of the first grants, incidentally, was £25,000 toward building the Shakespeare Festival Theatre in Stratford, Ontario.[48] Early in 1958 the Gulbenkian trustees launched an inquiry into the needs of the arts in Britain, and in the same year awarded a total of about £200,000, nearly half of which went to the arts. Altogether during the first four years of Gulbenkian activity the United Kingdom and the overseas Commonwealth profited by grants totaling over £850,000.[49]

The Isaac Wolfson Foundation, established in 1955 by the managing director of Great Universal Stores, Ltd., operates on a capital fund of over £6 million

[44] 2d Rept., 1956–58, p. 11; 3d Rept., 1958–60, p. 8.
[45] 1st Rept., 1937–56, p. 68.
[46] The others being Portugal, the Middle East, and the Armenian communities. (The Times, 14 Sept. 1956.)
[47] The Times, 14 Sept. 1956.
[48] Ibid., 27 April 1957.
[49] Ibid., 4 Nov. 1959 and 20 July 1960.

consisting largely of holdings in the company. Since Great Universal Stores controls a formidable list of retail establishments — among them Burberry's, Darling & Company (Princes Street, Edinburgh), Waring & Gillow, Penberthy's, Ltd. (Oxford Street), Jay's Ltd., and others, as well as a huge mail order business, travel agency, and merchant bank — and has been showing annual profits of upwards of £20 million, the future of the trust appears reasonably secure.[50] Wolfson, indeed, is the first of the group of fabulously successful entrepreneurs who have risen to prominence in postwar Britain to assign to philanthropy a share of his fortune. The late Lord Nathan was the original chairman, and among the trustees are such distinguished figures as Sir John Cockroft, first Master of Churchill College, Cambridge; Lord Birkett; and Professor Arthur Goodhart, Master Emeritus of University College, Oxford, and an eminent legal scholar.

The Foundation holds a relatively inclusive commission, and its announced policy calls for special attention to the advancement of health, education, and youth activities in the United Kingdom and the Commonwealth. The slightly over a hundred grants made thus far (to October 1962) show a considerable sweep of interest, and they vary in amount from £600 to £450,000. The larger amounts, however, have gone to established institutions for specific purposes — such as £250,000 to the Westminster Hospital for a School of Nursing, £200,000 for a research professorship in the Royal Society, £450,000 for a new headquarters building for the Royal College of Physicians, and £350,000 to the Imperial College of Science and Technology for a biochemical laboratory. In its first seven years the Foundation has awarded nearly £5 million in grants, over £4 million of these falling in the health and education categories.[51] Its best publicized benefaction — £100,000 toward the purchase price of £140,000 (the balance being provided by the Government) for the Goya "Duke of Wellington" came to an unhappy issue when the portrait was stolen from the National Gallery in one of the more sensational art thefts of recent years. There are, in sum, good reasons for believing that the Wolfson Foundation fills a genuine gap in the lines of British philanthropy. Less restlessly experimental than Nuffield but considerably more selective than, say, King George's Jubilee Trust, the Wolfson trustees hold strongly to the belief that to equip universities, hospitals, and research institutes with critically needed facilities may in the long run turn out to have been a pioneering service.

4

The Nuffield Foundation merits a special niche in the gallery of British trusts. Not only is it the most heavily endowed, but it was the culminating gift in a series of benefactions by the outstanding industrial philanthropist of modern Britain. As the business career of William Morris, Lord Nuffield, recalls the accomplishments of some of the great American entrepreneurs, so the Foundation

[50] *Ibid.*, 17 Oct. 1956 and 3 July 1958.
[51] The Foundation's mimeographed list of grants, 1 July 1955 to 31 Oct. 1962.

that he set up, with its far-ranging interests, seems to have more in common with the major American foundations than with the Pilgrim or King George's Jubilee Trust. And like some American multimillionaires, not only has he taken pleasure in applying his fortune to useful public ends but he has regarded it all as a kind of demonstration of the social value of free business enterprise. To Nuffield his philanthropies served to express his conviction that the resources built up by private economic activity "which are freely given in the service of the community are a vital factor in the growth of Commonwealth." [52]

When in June 1943 Nuffield created his Foundation, he had already given about £15 million to public causes.[53] His benefactions included over £4 million to Oxford and other universities — the cost of Nuffield College representing more than a million — which recorded their gratitude by awarding him an Oxford M.A., several honorary doctorates, and four honorary Oxford College fellow-ships.[54] Of his earlier trusts, aggregating about £7,600,000, the most original was one (1936) to help finance industrial enterprise, new or old, in the Special (De-pressed) Areas. This turned out to have been bread cast upon the waters, for repayments were such that by the end of 1954 the Trust had made over to King Edward's Hospital Fund a total of £1,600,000.[55] There was also a trust for the Forces of the Crown (£1,650,000), one for employees of Morris Motors (£2,125,000), and the Provincial Hospitals Trust (£1,200,000). Medical and related interests accounted for about £2,375,000, while miscellaneous wartime and other benefac-tions exceeded £1 million. To say the least, Lord Nuffield had cut his teeth as a philanthropist well before he was ready to establish the trust by which he is best known.

The Foundation, it appears, was designed to stand as Nuffield's final major bene-faction. Where the other trusts had been limited and specific, in some degree the philanthropist's response to a particular crisis or a reflection of his own current interests, the new one was admirably general. Here, especially since no one could foresee the configuration of postwar England, it would be imprudent to lay down too precise conditions. The trust deed did, in fact, specify the advancement of health, the promotion of social well-being (particularly through research and education), the care of the aged poor — and "such other charitable purposes as shall be declared in writing (a) by Lord Nuffield in his lifetime and (b) after his death by all the Ordinary Trustees and Managing Trustees." Such comprehen-sive objects assured the trustees of an ample field for maneuver and for the exercise of their discretionary judgment.

Unlike most individual philanthropists establishing foundations, Nuffield did

[52] Quoted in a memorandum by the Nuffield Foundation to the Nathan Committee.

[53] For beneficiaries and amounts see P. W. S. Andrews and Elizabeth Brunner, *The Life of Lord Nuffield* (Oxford, 1955), pp. 259–63.

[54] *Ibid.*, pp. xi–xii. Actually the Oxford D.C.L. antedated Morris' first major gift to the University.

[55] *Ibid.*, pp. 277ff. The Trust spent about £1,200,000 in loans, invested £1 million in shares in business enterprises, and gave £86,000 in free grants-in-aid. The excess in expenditure over the original £2 million capital is accounted for by repayments which were re-lent, interest, and so on.

not scorn the contributions of others. The trust deed provided for an auxiliary fund to receive gifts and legacies from other persons wishing to advance the purposes of the Foundation. The most dramatic response to this opportunity came from Captain Oliver Bird, who offered £450,000 for research into the prevention and cure of rheumatism. From the income of the Oliver Bird Fund the Foundation financed some of the early clinical testing of cortisone and ACTH, as well as fundamental research into the nature of rheumatic conditions.[56]

The Nuffield Foundation has been fortunate in the continuity of its leadership and consequently of its policies. The six Managing Trustees, presided over successively by two bankers, Sir William Goodenough (Barclay's) and Sir Geoffrey Gibbs, who had served as chairman of the Nuffield Provincial Hospitals Trust, have suffered few changes in membership other than those caused by death.[57] The roster has included such distinguished academic names as Sir Henry Tizard (at the time President of Magdalen), Sir John Stopford (an eminent neurologist and Vice-Chancellor of Manchester University), and Sir Hector Hetherington (Principal and Vice-Chancellor of Glasgow), and from the beginning the Director has been Leslie Farrer-Brown, who served also as Secretary of the Hospitals Trust. Nuffield has avoided the periodic internal upheavals which marked the first decade of the Ford Foundation and led to a succession of policy mutations.

The trustees throughout have been committed to the philosophy of the calculated risk, considering their main mission "to seek out the unique project and to try out the unique man."[58] But the search for "uniqueness," as we have already noticed, has not prevented the Foundation from prodding public authorities by launching experiments that might reasonably be regarded as statutory responsibilities. In general, according to standard foundation practice, pioneering ventures are carried on through grants to established organizations and institutions for limited periods. But, although Nuffield is primarily a grant-awarding rather than an operating foundation, occasionally it decides to proceed independently. The Foundation, for example, conducted a study on behalf of the B.B.C. on the effect of television on children. There appeared to be no practicable alternative, for the B.B.C. was an interested party, while conclusions drawn from an inquiry by commercial TV would have been suspect.[59]

During its first fifteen years (1943-58) the Foundation has awarded nearly £8½ million in grants, of which about £6½ million was spent in England, the balance in the Commonwealth.[60] Notwithstanding the essential continuity of policy, each quinquennium has brought modifications and adjustments. During the second five years the social sciences came in for greater play, as against the earlier almost exclusive stress on the medical and natural sciences. Not only was the allotment to the social sciences increased by 250 per cent but the Foundation

[56] *9th Rept.*, 1953-54, pp. 47-48.
[57] The trust deed provides for no fewer than five nor more than seven Managing Trustees.
[58] Memorandum by the Nuffield Foundation to the Nathan Committee.
[59] *9th Rept.*, 1953-54, pp. 66-68.
[60] *13th Rept.*, 1957-58, p. ix.

hopefully thought to assist "in promoting the closer integration of the social sciences where they have tended to diverge." [61] The trustees therefore determined to explore the relatively uncharted paths of cooperative research on contemporary problems to be carried on by specialists from various disciplines, an investment which those familiar with academic behavior might regard as an almost flagrantly daring employment of risk capital.

The balance among the Foundation's interests in the United Kingdom can be judged from the following table of grants made in the years 1943–55. To a preponderant degree, Nuffield grants went for the objects here listed (in £000's) :[62]

Care of the aged (chiefly through the National Corporation)	£970
Medical research (including £295,000 for rheumatism)	875
Social sciences	684
Physical sciences	614
Biological research	586
Scholarships and fellowships for U.K. residents	292
Miscellaneous projects	277

The Nuffield Foundation was intended to be more than a Little England philanthropy. Although not authorized, as was the Rockefeller Foundation, "to promote the well-being of mankind throughout the world," the overseas Commonwealth was expressly included within its sphere of operation. And over the years overseas projects have tended to gain at the expense of those based in the United Kingdom.[63] This shift was calculated. The trustees, surveying the field at home and abroad, concluded that the marginal return on their risk capital would be perceptibly greater if invested overseas. No doubt their decision was partly a response to the expanding sphere of state activity at home. As the *Ninth Report* put it: "With the increasingly generous provision for scientific and medical research in the United Kingdom, supplemented by growing support from industry, the Foundation thought it opportune to extend help to institutions and people in overseas parts of the Commonwealth, where private adventure money is more keenly needed, sought, and valued." [64]

It would be pointless to recall the variety of overseas projects financed by Nuffield. In general, grants have gone to established agencies — to pursue special investigations in the natural or social sciences. But by no means all grants conformed to this pattern. In the five years 1951–55, the Foundation set aside £250,000 for distribution among some of the university colleges in the (then) colonial ter-

---

[61] Memorandum to the Nathan Committee.
[62] *10th Rept.*, 1954–55, p. 10.
[63] *Ibid.*, pp. 9–11; *Report on Grants*, 1943–53, p. 10.
[64] *9th Rept.*, 1953–54, pp. 10–11.

ritories. It contributed to the Smuts Archive Trust in South Africa, to the improvement of medical services in the Aden Protectorate, and to the founding of an international library of African music. All this in addition to an imposing list of scholarships and fellowships, to and from the Commonwealth. In 1954–55 nearly £65,000 was allocated for the purpose, the bulk of it to finance twenty Dominion Traveling Fellowships.

The growing Nuffield emphasis on overseas needs may perhaps foreshadow moves in the same direction by other foundations — where these can be reconciled with the terms of their trusts. The Joseph Rowntree Memorial Trust, which, it will be remembered, was created in 1959 as an expansion of the old Village Trust, has developed a number of projects in Central Africa.[65] It would not be overventuresome to predict that British foundations will increasingly share in the almost universal concern for welfare in the underdeveloped areas. In fact, as social exigencies at home are, in an ever greater degree, met by statutory action, it is almost inevitable that they should turn to sections of the world where the demand for social pioneering is more insistent than at home. Conceivably the most promising field for the investment of the risk capital of social advance is now overseas or in projects which hold special significance for underdeveloped regions. Like the achieving of social welfare at home, the total task is plainly beyond private bodies, but also, as at home, these can make a contribution that is distinctive and, indeed, almost indispensable.

[65] *2d Rept.*, 1961–63, pp. 38–47, and information from Mr. L. E. Waddilove.

CHAPTER XXI

THE NATHAN REPORT
AND THE CHARITIES ACT

WHEN, in the summer of 1960, the Charities Act[1] received the
royal assent, the charitable realm acquired a new constitution. Although the preceding century had placed on the statute books a formidable volume of legislation having to do with charitable trusts, this was mostly
of an *ad hoc* character. Not since the Act of 1860 had there been a comprehensive formulation of the law of endowed charities. The demands for reform
associated with the names of Hobhouse, Hare, Kenny, and Trevelyan attained
only limited success, but the clamor had subsided. What dissatisfaction remained
was limited and occasional. As for the Charity Commissioners, they had discovered that too much initiative might be dangerous, and they increasingly confined themselves to the routine duties of their office.

The expansion of the public social services in the 1920's and '30's raised questions without dramatically altering the status of private philanthropy. But the
impact of the legislation of the '40's was of a different order of magnitude. Plainly
charitable enterprise would have to take stock of its position and perhaps lay
out a new course. In addition to the broader issues of statutory-voluntary relationships, the extension of the public services had created a series of immediate and
practical problems. What, for example, was to be done with endowments which
now faced unemployment owing to the State's assumption of the financial burden?
Possibly the clearest case was that of the Royal Surgical Aid Society, whose invested funds amounted to about £250,000. In 1948 the Society supplied 13,000
surgical appliances, in 1949 only 635. Fortunately the court order authorizing a
change in the objects of the Society went well beyond the normal scope of *cy-près,*
and it was permitted to establish homes for the elderly.[2] Although the Society's

---

[1] 8 & 9 Eliz. II, c. 58.

[2] *The Times,* 26 Oct. 1950. The situation of almshouse trusts (*Nathan Report,* Par. 318), though
less dramatic, was of broader significance. Many of these were obligated to provide rent-free accommodations and a small allowance to the inmates, even if their income was insufficient to keep
the premises in a habitable condition. But with residents receiving National Insurance pensions and
frequently supplementary National Assistance allowances, it was reasonable that trusts should be
altered so as to permit trustees to charge a small rent and devote their income to upkeep and improvements.

predicament was settled promptly and satisfactorily, not all obsolescent charities could count on Mr. Justice Parry's understanding treatment.

The question was not often presented in such sharp outlines. More generally, this was a situation that had been created by a complex of social and economic changes covering half a century. With state action so widespread in areas formerly reserved to voluntary effort, the relationship between the two had been radically altered. But, as Lord Nathan observed, the condition of the law was such as to inhibit the voluntary energies of the community, especially insofar as these were embodied in charitable trusts, from contributing usefully to the partnership.[3] There was, in short, a realistic argument for re-examining the legal basis of the charitable endowment and presumably for revising such parts of the law as might tend to immobilize trusts or otherwise limit their cooperation in the total welfare undertaking. It is not wholly fanciful, perhaps, to discover some analogy between the situation that produced the Nathan Committee and that which inspired the Brougham inquiry nearly a century and a half before. Both at least grew out of a conviction that charitable endowments could be a more creative force in English society and that in order to bring this about certain changes in their status, legal and administrative, were indicated.

Some of the queries about the future of the voluntary services were posed by Lord Beveridge in his book *Voluntary Action,* which appeared in 1948.[4] As the author of the Beveridge Report, he was a figure of commanding prestige and his views were assured of wide circulation. No one could suspect that his concern for the voluntary services reflected any lack of conviction with regard to the social responsibilities of the State. The situation, he insisted, called for "political invention to find new ways of fruitful co-operation," and he urged the State to "use where it can, without destroying their freedom and spirit, the voluntary agencies for social advance, born of social conscience and of philanthropy."[5] He was convinced that charity law was overdue for revision, and he included in his recommendations a demand for a Royal Commission to survey charitable trusts, with terms of reference which in truth bordered on the cosmic.[6]

Beveridge's book articulated the uneasiness that was already widespread in voluntary circles. Should not the Government be pressed to consider, officially and systematically, the role of voluntary effort in the Welfare State? A number of Liberal peers joined with Beveridge to bring the dilemmas of private philanthropy before the House. If the manpower of the Party in the Commons was thin, its brainpower in the Lords was impressive, and here was a highly con-

[3] *J. Royal Society of Arts,* 12 June 1953, p. 482.

[4] A second volume, by Beveridge and A. F. Wells, *The Evidence for Voluntary Action,* comprising a good deal of the data on which the first volume was based, appeared in the following year.

[5] Beveridge, *Voluntary Action* (London, 1948), pp. 10, 318.

[6] Beveridge contemplated a commission which would "make a survey of the existing charitable trusts [that is, 'do for the whole of Britain what the Royal Commission of 1878–80 did for the City of London'], and of the law and the administrative machinery concerned with such trusts" and would then "make recommendations for making charitable trusts at all times most beneficial to the community and adjusting their application to changing circumstances."

genial debating topic. In the end it was a motion by Lord Samuel — "to call attention to the need for the encouragement of voluntary action to promote social progress" — that the House debated on 22 June 1949.[7] He noted the financial hardships suffered by voluntary organizations, the drying up of their traditional sources of revenue — "the gentry have now become the indigentry" — and he called for an inquiry into possible new sources of support. The speakers were mainly Liberal peers — Samuel, Amulree (a distinguished physician), and Beveridge, in addition to the Labour peer Lord Nathan, a former Liberal — and they argued with vigor and conviction that voluntary effort remained indispensable and would still be needed, as in the past, "to pioneer ahead of the State." For them the notion of "a perpetually moving frontier for philanthropic action" was no mere pious aspiration but sober reality.

Lord Pakenham (now Earl of Longford) joined on behalf of the Government in the hymn to philanthropy. He enunciated the familiar thesis of the interdependent roles of the voluntary and statutory, and he committed the Government to encourage voluntary associations. But with some reason he boggled at Beveridge's proposal for a full-dress Royal Commission to survey charitable trusts. The spectre of the Brougham Commissioners, with their nineteen years of labor, made any comparable twentieth-century inventory a terrifying prospect. Instead, the inquiry was to be entrusted to a committee appointed by the Prime Minister, with terms of reference considerably less inclusive than Beveridge had contemplated. It would be the duty of this committee "to consider and report on the changes in the law and practice (except as regards taxation) relating to charitable trusts in England and Wales which would be necessary to enable the maximum benefit to the community to be derived from them." [8]

Another current which fed into the demand for an inquiry was a certain disquiet in legal circles over the condition of charity law, a domain not infrequently described as "a jungle and a wilderness." [9] Admittedly this was one of the more involved and technical branches of equity practice and one which, in the view of many laymen and some lawyers, badly needed clarifying and simplifying. Perhaps the time had come to attempt a new definition of the legal concept "charitable," for neither the enumeration in the preamble to the Elizabethan Statute nor Lord Macnaghten's classification in the Pemsel case established a precise line. Plainly, also, there was much to be said for a more flexible method of revising trusts, not merely those that had proved entirely impracticable but those that were thought undesirable or had become redundant, especially as a result of the expansion of the public services. By common consent this meant a relaxation of

[7] 5 Parl. Deb. (Lords) 163:75–136.
[8] Nathan Report, Par. 1.
[9] J. W. Brunyate, "The Legal Definition of Charity," Law Quarterly Review, 51:268 (July 1945). See also G. W. Keeton, "The Charity Muddle," in Keeton and Schwarzberger, Current Legal Problems (London, 1949), pp. 86–102, and the Law Journal: Annual Charities Review, 13 April 1940, pp. 3–6, and 3 May 1941, p. 16. For a more recent analysis see Keeton, The Modern Law of Charities, chap. II.

cy-près, though opinions varied as to the kind and degree of modification that was indicated.

The suspicion among equity lawyers that something needed to be done about charity law was strengthened by three decisions handed down during the 1940's. All three involved imperfectly drawn trust instruments (as a result of which substantial sums were lost to charity), though in only one was the draftsman obviously in error. The most sensational of these cases had to do with the will of Caleb Diplock, in which he left his residual estate of over £250,000 "for such charitable or benevolent object or objects" as his trustees and executors should select. These proceeded to establish an old persons' home in Sussex and to distribute the balance among some 139 institutions. After long and tortuous legal proceedings started by the testator's next-of-kin, the House of Lords held that "charitable" and "benevolent" were not synonymous (that "or" was used "disjunctively" rather than "exegetically"), and that, since "benevolent" was broader than "charitable," the trustees were empowered to apply the estate to objects beyond the range comprehended by "charitable." The Diplock will was therefore held void for uncertainty.

Within the legal profession there was little inclination to quarrel with the decision of the Lords. Their interpretation of the law as it stood was unimpeachable.[10] Although there was sympathy for the Diplock trustees, who suffered disastrously, most lawyers felt only contempt for the hapless solicitor responsible for the will. The point involved was not particularly obscure and should have been familiar enough to anyone who ventured to draw up a will for such an estate as Diplock's. Yet all agreed that the intentions of the testator had in fact been frustrated, and there was some feeling that his remote next-of-kin had done more handsomely than they deserved. Clearly he had intended to leave his property not to relatives but to such good works as his trustees might select. Neither lawyers nor laymen could be entirely happy over the outcome. One of the justices who sat on the appeal, Lord Goddard, was led to reflect, "When I find a rule which says that if property is left to trustees to give to charitable and benevolent purposes, that is good, but if it is for charitable or benevolent purposes, it is not, I regard it with some distaste." [11]

The two other cases were more novel and concerned issues which the courts had not hitherto been asked to decide. Both had to do with claims for tax relief by organizations whose principal objects were admittedly charitable. But did "charitable" mean wholly charitable? In the Memorandum of Association of one of the organizations (the Oxford Group) were included secondary objects not of a strictly charitable nature, and tax relief was denied.[12] The Ellis case involved land

---

[10] In re *Diplock,* No. 1, 1940. The case is discussed in the *Nathan Report,* Par. 520–21, with an interesting quotation from the evidence of Mr. Justice Vaisey which explains with admirable clarity the reasoning of the court.

[11] Quoted by Brunyate, "The Legal Definition of Charity," (n. 9), p. 268.

[12] The Oxford Group decision was less disastrous than might at first appear, for it was simple enough to rewrite a Memorandum of Association so as to exclude noncharitable objects. Meanwhile,

conveyed to trustees as a site for Roman Catholic buildings to be used for purposes which, the courts held, were too vague to be strictly charitable. Such a decision held grave implications for other religious bodies and for a variety of trusts whose right to tax exemption had never been questioned. Must such trusts, probably numbering into the thousands, look forward to a future of constant torment lest their defective legal basis be discovered by Inland Revenue? One of the manifest duties of a government committee on charity law would be to devise a method of validating such trusts, especially those already in existence at the time of the adverse decisions.

2

The personnel of the new Committee adequately reflected the diversity of interests concerned. Lord Nathan, an eminent lawyer and man of affairs with a distinguished record of public-spirited service, took the chairmanship. He had entered Parliament originally as a Liberal but in the mid-'30's had joined the Labour Party. Nathan brought to his assignment not only an acute understanding of the technical legal issues involved but a solid belief, based on wide experience, that both statutory and voluntary services were essential to British social well-being. As chairman of the Westminster Hospital, he had seen at close range some of the problems of private philanthropy in a world increasingly dominated by the public services. In addition to its chairman, the Committee numbered among its dozen members able representatives of the statutory services, voluntary social work, and the legal profession.[13]

During its three years of life — January 1950 to December 1952 — the Nathan Committee held 31 regular meetings, received written evidence from 75 organizations and 17 individuals, and asked more than 7500 questions of 92 witnesses. Those who were invited or offered to submit evidence were widely representative — government departments, foundations, voluntary associations of various sorts, church agencies — and, as is commonly the case, some of these the Committee was eager to hear, and others eager to be heard by the Committee. Taken as a group, however, they gave a reasonably complete picture of the interests connected with British philanthropy and provided an adequate basis for judgment. One might sample alphabetically the list of those who gave both written and oral evidence with, say, the National Association of Parish Councils, the National As-

---

section 3 of the Finance Act of 1950 provided an escape from liability for back taxes, and no permanent injury resulted.

[13] Some of the more active and knowledgeable members of the Committee were Donald (later Sir Donald) Allen of the City Parochial Foundation; B. E. Astbury of the Family Welfare Association; Sir William Brockington, a former Director of Education in the Midlands; Sir John Maude, barrister and Ministry of Health official; S. K. Ruck, a Welfare Officer of the London County Council; and Miss Eileen Younghusband, a leading figure among British social workers and at the time head of the Department of Social Science of the London School of Economics. The secretary of the Committee, Miss J. H. Lidderdale of the Office of the Lord President of the Council, earned the gratitude of the members for her tactful and skillful handling of the administrative and organizational side of the Committee's activities. The drafting of the report was largely her work.

sociation of Social Service, the Ministry of Pensions, the Pilgrim Trust, the Procurator General and Treasury Solicitor General, the Public Trustee, the Roman Catholic Hierarchy, and the Royal Patriotic Fund Corporation.[14] For the kind of issue which the Committee was instructed to consider there could be little complaint about the scope of its researches.

In the words of the chairman, the Committee's assignment was "to recommend ways in which the goodwill of the past may be more free to serve the changing needs of the present" — specifically, ways in which charitable endowments may "add their full weight to the whole drive of voluntary action for social progress."[15] Broadly speaking, two aspects of the charitable trust, the more technical legal side and the operational or administrative, engaged the attention of the Committee. It was expected, on the one hand, to canvass possible changes in the law of charities with a view to increasing the social utility of endowments, and, on the other, to suggest improvements in the agencies, such as the Charity Commission, and in the methods established by the State for dealing with them.

On one of the two most basic legal questions faced by the Committee, that of attempting a new definition of "charitable use," its answer left the matter about where it had been. To have come up with a more radical solution would have meant running counter to virtually all of the legal witnesses.[16] Although at the outset lay witnesses tended to be impatient with the archaic character of 43 Elizabeth and the vagueness of Macnaghten's residual fourth category and to demand a shiny new twentieth-century statement, even they came to recognize the difficulty.[17] For one thing, it was obvious that no single formula, however complex, would do, but that definition would have to take the form of an enumeration. Would such a list, in the long run, be any more satisfactory than existing formulations? As Mr. Justice Vaisey told the Committee, wherever the line was drawn, marginal cases would still exist, for the legal conception of charity "had its origin in the eccentricities of the benevolent."[18] Charity law, he implied, was decently clear save on the fringes, and the consequence of a redefinition would be to create new fringes.

Other arguments contributed to the Committee's decision to attempt no new statutory definition. There was always the possibility that such a formula might tend to freeze the legal conception of charity and inhibit growth in response to social change.[19] Most convincing of all was the fact of a mountain of case law,

---

[14] *Nathan Report*, pp. 181–82.

[15] *Ibid.*, Par. 60.

[16] In his article "The Legal Definition of Charity" (*Law Quarterly Review*, vol. 51), John Brunyate attempted a new definition and urged that one be officially formulated, though he inclined to a judicial rather than a statutory redefinition. Before the Nathan Committee he was even more doubtful of definition by statute. Other legal witnesses who opposed redefinition were Sir Cecil Dawes (Q. 1988), Lord Macmillan (Q. 2236), and Mr. Justice Vaisey (Q. 7468).

[17] See, for example, the statement of the Nuffield Foundation (*Nathan Report*, Par. 126). Memoranda submitted by the National Association of Parish Councils and by the National Council of Social Service also urged redefinition.

[18] *Nathan Report*, Par. 521.

[19] Lord Nathan, *J. Royal Society of Arts*, 12 June 1953, p. 485.

some of which would be rendered irrelevant by a change in the law. Redefinition, Mr. Justice Vaisey warned, would produce a fresh series of cases, "without, I think, doing any really substantial good to anybody except the legal profession." [20] Suspecting that any proposal which would render obsolete the existing mass of case law would only make a bad matter worse, the Committee decided against trying to hammer out a new definition.

Even so, could nothing be done to improve on the preamble of 43 Elizabeth? Here the danger was that even a cautious rephrasing might disturb case law. But to substitute Macnaghten's four categories (relief or poverty, education, religion, and other purposes beneficial to the community), which had in fact been accepted by the courts as the operative definition of charity, would presumably not prejudice the corpus of judge-made law.[21] The Committee therefore recommended the enactment of a statute based on the Macnaghten classification, "but preserving the case law as it stands." [22] To the Government, however, even such a discreet change was irreconcilable with case law. The choice, as the White Paper was to suggest, lay "between leaving things as they are and adopting a new definition which is different in substance." [23] The question of definition is therefore left untouched by the Charities Act of 1960, and the Elizabethan enumeration still remains the ultimate authority.[24]

Some of the demand for a fresh definition reflected an uneasy conscience over the outcome of the Diplock case. Why not devise a new formula which would include "benevolent" as synonymous with "charitable"? This kind of solution the Committee refused to countenance. If "benevolent" were admitted, was there reasonable ground for rejecting "philanthropic," "pious," or "patriotic"?[25] Less easy to ignore was the problem of trusts that (in the Oxford Group and Ellis cases) had been held void because they contained objects of a noncharitable nature. If these decisions were applied to all such imperfect trusts, the consequences for charity could be disastrous. Both lawyers and laymen looked to the Committee to discover a way out of an embarrassing situation. None relished the prospect of thousands of trusts' being left vulnerable to challenge in the courts. In the view of some, the proper course was to take a leaf out of the Australian

---

[20] Q. 7473. Professor Keeton, however (Modern Law of Charities, pp. 41–42), regards the preservation of existing case law as a doubtful benefit, since it "reveals in the plainest fashion the complete absence of principle governing this branch of the subject."

[21] The fourth category, "trusts for other purposes beneficial to the community," raised a complicated legal question. Not every trust beneficial to the community was "charitable." To be charitable a trust must be "beneficial to the community in a way which the law regards as charitable" — that is, in a way that can be squared with the preamble of 43 Elizabeth. See Brunyate, "The Legal Definition of Charity," p. 275, and Sir John Maude, J. Royal Society of Arts, 12 June 1953, p. 501.

[22] Nathan Report, Par. 140.

[23] Government Policy on Charitable Trusts (Cmd. 9538), 1955, Par. 3.

[24] Lord Nathan discusses the question in his volume The Charities Act, 1960 (London, 1962), pp. 8, 13, 23–28.

[25] There were hopes in some quarters for the extension of the definition in particular directions. The Roman Catholic hierarchy, to cite one instance, felt strongly that gifts to contemplative communities ought to be brought within the scope of valid charities, a claim that the Committee (Par. 129) could not accept.

and New Zealand statute books and authorize the courts, in effect, to strike out the noncharitable purpose and to handle the trust as though it contained only charitable objects.[26] One eminent legal authority suggested that in failing to recommend this solution the Committee must have been acting "largely with the interests of Inland Revenue in mind."[27]

The Committee's solution was moderately cautious. Admittedly in principle there were strong arguments against revising the law and applying it retroactively, but this was not chiefly a matter of legal principle. What the Committee proposed, in a word, was a virtual statute of limitations on defective trust instruments. Specifically Parliament was to be urged to declare that the funds of all trusts which had been in operation for six or more years "are and always have been impressed with a charitable trust."[28] Newer trusts would have to meet more searching tests but could still gain recognition, while those established since the Oxford Group and Ellis decisions (1949) must conform to the law as embodied in those cases. Though not a daring expedient, this formula disposed of the most critical problem, and a bill incorporating the Committee's recommendations in substance was promptly put through Parliament.[29]

3

By common consent the most important and complex legal issue before the Committee had to do with the revising of trusts. Of the 110,000 charitable trusts on the books of the Charity Commissioners and the Ministry of Education, all save about thirty thousand educational endowments (which came under the more liberal provisions of the Endowed Schools Acts) were still subject to the full rigors of the *cy-près* doctrine. Over half of these eighty thousand trusts, the Committee estimated, were intended to benefit the poor and sick, for whose welfare a whole network of state services had now been fashioned. Relatively few of them had failed in the technical sense, but many were thought to be in need of rescheming of a kind that was impossible under strict *cy-près*. The essential problem was not masses of "freakish or archaic trusts crying out for reform," the charities exploited by the reformers of the '70's and '80's, but rather of numbers from which the community was getting less benefit than would have been the case if the *cy-près* doctrine were relaxed. In short, the Committee purposed to readjust the rules governing the alteration of trusts so that they might contribute more productively to mid-century British life. But on this, to look ahead, the Government declined to go as far as the Committee, though the new Charities

[26] Memorandum by the Law Society.

[27] H. G. Hanbury, Vinerian Professor of Law at Oxford, "Charitable Bequests," *The Listener*, 53:146 (27 Jan. 1955). Another critic, Robert Pollard of the Arthur McDougall Trust, also was unconvinced by the Committee's reasoning. He urged (*J. Royal Society of Arts*, 12 June 1953, p. 504) that, if a charitable intention was clear from the instrument, bad drafting ought not to be allowed to upset the charity.

[28] *Nathan Report*, Par. 539.

[29] As the Charitable Trusts (Validation) Act, 1954 (8 & 9 Eliz. II, c. 58).

Act does, in fact, substantially extend the conditions under which trusts can be reschemed *cy-près*.

Proposals to modify *cy-près* were, of course, neither novel nor revolutionary. Not only had the charity reformers taken it as a main point of attack, but on more than one occasion eminent jurists, Lord Chancellors and others, had termed it excessively restrictive.[30] The doctrine no longer operated over the whole world of endowed charities, for by Act of Parliament some major categories of trusts, notably educational trusts, could be revised without reference to the founder's wishes. Thus for a quarter to a third of the nation's endowments *cy-près* no longer existed in any strict sense. Among the witnesses who appeared before the Nathan Committee or who submitted memoranda virtually none denied the need for some relaxation of the doctrine. The only exception that comes to mind was the National Association of Discharged Prisoners' Aid Societies, which, for rather special reasons, held that if there was to be a change, it should be in the direction of strengthening the *cy-près* principle![31] Other witnesses might imply that their organizations had not been seriously handicapped — but some of the older and more powerful charitable bodies, it appears, had given the doctrine an elastic construction in their own operations. An official of one of the Twelve Great Companies could suggest that "the wise trustee does not really adhere too closely to it" but interprets "his trust in the widest possible terms," though he conceded that greater legal latitude would be desirable.[32] The Jewish Board of Guardians also seemed in some instances to have followed a liberal, homemade version of *cy-près*.[33]

Yet there was general agreement that an easier method of varying trusts — trusts which lay outside the category of the technically "impracticable" — was essential. The issue was not so much "whether" as "under what conditions," "with what safeguards," "by what authority," and the like, and these could become fairly explosive matters. To tamper with the founder's intentions, the familiar argument ran, would "tend to dry up the springs of charity, and the overriding public importance of fostering charitable sentiments and the gifts which flow from them outweighs the occasional disadvantage of having endowments which serve a less useful purpose than they might do." [34] But such an argument, though it might suggest to reformers that they had best tread softly, was less convincing in the new situation created by the expansion of the public social services.

On the matter of revising trusts the ramifications seemed infinite. Assuming, for example, that in the future a trust could be altered without showing that it had

[30] For examples see the *Nathan Report,* Par. 301, and for a summary of the attempts of the Charity of Commissioners to broaden their powers of rescheming see Keeton, *Modern Law of Charities,* chap. X.

[31] Apparently the Association felt that a more stringent application of *cy-près* would give prison charities a larger share of the surplus income of the Old Society for the Discharge and Relief of Persons Imprisoned for Small Debts.

[32] Sir Ernest Pooley, Q. 2384.

[33] Q. 4088ff.

[34] Par. 316.

wholly failed, under what conditions ought this to be permitted? Should new endowments be assured of a period of immunity, perhaps a half century, before they could be legally revised — in other words, how long ought the founder's wishes to be respected? How drastic a revision ought to be permitted? Should not the particular interests of the founder be considered even though it might be no longer expedient to carry out his specific instructions? Some witnesses, including the Charity Commissioners, thought that revision ought to take place only within one of the four Macnaghten categories;[35] and in general, there was little enthusiasm for encouraging radical shifts — for converting, say, a trust for the relief of the aged into a prize for proficiency in classics at a nearby grammar school. Religious bodies were naturally concerned that charities intended to further religion should continue to benefit the specific religious community for which they were intended.[36]

Closely related to such issues was the question of pooling local trusts, especially small and obsolescent endowments, into common good funds, community trusts, or foundations with broad charitable objects. In its 1949 debate the House of Lords had displayed some interest in the creation of common good funds, and it was obviously a possibility on which the Committee would have to pass judgment. The City Parochial Foundation offered a magnificent example of what might be done with obsolete or redundant trusts, and within the Committee there was some sentiment for a positive policy favoring such amalgamations. But there were also misgivings. Conceivably the City experience was a special case with limited applicability. Certain witnesses doubted the wisdom of forcibly sweeping large numbers of small trusts into a central fund, urging that the interest of individual trustees in individual charities was too important a social value to be casually sacrificed. In the end, though conceding that large numbers of small trusts were inefficient and undesirable and that some merging would be useful, especially of the thirty-five thousand or so with incomes under £5, the Committee shied away from recommending a policy of wholesale consolidation.[37]

These did not exhaust the troublesome questions. What about changes in the area which a charity was established to serve? Here, although in some instances to extend the "beneficial area" was an obvious step and might be accepted without too much opposition, any suggestion that an endowment be transferred to a new district would inevitably stir up a hornet's nest. Founders often felt more strongly about benefiting a particular village or town than about a specific charitable object. Charity authorities had thus come to regard the shifting of endowments, in all but the most exceptional instances, as not only an inequitable but a self-defeating policy.

There were other issues, but this is enough to suggest how complex and slippery were the problems connected with relaxing *cy-près,* a reform which nearly everyone favored in principle. What was needed was a formula which would

[35] Q. 1067, 5736.
[36] London Diocesan Board, Q. 4718.
[37] Messrs. Sessions and Waddilove of York, Q. 1578ff, 1600ff.; *Report,* Par. 554.

combine flexibility with reasonable stability and would in some degree harmonize the various interests involved — which would, in short, furnish relief where required without unduly disturbing the charity world. As it turned out, a provision which, in the view of the Committee, met these conditions, was already on the statute book, but it applied only to Britain north of the Tweed. The Scottish Act on educational endowments — the only attempt of Parliament in the twentieth century to deal comprehensively with the revision of trusts — supplied the Committee with a basis for its own recommendation.[38] The Act conferred on the Secretary of State broad powers of rescheming charitable trusts, altering their purposes, amalgamating or dividing them, or changing the constitution of their governing bodies. Had this been all, such authority might have been fairly criticized as bureaucratic and arbitrary. But in exercising his sweeping powers, the Secretary was enjoined to consider a number of factors, including the public interest and "existing conditions" — and "to have special regard" for the spirit of the founder's intention, the interest of the locality, and the possibility of effecting economy by grouping, amalgamating, or combining endowments. Such language seemed to offer sufficient protection for the variety of interests involved, while allowing reasonable freedom of action to the authorities.

The Committee decided against trying to lay down in specific terms the circumstances under which trusts might be revised — that is, against enumerating objects to be regarded as obsolescent — and instead took its stand on the more general statement of the Scottish Act. In Scotland it was enough to justify revision that the purposes of a trust "have become obsolete or useless or prejudicial to the public welfare or are otherwise sufficiently provided for, or are insufficient in comparison with the magnitude of the endowment or are not substantially beneficial to the class of persons for whom it was originally intended." A critical phrase was, of course, "already sufficiently provided for," which would presumably provide an adequate basis for revising trusts whose functions had been taken over by the State. But were public authorities to be allowed to alter any trust they regarded as obsolescent, however recently established? The issue here was less simple than might at first sight appear. For, although ordinary prudence and simple justice might dictate a period of immunity against disturbance — fifty years was most frequently suggested by witnesses — the creation of a new state service could suddenly reduce numbers of trusts to obsolescence. Again, the Committee sought and reached a compromise: With the consent of the trustees and of the donor, if living, a trust might be altered at any time, but lacking that, the authorities must keep hands off for a period of thirty-five years, that is, for approximately a generation.[39]

[38] Education (Scotland) Act, 1946, Part VI (9 & 10 Geo. VI, c. 72). The suggestion came from Lord Macmillan, who gave evidence on behalf of the Pilgrim Trust (5 Parl. Deb. [Lords], 216:370.)

[39] The Committee (Par. 344ff) also had to reconsider the question of the scheme-making authority. Was the function primarily judicial or was it administrative and policy-forming in character? And should it be exercised by a court of law or by an administrative organ of government? The decision was in favor of the latter, and the Charity Commission and the Ministry of Education were to continue as the chief scheme-making authorities.

These, in brief, were the lines along which the Legislature was invited to proceed in providing for the revision of trusts. The Committee's aim had been "to strike a balance between regard for the spirit of the intention of the founder and the claims of the present," and no one could fairly condemn its recommendations as reckless, ill-considered, or destructive. Even so, the Conservative Government found them unnecessarily sweeping, and its own counterproposals, when these were issued, stopped short of the Committee's position.

A minor legal chore performed by the Nathan Committee had to do with the anachronism represented by the mortmain laws. Although their original severity had been whittled down, it was still presumably illegal for a corporation, save under a Crown license or statutory exemption, to acquire land in mortmain, and illegal for a charity to hold for more than twelve months land received by will, unless the period of grace were extended by court or Charity Commissioners. By mid-century, in fact, the situation had become almost unintelligible, so that among the witnesses before the Committee, none could discover any merit in the mortmain laws. On this issue the Committee's recommendation was unequivocal. The laws were serving no useful purpose and should be repealed at once, a view which the Government unhesitatingly endorsed.[40]

4

No doubt the problems connected with "the practice" of charitable trusts were less intricate and technical than those having to do with "the law." Yet these practical matters were of major importance, for, whatever adjustments might be made in the legal framework, their ultimate value would depend on those who formulated charity policy under the law and administered it. Specifically the Committee must scrutinize the record of the Charity Commission and the Ministry of Education (as the supervising authority of educational trusts), and must pass judgment on the adequacy of their performance.

Complaints about the Charity Commissioners were, of course, an old story. During their century of life they had been attacked, at various times, as tyrannical or timid, headlong or supine, unprincipled or legalistic. The witnesses who appeared before the Nathan Committee kept the tradition alive. Their criticisms covered a broad expanse of bureaucratic terrain, but two specific charges stood out. In the first place, there was the complaint, by no means novel, of intolerable delay in the office of the Commission. One agency stressed its reluctance to submit cases which required a decision "within a reasonable time." [41] The Royal Maternity Charity, founded in the mid-eighteenth century to provide midwives for poor married women, submitted over a hundred documents — letters, memoranda, and orders — bearing on its request to turn over its work and assets to the Central Council of District Nursing. An examination of the correspondence, which covered two years of negotiation, suggests that, although some of the

[40] *Nathan Report*, Par. 276; *Government Policy on Charitable Trusts*, Par. 16.
[41] Memorandum from the Methodist Board of Trustees for Chapel Affairs.

epithets applied to the Commission may have been excessive — "unimaginative departmentalism," "coercion difficult to distinguish from tyranny" — they were not entirely unmerited.[42]

Apparently experience with the Ryder Street office varied a good deal from charity to charity. Larger metropolitan foundations, whose officials were well known to the Commissioners, could get their business handled with a good deal of dispatch, sometimes by telephone. The City Companies reported their relations as "excellent" and the Commissioners as "most helpful," while the Clerk of the City Parochial Foundation defended them against charges of pettifogging delay.[43] But the Law Society thought that, in the large, inordinate delay marked the proceedings of the Commission, and supplied the Committee with specific examples.[44] The Commissioners had a ready and, within limits, a legitimate answer. Even more than most government offices, the Charity Commission was gravely understaffed and not only had not expanded with the increase of business but had actually shrunk. In 1860, with responsibility for about 32,500 trusts, the legal staff numbered twenty-five. Ninety years later, when registered charities had increased to perhaps 80,000, only twenty-one members made up the staff.[45] Yet, however genuine the disabilities under which the Commissioners labored, there is also reason to suspect that they had become addicted to their own routine and had made little effort to work out summary methods of handling their more mechanical duties.

A second criticism was perhaps more fundamental. This had to do with the Commissioners' conception of their function. On the whole, they tended to exaggerate the quasi-judicial side of the work at the expense of the administrative and, at least in the eyes of their critics, to be excessively legalistic and literal in their decisions. What seems clear is that they had long ceased to be actively concerned with the broader questions of charitable endowments and how to improve their social utility. To them the role of the Commission was chiefly "that of a Court to whom people resort rather than that the Commissioners themselves go out and find cases to remedy."[46] The inquisitorial function, which originally formed an important part of the Commissioners' mandate, was rarely exercised, and then only for a suspected breach of trust or other serious legal offense.[47] Their major obligation, as they saw it, was to answer inquiries, decide questions referred to them, and frame schemes in accordance with sound law. The senior staff was composed exclusively of lawyers, and these, their critics held, were inclined to sacrifice the spirit to the technical letter.[48]

One obvious handicap under which the Commission worked was that of faulty

[42] Memorandum to the Nathan Committee, with documents.
[43] Q. 5067, 5068, 6080ff.
[44] Memorandum to the Nathan Committee.
[45] *Nathan Report*, App. F. This figure includes only the trusts handled by the Charity Commissioners.
[46] The Chief Commissioner, Q. 43.
[47] Memorandum from the Law Society.
[48] *Ibid.;* Chief Commissioner, Q. 652.

liaison with the responsible agencies of government. To visit the Ryder Street office was to find oneself in a sleepy bureaucratic backwater, wholly cut off from the main currents. The isolation was not only spiritual but constitutional, for the Commission was affiliated with no government department. This was in sober fact an orphan agency. Its spokesman in the House continued to be, as for decades, an unpaid Parliamentary Commissioner, whose influence was necessarily limited by his back-bench status.[49] Certainly the Commissioners were entitled to have a Minister to whom they could present the needs of their office and their suggestions for improvements in the statutory basis of their work.[50]

The Committee's prescription was a radically reconstituted Charity Commission, larger and more varied in personnel, with a Minister responsible for representing it in Parliament. The Commission, however, would retain its semiautonomous character; it would not be absorbed into the departmental organization and would carry on its regular administration free of outside control. The most original recommendation of the Committee (not accepted by the Government) called for an enlarged Commission of between five and nine members who would serve part-time for not less than five years. The new body should not be restricted to lawyers but should include "men and women of standing and experience in public and charitable affairs."[51] The Committee left no doubt of its preference for an agency less pervaded by a narrowly legal spirit. In Welfare Britain scheme-making would impinge more directly on the domain of public policy and administration, and such a function, the Committee was persuaded, could be more satisfactorily discharged by a larger and more widely experienced Commission.

Before the Nathan Committee could formulate its plan for reconstituting the Charity Commission, a preliminary (but basic) issue of jurisdiction had to be settled. Since 1899 there had been in existence two central charity authorities, the Ministry of Education (earlier the Board of Education) and the Commission itself. Should not the precedent established in 1899 with educational trusts now be carried forward by turning over other specialized endowments to the departments most directly concerned? There was an attractive administrative logic in proposals to decentralize the authority — for example, to assign charities for the benefit of orphans to the Home Office (which under the Children Act of 1948 had been given responsibility for children deprived of normal family life) and those for the aged to the Ministry of Health. On balance, however, the Committee concluded that decentralization, though appealing enough in the abstract, was impracticable, and preferred rather to reconstitute and strengthen the Charity Commission.

Throughout their history one of the graver shortcomings of the Commissioners

[49] The Parliamentary Commissioner at the time, M. Phillips Price, formerly of the *Manchester Guardian,* was aware of the weakness of the position and urged that the Commission be provided with a guardian Minister to lay down broad lines of policy and to act as representative in the House (Q. 5795).
[50] *Nathan Report,* Par. 109.
[51] *Ibid.,* Par. 377.

had been their handling of public relations, both in a general and in a more specific sense. Plainly if the nation was to receive full value from its charitable trusts, information about them must be readily available to potential beneficiaries, social workers, and others. This condition did not in fact obtain. Although **guides** to local endowments had been issued in a few cities, there was no central, classified, easily accessible registry of the country's trusts. It was inevitable that among the Nathan Committee's more significant recommendations should be that of a serviceable scheme of charity registration.

This was a curious situation, and one which the Committee found more than faintly shocking. Although the statute book carried certain enactments out of which a satisfactory scheme of registration might have developed, these had never been enforced and for decades had been entirely disregarded.[52] It was any-body's guess how many trusts remained unknown to the Commission. Yet even if the records of the Commissioners and the Ministry of Education included most of the country's trusts (as the Nathan Committee believed), this was of little bene-fit to the ordinary citizen requiring information. In neither office had there been any attempt to arrange and classify the data, other than by areas.

To the Nathan Committee a more adequate registry was indispensable if charitable endowments were to reach their maximum usefulness as instruments of welfare. This involved no serious issue of principle. The critical questions had rather to do with details concerning the nature of the registry — should it be local or national or both, what data should it include, and who should be respon-sible for supplying the information? To require too many details would defeat the purpose of the registry and might produce from trustees complaints of being harried by bureaucratic requirements. Yet surely, given the concessions enjoyed by charitable trusts, it was not excessive to require trustees to supply the minimal information which would form the basis of the classified registry. A more dif-ficult question was that of local versus national registries, for a strong case was to be made for each. In the end, however, the balance of argument seemed con-clusively to favor the central authority as primary recording agency — but classified lists of regional trusts supplied by the central authorities to county and county borough councils would serve well enough as local registries.

The purpose of registration was to make more readily available information about endowed charities. Another proposed reform, intended to improve their income, had to do with broadening their statutory range of investments. There was obvious justification for the feeling among trustees, charitable and otherwise, that the choice of investments permitted by the Trustee Act of 1925 — almost wholly limited to the securities of public and semipublic bodies — was unduly restricted. Some of the securities no longer existed, and virtually all were of the sort that offered a fixed return and a fixed sum on redemption. As the Institute

---

[52] The Charitable Donations Registration Act of 1812, mentioned in an earlier chapter, required trustees to report certain details to the Clerk of the Peace of the County, but this obligation, never more than fitfully observed, had long since become a thoroughly dead letter.

of Chartered Accountants pointed out, though the regulations had been effective enough in protecting the principal of trust funds, these had "nevertheless caused great rigidity . . . and introduced a pattern of investment which a prudent business man would be unlikely to adopt in handling his own affairs." [53] What was called for, in the opinion of qualified financial men, was a policy sufficiently flexible to allow trustees to meet rapidly changing conditions in the investment world. In general terms, the Nathan Committee proposed extending the range of charitable trust investments to include, subject to certain safeguards, debentures and shares quoted on the Stock Exchange, though only up to 50 per cent of the capital of a trust. Trustees also should be authorized to acquire freehold or long leasehold property for investment as well as for functional purposes.[54]

The Committee, in summary, found conditions in the charity world to be less than shocking — better, one suspects, than had been imagined. Evidence showed fraud to be virtually unknown, likewise gross negligence.[55] Inefficiency in administration, being a relative notion, was more difficult to assess. The implied conclusion, however, was that trustees as a group were doing their job in a creditable fashion. Obsolescence and redundancy among the nation's charities also emerged as a less serious evil than had been assumed. The National Association of Parish Councils, for example, doubted "from our experience . . . that there are so many obsolete charities in the rural areas . . . as appeared to have been suspected." [56]

There were, of course, maladjustments, legal and administrative, and an obvious need for better considered and more positive government policies. In some branches the field for voluntary effort had been little affected by the extension of the statutory services; in others it had been drastically curtailed. Working arrangements between the two partners in the welfare firm were still being fashioned, and, although they could not be made by Committee or Act of Parliament, at least these might clear away some of the more formal and technical obstacles. The situation, in the view of the Committee, called for no revolutionary measures but rather for a number of specific reforms in law and procedure which would, among other things, establish a basis for more constructive cooperation between charity trustees and the statutory services. As Lord Nathan told a conference called by the Society of Arts, "We want to see these vast charitable resources marshalled behind the drive for social progress. We believe we have provided the means for doing so in a way which will ensure a future for charitable trusts as rich in variety and blessings as their past." [57]

5

The Nathan Committee completed its Report in the spring of 1952, and in December the Prime Minister presented it to Parliament. Comment followed

[53] Memorandum to the Committee.
[54] *Nathan Report*, Par. 295–98.
[55] Chief Commissioner, Q. 570–73.
[56] Q. 4437.
[57] *J. Royal Society of Arts*, 12 June 1953, p. 490.

predictable channels. Few qualified critics could dissent from the Committee's proposals for tidying up charity law and administration. Its more substantial recommendations — in the view of the Committee, moderate and middle-of-the-road in their purport — drew censure of a rather temperate sort from both those who inclined toward a more active public policy and those who were uneasy about further extending the State's authority over private charities. Not all of the latter were as agitated as the Master of one of the City Companies, apparently a gentleman of pre-glacial political outlook, who resented the intrusion of public bodies into the world of private philanthropy. He bleakly contemplated the creation of a gigantic charities bureaucracy with virtual nationalization of endowments as a probable consequence.[58] In certain voluntary circles, too, there was doubt whether in its recommendations the Committee had taken sufficient account of "the reactions and enthusiasms of private donors."[59] Might not some of its proposals have the effect of dampening their initiative?

On the more positive side, no informed reader could miss the fact that the Report had been drawn up on spacious lines. The Committee had not been content merely to iron out legal and mechanical details nor had it shrunk from the larger issues. The task had been conceived in part as one of social planning — of defining the place of private charity in the new semicollectivist society — and its conclusions, many were relieved to discover, seemed to vindicate the traditional values of English philanthropy. The title of the first chapter, "The Value of Charity in the Modern Social Structure," indicated well enough the "immense importance" that the Committee attached to voluntary action. "Indeed," the chapter concluded, "we think that those who deny its importance can have but scant understanding of the historical process or of the forces which make for social cohesion, enrich social life and deepen social responsibility."[60]

The preliminary debate on the Report, which took place in the Lords in July of 1953, once more brought into the open conceptions of private charity which had been in conflict at least since the time of Lord Brougham.[61] Broadly speaking, the cleavage lay between those who conceived of charity as a personal and voluntary act and those who were more concerned with maximizing the utility (to recall the Benthamite formula) of the nation's charity resources. These positions, both of which stopped short of rigid dogmatism, were ably enunciated by the Archbishop of Canterbury (Geoffrey Fisher) and Lord Samuel. The former, while joining in the praise of the Report, was doubtful about too much tidying up of the charity household. Husband and wife, he reflected, sometimes have different ideas, and "when, as here, the relation is between the robust, forceful partner of statutory action and the frail and delicate but gracious partner of voluntary charity, then one must be more than ever careful."[62] It was the old

[58] *Ibid.*, pp. 510–12.
[59] Liverpool Council of Social Service, *Ann. Rept.*, 1953, pp. 3–4.
[60] *Nathan Report*, Par. 61.
[61] 5 *Parl. Deb.* (Lords), 183:747–848.
[62] *Ibid.*, 761.

fear, echoed by several noble Lords, of rigidity, overcentralization, indifference to local interests and the wishes of benefactors — and thus, in the words of *The Times,* "loss of the grace and spontaneity without which charity, in the Christian sense, is no longer itself." [63] There was little enthusiasm in this quarter for common good funds, which Lord Samuel championed and the Nathan Committee had recommended, still less for any move to pool parochial trusts.

These conflicting points of view were not novel to Lord Nathan, and he summarized them in an incisive statement to the House. On the one hand, the myriad of trusts could be thought of as assets worth some £200 million, together with vast amounts of land, "to be disposed, reformed and diverted like so many military formations in the battle against want and wretchedness. Alternatively, they can be considered, as they have for centuries past been considered, as so many benefactions, each of whose peculiar characteristics must as far as possible be reverently protected against the ravages of time and the buffetings of economic change. The first is an argument for efficiency — efficiency for the sake of the beneficiaries. The second is an argument for piety, for respect for the wishes of the founders." [64] What had been attempted and what, in the opinion of most competent critics, had been accomplished with tolerable success was to strike a balance between the demands of efficiency and piety.

Those who viewed the Nathan Report through professional eyes regarded it, on the whole, as an admirable performance. Critics of less than iron-bound legal orthodoxy tended to find most fault with the Committee's cautious recommendations on the matter of imperfect trust instruments. The proposal (not unanimously favored within the Committee) was to validate past errors by statute but to require those which legal draftsmen might make in the future to run their chances in the courts. This solution, which might mean frustrating the clear intentions of the testator, seemed less resolute and imaginative than the Committee's other prescriptions. Competent legal advisers ought to know the law, but the fact remained that they did make mistakes. [65] The consensus of legal opinion, one critic insisted, would hold that where an obvious technical slip had occurred the court should have power to rectify it in the interest of the charity. [66]

The Government was in no hurry to state its official opinion on the Nathan recommendations as a whole, but it took only a few months to enact a measure validating trusts whose legality might have been called into question by the Oxford Group and Ellis cases. Here, as we have seen, the Government's prescription,

---

[63] *The Times,* 23 July 1953.

[64] 5 *Parl. Deb.* (Lords), 183:776–77.

[65] *Law Times,* 216:550 (30 Oct. 1953).

[66] D. W. Logan, "Report of the [Nathan] Committee," *Modern Law Review,* 16:348 (July 1953); see also H. G. Hanbury, *Listener,* 53:146 (27 Jan. 1955). In addition to the other complaints, there was some unhappiness over the failure of the Committee to deal more resolutely with the "nexus of common employment" issue. The question here (*Oppenheim* v. *Tobacco Securities Trust Co., Ltd.*) was whether a trust established for the benefit of the employees of a large limited company constituted a valid charity. See the *Nathan Report,* Par. 136; the *Law Times,* 216:550; and Keeton, *Modern Law of Charities,* pp. 71–73.

the Charitable Trusts (Validation) Act of 1954, followed the Nathan proposals in principle. Specifically, the Act accepted the Nathan thesis of distinguishing between trusts established in the past whose legal basis might be doubtful and those to be founded in the future. Obviously the former had to be given legal relief, but future victims of bad draftsmanship could expect no quarter.[67]

When, two and a half years after the appearance of the Report, the Government's White Paper was finally issued, it gave the Nathan position only a qualified endorsement.[68] This was natural enough. Not only was the Committee a Labour creation whose handiwork was now being judged by a Conservative Government, but since its appointment five years before there had been a palpable change in the public temper. By the mid-'50's planning had gone somewhat out of fashion — at least, as the *Law Times* suggested, confidence in what it could accomplish was less sanguine.[69] If the Committee had held that a touch of planning would improve the charity world, the Government inclined toward less comprehensive policies, and the White Paper tended to align it, though not unreservedly, with the Archbishop and other spokesmen for decentralization, local initiative, the rights of trustees, and the utility of small, individual charities. The Government, in short, was reluctant to disturb the existing charity structure even to the extent contemplated by the Nathan Report.

At the outset, though agreeing that there was no case for altering the legal content of charity, the Government rejected the Committee's more positive proposal. There was little merit, the White Paper implied, in drafting a new definition based on the Macnaghten categories but preserving case law. These two desiderata the Government held to be incompatible (even though such an eminent Chancery judge as Mr. Justice Vaisey had thought the Committee's position tenable) and doubted whether the corpus of case law, resting as it did on the preamble of 43 Elizabeth, could survive if the Statute were to be scrapped. Since to the Government either matters must be left as they were or a fresh statutory definition formulated,[70] the Charities Act of 1960, predictably enough, took the former course.

To the three major recommendations of the Committee — those having to do with the setting up of a usable charity registry, the reconstitution of the Charity Commission, and the relaxation of the *cy-près* doctrine — the Government gave a somewhat qualified approval. A central, classified record of charitable trusts was highly desirable, but the Charity Commission and Ministry of Education should not be required to transmit copies to local authorities. The Government agreed that the Commissioners ought to have a Minister, presumably the Home Secretary, to represent them in Parliament but flatly rejected the Nathan proposal to reconstitute the Commission as a part-time body of "men and women of standing in

---

[67] 5 *Parl. Deb.* (Lords), 185:278ff.

[68] *Government Policy on Charitable Trusts*, 1955. For a summary of the White Paper, see *Nathan on the Charities Act, 1960*, pp. 13–15.

[69] *Law Times*, 220:105 (19 July 1955).

[70] Paragraph 3.

public and charitable affairs." In holding to a Commission "with a predominantly legal composition," the White Paper implicitly accepted the Commissioners' own conception of their role as a quasi-judicial body "whose primary task is to deal with proposals initiated by trustees." [71] Still, the Government conceded, a nonlegal element could be usefully added, and the future Charity Commission should consist of three paid members, only two of whom, however, need be "legally qualified."

On the critical issue of altering trusts the differences between Government and Committee, broadly speaking, were matters of emphasis rather than of substance. The White Paper agreed that some relaxation of *cy-près* was indicated, while insisting that the Committee had underestimated the possibilities of revision under existing law. Obviously the Government was even less inclined than the Committee to sanction any wholesale reshuffling of endowments: initiative in revising schemes should normally lie with the trustees, with whom the words of the Commissioners "will carry more weight if they remain as they are at present, the friend and adviser of trustees and not their master." [72] Given this cautious approach, with its solicitude for trustees, local interests, and founder's wishes, it is mildly surprising that no exception was taken to the Committee's recommendation of thirty-five years as the assured period of immunity for new trusts. [73]

6

It was the conviction of the Nathan Committee that little could be accomplished until some order was introduced into the chaos of charity law. Tinkering with details would only confound the confusion. What was indicated was a new, simplified statute in place of the scores of enactments — as familiar and basic as the Charitable Trusts Act of 1853 and as obscure as the Seamen's Fund Winding-up Act of 1851 — bearing more or less directly on charitable endowments. At the time of the White Paper, the Government evidently thought it possible to avoid drafting a fresh, comprehensive statute, but the hope proved short-lived. Christopher Pascoe Hill, Assistant Under-Secretary at the Home Office, who was assigned to the Charity Commission "with the daunting brief of applying it [the White Paper] to existing law," concluded that patching was futile and that no alternative remained but to frame a new law. [74] This was a major undertaking in draftsmanship and justified what must have seemed exceedingly slow progress. Merely combing the statute book for acts and clauses which the new bill would repeal or "consequentially amend" was a labor of months. When the bill was

---

[71] *Government Policy on Charitable Trusts,* Par. 43.

[72] *Ibid.,* Par. 19.

[73] Common good trusts, which, the Committee believed, might in time become an important part of the welfare machinery, were regarded by the Government with only moderate enthusiasm. Local common good trusts, which might attract small and middling bequests, were to be encouraged, but they should always be "spontaneous in origin and unofficial in character." As for national common good trusts, created and subsidized initially by the State, to which might be transferred intestate estates (without next of kin) — this proposal had little appeal.

[74] *The Times,* 4 Aug. 1960.

finally introduced, the number of such enactments totaled about two hundred and covered the seventeen pages of the Fifth, Sixth, and Seventh Schedules.

To those most heavily committed to the reform of charity law the delay seemed ominous. When nearly four years had passed after the issuing of the White Paper, Lord Nathan precipitated a debate in the House of Lords with a view to prodding the Government. "During the past four years," he protested, "not only has there been silence; there also, to all outward observance, has been complete inactivity." [75] Obviously the Committee had viewed the White Paper with mixed emotions, though on the whole rather relieved that more of its recommendations had not been cast aside. For Lord Nathan the most disappointing decision of the Government was its refusal to enlarge and alter the character of the Charity Commission. The smaller Commission, predominantly legal in its make-up, which the White Paper favored, he thought would be less likely to take advantage of the new powers contemplated in the Report.

The debate in the Lords, though it brought no significant concessions from the Government, elicited the virtual commitment to introduce a bill in the course of the next session. Actually, when a little less than a year later a relatively short and relatively intelligible bill was brought into the Lords, there was general agreement that this was "a superb piece of drafting" (in Lord Nathan's words) and that the achievement justified the five years of delay. From the beginning it was clear that the bill, which followed fairly faithfully the lines blocked out in the White Paper, would go through without substantial amendment. Both Houses showed an awareness that the scope of private philanthropy had been radically altered — that, as the Home Secretary remarked in the Commons, the problem of what to do about private charity in a society where "the basic needs of the people are met by the people acting through the Government" was historically an entirely novel one.[76]

Not surprisingly, critics on both the right and the left discovered flaws, serious or trivial, in the plans for the new charity edifice. The former, broadly speaking, reflected the apprehensiveness of individual charities and local interests over what they pictured as increasing control by public authorities. They professed uneasiness lest the trend have an adverse effect on voluntary support. A Scottish peer recalled the sheaf of bequests received by the Royal National Life-boat Institution which were to become invalid "if the Government had the smallest finger in our activities." [77] And certain national charities which operated mainly through local units — the Boy Scouts, the Salvation Army, and Dr. Barnardo's Homes, for example — were apprehensive as they faced the complexities of compulsory registration.

Peers on the Labour and Liberal benches leveled more fundamental and interesting objections. Implicit in a series of motions (chiefly by Lord Silkin)[78] was the belief not only that the Government had dismissed some of the Nathan recom-

[75] 5 Parl. Deb. (Lords), 216:366.
[76] Ibid., 221:574.
[77] Lord Saltoun, ibid., 613.
[78] Deputy Leader of the Opposition.

mendations too readily but that in certain instances these proposals themselves had been overcautious. Labour critics could regard the Nathan plans for altering trusts as unduly timid, and they pushed for a less restrictive definition of "charitable purpose," a view which received some support from academic lawyers both within and outside the House.[79] Professor Keeton, for example, could (later) deplore the leaving to the courts the task of defining a charity, for their "intervention in this field is probably the worst exhibition of the operation of the technique of judicial precedent, which can be found in the law reports."[80] With such objections, however, the Government would have no commerce, and the bill passed with little change.[81]

To review the provisions of the Act of 1960, the new constitution of English charity, would be repetitious, since these had been foreshadowed accurately enough in the White Paper.[82] It brought a degree of order into the tangled jungle of charity statutes, and introduced reforms, of greater or less consequence, in the statutory procedures affecting endowed charities. Of these the most notable were, no doubt, a relaxation in the conditions necessary for varying trusts *cy-près* and the creation of a central register of charities.[83] To look ahead, this register may list a quarter of a million charities rather than the 110,000 of which the Nathan Committee was aware, and, contrary to the implication of the White Paper, the Commission is authorized to supply particulars of relevant trusts to local authorities wishing to establish a register.[84] Among charity administrators, social workers, and presumably a majority of charity lawyers, there was general satisfaction with the Act. As with most constitutions, however, the decisive test will be that of experience.

The reconstruction of the Charity Commission began almost simultaneously with the passing of the Act. In something of a departure from precedent, Christopher Pascoe Hill, the principal architect of the Act, was appointed Chief Commissioner, even though he had not come up through the hierarchy of the Commission. But, as a result of his five years in the Ryder Street office, he was not lacking in familiarity with its procedures and problems. The forecast of *The*

---

[79] Lord Chorley, a distinguished legal scholar and professor in the London School of Economics, joined in Silkin's complaint over the narrow construction which the courts had tended to put on "charitable purpose."

[80] *Modern Law of Charities*, p. vi.

[81] A special and under some circumstances a trying problem was presented by surplus charity funds, especially disaster collections which were no longer needed for their original purpose. What could be done with such excess funds? As a rule, the courts looked for a "general charitable intention" on the part of the donors before permitting such surpluses to be put to other charitable uses. What was needed, the critics urged, was a provision in the Act which would make it possible to turn such excess funds over to other charities without a clear general charitable intention.

[82] For a summary of the Act, see *Nathan on the Charities Act, 1960*, pp. 17–22. The Charities Act itself left untouched the question of trustee investments. In the following year, however, the Trustee Investments Act (9 & 10 Eliz. II, c. 62) opened a much wider range of investments to trustees, charitable and otherwise.

[83] These are laid out in Section 13 of the Act and explained in *Nathan on the Charities Act, 1960*, pp. 73–82.

[84] *110th Ann. C.C. Rept.*, 1962, p. 19.

Times was only a simple statement of fact: "After four years of hard work, which included the drawing up of a new constitution of his office, the chief commissioner faces a lot more." [85]

If the Act of 1960 marked a stage in the rationalization of charity law and administration, it had another and partly symbolic significance. The enactment made official and statutory what had been stated occasionally in and out of Parliament and had been asserted by the Nathan Committee — that is, it recognized voluntary action as an integral part of the machinery of the Welfare State. A major aim of the legislation, as the Lord Chancellor observed in introducing the second reading, was to establish a statutory basis for cooperation between the public and voluntary welfare services. [86] In the course of the debate Lord Pakenham reminded the House of the enormous advances made during the previous decade in defining and developing the relations between the two. In 1949, when Lord Samuel's motion on voluntary action was discussed, no one could be entirely certain how the Conservative Party was going to take to the Welfare State or how Labour would deal with the voluntary services. "Today," he went on, "the danger of a conflict on Party lines between the principle of the Welfare State and the principle of voluntary action has disappeared." Nothing would do, he asserted, but partnership between the two, for "the Welfare State without voluntary action loses its chance of realising its vision of national welfare in freedom." [87] To that partnership the Charities Act of 1960 gave statutory ratification.

Though this partnership has never been as consciously defined as in recent years, it was not, of course, a new notion. What had changed was the division of responsibility between the two partners. From the time of the Elizabethan Statute of Charitable Uses, the State had laid great store by voluntary action and, indeed, had thought of it as the major instrument for relieving suffering, educating the young, and dealing with social malaise. The Statute itself was an attempt to guide the generous impulses of Englishmen which in the past had been applied to more directly religious purposes. Clearly it was the intention of the Government that charitable individuals should take over and that the State should act only where there was no alternative. To repeat what has been said more than once before in the course of this study, the function of the State was to fill gaps in the network of private charity.

For the next three centuries this thesis was accepted with little question. And, whatever their weaknesses and blind spots as philanthropists, many Englishmen responded with eagerness and a powerful sense of obligation. With the passing of the years they faced new needs and developed new techniques for meeting

---

[85] 4 Aug. 1960.

[86] 5 *Parl. Deb.* (Lords), 221:563. The relevant sections (10–12), Lord Nathan points out (*Nathan on the Charities Act, 1960*, p. 19), "do little more than confer power on local authorities and charity trustees to co-operate if they wish to do so." Their essential purpose, according to the Lord Chancellor, was "to remove the last obstacles, the last suspicions, the last argument that Parliament does not really approve co-operation."

[87] 5 *Parl. Deb.* (Lords), 221:637, 639.

them, in some cases, admittedly, too late and to little effect. The eighteenth
century saw imposing efforts, through the charity schools, to grapple with the
problem of child training and, through the hospitals, to improve the care of the
sick. Both of these employed, in a large degree, the method of the voluntary
society, "associated philanthropy," with the standard devices of subscription list,
charity sermons, and collections. It was this mechanism that presently became a
principal vehicle for philanthropic action, and the mass of voluntary societies one
of the distinguishing marks of the British community. Point to a need and an
organization would promptly rally to deal with it, sometimes effectively, sometimes merely hopefully.

What sharpened the problem was, of course, the economic and social revolution.
With the transformation of the old, predominantly rural community into an
urban society and with population mounting in catastrophic proportions, the
philanthropist faced a situation far more baffling and complex than in the earlier
days. As the terms of the problem changed, the impulses also altered. In some
areas of Victorian life, good works took on a pronounced evangelical tone; in
others they continued to reflect the compassion or sense of social obligation of
men of goodwill; and in some instances they hinted at less exalted motives. But
almost universally among Englishmen it was taken for granted that social welfare
— if such it can be called — was the proper field for philanthropy and not for the
State, which would intervene only where the crisis lay plainly beyond the capabilities of private agencies.

This division of responsibility had its effect on English life. On the one hand,
the acceptance of public obligation by a multitude of Englishmen, great and
humble, not only produced societies and organizations and charitable trusts for
hundreds of more or less estimable purposes but also imparted a special flavor
to English society. The determination of Englishmen, in the words of the *Edinburgh Review,* to "conduct our affairs without the interference of the State" [88]
resulted in a vast number of associations, charitable and otherwise, standing
between the State and the individual and has helped to maintain in Britain a
conspicuously pluralistic commonwealth. Englishmen have taken responsibility,
individually and collectively, for their community in a way that, whatever their
failings, is almost unique in the Western world. Certainly charitable enterprise
was one of the schools in which the public-spirited citizen received his training.

Yet, on the other hand, it became increasingly obvious that private charity had
left the essential problems of urban-industrial life only slightly altered. Housing
congestion, ignorance, unemployment, and poverty remained about what they
had been. Both by its successes and its abysmal failures, philanthropy helped to
reveal the real outlines of the problem. However hesitant the State may have been
in embarking on a positive social policy, very likely Victorian public authorities
accomplished more toward creating a basis for civilized living than did all of

[88] 114:10 (July 1861).

the voluntary societies. In the late century, especially, new currents — advancing democracy, an adequate civil service, reformed local government, and the more extensive data collected by Charles Booth and others about the facts of poverty — opened the way and, indeed, created an irresistible demand for state action.

The intervention of the State extended rather than reversed the long tradition of voluntary effort. In no sense a monolithic structure, the Welfare State of the 1960's depends, in an extraordinary degree, on voluntary resources, human and financial. The Nathan Committee was not overstating the point when it urged that democracy "as we know it, could hardly function effectively" [89] without making wide use of voluntary activity. Ancient donors and pious founders, devoted evangelicals, humanitarian promoters of organizations, and the rest of the charitable host would, no doubt, be mystified by the welfare world of modern Britain. But they could hardly miss the ineffaceable stamp left on the British community by their own labors and gifts.

[89] *Nathan Report,* Par. 53.

INDEX

Abbey Mills, 513

Abuses in charity administration, 72–73, 185–86, 190–91, 307, 324–25; reported by Brougham Commissioners, 193–97; Nathan Committee, 588

Acland, Sir Thomas Dyke (1809–98), 250

Acland, Sir Thomas Dyke (1842–1919), 497–98

Adams, Serjeant, 145

Addenbrooke, Dr. John, 41

Addenbrooke's Hospital, 41, 42, 46

Adderley, C. B. (Lord Norton), 155, 156

Addington, Lord, 334

Addison, Joseph, quoted, 54

Aikin, Dr. John, 37, 49

Akroyd, Edward, 382–83

Albert, Prince, his model dwelling, 376–77

Aldgate Freedom Foundation, 294

Alex, Ephraim, 421, 422

Allen, A. W. G., 350, 353

Allen, Matthew, 379

Allen, William, philanthropist, 102, 103, 111, 117, 152

Almshouse and pension charities: statistics on, 74, 507; York, 445; impact of Welfare State, 547ff; National Association of, 551–52

Amulree, Lord, 575

Annual Charities Register and Digest, 235, 242, 244, 476, 477–78

Anti-slavery movement, 129ff; Committee for the Abolition of the Slave Trade, 129; Anti-Slavery Society, 131–32; *Anti-Slavery Reporter*, 132

Arch, Joseph, 405, 407

Armstrong, Dr. George, 122

Armitage, Dr. Thomas Rhodes, 491

Arnold, Matthew, 250

Arnott, Dr. Neil, 374

Arts Council, 555, 557

Ash, Dr. John, 41

Ashley, Lord, *see* Shaftesbury

"Associated philanthropy," 3, 11–12, 71–72, 181, 596

Association for the Relief of the Manufacturing and Labouring Poor, 97, 110

Astbury, B. E., 246

Bagehot, Walter, quoted, 167–68

Baird Trust case, 334

Baker, Barwick, 155

Balfour, Gerald, 517

Barbauld, Mrs. Anna Letitia, quoted, 94

Baring Brothers, 494

Baring, Thomas, 141, 356, 493

Barnardo's Homes (Dr. Thomas), 151, 157–58, 543; and C.O.S., 230–31

Barnett, Mrs. Henrietta, 240, 504

Barnett, Canon Samuel, 218, 240–41, 390, 431, 504, 514

Barrington, Bishop Shute, 128

Bartlett, William Ashmead, 414

Bath Society for the Suppression of Common Vagrants, etc., 111

Baths and washhouses, 175, 455

Bawden, E. G. (Bawden Trust), 490

Bedford, (4th) Duke of, 53

Bedford, (8th) Duke of, 494

Bedford Grammar School, 251, 256

Beit, Alfred, 472

Beit, Otto, 490

Bell, Dr. Andrew, 116, 117, 118

Bellers, John, 38

Benson, A. C., 351–52

Bernard, Sir Thomas, 92–93, 117; career and philanthropic work, 105ff; School for the Blind, 119–20

Berridge, Richard, 490

Besant, Walter, *All Sorts and Conditions of Men*, 293

Bethel Hospital, Norwich, 75

Bethlem, 52, 333, 341

Bevan, Aneurin, quoted, 547

Bevan, Mrs. Bridget, 29

Beveridge, Lord (Sir William), 246, 488, 514, 575; *Report*, 525, 531; *Voluntary Action*, 574

Beyer, Charles Frederick, 364

Birkett, Lord, 568

Birmingham, University of, Mason College, 412–13

Birmingham General Hospital, 41

Bishopsgate Institute, 294

Bitter Cry of Outcast London, 385–86, 503–4

Blackley, Canon W. L., 505–6, 508